YOUNG EDWARD GIBBON

YOUNG EDWARD GIBBON

GENTLEMAN *of* LETTERS

Patricia B. Craddock

THE JOHNS HOPKINS UNIVERSITY PRESS
BALTIMORE AND LONDON

This book has been brought to publication with the generous assistance
of the Andrew W. Mellon Foundation

The Johns Hopkins University Press, Balitmore, Maryland 21218
The Johns Hopkins Press Ltd., London

Frontispiece: Portrait of Edward Gibbon.
Reproduced from Meredith Read's
Historic Studies in Vaud, Berne, and Savoy
(London, 1897)

Library of Congress Cataloging in Publication Data

Craddock, Patricia B.
  Young Edward Gibbon, gentleman of letters.

  Includes index.
  1. Gibbon, Edward, 1737–1794. 2. Historians—
England—Biography. I. Title.
  DG206.G5C73   937'.06'0924   81–13726
  ISBN 0–8018–2714–0   AACR2

For Peggy, the best of sisters,
and in memory of the dearest of parents

Contents

Preface

Gibbon himself wrote the perfect account of Gibbon-the-historian, from illustrious ancestors to "luminous pages," in the fifth and only completed draft of his *Memoirs*. But he was not satisfied with that view of himself; after almost doubling its length with notes, he abandoned it and began a sixth draft of his autobiography on a new plan, one that had room for his human inconsistencies and irrelevancies. Nevertheless, all previous biographical studies of Gibbon, even D. M. Low's admirable portrayal—the only one entirely based on original research—have in effect accepted the image of Gibbon's life represented in that rejected draft. The present study adopts instead the ideal implicit in the abortive sixth version and attempts to portray the man as well as the historian.

When Low wrote his biography in 1937, moreover, the only primary source for Gibbon's life to have received a modern edition was his first journal (to January 1763), which had been splendidly edited by Low himself. Since then, all the primary sources have enjoyed exemplary editions: his journals both in French and in English, his letters, and the autobiography itself. Furthermore, virtually all the remaining manuscript materials relating to Gibbon's life have now found their way into public or university collections.

The reader of Gibbon, therefore, has available a wealth of materials about him. One purpose of the present work is to provide a guide for such a reader through the riches of Gibboniana; the other, of course, is to propose my interpretation of them, to offer a new view of Gibbon's life and character before he became the historian of Rome.

In Gibbon's early life, three themes, in particular, seem to require attention: (1) His infancy, childhood, and adolescence are marked by a series of painful and destructive experiences connected with family ties; after this period, he channels all passionate feelings into two activities, friendship and scholarship, which cannot lead to such ties. He seems to search for a less dangerous alternative to blood ties and enthusiasm. But his temperament is by no means innately tepid. (2) His self-education as a scholar, as a historian, and as a mediator of the quarrel between the *philosophes* and the *erudits*, the fruits of which have been admirably studied by a number of modern scholars, is a process much richer and more complex than he or his biographers have suggested. It is recoverable from his forgotten and neglected apprentice works. (3) His definition of himself as an adult wavered for a long time between two possibilities. Success in life as his father defined it was that of the "country gentleman": Tory M.P., landowner, gentleman of leisure and social grace. Gibbon found this program, or at least the parental approval to which it led, persistently attractive. But still more compelling was the urge to become a scholar and writer—and in the event, his father approved, though he did not sponsor, those fledgling efforts. Could he have both worlds, and if not, which should take precedence? This is the question that is resolved at the end of the present study, when he sets up his own house, catalogues his library, and settles down in earnest to the writing of the *Decline and Fall*.

In addition to my great and constant debt to my predecessors and contemporaries in Gibbonian studies, I have enjoyed the inestimable advantage of loving and supportive friends and family members. Lest I too produce six massive volumes, I must thank most of them in this general way. But three friends, Evelyn Barish, Martine Brownley, and Margaret C. Huff, have read substantial portions of this work in draft, and one heroic friend, Joan Hartman, read the whole manuscript. To all four I am grateful for astute criticisms and kind encouragement. Nevertheless, I fear that I have ingeniously contrived to preserve many of my faults and weaknesses.

The reader of the present volume will observe that virtually all the quotations are in English. Many of them are, however, translations—my own, unless otherwise noted. Many persons interested in Gibbon will, of course, wish to read these materials in the original languages (provided in the notes), but the needs of other readers seemed to require translation. My translations are intended to be neither literal nor literary. Young Gibbon, writing in French, does not sound like "the grand Gibbon," and it seemed inappropriate to attempt to imitate the Gibbonian manner before it existed. A strictly literal translation would, on the other hand, be unduly awkward and unpleasant for the English reader. Hence the compromise, which, like every compromise (and every failure to compromise), has its faults. The present translations would be still more faulty, were it not for the kind assistance of my friends Nelly K. Murstein, professor of French at Connecticut College, and Gerald P. Fitzgerald, professor of English and Italian at Boston University.

I should note also that in quoting in English I silently modernize long *s*. Otherwise I have attempted to transcribe faithfully the spelling, punctuation, and capitalization of the originals. The same procedure is followed for foreign languages, in which Gibbon's accents, however peculiar, are preserved.

No work of mine will ever be complete without grateful reference to two of my teachers: F. A. Pottle, Sterling Professor Emeritus at Yale University, who introduced me to Gibbon; and Irvin Ehrenpreis, who introduced me to the eighteenth century and sustains me with his counsel and friendship in the twentieth.

Besides Gibbon and Low, many people have written thoughtfully and interestingly about Gibbon's life. I have profited from the insights of my predecessors, as my notes record. I should like to call my reader's attention to one valuable study of Gibbon's character (as revealed by the changes in his *Memoirs*) with which I became acquainted too late for adequate acknowledgment in my notes, that by Patricia Spacks in her *Imagining a Self*. Her Gibbon is the Gibbon I know. I hope the readers of the present volume will enjoy furthering their acquaintance with him.

Acknowledgments

I am grateful to the following organizations for support during the research for this volume and during its composition: in 1971-72, the John Simon Guggenheim, Junior, Foundation; in the summer of 1977, the American Council of Learned Societies; in 1978-79, the National Endowment for the Humanities.

I also wish to thank the following for permission to consult and to quote manuscript materials:

Archives Cantonales Vaudoises
The Trustees of the Beinecke Library, Yale University
The Trustees of the British Library
The President and Fellows of Magdalen College, Oxford
John Murray
The Trustees of Dr. Williams's Library, London

Abbreviations

ACV	Lausanne. Archives Cantonales Vaudoises
Add. MSS.	London. British Library Additional Manuscripts
B.L.	London. British Library
BU	*Biographie universelle ancienne et moderne,* nouvelle édition. Paris, 1843–65.
CPB	Gibbon's manuscript commonplace book of 1755–57
DF, Decline and Fall	Edward Gibbon. *The History of the Decline and Fall of the Roman Empire.* 6 vols. London, 1776–88.
DGP	New Haven. Yale University. Beinecke Library. Dorothea Gibbon Papers
DNB	*Dictionary of National Biography.* London, 1885–1901.
EE	*The English Essays of Edward Gibbon.* Edited by Patricia B. Craddock. Oxford, 1972 [1973].
Journal A	*Gibbon's Journal to January 28th, 1763.* Edited by D. M. Low. London, 1929.
Journal B	*Le Journal de Gibbon à Lausanne.* Edited by G. A. Bonnard. Lausanne, 1945.
Journey	*Gibbon's Journey from Geneva to Rome.* Edited by G. A. Bonnard. London, 1961.
Letters	*The Letters of Edward Gibbon.* Edited by J. E. Norton. 3 vols. London, 1956.
M	*The Autobiographies of Edward Gibbon.* Edited by John Murray. London, 1896.
Memoirs	Edward Gibbon. *Memoirs of My Life.* Edited by Georges A. Bonnard. London, 1966.
MG	*Miscellanea Gibboniana.* Edited by G. R. de Beer, G. A. Bonnard, L. Junod. Lausanne, 1952.
ML, 1	Edward Gibbon and Georges Deyverdun. *Mémoires littéraires de la Grande Bretagne pour l'an 1767.* London, 1768.

ML, 2	Edward Gibbon and Georges Deyverdun. *Mémoires littéraires de la Grande Bretagne pour l'an 1768.* London, 1769.
MW 1796	*The Miscellaneous Works of Edward Gibbon.* Edited by John, Lord Sheffield. 2 vols. London, 1796.
MW 1814	*The Miscellaneous Works of Edward Gibbon.* Edited by John, Lord Sheffield. 5 vols. London, 1814 [1815].
NBG	*Nouvelle biographie générale.* Paris, 1852-56.
N.S.	New Style
O.S.	Old Style
Tour	Gibbon's journal of a tour of Switzerland, in *MG*, above

CHAPTER 1

A Love Tale
at Putney

THE POLITICAL consciousness of
the average four-year-old boy, whatever his time or country, can safely be
estimated as nil. But the little boy whose father had just administered to
him the unusual indignity of a whipping, somewhere in the rooms or on
the lawns of Lime Grove, at Putney, in the spring of 1741, was not an
ordinary four-year-old. Undaunted by the superior physical force that
Edward Gibbon, Esq., had just demonstrated, Master Edward Gibbon
sought revenge with words, running after his father to shout, "Dumner,
Henley! Dumner, Henley!"[1] These cryptic words were well and precociously designed to annoy the elder Gibbon: Dumner and Henley were the
Opposition candidates in the parliamentary election for which he was
then standing.

The furious little figure, frail, red-haired, with a head far too large for
its body, must have amused as well as surprised its elders.[2] In later years,
though Gibbon remembered the episode itself, he also remembered being
told about it. Typical of his precocity, it is atypical in that for once, open
defiance of his father did not lead to disaster. Perhaps, however, the boy
observed with chagrin the laughter of the adults he had tried to punish.
It was the earliest memory he retained as an adult.

That it is not a memory of terror, guilt, love, happiness, or some feat or
failure in the occupations of childhood seems appropriate to the placid,
even tepid, quality of Gibbon's emotional life as an adult, though it does
not prepare us for the warmth and strength of his friendships. That it *is*
a moment of impetuous anger, directed against his father, reminds us that
the coolness of the mature man followed episode after episode of passionate, impulsive conflict with that passionate, impulsive father—with the
younger Gibbon constantly suffering defeat until he adopted, and even
came to feel, the suave, measured, reasoned, temperate view of life characteristic of much of his later life and work.[3] After Gibbon's death,
Edmund Malone remarked of him:

Independent of his literary merit, as a companion Gibbon was uncommonly agreeable. He had an immense fund of anecdote and of erudition of various kinds, both ancient and modern; and had acquired such a facility and elegance of talk that I had always great pleasure in listening to him. The manner and voice, though they were peculiar, and I believe artificial at first, did not at all offend, for they had become so appropriated as to appear natural.[4]

A similar deliberate, but not altogether voluntary, re-creation of the passionate boy as a dispassionate man is another thread, like that of the development of the historian of Rome explored by Gibbon himself in his *Memoirs*, to link and explain the events of the life of Edward Gibbon the man. Latent and open conflicts with his father and his father's aims for him characterize most of young Gibbon's experiences not only before his father's death, but even for the two years required to untangle his father's affairs after his death. Only in 1772 does he emerge as "the historian of the Roman Empire," as he liked to call himself. This book is a study of the prehistory of the historian, an account of a baby, a child, an adolescent, a young and then an older man, learning to love, to fear, to learn, to trust and distrust, in short, to be a particular human being. This person's history was from the beginning marked by deprivation and pain. His choice of the life of the mind, rather than that of the body or even the emotions, was neither innate nor fortuitous. It was influenced and to some extent determined by persons and conditions that existed before and at his birth.

In his youth, moreover, it was a choice that had a rival. He might have been, or so it seemed, simply a gentleman—a man of means, culture, and leisure, ready to serve or lead his country and to manage his hereditary property. His early years are indeed the history of his becoming the historian of Rome, but they are also the history of the roads not taken, some Edward Gibbons who might have been, and whose rejected alternatives and accepted limitations helped to form the man who, for five drafts of his memoirs, thought that he could wholly define himself by his role as historian, and who, having at last rejected that definition, was unable to complete a richer portrayal of himself. Such a portrayal is the object of the present study.

Gibbon began most of his accounts of his life by discussing his ancestors. In an autobiographical fragment he justified this pursuit:

A lively desire of knowing and recording our ancestors so generally prevails, that it must depend on the influence of some common principle in the minds of men. Our imagination is always active to enlarge the narrow circle in which Nature has confined us. Fifty or an hundred years may be alotted to an individual; but we stretch forwards beyond death with such hopes as Religion and Philosophy will suggest, and we fill

up the silent vacancy that precedes our birth by associating ourselves
to the authors of our existence. . . . The Satirist may laugh, the Philosopher may preach; but reason herself will respect the prejudices and
habits which have been consecrated by the experience of mankind.[5]

The only completed autobiographical sketch began without apology or
explanation, "My family is ancient and honourable in the county of
Kent" (M 293). The thought of his ancestors seems, in fact, to have
inspired the writing of the *Memoirs* in the first place: Gibbon encountered
a book by John Gibbon, Bluemantle Pursuivant, who could trace his
ancestors to 1326, and mistakenly concluded that this John Gibbon was
a brother of his Great-grandfather Matthew.[6] It is, however, only with
Matthew that we can begin the authentic series of Gibbon's ancestors, and
it is also Matthew whose character and achievements leave discernible
traces deep enough to affect his great-grandson. For the characters and
fortunes of Matthew and his wife affected the redoubtable character of
the first Edward Gibbon, a director of the infamous South-sea Company,
who in turn affected the life of his son, who in turn influenced the personality and development of his son the historian. History and psychology,
therefore, lead us to begin with Matthew.

On February 23, 1642, Matthew Gibbon, a younger son by a second
marriage of a Kentish landowner, Thomas Gibbon, was baptized in the
parish church at Westcliffe, Kent. His father had twelve children. An
older half brother is known to have had £4,000 as his portion of his
father's estate, but we do not know whether the children of Alice Sel-
hurst, Matthew's mother, were provided for equally well.

The family estate went, of course, to the eldest brother, and Matthew
went to London to become a linen draper in Leadenhall Street. Though
his parish was St. Andrew Undershaft, it was at St. Helen's Bishopsgate
that he married, on October 17, 1667, Hester Abrahall of Allhallows,
Barking.[7] They prospered. Their eldest son, another Thomas (born
1668/69), was sent to St. Paul's School, London, and then to St. John's,
Cambridge.[8] One daughter, Elizabeth, married Sir Whitmore Acton,
grandson of a Shropshire baronet, Sir Walter Acton of Aldenham, whose
younger son, Richard Acton, also figured in the Gibbon family history.[9]
Another daughter, Hester, married Oliver Elliston on June 11, 1692. The
family was then living in St. Olave's Heart Street.[10] There was one son,
Matthew, who was "not right in his head."[11]

It was their second son, Edward, born in 1675, who proved to be of
interest to history. Probably he too was sent to St. Paul's School in his
turn, for an Edward Gibbon was there sometime between 1672 and 1697
and was a Steward of the Feast in 1701.[12] When Edward was almost
eleven, his father was petitioning for a place in the customs commission
and was receiving serious consideration for it, a sign of prosperity.[13] So

far we seem to have a typical mercantile success story. Edward the future South-sea director would seem to be simply the more successful son of a successful father. But the story is a bit more complicated than that.

When Edward was fifteen, his father's name vanished from the Treasury books. Hester Gibbon, his mother, late in 1690, suddenly appeared there in her own name, lending considerable sums to the government.[14] We might infer that the reason Edward did not follow his brother to Cambridge, and that Matthew did not figure any longer in the Treasury books, was that Matthew had died (the date of his death is unknown).[15] But that inference would be incorrect at least until 1692, for in a letter to her "Dear Ned" of July 19, 1692 (Old Style, of course), Hester wrote, "I pray God give you health, yr father is still Ill, I hope in a fortnight to gett time to see him, the Bord have given you order att my Request, to Draw Bills upon them for 400011 . . . I hope your Creditt will not faile you, for if it shd. it would be A Reflexion on me as if I imposed a fallicy on them, but I hope these fears are Needless." She went on to discuss war news and rumors very capably and concluded, "You have services from all yr fds. & all ways the Blessing My D. N. of Yr very Affectionate Mother H. G."[16] The envelope was addressed to Mr. Edward Gibbon, Paymaster to the king of Great Britain's train in Flanders. This paymaster, it will be remembered, was no more than seventeen years old. That he held so responsible a post is a tribute not only to his ability but also to his mother's powers of persuasion, including her financial resources. Perhaps it is not surprising that she saw her ailing husband so infrequently, or that he faded out of her life and her son's so inconspicuously. It prepares us, however, for the ruthless energy and capability that characterized her activities and those of her second son, and that both expected in vain from the son's son, Edward, father of the historian.

Though in 1692 a Mr. Gibbon was humbly petitioning the government for any employment for which he was deemed fit, if that Mr. Gibbon was Edward, aged seventeen, both his need and his tone soon changed drastically. As early as 1696 he was the government's creditor, figuring in the Treasury records for larger and larger sums, owed for supplies either of goods or of money.[17] By now holding the rank of captain (in the militia), the young entrepreneur spent much of his time abroad while, we are told, his mother handled the business at home.[18]

By October 1698, Matthew Gibbon was certainly dead; in that month his widow remarried, one Richard Acton, a widower, younger son of a baronet but, like Matthew, a linen draper by trade.[19] Richard had a daughter, Katherine, who was about nine years old at the time of the marriage. He died in March 1704, and his brother Francis became his daughter's guardian, though she continued to live with Hester Gibbon Acton. On May 9, 1705, in St. Paul's Cathedral, Katherine, aged sixteen, was married to her stepmother's son Edward, now thirty. The groom gave the bride jewels valued at £500.[20]

Was this a love match? If so, it was one very convenient for the families concerned. One is tempted to doubt whether the young bride was given any option. Her son, Edward Gibbon II, was later sure that his father had never known what it was to be in love, but Edward's was interested testimony—his father was unsympathetic to his love affair at the time. At any rate, the couple went to live in Mr. Gibbon's house in Crosby Square and began promptly to produce grandchildren for Hester. This house—still owned by him in 1720 when, as a director of the collapsing South-sea Company, he was required to enumerate his assets—was that of a successful merchant but not of a merchant prince. Each floor contained two rooms and closets; probably the cellar contained the kitchen and a "hall" used for storage. On the ground floor one found the parlor, containing "three Tables, a Looking-glass, two Sconces, eight Chairs, two Cushions, two Prints, a Stove Grate and [its] Furniture," and the "Compting House." Presumably the family plate was kept in the parlor; still there in 1720 were "three small salvers, a mug, two salts, one soup spoon, eight spoons, and six teaspoons, weight seventy-two ounces." Up "One Pair of Stairs backward" there was a bedroom; the front room on that floor was also a bedroom—quite large, perhaps, because it contained, in addition to the bed and bedding, two tables, two looking-glasses, eleven chairs, two stools, a close stool and pan, etc. Up another flight of stairs, there were two more bedrooms. Above these, there were garrets.[21]

Did Hester live with the young couple? Had they all lived in that house before the marriage? Crosby Square was in the parish of St. Helen's Bishopsgate, from which the bride was married. There was plenty of room, even with the children, who soon began to arrive and to be baptized at St. Helen's. Whether or not she lived in the same house, Hester's overpowering presence is pointed to by an odd error in the baptismal records. Each of the seven children born to Edward Gibbon and his wife was said to be the son or daughter of Edward and *Hester*, his wife.[22] The spellings are various but the name is clear. One cannot escape imagining that the slip reflects the relative power and importance of the two women in Edward's household—or households, as they were soon to become.

The first child came promptly in 1706, a daughter, inevitably called Esther, that is, Hester. According to the parish register, she was baptized on May 29, 1707. This odd delay or discrepancy is even more noticeable in the case of the second child, a son, Edward, born, according to *his* son, in October 1707, but baptized, so say the parish registers of St. Helen's, October 21, 1708. The father, Edward Gibbon I, did not, however, spend all his time begetting children and having them baptized. We may track him everywhere in the Treasury books; by 1716, he was worth £60,000, though his mother retained her own property.[23]

The parish registers list the baptism of his third child—the last to survive childhood—on May 11, 1710. Her name was her mother's, Catherine. Soon after, her father became a commissioner of customs, the post his father had failed to obtain:

> Under the Tory administration of the four last years of Queen Anne (1710-14), Mr Edward Gibbon was appointed one of the Commissioners of the Customs; he sat at that board with Prior, but the merchant was better qualified for his station than the poet; since Lord Bolingbroke has been heard to declare, that he never conversed with a man who more clearly understood the commerce and finances of England (13).[24]

Between 1710 and 1714, at least four more children were born to the Gibbons—five, if the dates of baptism are still a year later than the dates of birth. Dorothy was baptized September 6, 1711; Acton, July 20, 1713 (he was buried February 14, 1713/14); Hannah, September 7, 1714; and Elizabeth, October 21, 1715. Though Dorothy may have died early (her burial is not recorded at St. Helen's or other parishes in which the Gibbons lived), the Crosby Square house was now surely rather full. Hester was nine, old enough to help her twenty-six-year-old mother with the younger ones, but still there were Edward, aged eight, Catherine, about five; Anne or Hannah, a year old, and the new baby, not to mention Grandmother Hester and possibly her weak-minded son, Matthew, who may have lived with the commissioner and his wife.

It was in the next year, 1716, that Edward I became a director of the South-sea Company. Clearly a man of substance, he was now also a man of property, that is, of land. When, four years later, he was required to enumerate his assets after the South-sea Bubble burst, he was the owner of considerable real property, the most important piece of which, to his young family, was undoubtedly his house, "Gardens, Stables, Coach-House, Brew-House, Barns, and other Out-Houses, with about sixty-five Acres of Land" at Putney, in Surrey, "purchas'd in fee-simple"—but when? Since he owned it in 1720, obviously not in 1736, as the Victoria County History, following a "deed in private hands," says.[25]

We can infer that the family was living in Putney at least part of the year as early as 1718, for the Putney Parish Register records the burial, June 28, 1718, of "Anne and Elizabeth, daughters of Edw. Gibbon, esq." The little girls would have been about three and four; the house must have been very quiet after their deaths. Edward Gibbon II, not yet eleven, had been sent to Westminster School in 1717 and so may not have been at home to catch whatever killed the little girls.[26] In the same year, 1718, the South-sea director bought the "Manor and Mansion House of Lenborough," in Buckinghamshire, as well as a farm there.[27]

Yet the family was still in residence at Crosby Square at times, for Edward and Katherine's last child, Francis, was baptized at St. Helen's on February 28, 1718/19. Edward continued to buy land—notably the "Manors of Buryton and East-Maple Derham, in the Parish of Petersfield" in Hampshire.[28] Francis, for whom perhaps one of these manors was intended, was buried at Putney on April 22, 1719.

The South-sea Company, meanwhile, no longer content with its highly successful monopoly of the British trade with South America and the Pacific islands, proposed, at the end of 1719, an even more ambitious scheme. In return for various rights, the company offered to pay £3,500,000 and take over the national debt (£31,500,000). The people who owned state annuities were to be persuaded to exchange them for South-sea stock, which would be issued at a high premium. Then the company would get the interest from the debt annually. After raising its bid to more than £7,000,000 (in competition with the Bank of England), the company achieved this arrangement in 1720 and soon persuaded more than half the annuitants to accept its stock. Naturally the stock rose precipitously, and the directors flourished. From 129 at the beginning of the year, the stock rose to 1,000 in July; 5,000,000 shares were sold. In August the fall began, by November the stock was back to 135, and in February 1721, a committee of the House of Commons reported on the machinations of the directors and the government. Some few investors had astutely taken their paper profits and sold out of the company; many more were ruined.[29] Although Edward Gibbon I retained his stock because he was a director, he was astute.

By a curious coincidence, on March 28 and 29, 1720, he suddenly decided it was time—after fifteen years of marriage—to make some Marriage Articles, settling his Hampshire, Surrey, and Buckinghamshire properties, as well as 1/36 share in the New River Company, on his mother, Hester, and on Francis Acton, in trust, for Katherine's jointure.[30] Just in time, because June 1 was to be the reckoning date for the inquiry into the property of the South-sea directors: Parliament decreed that the properties of the directors should be confiscated and used to compensate the sufferers under the South-sea scheme, when it was discovered that government favors had been purchased by bribes, and fake shares of stock issued.

Although 1720 was Edward II's last year at Westminster, presumably because of the bursting bubble (he was only thirteen and might have continued at the school), it is not likely that he was precociously interested in his father's financial affairs. Perhaps he was more conscious of the pleasures of a country house in which to spend his holidays, or even of some new playmates, also children of a London merchant, but next-door neighbors in Putney. These were the daughters of one James Porten and his wife, Mary Allen (a Putney girl): Mary, born in 1704; Catherine, born in December 1705; and Judith, born in 1709 or 1710.[31] When the Gibbons arrived in Putney, the Portens would have had a young son, Stanier (baptized June 26, 1716).[32] The children would have been socially suitable playmates for the young Gibbons, because Mr. Porten was apparently successful in business,[33] and their Uncle Francis was an alderman and a director of the Bank of England.[34]

Gibbon's account of his grandfather's fate in the South Sea debacle need not be much expanded. Edward I in 1721 declared his net worth to Parliament, including an inheritance of £1500 from Hester, who had died before May 19, 1721, at £106,543/5/6, even after the hasty provision for his wife.[35] This admitted net worth was some £45,000 more than he had had when he became a director of the South-sea Company and excludes, of course, all the value of the real property settled on his wife except a ten-year life interest. Still, to leave him only £10,000 of his £105,000, as Parliament voted to do, may indeed have been almost as unjust as his grandson, the historian, was to consider it.[36]

Other events more immediately important to his fifteen-year-old son soon followed. Early in 1723, Katherine Gibbon, his mother, died—after almost eighteen years of marriage—at about age thirty-four. Three of her seven children survived her. Later in the same year the household acquired a new member, ultimately far more influential than poor little Katherine. William Law, nonjuror and author of the *Serious Call*—the book of morality and devotion that most impressed and influenced Samuel Johnson—became Edward's tutor and "the much-honoured friend and spiritual director of the entire family" (17).

With undiminished skill and knowledge, and with the residue of his first fortune preserved by his own machinations and Parliament's decree, Edward Gibbon I set to work to rebuild his fortune. Meanwhile, his children were growing up. Under the influence of Mr. Law, Hester (sixteen when her mother died) seemed to prefer to concentrate on her reward in heaven, choosing a life of celibacy and piety. Hester Gibbon's virtues—even her charities—were not of a sort to attract favorable attention from her nephew the historian, or from the historian's admiring readers, but as a girl she may have had more endearing qualities. Her father was certainly fond of her, if we may judge from the tone of the notes from him that she happened to keep, addressing her as his "Dr Child," and he took the trouble to consult her about what she wished him to do for her in his will, that is, about how she wanted her portion left, assuming that she might not marry.[37] Her draft letter of reply to his inquiry is among the Walton manuscripts in Dr. Williams's Library, London. She wrote:

> At present I have no intention of Marrying & therefore am Obliged
> to you for thinking how to make my Fortune as secure to me as you

can. But if it should please God, that I live to see my Self deprivd of your care of me, should be Glad if you would not leave me dependent on anyone else. Whatever fortune you are pleased to bestow upon me I shall be thankfull to you for, & only desire to be this much Mistress of it, that if I don't bestow it upon a husband, I may have the liberty of chusing such persons for my heirs, as my affection or Judgment shall direct me to.[38]

As we shall see, her father honored this request. The younger sister, Catherine, grew up to marry her first cousin Edward Elliston (December 27, 1733) and to die some ten years later, after the birth of one child, another Catherine.[39]

And what of the South-sea director's only son? Between 1720 and at earliest 1723, he had been at home in Putney. There, he could have renewed his acquaintance with James Porten's daughters, however little he recognized its importance at the time. In 1723, Mr. Law accompanied the reluctant young scholar to Cambridge where, at sixteen, he entered Emmanuel, Mr. Law's college, as a pensioner, becoming a fellow commoner in 1727 and leaving without a degree in 1730.[40] We can infer from these dates alone that Edward II was not an industrious or a successful student, but there is more direct evidence of his character and behavior at Cambridge in the diary of one John Byrom, an expert in shorthand, who was engaged to teach him that art.[41] Family tradition identified Edward with the character Flatus, in Law's book, always with "some new project in his head," but promised so much happiness by his "sanguine temper and strong passions" that he is "satisfied with nothing."[42] Certainly Edward was neither quick nor eager to accept adult responsibilities and attitudes. When Byrom first met him (at his father's house in Putney), young Gibbon—then twenty-two!—"left [Byrom and Mr. Law] after a little while over a bottle of French wine."[43]

Byrom, a great admirer of Law's, was particularly pleased to hear of the interest that Law's pupil had in learning shorthand. His enthusiasm soon waned. The lessons began on Candlemas day, 1730. Two days later Byrom called on Edward in his rooms to give him a second lesson. He found that his pupil "had been playing, he said, at quadrille, had writ a little, but very ill, for he makes his letters wretchedly, but reads pretty well. Mr. Law came in while we were at it. . . . He said I should have more pains with Mr. G., because he wrote a very bad hand. . . . Mr. Law made Mr Gibbons go to the porter's with me to let me out." The next day, going to Emmanuel by appointment, Byrom found Gibbon leaving just as he arrived. The appointment was put off until the next day. On that day, February 6, "to Gibbon after five, but Mr. Law said he was gone to the West[minster] Club; I asked who taught him writing? He said it had cost much money, that he had learnt also of Leech the famous clergyman."[44]

Four of the other six appointments with Gibbon noted in Byrom's diary in February were not met by the student: on the 7th, Law reported that Gibbon was gone to Huntingdon; on the 9th, Byrom "began to have some hopes of his writing"; on the 11th, however, he had to be sent for from "the Combination"; and on the 18th there was not even a message. All went well on the 25th, but the next entry about this wayward pupil is March 11 and reads, "Mr. Gibbon went to London on Wednesday last I think, without telling me, and a gentleman of his acquaintance gave me five guineas at the Music Club March 18th."[45]

Perhaps Edward thought that there was no significant discourtesy in breaking an appointment without notice when he was to pay for the other's time, but one can sympathize with Byrom's annoyance in the last three-week interval in particular. Edward Gibbon II had now left behind not only his study of shorthand but also his university career. During his university days, he had, of course, spent the long vacations in Putney, and there he had discovered that the youngest of the Porten girls, "Miss Judy," had grown up to be beautiful. Thanks to his father's acumen, young Edward was a most eligible bachelor: "on [his former fortune's] ruins, with the skill and credit of which Parliament had not been able to despoil him, [Edward Gibbon I] at a mature age erected the edifice of a new fortune. . . . The second structure was not much inferior to the first" (16). The Portens had not fared so well. The uncle Francis who had been an alderman had died three years earlier. The eldest daughter had married a Robert Darell in 1724; hers was a respectable but not a spectacular marriage.[46] The former South-sea director could see symptoms of impending ruin in the commercial activities of James Porten himself. Soon he removed his son from the dangers of Putney and sent him off to Paris, without Mr. Law. There he was supposed to learn French and to forget Judith. He did neither. He did not even see much of France, beyond the obvious attractions of Paris itself. Instead, he fell ill, requested the care of his mother's first cousin's son, Edward Acton, who was studying medicine in Paris, and recovered. A letter to his oldest sister during his convalescence (March 19, 1732) is playful and affectionate; it also suggests a difference of opinion between ascetic sister and pleasure-loving brother about the latter's diet, and a resemblance between Edward Gibbon II and his son the historian: "I believe if you was to see me you woud say [the fever] has brought me down some Degrees lower than you your self woud have me, my Double Chin to a Sharp Point, & my Belly to the Shape of a couple of Lathes."[47] Soon, however, he recovered completely from the fever; love was not so easily cured. In fact, it proved to be contagious: "During the slow recovery of his patient, the Physician himself was attacked by the malady of love: he married his mistress, renounced his country and religion, settled at Besançon, and became the father of three sons" (18). The patient seems to have been an attractive companion;

thirty years later he was still remembered with affection by those who had known him during his convalescence, even by his physician's bride, who had a reputation as a termagant.[48] Perhaps the example of his cousin-physician helped the usually changeable Edward adhere firmly to his love for Judith.

Finding the Continent an ineffective antidote to love, and unable to refuse to allow the convalescent to come home, Edward Gibbon I tried a new distraction. He saw to it that as of April 27, 1734, the new M.P. for Petersfield was his son.[49] The scheme succeeded to some extent; as we shall see, Edward II was quite impressed with his own importance as he ran the country, and the romance obviously suffered delay. Perhaps the stern father was actually unaware of the extent of the attachment between Edward and Judith; they thought they had concealed it from him, despite the warnings he received from at least one of his daughters, Catherine Elliston. Mr. Gibbon could not readily prevent accidental meetings in the park or on the bridge, in the course of an evening's walk, but he was unaccustomed to disobedience; "his children trembled in his presence." Tradition further informed his grandson that "the independent visitors, who might have smiled at his anger were awed by his frown; and as he was the richest, or wisest or oldest of his neighbours, he soon became the oracle and the tyrant of a petty Kingdom" (16). Certainly Edward and Judith dared not defy him openly. But constancy despite opposition "is the beginning of a love tale at Babylon or at Putney" (19).

Furthermore, they could not count on the cooperation of Judith's parents. They would have welcomed the match had Mr. Gibbon not objected to it, but when it came to the point, her father had his pride. And Mr. Porten could not be unjust to his other children in order to give Judith a portion that would satisfy Mr. Gibbon's reasonable or unreasonable expectations. So, as the lovers' son summed it up, "The usual consequences ensued: harsh threats and tender protestations frowns and sighs; the seclusion of the Lady, the despair of the Lover; clandestine correspondence and stolen interviews" (19).

The best evidence of all these consequences is the extant remains of the clandestine correspondence, the very existence of which, as all readers of Richardson and Jane Austen know, was tantamount to an engagement, unless one of the parties were a Lovelace or a Willoughby.[50] Like Clarissa's, however, Judith's first letter appears to have been one of demurral, or even denial. It was not preserved, but Edward's answer, endorsed "1" and carefully saved by Judith, begins, sternly and indignantly:

Madm/
    The Pleasure your Favour gave me was very short, and lasted no longer, than till I had read the Contents of it, for then I felt the Contrary Passion in the highest manner, & shall feel it; for since the reading over & over again of your Letter won't cure it, I am sure nothing will;

I tryed it several times both last Night & this Morning, in hopes it wou'd bring me to that same degree of Indifference it was wrote with, but all in vain, my Passion has taken too deep Root, & I will say it to, has the strongest Foundations. I don't mean so much your External as your Internal Beauties:—It has had too, Madm. pretty strong Tryals, For I have refused thousands, & ten Thousands [he presumably means to refer to the amounts of the ladies' fortunes, not to the number of ladies], for Love of you, & if repeated Perswasions that you tell me of, cou'd have prevailed, shou'd not be now in the state I am in.

His mood, pride satisfied, mellowed somewhat in the next part of the letter, in which he asked why he flattered himself that "so great Merit" as hers might be his and supposed that she had made a worthier choice. But "you had only a Mind to divert your self a little, & as you now see how serious a thing it's become to me, you advize to break off, as it seems attended with so many Difficulties."

One suspects that much of this is fustian, or at least self-dramatization, but surely there is a touch also of genuine hurt, albeit not despair, when he asks, "You insists upon my giving my Sentiments without Reserve, why did not you give yours at once, Without that going abt., & tell me fairly you did not coud not love." His further protest, that he should then have tried to endure his misery philosophically, even to be comforted slightly by the prospect of Judith's being happier, is less convincing.

From this sublime rhetoric he descended immediately to some comically practical considerations: "You are certainly right in your Conjecture with regard to my Sister, & so am I too, that you knew it as well as I did, My Father highly approves her Conduct in it, so that you may imagine how I am Worrited."

This first letter is dated January 18, 1734/35. It concludes, "my future Happiness or Misery . . . I protest, Dr. Mis Judy, entirely depends upon you." Judith's reply makes evident not only her grateful and affectionate nature but also her possession of some wit and spirit of her own:

[W]hen I consider what I'm abt, I cant help being under some uneasiness least I shou'd act wrong, for 'tis reckon'd an indiscretion to proceed, in such an affair, without the knowledge of ones family, but whn I reflect upon the honour & character of the person I corrispond wth, and the many obligations I have to him, solve it to my self, ths way, tht I'm going on in the only way to bring tht abt wch will give me the greatest satisfaction, provided tis wth their approbation. . . . I'm affraid you think none of our sex can keep a secret, by yr asking whether I have told Miss Kitty, & sister french, but however I will satisfie yr Quere, in the clearest manner I can . . . I have found it the best way neither to deny, nor own it . . . since I agree with you, tht we may ask questions without reserve, give me leave to ask, whether, yu ever talk'd with yr father, upon the Subject, or whether he has all his intelligence from Mrs. E— also who first put it in her head, & who has influenced Ldy A, & if Mrs T— is at the bottom of it.

Sauce for the goose, she implies, is sauce for the gander. Although her letters never fall into the self-important posturing that Edward's sometimes betray, she too enjoyed at times the game of secret courtship: "You wou'd hardly guess how difficult I find it to conversse, in ths way [i.e., by letter], and cou'd never do it, but for learning french, wch they think I apply much too, but you may guess, how I'm likely to improve."

Indeed, though Edward II is more attractive in this correspondence than in any other role in which posterity can observe him, it is Judith who comes alive in these letters and whose sweetness and simplicity are appealing in them. Several weeks after the letter just quoted, for example, in obvious reply to an Edward not content with the compliment of a secret engagement and the praise she had already bestowed on him, she says:

Had you been Equal in circumstances I might have said more, but now am so afraid you shou'd think fortune has any weight wth me, that I have been cautious upon tht account, & no other, but Since you press me to speak more plainly, you must not think the worss of me for dealing ingeniously, & owning freely, that I shou'd be quite happy, in spending my life with you, I think ths is telling you no more, than you knew before, for beleive me, I shou'd never have behav'd in ths manner, unless I had prefer'd you before all others, I suppose what you said of yr person, you meant in banter, & as for yr temper, & behaviour, they must suffer by an alteration.

It is not surprising that Edward, vain and yet in need of the constant reassurance of open and whole-hearted admiration, loved her.

His gaiety and his attachment to her are attractive qualities, and his vanity and thoughtlessness seem naive and relatively inoffensive at this stage of his life. He is a statesman:

We [the House of Commons] sat last Night till Eight o'Clock, & I was obliged to be out this Morning by Seven, & have been abt. ever since, I steal this at a Coffee House where I am Waiting for a Gentleman for tho' my Business is no less than the Good of the Nation I am quite miserable If I can't find an Oportunity of writing to you. . . . I expect to see you to morrow Night at the French Play House, where I shall certainly attend.

Or he is a philosopher:

What are Riches, what's a great Fortune, to the Real Satisfaction & true Enjoyment of Life, we may have in each other, I remember a Character in the first Volume of Spectators (which as you are conversant with, must have occurred to you,) it's under the name of Aurelia,[51] I wish I cou'd make it answer as well on my side, as it does on yours, but however I propose it as worthy the highest Imitation. If we consider Life in the same Situation they did, & indeed there is not a great Deal of Philosophy required to do it, for if we reflect at all, we shall naturaly fall into the same Way of thinking, & then what signifyes it whether we have five hundred a year, or five thousand.

One's impression is that he, the pampered only son of a rich albeit stern and forbidding father, does not really fear any serious barrier to their happiness, while she, despite her closer relationship with more affectionate parents, rather hopes than expects that she and Edward will have their way.

By May 29, Edward had become impatient:

> The Pleasure My Dearest Mis Judy, your Letters give me, make amends in a great Measure for the Many Crosses & Disapointments I meet with as well from your Folks, as my Own, What can be the Meaning of yours, for as they always before treated me with the greatest good Manners & Complaisance in the World, it's now truly I see it is with the greatest Difficulty they can be tolerably civil to me.

None of his impatience was directed against her, however:

> I find the greatest Benefit from your Letters in ye World, for when ever I find my self low spirited, or in the Vapours, I have nothing to do, but go to my Desk & there am sure of a Certain Specifick, they give such a fine Turn to the Spirits, & Create such pleasing & Charming Ideas, that I'm well presently.

His mercurial spirits actually required more solid support, however, as the remainder of the letter makes clear; until she was actually his, his depression would return—perhaps his metaphor suggests that her letters were not his only remedy for it:

> But even this too, like all other joys, has a Damper comes after it, for as the more I read the more I love, & this reading naturaly brings a Reflection, but when shall I be in possession too, of the Sweet Author. The thought of that *When*, makes all my Spirits subside again, & tho' at the Beginning I said I found the greatest Benefit, Yet it's only like drinking Drams, which flatter & raise ones Spirits a little at first, but afterwards depress you ten times more than they were before, & will at last as effectualy destroy me as the other wou'd.

It was his own father who was the most significant obstacle, as Edward fully realized, despite his rhetorical questions and maledictions against fate. The letter continues:

But be assured that to my latest Breath I shall always love & esteem My Dearest Judy Porten, Oh! Why can't I alter that Name? But on the Contrary I find all my Endeavours to do it, by some Curs'd Fate, rendre'd abortive, My Father taking all Methods & trying by a thousand Subtleties to put it of, but the greatest Farce of all is his having me apply for two or three Months to my Studys [Edward, never scholarly, was now twenty-eight years old and an M.P.!] It's Plain he never knew what it was to be in love so can easily excuse his talking in that Manner, but however I tryed his Expedient, (but dont infer from thence I wanted to be cur'd of my Passion) & have attempted to read a little but alas! I can see no other Letters in the Book but those that spell your Dear Name
At other times My Pen & Ink I take
But still no Marks but J & P. I make.
I was in your Debt some Poetry, but now I beg we may quit Scores, for I can't go on with you. I'll be no longer impertinent, but haste to give you this which perhaps you may be tired of before you have got half thro'.

It is clear, on the whole, that he was annoyed but not seriously afraid of being permanently thwarted. A series of undated letters from Judith are very different in tone. The postscript of Edward's letter of May 29 promises to send to "JT," whom Judith recommends as a go-between in the second of these undated letters, which may therefore be assigned to late May and early June of 1735.[52]

She had begun by approaching her mother, on Thursday morning, perhaps May 22. She told Edward,

[E]xactly at ten, I went to mamma, told her what you bid me & in the manner you directed, she heard all I had to say, look'd very serene, & only said, she thought I was much oblig'd to you, for yr good opinion of me, but that she fanc'd yr family wou'd never come into it, neither cou'd she judge, what pappa wou'd do, that I ought to be quite pasive in it, & make my self Easey, either way. . . . I am determin'd to hope the best, & not anticipate misfortunes, for tho pappa's answer shou'd not be quite so favourable as one cou'd wish, tis possible, a little time & reflection, may alter his resolutions in our favour, Especially when he finds my happiness intirely depends upon it. . . . Adieu dear Mr Gibbon it may be the last time, it is ever proper to call you by that name.

A few days later she had "a long Conference" with her father:

He told me you had been with him in town, upon this affair, & that he had given you no direct answer, for it requir'd some time to consider it, that it was a very great offer, & paying our family a compliment, we cou'd no ways expect, but bid me not think too much of it, least it shou'd never be Effected, I answer'd, that I alwais thought you

an agreable companion, I knew you to be perfectly well temper'd,
& Every body Esteems you a person of good sense, all wch qualifi-
cations render'd you agreable to me, but that now, I had a still stronger
motive to Esteem you, Since you have shown yr Value & regard for me,
by this offer, which in point of fortune is so greatly below you, that
Gratitude, joyn'd to the good opinion I have long had of you, wou'd
make me very uneasy, if this shou'd not be finish'd, & therefore I
hoped he wou'd contribute all in his power, to bring it about, he again
bid me not think too much of it, for he cou'd not answer for the Event,
adding you told him, yr father wou'd not stand upon an Equivalent,
but still he might insist upon a great deal more then he cou'd part with,
for he had other children to provide for, who he wou'd not injure to,
enlarge my fortune, this was the cheif of our conversation, & he argued
so calmly, that I thought it better to give my sentiments in the cool
manner above mention'd, than to put them in Stronger terms, till I
find it necessary, I asked him if he intended to speak to yr father, he
said he must consider, & seem'd to hint as if he wou'd Employ a third
person, Now I think this wou'd be much the best way, for it wou'd
prevent any passion, that might arise between the two old Gentlemen . . . in my opinion JT: is the only one, that wou'd do in this affair,
you know I cou'd not Name him, but I hint'd it to you, who may
possibly have an opportunity of advising.

In this and in other letters she displays some talent for scenic narrative,
the only hint of literary ability among Gibbon's forebears.

Edward's letter of May 29 seems to respond to this letter. Then, an
evening or so later, having failed to meet him during her evening walk, she
wrote in breathless agitation, "[P]apa . . . desir'd me . . . to tell you he
shou'd be much Oblig'd to you, if you will come down to him, any time
to Morrow Morn. . . . Adieu I shall hardly sleep more then did last night
do God bless you write to kensington, & let me know the Success at this
Meeting I am more than can Express Yrs JP."

But the hoped-for interview was not the end of their troubles. Judith's
last extant letter of 1735 tells the story very clearly:

You shall judge my dear Mr Gibbon, how different their account is
from yrs by the following, particulars. my Aunt last night walk'd with
papa, & she assures me, she represents the case to me, exactly as he did
to her, that he went to Mr T: & did absolutely talk, with the utmost
freedom to him, told him what he cou'd give, wch he Assures my Aunt
shall be to the utmost of his power, but he wont injure his other
children for any advantage, or consideration whatever, this you must
allow reasonable, tho' unhappy for us, he also told Mr T: that he wou'd
do all he possible cou'd to forward it, that he had an extream good
opinion of you, & was sensible of the honour you did him, & wou'd
act in this affair, (in regard to yr father), in the manner he shou'd
direct, as knowing his temper best, & by what I can understand, Mr. T:

has promis'd to tell yr father, what mine has said to him, & Papa is
to wait his answer, & will at any time if tis thought proper, talk or
write to yr father, this is the light they set it in to me, but how different is what you say. how cou'd Papa be so imprudent, to talk to Mr. T:
in a way he knew wou'd provoke him? why wou'd he raise any difficulty's when there are too many already? what cou'd make him object
against an Income, that we are to live upon, not him? in short I am
quite in the Vapours, & Vex'd till I was quite ill last night, & cou'd
intirely give my self up to despair, only I think there may be turns in
our favour, & that tis wrong to anticipate Misfortunes, let me beg you
therefore to have a little patience, & make yrself Easey, I own I am giving
you advise I cant take, but I think we shou'd both Endeavour it, consider, tis not in their power to make us alter our Sentiments, that neither
Fate, nor Fortune, distance, nor absence, can ever change my affec-
tions, & when you give me the same kind assurances, I cant help reflecting, that tho' we may be perplex'd for a time, it may not be for Ever.

Most revelatory of her feelings, perhaps, is the postscript of this letter,
the last written while their affairs were still in suspense: "for Godsake
take care of this, for shall never be forgiven, if tis seen." But all "their
acquaintance, the whole neighbourhood of Putney was favourable to their
wishes," and eventually even Edward's father "yielded a tardy and ungracious consent" (19). Two letters of the subsequent spring, 1736, survive;
in them, Judith shows the lovers subject to no more serious mortification
than a missed meeting or a week's separation caused by an engagement in
town: "I shou'd be very unhappy if I thought, a more agreable Engagement prevented yr coming, but I'm quite Easey in that regard . . . so look
upon this disappointment in no other light, than that Fortune was in an
ill Humour, & hinder'd you from Complying with your inclinations . . .
this you'll say is answering for yr Sentiments, & taking it for granted, tis
very true, I think I do know them, & it makes me inexpressably happy
being much more than I can Express yours Unchangably." Similarly, in
the last preserved letter, she wrote, "My . . . only Mortification, is to
know, that by being in town I'm prevented seeing my dear Mr Gibbon,
whose company it is, makes these Amusements delightfull, & Every
place Equally Agreeable. . . ."

> I wish I cou'd Convey my self to putney, as Easily as I do this letter,
> & Assure you it requires some philosophy, not to be Vastly Envious
> of those that are, there, I would Even have been Content, to have been
> my Grandmother, for the week, Only perhaps you wou'd not have
> Visited me Then . . . Adieu Love me & let me flatter my self, you won't
> spend this week, so much to yr Satisfaction, as you did last, when you
> was with your faithfull & unalterable—JP.

Their period of betrothal was not extraordinarily long by eighteenth-
century standards: they were married on June 2, 1736, less than a year

after they had approached their fathers for permission to marry. The ceremony took place at St. Christopher-le-Stocks in London, and William
Law, Edward Gibbon I's friend and Edward II's former mentor, offi-
ciated.[53]

The senior Gibbon received the young couple into his house "on the
hard terms of implicit obedience and a precarious maintenance" (19) (perhaps the £500 per annum mentioned in one of the letters—if so, not so
precarious a provision as Gibbon implies, unless they were charged for
their board and rent). The historian's account, just quoted, is presumably
based upon family tradition, and continues:

> Yet such were the charms and talents of my mother, with such soft
> dexterity did she follow and lead the morose humour of the old Tyrant,
> that in a few months she became his favourite. Could he have embraced
> the first child of which she was pregnant at the time of his decease, it is
> probable that a Will executed in anger would have been cancelled by
> affection; and that he would have moderated the shares of his two
> daughters, whom, in resentment to his son he had enriched beyond the
> measure of female inheritance. (19-20)

However warranted by the accounts he had received from the surviving
witnesses, his father and his Aunt Porten (both of whom had doted on
Judith), this sanguine description and hypothesis is not supported by the
facts, because the angry will was executed on December 1, 1736, just a
month before the "Tyrant's" death and after six months' operation of
Judith's charms.[54]

Some of Gibbon's biographers have concluded that Gibbon (and presumably his father) erred or exaggerated in regarding the will as injurious
to Edward Gibbon II. Thus Low:

> The grandfather's will was not so unfavourable as Gibbon subse-
> quently tried to make out. . . . The residue of his personal and real
> estate was to be held on trust for his son, with remainder to his sons
> and grandsons, and with powers to make jointures for his wife or wives
> up to £100 a year for every £1000 he received.
> It does not seem too bad.[55]

Low's account of the will is somewhat inaccurate, however, and he over-
looks several grievances for Edward II, even if we agree to discount the
view that the amount of the daughters' provision was unusually large.

1. The real property left in trust to Hester and her heirs (male or
female) went, in default of such issue, to "such Person or Persons Descendant or Descendants of my body or to my said Nephew the Reverend
Williams Gibbon to such person or persons Descendant or Descendants of
his body . . . as my said Daughter Hester Gibbon . . . shall direct limit or
appoint."[56] The daughter was permitted, if there were no heirs of her
body, to select heirs for her property from the designated group of direct

and collateral descendants according to her own affection or judgment, more or less as she had requested in the letter to her father mentioned above. Her brother was given no similar authority and was, moreover, the heir who would have succeeded automatically under the entail if Hester had not been given that authority. Hester's income, incidentally, has been estimated at £500, which implies that the value of her inheritance was indeed considerable, say £10,000.[57]

2. The entailed property to which Edward was heir was to go to the sons and their sons of any of his *subsequent* marriages; only failing such issue did it go to the sons and grandsons of Edward by Judith. Edward was allowed to appoint property for jointures for his future wife or wives, as described by Low, and was to enjoy his life interest in the real estate "without impeachment of wast." He was, like Hester and his married sister's husband, an executor, with the trusted Joseph Taylor, of the will. But he was given no other authority over any real property or cash whatever.

3. Hester, on the other hand, received £500 outright. This legacy might have been meant as equivalent to her sister's trousseau and to the household effects at Putney, the only bequest to Edward that was not left in trust. Or it might have been, or have seemed to be, yet another sign of the father's superior confidence in his elder daughter. The other sister, Catherine, had received a dowry of only £2,000, and that portion was not increased by the will. The implication that Catherine was unduly favored is certainly not justified. But that Hester was more trusted than Edward, and that Edward's present wife was slighted, seem quite justified inferences.

The opposition and even the testamentary dispositions of the old man were to have no adverse effects on the marriage he opposed, or on the unborn grandchild he was willing to disinherit. The devotion of the young lovers to each other, on the other hand, would strongly, if unwittingly, affect that child in three ways, and not for his good.

Their love for their child, or so it was to seem to him, was, in the first place, distinctly inferior to their love for each other. Instead, he was the charge of his mother's unmarried sister; "My mother's attention was somewhat diverted by her frequent pregnancies, by an exclusive passion for her husband, and by the dissipation of the World in which his taste and authority obliged her to mingle" (28). The boy was, at least in his judgment, clearly a loser in the Oedipal conflict. Perhaps we can sense some remaining bitterness in the account of his reaction to her death in 1746—he was nine years old: "As I had seldom enjoyed the smiles of maternal tenderness she was rather the object of my respect than of my love" (34). And he was similarly aware of the exclusiveness of his father's passion for her; the most dramatically recalled of his youthful memories is the first interview with his father "some *weeks* [emphasis mine] after the fatal event [of Judith's death]." The boy was never to forget the "fervour with which he kissed and blessed me as the sole surviving pledge of their loves" (34).

Second, his parents' way of life was dictated by the frivolous tastes of Edward, unmoderated by Judith's simpler preferences, because, as her letters lead us to anticipate, she was unwilling or unable to oppose his choice of pleasures. Gibbon thought she "vainly attempted to check with a silken rein the passions of an independent husband" (26); the letters suggest that she may not even have tried to set up her judgment in opposition to a husband she loved so deferentially and so gratefully. Even her children's illnesses need not have seemed a superior duty to her, for their father was also frequently ill, or thought himself so. After her death he wrote to his sister, "What will become of me now God knows, for as am often ayling, & have my fever continuosly, [and] from having the tendrest best Nurse in the World have nobody even to speak to at Putney." [58]

Finally, the biological result of their devotion was a constant succession of pregnancies. Judith died after fewer than 127 months of marriage; during at least 63 of those months, she was pregnant. She would have been distracted from her eldest son not only by her pregnancies and by the needs of the younger children but also by their final illnesses and deaths: only her oldest child survived her. Love tales at Babylon do not end so, but this was Putney. Although the last Edward Gibbon survived to tell the story, his infancy and boyhood could not be unmarked by it.

CHAPTER 2

Death-Filled
Infancy

M Y BODY," Gibbon remarked in
the *Memoirs*, "is still marked with the indelible scars of lancets, issues and
caustics" (29)—the doctors' contributions to the physical sufferings that
beset him from birth to puberty. He noted also that "in this early period,
the care of my mind was too frequently neglected for that of my health,"
a form of neglect not painful at the time, but acutely felt later. On the
other hand, the psychic scars he must also have suffered, not only from
these illnesses and their treatments but also from other terrors and losses
in his infancy, he did not remark. He escaped one physical trial, smallpox,
and he had one important source of emotional support, intellectual development, and physical care. That source was his mother's sister Catherine
Porten, one of "the world's perfect aunts."[1] Her loving and unselfish
support had begun with the courtship of Edward II and Judith.

Catherine Porten was the second surviving child of James and Mary
Porten of Putney. She was born December 6, 1705, approximately four
years before her beautiful sister Judith.[2] When the clandestine correspondence between Judith and Edward Gibbon began, "Miss Kitty"
was twenty-nine. Strictly, she was not "Miss Kitty" or even "Miss Catherine," but "Miss Porten," because her elder sister, Mary, had been ten
years married. Yet Catherine was "Miss Kitty" to both lovers. That she
was accorded the affectionate diminutive by Edward as well as by her
sister Judith suggests that she was not a woman who stood much upon her
own dignity; in the eighteenth century, at twenty-nine, she had probably
given up hope of marrying, but she was neither envious nor censorious.
Instead, she was observant, but sympathetic and loyal, teasing her younger
sister with acute questions, yet never betraying her. "You say . . . Miss
Kitty Guesses Most, (I hope it's all Guess)," Edward had commented in
his third letter to Judith, "& I have remarked, she takes all oportunities
of leaving us alone. Your sister French too has been very favourable to
me that Way."[3] ("Sister French" was probably a sister-in-law, perhaps a
married sister of Mary's husband, Robert Darell.)

Judith had replied, "they have both tax'd me wth it a thousand times, not only lately, but long ago, and have both observ'd so much, that they positively beleive it, & put it to me so closely, tht I have found it the best way neither to deny, nor own it, for whn I offer to deny it, they bid me say no more, I need not tell a lie, for they know it is so," but pausing only for a comma, Judith added, "this opinion of theirs, has I conclude, occation'd the opportunity's you mention, but they keep their sentiments to them-selves, never giving the least hint tht way, to any body but my self."[4] Catherine's discreet teasing is alluded to until the lovers have approached their parents. Then it is "Miss Kitty is quite on our side" and "at the distance of forty years my aunt Catherine Porten could relate with pleasure the innocent artifices which she practised to second or screen her beloved sister" (19).[5] No wonder Edward and Judith willingly entrusted their son to so reliable and affectionate an ally; not surprisingly, Catherine considered the children of their marriage as almost her own.

Gibbon's secure possession of the love and attention of this maternal substitute may have made him considerable amends for his failures with his parents, but the compensatory effect would have been limited by one trait in Catherine Porten's character: she was extremely deferential to his parents, so much so that his stepmother later criticized her failure to intervene between Gibbon and his father's wrath in a crisis of his adolescence (see Chap. 5), calling her an "old Cat."[6] Following his aunt's own lead, then, Gibbon would have rated her below his parents and would therefore have felt that he himself had won only a lesser prize. With this limitation, however, she mothered him—mind, body, and spirit—most truly and quite satisfyingly.

As for the young couple, their son wrote, "About four months before the birth of their eldest son [i.e., himself] my parents were delivered from a state of servitude [by the death of Edward Gibbon I], and my father inherited a considerable estate, which was magnified in his own eyes by flattery and hope" (25). Though the house was officially in mourning when Gibbon was born, "the tears of a [Gibbon] son are seldom lasting" (150), and resentment of the old man's will helped to banish grief. Decorum, however, was necessarily maintained, for both William Law and the formidable elder sister, Hester, worthy grandchild of the first Hester, were still resident in the Gibbon house at Putney. When John Byrom called on April 13, 1737, he arrived shortly after 2 P.M., as "the dinner was just going up":

> Mr Law was in the dining Parlour by himself, I went in and came out again, and upon Miss G telling me it was he, I went in again, and he said, Are you but just come in? and I sat down by the fire and they came in to dinner, and being asked, I excused myself and said that I had dined, and Mr. Gibbon saying Where? I said. On the other side

the bridge. . . . After dinner I sat to the table and drank a few glasses of champagne. Mr. Law eat of the soup, beef &c. and drank two glasses of red wine, one Church and King, the other, All friends; Mr. Gibbon fell asleep.[7]

The mixture of country hours and afternoon champagne perhaps epitomizes the varying strands in the household. That Hester, not Judith, functioned as hostess was not surprising; Judith's first child was born just two weeks later.

An eighteenth-century child's first hours of life seem perilous at best to us. A would-be reformer in 1768 described the treatment of the newborn then usual: "As soon as a child is born [the practice is] to cram a Dab of Butter and Sugar down its throat, a little Oil, Panada, Caudle, or some such unwholesome Mess"—or, in some circles, a little roast pig(!)[8] During the six or seven hours between birth and being put to the breast, a fashionable infant would be given "a teaspoonful every 2–3 hours of honey wine," or, if older ideas prevailed, of "pap"—bread soaked in water or in milk and water.[9]

Nor were the attacks upon his or her digestion the newborn infant's only problem. "They think a newborn Infant cannot be kept too warm: from this Prejudice they load it and bind it with Flannels, Wrappers, Swathes, Stays etc commonly called Cloathes, which all together are almost equal to its own Weight."[10] Gibbon, who was small-boned and frail, had (or soon acquired from the ponderous wrappings) a "crazy frame . . . crooked and deformed" (28), but the anxieties about his survival cannot have been acute at first, because his baptism was deferred for a not uncommon period of two weeks, to May 13 (O.S.)[11] On Sunday, May 15, Byrom recorded: "They have had great doings here at the christening of Mr. Gibbon's son. I called there last night to ask how they did, and [they] asked me to take a bed there, but I excused myself. . . . Our landlady says that his lady had no fortune, but was a young lady of good family and reputation, and that old Mr. Gibbon led her to church and back again. It is a most charming day."[12]

The sunshine of that day was a brighter interlude than most in the infant's life. Put to a wet nurse for the three or four months it was then fashionable to allow before weaning, he suffered the unusual additional distress of his nurse's losing her milk, which brought upon him the psychological as well as physical misfortune of abrupt deprivation of the breast. Perhaps, like Samuel Johnson, he acquired some of the diseases that beset his infancy from his nurse, although Johnson's worst disease, scrofula, is not mentioned in the long and nearly comprehensive tally of Gibbon's childhood ailments. Moreover, his nurse may have been negligent as well as unfortunate, because his Aunt Kitty later told him "with tears in her eyes, how [he] was starved by" the nurse (28). In a letter he wrote when his aunt died, Gibbon recalled, "I was a puny child neglected by my Mother, starved by my nurse, and of whose being very little care or expectation was entertained; without her [i.e., his aunt's] maternal vigilance, I should either have been in my grave, or imperfectly lived a crooked ricketty monster a burthen to myself and others."[13]

Where was his mother, Judith? Wherever his father was, and that might be anywhere where there were convivial companions, but was not likely to be Putney, where he fell asleep after an early dinner. As an M.P., he had a good excuse for the London life he enjoyed and apparently ornamented:

> The World was open before him: his spirit was lively, his appearance splendid, his aspect chearful, his address polite: he gracefully moved in the highest circles of society, and I have heard him boast that he was the only member of opposition admitted into the old Club at White's where the first names of the Country were often rejected. Yet such was the pleasing flexibility of his temper that he could accommodate himself with ease and almost with indifference to every class; to a meeting of Lords or farmers, of Citizens or Foxhunters: and without being admired as a wit, Mr Gibbon was every where beloved as a companion and esteemed as a man. (26-27)[14]

Before their sickly son was nine months old, moreover, Judith was pregnant again, and perhaps the young parents did not worry about a succession apparently so easy to secure.

The new baby was also a boy and was named for his Porten grandfather, James. He was baptized at Putney, on October 20, 1738, fifteen days after his birth. We know nothing about the illnesses of this child, but he did not simply pine away, as Gibbon and his biographers state or imply. He lived fifteen and one-half months, quite long enough to give his older brother (who was seventeen months old at James's birth) the experience of a rival sibling, although Gibbon, less than three when James died January 22, 1739/40, did not consciously remember him. This first death among their offspring must have upset the young parents, however absorbed in each other they were, and however inured to infant mortality we may imagine eighteenth-century people to have been. Presumably they avoided discussing James's illness and death in front of "Ted" (as they called their older baby), but the child could not have been unaware of the upheaval in the house and the distress of his elders.[15] Soon the household experienced another change: Hester Gibbon and Mr. Law decided to move out.[16] They did not immediately take up residence in the same house, so the debate, if any, about the propriety of that decision would not yet have arisen.[17] Probably neither had spent much time in the children's section of the house. At family prayers and meals and gatherings, however, they had been a part of the little boy's experience for a lifetime; his little brother's birth and death, and the adults' departure, were his first intimations that the population of his own world was unstable. He soon had reason to suspect that he himself was vulnerable also.

The anxieties, at least of Aunt Kitty, about Gibbon's own health, were apparently continuous, though of course the various maladies cannot be dated, except the continuing problem of his "deformed" frame. His ills from infancy to puberty he later enumerated, not failing to note his preservation from *one*, smallpox, by the innovative precaution of innoculation:

> I was successively afflicted by lethargies and feavers; by opposite tendencies to a consumptive and a dropsical habit; by a contraction of my nerves, a fistula in my eye, and the bite of a dog most vehemently suspected of madness. . . . From Sir Hans Sloane and Dr Mead, to Ward and the Chevalier Taylor every practitioner was called to my aid: the fees of Doctors were swelled by the bills of Apothecaries and Surgeons: there was a time when I swallowed more Physic than food; and my body is still marked with the indelible scars of lancets, issues, and caustics. (29)

Dramatic as this description is, we who read it in the twentieth century can have no very vivid sense of the actual misery of the boy who experienced the "torture" of the physicians as well as of the illnesses. The remedies were at best useless. One of the less appalling treatments, for example, prescribed by one authority for *all* infantile illnesses, on the theory that they all arose from hyperacidity, was calcium carbonate, for example, powdered oyster shells, "½–1½ drachms suspended in syrup every two hours, or every four hours for two days," followed by an aperient; rhubarb was recommended.[18] Though hardly the cure-all it was thought to be, this treatment would not in itself be unpleasant or harmful and might occasionally even work. But the most advanced writer on rickets still held to the humor theory, though he was humane enough to recommend against one treatment dictated by that theory, the application of a cautery "between the Second and Third turning Joynt of the Neck," on the grounds of the "vehemence of the pain . . . therefore we allow rather of incision with a sharp Penknife."[19] We may hope that Gibbon was treated for his "ricketty" frame by a physician with such advanced views, but the terror of the approaching knife might have been as disturbing as that of the hot iron.

Whatever the treatment, he was subjected to pain he could not possibly understand, by overwhelmingly powerful adults, in the presence of, or at least with the consent of, those to whom he turned for love and nourishment. Among his other sufferings, blistering should be included, for it (in addition to the use of the penknife) was allowed in the treatment of rickets. Furthermore, Gibbon's reference to lancets indicates that some of his physicians considered bleeding an appropriate treatment for children, though that was and remained a matter of controversy.[20]

Except for the oyster shell and rhubarb regime (if Gibbon was ever lucky enough to receive so mild a treatment—we do not know whether any of his doctors accepted this approach), the taking of "physic" was also a far more distressing experience than we may realize. "Physic" consisted primarily of emetics, purges, and opium drafts. When adults "took physic" they often resigned themselves to a day unfit for any other activities; children experienced the same discomfort, with the added distress of not understanding why they were being so tortured by their loving elders.

That Gibbon actually felt at least some of the rejection and insecurity a prolonged period of illness and such treatment might be expected to produce is suggested by a revealing error in his memoirs. Although he had sent for information about his family from the Putney Parish Register and had means to correct his faulty memory, he persisted in saying that his brothers were *all* successively christened Edward. In fact, however, only one brother was given that name—James Edward, born July 18, 1740, and christened August 15. Only once, therefore, and that at the age of three, did Gibbon experience this sign that his elders despaired of his life and treated him as in some respect replaceable. Though it seems improbable that the sick child would have been taken to James Edward's christening— perhaps he was not even told of his new brother's name at the time—the event obviously impressed him strongly, or he would not have generalized it.

Although it was his aunt who, he believed, spent "many wakeful nights" beside his bed "in trembling expectation that each hour would be [his] last" (28), his parents spared no ingenuity or expense in procuring medical care for him. Sir Hans Sloane was one of Queen Anne's physicians (albeit a Whig) and an authority on diseases of the eye; he may have been consulted about the fistula Gibbon mentions.[21] Richard Mead, who had studied at Leyden and held M.D. degrees from both Padua and Oxford, "commonly charged a guinea as an office fee, two guineas or more for a visit to patients in good standing and . . . wrote half-guinea prescriptions for the apothecaries while sitting in his coffee-house, without seeing the patient. His average income was between £5,000 and £6,000 per annum, which had a purchasing power of over three times its equivalent in modern [1929] money."[22] That would mean at least $75,000 in 1929 dollars. Sloane was seventy-seven in the year of Gibbon's birth, and Mead was sixty-four, so, although they did not die until 1753 and 1754 respectively, it may be inferred that they were consulted earlier than John Taylor (who was only thirty-four in 1737), and we know that Joshua Ward was first consulted in 1750.[23] Of course Gibbon was also attended by numerous nameless local apothecaries and physicians.

"Of the various and frequent disorders of my childhood my own recollection is dark," Gibbon tells us, "nor do I wish to expatiate on so disgusting a topic" (29). Allowing for the eighteenth-century force of "disgusting" (distasteful), we may still speculate that the memories were lost because they were so painful. His remembering nothing about them before the age of four requires no explanation, for it is not uncommon; but his childhood disorders continued until he was about fourteen, and therefore they might have been remembered, if they had not been suppressed. Simply too early to remember, however, was his first induction into learning; there is no reason to suppose it painful.

In the *Memoirs* Gibbon says that he was taught "the arts of reading writing and vulgar Arithmetic" as soon as he had learned to talk, but "So remote is the date so vague is the memory of their origin in myself, that were not the error corrected by Analogy I should be tempted to conceive them as innate" (30). He acquired these rudiments "at home *or* at a day school at Putney" (emphasis mine; most biographers misread "or" as "and"); that he does not know which, supports his claim that he does not remember a time when he did not have these elementary skills, a claim that Low found incredible. [24] But if Emerson's father could complain that Ralph, aged three, was a "dull scholar" because he did not read "very well," it is not surprising that Gibbon's introduction to the rudiments was equally early. [25]

In a letter of 1786, Gibbon appears to attribute his earliest lessons to his faithful Aunt Kitty: "To her instructions I owe the first rudiments of knowledge, the first exercise of reason, and a taste for books which is still the pleasure and glory of my life, and though she taught me neither language nor science, she was certainly the most useful praeceptor, I ever had." [26] This may, however, refer to slightly more advanced studies; in the *Memoirs* he put it, "Pain and languor were often soothed by the voice of instruction and amusement: and to her kind lessons I ascribe my early and invincible love of reading, which I would not exchange for the treasures of India" (36). Obviously she patiently read favorite stories to him, over and over, as children have always preferred. As he noted, "I should perhaps be astonished were it possible to ascertain the date at which a favourite tale, was engraved by frequent repetition in my memory; the cavern of the winds, the palace of Felicity, and the fatal moment at the end of three months or centuries, when Prince Adolphus is overtaken by Time, who had worn out so many pair of wings in the pursuit" (36). Gibbon's fragmentary note to this passage, as expanded by Bonnard, indicates that this tale is from Catherine La Mothe's romance, *l'Historie d'Hipolite, Comte de Duglas* (English translation 1708). [27] One may wonder whether it was a book from the Porten children's nursery and doubt that the South-sea director's children were supplied with such fanciful entertainment.

Most of the time, "as far back as [Gibbon could] remember," aunt and nephew were together in the house, not of his father, but of hers. It was next to Putney bridge and Putney churchyard, "an old brick house, surrounded by trees."[28] "It was there that I was allowed to spend the greatest part of my time, in sickness or in health, during . . . my parents residence in London" (36). Presumably he was also left or sent there during the crises of the births and deaths of his siblings. James Edward did not survive his first winter: he was buried at Putney on December 26, 1740. In 1741 came all the excitement of the election campaign, and another, even frailer brother: William, born September 1, was buried September 4. The exhausted Judith then had a respite from childbearing of a little more than two years (unless there was an unrecorded intervening miscarriage). Perhaps the parents found a little more time for their surviving child in this interlude; he remembered that he was at some point "praised for the readiness with which [he] could multiply and divide by memory alone two sums of several figures: such praise encouraged [his] growing talent" (30-31).

In November of 1743 the only one of his siblings of whom he later had any memory was born, his sister, Judith. Compared to the boys, she appeared quite healthy, and the parents must have felt cautiously encouraged about their offspring as they promoted their son to the dignity of a tutor and saw their daughter survive the first perils of infancy. On or about Gibbon's seventh birthday (April 27, 1744, O.S.), Mr. John Kirkby joined the household. Well educated, impoverished, and holding (like his new patron) strong political views favoring the Stuarts, Kirkby was apparently a kind and knowledgeable instructor.[29] It was he who introduced Gibbon to Latin, and he was the author of an English and Latin grammar, dedicated to Gibbon's father, which Gibbon praises in his memoirs: "The Grammar is executed with accuracy and skill, and I know not whether any better existed at the time in our language" (32).

Gibbon does not appear to have retained a very clear memory either of Kirkby or of his instruction, though he did remember, not merely discover through records, his tutor's name and the date on which he entered the household, for this information is included in a list of significant events in his early life that Gibbon later wrote down from memory, possibly in preparation for the writing of his memoirs.[30] Gibbon had pleasant memories of little Judith, an "amiable infant," who lived a little more than sixteen months. She died in March 1745. Kirkby's presence in the household lasted a little longer (eighteen months), until, in the delicate days after the abortive uprising in favor of the Stuarts in 1745, he either forgot or refused to include King George when he was reading prayers in the parish church. In the autumn of 1745, this was an offense that could not be condoned, whatever the secret sentiments of his patron, and he was dismissed.[31] Gibbon was between eight and nine years old. Between the loss of his sister and the loss of his tutor, he had acquired another brother, Stanier (baptized May 15, 1745). Although Stanier's life was, like little Judith's, "somewhat prolonged" (24), Gibbon did not later remember him, whether because his internal censor deleted this new rival, as it had not deleted the sister, or because the dismissal of his tutor and an interlude of comparatively good health had led to a family decision of far more moment to him: he was to go to school.

The early childhood of Gibbon, like that of most people, is only imperfectly recoverable, even by the subject himself. Gibbon himself was bemused by the inaccessibility of our early years: "Of these public and private scenes and of the first years of my own life, I must be indebted not to memory, but to information" (27). There is inevitably a disproportionate emphasis on crises. No doubt Gibbon had pleasant days playing in the fields and barns at Lime Grove, or watching the traffic on the river; somehow he had to encounter that dog suspected of madness, and despite the encounter, he loved dogs all his life, so he must have had animals to play with. In his *Memoirs*, he went on to note how different we are from Adam, with his instant and perfect consciousness:

> I may confidently apply to myself the common history of the whole [human] species. . . . Of a new born infant it cannot be predicated "he thinks, therefore he *is*;" it can only be affirmed "he suffers, therefore he feels." . . . . Slow is the growth of the body: that of the mind is still slower: at the age of seven years I had not attained to one half of the strength and proportions of manhood; and could the mental powers be measured with [the] same accuracy, their deficiency would be found far more considerable. The exercise of the understanding combines the past with the present; but the youthful fibres are so tender, the cells are so minute, that the first impressions are obliterated by new images; and I strive without much success to recollect the persons and objects which might appear at the time most forcibly to affect me. . . . In the entire period of ten or twelve years from our birth, our pains and pleasures, our actions and designs, are remotely connected with our present mode of existence; and, according to a just computation, we should begin to reckon our life from the age of puberty. (M 33–35)

What he remembered, and what the records show, is a constant series of deprivations and threats of annihilation, if a melodramatic word may be used. He loses breast and milk, he loses his mother to his father, he is constantly deprived of the contents of his own stomach and intestines, and even of his blood, his name is appropriated to another, new brothers are constantly produced first to rival and then to abandon him. His very habitation is moved whimsically from the Porten house to Lime Grove and back again. Only his aunt and the stories to which she and his books give him access are constant. Throughout his childhood and into his early adolescence, the premises thus established in his infancy apply: the body was a source of pain and weakness; the nuclear family, a collection of deserters or rivals; the mind—with its reliable ally, the aunt who functioned as friend or at least as contemporary as much as parent—the sole means of escape, and escape was directed to remote times and places. If his aunt had chosen to read to him tales of everyday reality, *The Spectator* or even *Pilgrim's Progress*, perhaps Gibbon would not have found the faraway lands and long ago times of the *Universal History* so instantly congenial. Instead, Gibbon enjoyed French romances, the *Arabian Nights* tales, and the "phantom of Homer" (Pope's translation). "To youthful minds . . . the marvellous is most attractive," Gibbon generalized, obviously from his own experience: "the decoration of the imaginary world is more splendid, its events more interesting, its laws more—more consonant to justice and virtue, and our ignorance is easily reconciled to the violation of probability and truth" (M 118).

In his maturity Gibbon would observe that his temper was "not very susceptible of enthusiasm" (134); he apparently thought this was an innate characteristic. But as a child, he revelled in marvels and romance as much as any born romantic. If he was skilled at arithmetic and prematurely logical, it might well be in a cause worthy of an enthusiast, even a religious enthusiast:

> Travelling one day with his aunt Mrs K Porten He said I have a great mind to Kill you. She enquired Why he should think of such a thing— He said you are a very good woman and if you die now, may go to heaven, but if you live longer you may grow wicked and go to Hell— she remonstrated that he would certainly incur great guilt by such an action & be punished for it; & go where he wished to save her from going. he instantly replied. my Godfather will answer for it—as I am not confirmed.[32]

The anecdote may well be apocryphal; neither Gibbon nor his aunt remembered the episode, which was probably recounted by his father. Yet the family found the anecdote characteristic of the boy, and its matter reminds us that extravagant fancy was not always foreign to Gibbon's character. Skepticism, as well as moderation, was thrust upon him.

These youthful traumas do not, of course, explain the emergence of Gibbon as a great writer. They do make it easy to see some of the attractions the writing of history, containing and controlling the past, would have had for him, the victim of a death-filled infancy. It is easy, too, to see why it was in remote times and places that his imagination chose to dwell, then and always. It is even predictable that he would write an autobiography, the ultimate gesture toward control of one's own past. Meanwhile, however, he had to face a new kind of trauma for the first but not the last time: exile. Not yet nine, sickly, imaginative, sheltered, indulged, and neglected, he found his journey across Putney Common to boarding school to be, in his own image, like crossing a vast ocean into a different world.

CHAPTER 3

Top and
Cricket-Ball

ONE OF GIBBON'S few specific memories of his mother concerned his removal to his first grammar school, which was at Kingston-upon-Thames. It was January of 1746. As they drove across Putney Common, she turned to him and admonished him "that [he was] now going into the World, and must learn to think and act for [him]self" (33). The boy was so impressed by this admonition that he always thereafter remembered the very spot where it occurred, perhaps because the truth of the implicit warning was to be vividly enacted for him.

The grammar school at Kingston-upon-Thames, founded in 1561 by Queen Elizabeth I, had about eighty boys in Gibbon's day, none of them supported by the foundation.[1] It functioned as a private preparatory school and enjoyed, under the then master, the Reverend Mr. Richard Wooddesdon, an excellent reputation. Wooddesdon was in his early forties when Gibbon entered the school and had been master there for some twelve years. Gibbon's notes about him, compiled for the *Memoirs*, are encouraging: "beloved by his boys who were numerous . . . a good scholar but within a narrow compass . . . choice of books, proper, good distribution of time." But these are notes not of Gibbon's own memories, but of Gilbert Wakefield's.[2] For eighty boys, Wooddesdon required several assistants, and Gibbon, as a beginner, was probably confided to the tuition of one of these. Whatever the reason, his personal experience was much less happy than Wakefield's. Gibbon writes feelingly of the terrors of the removal of a child from

> the luxury and freedom of a wealthy house to the frugal diet, and strict subordination of a school from the tenderness of parents, and the obse-quiousness of servants to the rude familiarity of his equals, the inso[le]nt tyranny of his seniors, and the rod, perhaps, of a cruel and capricious pædagogue . . . my timid reserve was astonished by the crowd and tumult of the school. . . . By the common methods of discipline, at the expence of many tears and some blood, I purchased the knowledge of the Latin syntax. (33)

The common method was of course the committing to memory, under threat of corporal punishment, of the rules and paradigms of Latin grammar, with the mnemonic verses containing exceptions. Gibbon's excellent though not minutely precise memory should have made these exercises easy for him, insofar as the mere repeating of rules and set passages was concerned.

Perhaps, like Samuel Johnson, Gibbon had trouble when what was required was not the exact repetition of material from the grammar, but applications such as going "through the same person in all the Moods and Tenses";[3] certainly "construing" presented its difficulties. Perhaps he was simply too frightened to remember. A kind master enforced his instruction with the rod only when there was negligence, when a boy had failed to learn his lessons. A capricious master, however, might punish him for any error or ignorance, however inescapable. Johnson's schoolmaster, Hunter, "would beat a boy equally for not knowing a thing, as for neglecting to know it. . . . For instance, he would call a boy up and ask him Latin for a candlestick, which the boy could not expect to be asked."[4] Gibbon recalled no such arbitrary punishment as that, but he may have been punished for failing to understand a corrupt text: "a schoolboy may have been whipt"—he complained, possibly concealing the personal in the universal—"for misapprehending a passage, which Bentley could not restore, and which Burman could not explain" (34).

The texts chosen for Kingston school were Phaedrus and Cornelius Nepos, and Gibbon long possessed the "dirty volumes . . . which [he] painfully construed and darkly understood" (33). These works were, in themselves, well selected, he was later to think:

> The *lives* of Cornelius Nepos . . . are composed in the style of the purest age: his simplicity is elegant, his brevity copious: he exhibits a series of men and manners; and with such illustrations, as every pedant is not indeed qualified to give, this Classic biographer may initiate a young Student in the history of Greece and Rome. The use of fables or apologues has been approved in every age from ancient India to modern Europe. . . . A fable represents the genuine characters of animals, and a skillful master might extract from Pliny and Buffon some pleasing lessons of Natural history, a science well adapted to the taste and capacity of children . . . when the text is sound, the style is perspicuous. (33-34)

But the promising possibilities of the texts were not realized in his own experience. The din of the schoolroom, the terrors of failure, and the insoluble mysteries of the faulty texts made him remember all his life the "daily tedious labours of the school, which is approached each morning with anxious and reluctant steps":

> Degrees of misery are proportioned to the mind, rather than to the object; parva leves capiunt animos:[5] and few men, in the tryals of life, have experienced a more painful sensation, than the poor school-boy, with an imperfect task, who trembles on the eve of the black Monday.

A school is the cavern of fear and sorrow: the mobility of the captive youths is chained to a book and a desk: an inflexible master commands their attention, which, every moment, is impatient to escape: they labour, like the soldiers of Persia, under the scourge; and their education is nearly finished before they can apprehend the sense or utility of the harsh lessons, which they are forced to repeat. (44)

In these sentiments Gibbon differed markedly from his great contemporary Samuel Johnson, who, however, enjoyed more success and suffered fewer difficulties in his youthful studies than did Gibbon. According to Johnson, a man's terror of failure is much worse than a schoolboy's terror of the rod.[6] W. Jackson Bate convincingly argues that this opinion is indicative of the almost obsessive need for preeminence that drove Johnson and that made unsuccessful competition the greatest of pains for him.[7] From Gibbon's reaction, we may make the complementary inference: victory was not so necessary to him as was self-direction. The images of immobility and incomprehension in his description of school life are striking and individual; perhaps we can compare his adult habit of pacing around his study as he composed the paragraphs of his history. It was the constraints suffered by the boy that made him reject the "trite and lavish praise of the happiness of our boyish years" (43). The schoolboy's "blind and absolute dependence may be necessary, but can never be delightful: Freedom is the first wish of our heart; freedom is the first blessing of our nature: and, unless we bind ourselves with the voluntary chains of interest or passion, we advance in freedom as we advance in years" (45).

The hours of recreation were, moreover, even worse for young Gibbon than the hours of labor. Unaccustomed to the society of other children, especially to the "tyranny" the older students exercised over the younger ones, he was too frail to join in the games and never forgot "how often in the year forty six [he] was reviled and buffeted for the sins of [his] Tory ancestors" (33).

He was a resident student and thus subject to the further peril of the well-intentioned ministrations of Mrs. Wooddesdon. According to William Hayley, she "had a dangerous propensity to dabble in medicine, and thought herself perfectly able, with the aid of an ignorant apothecary, to manage the most formidable disorders. Hence, she was apt to conceal or misrepresent the illness of the children, from an unwillingness to alarm their parents."[8] Hayley, who was eight years younger than Gibbon, was of course not his contemporary at the school, and Mrs. Wooddesdon might not have been quite so dangerously self-confident in Gibbon's day. Perhaps his established bad health helped to protect him from her ministrations; he was remembered as a particularly sickly child by at least one of his fellow students.[9] In any event, because of his illnesses his residence at Kingston-upon-Thames was as much nominal as real. He spent much of his time on the Putney side of the common, suffering his usual illnesses and enjoying the care of his usual nurse, Aunt Kitty. At home there was soon another death to mourn: Stanier died in March of 1746. Eight months later, on November 18, Gibbon's mother gave birth to her seventh child, another James.[10] All went well at first, but "at the end of her Month, [Mrs. Gibbon] was taken with a Pain in one of her Breasts, which was obliged to be opened, & every body was in great hopes, it wou'd have done her a great deal of good by the great Discharge that came from it."[11] Meanwhile, the baby grew desperately ill; he was baptized on December 20 and died on December 21, aged one month and three days. He was buried on December 23, and, on Christmas day, his mother "was taken Speechless, & Senseless, & so Continued, till the next Day she Dyed."[12] She was buried at Putney on January 3, 1747. Gibbon was not yet ten.

The boy, who was of course home from school, did not remember a final interview with his mother. What he did remember was his father's "transport of grief," his "storm of passion." His aunt "bewailed a sister and a friend" (and presumably his maternal grandparents grieved for their lost daughter), the boy himself shed "some natural tears,"[13] the house was draped in black and plunged into midday gloom by drawn curtains, but most of all, "my poor father was inconsolable: and the transport of grief seemed to threaten his life or his reason" (34). When, somewhat later, Gibbon read the translation of Prévost's *Mémoires d'un homme de qualité*, "the grief of the Marquis on the death of his beloved Selima most forcibly brought to my mind the situation and behaviour of my poor father" (M 378-79)—sensibility run rampant.

For some weeks the boy did not even see his father, but the interview, when it finally came, was memorable: " . . . the awful silence, the room hung with black the mid-day tapers, his sighs and tears; his praises of my mother a saint in heaven, his solemn adjuration that I would cherish her memory, and imitate her virtues; and the fervour with which he kissed and blessed me as the sole surviving pledge of their loves" (34). This "storm of passion" gradually calmed, but Mr. Gibbon "persevered in the use of mourning" for at least three years, "much beyond . . . decency and custom" (34). Hester Gibbon apparently did not visit her brother on this occasion, but she did send Mr. Law. The grief-stricken widower wrote to thank her from Dover Street, London, January 20, 1747:

My Nerves & Spirits are (thank God) much better, tho' am far from having got over the Shock, the Loss am sure can never, as there never was truer Love & Affection, what will become of me now God knows . . . have nobody even to speak to at Putney, but miserably stalk about my great House by my self, when there, tho' indeed have not been much there, as it is not to be born, I hope & pray to God & beg you will do so for me that now am left destitute, I may not fall again into any of my Old Vices, which for want of my Dearest Companion, & thro' evil Company I may be led into.[14]

Both the self-centeredness and the sincerity of this grief are obvious; it is also obvious that his young son was, in Mr. Gibbon's mind, "nobody."

The widower, urged both by grief and by the embarrassment of his affairs, "renounced the tumult of London and the hospitality of Putney, and buried himself in the rural or rather rustic solitude of Buriton from which during several years he seldom emerged" (35). When he did emerge, it was sometimes for very uncharacteristic activities, such as visiting the pious household at King's Cliff—his sister Hester, Mr. Law, and Mrs. Hutchinson. In an undated letter written after he had ceased to be an M.P., that is, after 1748,[15] Edward Gibbon II thanked Hester for her "favors at Cliff" and observed that "If I am not something better for Cliff Spaw, certainly am from the good life I led there, as so much regularity must be the best preservative." His grief for Judith was still fresh: "Hardly an hour passes without thinking of my Dearest Wife, I pray God I make a right use of it, but fear it will always lye too heavy upon my Spirits, as can't think of it with that Resignation of mind I ought to do, I know Dear Sister you will pity me & excuse me, I can't go on any further so Adieu."[16] There is no further mention of his bad companions. Beriton, the family estate in Hampshire, allowed Mr. Gibbon to exercise his inconsiderable business talents in the relatively safe role of gentleman farmer. Passing hunts and visiting neighbors could gently enliven his melancholy solitude. His son thought his retreat was motivated not only by grief and prudence but also by "a secret inconstancy, which always adhered to his disposition" and might make the sudden transition from man of fashion to Hampshire farmer attractive to him by its very suddenness and variety (35).[17] This opinion of sudden reversals of role suggests another source of Gibbon's reluctance to be "enthusiastic" or impulsive in his adulthood: repelled by or sceptical of such extreme changes in his father, he avoided them in himself.

His father's retiring from London might have given the boy an opportunity to enjoy his parent's companionship (for Gibbon was not sent back to Kingston), but the removal from Putney meant that Gibbon could not be with his father without leaving his aunt and vice versa. It was with his aunt that he remained. His father, meanwhile, acquired a share in a new responsibility. His deceased sister's child, Catherine Elliston, who was only thirteen, was orphaned: her father died in June 1747. It was at first assumed that her closest surviving female relative, Hester Gibbon, would care for her, but Hester declined even to come to the funeral. Mr. Lockwood of Dewshall, friend and agent for the orphaned heiress, though not an executor, wrote to Hester:

> You'l Pardon me for Telling you, as I know you have th'utmost regard & affection for her, on this occation In my opinion, its absolutely Necessary, & this is th'opinion of both Mr Ellistons Executors as well as Yr Brother Gibbon who all dined wth toDay. I hope therefore you'll

not Delay this Necessary journey Miss Elliston is wth us & if you'l do us the favour to make this in yr way you'l make her very happy.[18]

Despite this appeal, Hester did not come. Instead, she invited her niece to visit her and gave her good advice about her choice of companions. Mr. Lockwood was still concerned with Catherine's affairs two and a half years later (December 1749), though it is not clear with whom the young heiress was living. It may have been with her uncle Edward, for when, several years later, she chose to move in with his friends the David Mallets, of whom Hester Gibbon disapproved, Hester blamed her brother for her niece's decision.[19]

Catherine does not mention her cousin Ted, only two years younger than she, in her letters after her father's death. They were, however, sufficiently intimate that Gibbon regularly referred to her in his letters.[20] Whether or not she lived with her uncle, Gibbon's staying with his maternal relatives, to whom she was not related, would of course have prevented their seeing much of each other.

The Portens must have been truly fond of their Gibbon grandchild, for they had other problems to occupy their minds. Three months after Judith's death, "the commercial ruin of her father . . . was accomplished and declared" (36). Mr. Porten did not become formally bankrupt (bankruptcy required the consent of one's creditors), but took the only other possible course: he absconded.[21] We do not know where he went, or exactly how long he had to stay away in order to allow his representatives time to negotiate with his creditors; he was, however, in London and at Putney in 1750.[22] In the interlude, his daughter Catherine, an untrained spinster of forty-one, was left to care for the boy, her mother, the house, and the creditors. Her brother, Stanier, who was thirty years old and a responsible person, no doubt dealt with the financial matters;[23] her mother may have been able to assist her daughter at first in other respects, but Mary Porten died less than a year later, and Gibbon says nothing about his grandmother, so it is probable that she was unable to make a very effective contribution to the household.

It certainly took many months to settle James Porten's tangled affairs. For the first eight months or so, that is, until after Christmas, 1747, his family continued to occupy the red brick house in Putney. For his grandson, the primary effect of the whole experience was that, by leaving him to range uncontrolled and often unsupervised in his grandfather's house, it "unlocked the door of a tolerable library, and [Gibbon] turned over many English pages of Poetry and romance, of history and travels" (37). The precocious ten-year-old was clearly a bright spot in Catherine's life; "more prone to encourage than to check, a curiosity above the strength of a boy," she, or, as Gibbon characteristically puts it, "her indulgent tenderness, the frankness of her temper," together with that curiosity on his part, "soon removed all distance between [them]: like friends of an equal age we freely conversed on every topic, familiar or abstruse: and it was her delight and reward to observe the first shoots of my young ideas" (37, 36). He did not, however, share her "enthusiasm for The characteristics of Shaftsbury" (M 119).

She was ignorant of the learned languages, of course, but her "natural good sense was improved by the perusal of the best books in the English language" (36). Even before Gibbon left Kingston school, she had kept alive his taste for the classics by seeing that he was "well acquainted with Pope's Homer":

> The verses of Pope accustomed my ear to the sound of poetic harmony: in the death of Hector and the shipwreck of Ulysses I tasted the new emotions of terror and pity, and seriously disputed with my aunt on the vices and virtues of the Heroes of the Trojan War. From Pope's Homer to Dryden's Virgil was an easy transition: but I know not how ... the pious Æneas did not so forcibly seize on my imagination, and I derived more pleasure from Ovid's Metamorphoses [several translations were available], especially in the fall of Phaeton, and the speeches of Ajax and Ulysses." (36-37)

It is notable that he thinks he had not experienced pity or terror until he had experienced them in books, and it is tempting to see, in his delight in the story of Phaeton, some response to the father-son relationship there depicted, and perhaps to the dangers of presumption and excess.

Whenever his aunt was required for other duties, because his father was elsewhere, preoccupied with mourning, Gibbon's reading seems to have been left entirely to his own choice, and he was not even required to continue his study of Latin, much less to begin Greek. Indeed, he disliked the study of languages and "argued with Mrs. Porten, that, were I master of Greek and Latin I must interpret to myself in English the thoughts of the Original, and that such extemporary versions must be inferior to the elaborate translations of professed scholars; a silly sophism, which could not easily be confuted by a person ignorant of any other language than her own" (42). Despite, or because of, this failure to advance in the usual rudiments of a liberal education, Gibbon regarded this year (he calls it "1748, the twelfth of my age," but it was actually 1747) as "the most propitious to the growth of [his] intellectual stature" (37).

His aunt, after the creditors had been satisfied and an annuity for her father's subsistence had been arranged, was left, in her nephew's dramatic words, "naked and destitute. Her more wealthy relations were not *absolutely* without bowels: but her noble spirit scorned a life of obligation and dependence; and after revolving several schemes, she preferred the humble industry of keeping a boarding-house for Westminster school, where she laboriously earned a competence for her old age" (37). Or, in a more temperate account probably attributable to Gibbon's stepmother, "finding herself in confined circumstances with her mother to take care of determined to fix herself as a Dame at Westminster & take Mr. Gibbon with her."[24] According to Lord Sheffield the family tradition was that she was "principally induced to this undertaking by her affection for her nephew, whose weak constitution required her constant and unremitted attention."[25] After Christmas, therefore, in January 1748, Gibbon and his aunt went to "her new house in College-street," and he was immediately entered in the school (37). He was in the second form, almost as low in the school as it was possible to be, but at least he had retained something from the instructions of Kirkby, or the sufferings at Kingston.

It must have been something of an ordeal for the weak and sheltered boy, whose sole experience outside his home had not been a happy one, to enter the great school. The schoolroom had once been the monks' dormitory. It was 96 feet long and 34 feet wide, and it held all the three hundred students except the sixth form. On one of the long sides there was a deep alcove, known as the "shell," containing a semicircle of seats and desks and one long table with benches. In front of the shell stood the headmaster's table and chair. On the right of the shell was a low door leading into the rod room. Desks extended down each side of the room and across the lower and upper ends. On the right, in the midst of the room, there was a heavy oak chest, the "lost box," and on the left, the examination table. The assistant masters had "old rough oak armchairs, each in front of his form."[26]

Another old Westminster recalled his first day vividly: "When school commenced [about 6 A.M.] I was told to take my place behind the 'examination table.' After prayers I stood up behind the table: the Headmaster and the under-master then came up, leant over the table, and examined me as to my classical knowledge."[27] Then he crossed the school to join his form. Because the school was arranged with the lowest form at one end, the highest at the other, Gibbon would have had to pass by one form to reach his assigned place.

There he would have found, by Westminster custom, an appointed helper. "For his first week every new boy was a shadow. His substance was a boy in the same form, by whom he was initiated into the day's routine, and who was responsible for his error in it. In form the shadow sat next to the substance, and they rose and fell together. The shadow [however] could not take down the substance."[28] The substance had to see that the shadow "brought the correct books up school, to take him to the bookseller's and to see him properly served out with pens, quaterns, dip, and the class books of his form; also to instruct him as to 'fagging,' 'lock-hours,' 'bounds,' 'check,' 'dress,' hours for 'school,' 'green,' 'fields,' and 'water,' and all the minutiae of school life."[29] Heavy duties.

The boys in the lower school wore black jackets and waistcoats, black or gray trousers, turn-down collars, and black "sailor's knot" ties. The week was divided into "whole-school" days (Monday, Wednesday, Friday) and "half-school" days (Tuesday, Thursday, Saturday). On half-school days there was no afternoon school, but instead, except on the Saturday half-holiday, boys were required to be in the college or their boarding-houses from 2 to 4 P.M. for study. These hours were called "lockers," and one was allowed out for such optional frills as arithmetic, French, or drawing.[30] Gibbon probably learned a little French and may have continued his arithmetical studies.[31]

The boys had to be in their places well before the lessons began, for there were morning prayers and inspection before the headmaster arrived. Monitors checked not only lateness and absences but also clean hands and faces. When the headmaster arrived, "repetition" began: the whole form recited in unison the lines they had been set to memorize, led by the *custos*, who held his office of disagreeable prominence as a punishment. After repetition, there was a breakfast hour, followed by other kinds of exercises.[32]

These included set passages. The head set a passage for the upper forms, which was "translated by the fourth, varied or controverted by the fifth and versified by the sixth and seventh";[33] the lower forms, including that of young Gibbon, had briefer passages set by the second master and of course did not aspire to the dignities of variation, controversion, or versification. On the first four days of the week there were themes, in Latin and Greek verse as well as prose for the upper forms, but in Latin prose only for Gibbon's level. Themes were followed by the appointed authors, which for the second form, where Gibbon began, were Terence, Aesop's *Fables* (in Latin, of course), *Dialogi Sacri*, and Erasmus's *Colloquies*. For the third form, to which he eventually rose, the set books were again Terence and Aesop, plus Sallust and Sturnmer's selection of Cicero's letters. Greek was begun in the fourth, to which, in his brief and interrupted stay, Gibbon did not advance.[34]

Morning school ended at noon. After dinner, school or "lockers" and compulsory games occupied the boys until 6 P.M. or later. Afternoon lessons included construing and translating from verse to prose and from prose to verse and, twice a week, an hour of music. Gibbon, who never liked music, no doubt found these two hours less of a respite than did the other boys. The traditional games were cricket—at which the younger boys had to fag for the older ones as well as carry on their own games—and, in the autumn and Whitsun halves, "Green," a form of football played in Great Dean's yard. "Green" was daily and compulsory before Christmas. The small boys were the goal keepers; there were twelve or fifteen at each end. They "had a cold time of it, poor little beggars! jackets on, but no caps, and hands deep in their pockets."[35] No wonder that the "violence and variety" of Gibbon's illnesses continued, even though, in living with his aunt, he in effect lived at home—he says, "was *cherished* at home" (39; emphasis mine).

Although at first he was her only boarder, she gradually acquired the care of a full household.[36] One effect was that, apparently for the first time, Gibbon demonstrated the capacity for warm friendship that was so marked a characteristic of his adult life. This first friend was Lionel Tollemache, third viscount Huntingtower, two or three years older than Gibbon and, of course, of higher social rank.[37] Gibbon thought that his new friend, a fellow boarder at Mrs. Porten's, would be a permanent acquisition, on the model of Achilles and Patroclus: "I formed . . . an intimate acquaintance with a young nobleman of my own age, and vainly flattered myself that our sentiments would prove as lasting as they seemed to be mutual" (39). This remark, brief as it is, reveals several interesting points about Gibbon: the indifference to an age difference (eleven and fourteen) that would usually be significant; the self-mockery for his trust in the other's feelings; the sense that Lord Huntingtower's withdrawal was a betrayal or deception, and unilateral; and perhaps a certain bourgeois snobbery, in the emphasis on his friend's rank. Gibbon first wrote that he formed *one* intimate acquaintance; the pattern of close rather than numerous friendships was to continue throughout his life.

The school year was divided into "halves," punctuated by holidays: a long weekend at Easter, three weeks at Whitsuntide (i.e., seven weeks after Easter), six or seven weeks at Barthelemy-tide (August 24), four weeks at Christmas. Although Gibbon's birthday (April 27, O.S.) never fell during a holiday while he was at Westminster, he had occasion to remember its celebration in 1749, when he was taken to see the fireworks for the Peace.[38] His first winter term—Christmas to Easter—was a long one, for Easter was fairly late (April 10). The winter term of 1750 was again a long one, but Gibbon did not experience its slow length, because in March he became desperately ill. The "regular physicians," indeed, despaired of his life. Fortunately, a Miss Dorothea Patton, a friend of the family, recommended that they turn to "Dr." Joshua Ward, a quack whose ministrations found favor with George II, Lord Chesterfield, Fielding, and other notables, as well as with the Gibbons. Though lacking in education, Ward is said to have been "well acquainted with the practice of chemistry and pharmacy" and to have "possessed considerable natural powers, with an abundant share of . . . common sense." He relied on three sorts of pills—blue, red, and purple—all thought to have contained antimony, and two of the three, arsenic.[39] The common sense was helpful, whatever the effects and contents of the pills, and Gibbon improved under Ward's care.

Gibbon's aunt, concerned about him and busy with her other boarders, may also have had to shelter and care for her ailing father. His will, dated London, April 19, 1750, mentions her with pathetic confidence and affection. "Reflecting on my Great age [about 85] and Infirmities," he says, although

in the present posture of my affairs . . . I can make no regular Will I
desire my beloved Daughter Catherine Porten to take Care to See me
Buryed wherever I Dye in the very most Private Manner leaving her to
Consult Mr ffotherby Baker my Attorney who knows all or most of
my Concerns in what Manner to divide my Effects as far as they will
goe and that she have the rest of what lawfully remains or Custom or
Charity may be deemed just to those whose affairs are entangled thro
Losses and Disappointments. . . . I wish could do for her as she highly
deserves and of all my Children has had nothing of me.

Later he added a postscript:

Upon further Reflection Should rather Choose if dye within Ten Miles
of London to be buryed . . . at Putney in the same private manner as
my Poor dear Wife . . . if I dye at any distant Place my Daughter will
order my Private Interrment Lett the tree lye where it ffalls—Signed at
my Son in Laws Edwd Gibbon Esquire Putney Thursday Seventh
June.[40]

On June 7 the Whitsun holidays were in progress, and presumably Porten
had removed with his daughter and grandson to Putney.

Despite Ward's ministrations and his escape from his most perilous condition, Gibbon was still, or again, very ill, with a "strange nervous affection which alternately contracted my legs, and produced without any
visible symptoms the most excruciating pain" (39). When the long vacation of August-September made it possible, his aunt took him to Bath
to try "bathing and pumping"—both ineffectual. At the end of the vacation she had to return to her Westminster duties, but the thirteen-year-old
Gibbon was left in Bath for "several months [until December] under the
care of a trusty maid-servant" (39). When his grandfather died (he was
buried at Putney, October 20, 1750), Gibbon presumably was not brought
home.[41]

In December a new pattern of life for the ailing boy began. He was
alternately "carried about" by his father and placed in various unsatisfactory temporary havens for the care of his mind and/or body. His first
remove must have coincided with an interlude of health, for in addition to
going to London with his father, at the end of December he was able to
make a visit to the Edward Southwells at Kings Weston, Bristol. He wrote
to his aunt: "I like the place Prodigously, I Ride out very often and Sometimes Go in Mr. Southwell Coach which Last I infinitely prefer to the
former. Kings Weston is a Most Grand House and Mr Southwell has a
Great Many Books. yesterday I went to a Chappel (it being Sunday) and
after Church upon our Return home we Veiwed the Remains of an
ancient Camp which pleased me vastly."[42] Obviously he was capable of
ordinary occupations, and probably it was when the January term began
(January 17, 1751) that he made the last "short unsuccessful tryal"

of Westminster School, although he elsewhere (M 221) says that he was removed from the school in August 1750.[43]

His illnesses allowed him only "a very small share of the civil and literary fruits of a public school"; nevertheless, Gibbon professed to approve of such schools: "A boy of spirit may acquire a prævious and practical experience of the World, and his playfellows may be the future friends of his heart or his interest." As for the secondary question, the education itself, Gibbon gave it qualified praise in a well-known passage of the *Memoirs*:

> Our seminaries of learning do not exactly correspond with the precept of a Spartan king 'that the child should be instructed in the arts which 'will be useful to the man' since a finished scholar may emerge from the head of Westminster or Eaton in total ignorance of the business and conversation of English Gentlemen in the latter end of the eighteenth century. But these schools may assume the merit of teaching all that they pretend to teach, the Latin and Greek languages: they deposit in the hands of a disciple the keys of two valuable chests; nor can he complain if they are afterwards lost or neglected by his own fault. The necessity of leading in equal ranks so many unequal powers of capacity and application will prolong to eight or ten years the juvenile studies which might be dispatched in half that time by the skillful master of a single pupil. Yet even the repetition of exercise and discipline contributes to fix in a vacant mind the verbal science of grammar and prosody: and the private or voluntary student who possesses the sense and spirit of the Classics, may offend by a false quantity the scrupulous ear of a well-flogged Critic. (38)

In 1751 his family finally realized that school life was not suitable for Gibbon, even under the protection of his aunt: "my infirmities could not be reconciled with the hours and discipline of a public seminary"; but unfortunately, "instead of a domestic tutor, who might have watched the favourable moments, and gently advanced the progress of my learning, my father was too easily content with such occasional teachers as the different places of my residence could supply" (39–40).

The picture of Gibbon's education for the next sixteen months is, as we might expect, somewhat confused. In the note of dates in his early life that is fullest and most often reliable, he says that it was in February 1751 that he was "put under the care of Mr. Philips," that is, of Philip Francis.[44] In the *Memoirs*, however, he places that event in January 1752, and although the dates in the *Memoirs* tend to be unreliable, he also says that it was the failure of this scheme that led to his father's entering him at Magdalen College, Oxford, in April 1752, a causal connection he might well have remembered accurately. The details of the manuscript note, however, are self-consistent, and it was therefore probably shortly after his visit to Bristol that he found himself at Esher in Surrey:

[That] pleasant spot . . . promised to unite the various benefits of air, exercise, and study. . . . Mr Francis was recommended . . . as a scholar and a wit. . . . Besides a young Gentleman whose name I do not remember, our family consisted only of myself, and his son. . . . It was stipulated that his father should always confine himself to a small number; and with so able a præceptor, in this private academy, the time which I had lost might have been speedily retrieved. But the experience of a few weeks was sufficient to discover that Mr Francis's spirit was too lively for his profession: and while he indulged himself in the pleasures of London, his pupils were left idle at Esher in the custody of a Dutch Usher, of low manners and contemptible learning. From such careless or unworthy hands I was indignantly rescued. (40-41)

In March, he was sent to Bath again, where he again tried the waters. Many years later, he noted in a journal that he there read, for the first time, about the Macedonians, in the *Universal History*.[45] It may also have been in this stay that he "voluntarily" (he was "never forced, and seldom . . . persuaded") "read with a Clergyman at Bath some odes of Horace, and several episodes of Virgil which gave [him] an imperfect and transient enjoyment of the Latin Poets" (40).[46] That summer he was well enough to accompany his father on a visit that had memorable consequences, to a Mr. Hoare's, in Wiltshire, where he discovered the continuation of Echard's Roman history (i.e., vols. 3-5), dealing with the successors of Constantine, material then "absolutely new" to the future historian. History had, however, long been a favorite subject for his reading:

Instead of repining at my long and frequent confinement to the chamber or the couch, I secretly rejoyced in those infirmities which delivered me from the exercises of the school and the society of my equals. As often as I was tolerably exempt from danger and pain, reading, free desultory reading, was the employment and comfort of my solitary hours: at Westminster my aunt sought only to amuse and indulge me; in my stations at Bath and Winchester, at Buriton and Putney a false compassion respected my sufferings, and I was allowed without controul or advice to gratify the wanderings of an unripe taste. My indiscriminate appetite subsided by degrees in the *Historic* line. . . . In my childish balance I presumed to weigh the systems of Scaliger and Petavius, of Marsham and Newton. . . ; the Dynasties of Assyria and Egypt were my top and cricket-ball. (41, 43)

While playing with this "top and cricket-ball," ancient chronology, he "engraved the multitude of names and dates in a clear and indelible series" (43), and a written record of such a series, a comparative chronology from the years 6000 to 1590 B.C., seems to have survived.[47]

He did not stop with chronology, however. He read all the Greek and Roman historians to whom he was led by the *Universal History* or by Hearne's *Ductus Historicus*, provided that they were available in English.

Oriental history particularly intrigued him. After discovering the successors of Constantine, he sought out more information as soon as he was taken back to Bath. First he read Howell's seventeenth-century history of the world (from the beginning to the fall of Augustulus), but then "some instinct of criticism directed [him] to the genuine sources." Before he was sixteen he had absorbed all the oriental lore available in English, as well as the French of d'Herbelot's *Bibliothèque orientale* and the Latin of Pocock's translation of a thirteenth-century Syriac chronicle (43).[48] His passionate delight in this feast of learning can hardly be overstated. In his own account, a striking series of food metaphors dramatizes the eagerness and nourishment he found in this reading. The conventional "taste" and "appetite" of his general statement become "greedily devour," "crude lumps . . . swallowed with . . . voracious appetite" when he ruminates upon the specific works and writers he consumed. When he discovered the successors of Constantine in Mr. Hoare's library, it was ironically the "summons of the dinner-bell [that] reluctantly dragged [him] from [his] intellectual feast" (42).

Gibbon later deplored the neglect of his mind that made all this gluttony possible, but he recognized that it left alive his intellectual curiosity, and, we may add, his delight in both imaginative and informative literature, in a way that might have been lost had he been well enough to receive the usual education. The passage previously quoted in which he overtly praises a school education, gives covert preference to the "voluntary student," who responds to the human and literary qualities of the classics, in spite of an occasional false quantity. He was thinking not only of Burke, to whom his fragmentary note to this passage refers, but of himself. According to Low, "Gibbon's Latin is fluent but faulty. . . . The reader gets an impression of spontaneity and animation."[49] That was after his years at Lausanne had yielded their fruit. That Gibbon never lost the spirit of the ancient works he read, and never acquired the accuracy of detail of the pure scholar, his manuscripts to the end of his life sufficiently show.[50]

More importantly, he thought of all this learning as his own domain, his entree into realms of gold, successor to the Arabian Nights adventures that had delighted him earlier. It was not the property of his masters or his elders, but his own toy, his only "top and cricket-ball." This learning became and remained an outlet for the passion, the "enthusiasm," for which he had few other outlets. H. A. Mason has argued that there is a significant sense in which Pope understood Homer better than Bentley did, for if a case or breathing escaped the poet, he never missed a characterization or an image.[51] Gibbon's earliest and most fundamental relationship with classical texts and the world from which they emerged was that of the poet, not that of the philologist.

CHAPTER 4

Oxford and Exile

T HE PROBLEM of Gibbon's illnesses had been difficult for his father; the problem of the health of the ill-educated prodigy was even more awkward for him. Though with puberty Gibbon's good health seemed established, he was still too small and slight to profit from the buffeting of games and sport, and both too clever and too sensitive to respond well to the regimentation of school instruction. A fervent patron of the circulating libraries, Gibbon was already an eager book purchaser: "My litterary wants began to multiply; the circulating libraries of London and Bath were exhausted by my importunate demands, and my expences in books surpassed the measure of my scanty allowance" (M 120). When Mr. Gibbon's friends visited the house, they "were astonished at finding [the boy] surrounded with a heap of folios, of whose titles *they* were ignorant and on whose contents *he* could pertinently discourse" (42). After two failures, the impatient father was unwilling to try again to find an adequate tutor; perhaps he felt also that Gibbon was too exclusively absorbed in his studies. And so, Mr. Gibbon's "perplexity rather than his prudence," determined his "singular and desperate" decision: on April 2, 1752, he entered his son, not yet fifteen, as a gentleman-commoner at Magdalen College, Oxford (41).

Very young university students were not unusual in the eighteenth century, and of course there were no entrance examinations or required diplomas to prevent a gentleman's entering his son whenever he chose. The choice was nevertheless far from obvious for a boy so small, so sheltered, and so unevenly prepared, despite his brilliance, as Gibbon. It is improbable that academic considerations were primary in Mr. Gibbon's choice, either of the university in general, or of Magdalen in particular. He had no great interest in scholarship, then or at any time of his life, and no reason, from his own experience, to associate a university with the actual acquisition of learning. Like Kingston School, like Westminster, like the Grand Tour, it was simply a way for a young gentleman to occupy his time in the company of his equals until he was old enough to leave his

45

father's house. Mr. Gibbon might have chosen Magdalen for its politics; the fellows were as "devoutly attached to the Old interest" (53) as he. But most probably he chose it to give his son a taste of the world he wanted him to enter, which was certainly not that of scholarship.

This is not to say that Magdalen was notably less intellectual than other colleges, but it did have a reputation for students of social, or at least financial, eminence. Daniel Parker, Gibbon's bookseller at Oxford, remarked in a letter to the *Gentleman's Magazine,* "They admit at Magdalen only men of fortune; no commoners."[1] Mr. Gibbon, perhaps remembering the unflattering care of his own father in delivering him to the university, at a greater age, under the special guard and ward of William Law, reacted to the opposite extreme with his own son. Three-and-a-half weeks before his fifteenth birthday, Gibbon became, by fiat, an adult:

> In my fifteenth year, I felt myself suddenly raised from a boy to a man: the persons whom I respected as my superiors in age and Academical rank entertained me with every mark of attention and civility; and my vanity was flattered by the velvet Cap and silk gown which discriminate a Gentleman-Commoner from a plebeian student. A decent allowance, more money than a school-boy had ever seen, was at my own disposal, and I might command, among the tradesmen of Oxford, an indefinite and dangerous latitude of credit. A key was delivered into my hands which gave me the free use of a numerous and learned library: my apartment consisted of three elegant and well furnished rooms in the new building, a stately pile, of Magdalen College. (46-47)

He probably enjoyed, for the first time, the "indispensable comfort" of a valet, for not having one was one of the most painful deprivations of the regime imposed on him in Lausanne, fourteen months later. No wonder he was never to forget his "first emotions of surprize and satisfaction" (46) at Oxford.

Whatever the expectations of his father, Gibbon himself eagerly approached Oxford as a place of learning, renowned especially for oriental scholarship,[2] and, he assumed, full of wise and learned men, who would, in the common room and dining hall to which his status as a gentleman-commoner admitted him, make "questions of litterature. . .the amusing and instructive topics of their discourse" (53). He was, of course, mistaken.[3] Young Gibbon was deeply disappointed when he found that the dinner table conversation of the Tory dons was hardly distinguishable from that he had heard among his father and his fellow Tory squires. "Their conversation stagnated in a round of College business, Tory politics, personal stories and private scandal"; they also drank so much that they encouraged still greater intemperance in the students (53).

It was not only at table that they disappointed Gibbon. Oxford professors, to his considerable indignation, were not then either required or inclined to give lectures; as a result, all the instruction devolved upon the tutors.[4] His first tutor, however, was one of "the best of the tribe":

> D[r] Waldegrave was a learned and pious man, of a mild disposition, strict morals and abstemious life, who seldom mingled in the politics or the jollity of the College. But his knowledge of the World was confined to the University; his learning was of the last, rather than the present age, his temper was indolent; his faculties, which were not of the first rate, had been relaxed by the climate; and he was satisfied, like his fellows with the slight and superficial discharge of an important trust. (54)[5]

Perhaps his conscientiousness deserves rather more credit than Gibbon gave him, yet despite the tender age of his pupil he felt no obligation to direct or control his work, but left him largely to his own devices.[6] He was also perhaps somewhat tactless: instead of challenging this ardent mind, which even proposed the study of Arabic, Dr. Waldegrave set Gibbon to construing the comedies of Terence, an exercise perhaps quite suitable to the insufficiency of Gibbon's Latin, but humiliatingly familiar as a Westminster task.

Although the daily hour so spent was dull and Gibbon soon and frequently absented himself from it, to it he owed "the sum of [his] improvement at Oxford" (54). The warmth of his retrospective contempt is well known; perhaps some of his ire derived not from the failings, great though they were, of the college and university, but from two other institutions to whose failures, as we shall see, his misdirected intellectual curiosity there exposed him: his family, that is, his father, and the Roman Catholic Church.

At first, after his initial surprise and disappointment at the mundane conversation of the fellows and the less than schoolroom quality of the intellectual atmosphere, his prime concerns were probably his lack of friends and a desire to appear adult. A visit to Dorchester to see the Progress on his birthday, when he had been at Oxford less than a month, was his first, innocent excursion away from the university.[7] The first of the debts he was allowed to incur included a purchase equally innocent, the *Bibliothèque orientale* of d'Herbelot, hardly the choice of a boy whose intellectual curiosity had been quenched.[8] His purchases may also have included new clothes; he affected the wearing of black in Hall and admired himself in his academic finery.[9] The other gentlemen-commoners (there were only five or six at Magdalen in the years 1750-52)[10] were disposed to laugh at him for his large head, his unfashionable erudition, perhaps for his errors in the classical languages and his ignorance of the world, certainly for that affectation of dress and another of arriving (dramatically?) late in Hall.[11] Finden, a fellow of the college, tartly rebuked them with the observation "that if their heads were entirely scooped, Gibbon had brains sufficient to supply them all."[12]

The talent for friendship that had first appeared at Westminster was apparently temporarily lost in the "awkward timidity" of Gibbon's adolescence. According to his own account, he "preferred his [tutor's] society to that of the younger students" (55) and walked in the evening with him to the top of Heddington Hill (about a half-hour walk).[13] According to the Reverend Samuel Parr, Gibbon entered the university "with a weakly frame of body, with a coldness of temperament, which made him stand aloof from the gaiety of companions, and from the generous sympathy of friends,"[14] but Parr was ten years younger than Gibbon, and if his account was derived from witnesses, rather than speculation, he does not so indicate. Shy, among school fellows older, larger, and more accustomed to each other's company, he certainly was; but instead of feeling physical weakness, he seems rather to have celebrated his newly acquired health, and if he was cold of temperament and aloof from friends, it was the only time in his life when he had such responses.

Instead, in all his splendor of independence, Gibbon seems to have been rather lonely; he soon sought out a friend away from the university. Early in June, he went to visit his contemporary Lord Nuneham, whom he had probably met at Westminster, at the Oxfordshire house of the latter's father.[15] Then, on July 22, the Trinity term ended, and Oxford emptied. Gibbon went to Buriton, where, "unprovided with original learning, unformed in the habits of thinking, unskilled in the arts of composition, [he] resolved—to write a book" (55). His description of his "infant labours," with their title ("The Age of Sesostris") "perhaps suggested by Voltaire's Age of Lewis XIV which was new and popular" and their contents inspired by Marsham's *Canon Chronicus,* the chronological treatise of which he was then "enamoured," makes it clear why the boy, with his small Latin and less Greek, was nevertheless recognized if not encouraged for his intellectual precocity. In the *Memoirs* Gibbon treats this first "book" with lofty patronage and rejoices that it was first relinquished and finally burnt (in 1772), but confesses or boasts that his solution of a chronological crux "for a youth of fifteen is not devoid of ingenuity" (56). The long vacation, which would ordinarily have lasted two full months, was not interrupted by "company or country diversions," but was shortened by eleven days, to the learned young chronologist's "great surprize," by the reform of the calendar. It concluded with a visit to his beloved Aunt Kitty in London.[16]

When Gibbon returned to Oxford, not yet in any serious difficulties, Dr. Waldegrave, who had accepted a college living in Sussex, was gone (55). Gibbon had a new tutor, and no friend. His feeling about being transferred unceremoniously to a new master is clear in his metaphor: he and the others were "live stock" (56). The new tutor, Dr. Winchester, totally neglected his new pupil; "except one voluntary visit to his rooms, during the eight months of his titular office, the tutor and pupill lived in the same College as strangers to each other" (57). If this observation is literally accurate, considering the size of the college and the opportunities open to gentlemen-commoners, Winchester must have almost openly avoided his duties, not merely neglected them.[17] Or Gibbon may exaggerate, betrayed into error by the rejection of another parent figure, or rather of two, for Waldegrave's unexpected departure must have been experienced as a rejection, whatever Gibbon's reason told him.

The results of the change were certainly negative. Gibbon had to find someone or something to occupy his time and attention. Instead of being driven by the "fatigue of idleness" to reading or writing, however, Gibbon was "betrayed . . . into some improprieties of conduct, ill-chosen company, late hours and inconsiderate expence" (57). His "chief pleasure was . . . travelling," and he went to London with one of his new companions, perhaps ill-chosen, from December 16 to January 8. There he was fortunately too young and bashful to enjoy the taverns and bagnios of Covent Garden (he tells us), but he certainly did not return to the safety and shelter of his aunt's house.

His companion on this and other jaunts was Thomas Powys, from Salisbury. He was seventeen when he entered Magdalen in 1750, that is, four or five years older than Gibbon; he received his M.A. degree on July 2, 1754.[18] Though he did not achieve a listing in the DNB, his prompt completion of his studies perhaps suggests, even at eighteenth-century Oxford, some intellectual ability. But he was at most only a companion, not a lasting friend, for Gibbon.

One of Gibbon's unauthorized expeditions took an unexpected turn, whose drama is concealed in the laconic entries in his note of dates:

Feby 16   went again to London with Powis
Feby 21   I saw my father in London.
Feby 24   I again returned to Oxford.[19]

Was his father amused by this illicit excursion, similar to his own when he was up at Emmanuel? Or did his wrath descend on his erring son? We cannot be sure, but the former is perhaps the more probable, despite Mr. Gibbon's irascibility, not only because Gibbon was not hurried off to Oxford instantly, but because his expectations about his father's attitude remained, in his later escapades, sanguine, as surely they could not have been had his father been harsh on this occasion.

Soon there were more "elopements." On March 27, "Buckingham & from thence to My Lord Cobham's Stow"; from April 18 to 30, another London expedition, this time alone (April 22 was Easter Sunday); on May 10, an unauthorized week at Bath.[20] "Powis" and "Cobham" indicate that Gibbon was not quite friendless, although Cobham was of Mr. Gibbon's generation (b. 1711) and his fellow M.P. (from 1732) and was therefore presumably as much or more the father's friend. In any event, Gibbon now acquired or became influenced by a more dangerous friend, a young man at Oxford with secret leanings to the proscribed religion. Gibbon omitted his name from the *Memoirs*; Lord Sheffield said he was a Mr. Molesworth.[21] From him Gibbon borrowed works of religious controversy and "bewilder[ed] [him]self in the errors of the Church of Rome" (58).

The seeds of this unexpected and unwelcome shoot had, however, according to Gibbon's own account, been planted long before, when his pious but not disputatious Aunt Kitty had been hard put to answer some of his boyish "objections to the mysteries which she strove to believe" (58). But as he chose to "grope [his] way" ("by the dim light of [his] Catchism") "to the Chappel and communion-table," which he was not obliged to seek at all, her success or her influence must have been greater than he admitted. At the same time, his spirit of controversy was spurred by hearing of two recent recipients of honorary doctorates (in 1749 and 1750) who had combatted a single antagonist: "The name of Middleton was unpopular; and his proscription very naturally tempted me to peruse his writings and those of his antagonists" (58).[22]

For young Gibbon, Middleton's attack on primitive miracles proved far more than it was meant to prove: either all miracles were false, or all were true, and it had the paradoxical effect of convincing the young reader not of the falsity of miracles, but of the truth of the Church confirmed by them. "In these dispositions, and already more than half a convert," he formed the friendship that gave him access to the Catholic apologists. He told Lord Sheffield that it was the famous Elizabethan Jesuit Robert Persons (or Parsons) whose writings he found most convincing, but in the *Memoirs,* with a certain poetic license perhaps, he gives the blame or credit to a "noble" hand, Bossuet's, whose works, in English translation, were no doubt among those that he read.[23]

Gibbon apparently began this consideration in March; if so, his solitary visit to London during Holy Week may readily be understood.[24] Though in 1792-93, when he wrote his *Memoirs*, it seemed to him "incredible that [he] could ever believe that [he] believed in Transubstan[tia]tion" (60),[25] without any discussion with a priest, and perhaps before he had met a Catholic, he had "resolved to profess [him]self a Catholic: Youth is sincere and impetuous; and a momentary glow of Enthusiasm had raised me above all temporal considerations" (60). During his "last excursion" to London (June 8, 1753), therefore, he "addressed [him]self to a Roman Catholic bookseller in Russell-street, Covent Garden," who recommended him to a priest, by whom he was received into the Church.[26]

In the first version of his memoirs Gibbon said that "the sincere change of [his] speculative opinions was not inflamed by any lively sense of devotion or enthusiasm, and that in the giddyness of [his] age [he] had not seriously weighed the temporal consequences of this rash step"

(M 130). This is almost self-contradictory, for to act without weighing the temporal consequences was surely a form of enthusiasm. What he means to suggest, of course, is that it was his mind, not merely his emotions, that converted him. His report of Chillingsworth's case may well have an unconscious touch of autobiography, even though the words are borrowed: "His doubts grew out of himself, he assisted them with all the strength of his reason: he was then too hard for himself; but finding as little quiet and repose in those victories, he quickly recovered by a new appeal to his own judgement; so that in all his sallies and retreats, he was, in fact, his own convert" (63).[27]

Whatever the relative strength of his thoughts and emotions, the new convert immediately addressed an "elaborate controversial epistle" to his father, which, though the letter had been approved by his spiritual director, he remembered, or at least described to Lord Sheffield, as "written with all the pomp, the dignity, and the self-satisfaction of a martyr."[28] His father's displeasure "rather astonished than afflicted me: when he threatened to banish and disown and disinherit a rebellious son, I cherished a secret hope that he would not be able or willing to effect his menaces, and the pride of conscience encouraged me to sustain the honourable and important part which I was now acting" (M 131). It is clear that despite his exclusion from the closeness of his parents, despite his experiences of illness and of death, despite his loss of his mother, and his various dismissals from his father's residences, Gibbon had not really expected that his father would abandon him completely. Sixteen is a relatively late age for an experience traumatic enough to alter one's personality, but in this episode we see a boy capable of quixotic, disinterested, impulsive acts, of acting out a role comparable to that of the heroes of far away and long ago on whom his imagination had fed. The man that boy became had no such desire or capacity.

Although Gibbon's potential for romantic action was not yet completely extinguished and would later manifest itself again, with further painful results, the pain of this rejection of an act of conscience, made with ardent emotional commitment; the revelation of his own impotence in the determination of his fate, and of the limitations of his father's affection, was surely of great significance. Young Gibbon had claimed a man's liberty of conscience; the penalty was reduction to the humiliating dependence of childhood, and even to babyhood, as he was, almost literally, "deprived of the use of speech and of hearing" (69). This worst of penalties was reinforced with physical discomfort, with ridicule and contempt, and with loneliness and exile.

Ridicule and contempt, together with his father's "sally of passion" (61), were the first effects. Mr. Gibbon took his son to the Mallets, at Putney, where the freethinker David Mallet plied him with philosophy by which the young convert was "rather scandalized than reclaimed" (68).

But stronger measures were in store. Eleven days after his avowal of the Church of Rome, Gibbon was dismissed from his home and country to Protestant, French-speaking Switzerland. He was sent not to Geneva, which was rather too fully populated with idle, wealthy, young Englishmen, but to Lausanne. It was the recommendation of Edward Eliot, soon to become Gibbon's cousin-in-law, who had visited Lausanne in 1746 (*Memoirs*, 68).[29] Considering Mr. Gibbon's later attitude toward Gibbon's expenditures, it is probable that the lesser cost of life in the smaller city affected his choice; there is no evidence that Mr. Gibbon made any inquiries about the variety of Protestantism to which his son would be exposed.

For the journey into exile, Gibbon was placed under the care and control of a Swiss stranger, Henri Frei. At first his "spirits were raised and kept alive by the rapid motion of the journey, the new and various scenes of the continent, and the civility of Mr Frey, a man of sense and who was not ignorant of books or the World" (69). After all, Gibbon liked traveling, and Frei, experienced in conducting young gentlemen in their travels, so far treated the expedition as one of pleasure that he bought Gibbon a knife.[30] The journey required eleven days.

At Lausanne, Frei turned him over to the care and control of one of the four "pasteurs" of the city, Daniel Pavillard.[31] The excitement of travel was over, and Gibbon found himself alone in a small room, with no fireplace (only a stove) and no servant, surrounded by a foreign language and thus unable to use speech or hearing effectively (a condition that can dismay even adults when they first encounter it, even those who enjoy the security of an early return to the linguistic and emotional familiarity of their homes), in an "old inconvenient house" in "a narrow gloomy street the most unfrequented of an unhandsome town" (70). The weather was hot, and he had to approach his unknown tutor to ask for appropriate clothing (Pavillard allowed it, on a modest scale). The food was bad, there was not enough of it, it was served at noon and seven (times to which Gibbon was unaccustomed), and, worst of all, the table linen remained unchanged for eight days at a time, offending not only sight, but smell. "My condition seemed as destitute of hope as it was devoid of pleasure: I was separated for an indefinite, which appeared an infinite, term, from my native Country; and I had lost all connection with my Catholic friends" (69–70). For a time he was even deprived of his books, which were seized at Calais and sent to Paris to be examined.[32]

Nevertheless he wrote with courage as well as bravado to his father, a month later:

> Knowing that Mr Frey had given you an account of my safe arrival . . . I chose to stay . . . to give you a more exact account of my present situation. . . . have been treated by [Mr. Pavillard], with the greatest civility

imaginable: I read French twice every day with him, I already understand almost all that is said and can ask for any common things I want.
with regard to other things the people here are extremely civil to
strangers and endeavour to make this town as agreable as possible. the
English here are Mr Townshend . . . Ld Huntingtower, Mr Crofts, and
Mr Umberstone. I have also been introduced to the Earl of Blissington
. . . as well as to Madame de Bressonê, to whom you gave me a letter
of recommendation and who is an extremely agreable woman. this
is the chief I have to say of the place, as to the climate I have reason to
think it will agree extremely well with me.[33]

His effort to appear not merely adult but urbane, a part of a distinguished
social circle, is obvious; it was his only possible defense against his reduction to childhood. If it had no effect on his father, it may at least have
enabled him to retain his self-respect, in spite of not being *quite* able, even
after a month, to ask for what he wanted or understand common conversation.

Pavillard had written to Mr. Gibbon a few days earlier, apologizing for
having let one courier depart without a letter, to tell him of his son's health,
politeness, and sweetness of character, and about the summer suit and shirts
he had allowed him. On August 15, Pavillard wrote again, praising Gibbon's progress in French, and remarking that Gibbon's friend of Westminster days, Lord Huntingtower, was in Lausanne: "He is particularly attached to my lord Huntingtower . . . who seems to like him
very much."[34]

Mr. Gibbon, however, had meanwhile written to order that his son be
kept close to the house and to his studies.[35] As all Gibbon scholars remark,
Pavillard's tactful reply gives us a high opinion of his kindness and psychological insight. Pavillard pointed out that, given Gibbon's serious character, if he were left alone in his room with his books and thoughts, his
opinions would simply harden. Gibbon would suspect Pavillard's discussions of religion of "coming from a man attached to the ideas he disap-
proves of, who wishes to make him accept them because that is what he is
paid for."[36] Pavillard believed it would be better to distract the boy, to
make him more cheerful; good company would accustom him to give-and-
take and he would see that he was not hated because of his sentiments, so
that he would have more confidence in the religious views expressed to
him. Of course it was for the father to decide.

Mr. Gibbon had also decreed that his son was to be allowed only one
Louis neuf per month in pocket money, that is, about half a guinea. Gibbon was accustomed to much more. A few days after his arrival, Gibbon
had asked for some money; not knowing Mr. Gibbon's wishes, Pavillard
had asked how much he wanted. "Two Louis neufs," was Gibbon's reply.
"Is that what your father usually gave you?" asked Pavillard. "Yes, and
even more."[37] So Pavillard had given him that amount in June and July,

but having received Mr. Gibbon's instructions, had given him only one Louis in September and October.

Mr. Gibbon's stern letter was written before he could have heard from Pavillard or Gibbon; it was dated July 21 and reached Lausanne on August 18. If Frei managed to get off a letter by the courier that Pavillard had missed (on June 30), or went back to England immediately after going to Geneva (which is unlikely), Mr. Gibbon might have heard from him about Gibbon's new suit, but none of his other repressive instructions can have had any inspiration other than his own thoughts and anger.

Despite Gibbon's brave references to English acquaintances, the English travelers passing through the city, free from constraints on time or money, could not be companions for the young exile. Instead, he made friends among the residents of Lausanne, especially as his French improved. A sign of his own good sense and healthy pride, this choice was also in keeping with Pavillard's plan for the health of Gibbon's mind, body, and soul. On August 13, although he had not had Mr. Gibbon's consent to the expense, Pavillard permitted Gibbon to begin riding lessons. Even after receiving Mr. Gibbon's letter making clear his determination to allow his son as little money as possible, Pavillard permitted Gibbon to continue the lessons.[38] Presumably about this time the twice-daily French lessons gave way, on one hand, to constant practice in daily life, and on the other, to the program of "modern history and Geography, and . . . critical perusal of French and Latin Classics" (72) that effectively began Gibbon's true education. And of course, at first only by books, but later by discussion as well, Pavillard, a sincere and relatively liberal Protestant, was alert to refute the "errors" of his pupil's chosen religion.[39] Gibbon was from the first willing to consider the arguments against his position, and of course he was on his own in countering these arguments; Pavillard's library would not have included the Catholic apologists, and the Swiss Catholics could not violate for an unknown English boy the "tacit understanding that the Protestants would abstain from any propaganda in the Catholic Cantons, and the Catholics in the Protestant ones" (272). This routine—study, controversy, exercise, society (mostly French-speaking)—characterized, not unpleasantly, not only the remainder of 1753 but 1754 as well.

We can, however, distinguish some important acquisitions in his experiences and in his "friends, among books and men" (98), attributable to this period. After "a few months, [Gibbon] was astonished by the rapidity of [his] progress" in French—he, who had never been good at languages and who had denied the value of learning them. On October 8, Lord Blessington left Lausanne; on November 15, Mr. Townshend and Mr. Crofts also left the city, and Gibbon was permitted to accompany them as far as Geneva, a little expedition neither countenanced by nor revealed to Mr. Gibbon.[40] Thereafter, Gibbon "felt the impossibility of associating with [visiting Englishmen] on equal terms, and . . . held a cold and civil correspondence" with those who came later (71).

Nevertheless he remembered one English traveler, otherwise unconnected, so far as we know, with his life. William Stewart, Viscount Mountjoy, was just two years older than Gibbon, who, recording the significant dates in his early life years later, included, "1754 March 27 Death of My Lord Mountjoy." Lord Mountjoy died in Paris on February 2, 1754, but the news would have taken some time to reach Gibbon in Lausanne.[41] It was the first time since his early childhood that Gibbon had experienced the death of a contemporary, and his remembrance of it, in view of Lord Mountjoy's not being a particularly close friend, is a sign that he was disturbed by it.

Most of his emotional energy was directed into a new channel. He tells us, "As soon as I was able to converse with the natives, I began to feel some satisfaction in their company: my awkward timidity was polished and emboldened, and, I frequented for the first time assemblies of men and women" (71). Not since the death of his sister had Gibbon enjoyed any female companionship of his own generation, except for the few days he and Kitty Elliston might have been together under his father's roof. In Lausanne, he is said to have attended a coeducational catechism class, and Pavillard had many young friends of both sexes to whom he could have introduced Gibbon.[42] Among them was a young man who regarded the pastor as "l'homme le plus honnête" that he knew and who would have seen him frequently were it not for Pavillard's many occupations and his "barbouille" wife.[43] The young man's name was George Deyverdun. He was the nephew of one of Lausanne's most illustrious scholars, C. G. de Loys de Bochat, and lived with his uncle and aunt. The date of Loys de Bochat's death (April 4, 1754) was entered in Gibbon's list of memorable dates; probably, therefore, Deyverdun was already among Gibbon's friends when his uncle died.[44] Certainly they had become acquainted before June 1, 1754, when Deyverdun noted in his diary that during his afternoon walk on the Terrasse he encountered "M. de Guibon."[45] The acquisition of such a friend as Deyverdun—especially one who, separated from a sometimes trying father, made his home with an aunt, and loved literature as much as good company—must have been, from the beginning, invaluable to the young exile.[46] This was the first in the life-long series of enduring friendships into which Gibbon channeled his capacities for warmth, generosity, and affection. Such friendships, despite one or two misjudgments in his choices, filled the space in Gibbon's emotional life that was left vacant by his immediate family, by death or by rejection.

Only Mr. Gibbon came into the latter category, and he not only sent his son away but also excluded him even from information about his own activities. It is not Gibbon's memoirs or letters, but other people's archives, that provide our scanty information about Mr. Gibbon's activities while his son was in exile. Early in 1754, for example, he thought of standing again for Parliament. He discovered, however, that "Lord M" had already promised his votes elsewhere, and complained rather petulantly:

> . . . strange behaviour sure! but there seems to be such infatuation upon this poor Country, that even a *good Catholick* shall joyn with a Dissenter to rivet on her chains. There are several of the Independents would have me stand it out, but I would not upon any account, for I find . . . it would lessen him in the opinion of a *great many people* to have him making interest for the two *present worthy candidates* against me [emphasis his or the recipient's].[47]

He hoped that this magnanimity would gain him credit for some future election. Meanwhile, he was engrossed by dreams of wealth—several memorials and letters record speculative investments and efforts to recover Edward Gibbon I's investments in Spain; farm duties—"I . . . wanted to have taken [the manor] farm in hand"; and fox hunting—"I must own I shou'd be very sorry to have any foxes killed at this time of the year [mid-April] as I design hunting nothing else for the future."[48] More ominously, he "did not enjoy with impunity the honour of being a member of the old club at White's . . . some large and nameless charges in his books must be placed to the Debtor side of play" (M 382). These debts were probably incurred (or so his son thought later) before his wife's death and his retirement to Hampshire, but the Spanish scheme failed, and thus the estate and farm had to be made to repay the loans. This demand might have been beyond the most skillful man of business; it was decidedly too much for Mr. Gibbon.

He found distraction and solace in the company of his Putney neighbors the Mallets. "The Poet's conversation . . . was easy and elegant; and his wife . . . was not deficient either in wit or cunning" (M 379). This portrayal reflects Gibbon's dislike of Mrs. Mallet and does not do justice to the Mallets' helpfulness. For "several years" they had provided a home for Mr. Gibbon's heiress niece, Catherine Elliston, thus relieving him of the obligations of guardianship, as he had relieved himself of those of parenthood (M 385). Though an "intimate friend" of his deceased wife "secretly aspired to supply as well as to alleviate the widower's loss" (M 379), Mr. Gibbon appeared to have no desire to set up a second family.

His son sought "intimate friends," characteristically, not only among his contemporaries, but among books. In 1754, two of the latter were of permanent importance:

> By a singular chance the book as well as the man [i.e., Pavillard] which contributed the most effectually to my education, has a stronger claim on my gratitude than on my admiration. Mr de Crousaz the adversary

of Bayle and Pope is not distinguished by lively fancy or profound reflexion, and even in his own country at the end of a few years, his name and writings are almost obliterated. . . . [But] his System of logic . . . may be praised as a clear and methodical abridgement of the art of reasoning from our simple ideas to the most complex operations of the human understanding. This system I studied, and meditated and abstracted, till I have obtained the free command of an universal instrument which I soon presumed to exercise on my catholic opinions. (73)

If it were exercised on his catholic opinions, of course its study must have been begun while he still had catholic opinions, that is, before December 1754, though he undoubtedly continued his work on Crousaz and engaged with Crousaz's "master Locke and his antagonist Bayle" (78) in the ensuing year. And it is probably to 1754, or at latest to the first two months of 1755, that we should attribute "a copious voluntary abstract of the *Histoire de l'Eglise et de l'Empire* by le Sueur," which Gibbon placed "in a middle line between [his] childish and [his] manly studies" (71).

Only one letter between Lausanne and Buriton survives from 1754; probably few existed. In that one, written on June 26 by Pavillard to Mr. Gibbon, the pastor enumerated in detail the popish doctrines he had "renversé" in Gibbon[49] and explained that he had expected that, with the basic tenets exploded, he could leave subordinate ones to fall without argument, but it had not proved so. Each article required particular debate; after having apparently renounced the central tenets of Catholicism, Gibbon had resumed the practice of fasting on Friday, and, Pavillard wrote, "A considerable time has been required to disabuse him and to make him understand that he erred in submitting to the practice of a Church which he no longer considered infallible."[50] Loving creature comforts, Gibbon perhaps needed to assure his conscience that he was not renouncing his chosen faith for mere bodily convenience. Or perhaps he was not so convinced as he had allowed Pavillard to believe; in the *Memoirs* he credits Pavillard with being "acute and learned on the topics of controversy," and Gibbon may have been silenced at times without having been convinced. "I was willing and I am now willing to allow him an handsome share of the honour of my conversion: yet I must observe that it was principally effected by my private reflexions" (73).

The climax of Pavillard's efforts and Gibbon's reflections was Gibbon's reception of the sacrament of Holy Communion in the church of Lausanne, Christmas Day, 1754. As Low persuasively argues, it is probable that the statement in the *Memoirs* that he "acquiesc[ed] with implicit belief in the tenets and mysteries which are adopted by the general consent of Catholics and Protestants" (74) is not ironic (except retrospectively), but literally true of the period in question.[51] Such acquiescence could seem to answer the desire for the most reliable and best supported religious position that had led him to his first change of religion, and his lengthy resistance—he had been in Lausanne for nearly a year and a half—allowed him to change his convictions without sacrificing his pride or his conscience. Although there is no evidence that any of the strictly emotional reasons for religious conversion—a sense of sin, a longing for consolation, a need for security—played a conscious role in his religious considerations, "mere Christianity"[52] would have been much more consistent with any unconscious emotional motives than would skepticism or indifference. That at least two disinterested friends, Pavillard and Deyverdun, were sincere and intelligent Protestants undoubtedly had its effect. His father's wrath, which had strengthened his heroic opposition, had turned to silence. The neglect he feared more than anger, the approval and acceptance he desired, and his newest intellectual skill, logical argument, all contributed to make him, not a disillusioned agnostic or disdainful atheist, but a relieved Protestant.

He had thus accomplished the purpose of his banishment to Switzerland. But he had done much more: he had begun to lay a solid groundwork of learning on his revived love of reading, he had discovered society, and he had made a friend. His romantic excursion into a forbidden church had ended neither in triumph nor in tragedy, but in the anticlimax of comfortable commonplace. Heroism was supplanted by moderation, at least in spiritual questions.

But Gibbon did not settle down in the placid peace of this emotionally temperate zone. Quite the contrary—he immediately involved himself in another rash escapade.

CHAPTER 5

Of Most Extraordinary Diligence

T HE LAST eight months of the year 1755," wrote Gibbon, was for him "the period of the most extraordinary diligence and rapid progress," in "the most important part of [a man of letters'] education . . . that which he bestows on himself" (74). But what of the first four months? Rapid progress might seem a natural response to Gibbon's "suspension" of the burden and distraction of personal religious inquiry at the end of December 1754. In February, indeed, he wrote to his Aunt Kitty with obvious relief, "I am now good protestant & am extremely glad of it." He summarized for her the "different mouvements of my mind, entirely catholic when I came to Lausanne, wavering long time between the two Systems & at last fixed for the protestant."[1] Low suggests that the process had been relatively swift and easy once Gibbon had enough French (and logic) to appreciate the books of controversy with which Pavillard provided him, and time enough to imagine that he had found a new "philosophical objection" to the doctrine of transsubstantiation. Says Low, "In truth it was not philosophy but weariness of what was seen to be nonsense."[2]

Weariness no doubt played a greater role than philosophy, but there is surely more evidence that Gibbon wearied of disapproval, isolation, punitive living conditions, and futile argument than that he already regarded revealed religion as nonsense. He had been sustained by "pride of conscience" (69) in his initial fervor as a convert; the "solitary *transport*" (73, emphasis mine) he recalled at his philosophical discovery suggests the role of some intellectual pride in his second change of religious opinion. To have a philosophical excuse to abandon his philosophical choice was surely helpful to his damaged self-esteem. That it was an excuse rather than a reason is indicated not only by the weakness of the argument but also by his having already read the answer to it in Bossuet (59).[3]

Thus, as Low indeed acknowledges, there is no reason to think Gibbon insincere in professing himself a Protestant, rather than a skeptic, at this point in his life.[4] Indeed the next part of his February letter to his aunt

records scruples about varieties of Protestantism. His *profession* of these
scruples might be thought insincere or self-serving; but the delay that they
had occasioned in his return to the Protestant communion and thereby
to the hope of parental approval could only have injured him and therefore could not have been self-serving. We may readily believe Gibbon at
seventeen when he speaks of doctrinal scruples, unless we are determined
to insist that great Infidels are born, not made:

> Brought up with all the ideas of the Church of England, I could scarce
> resolve to communion with Presbyterians as all the people of this coun-
> try are. I at last got over it in considering that whatever difference
> there may be between their churches & ours, in the government & disci-
> pline they still regard us as brethren & profess the same faith as us.
> determined then in my design, I declared it to the Ministers of the
> town . . . who having examined me approoved of it & permitted me to
> receive the communion with them which I did Christmass day from the
> hands of Mr Pavilliard who appeared extremely glad of it. I am so ex-
> tremely myself & do assure you feel a joy pure, & the more so as I know
> it to be not only innocent but laudable.[5]

Those two "extremelys"—he had marked out a third—may justly make
a reader suspicious, but the reason for his nervous excess is soon clear:
not irony, but guilt. Gibbon had celebrated his restoration to the accepted
fold by what must have seemed at the time an act of folly almost as
extreme as, but even less defensible than, the original fall into popery.

Though visiting Englishmen by now played little part in his social life,
in the cheer of the new year and the security of his renewed religious
respectability, he made an unfortunate exception:

> One Evening I went to Mr Gee one of the English now here. I found
> him in his room playing at Pharaon with some other Gentlemen. I
> would have retired but he desiring me to stay I took a chair & set down
> by the fire. I continued to look at the Gamesters about half an hour
> till one of them going away Gee desired me to take his place; I refused
> but on his assuring me that I might punt as low as I would at last
> complied & soon lost about half a Guinea, this Vexed me & I continued
> upon my word, the play warmed & about three a clock the next morn-
> ing I found I had lost only forty Guineas. Guess my situation (which
> I did not dare communicate to any one) such a loss & an utter impossi-
> bility of paying it. I took the worst party I could I demanded my
> revenge. they gave it me & the second meeting was still worse than the
> first. it cost me 1760 Francs, or 110 Guineas.[6]

His pocket money was one guinea a month at most, and his father's
reluctance to meet even legitimate extraordinary expenses was only
too well established. Pavillard was kind but not rich, and, in any event,
it was Madame Pavillard who held the purse strings, and she was "ill-
tempered and covetous" (69). Aunt Kitty herself, to whom he was writing

this history, did not immediately occur to him as a resource; she had at least pretended to concur in his father's harsh judgment of the young apostate, and would in any event have found such a sum almost as enormous in proportion to her income as did young Gibbon himself.

He could think of but one thing to do, and he did it. Explaining to Gee that he would have to go to England to fetch the money, he proposed to finance his journey (it had taken eleven days to travel from London to Lausanne and had cost more than £40 for him and Frei)[7] by selling his horse and watch en route—a horse and watch, however, which he had first to purchase, on credit of course, from Gee himself. Gee agreed, and "Gibbon escaped from Pavillard's house and set off in the middle of the Swiss winter. He rode as far as Geneva."[8] It must have taken at least four or five hours for a good horse and a good horseman, with good road conditions, and, whatever the state of the horse and the roads, Gibbon was no horseman. Nevertheless, he managed to get to Geneva, but there he found an insuperable difficulty: nobody would buy the horse. He tried for "some days," although his courage must have been ebbing; he had "not forgot that step would expose [him] to all the indignation of [his] father but . . . shut [his] eyes on all those considerations." When, perhaps a week later (Gibbon's estimate of the date some six years afterward), Pavillard "ran after" him, it is not surprising that with "half entreaties, half force" he could bring Gibbon back to Lausanne.[9] What had the awkward boy been living on in Geneva, and where? We do not know. He had not sold the watch, as we shall see.

Back in Lausanne, Pavillard had helped him by writing a tactful letter, on January 28, to Aunt Kitty, hinting for money:

> His behaviour has been very regular & [he] has made no slips, except that of Gaming twice & losing much more than I desired. . . . As his father has allowed him the bare necessaries but nothing more, I dare to beg you to grant him some tokens of your satisfaction. I am convinced he will employ them well & I even flatter myself he will give me the direction of them, for he has promised me never to play any more games of Chance.[10]

But March 15 was the date on which his creditors required settlement; hence the more open and frantic letter we have been reading:

> I Am there [at Lausanne] at present not knowing what to do. . . . Should I acquaint my father with it. What first-fruits of a conversion should I give him? I have then no other ressource than you; tell me not you are poor that you have not enough for yourself, I do not address myself to you as the richest but as the kindest of my relations nor do I ask it as a gift but as a loan. if you could not furnish me the whole sum let me have at least a part of it. I know you have thoughts of doing something for me by your will I beg you only to anticipate it. . . .

I am too much agitated to go on. I will tell you something of myself in my next, i e very soon. I am Dear Kitty your unfortunate nephew

E. Gibbon

PS. I have enclosed a carte Blanche, write there a promise for what you send me it may serve you with my father in case of my death.[11]

The agitation is very clear, especially in that for "death" he first wrote "debt"—two words nearly synonymous for him at the moment, perhaps.

His aunt revealed the matter to his father, much to Gibbon's indignation. Perhaps she interpreted Gibbon's "should I acquaint my father with it" as a veiled request for her to do it for him, but even given the slow communications and the need for haste, her revealing it without his consent seems a breach of trust. But at least she apparently did not make matters worse, and perhaps, not having the money herself, and knowing Edward Gibbon II better than we can, she had reason to think that telling him the whole story was the best available means of assisting her nephew. If a letter from Gibbon to his father of March 1 was written after the revelation, perhaps the wrath of Mr. Gibbon had not been so extreme as his son had expected. Though the letter "demands" the "return of your paternal tenderness, which I have forfeited by the unhappy step I have made," it continues with a hope to merit that return and a request for lessons in riding, fencing, and dancing, together with the news of the arrival of Voltaire.[12] The "unhappy step" was probably his gambling, rather than his old fault, the conversion to Catholicism, because if it were the latter, he could and would point to his happy renunciation of the error. But the calm of the letter may be a pretence, or founded in despair. The letter ends, "If I could hope to hear from you I should think myself compleatly happy." Perhaps the father's wrath was as great as Gibbon had feared, and he was punishing his son with silence.

Eventually, matters were patched up. Part of his debt was not with Gee, but with a person of Lausanne, who "heard reason easily enough [and] ... consented to receive a note by which I own the debt, and promise to pay him when I can." Gee was less obliging, but he was forced to take back the watch and the mare and consented to accept a watch worth twenty guineas, which Gibbon could buy on credit, in partial payment of the fifty Gibbon owed to him. Gibbon does not explain where the other thirty came from; perhaps from his father? The payments on the watch (two guineas per week) were to be met by retrenchment from his other expenses.[13] Perhaps Mr. Gibbon, conscious of his own weakness for gambling, was more understanding than usual; perhaps Pavillard's tact won another victory. In any case, the fatal deadline of March 15 came and went, and Gibbon not only survived but entered upon a new way of life, the eight months of extraordinary diligence upon which he remarks in his memoirs. It is notable, however, that the entire episode with Gee is suppressed in the drafts of the memoirs—suppressed, not forgotten, for it was recorded in his early journal. The episode, which showed not only naïveté and poor judgment in the loss itself but also pure folly and panic in the flight to Geneva, apparently continued to embarrass Gibbon when he remembered it as an adult, unlike his more heroic youthful escapades. Yet we can see, in the unthinking gambler, the misguided effort at "revenge" (or rather, confidence that luck would change), and the attempt to meet his problem with impetuous action rather than prudent deliberation, that Gibbon was by nature his father's son in some ways. We can also understand that in Lausanne he was again seeking to relieve his emotional discomfort by flight, just as he had done when he read romances, became ill at school, or "escaped" from Oxford. This time, however, he was brought back and aided to face and solve the problem. It is perhaps not coincidental that the next phase of his life was that in which "his mind . . . expanded to its proper form and dimensions" (M 231).

Not in the *Memoirs*, but in contemporary letters—Pavillard's as well as Gibbon's—and early journals, we are given accounts of the work of this year of greatest progress.[14] Yet if Gibbon is correct about the importance of this period to the growth of his mind, we must be surprised by the relatively limited picture he and Pavillard gave in their letters. Gibbon wrote to his father, in French:

1. My French. I know that I am far from knowing this language as well
as I might. But I may say, without fear of being contradicted by M.
Pavillard, that I know it better than most of the English I have seen at
Lausanne. 2. My dead languages. You know better than anyone my
weakness at Latin when I left England. There was then no author whom
I could read with ease, or, in consequence, with pleasure. At present
there is none I do not read fluently. I have read several recently, such as
most of the works of Cicero, Virgil, Sallust, Pliny's epistles twice, the
comedies of Terence as often, Velleius Paterculus, and I propose to read
all of them in time. As for Greek, having begun to study it only a
month or six weeks ago, I am still at the elementary rules, as you can
well understand. 3. My philosophy. I have completed the Logic of
Monsieur de Crousaz, which is highly esteemed in this country, in part
with M. Pavillard, in part by myself. I am going to read the Human
Understanding a second time, and as soon as I have finished it I will
begin the algebra that you so much recommend. 4. My dance and my
drawing. I believe that you will not be dissatisfied with my progress
in the latter subject. For the former, I do what I can.[15]

Gibbon's retrospective account of 1755 in his journal, written in 1762, differs from, but does not contradict, this account:

In the space of 8 months from the beginning of April I learnt the
principles of drawing, made myself compleat master of the French and
Latin languages which I was very superficially acquainted with before,
and wrote and translated a great deal in both. Read Cicero's Epistles ad

familiares, his Brutus, all his Orations, his dialogues de Amicitia and de Senectute, Terence twice and Pliny's Epistles; in French Giannone's History of Naples & Abbé Banier's Mythology and M. de Bochat's Memoires sur la Suisse, and wrote a very ample relation of my Tour. I likewise begun to study Greek and went thro' the Grammar. I begun to make very large collections of what I read. But what I esteem most of all, from the perusal and meditation of De Crousaz's logic, I not only understood the principles of that science but formed my mind to a habit of thinking and reasoning.[16]

We seem, then, to have a picture of these eight important months as spent in mastering Latin and French, in learning to think through the study of logic, and in studying the elements of drawing and Greek. But there is something out of focus in this picture. De Crousaz, a central figure, must, if we trust the memoirs, have been mastered to a significant extent well before the year began, for Gibbon exercised his logic on his *"catholic opinions"* (emphasis mine), which were entirely abandoned, as we have seen, before 1755 began. Therefore, at least a substantial portion of the study of the helpful logician must be attributed to 1754, and we must not see it as a sufficient occupation for eight industrious months in 1755.

His earlier language study, too, or at least his study of French, can have been superficial only in comparison to his later achievements. Perhaps the key change was that he was now teaching himself, by an arduous method he recorded and recommended in his memoirs—that of double translation. Aimed not at mere correctness but at stylistic merit, the method was far more thorough and demanding than Pavillard's lessons. Gibbon describes his practice as follows:

> I chose some Classic writer, such as Cicero and Vertot the most approved for purity and elegance of style. I translated for instance an Epistle of Cicero into French, and after throwing it aside till the words and phrases were obliterated from my memory, I re-translated my French into such Latin as I could find, and then compared each sentence of my imperfect version with the ease, the grace, the propriety of the Roman orator. A similar experiment was made on some pages of the Revolutions of Vertot; I turned them into Latin, re-turned them after a sufficient interval into my own French, and again scrutinized the resemblance or dissimilitude of the copy and the original. (74-75)

It is easy to see what progress in the languages this demanding method would require and facilitate and to believe that it "filled several books" (though none survives), but, even though Gibbon added that "this useful exercise of writing was accompanied and succeeded by the more pleasing occupation of reading the best authors," who would infer from this evidence that in the course of the same year he would be able to write a thousand-word essay correcting in Vertot "two or three mistakes of this celebrated historian"?[17] Yet he certainly did so.

The memoirs inform us also that one of the modern books attributed in the journal to this year's study, Giannone's history of Naples, in which Gibbon "observed with a critical eye the progress and abuse of Sacerdotal power, and the Revolutions of Italy in the darker ages," "may have remotely contributed to form the historian of the Roman Empire" (79). But the journal does not inform us that another book to which the memoirs attribute that important role, the life of Julian the Apostate by the Abbé de la Bletterie, was also studied in this important year. Yet it certainly was.

These facts, and a great deal of other information about Gibbon's studies in his eight months of "most extraordinary diligence," have been preserved through the survival of a "large Commonplace book," in which "this various reading which I now conducted with skill and discretion was digested according to the precept and model of Mr Locke" (79). This book, labeled by young Gibbon (in both English and French) "Common Place Book/In which I propose to write what I find remarkable in my Readings"—changed immediately to "Historical Readings"—"Begun at Lausanne March 19 1755," contains some 235 entries from at least 62 sources and is arranged, as Locke recommended, in a kind of alphabetical order. The order, however, is such that the approximate chronological order of the entries can be established. (See the Appendix.) Few of these entries have been published, but the manuscript can be used, as J. E. Norton once hinted, to determine the order and examine the range of Gibbon's reading in the last eight months of 1755, and to see first-hand evidence of how and how much his mind was growing. [18]

The picture of Gibbon's self-education in this period, exclusive of the month (September 20 to October 19) that he toured Switzerland, that we obtain from the commonplace book is one of remarkable but not linear development. It is possible to distinguish some five categories of entries in the book: translations, quotations, summaries, independent comments and brief essays, and lists of references. The first category is almost entirely confined to the early entries, more specifically, probably to entries made before April 3. The last category occurs only after Gibbon had begun writing essays in another notebook, that is, after January 19, 1756. The relations among the middle three types are more complicated, as we shall see.

But we must note the development not only in his use of his reading but in his selection of it. His selections eventually confirm his estimate of his "skill and discretion." No discretion is, however, apparent in the earliest entries, those translated into English, or more precisely into "Frenglish" (for after a year and three-quarters in Lausanne, Gibbon's English was suffering from neglect and contamination). [19] These translations are almost literal; the only liberty he takes is that of deletion. He was reading a book itself cheerfully desultory in organization, Amelot de la Houssaie's little two-volume alphabetical compendium of historical tid-bits, and he recorded romantic or sensational data about knights, duels, illustrious bastards, and the like, more or less in the order in which he encountered them in Amelot, although translation of course changed the relation to the alphabet. He moved on to a similar haphazard treatment of other popular historical works—Voltaire's *Annals de l'Empire,* Sir William Temple's history of the Netherlands, de la Hontan's *Voyages en Amerique.* He consulted Bayle's *Dictionnaire* and inserted obituary notices of Marsham and Sarpi from Rapin's well-known history of England and from a journal, the *Bibliothèque raisonnée.* All these entries were probably made before or in the early part of April, if we may trust a tempting inference from one of the last English entries, an obituary notice of Gibbon's friend Deyverdun's uncle, M. Loys de Bochat, who had died April 3, 1754. The entry was probably made on the anniversary of his death.

The earliest entries have little other interest for the student of the historian, with one important exception: surely we hear the germ of the Gibbonian ironic manner in such a passage as the following: "Tis far from this to the Tiara ["this" is the humble position of the seventh- and eighth-century popes] ; But tis far too from the first monk who preached on the banks of the Rhine to the Electoral Bonnet, or from a chief of wandering Salians to a Roman Emperor. Every grandeur is formed by little and little and every origine is inconsiderable."[20] These Gibbonian lines are a literal translation from Voltaire: "Il y a loin de-là à la Tiare. Mais il y a loin aussi du premier Moine qui prêcha sur les bords du Rhin au bonnet Electoral; & du premier Chef des Saliens errans à un Empereur Romain. Toute grandeur s'est formée peu à peu; & toute origine est petite."[21] Little as Gibbon, when older, was to respect Voltaire's practice as a historian, it is likely that Voltaire's style was one of the formative influences on the style of young Gibbon, in English as well as in French, even though Voltaire was not the model Gibbon consciously chose to emulate.

It is only with his next project that we see Gibbon undertake a more ambitious and consecutive study, of a more ambitious work, the Abbé Banier's *Mythologie et les fables expliqués par l'histoire.*[22] Gibbon's excerpts from this work appear to have been chosen by a discernible principle, and his treatment of the excerpts has also matured: the quotations are cited in the original language, and many entries are highly selective summaries rather than mere quotations. But none is a critical essay, pointing out errors or omissions in the modern scholar and derived from a comparison of the modern with classical sources; later, Gibbon's entries often take the form of such essays. It seems probable that Gibbon decided how to select his entries when he had completed the first volume and read part of volume two; the entries from this portion of the work do not occur in consecutive order, and, because Gibbon hardly read backward, it seems probable that he retraced his steps to make his entries.[23]

Banier's thesis was that fables and mythology preserved, in distorted form, historical facts. He tried to explain myths in historical ways and to relate his conclusions to known historical evidence. One characteristic of Gibbon's excerpts is their close connection to the evidence of historians and poets. At first his own contribution to the entry was simply selection: he reduced long passages to their gist by deletion and paraphrase. Banier's work begins with discussions of preliminary questions necessary for the study of mythology, moves on to theogonies, and then to "Idolatry" (vol. 1, bk. 3) and "Superstitions authorized by Idolatry" (vol. 1, bk. 4). Three of Gibbon's five entries from volume one came from these third and fourth books; none came from the first two. Evidently Gibbon was not yet interested in mythology for its own sake, or in a past too remote to be accessible to history in any form other than myth (in those pre-prehistorical times).[24]

The entries he chose dealt with cities of asylum, the sibyls, and the distinction between *Théurgie* and *Goétie* (white and black magic).[25] The other two entries from volume one, from books six and seven respectively (book five is short and transitional), record the scholarly debate about Serapis and information about the meaning and significance of the name Beelzebub.[26] Gibbon did not quote verbatim from the text in either entry, but both were substantially quotations, except that by adroit omission he compressed more than two pages about Serapis into a single paragraph.

From Banier's second volume, Gibbon abbreviated a passage about the princes who have been given the name of Mars, that is, the historical or quasi-historical persons identified with that archetype (beginning with Belus, alias Nimrod, according to Banier) and quoted (with both deletions and parenthetical comments) from Banier's account of the Salii, a sacerdotal order associated with Mars.[27] Gibbon's comments, however, were not yet critical; they merely added information. The abbreviation was both drastic and skillful. Gibbon reduced Banier's thirteen-page discussion of giants to two paragraphs. The difference in approach is apparent in the opening words of Gibbon's entry, "M. l'Abbé Banier gives us the precis of what has been said for and against the existence of giants."[28] But it is Gibbon himself who achieves the brevity at which he assumes Banier was aiming. All subsequent entries from Banier followed this pattern; substantially quotations, they were effectively abbreviated by the selection of securely historical material only.

Gleaning historical facts from Banier's melange was not Gibbon's only intellectual activity at the time, of course. In addition to his double translations and his study of logic, he continued to read the classics, especially Cicero. He also refreshed himself by dipping into a volume of the *Journal universel* and by reading Frederick of Prussia on himself, as well as the reminiscences of famous scholars in Jordan's *Voyage littéraire fait en 1733*. References to all this reading (including Cicero on Brutus) intervene in the commonplace book between entries from Banier's second and third volumes.

The entries from that third volume illustrate the progress Gibbon had made in selecting and editing his reading. The two quotations record the best available evidence about two phenomena, an astronomical event reported by Augustine from Varro, and a geographical and zoological explanation of the chimera. Clearly Gibbon's taste for the marvelous had not vanished, but he now sought a factual or rational basis for the marvels that intrigued him. Another entry was made to supplement other reading: he added to notes from an article in the *Mémoires de l'Académie des Inscriptions* a close paraphrase of Banier's views on the topic (Orion). Another entry is not only abbreviated but capably reorganized, an evaluative summary of Banier's long chapter defending Medea. This capacity to separate wheat from chaff was of course to prove invaluable to Gibbon; indeed, it did so before the year was out.

If Gibbon had learned from de Crousaz *how* to detect, expose, and correct weaknesses in historical as well as abstract arguments, he had not yet begun to put this critical skill to work. He could select relevant and relatively reliable data and disentangle the meat of an argument from its sauces, but he had not demonstrated that he could either criticize or construct a historical argument. From, or at least at the time of, his next major reading project, he learned just that. The project was Giannone's *Histoire civile de Naples* (i.e., the French translation of Giannone's Italian work).

Virtually every step in this major period of Gibbon's self-education may be retraced. First, we learn how Giannone came to Gibbon's attention. The *Journal universel* carried a fourteen-page notice of Giannone's book on the occasion of its French translation. The emphasis of Gibbon's skillful condensation of the notice[29] is on Giannone's position as combatant and probable victim of the Catholic Church, at least as much as on his accomplishments as a historian. Perhaps for biographical reasons, then, Gibbon sought out the book and added, from its preface, another biographical fact to his entry, "The author of the preface to the French translation of his history says that this event [Giannone's being seized, bound, and taken to Chamberry] occurred in 1736."[30]

Before Gibbon began making entries from Giannone's book, however, he completed the reading of Banier, showing either self-discipline as a scholar or delay in obtaining Giannone's book. Once he actually began reading the history, he ceased to think of the book as a mere adjunct of its author's sympathetic career and no longer made new entries under the heading "Giannone." Instead, each was placed under the subject it illuminated.

Though the entries from Giannone sometimes consisted of quoted data or commentary, more often they took the form of appreciative summaries of Giannone's arguments, almost as much for the sake of the pattern of argument as for the conclusion. For example, the following:

> M. Giannone solidly refutes the fabulous donation of Italy to Silvester, Bishop of Rome, which some writers pretend that Constantine made in 324, four days after having been baptized by him. It is demonstrated to be false by the following arguments:
>
> Irst. Because neither Eusebius, nor the authors writers [sic] who have written the life of Constantine in so much detail spoke of it at all.
>
> II. Because Eusebius informs us that Constantine had himself baptized at Nicomedia a few days before his death (according to a bad custom rather frequent among the nobles of that century) and not at Rome in the year 324.
>
> III. Because we know by the dates of the edicts of Constantine that during the whole course of the year 324 in question, he did not set foot in Italy, but spent it entirely in Thessalonica.
>
> IV. But what proves beyond all doubt the falsity of this donation is that all the provinces of Italy remained subject to the successors of Constantine, who commanded them as their master until the destruction of the Western Empire.
>
> *Giannone. Civil History of the Kingdom of Naples Vol. I. p 123* [31]

The key to the new value that Giannone's argument had for Gibbon is the word "solidly." Banier's arguments were sometimes persuasive, but never "beyond all doubt," largely because they represented speculation about what must have been true *if* there was a historical basis for a particular fable, but also because Banier lacked merits that Giannone possessed; here, the ability to argue from different sources (Eusebius, the other biographers, the edicts, the subsequent legal conditions in Italy) against different corollaries of the disputed point, and not just from probabilities about human nature (arguments that were endemic in, say, Voltaire and Temple).[32] Gibbon's choice of a favorite argument here may be partially attributable to his study of formal logic, for he chose the one that is in a formally valid form, *modus tollens* (the denial of the consequent of a hypothetical syllogism disproves the antecedent as well). His enthusiasm for the form, with the undeniable truth of the minor premise, permits him to leave the truth of the major undiscussed. The tempting argument from the interestedness of the witnesses is not used by Giannone, and Giannone's example may be one reason that Gibbon avoids addiction to that argument in his subsequent historical writing, recognizing instead that even interested witnesses may sometimes tell the truth.[33]

Because there are more than forty entries from Giannone—clearly made not only in the course of Gibbon's reading of that history but also as his further reading recalled Giannone's testimony or arguments to his mind—it is impossible to examine each of them here. But it was while he was reading Giannone that an entirely new category of entry appeared in the commonplace book, the independent historical argument by Gibbon himself, combining or analyzing evidence from his reading of other authors, as well as the one at hand. A relatively well-known instance, written, atypically, in English, takes issue with the master Giannone himself as to when Naples became a Roman colony:

> M. Gianone asserts that Naples did not become a Roman Colony before the reign of Vespasian or at most before Augustus: a passage of Cicero well considered will convince us that Naples lost the state of an Allied City before the Consulat of Cicero or AUC. 690. Cicero speaking against the Agrarian law of Rullus, . . . [Gibbon quotes and gives the reference to a passage in which Cicero speaks of a power applicable only to *municipia* and *coloniae* and lists Naples as affected by it.] By this passage, we see that as power was only granted to the Decemvirs over the Municipal towns, and the Colonies; that Naples was one of the two but we know that Naples was never a Municipal city she must then have been a Colony in that time.[34]

This entry is typical in its deductive structure, in its preference for evidence from primary sources (and a still uncritical confidence in such evidence), in its alertness to chronological incongruity, and in its combination of information from more than one source. There are a number of such miniature essays in the commonplace book, but all the others are in French.

Indeed, Gibbon frequently selected material from Giannone that enabled him to write such commentaries, either by providing additional data, which Gibbon could use to settle discrepancies between or within modern and ancient writers, or by calling attention to discrepancies, which Gibbon found he could settle by means of data he already possessed. Other entries were selected by topics or type, for example, nine brief biographies of important writers, lawyers, or political figures (including Roger Guiscard; this material on Guiscard was used thirty years later in the fifth volume of the *Decline and Fall*), and ten entries concerning various encroachments of the Church. Ten entries dealt with language and particularly with the significance of honorific titles. Only one entry seems essentially random.[35]

The study of Giannone was of permanent value to Gibbon, not only in training his mind but also in providing information and insights he would use in the *Decline and Fall*. There are at least twenty quotations from Giannone in the *Decline and Fall,* and Gibbon often comments on his admired predecessor. For example, in the earliest reference I have found in the history, Gibbon writes:

> The subject of ecclesiastical jurisdiction has been involved in a mist of passion, of prejudice, and of interest. Two of the fairest books which

have fallen into my hands are, the Institutes of Canon Law, by the Abbé [Claude] de Fleury, and the Civil History of Naples, by Giannone. Their moderation was the effect of situation as well as of temper. Fleury was a French ecclesiastic, who respected the authority of the parliaments; Giannone was an Italian lawyer, who dreaded the power of the church.[36]

Gibbon's high regard for Giannone was not uncritical. For instance, a recurring subject, in the commonplace book and in Gibbon's career, is Roger I, king of Sicily. In the *Decline and Fall*, Gibbon's account is not very favorable to Roger; "the ambition of the great count . . . was gratified by the vulgar means of violence and artifice." Gibbon, who was already skeptical, reported in the commonplace book that "M. Giannone gives us a very flattering [*avantageuse*] idea of Roger I."[37]

Generally, however, Gibbon's reading of Giannone gave him a useful model for historical inquiry within printed sources. It inspired in him a new tendency to juxtapose the miscellaneous materials of his readings to make them illuminate each other. The next step was perhaps obvious: the reading of related works at or near the same time. Gibbon took this step, but the commonplace book reveals much miscellaneous reading both before and during these projects, perhaps as a relaxation, perhaps on the recommendation of Deyverdun or Pavillard.

For example, Cicero, the object of the double translations, continued to be a constant companion. Gibbon also frequently recorded material from the *Journal universel*, occasionally from other journals or works of current interest. Indeed, where there is only a single citation from a work, we sometimes cannot tell whether Gibbon read the book itself or only an abstract in a journal. More often it is clear that he has read the book itself. For example, soon after completing Giannone, he seems to have read Baratier's French translation of the itinerary of Benjamin of Tudela, a twelfth-century rabbi. I suspect that Baratier, an intellectual infant prodigy, was the attraction, rather than Benjamin, though Benjamin was to be of use to the historian of the Roman Empire. The entry begins, "I shall note two [marked out] three [marked out] two little mistakes of this young savant."[38] Giannone is one source for Gibbon's superior erudition in this case, but his other correction comes from Ockley, reminding us of Gibbon's remarkable memory (he cites Ockley by volume number only, which suggests that he did not have the book before him). Not for nothing were the dynasties of Assyria and Egypt his "top and cricketball." In the *Decline and Fall*, he goes on to remark, "The Hebrew text [of Benjamin] has been translated into French by that marvellous child Baratier, who has added a volume of crude learning."[39] Baratier's youthful success could not have been so patronizingly regarded by the other young savant, who was only just in the process of educating himself. And who never learned Hebrew.

The entries from the *Journal universel* are for the most part notices of deaths in the year 1744. Although there is a long transcription from some modern Latin verses, which are presented in the *Journal* as if they were ancient and are acknowledged as modern only on the fourth page of the poem, I suspect that Gibbon was not interested in modern Latin verse, but began his transcription thinking that the poem was really "from a most ancient manuscript recently found in the Ambrosian library."[40] The obituaries he selected for notice seem to reveal something of his own ambitions, or at least of the achievements he admired. They included Cantemir, credited by the *Journal* with being the first to make poetry "speak Russian"; Barbeyrac, Celsius, Vignoles. Two obituaries were recorded at length; one was Giannone's; the other was the following:

> The reverend father Souciet was born at Bourges in 1671. His father was an advocate in the Parliament of Paris . . . he entered the Society of Jesus at the age of nineteen . . . and he died at Paris in 1744 in the 73rd year of his age.... His vast and extended spirit did not permit him to limit himself to a single type of study; he embraced all fields of knowledge and made himself equally skilled in each: sacred and profane learning, ancient and modern history, geometry, astronomy, chronology, geography, mythology, medals, inscriptions, etc. all this knowledge was within his competence, he has given us proofs that he mastered them all.[41]

Journal universel and Gibbon continued by enumerating some of Souciet's publications. It is clear that this universality of scholarship attracted Gibbon; perhaps it encouraged him to think that he might pursue his own multifarious interests *"en Maître."* It did not lead him to a scattering of attention, however, for the next stage in his self-education was the reading of two or more books on a given subject in sequence.

The first signs of Gibbon's new plan may be his references to Labat's *Voyages d'Espagne et d'Italie*. Italy was clearly the object of Gibbon's interest in this book: only one entry from it refers to Spain, and it deals with the excessive number of nobles or titles of nobility that Spain exported to Sicily. All the other entries function as statistical or geographical or descriptive supplements to Gibbon's reading in Giannone. It is not certain, however, when the Labat entries were made.

The earliest clearly datable project was that related to the apostate Roman emperor Julian, who of course would become one of Gibbon's quasi-heroes in the *Decline and Fall*. Gibbon mentions La Bletterie's *Life of Julian* in his memoirs, as one of the formative books of his intellectual life (79); he does not mention that the reading of Julian's *Caesars*, not the original but the translation of Spanheim, was the occasion or at least the accompaniment of his interest in Julian's life. The edition cited in the *Decline and Fall* was often Spanheim's, for Gibbon spurned the pedantry (as he called it) of refusing to avail oneself of translations.

Although three of the seven citations from Spanheim's Julian in the commonplace book record Julian's comments on his predecessors, the others are from Spanheim rather than Julian, especially a lengthy precis of the scholar's argument about the relation between Greek and Latin satire.[42] Perhaps the most revealing selection from Spanheim is about neither church nor emperor, but the absorbing topic of flowered clothes. With scholarly integrity, Gibbon recorded the censure that pagan and Christian alike addressed to males who wore this effeminate garb, but we can imagine that he was glad to be able to add a subsequent note from Donatus implying that "young gentlemen [*jeunes Gens*] " wore multicolored clothing without censure.[43] Gibbon's tailors' bills make it clear that he himself loved a lively waistcoat.[44]

Gibbon's notes from La Bletterie suggest an interest in Julian's conversion and his relation to Christianity; although one selection is devoted to the civilized state of Paris in Julian's time, the others deal with the role of Maximus of Ephesus in converting Julian, the occult lore of such Platonists, Julian's attempt to purify paganism, the miraculous fire at the rebuilding of Jerusalem, Julian's death, and Julian's methods of combatting Christianity.[45] Each of these subjects reoccurs in chapter 23 of the *Decline and Fall*. The account there of the "artful system by which Julian proposed to obtain the effects, without incurring the guilt, or reproach, of persecution" includes, but is not limited to, six of the seven methods Gibbon extracted from La Bletterie in the commonplace book. Of course, in the *Decline and Fall* Gibbon relies on the original authorities as La Bletterie had done, but the reader of the history can readily see how similar Gibbon's interpretation is to the following entry in the commonplace book:

Christianity

The great end of Julian the Apostate was to destroy the Christian religion, and he certainly went about it well. He was the mildest and most systematic of the Persecutors and at the same time, the most dangerous. He was aware that the ten Great Persecutions had only caused the number of Christians to increase; he resolved to act otherwise in order to decrease them. Here are some of his measures, which I have drawn from the new historian of Julian's life.

I.   He pretended to speak of the Christians with pity sometimes (1) with contempt sometimes (2) never with hate, and often made a show of great moderation in regard to them (3)

II.   All civil and military employments were given to pagans, all converts were readily received and well rewarded. (4) and to force all those who came near his person to be pagans he brought in acts of idolatry everywhere. (5)

III. He forbad the Christians to maintain schools and to teach the pagan authors to their children, whom he permitted to attend pagan schools (6)

IV. He recalled all the bishops, whether Arian or Orthodox (who
had been banished from their Sees), and under a mask of moderation,
sought to foster the division between them. (7)

V. He worked to reform the customs and worship of the pagans. (8)

VI. He sometimes permitted the inhabitants of the provinces to
commit violences against the Christians, but always tacitly, and claiming
credit for the pardon which he granted them. (9)

VII. When he put some Christian to death he would always use some
argument to prove that it was not because of his religion. (10)

[Gibbon supplied references to La Bletterie for each of the numbers
in parentheses.] [46]

Point 7 is the one not ratified by Gibbon in the *Decline and Fall*, where
he argues that the fears and suspicions of the Christians led them to interpret even the "ordinary administration of justice" as persecution of the
innocent. "They expected that, as soon as he had triumphed over the
foreign enemies of Rome, he would lay aside the irksome mask of dissimulation . . . and that the Christians . . . would be deprived of the
common benefits of nature and society. . . . It is impossible to determine
how far the zeal of Julian would have prevailed over his good sense and
humanity."[47] Gibbon had not, at eighteen, come to doubt the numbers
and even the existence of martyrs as he was later to do.

Indeed, although ready to believe the worst of the particular church
to and from which he had been so futile an apostate, at eighteen Gibbon
had not yet suspected that the events as well as the significance of church
history were open to question, except in the crucial instance of miracles.
As we have seen, an unwillingness to dismiss all miracles once led him to
embrace them all, and now, nearly two years later, an entry betrays his
uneasiness at an apparently well-supported and unrationalizable miracle,
as he quotes La Bletterie's account of the fire at the rebuilding of the
temple of Jerusalem:

Jersusalem (Temple of)
Julian, wishing to deprive the Christians of the arguments that they
drew from the dispersion of the Jews and the destruction of their
temple, ordered that it be rebuilt. For this purpose a prodigious quantity of materials was assembled; they worked day and night to clear
the site of the ancient temple and to demolish the old foundations. . . .
The demolition was completed and unintentionally they had fulfilled
in the last rigor the saying of Jesus Christ, "that there shall not be left
one stone upon another." They tried to set the new foundations.
But from the very spot came ghastly clouds of flame, whose redoubled
jets consumed the workers. The same thing occurred at various times,
and the obstinacy of the fire making the place inaccessible, forced the
abandonment of the work forever. This fact is certain because of the
testimony (to say nothing of that of Rufin, Theodoret, Sozomen,
Socrates, and Philostorgus, and of St. Gregory Nazianzen, St Chrysostem

and St Ambrose) of that (I say) of Ammianus Marcellinus, pagan and contemporary (1), it is even insinuated, by Julian himself (2).
(1) Ammian. Marcell. Lib: xxx. C. 1.
(2) Julian: fragm. : Ep.
V. *Life of Julian L. v. p 251.*[48]

The conclusion of this excerpt gives an indication of Gibbon's views on historical evidence. Essentially, he seems already to hold the view that he expounds in the *Vindication*: the reluctant testimony of someone who had an opportunity to know is honest and, to that extent, reliable (the witness may of course have been deceived.)[49] Neither Hume nor Voltaire had convinced him that a priori notions of impossibility were more reliable than testimony of this kind. Of course, he later returned many times to the problem of historical skepticism. This youthful evaluation of evidence is, however, particularly interesting because it was entirely unselfconscious: he was not yet a participant in the scholarly debate on the topic.

After completing the project dealing with Julian, Gibbon managed to obtain a copy of Voltaire's recent *Abrégé de l'histoire universelle* (London, 1753). He selected only two passages from this work for his commonplace book, however; and one is Voltaire's statistics about the European losses in the crusades, with the conclusion that France's only real gain was the liberation of a few serfs who took part and survived.[50] The other selection, reported without comment, was Voltaire's argument against an inscription reported by the Jesuits as recording the history of Christianity in China from the year 636. In this instance Voltaire did not simply dismiss out of hand the testimony of an interested (especially a Christian) witness. Instead, his arguments resembled those that the young Gibbon was in the habit of bringing against historical discrepancies he detected in the authors he was reading: the bishop alleged in the inscription to have come to China in 636 has a Spanish name, he is represented as having received honors in a country notoriously hostile to foreigners, and the monument is dated in anno Domini, contrary to eastern custom, or western custom before Charlemagne, says Voltaire.[51] Young Gibbon recorded this as Voltaire's opinion, not as his proof, but he did not reject or apparently even doubt it. Some ten years later, in his Index Expurgatorius, he had learned enough about Chinese history to reject Voltaire's conclusion, and enough about historical method to reject Voltaire's tone in argument.[52]

At eighteen, however, Gibbon, delighting in his new powers of cross-examination, was quite ready to launch similar attacks on errors by the French translator of Pliny's letters, on the Abbé de la Pluche's ignorance of the date of Cromwell's death, and on a scholar cited by Voss in his life of Velleius Paterculus. In this last instance, Gibbon rivals Voltaire in arrogance as he calmly begins, "Never having seen Velsirus' works, I do not know what arguments he has used, but here are four that demonstrate their falsity."[53] But after adducing his four arguments, Gibbon remarked, with an un-Voltairean naïveté, "Is it imaginable that Velleius Paterculus would have made such gross blunders about events so close to his own time [about a century before it] ?"[54] Alas, only too easily.

None of these excursions, however, led to Gibbon's next major project. The unlikely generator, or at least sponsor, of that project was Gibbon's father. Late in July or early in August (the letter is missing), Gibbon had written to ask his father for permission to make a "little tour about Swisserland." Writing to his Aunt Kitty on September 20, Gibbon reported: "About a fortnight ago I received a vastly kind letter from my father of the 18 of August. . . . he forgave me in it all my past faults . . . allows me to make a little tour about Swisserland . . . and tells me that after having completed my studies and my exercises He would make me make that of France and Italy."[55] This permission would of course have spurred Gibbon's interest in all things Swiss, and especially in the points of interest of places he was to visit. Predictably, his next reading project was a group of books about Switzerland, beginning with a work by his friend Deyverdun's late uncle, Loys de Bochat.

Although the second book in his Swiss group, that by Watteville, was probably not read until after the tour, Loys de Bochat may have been his study during the two weeks between his reception of his father's permission and his departure, or even during the six or seven weeks since he had sought it.[56] If so, we have Gibbon's extensive comments on this substantial work to add to our account of his six months of work. Since March 19, he had spectacularly improved his mastery of French and Latin (at some cost to his English); he had learned to detect inconsistencies in the use of scholarly evidence, to compare moderns with their sources, and actively to seek occasions for such corrections; he had found a great model in Giannone, and he had rejected some of the faults of a specious one, Voltaire. There is no trace of his reading of Pascal or de Crousaz in his records in the commonplace book, but his study of Cicero had yielded much more than a mastery of the Latin language. Most recently, he had discovered the advantages of reading two or more works dealing with the same subject at the same time. Was there anything left for Loys de Bochat to teach him?

Perhaps. The *Mémoires sur l'histoire ancienne de la Suisse* is not an easy book to use as the basis of methodical study, because its three volumes, each more than six hundred pages long, have neither an index nor a table of contents and deal with a multitude of subjects of antiquarian and historical interest.[57] Loys de Bochat's method is usually to propose a subject, such as, What are the origins of Switzerland's place-names?; refute the positions of previous scholars who disagree with him, often with elaborate academic humor, always in a clear but somewhat periphrastic style; propose his own position; list all the evidence and illustrations that pertain to it; bring in, via graceful compliments, the views of the scholars who agree or almost agree with him; point out how they too just failed to hit the mark; and then ostensibly appeal to the reader's unbiased and doubtless reliable judgment. As a good Swiss Protestant, Loys de Bochat is urbanely scornful of religious credulity, though he reports relevant miracles with an objective pose. It is clear that data were not the only things Gibbon found valuable in Loys de Bochat at the time. Indeed, moderation, or its appearance, remained more congenial to Gibbon than open attack or passionate contempt. But Gibbon does not mention Loys de Bochat as one of the formative influences of his youth. Perhaps that is because Loys de Bochat, big frog though he was in the puddle of Lausanne, seemed unlikely to be known to the audience to whom Gibbon addressed his memoirs thirty-odd years later.[58] Perhaps it is because, despite Loys de Bochat's virtues, there was so much for Gibbon to discard or revise before finding him a useful model.

The most pressing flaw in Loys de Bochat's work was his lack of selectivity and the maddening inconsequence of his organization. Loys de Bochat appears to have been trying, perhaps unconsciously, to combine the industry and information of the other *érudits* with the graceful ease of the *philosphes*. This was later to be Gibbon's goal and achievement. But Gibbon realized that the two traditions must serve rather than compete with each other and that their harmony required the principled overview of the truly philosophical historians and the capacity to find and weigh evidence properly characteristic of the best of the antiquarian scholars. We can see something of this discovery foreshadowed in the use young Gibbon made of Loys de Bochat's essay, though his first entry and several others simply preserved some useful data from Loys de Bochat. Even these, however, are well selected and edited.

Gibbon was clearly interested, as he read Loys de Bochat, in understanding the scope and antiquity of the Swiss nation and the particular places included in the Swiss tour he had taken or was going to take, in the way the Swiss colonies were governed by the Romans, and in how the savants used the evidence of Roman inscriptions to determine issues of Swiss history. Except for recording in the text the Latin originals that Loys de Bochat had placed in notes, Gibbon preserved Loys de Bochat's strong arguments without comment, but in a summarized and often in a reordered form. For instance, Gibbon condensed a twenty-eight-page article on the curators, one kind of Roman official, to a single page without omitting a cogent point. He used two quoted sentences, but his own words, his order, and his brevity gave his version a considerable advantage in clarity. Loys de Bochat began with a flourish of prologue, chattily inquiring whether it would not be interesting to consider some of the officials of Roman government and answering his own question affirmatively (to no one's surprise).[59] He then explained how he would order his essay by posing a series of rhetorical questions. Two-and-a-half pages were filled without his producing a topic statement, much less an interesting thesis.

Gibbon began his abstract, on the other hand, as follows:

> The curators (according to the idea that M. de Bochat has given us on this subject) were the magistrates of municipal towns at the time of the Roman empire. It is difficult to determine exactly their functions and their power; it varied according to the constitution of different places. In some towns they had jurisdiction, in others, none. Here they were principal magistrates, there they were only subordinate.[60]

This summarizes Loys de Bochat's introduction and the functional point of his first section (called "By whom were they established"), which Loys de Bochat never even seems to see; that is, he represents his catalogue of differing establishments of magistrates as of obvious antiquarian interest, but does not state its relevance to his conclusion (in section 4) that a single function for the office cannot be determined. Similarly, Loys de Bochat discusses the terms of office of the curators in one section and the way they were elected in a different place. Gibbon put all the information about how someone became a curator first, then discussed the tribulations of the office (it cost a fortune to be a curator) and the consequent rule that no man was forced to serve as curator for more than one year. He concluded his abstract by stating that:

> They were not obliged to serve more than one year, and Citizens who had accepted the office more than once took great care to put it among their titles on the public monuments. Some scholars have believed that it was necessary to be a Roman citizen to exercise the office, but both by authorities and by arguments, M. de Bochat shows that very probably provincials enjoyed it equally.[61]

One perhaps hears some latent Gibbonian irony in the "enjoyed" ("*jouis-soient*"); in the abstract as a whole, one certainly perceives his gift for lucid argument in narrative order.

Both by positive and by negative example, then, Loys de Bochat contributed something to the formation of the historian of the Roman Empire. He also contributed something to Gibbon the young traveler. The commonplace book records Loys de Bochat's remarks on the antiquity of Baden, and Gibbon's language in his journal of the tour suggests that he accepted Loys de Bochat's conclusion that instead of being founded by the Romans, Baden was flourishing in their time.[62] Loys de Bochat, however, was not Gibbon's only source in that instance; Gibbon is more clearly dependent on him in his remarks on Avenches: "It is supposed, indeed with great probability, that it was the Aventicum of the ancients, which Tacitus calls the capital of the nation. . . . M. de Bochat, of whom

I have already spoken to you as a learned antiquarian, derived the name of Aventicum from that of the Avantici, a people of the southern provinces of France, who, according to him, founded Avanche."[63] In his commonplace book entry, Gibbon abridged and summarized four pages of Loys de Bochat's argument to this effect and related it to his larger thesis, "that 'Helvetia' was populated by colonies of southern Gauls," an argument that Loys de Bochat had made some four-hundred pages earlier. One important point was drawn from Cicero's oration on behalf of Cornelius Balbus, and Gibbon concluded the entry with pardonable pride, "This remark is from M. de Bochat, but I had made the first part of it before having read his book."[64]

Gibbon did, then, relate the learning he derived from books to that he derived from travel. When he was about to set out, however, as his letter to his Aunt Kitty suggests, it was the excitement of change that was uppermost in his mind; "I have been the whole day writing you this letter, the preparations for our voyage gave me a thousand interruptions."[65]

About 6 A.M. the next day (a Sunday), M. and Mme. Pavillard and their eager young charge set out for Yverdun. They arrived about noon; in his journal, Gibbon reported to his father, like a dutiful geographer, Yverdun's size, appearance, situation, principal products, and means of government. Perhaps there is a personal note when he remarks, "although no one is very rich, everyone is comfortably off."[66] After dinner they traveled for another hour before passing through Grandson, the extraordinary government of which (it owed allegiance to, and received bailiffs from, two states, Bern and Fribourg, in alternate years) interested Gibbon. He turned to history, noting Grandson's claim to fame, the battle in 1476 against Charles the Bold of Burgundy, a day honored in the annals of the Swiss no less than "Marathon, Salamis, Plataea, Mycale in those of the Greeks."[67] The party slept at Concise.

The historical and political enthusiasm aroused by the first day was surpassed by the scenic pleasures of the second, when they traveled the twenty-odd kilometers from Concise to Neufchatel, along the lake of the same name:

> We arrived at Neufchatel after having passed across one of the most beautiful countrysides I have seen. One sees there a happy air that marks the wealth and prosperity of its inhabitants. Everywhere there are factories, the villages, so to speak, touch each other, and except for the environs of London, I have never seen in a similar extent of land so great a number of country houses, most of them very pretty.[68]

Unimpressed, it would seem, by mountains in the distance, he looked at landscape like Jane Austen's Edward Ferrars, who had "more pleasure in a snug farmhouse than a watch-tower—and a troop of tidy, happy villagers pleases me better than the finest bandetti in the world." Both Edwards met with Romantic contempt for their insensibility.[69]

The Pavillard party visited Neufchatel and Bienne, where they spent a full day and two nights. Gibbon called the city "extremely ugly. Its town hall [*maison de ville*] is thoroughly pitiable."[70] Here again Gibbon's taste is shocking to the Romantic sensibility, for the town hall is Gothic, and the town itself contains a well-preserved medieval arcaded square considered an "architectural gem" by modern experts.[71]

Gibbon, blind to Gothic beauties, had no voice in determining the length of the stay the party made in various places; he would have preferred more time in Soleurre (Solothurn), to which they traveled on Thursday morning, leaving after dinner on Friday. His journal entry for Soleurre describes the nature of the Swiss cantons as well as the local government, and what, in his view, was most worthy of curiosity included the Jesuit college and the arsenal (which contained an interesting representation of the thirteen cantons seated at table, an early example of Gibbon's marked preference for paintings with literary content).[72] He also considered notable the town hall, the Church of St. Joseph, the "Grand Eglise," the fine (*"jolies"*) city fortifications, and the residence of the French ambassador. Only the fortifications are listed as points of interest in a brief modern guide, and such a guide, unlike Gibbon, stresses the antiquity of the town, a remarkable omission for the historian-to-be. We may be surprised, too, that Gibbon failed to comment on the change of language; he was then in German-speaking Switzerland.

On Sunday the 28th, he and Pavillard traveled on to Baden, where they met "His Excellency M. l'Avoyer Tillier," the first confirmation in the *Journal* of Gibbon's claim in the *Memoirs* that during this journey, "in every place we visited the Churches, arsenals, libraries and all the most eminent persons" (80). The government interested him, and the Roman associations, but he saw "nothing much worthy of the traveller's attention" except the "famous dice," about which there was scholarly debate: they might have been products of nature, leftovers from the Romans, or modern fabrications.[73] Gibbon did not take a stand, but he did buy a pair (his pocket money had been increased for the journey).[74] What was best about Baden was clearly the attention of Tillier and the other Bernese deputy, M. Ougsbourger, who "did us a thousand kindnesses during the day and a half that we spent there. They did not wish us to have any table other than theirs."[75] They also supplied recommendations for Zurich and elsewhere.

Gibbon and Pavillard spent the 28th and 29th of September in Baden and the morning of the 30th in traveling to Zurich by "very bad" roads. The next day they made their excursion to Einsiedeln, only eight leagues away (roughly thirty-eight kilometers), but on a road so terrible that they took a litter rather than a carriage. Gibbon says that he was surprised by the bad roads, but then reflected that the Republic of Zurich was like that of Genoa: the public treasury was empty but the citizens' pockets were full. [76]

He had looked forward to the "famous Raperswyl bridge" and was disgusted to find that it was only boards thrown across pilings, not even attached, lest the wind blow the whole thing away, and suitable only for foot traffic or an occasional foolhardy horseman. In the Canton de Schwitz, "instead of this cheerful, peopled, cultivated hillside, we found ourselves in a country equally abandoned by art and by nature." In this journey, Gibbon's unromantic view of wild nature is very obvious: "The slightest false step of a horse could have precipitated us into the precipices [*precipiter dans les precipes*] alongside which we could not look at without trembling. This road was bordered with firs which by their thickness and blackness heightened the horror of the prospect. If sometimes we discovered objects beyond this wood, it was only to glimpse some barren rocks and the huts of miserable cowherds." [77] So much for the sublime.

Nevertheless he decided that he knew why the monks had placed their hermitage in so isolated a spot: good politicians that they were, they knew the effect the setting would have in preparing the credulous for veneration. "In fact a mind well armored by good philosophy is necessary in order not to feel there a certain fluttering, a certain—in English I would say Awe—more easily felt, than defined. Such is the force of prejudice and so great the power of our imagination." [78] Thus speaks a reluctant or *manqué* romantic.

It was Einsiedeln that he remembered thirty years later in his memoirs, and the architecture of which aroused the most enthusiasm at the time. Perhaps the combination of the elaborate, practical, impressive modern architecture and the crude, antique, superstitious worship he thought it housed fascinated him; he describes both at length, giving more than four pages of his forty-page journal to Einsiedeln, where he spent one night.

The next five days were spent in Zurich. As usual, he had much to say about its real and theoretical political role and organization. The visual impression of the site seemed to produce real enthusiasm, as well it might: "The city of Zurich is situated in one of the most beautiful locations in the world, at the head of a beautiful lake, which brings all the commodities of the country to it, very cheaply. . . . All the shores of the lake are strewn with houses and villages and the sight is halted by the high Swiss mountains only when it can extend no more." [79] His pleasure, obviously, was at least as much in its convenience for culture and commerce as in its intrinsic loveliness. With slightly comic solemnity, the young man praised the people and the interior of the houses, as well as the situation. It seems odd that he objected to one street, which was broad, straight, and ornamented with fine houses, for having too many gardens: "This street, lovely as it is, has too much the appearance of a fine village." [80]

He described among the most curious sights of Zurich the town hall, the arsenal, the fortifications, M. Escher's silk factory (where Gibbon noted the problem of unemployment caused by technological progress), and the library. In the biblical manuscript there, he particularly noted (and verified) the absence of the passage in 1 John 5:8 about the three divine witnesses. He was careful to point out that Lacroze had previously noted this absence. He was most interested in the library's many holdings related to the Reformation in England. Reporting this to his father, he anticipated briefly his mature ironic manner—he had, after all, already read Giannone and Voltaire, not to mention Pascal: "While our good king Henry VIII was hanging the Catholics for not wishing to recognize him as head of the Anglican Church, and burning the Protestants for refusing to subscribe to the Five Articles, many of each communion . . . withdrew into foreign lands."[81] Obviously the five days in Zurich were well spent. By the way, Gibbon noted the excellent natural fortifications of the Canton of Basle but drily observed, "It is open only on the side of France, the only one, in truth, where there is something to fear."[82] Next they returned to Aarau, where they stopped again, for two-and-a-half days, to Gibbon's evident irritation. "Why did we stay so long in a place I had already seen enough of," he rhetorically asked his father. Because Mme. Pavillard, "wife of the person to whom you have confided me, Madame, I say, . . . wished that her husband should spend some time with his sister-in-law."[83] Finally, they set out again, dining October 13 at Aarbourg, where they inspected the fortress.

The fortress was used to hold prisoners of state, which gave Gibbon an occasion to tell the history of the one it then held, M. Micheli du Crest, "grand partisan de la Democratie." The degree of Gibbon's own youthful enthusiasm for democracy is a matter of some scholarly debate, so it is interesting that his report on this "famous Genevois" to his Tory father was carefully neutral: since 1735, Micheli du Crest, "who certainly has a great deal of genius, . . . has always prowled about the world setting the spark of discord (according to his enemies) everywhere." Because he was a great partisan of democracy, and as several Swiss states had "ceased to be such," these sentiments only rendered him odious everywhere.[84] Gibbon added that Micheli du Crest had been well treated as a captive and had amused himself with mathematics.

If Gibbon's "Lettre . . . sur le Gouvernement de Berne" was written little more than two years later, as Lord Sheffield, Low, and Giarrizzo believe, we might expect an anticipation of its stern attack on both the theory and the practice of Bernese government.[85] But the Swiss editors and historians are probably right in attributing it to his second (1763-64) stay in Lausanne, not only because, as they note, Gibbon's penmanship is clearly that of the later period, and the attitudes and occasions of that period are suitable for its composition, but also because Gibbon remarks in the "Lettre" that Stanyon's estimate of the Canton's treasury "il y a quarante ans" was made in 1722, and 1763 is certainly closer to forty years after 1722 than is 1758.[86] In 1758, Gibbon did have much to say about the government of Berne, but his reservations about it, if any, were too well hidden for him to fear the censor's eye, as we shall see.

October 15 was—not for the last time—remarkable for scholar Gibbon, because he saw in Fraubrunnen an inscription commemorating the victory of the Swiss over an English army in 1375 in which he was able to point out, using his knowledge of English history, "two mistakes." That night, and the next three days, he and the Pavillards spent in Berne. The key element of the Bernese government, according to Gibbon, was the status of citizen. Recounting to his father the history of this responsibility and privilege, Gibbon noted with pleasure the close resemblance to the history of the attitude toward Roman citizenship. He wondered, "The Bernese have read history, why have they not noticed that the same causes produce the same effects? The reply is easy but delicate, it is that private cupidity extinguishes the light of reason."[87] Later, of course, he would know that the relation between causes and effects was not invariable in questions of history, but the ironic combination of generalized abstraction and deadly dying metaphor in the explanation foreshadows the manner of the "grand Gibbon."

But the only possible foreshadowing of the argument of the "Lettre" is his description of the Conseil Secret, the members of which were, for a week after Easter each year, the "sole masters of the State. . . . They have even the power to depose a Councillor without giving a reason. . . . The Conseil Secret of Berne is quite similar to the Council of Ten at Venice, except that it does not exercise its authority with the severity of the latter."[88] This council was a danger to Bernese, not Vaudois, liberties, and is not discussed in the "Lettre," but its discussion here is an indication that in 1755 Gibbon was aware of a power in the Bernese constitution inconsistent with the freedom of the citizens. He did not yet say, as in the "Lettre," that the benign exercise of such a power was no corrective of the malignity of the institution.

After no fewer than eight pages devoted to the government, history, and politics of Berne, Gibbon turned at last to the description of its appearance and places of interest. He admired, like other travelers, the convenience and appearance of its arcades, and he dutifully described the town hall, the library, the arsenal, the great church, with its spectacular terrace, and the hospices. He found the "Grand Hôpital" the most beautiful building of its type he had ever seen—and disapproved. "A hundred poor people maintained according to their state, please me very much more than fifty in a palace." Moreover, the objects of its luxurious charity were restricted: "It is necessary to be Bernese [*Bourgeois de Berne*] to be worthy of not being left to die of poverty or sickness." He preferred the less sumptuous but more useful "hôpital de l'Isle": "In it, whatever country, whatever religion you may be, the title of Poor Person or Sick Person suffices."[89] These judgments were clearly not merely perfunctory, conventional, or politic. Gibbon was not, like Johnson, remarkable for empathy with the sufferings of the unfortunate, but his practical concern about the needs of those sufferers he happened to encounter was lifelong and real. There is a quiet enthusiasm in his response to the unstinted and effective work of the Hôpital de l'Isle, "even to having a country house for those for whom the physicians advise a change of air."[90]

Gibbon's visit to Berne also provided him with a chance to meet an extraordinary scientist and poet, Albert de Haller, then employed as "Rathausmann" there. Gibbon's response to the meeting shows no great insight: "He is a man of rather good appearance, but excessively fat."[91] This despite Haller's showing Gibbon and Pavillard some of his work in progress. More interesting is Gibbon's description of a M. Schmidt, a rising young scholar just Gibbon's own age. Gibbon does not seem to have met young Schmidt, but mentioned him apropos of the elder Schmidt's collection of medals. Gibbon went out of his way to comment on the young man, "who will one day make a figure in the Republic of Letters." Did he hope to convince his father that such a man was admirable and such a career acceptable? Clearly it did not occur to him that his father might make invidious comparisons between young Schmidt and his own son. At any rate, he devoted several lines to this "jeune savant": "Since his childhood he has continually shown a decided taste for studies of antiquity. At the age of fourteen he composed a Latin dissertation on the monuments discovered at Avenches, in which he dared to attack the views of M. de Bochat, the most learned antiquarian in Switzerland at that time, and attacked him so well, that M. de Bochat himself . . . was very happy to have found so learned an adversary. This year he won the second prize at the academy of Besançon."[92] What Gibbon certainly observed was that at least one father could regard precocious scholarship in his son as worthy of pride and praise.

Gibbon concluded with a description of the livelier aspects of Berne, the splendid new roads and the innkeepers. He had not intended to mention the latter, he tells his father, "for fear that you would reproach me for making no other profit from my journey," but he broke this rule to note that "the profession of innkeeper is very much more honorable in Switzerland than anywhere else. . . . At Zurich, Basle, Berne, our innkeepers were always persons worth five hundred thousand francs or two hundred thousand ecus, persons honored and considered by everyone."[93] *Plus ça change . . .*

The journey was almost over. On the 19th, five leagues from Berne, Gibbon and the Pavillards saw the pretty little city of Morat, where Charles the Bold suffered a famous defeat. ("For at Grandson he lost his treasures, at Morat his troops, and at Nancy his life."[94]) In Avenches they saw Roman ruins, and Gibbon had an opportunity to mention to his father the antiquarian learning he had acquired from Bochat. They spent the night in Payerne. The next day, by way of Moudon, they returned to Lausanne.

Gibbon was soon back in his industrious routine. The excursion had given him not only pleasure but also some valuable encounters with other scholars and with environments outside the small world of Lausanne, in which, as in Lausanne, learning was not relegated to schoolboys and pedants. He had met Haller, Breitinger, Tscharner, and Watteville.[95] He immediately resumed his Swiss reading with Watteville's book.

His life was not entirely devoted to study, of course. As he had told his aunt, he had lessons in more frivolous fields as well—not only riding, but dancing and drawing. Though he often spent "ten or twelve hours a day" reading and writing, he could tell her also, "I find a great many agreable people here, see them sometimes and can say upon the whole without vanity, that tho I am the Englishman here who spends the least money, I am he who is the most generally liked."[96] Soon he would be able to persuade one of those friends, George Deyverdun, to join him in his studies, but during 1755 we must picture him as spending nearly every morning privately at work, sometimes getting up early in his eagerness, or devoting the afternoon to his studies as well.

> As soon as [Pavillard] felt that I advanced beyond his speed and mea-
> sure he wisely left me to my Genius; and the hours of lesson were
> soon lost in the voluntary labour of the whole morning, and sometimes
> of the whole day. The desire of prolonging my time gradually con-
> firmed the salutary habit of early rising to which I have always adhered
> with some regard to seasons and situations: but it is happy for my
> eyes and my health, that my temperate ardour has never been seduced
> to trespass on the hours of the night. (74)

Those hours were available for social pleasure, though not for card parties, because much of his pocket money was still used to pay his gambling debt.

Most of his friends were Swiss, but he naturally saw the visiting English-men as well. One of them, Mr. Hugonin, son of a Hampshire neighbor, had supplied Gibbon with a powerful distraction from his studies. Early in September he had happened to mention to Gibbon something about Mr. Gibbon's new wife. He provided no particulars. His father's having remar-ried was entirely unknown to Gibbon, and he was unable to imagine why so aged a man (Mr. Gibbon was forty-eight) would remarry unless he were offended with his son. Gibbon had therefore begged his Aunt Kitty to find out what she could about his financial situation and his new step-mother: "You know he had always protested that he never would marry again; at least had he done it in the time he was angry with me, I should have been less struck, but now, what can he mean by it!"[97]

What he meant by it is not so difficult for us to understand as it was for his son. Mr. Gibbon was not so near the grave as his young son naturally imagined, and the beloved Judith had been dead for more than eight years. Mr. Gibbon, an eminently clubbable man, by all accounts, could not safely return to the life of the London clubs while he could not afford to gamble, and he had no companion at home. He had cause to be grateful to one Dorothea Patton, a distant cousin of his friends the Mallets, first because in 1750 she had recommended the doctor whom he credited with saving his only son's life, and second because she obviously, whole-heart-edly, and unselfishly admired him. Nearly his own age, she could give him no more children, and she brought him little or no more dowry than had Judith, but on May 8, 1755, they were married.[98] It was his son's eigh-teenth birthday, but even that did not remind Mr. Gibbon to tell the boy of his new stepmother, much less to reassure him of his own place in his father's affection and plans.

True, he had his own problems. The marriage, or Hester Gibbon's sud-den realization that her niece was living with the ungodly Mallets, brought down her wrath upon her brother, his bride, and young Catherine Elliston. A letter from Edward to Hester, dated May 18, 1755, indicates how angry or hurt he was. He would have called on her (Hester was staying in Lon-don) to take leave,

> but I thought to my mortification, it wou'd be no kind of pleasure to you, as I am too sensible you have little or no affection left for me, from your behavior in town to me; whatever you may think, I have had very little to do with Kitty's living with the Mallets, which step she took without at all consulting me about it, and which she was by no means drove to, as she was wellcome to have lived on with me as long as she pleased, I hope it will not be attended with any bad consequences to her, but if it is, I cannot help it as I had no other hand in it, than acci-dentally bringing her acquainted with them . . . whatever little affection you may have towards me, be assured I shall allways retain that of a loving Brother toward you—[99]

Hester was, of course, still a rich spinster, and affection or prudence advised an effort to mend the breach. The new Mrs. Gibbon, who brought not only her housekeeper, Phoebe Ford, but a considerable degree of tact and common sense, into Mr. Gibbon's household, wrote a conciliatory let-ter to Hester on June 1.[100] In it she explains that it is all a misunder-standing:

> . . . as I guess from the purport of your letter, & from knowing that the intimacy between Mr. Gibbon and the Mallets is at an end. . . . I trust whenever you hear me mention'd you will be convinc'd that a distant

alliance, give no more similitude of sentiments than Likeness of face but . . . I could not help owning . . . [that] the Secrecy we so strictly kept might give occation for such surmise [i.e., that her principles were no better than those of her free-thinking cousins, the Mallets]. . . .

As to Mr Mallet he is a distant relation of mine . . . & I as much Condemn the influence he & his Wife have over Miss Elliston as you can . . . but now their power over her mind, is I fear too strong, for her Uncles.[101]

On June 12, Kitty Elliston herself wrote to Hester, a letter by no means conciliatory, but indignantly defending her friends the Mallets. The outraged Hester, offended as much or more by Catherine's impertinence than by her alliance with those of the devil's party, required the aid of William Law to compose a sufficiently severe rebuke.[102]

Somehow, familial peace was eventually restored, even between Catherine and her aunt. Whether or not with the aid of Dorothea Gibbon's letter, it had been restored, so far as the Edward Gibbons were concerned, by 1758.[103] Perhaps it is not surprising that in the midst of this turmoil, Mr. Gibbon shirked the task of telling his son about his marriage when he wrote to him in July.

Indeed, he did not mention his marriage to his son until a letter written on December 24, nearly eight months after the wedding. In the interim, Gibbon had devoted himself to two new tasks. He wrote the extensive account of his recent tour (it was finished and professionally copied in time for his father to have received it and subsequently to have "paid a bill for the Expences of [his son's] Tour amounting to 35 louis" when he wrote in December).[104] Because letters took two or three weeks en route, and the copyist must have needed time for his work, the journal of the tour was probably completed by the end of November at the latest.

The second new task was the study of Greek. In mid-November or early December he turned again to M. Pavillard for aid: "The lessons of Pavilliard again contributed to smooth the entrance of the way, the Greek Alphabet, the grammar and the pronunciation according to the French accent" (77). But even Greek was not a full-time occupation for him. He also continued to study the Latin authors and to record that study in his commonplace book. Of course, he had first completed his Swiss reading—Watteville and B. Barnard's *Mémoires sur les troubles à l'occasion du consensus*.[105] Then he "finished" reading Cicero, "a library of eloquence and reason" (76), and turned once again to Terence. He also finished his other tutor in the double translation process, Vertot; the little essay about Vertot's faults can be dated as written while Gibbon was completing his Swiss studies. The emancipation from Vertot, and the treatment of Cicero as source and pleasure rather than language master, show that Gibbon had completed at least one important phase of his growth by the end of 1755: he had mastered two of the four or five languages that would be required for his life's work.

In another sense, too, his growth was complete. He had reached his full adult height and had to accept the fact that, even by the standards of his day, he was a little man. He was not yet fat, and his large head, despite its delicate features, seemed even larger atop his small body. He was less than five feet tall—only four feet seven or eight by one account—and the same account adds that his feet were too large and acutely pigeon-toed.[106] Whether or not he suffered those additional defects, we know that he was conscious of his lack of stature. There is a note in the commonplace book, recorded in its original Latin without comment, from Casaubon's edition of Suetonius, on the subject of the "justa statura." Several authors held, Casaubon informed him, that a man's proper stature should be no more than seven feet; some said five feet ten was ideal, others that five feet seven was usual. Casaubon concludes that "the ideal height, therefore, in the estimation of the Romans, was about six feet."[107] Gibbon, who was more than a foot shorter, had to draw what consolation he could from Casaubon's additional comment that many Italians must have been below that height and that to exceed it was evidently unusual; seven feet was considered the height of a giant. It is rather sad, but perhaps typical, that this young man, confronting what probably seemed an inadequacy of his own body, turned for counsel to an antiquarian note to a classical author.

These studies—the Swiss books, the journal of the tour, the Latin authors, and the elements of Greek—occupied his working hours throughout December and into January. On January 9, he received his father's curt letter of December 24. It told Gibbon, "you may as well make yourself easy for I am determined you shall stay abroad at least two years longer" and coolly remarked: "The news that you heard of my being married again is very true . . . but if you behave as you ought to do, it shall not make any difference to you."[108] On January 10 Gibbon wrote a tactful reply in French, which included the account of his 1755 studies discussed above. Then, on Monday the nineteenth, he was ready to begin a systematic program of classical studies, the occupation not only of 1756 but of 1757 and the first months of 1758 as well. It is as if, realizing that his exile was destined to last two more years, he determined to fill them well. The most extraordinary year of his education was over, but it had indeed established the level from which he would soar "with his own wings to his proper height" (75).

CHAPTER 6

A Young Man
of Letters

Gibbon's OUTLINE for the chapter dealing with his sojourn in Lausanne in the final draft of his memoirs—a chapter never actually written—shows that he thought of the period as having three parts, with the year 1755 and its extraordinary diligence in the center.[1] Just as the initiatory period (June 1753-December 1754) was, in his view, a distinct unit within the experience, so too the period of happiness and success in that paradise of exile, the period from January 1756 to April 1758, was to form a single chapter.

The outline notes the topics for that chapter (numbered continuously with the topics for the previous sections of the outline):

1756, Janv.-1758, April
10. My series of Latin Classics—criticisms—Greek fragment.
11. Mathematics—Metaphysics—Ethics public and private
12. Correspondence, with Breitinger, Allamand, etc.
13. Taste and compositions—seeds of the Essay
14. Love
15. Friendship and society
16. Voltaire Theatre
17. The World
18. Recall and Estimate

The outline indicates the two but not parallel lines of development that characterized this season of accomplishment, that of the man of letters and that of the youth entering a social world. He had come to Lausanne a precocious but ill-instructed schoolboy, despite his premature university experience. He left as a fledgling author, a trusted friend, and a hopeful lover. As he had planned to do, we can look first at the scholar.

Midway through January 1756, Gibbon took a new sheet of paper and headed it, in a bold hand, "January the 19 of the year 1756." It began: "I have resolved to read in sequence all the Latin classics, dividing them by subjects into 1rst. The Historians 2nd. The Poets 3rd. The Orators, in which class I shall include all prose writers who were neither philosophers nor historians. 4th. The Philosophers."[2] It is clear that this scheme was an enlargment of the approach that he had learned from his reading on selected topics in the previous year. New scholarly acumen or instinct was immediately demonstrated in it, however. Without pausing for breath after announcing the project, he began it by next recording on the same sheet the heading "1me Classe Les Historiens" and listing, as a prerequisite to his study of Sallust, the scholarly editions of the author that were available to him. Neither edition (that of Thysius, Leyden, 1649; and of an unnamed editor, Paris, 1744) merited inclusion in Gibbon's library later in life, when he was able to select his own books, and neither is listed in J. W. Moss's *Manual of Classical Bibliography*.[3] Thys's edition is, however, the one cited in Gibbon's *Essai sur l'étude de la littérature* of 1761, and the very fact that he was concerned about his texts and commentators marked a new state in his erudition.

The structure of his comments on Sallust clearly indicates how he was now approaching his studies. After a quick survey of Sallust's life derived from the biographical notice (by one M. Philippe)[4] prefixed to the Paris edition, Gibbon discussed the question of the dates of Sallust's works. He thought that both must derive from the period of Sallust's retirement, but for different kinds of reasons. *Catiline* could not have been written in Caesar's lifetime by a flatterer and dependent such as Sallust because he would not have dared to compare a living Caesar to his enemy Cato.[5] The history of the Jugurthine War must also date from Sallust's retirement (1) because of certain materials that it contains, for example, evidence of Sallust's visiting the celebrated sites of that war while he governed the province (Gibbon cites La Mothe le Vayer to verify this); and (2) because his citations of the Punic books are reconcilable only with this period. Gibbon seemed to regard these two or even three different modes of argument as equally conclusive or at least as equally adequate.

His final preliminary was to note the extant *oeuvre*. Then he turned to evaluative criticism. First he raised the issue of style, and we are reminded that he still thought of scholarship as fundamentally a matter of restoring texts and solving or observing grammatical cruces and niceties. "Everyone knows that Sallust distinguished himself in the concise manner [*genre*], but perhaps not everyone has remarked that his frequent use of absolute infinitives contributes greatly to it."[6] A long way, this, from the Westminster struggle to climb into the third form! The reader of the *Decline and Fall* might be surprised to discover that Gibbon not only admired the beauties of this brevity (despite the dangers of obscurity and harshness) but also found it "quite suitable for history, since it hides . . . the trivial circumstances that at one time or another weigh down the historian's pen."[7] Gibbon also noted with approval, however, the distinction made by La Mothe le Vayer between the conciseness of Sallust and that of Tacitus: Tacitus is concise in matter as well as manner; Sallust is as diffuse with respect to material as Livy.

From style the future historian soon moved on to "what is fundamental to history." He reproached Sallust for allowing "passion" to appear in what he says about Cicero and Caesar.[8] Gibbon observed disapprovingly that Sallust allowed his own opinions to be observed and was "charmed" to portray the atrocities committed by the other side, but was silent about those of which his own party was guilty. While this is obviously a naïve view of the objectivity a historian can achieve, it is the naïveté appropriate to a historian-to-be.

In the pattern of his commonplace book entries, Gibbon then singled out "un couple d'endroits" that required remark. Gibbon first discussed two "contradictory" passages close together, in one of which Sallust says that corrupt people desired money first and then power, and in the other, that they were more moved by ambition than avarice. Gibbon was surprised that Sallust's commentators had nothing to say about this striking inconsistency, but (assuming without question that a textual emendation was necessary) he was ready to cut the Gordian knot (cliché his). He would emend the first passage by the second, for the sensible reason that in the second, Sallust explains his point, which therefore cannot be a textual corruption. At this stage of his scholarly and critical career, Gibbon tried to explain almost every difficulty as a textual flaw, but in the other instance from Sallust, Gibbon's discussion was not limited to philology, although the issue was a word. He wondered why Sallust, "whose writings express nothing but severity and virtue," had said of Catiline's companions' character, "Quicunque impudicus, adulter . . . pene bona patria laceraverat."[9] The expression "pene" was not "one of those words that decency allows for the naming of things contrary to it," for a passage of Cicero indicates that it was obscene, not euphemistic, in his (and therefore Sallust's) time. Gibbon suggested that Sallust might have been a Stoic, a sect, he said, that believed in calling "un chat un chat."[10]

After rising to this flight, Gibbon contented himself with a few comments on Thyon's French translation, including the confident correction of an error: "M. Thyon errs when he tells us that Pompey's father died during his consulate. Nothing is more certain than that he did not die until two years later."[11] The essay ends anticlimactically with a comment on Sallust's allegedly archaic spelling.

This essay is the pattern for Gibbon's commentaries, recorded on the next few pages of his manuscript, on three other Roman historians: Caesar, Cornelius Nepos, and Livy. The writing of these commentaries must have occupied the remainder of January and February, at least: the commentaries amount to some 30,000 words and, of course, required the rereading of a substantial quantity of Latin prose, not to mention the commentators. The essays are, however, significantly distinct from one another, despite their similarity of pattern. The second essay, for example, begins with a quotation from Montesquieu's *Considérations sur les causes de la grandeur et la decadence des Romains*. Although in one draft of the *Memoirs* Gibbon mentions his "delight in the frequent enjoyment" of Montesquieu, the work he speaks of there is the *Esprit des lois*, and the context is his study of legal theory and law, not begun until 1757 (78). This is therefore our only evidence of Gibbon's earliest acquaintance with the work that was the one most significant precursor of the *Decline and Fall*. [12]

Despite the essay's intriguing beginning, its structure closely resembles that of the one on Sallust: Life and Works, Particular Observations, Points from the Commentators. The quotation from Montesquieu deals with Caesar the man, to the effect that this extraordinary man had so many great qualities, without a defect though with numerous vices, that he would have conquered with whatever army he led, and governed whatever republic he was born in. Stressing Caesar's accomplishments as a writer (and pausing to heap scorn on the continuator of his Gallic Wars), Gibbon praised the style of Caesar's work and its modesty about himself, as well as the rapidity with which it was written. This point led him to a significant digression. "I have spoken," he wrote, of this rapidity as "a great merit of the writer . . . and not of the *Memoirs* themselves." He had chosen the expression advisedly, for author and work may have different merits. The merit of a *work* consists in teaching the reader something that he or she did not know, or in telling the reader something known in a "just and elegant manner." Books may acquire such merits accidentally; a derivative work may take over the functions of its sources if the sources are lost, but that merit pertains to the book only: "Plagiarisms may well give merit to a book, but never to its author." On the other hand, when we have made due allowances for the prejudices, age, problems, distractions against which the author has struggled, we may find that the less admirable book was produced by the greater genius. "Unfortunate reflection for the self-love of authors!"[13] From this impressive demonstration of independent thought in the cause of a useful distinction, Gibbon sank instantly, unfortunately, to the depths of a cliché; "Revenons à nos chevres."[14]

The "couple d'endroits" of Caesar that Gibbon selected for discussion were not mere verbal quibbles. One was Caesar's lack of candor about his treatment of the enemy chiefs in the war with the Usipetes and Tencteri. The other was what Gibbon considered the remarkable resemblance between the Druid priests and the Catholic clergy.[15] One might expect Gibbon to demonstrate the bitterness or uneasy wit of the ex-convert here, but except in a phrase deleted by Lord Sheffield ("The clergy of every sect are always deceitful, and the people of every age always stupid"),[16] the parallels are objective and have to do with powers and privileges, for example, exemption from military service.

But verbal criticism had not lost its interest: the last section of the essay discusses two such points raised by Lipsius. Not in the organization or purpose, but in the quality of some of its incidental points, then, the essay shows Gibbon's scholarly growth. The tone, furthermore, is that of a man doing his work, rather than that of a schoolboy trying the man's role.

This change is still more striking in the third of these studies of Roman historians. That essay neatly dispatches the villain of Gibbon's Kingston school days, Cornelius Nepos. The edition Gibbon used (Leyden, 1728) might have been the very copy he suffered over as a schoolboy and long retained,[17] except that it is improbable that the young scholar would have settled for a school text if he had any choice at all, or that the British school would have selected a foreign edition. The interest of the essay is, however, not its source but its implied audience. Gibbon now wrote as if for a learned journal, not for a master or even for his own instruction. His point required the interpretation of some verses found in many manuscripts but not all. Gibbon remarks, "As I do not know whether these verses are found in all editions, here they are," and copies them out.[18] Of course, this might have been a precaution against his later having no access to the verses himself, but they are of no interest except in proving his point, and the point, once established, requires no rereading. He therefore seems to have been thinking of the essay as it might appear in a scholarly journal, to be read by scholars possessing other editions of the work with which it deals. The Nepos essay, briefer than the others, shows a tendency to combine the portrayal of the man and that of his work. While apparently contrary to the critical principle Gibbon established in his essay on Caesar, this approach was required because little was known about Nepos except what could be inferred about his opinions from the works.

The fourth essay was never finished. After a prefatory paragraph about Livy's greatness, Gibbon wrote:

As I anticipate that the subject of his history, which I am now beginning, will take me somewhat further than the others, I shall divide what I have to say into several sections; I shall have four: I. In the first, I shall say something about the person and work of Livy. II. In the second, I shall indicate some of the qualities that distinguish his history from most others. III. In the third, I shall consider the objections and accusations that have been made against him; and IV. In the last, I shall make some detached remarks on some passages of this historian.[19]

This is, of course, the pattern he had used for the other historians made explicit, except for the separation of Livy's distinguishing qualities from the objections to and accusations against him. In the event, however, Gibbon did not finish even the first section, because it developed into an essay on the lost books of the history and on why the works of the great Roman historians were so incompletely preserved. After briefly examining the facts known about Livy's life and enumerating the extant books (35 out of 140 or 142), Gibbon, musing on the magnitude of our loss, remarked that he seemed to remember Bolingbroke's somewhere making more of the lost books than of the surviving ones, saying that he would willingly have given what we have to recover what we have lost. He might be right, said Gibbon, but it would be hard to part with the treasure we have, even for so rich a reward. There were, however, other ancient authors Gibbon would willingly sacrifice for Livy's account of the years 90–30 B.C.

The enthusiasm with which Gibbon imagined the prospect gives us insight not only into his judgment of Livy but also into the contribution Livy's example made to his own practice:

> One can scarcely conceive a more magnificent prospect than that one, where all the known world was the theatre, and a crowd of great men, such as nature ordinarily produces only in the course of several centuries, but which she had then made contemporaries, were the actors. . . . A brush like his, without flinging itself, like Sallust, into continual declamations against the manners of his age, and without, like Tacitus, attributing to men's minds what was of their hearts, would have depicted the manners of the age of Lucullus with the same calmness with which he had portrayed those of the age of Fabricius, seeing that both were different states of the republic and that to desire that a people who were masters of the world should be animated by the same spirit as the inhabitants of emerging Rome, was to desire a Platonic republic. Like the naturalists he would have recognized that experiments [*les experiences*] were worth more than systems, and . . . he would have interpreted a man's character by means of his actions (. . . with many precautions) not his actions according to a preconceived idea of his character. He would have seen that, far from a character proposed as the foundation of a narrative's being uniform, . . . nothing is more unlike the man of yesterday than the man of today.[20]

In this eager comment we can easily see germs of the *Essai sur l'étude de la littérature*, not to be begun for two more years, and even the first impulses of a great narrative historian. Of course, in the *Essai* Gibbon would dethrone Livy in favor of Tacitus: "One wrote history as an orator, and the other as a philosopher."[21] Although Livy makes us experience horror, wonder, pity, each in turn, he does not show us the laws made for a small, poor, half-savage republic overturned when the power of its greatness would have carried it to the height of its institution.[22] Even in the *Essai*, however, Gibbon's admiration for Livy is diminished only by comparison with that for Tacitus.

Such admiration made him very indignant with our barbarous ancestors, who had allowed Livy's works to perish, or had even willfully destroyed them. Gibbon's prejudice against the Eastern Empire shows itself full-grown already: "Yet patience with the thousand years their reign endured without their having advanced knowledge at all—if they had left, in the state in which they found it, the literary world of about the year 400, when they commenced their inundations in earnest."[23] That complaint led him to note that the works of poets have been much better preserved than those of historians and to speculate about the cause (assuming equal merit). He noted the universality of the interests of poets and suggested further that selfish motives might have prompted the conquerors of the Romans to conceal or destroy the factual testimony to past Roman glory and barbarian weakness contained in the Roman histories.

He also speculated about whether some of the lost books might have survived, if not in the seraglio of the Grand Turk, perhaps in the monasteries of Mt. Athos. One M. des Cloires,[24] familiar with Greece and belles-lettres, had apparently discussed this with young Gibbon, telling him of various fruitless efforts to obtain old manuscripts. Gibbon concluded that the "modern Greeks are at the same time so ignorant and so poor" that if they had such manuscripts, they would produce and sell them.[25]

He then turned to the faults of Livy's epitomisers, but broke off in the middle of his first point. Probably he realized that his great plan of reading the whole series of Latin classics could take years to complete if he wrote at such length as this.

Very little of the work of the next few months has been preserved. This was the period during which Deyverdun joined him in his studies. Although Deyverdun, like Gibbon, was "addicted to early rising" and delighted in literature, he had responsibilites to his widowed aunt to distract him, and considerably less austere tastes than Gibbon; he "joined with equal zeal, though not with equal perseverance" (76) in the project.[26] "To him every thought, every composition was instantly communicated; with him I enjoyed the benefits of a free conversation on the topics of our common studies" (76). Their common studies were impressive. We know from Gibbon's journal and Pavillard's letter that Gibbon read and "digested" Locke's *Essay on Human Understanding,* and the journal contains a list of the classical authors Gibbon read in 1756: "Virgil, Sallust, Livy, Velleius Paterculus, Valerius Maximus, Tacitus, Suetonius, Quintus Curtius, Justin, Florus, Plautus, Terence and Lucretius."[27]

This is not a chronological list. For example, in a letter to his father, dated June 14, 1756 (now lost), Gibbon mentioned that he had begun Tacitus. When he wrote to his father again, he had finished Tacitus, Suetonius, Quintus Curtius, Justin, and Florus, and thus had completed his planned reading of historians. It was late October by that time.[28] Between Livy and Tacitus, he had apparently reread Velleius Paterculus and Valerius Maximus, and then, between June and November, the last five historians. Traces of this reading are visible in the commonplace book, which also acquaints us with at least some of his by no means negligible incidental and ancillary reading. It included Du Bos's *Histoire critique de l'etablissement de la monarchie Françoise dans les Gaules*, La Mothe le Vayer's *Jugement des anciens historiens*, and consultations of Tillemont and Crevier, Diderot, Fontenelle, and others.

Several of these references occur in organized lists that look like notes for essays either never written or now lost. For example, there is a list of quotations or paraphrases from various authorities on the topic of Marcellus's exact relationship to Augustus, and others dealing with references to Homer in the "Ancients and Moderns"—evidently incomplete because it contains no moderns—and to Britain in Latin literature.[29] The last two, however, must be attributed at least in part to 1757; Gibbon was well advanced in his "poets" category when he made these entries.

Perhaps the reason for not writing or not preserving any more solitary essays was that Gibbon not only had Deyverdun with whom to share his views of his reading but also now began to enter the wider community of scholars, by means of letters. While reading Livy, he had noticed a passage in a speech of Hannibal's which could not be "reconciled with his character or argument" (81) and had thought of an easy emendation to correct it. He bravely communicated his suggestion to a recent editor of Livy, J.B.L. Crevier, whose reply, dated "Paris, 7 Aout, 1756," must greatly have gratified the young critic, for Crevier not only adopted his suggestion but wished "to have such assistance often."[30]

Emboldened by this success, Gibbon went on to challenge an admired acquaintance to epistolary debate. "Mr [François-Louis] Allamand, Minister at Bex was my personal friend . . . a master of language[,] of science, and above all of dispute" (81). Their subject was Locke's *Essay on Human Understanding*, "which he attacked and I defended." In a letter dated September 14, 1756, Allamand wrote, "With joy I seize some moments of repose to converse with you, Monsieur: without, if you please, making any very great effort about the topic that you propose, innate ideas."[31] The tone of Allamand's letters confirms Gibbon's claim of friendship, because it is indeed warm and friendly.

Gibbon's next step was to solicit a correspondence on topics of more general literary and historical import. He did so with rather touching personal diffidence, albeit with a brave show of scholarly confidence. He addressed himself anonymously to a distinguished scholar of Zurich to whom he had been introduced during his tour. Before the end of 1756, Gibbon had written twice to this scholar, J. J. Breitinger, and Breitinger had twice replied. This was indeed to be taken seriously as a scholar.

The correspondence was, of course, carried on in Latin. In his first letter, Gibbon questioned four received readings of Justinus, the third-century epitomist of the Augustan historian Pompeius Trogus. As D. M.

Low points out, the very slight value of so late an "ancient" authority had not yet been appreciated when Gibbon and Breitinger carried on their discussion of how and whether it was necessary to change Justin's text in order to make it intelligible, self-consistent, and consistent with other historians. It is therefore not surprising that they did not regard the question of Justin's text as a dead issue, as modern scholars do.[32]

In addition, Gibbon raised two questions of fact: First, how could the Romans send one set of ambassadors to Antilochus demanding that Egypt be returned to the infant Ptolemy, their ward, and a second set demanding it by right of war? Breitinger's answer persistently missed the problem of illogic that troubled Gibbon (right of inheritance is not right of war; Ptolemy's right is not Rome's); he suggested only that the Romans might mean to say that Egypt was Rome's by reason of the right to make war. Dissatisfied, Gibbon finally put the same question to another scholar, Johann Matthias Gesner, with whose solution Gibbon professed himself satisfied.[33] Second, why would the Senate, according to Justin, instruct their general to free Greece from Nabis, as he had freed Macedonia from Philip, when they had freed not Macedonia, but Greece, from that king? Even his matters of fact, it will be seen, assume that there is or ought to be some concord between Justin's words and historical facts, just as, when he questioned various readings in Justin's text, he was troubled by apparent historical absurdities that resulted from them. In later letters to Breitinger, he pursued most of these points further, but when he introduced new topics, they were for the most part of the factual, rather than the textual, type.

Low's evaluation of the evidence this correspondence gives us about young Gibbon's accomplishments as a scholar can hardly be improved upon—certainly not by the present writer:

> The letters indeed abundantly confirm the breadth and thoroughness of Gibbon's reading. They reveal him as pertinacious ... in argument, and ambitious, as young [classical] scholars commonly are [were?], to distinguish himself as an emender of texts. With all his pertinacity he treated Breitinger with a flattering deference and it is indeed strange that in one passage where Gibbon was clearly right he humbly accepted an interpretation from Breitinger which was quite egregiously wrong.[34]

It is also notable that Gibbon the mature and distinguished scholar, looking over these letters as he wrote his memoirs, did not make Low's observation. Quite possibly he did not even then realize that he had been right and Breitinger wrong, for in textual scholarship, Gibbon never became, or thought himself to be, the epitome of correctness.

Many present-day readers, however, acquainted with Gibbon only in the silently corrected and polished editions of J. B. Bury, have a false impression of the precision and accuracy of Gibbon's hard-won classical scholarship. It has aptly been described as "massive rather than minute," and Low points out that "Gibbon's Latin is fluent but faulty. . . . The chief weakness . . . is an uncertain grasp of the syntax of the Latin moods. . . . He has a ready command of vocabulary and of some idioms, especially those of Cicero's letters. At the same time, post-classical words are freely employed." Low goes on to note that Gibbon shared the error of his age in not enforcing the metrical rule that a vowel "cannot stand short before two consonants."[35] Although Gibbon would no doubt have been pleased if his scholarship had been literally precise as well as comprehensive in range, it is clear even in the sometimes pedantic propositions of these youthful letters that he never lost sight of the larger meaning of the passages he examined, whatever his weaknesses in grammar, metrics, or idiom.

Besides his correspondents and Deyverdun's flagging zeal, Gibbon had another source of scholarly companionship: he continued his Greek studies with Pavillard. Pavillard's Greek was New Testament, of course, and they had used the Gospel of St. John as their first text, but Gibbon soon persuaded Pavillard to turn to Homer. Pavillard was able to report to Mr. Gibbon, in a letter of January 1757, that Gibbon had read "half of Homer's *Iliad*."[36]

Despite Gibbon's taste and obvious talent for belles-lettres, his father continued to insist that he study algebra. Gibbon's activities in the winter of 1756-57 (and Pavillard's bills) therefore included private lectures in mathematics.[37] His progress in that subject pleased Pavillard very much, but Gibbon felt that he learned only passively, accepting what he was told "without any active exercise of [his] own powers." He remained glad that he did not pursue mathematical studies so far as to demand "rigid demonstration" in questions of "moral evidence" (78). This view was not arrived at in middle age, but in youth—by 1758, when he argued, in his *Essai sur l'étude de la littérature*, that criticism had an even better title than geometry to be praised as a logical system, because "geometry is concerned with proofs that occur only in its own domain; criticism balances different degrees of probability, and it is in such comparisons that we regulate our actions every day."[38]

Although in 1757 Gibbon had given up his lessons in drawing, dancing, and riding, he entered his name at the Academy of Lausanne and considered attending the series of lectures being given there on "the law of Nature and Nations . . . by Mr Vicat a professor of some learning and reputation" (78). Instead, Gibbon decided to work on his own, studying Grotius and Puffendorf with the aid of their commentator, Barbeyrac, reading Locke's *Treatise of Government*, "delighting" in Montesquieu, and—prepared by de Crousaz—"engaging" with Locke and Bayle, respectively "bridle and . . . [spur] to the curiosity of a young philosopher" (78). This metaphor, incidentally, was employed by Breitinger in his letter to Gibbon of March 1, 1757, to describe Gibbon's sagacity and ingenuity "quæ non *stimulo* [spur], sed *fræno* [rein] potius opus habere videtur" (emphasis added).[39] Gibbon's study of law might have been begun in 1756 but seems more likely to have occurred in 1757.

In addition to the studies recorded in the commonplace book, Gibbon reported two other important intellectual activities in a letter to his father dated October 30, 1756. While reading the Latin authors and writing his remarks upon them (and these remarks "sometimes have the happiness of pleasing the people to whom [he] showed them"), he had consulted Pitiscus's lexicon of Roman antiquities, trying to "grasp the distinctive characteristics of each age and . . . country."[40] This attempt to transfer himself imaginatively into that world and country is characteristic both of the boy who loved the *Arabian Nights* tales and of the man whose great history, as has often been noted, is narrated from the geographical and emotional perspective of Imperial Rome. This imaginative journeying is also the quality of the study of Greek and Latin writings that, according to Gibbon's *Essai*, makes the study of classical literature the best means of developing one's "esprit philosophique."[41]

His other important achievement had been the reading, in Greek, of two books of Xenophon. In the *Memoirs* he comments, "Cicero in Latin and Xenophon in Greek are indeed the two ancients whom I would first propose to a liberal scholar, not only for the merit of their style and sentiments but for the admirable lessons" they provide for both public and private emulation (75–76). His "gratitude" to Xenophon was one of the topics Gibbon proposed to discuss in the outline for the continuation of the final draft of his memoirs, and, of course, Spelman's admired translation of the *Cyropedia* had been one of the favored works of Gibbon's boyhood. Like the attempt to seize imaginatively the spirit of faraway places and times, this study of Xenophon in 1756 had long-lasting effects. Indeed, as we shall see, Gibbon returned to Xenophon in one of the apprentice works through which he prepared himself to write the *Decline and Fall*.

Even in the industrious period of 1756–57, all work and no play would have been unhealthy as well as unpleasant, and Pavillard assured Gibbon's father that Gibbon "saw company." Gibbon mentioned to his father meetings and conversations with visitors from other countries and requested an increased allowance and a valet on several occasions. For the lighter side of Gibbon's life, however, a cheerful and charming letter to his Aunt Kitty is the best evidence. For example, a figure out of his Westminster past, George Simon Harcourt, Lord Nuneham, to whom Gibbon had paid a visit in the crucial period while he was meditating his first change of religion, had come to Lausanne. Gibbon's scenic talent is already evident in his account to his aunt, as is a sense of good-humored comedy, of which some readers of the *Decline and Fall* apparently remain unaware:

I was some hours with him in this place, that is to say almost all the time
he was here. I find him always Harcourt, always good natured always
amusing, and always trifling. I asked him some questions about Italy,
he told me he hurried out of it as soon as he could because there was no
French Comedy, and that he did not love the Italian Opera. I let slip
some words of the pleasure he should have of seeing his native Country
again, on account of the services he could render her in Parliament.
"Yes says he I want vastly to be at London, there are three years since
I have seen Garrick."[42]

The warmth and ease of his relationship with his aunt does not seem
dimmed by distance, by her failure to aid him in some crises with his
father, or by his adolescent superiority—at nineteen, perhaps he had
already outgrown the last. She had asked when he would come to England; "How should I know it?" he replied with wistful asperity. He would
try for the following spring; he told her his plan for obtaining his father's
permission to return. "If all that produces no effect I do not know what I
can do." He asked her about friends and neighbors, and added, with unintentional pathos: "Tho you have not seen my father [since his marriage]
yet I suppose You have heard of him. How was he in Town? his wife was
she with him? Has Marriage produced any Changement in his way of
living? . . . Pray have you ever seen my Mother in law. Or heard any thing
more of her Character."[43]

He concluded with the affectionately pert question, "Do you never
read now?" He urged her to read *Sir Charles Grandison*, for his sake
(Gibbon's, not Richardson's); he found it "much superior to Clarissa."
Then she should read Mme. de Sevigné's letters to her daughter, which he
is sure must have been translated into English:

> They are properly . . . letters of the heart, the natural Expressions of a
> Mother's fondness regrets at their being at a great distance from one
> another and continual schemes to get together again. All that won't it
> please you, there is scarce anything else in six whole Volumes. And
> notwithstanding that, few people read them without finding them too
> short. Adieu My paper is at an End. I don't dare tell you to write
> soon. Do it however if you can. Yours affectionately,
> E. Gibbon.[44]

No wonder she saved the letter.[45] But such distractions, and the light-
hearted mood of most of this letter, by no means interrupted his intellectual progress.

In Gibbon's self-education, 1757 is indivisible from 1756. He continued
his reading of Homer, his study of law, his series of Latin writers, his critical remarks. He added Gesner to his collection of learned correspondents;
in his mathematics course, he progressed to the conic sections. In 1757 we
do not so much see him taking new steps toward scholarly maturity, as

perfecting by exercise and experience the scholarly abilities of which he was already possessed. The fruits of that exercise have to some extent been preserved. He kept a collection of dated and numbered critical essays, and while there may have been others not in this collection, and there are discrepancies between the dates on the manuscripts and the dates ascribed to some of the pieces in his journal, they contribute to the following picture of his studies in 1757.

Geometry, Latin poets, and learned disputation with Breitinger occupied January, February, and March. He read Tibullus, Catullus, Propertius, Horace (with the commentaries of Dacier and Torrentius), Virgil, Ovid's *Epistles* (with the aid of Meziriac), *Ars Amandi,* and *Elegies.* Possibly in March, or more probably in April, he began to undertake essays discussing various historical and geographical cruces in the text of the poets. For example, in Plautus he had noted a character who claimed to come from Sparta in the time of *Regem Attalum*—a historical inconsistency. Gibbon proposed that we identify the time as in the reign of the *Regem Aetolum*—an easy error for the copyist, he assumed. He admitted, however, that the historical mistake might easily have been made by Plautus rather than a copyist. That essay is dated May 4, 1757, in the manuscript but attributed to March in the later record in his journal.[46]

According to both journal and manuscript, he wrote an essay on April 1 to resolve the debate about whether the "Indians" mentioned in Virgil's *Georgics* were the Ethiopians or the inhabitants of Hindustan.[47] On May 13 (or May 8—the journal date), he wrote another "remark" on the *Georgics,* to which he refers in the *Memoirs:* "I can still read without contempt a dissertation of eight folio pages on eight lines (287-294) of the fourth Georgic of Virgil" (76).[48]

In this essay the issue is whether the verses in question should be emended or explained, in view of their appearing to place the Nile and Persia in same vicinity. Those who have explained the passage have "followed different routes; some have brought Persia forward to the Nile; some have pushed the Nile back to Persia. Let us see which view we may more conveniently accept."[49] Gibbon then accepted Huet's refutation of a proposed emendation, refuted Catrou's support of the first of the alternative interpretations and Huet's of the second by means of chronological and geographical evidence as well as critical arguments, and tentatively proposed a resolution of his own, which requires a metaphorical sense of a key term but otherwise does not strain the evidence.

This argument contains several interesting passages from which the reader can easily perceive Gibbon's growing intellectual maturity. In refuting one of the previous hypotheses, which rested in part on a supposed allusion to a tradition reported only in Sallust's then-recent history, Gibbon pointed out that allusive use of historical traditions requires that they be familiar to one's readers, as this one could not have been to Virgil's readers.[50] This is a motif later to reoccur and be developed in the *Essai*, in which Gibbon digresses to the (to him) significant question of the legitimate limitations on a poet's departure from historical truth (*Essai,* chaps. XXXVI–XXXVII). As in 1755, Gibbon's critique of 1757 marks the faults of the works he is reading, but the spirit of the criticism has become significantly different, for example, apropos of Huet's treatise, "I would have wished for more selectivity in his quotations, more clarity [*netteté*] in his ideas, more method in his plan; I sought here the philosophic spirit that assembles material; I found only the compiling spirit that amasses it."[51] Huet had written a work, said Gibbon, which might have nourished an emerging reputation but could add nothing to an established one. In 1755 he would hardly have sought, much less ventured, such a generalization.

Also interesting is a clue to his emerging principles as a historian. Although, when graveled for want of matter, he himself was occasionally guilty of the "crime" of combining evidence from different periods in a composite picture,[52] he did so with some chronological restraint, and he knew that it could be a crime: "M. Huet neglects a very essential precaution. He cites indifferently all those who might appear to contain something favorable to his cause, without paying attention to the time in which they lived, as if it would make Virgil's error more plausible to unearth something similar in a writer who lived six centuries before or after him."[53]

Even if one can no longer become exercised over the question of Virgil's geography, one can understand why Gibbon, who always retained his acute sense of the order of time and the divisions of space, approved of this essay in his maturity. Stylistically, it is much more like the mature Gibbon, allowing for differences of subject, tone, and occasion, than the imitation of Montesquieu in the *Essai* of 1758–61. For instance, the organization and rhythm of the following is characteristic not only of this essay but—with greatly lengthened periods, of course—of Gibbon's mature English style: "Travels, conquests, trade extend them; migrations, division of states, barbarism, contract them. The westerners have had there their dawn, their noon, and their sunset."[54] The combination of abstraction and concrete imagery in the presentation of the same point is also characteristic, though in later works the concrete element is likely to be evidence, or at least literal, not metaphoric.

None of Gibbon's extant writing is dated in the summer of 1757, but an undated essay on the date of Catullus's death (unpublished by Sheffield because the substance of it is incorporated in Gibbon's 1758 correspondence with Gesner) may have been written in this period.[55] According to Gibbon's recollection, his reading in 1757 included Suetonius on Augustus and Tiberius, and a Latin translation of Dion Cassius.[56] On September 15 he went to Geneva for a month, to see a traveling troupe of French actors and enjoy a holiday on the model of, but less ambitious than, the tour he had been allowed in 1755. Less expensive than the earlier journey, this one was not succeeded by a similar elaborate journal.[57]

During the last two-and-a-half months of the year his pen was busy again. In addition to an (unpublished) essay on a census of the Romans during the republic and one refuting certain alleged prodigies, for example, omens of greatness at the birth of Augustus (one is reminded of his letter to Hurd in 1771), there is an undated essay dealing with Caesar's sacerdotal offices, which must have been written prior to the beginning of the *Essai* in 1758, in which it is echoed and developed.[58] He also wrote long letters to both Breitinger and Gesner. That even his literary interests were essentially historical by this time seems obvious in retrospect, but of course he did not enjoy the advantages of hindsight and did not yet know himself to be a historian.

Even more impressive than the reading and writing that he recorded are the works that the notes to these essays show him to have read, consulted, and taken for granted. Gibbon distinguished, in his youthful manuscripts, between the works he had read and those he cited secondhand by underlining his own sources and quoting the others without underlining. If he errs, therefore, it is likely to be in failing to credit himself with work that he actually did, rather than in claiming credit for another's reference. The number and range of these works would be impressive even if he had read nothing else, and of course it is probable that he read some works he had no occasion to cite.

The authors he did cite included those whose works he had recently been studying, others he had been reading but of which we would not know had he not cited them, some he bravely attempted in Greek, and some he had to read in translation; his citations also included works and authors he had read when he was much younger, but that his extraordinary memory recalled when necessary. These include passages not entered in the commonplace book from works read in 1755, such as Banier and Spanheim's *Julian*, as well as some read in his childhood—Marsham, Petau, Dodwell, Cellarius, Prideau, for instance. Gibbon's memory was not only remarkably well stocked but also remarkably well indexed throughout his life. Such a memory was certainly a prerequisite to, if not the cause of, the great synthesist he became. But from his perspective, the most momentous event of 1757 was, though unforgettable, not intellectual. It was the life of the heart, not the life of the mind, to which he planned to dedicate his autobiographical account of his last months of exile in Lausanne.

CHAPTER 7

The Warm Season of Youth

"E XILE" is a harsh word for a place of so much growth and recognition as Lausanne had proved for Gibbon. He always allowed full credit to Lausanne for the pleasantness of his life there and its absolutely essential contribution to his development and accomplishments. To it he owed his first friend and his first love. But if Lausanne was (relatively speaking) paradise, nevertheless he was confined there, and it was not home. The emotional demands of the fourteen months from June 1757 to August 1758 were the last by which Gibbon was overcome (i.e., not the last that he experienced, but the last he found overwhelming) until long after the death of his father. In the *Memoirs*, his retrospective view of the first stay in Lausanne, after two happy periods there as an adult, gives a spurious tranquillity to his first experience there, particularly to the final months. But between the lines, and in his letters, the real turmoil may still be read.

In Gibbon's letter to his Aunt Kitty explaining his schemes for returning to England, we have seen signs of the strength of his desire to come home, signs confirmed and emphasized by a letter of June 4, written in French, to his father:

When could I hope to testify these feelings [that he has for his father] to you in England. Four years have already slipped by since your sentence placed me in this country. They have appeared to me as so many centuries. It is not that I complain of the country itself or of its inhabitants. I have essential obligations to them. To my sojourn here I owe my taste for the development of my mind, the progress, such as it is, that I have made in various kinds of study. I have even acquired a small number of friends who merit my esteem and whose memory will always be dear to me. But what are these friends compared to the value of a father . . . of a mother who has an equal right to my gratitude and to my respect, of an aunt whom I have loved since I have known her. . . . I shall not repeat all the arguments I have already used to make you see that, whatever your intentions may be, a longer stay in Lausanne can only be injurious to me. . . . But permit me, my very dear father, to beg you to consider seriously what effect the various uses of my best years can have on the rest of my life.[1]

Surely the serious and sincere tone of this passage is unmistakable.

Yet his objection to staying longer in Lausanne does not imply dissatisfaction with his way of life there. As he acknowledged, it was in fact both profitable and pleasant. In addition to the companionship of Deyverdun and the visiting foreigners. Gibbon enjoyed (as Pavillard's bills indicate) several brief excursions away from Lausanne during the year, and the recreation of several billiard parties.[2] Moreover, it may well have been early in 1757 that Gibbon first met Lausanne's most famous resident, Voltaire, an honor and pleasure Gibbon valued even more highly at the time than he did in retrospect. In later years Gibbon remembered that first meeting with some complacency despite a fear of having displeased the great man: having been allowed to read an unpublished poem through twice, Gibbon indiscreetly revealed the text to others ("my discretion was not equal to my memory" [83]).

Young Gibbon particularly enjoyed the "uncommon circumstance of hearing a great poet declaim his own productions on the stage" (83). Although it was obviously his sense of history that was most gratified in this entertainment, Gibbon acquired in Lausanne a taste for the theater in general, and the French theater in particular, that endured throughout his life. After the theater, moreover, his taste for social life could be indulged. The elite of the Pays de Vaud gathered at Mon Repos to applaud and to weep.[3] Gibbon's

> ardour which soon became conspicuous seldom failed of procuring me a ticket . . . and however addicted to study [he was so notoriously studious that some of his contemporaries thought him "fou"], I enjoyed my share of the amusements of Society. After the representations of Monrepos I sometimes supped with the Actors: I was now familiar in some, and acquainted in many houses; and my evenings were generally devoted to cards and conversation either in private parties or numerous assemblies (84).

Thus life in "exile" had in itself few pains and many pleasures, and Gibbon always considered that the inhabitants treated him like their fellow citizen. Deyverdun, who moved in the best circles of Lausanne society, was, of course, Gibbon's most valued friend; he "was a young Gentleman of high honour and quick feelings, of an elegant taste and a liberal understanding: he became the companion of my studies and pleasures; every idea, every sentiment, was poured into each other's bosom; and our schemes of ambition or retirement always terminated in the prospect of our final and inseparable union" (M 238). Deyverdun was a few years older than Gibbon and somewhat similarly detached from his father's house.[4] Gibbon indeed may have enjoyed some sense of paternal support and protection from the friend who sponsored his entry into the world around them. But he himself offered support and even leadership to the intellectually less powerful Deyverdun, whose willingness in later years to serve as a sometimes humble assistant in Gibbon's literary projects suggests that he recognized and accepted his intellectual subordination. But despite the terms of Gibbon's description of Deyverdun, and despite the fact that neither of them married, it seems unlikely that their relationship was in any conscious way sexual. Both sought marriage, and Gibbon's comments on Greek and Roman tolerance of homosexuality have a tone of incredulous distaste that is unlikely, especially in private notes, to have been feigned, whatever may have lain beneath that reaction.[5]

In the *Memoirs* Gibbon was not unwilling to confess to his sexual feelings, although readers of Lord Sheffield's editions were not allowed to know it. As a bachelor in his fifties, fat and famous, Gibbon took pains to do so with dignity:

> I hesitate from the apprehension of ridicule, when I approach the delicate subject of my early love. By this word I do not mean . . . the gallantry without hope or design which . . . is interwoven with the texture of French manners. I do not confine myself to the grosser appetite which our pride may affect to disdain, because it has been implanted by Nature in the whole animal creation. . . . The discovery of a sixth sense, the first consciousness of manhood is a very interesting moment of our lives: but it less properly belongs to the memoirs of an individual, than to the natural history of the species. (84)

It was, of course, to gallantry that he had confined his attentions to the other sex in later life, and there seems no reason to doubt that he spoke from experience of the "grosser appetite," however restricted his indulgence of it. But love, he believed, was something different from either: "the union of desire, friendship and tenderness, which is inflamed by a single female, which prefers her to the rest of her sex, and which seeks her possession as the supreme or the sole happiness of our being" (84). As a definition this is both cautious and as comprehensive as is consistent with an exclusively masculine and heterosexual perspective, though a modern reader may raise an eyebrow at the expressions "single" (for "particular"), "possession," and "our." More subtly revealing is the expression "the supreme or the sole happiness." One of Gibbon's characteristic rhetorical habits is to couple two unlike terms with "or" as if they were equally plausible alternatives, for ironic effect, usually with the more probable alternative second, for example, "restrained by modesty or timidity." Here, probably unintentionally, the construction "supreme or sole" ironically reveals the key problem with love as Gibbon experienced it. Prepared to seek and regard it as the *supreme* happiness, he was offered it only as the *sole* happiness he could thenceforth expect. And the alternatives were not, after all, equivalents.

No such expectation distressed him on the June day in 1757 when he was taken to meet the latest belle of Lausanne society (or at least of the portion called the Cité). Not only was she blond, blue-eyed, and beautiful, but she was liberally educated, sensitive, and intelligent. Her father was an obscure but well-read minister in the mountain parish of Crassy, not far from Lausanne; "in her short visits to some relations at Lausanne, the wit and beauty, and erudition of Mademoiselle Curchod were the theme of universal applause. The report of such a prodigy awakened my curiosity; I saw and loved" (85).

Suzanne was a few weeks younger than Gibbon; she had just celebrated her twentieth birthday in June, whereas his birthday had occurred a month earlier. As he said in his journal, when he saw her *"omnia vincit amor et nos cedamus amori."*[6] The young people of Lausanne made a fad of writing verbal portraits of themselves and each other; Suzanne's self-portrait is both informative and frank. She emphasizes her gaiety, the smile in her eyes and on her lips, the sweetness of her voice, but she acknowledges that her "form, tall and well-proportioned, lacks that enchanting elegance which increases its value" and accuses herself of having "the air of a villager" and a certain abruptness in her motions.[7]

Gibbon found her learned but not pedantic, lively, elegant, ingenuous, and sincere. He seems also to have found her coquettish, because it was not until they were at Crassy, where "the gay vanity of youth" no longer distracted her with the attentions of her many admirers, that he began to feel that she had listened to him. But he was attracted to her from the first; he alludes to the "first sudden emotion" that he had felt then, even when, in his maturity, he did not desire to stress his impetuous passion. Perhaps only two other events are treated in the *Memoirs* with equivalent fullness and feeling: the reconversion from Catholicism to Protestantism and the dawning of the idea of the *Decline and Fall.*

When Gibbon wrote his memoirs, having become "Augustan,"[8] he stressed Suzanne's balance and reconciliation of extremes in his description of her. He praised her combination of social, personal, and intellectual merit in her youth, and the steadfast character she manifested throughout her life in the extremes of fortune she experienced. Certainly she deserved such praise. But at the time the two young people met and loved, extremes were much more appropriate to her description than moderation. An only child, conscious of her unusual accomplishments, informed of her beauty not only by her mirror but by a series of theology students who came to study with her father, Suzanne was also carefully educated in moral matters. She was very conscious of at least some of her own shortcomings, even exaggeratedly so, and a person of exceptionally strong feelings, if we may judge from her letters and journals. While this sensitivity and an accompanying irritability of nerves sometimes caused her pain or embarrassment, it probably played a role in preventing her becoming vain and

smug, as her treatment in her girlhood as "la belle Curchod" might have
encouraged her to be. A contemporary once wrote to her:

> When I was a student of literature at Lausanne, M. Darney, our pro-
> fessor, used to tell us that you were an exception to your sex in your
> understanding [*lumières*] and proposed you to us as our model. When
> you passed in the street, always surrounded by a train of admirers,
> I would hear the public saying, "There goes the beautiful Curchod,"
> and I would immediately run along your route, where I would remain
> as long as I could. I even had the honor of dancing with you, at a
> student ball, of which you were the queen.[9]

It is to her credit that she was not spoiled by such adulation.

In her journal, indeed, Suzanne went so far as to load herself with
bitter reproaches. For example, after her father's death, Suzanne helped
to support herself and her mother by giving lessons in Geneva. Three
years later, her mother also died. Many years later still, Suzanne wrote in
her journal, addressing her memory of her mother, "during those three
years . . . I had these petulant outbursts [*acces d'humeur*], even, alas!
towards you, because you were the source of all my happiness on earth."
The force of her feeling is clear not only in what she says but also in her
efforts to excuse herself to herself in the same passage ("What tears, what
tenderness, what feelings, what transports, have paid for these instants of
ill-humor") and in the very persistence of her feelings of guilt.[10]

This irritability occurred when she was under great stress. The task by
means of which she contributed to her own and her mother's support was
extremely uncongenial to her, or at least extremely painful to her pride,
which was injured further by the reaction of Genevan society. She wrote
later to an intimate friend: "Your Genevans are indeed unjust, and I
would never have believed that the greatest effort of virtue of which I was
capable would have been regarded as degrading. I speak of those lessons;
no one knows all they cost my pride."[11] So Suzanne might well have
forgiven herself a few cross words to her mother, but she could never
do so.

Similarly, when she became mistress of her own salon in Paris, hostess
to a glittering array of believers and freethinkers alike, on one occasion
she was sufficiently poised to say, when reproached by a believing friend
for admitting the nonbelievers to her company, "I have atheistic friends—
why not? They are friends who are unfortunate."[12] But on another
occasion, when such a friend urged a controversial point that wounded
her religious sensibilities, she "replied to him with vivacity at first,
then . . . she lost all control of her nerves and burst into tears in front of
all her somewhat discountenanced guests."[13]

Once she met her eventual husband, Jacques Necker, her love affair
with him was lifelong, a highly romantic circumstance; and if her love for

him had its origin in his position as well as his character, it was nonetheless sincere and fervent, according to the convincing evidence that her biographer collected from her private papers.[14] Somewhat hasty of temper, capable of strong devotion and great distress, proud but not vain, Suzanne in her youth was in both character and person, a reasonable facsimile of the heroines of romance that young Gibbon had so long admired. He seems to have recognized this resemblance.

Early in August 1757, Pavillard and the Curchods consented to Gibbon's paying the first of his visits to Crassy (in the accounts Pavillard sent to Gibbon's father, these expeditions are tactfully entered only as a lump sum for hiring horses; as the item amounts to a mere seven livres, it is possible that Gibbon rode rather than taking a carriage).[15] Soon he could "presume to hope that [he] had made some impression on a virtuous heart" (85); by mid-October, he and Suzanne probably had her parents' consent to their eventual marriage, for they were carrying on a correspondence, and Suzanne, who was not merely a dutiful but a devoted daughter, would not have corresponded with a young man without her parents' consent. (Clandestine correspondence was, however, not without precedent in Gibbon's family!)

The first letter followed several months of friendship, or rather courtship, but it was, of course, eighteenth-century courtship, and that of two intellectually gifted but innocent and even cloistered young people. Gibbon began his first letter by addressing himself (his familiar spirit), a device that permitted him to establish a playful tone, express some compliments, confess that he had found it difficult to know what to say, and use the intimate "tu" without presuming to use it to her. One is tempted to compare another Swiss lover, St. Preux (in Rousseau's *La Nouvelle Héloïse*), though Gibbon seems considerably more sincere.

Letters were, of course, the supplement to Gibbon and Suzanne's courtship, not its center, and, as J. E. Norton notes, Gibbon's proposal of marriage, even if it did not precede the permission to correspond (the English convention, that correspondence invariably implied an engagement, does not seem to have held in Switzerland), cannot have been later than the second week in November, that is, little more than five months after their first meeting.[16] She was a penniless foreigner; he had ignored the possible commands of a dictatorial father, on whose whim his livelihood (until the father's death) depended, and he was prepared for no profession. To seek marriage under such conditions may not be love in the "high, romantic fashion," but it is far from rational, restrained, and temperate.

Every admirer of Gibbon should be acquainted with Low's full, well-balanced, and judiciously sympathetic accounts of this affair (in his introduction to Gibbon's journal and in his biography of Gibbon),[17] but for a full appreciation, we must look also at the lovers' own words.

Suzanne painted a word-portrait of her English admirer, similar to the one in which she had described herself.[18] Although Gibbon was short, frail, and certainly not conventionally handsome, Suzanne found him attractive. Her sincerity, or at least a remarkably shrewd tact in its stead, is evident in her singling out for praise qualities that he actually had, instead of being loosely flattering in her description. She spoke of his beautiful hair, his fine hands, his gentlemanly air. His countenance was what most attracted her. It was "so clever [*spirituelle*] and unusual" that it was like no one else's. There was always something new in its expression, and his gestures were expressive also. (They had not yet been stylized into mannerisms.) "In a word it is a physiognomy so extraordinary that one does not tire of examining it, of painting it, of copying it."[19] Obviously Gibbon, who was shy, awkward, even pompous (or silent) with strangers, had unbent sufficiently to show Suzanne the good companion so much enjoyed by his friends, so inconceivable to his enemies. Suzanne's absorption in his play of countenance suggests a more than casual interest on her part. She turned quickly to more objective features; his manners were good. He knew how to treat women and achieved politeness that was easy without being familiar (a Chesterfieldian standard). His dancing, however, was mediocre, and the "graces" of a fop he lacked. She then began to describe his mental qualities with "His mind [*esprit*] has prodigious variety," but the sketch breaks off there, as if, suggests d'Haussonville, she was fearful of betraying too great an interest in the model, or as if, we might add, his intellectual range and brilliance defied description.[20]

Other perceptive people also recognized young Gibbon's gifts despite his handicaps in society, as various observers similarly saw past the greater handicaps of young Sam Johnson, but if it is fair to see in Tetty's praise of Johnson as "the most sensible man I ever saw in my life" the proof and source of her genuine fondness for him, it is certainly fair to see this portrait as evidence of similar sincerity in Suzanne.[21] Suzanne's motives may not have been entirely disinterested, however; when writing the *Memoirs*, Gibbon seemed to feel or fear that the hope of a good establishment had been at least contributory to her feelings toward him. He found her easily consoled by other equally good prospects. But this judgment is doubly suspect; at the time, it would have been painfully easy for an insecure young man, uncertain of his own loveableness, to believe himself unloved, and later it relieved the conscience of the man who had been accused of relinquishing her with heartless ease to assume that her feelings had not been deeply engaged.[22]

Yet her reply to his first letter shows no anxious desire to please a good catch, and considerable pleasure in the verbal games he had begun. Most of the letter is devoted to elaborate play with the notion of their familiar spirits—not to be confused with themselves—and the enchanted land or lands where those spirits live. The Arabian Nights setting evoked in

Gibbon's letter is developed by Suzanne with hints of allegory: "The place where your Genie [*votre genie*] lives is prodigiously stormy, subject to hail, fogs, winds, thunder, and lightning; a country enchanting, however, when it is peaceful, a country which can produce in an instant flowers of astonishing beauty (these regions were in precisely this enchanted state when you were composing your letter—absurd parenthesis!)"²³ Her ready fancy and this pleasant self-interruption suggest something of the vivacity and charm that appealed to Gibbon. Some modern readers find these exchanges stilted and unfeeling, but only a little imagination is required to be touched by the awkward bookishness of these brilliant but isolated young people, making their first hesitant steps in the old dance.

On a serious note, Suzanne went on to ask Gibbon not to come to Rolle when she went there; her mother objected and had made Suzanne see her point of view. Like a good lover, Gibbon knew when to disobey. He had told her that the meeting was his only consolation and had described the pleasures he would derive from it. At Rolle, unlike Geneva, he could see her without so much constraint, without being banished from the door at 6 P.M.; he could be at her feet, could talk of love, and—so his bold imagination proposed—she would not be angry.²⁴ She had not replied to *this* passage. So of course he went to Rolle, though he managed to adhere to the spirit of the prohibition by making his destination officially Loin, and Rolle only a stop on the way home (it was November 1—Watteville was the ostensible object of his visit).²⁵ Except at her command, however, Gibbon wished neither to absent himself from her nor to conceal his attachment. A story is told of his roaming the fields around Lausanne with his newly purchased sword, forcing the peasants, who perhaps were amused at this belligerent Tom Thumb, to agree that Mlle. Curchod was the most beautiful person on earth.²⁶ However improbable the story, it would not have been told had he not been an enthusiastic, open, whole-hearted lover, little concerned about appearances except those his bookish study of love made him think requisite to the lover's role. He might even have recalled his father's extravagant grief for his wife and felt that a certain theatricality was a part of love.

After the November meeting at Rolle and a longer visit to Crassy, Gibbon's letters occasionally set aside all masks and revealed a touching admiration for the mutual love of Suzanne's family, as well as a wistful desire to offer at last the warmth of his own feelings without fear of rejection or neglect. In his letter of November 30, for instance, he wrote:

> Do you wish me to speak naturally to you, Mademoiselle? I have always valued you infinitely, but the happy week I spent at Crassy, put you in relief in my mind in a new way. I saw all the treasures of the most beautiful soul I know. A mind and temper always the same, and always proof of a soul content with itself. Dignity even in jest [*badinage*], graces even in serious matters. I saw you do and say most impressive

things, without being conscious of them, beyond what was necessary to say and do them with deliberation. Your ruling passion. One sees it well enough; it is the most lively tenderness for the best of parents. It breaks out everywhere and makes everyone who comes near you see how susceptible your heart is to the noblest feelings. Every time that this reflection came to my mind, it always carried me very far from the objects that prompted it. I reflect in this very moment on the happiness of a man who, possessor of such a heart, found you responsive to his tenderness, who could assure you a thousand times a day how much he loved you and who would cease to assure you of it only when he ceased to live. [27]

To some moderns such praise from a lover seems stiff or tepid, but if we care about the marriage of true minds, it may seem more deeply felt than explicit recognition of her physical attractions or boasts of the fervor of his appetite for her. It is striking that he admired her combination of deep feeling and tranquil disposition, because it was such a combination of virtues that he had sought in vain in his parents. He admired not only her "grand" actions and speeches but also her apparent unselfconsciousness in them. Thus his praise of her, like hers of him, was not just pleasant generalization or a conventional catalogue. We should also note that the hope of familial tenderness was no small or taken-for-granted delight for Gibbon.

Similarly, in a December letter, there is obvious, even remarkable, honesty and strength of feeling:

Formerly my lot was more dull than distressing. A decent fortune, a few friends, a certain reputation; there perhaps is what I should have looked forward to, but all these benefits, undoubtedly real, were not accompanied with the power of enjoying them. I had a heart capable of much feeling; I experienced none. And all made me conscious that the most painful feelings are not so vexing to the soul as this void, this total inactivity in which it languishes isolated in the universe. . . . That is a frightful picture, Mademoiselle. That, however, is an idea of the state I have often experienced, a state the more painful in that one has not even the consolation of pouring it out. . . . I met you, Mademoiselle; everything is changed for me. A happiness above Empire, even above Philosophy, may await me, but also, a torture repeated every day, and always increased by the consideration of what I have lost, may fall to my share. However, Socrates thanked the Gods every day for "having made him be born Greek"; I will thank them always for having given me birth in a century, for having placed me in a country, where I have known a woman whom my mind makes me respect as the most estimable of her sex while my heart makes me feel that she is the most enchanting. Here, you will say, is solemnity, melancholy, even tragedy. What a tedious person—can one avoid yawning as one reads him. Yawn, Mademoiselle; I am aware that I have deserved it, but I have also deserved that you add, It would, however, be desirable that all preachers be so convinced of what they say.[28]

At the end of this long and heart-felt passage he begins, obviously, to cover his tracks a little, to prevent embarrassment for himself or for her, and the remainder of the letter, equally long, is self-mockingly extravagant. But it is not a disavowal of what we have just read. In later years, circumstances or choice led him to accept, in his emotional life, something like the vacant tranquillity he here rejects. This passage reminds us that the choice cost him something, and that he was aware of that cost.

As the year 1757 came to an end, Gibbon looked forward to a happier, more rewarding new year, one with more emotional risks but more emotional delight than he had ever known. He anticipated no change, however, of domicile, companions, or purpose. He failed to appreciate a crucial fact: on May 8, 1758, he would be legally of age.

The month of January did not seem unusual. It began with an expedition to Catholic Fribourg for the feast of the Epiphany—not, of course, for the religious observance, but for the festival, although Gibbon assured Suzanne that it was the others with whom he was traveling, not he, who wished to stay for the ball. From Fribourg it was an easy trip to Berne, and Gibbon also told Suzanne that they went on to Berne after the festival, staying there till the end of the month. He wrote to her on February 9, having just returned (he said) to Lausanne, where he found her letter of January 10 and another letter from her (now missing), which reproached him for his neglect.[29] There is, however, evidence that Gibbon was in Lausanne during at least part of January. Some critics believe that he did not go to Berne at all, but if he did not, his statement to Suzanne would be not only a lie, but a gross, easily detectable, and therefore stupid lie. Gibbon might have lied, but not stupidly, and if he had, she would certainly have reproached him with the lie when she discovered it. She did not, and it seems therefore improbable that he lied.[30]

On the other hand, there are manuscripts in which Gibbon discussed Newton which are dated, respectively, Lausanne, January 13, 1758, and January 20, 1758. These dates, moreover, look as if they were placed on the manuscripts at the time they were written, not added later from memory.[31] Furthermore, Pavillard wrote to Gibbon's father on January 14 as if Gibbon were present and mentioned no journey.[32] But Pavillard did not expose Gibbon to his father's possible displeasure when it was avoidable, so that omission may mean nothing.

The most probable reconciliation of these conflicting pieces of evidence is to suppose that the journey took place—as Gibbon told Suzanne—but was interrupted—as he did not admit to her—by a brief return to Lausanne. There he was busy with Newton, and although he saw her letter of January 10, which gives no impression of urgency, he failed to answer it before going back to Berne. On horseback, he could have traveled directly between Berne and Lausanne in a day. On his second return, he would have found her later letter, full of urgency; at that point he would have been sadly tactless to suggest that the earlier letter had been read without receiving an immediate answer. Or conceivably Gibbon was working while on holiday, dating his manuscripts from "Lausanne" because that was his permanent address at the time. Neither of these hypotheses can be proved, but either is more likely than that Gibbon took the pointless risk of inventing trips to Fribourg and Berne she would soon have known he never took.

However that may be, a letter from his father (also delayed, Gibbon said, by his absence from Lausanne) offered an unexpected complication with which he had to deal in his letter to Suzanne of February 9.[33] It brought both new hopes and new fears. It was an affectionate letter, and Gibbon could not help hoping that the affection was sincere, however skeptical his father's past behavior might have made him. Astonishingly, the letter spoke of Mr. Gibbon's desiring his son's happiness—and called him home to England. Gibbon had long wondered whether his father ever intended him to be a son indeed, to lead the kind of life usual for his class. His hopes may have extended no farther than to receive into his own hands the money it cost to maintain him at Pavillard's, perhaps slightly increased, when he attained his majority. Remembering his father's absorption in Judith Gibbon, Gibbon could not know whether there would be room for him in his father's life, now that Mr. Gibbon had a new wife. Perhaps his father would never again require or allow his presence in his household. Thus a letter affectionately recognizing his rights and expectations as an adult son and heir, and making a place for him in the home of a family, was a surprise and in some ways welcome.

On the other hand, if his father wanted him in England, what became of his plans to marry Suzanne, to which she had agreed on condition of their living in Switzerland? His father's new plans for him, which would once have been entirely gratifying, raised a crowd of obstacles to his happiness, of an entirely different nature from the one obstacle he had expected, that of "the Inequality of fortune," he rather tactlessly told Suzanne.[34] His living in Switzerland, it now appeared, would shock equally his father's "tenderness" and his ambition for his son. But, he assured Suzanne, love would make him eloquent; he himself did not desire riches, and he would be able to persuade his father: "He desires my happiness and if he desires it, he will not think of separating me from you. . . . The love of study was my only passion until you made me know that the heart has its needs as well as the mind, that they consist in reciprocal love."[35]

Suzanne's reply is one of her most appealing letters.[36] She would not affectedly pretend that she had not been anxious for, and pleased with, his letter; of course she understood what his duty to his father was and would have been shocked herself "to send his white hair down to the grave in sorrow" (to her, Mr. Gibbon's fifty years were antiquity). She had a project that she believed might make both families content and hoped to discuss it with him when the roads became passable. Her dignity, we may infer, had been slightly injured by his remark about the inequality of their fortunes, for she reacted somewhat stiffly both to that and to his under-estimating her sensibility by imagining that she might hope to hear that he was indifferent to her.

In the next month, March, when the roads were clear enough, he did visit her—the last visit, he calls it in his retrospective journal.[37] It was apparently a happy visit, not only for the lover but also for the scholar. He had a new project for literary fame, perhaps inspired during the visit itself.[38] There is even a draft of a dedication of this project to her.[39] It was to become his first published book, the *Essai sur l'étude de la littérature.*[40]

Between the time of the letter and the visit, Gibbon had turned his attention to Suzanne's only rival in his passions, scholarship. He produced an extract of M. de la Barre's treatises on the units of measurement of ancient geography (dated February 11), and a discussion of M. de la Bletterie's account of the succession of the Roman Empire (February 20).[41] Much later Gibbon returned to both subjects. He had read the articles of both scholars in the *Mémoires de l'Académie des Belles-Lettres et des Inscriptions,* to which he also returned. These extracts are more important as prophecies of things to come than as immediate evidence of scholarly achievements.

The La Barre extract contains very little original material, although the tabular presentation of the scholar's findings no doubt required a good deal of labor on Gibbon's part. Probably the most interesting aspect of this piece is its motive: "I want to form a clear idea of M. de la Barre's system. It is worth the trouble, as it is useful in throwing light on the ancients. It requires the trouble, for the author's mind is not so clear as it is profound, and besides, his great learning everywhere suggests to him digressions which he does not have the fortitude to deny himself."[42] The author of the *Essai* is obviously nascent there.

Despite its modesty, the study of La Bletterie is more than an abstract; it is a scholar's response to another scholar's hypothesis. The views Gibbon later expressed in the *Essai* were anticipated in his prefatory remarks: "To bring a spirit of clarity into the shadows of antiquity suffices for the man of letters who wishes to instruct himself; to scatter flowers on the thorns of knowledge is the plan of the wit who seeks only to amuse himself. To unite the useful and the agreeable is all the most demanding reader can ask: let him ask it of M. de la Bletterie without fear."[43] La Bletterie's thesis is that the Roman Empire was always in law (though not, of course, in fact) elective, rather than hereditary. After recapitulating his arguments and the objections that La Bletterie himself anticipated, Gibbon proposes others. He begins by stating an important principle regarding historical evidence, "which would appear unquestionable": "The testimony of a contemporary historian has an entirely different authority in these matters from the inductions that we French can draw from the facts encountered in their writings. The reason is clear. We see the history of those times only in gross, while they saw it in detail: and it is on this detail that everything depends in discussions as delicate as these."[44] We see the empire full-blown, all of a piece; contemporaries saw how it was established and believed it to be hereditary, at least in the beginning. But after two or three pages of counterarguments, directed against La Bletterie's hypothesis, Gibbon turns abruptly: "While awaiting M. de la Bletterie's clarification of these difficulties, let us continue to adopt his system . . . clear, plausible, and well tied together. If it is an error, it is one of those errors that enlighten the mind as they deceive it. Supposing the system proved, I shall hazard some ideas on the soldiers' part in the choice of emperors."[45] And so he does, to the end of the "extract." Having observed as a final point the difference between the significance of "Imperator" in the Republic and in the Empire, Gibbon comments, in closing, that the retention of the word is "A new example of men's attachment to names, and their negligence of the ideas that they contain."[46] At the end of this dissertation, Gibbon added, probably in 1760, a paragraph from another of La Bletterie's works, on the name or title of "Augustus"; Lord Sheffield printed it as a part of this extract.

Writing the two abstracts and paying the visit to Crassy were not his only activities in early March of 1758; he also wrote a final letter to Gesner, continuing his arguments about the date of Horace's *Art of Poetry* and the identity of Piso, and proposing an emendation to Velleius Paterculus.[47] Neither amatory nor filial preoccupations distracted him from such scholarly pursuits.

"About the 20th of March" (clearly the date is a later estimate, not contemporary with the beginning of the manuscript), or perhaps as early as March 8, he began the work that eventually became his first published book.[48] Between beginning that *Essai* and departing for England on April 11, he had, of course, to plan and arrange for his journey and to take leave of his friends, in addition to writing. The first of these tasks was by no means simple. He wrote to his father, anticipating his new life by writing in English:

> With regard to the road the war renders almost all roads almost impracticable [he pointed out tartly in the *Memoirs* that "our taking (the
> French) ships without a declaration had rendered that polite nation
> somewhat peevish"], however after having consulted the persons the
> most used to travelling they all agree that that of France will be the least
> dangerous. I shall pass for Swiss, Officer in Holland, I shall have Dutch

Regimentals, and a passeport from the Canton of Bern. I am pretty sure that my Tongue won't betray me. I think of setting out the 8th or 10th of next month and if I stay a few days in Holland to look a little about me I may be in London the 2d or 3d of May.[49]

It is clear that traveling under a false name with false regimentals in an enemy country held no terrors for him, perhaps because he had already embarked on a dangerous undertaking in another sphere: he had coolly begun to engage in the most significant literary debate of the age, on the less fashionable side, and in a foreign tongue. At first he called his book "Réflexions sur l'étude des Belles-Lettres" (it was later "de la littérature"), and in the three to five weeks before he left Lausanne, he wrote sixteen chapters of it. These chapters are no longer than paragraphs, and he did not immediately write all the notes, so that the material produced amounts to some 3,000 words, a respectable but not overwhelming quantity. More significant, perhaps, is that although there were numerous minor revisions before these words saw print, the first effort was quite close to "publishable" state.[50] Perhaps he was already in the habit of forming his sentences in his mind before committing them to paper, though the sentences so committed are very different from those that characterize his mature style.

In the *Essai*, whose style is consciously modeled on Montesquieu, the sentence is the organizing unit: the rhythmic and even the logical sequence among the sentences is relatively unconsidered, and the sequence of sequences, in paragraphs, chapters, and finally a unified work, so triumphantly achieved by Gibbon in his maturity, is of course even more neglected. In this youthful work, Gibbon aimed to produce polished apothegms, dazzling even, if necessary, at the cost of clarity. Connections are rarely explicit and sometimes difficult even to infer. In revising the work, moreover, he tended to insert new material or substitute whole arguments or illustrations for their equivalents, instead of smoothing and clarifying the unity of his argument. But as conceived and begun at Lausanne, the work did have a unified theme and a fairly coherent structure.

Its motive, and therefore its theme, was, according to Gibbon's *Memoirs*,

the desire of justifying and praising the object of a favourite pursuit . . . the learning and language of Greece and Rome. . . . The guardian of those studies the Academy of Inscriptions was degraded to the lowest rank among the three Royal societies of Paris: the new appellation of *Erudits* was contemptuously applied to the successors of Lipsius and Casaubon; and I was provoked to hear (see Mr d'Alembert's Discours preliminaire à l'Encyclopedie) that the exercise of the memory, their sole merit, had been superseded by the nobler faculties of the imagination and the judgement. I was ambitious of proving by my own example as well as by my precepts that all the faculties of the mind may be exercised and displayed by [the] study of ancient litterature. (99)

The first version of the *Essai* included the materials published as chapters I-X, XIV-XVII, and XXIII, with the long note on the term *erudit* in chapter VI of the published version treated as a separate chapter "7." If these sections are read without the additional chapters Gibbon later inserted, the relative clarity of the original structure emerges.

After an introduction describing and deploring the current neglect of classical studies ("in France, to which [his] ideas were confined" [99]), he moved on to a section on Taste, in which he defined three sources of beauty and showed that response to one of these required erudition.[51] He then examined Criticism, by which, despite an appeal to Aristotle, he clearly meant the reasoned use of general principles and particular evidence to interpret any document, whether belletristic, in our sense, or not. Gibbon sometimes pursued too ardently the oracular manner of his model Montesquieu in this portion of the *Essai*, but its argument is clear in spite of its apothegms. In manuscript, it is free from the digressions that later obscured its structure while enriching its content.

The first section (chaps. 1-9 of the draft, or I-VIII of the published version) is directly addressed to winning an audience for his subject in a hostile age. He uses four arguments:

1. Classical studies are a part of cultural history, which is intrinsically valuable because it shows man at his best.

2. Their neglect is a matter of fashion, to which other studies have also been unjustly subject.

3. They also suffer, in our age, from the excessive favor in which they were once held.

4. But they have never been incompatible with the kind of greatness we now admire; great men of the past have often pursued and have never despised classical studies, whereas great classicists have sometimes had qualities we can admire and should not be condemned with their fellow classicists who are mere compilers.

This set of arguments is clearly designed to shame and flatter a *philosophe* reader into continuing to read. This portion of the *Essai* is essentially defensive, though there are hints in it of the positive case that is to come, for example, in the ironic recognition that "wits" have profitted from their readers' ignorance of the classics (chap. VI) or in the parenthetical assertion that the labors of even the worst of the compilers may demand our esteem for their usefulness (chap. VIII).

The youthful admirer of Montesquieu did not condescend to make explicit the connection between his thesis and the two remaining subsections, Taste and Criticism, but the unspoken premises of his argument may safely be inferred. It is agreed, the argument implies, that classical literature offers us beauty, but it is not agreed that antiquarian studies of classical language or artifacts (including literary texts) are necessary to our possession of that beauty. Response to beauty is, however, as we know, governed by taste and criticism. At this point the argument becomes explicit. Beauty comes from three sources: images of nature, images of human nature, and "artificial" images. The first two are indeed independent of knowledge of the past (Gibbon clearly assumes, in common with his age, the doctrine of unchanging human nature), and portrayals of the human heart are indeed the surest road to immortality. The images of external nature are not, however, an adequate resource, because a few geniuses have already exhausted the pictures of its surfaces which are all that we accept. All great writers, therefore, have wisely made use of images of art: by art, Gibbon means anything made by man—for example, religions, governments, customs (chap. X). But beauties drawn from these sources can be appreciated only if we have a knowledge of antiquity sufficiently thorough to enable us to view them as the writers' contemporaries did: "The knowledge of antiquity—that is our true commentary: but what is still more necessary is a certain spirit that results from it, a spirit that not only makes us acquainted with the past but makes it familiar to us, and gives us, with respect to matters of the past, the eyes of ancients." [52]

This point actually completes Gibbon's argument in favor of the study of the past as necessary to achieve a taste for ancient literature. But he raises and answers a possible objection to his thesis in the next three chapters (XIV–XVI). Writers, he observes, may either seek fame from their contemporaries or hope for enduring praise. Some works and genres deal primarily with manners; others, with passions. Writers who hope for the applause of posterity and who write in genres concerned with passions rather than manners make less use of artificial images; their works require proportionately less classical scholarship in their readers than, for example, Horace and Plautus, who are "almost unintelligible to anyone who has not learned to live, to think, like the Roman people." [53] Nevertheless, even high poetry such as the epic uses artificial images to ornament its background and cannot be fully appreciated without being "profoundly instructed" about antiquity. [54] Gibbon gives an illustration from Virgil, remarking that this picture, so striking for those who know antiquity (as it was for Virgil's original readers), is "dull in the eyes of a man who brings to the reading of Virgil no other preparation than natural taste and some knowledge of his language." [55] Thus even where classical learning is least necessary to taste, it is still essential.

The third and final section of the Lausanne *Essai* was incomplete; it broke off in mid-sentence, but it was clearly intended to show how scholarship was essential to the other division of literary appreciation—criticism. Gibbon pointed out that Aristotle, who had been superseded in other disiplines because of the imperfect evidence on which he based his discussions of them, drew his critical precepts, which have endured, from "the nature of things" and "the knowledge of the human heart. He illustrated [his precepts] by means of the examples of the greatest models."[56] Perhaps because Gibbon was conscious of how little he himself knew about Aristotle's models, he did not go on to describe the history of criticism but rather its results. Its methods had been perfected, he said, but no definition of criticism had been agreed upon. For him, criticism was "the art of judging writings and writers—what they have said, whether they have said it well, whether they have spoken truth." He explained in a note that the truth he had in mind was that of writers' "testimony, not of their opinions"; he labeled truth of testimony as "Historic Truth."[57] This note cannot be dated and therefore may not have been written while Gibbon was in Lausanne. It is certain, however, that at Lausanne his impulse was to move on from this definition of criticism, via the confident assumption that "one knows" what powers of mind are necessary to the use of this "Instrument of reason," to argue that no study is better suited to the development of those powers of mind than is criticism. Even geometry, justly called an excellent system of logic, is not better for that purpose. The page on which he was writing, and the Lausanne portion of the *Essai*, ended in the midst of his support of this conclusion. It was time to depart for England.

When, with Deyverdun's passport and his two Swiss friends who served in the Dutch army, Gibbon set off in a hired coach for Toigne in Franche-Comté, the first step in his journey, he hardly felt English any more, he tells us (86). Certain evidence suggests a lingering identification with his native land of which he himself may not have been conscious, for example, his personal charities at Lausanne were directed to indigent "Englishman" (one was in fact Irish.)[58] He recognized that the speed of his journey resulted from his own impatience. Further, he had not experienced in Lausanne, except perhaps as a guest on some of his excursions, the homely comforts and conveniences he had always enjoyed in England—clean table linen, good food, a plentiful supply of books, warm and handsome rooms. And although Gibbon admired the topographical beauties of Lausanne, he had no taste for Alpine scenery and always remained English enough to take pleasure in the less dramatic landscape of his homeland. Despite these touches of Englishness, however, we might expect as solemn a sense of an era's end as young Boswell felt when he left Scotland— though at no age would Gibbon have indulged in public ceremonies of leavetaking.[59] Most unromantically, however, when Gibbon left his place of exile and redemption, it was with the escort of a number of friends, who accompanied the travelers to Toigne and with whom they "made a debauch of it."[60] If it was not an appropriate farewell to the nursery of his scholarship, it was suitable that he so conclude this phase of his youth, for upon leaving Lausanne, he wrote as a scholar, but he traveled as a young man of fashion.

CHAPTER 8

The Young Squire

HE YOUNG MAN of fashion tra-
veled light-heartedly north in disguise. Poring over a map three years
later, he could remember nearly every stop for dinner or for the night:
Pontarlier and Ornans on April 12, then Besançon, Vesoul, Luxueil,
Epinal, and finally (on April 17) Nancy. There Gibbon's lifelong taste
for the neat and modern was predictably gratified by Stanislaus's newly
built and well-planned town center (though he does not mention the
famous iron railings): "a large Square surrounded by a Playhouse town
house and handsome uniform private houses, with a statue of Lewis XVth
in the center, and handsome streets issuing out of it, one of which is terminated by an elegant palace of Stanislaus."[1] At Nancy he could post the
letter to Suzanne that he had written the night before at Bayonne. To her
he wrote "the language of the Heart [and] of the Mind," both of which
were, he complained, unknown to his companions. He told her about the
poverty and superstition of the country, about his being limited by his
companions' tastes to seeing "streets, carters, and taverns." He has had,
nevertheless, a very easy journey, and in a few days he will be the happiest
of men, or—"do not require me to go on."[2]

From Nancy to Metz to the "wild country of the Ardennes" the travelers continued, arriving about noon on April 23 at Maestricht, where
Gibbon posted another letter to Suzanne, this one destined never to reach
her.[3] At Maestricht they dined with the officers of the garrison, and Gibbon had the pleasure of meeting a well-known savant, Louis de Beaufort,
known to Gibbon by "his specious arguments against the five first Centuries of the Roman history" (87) and later discussed in the *Essai* (chap.
XXVII).

Moving across Brabant, Gibbon left his companions at their garrison at
Bois-le-Duc and continued by ship toward Rotterdam. On the 27th, however, instead of traveling on to Brielle, he went through Delft to The
Hague. "I wished to have observed a country, the monument of freedom
and industry," he tells us, "but my days were numbered, and a longer
delay would have been ungraceful" (87–88). From The Hague, April 29,
he wrote to his father about his plan to embark for England on Wednes-

day, May 3.⁴ About 4 P.M. on that day, he set out for England and, forty-
four hours later, reached London, having been absent from his native
country for "four years, ten months, and fifteen days."⁵ He was appre-
hensive about his reception from his father and unknown stepmother and
went directly to "the only person in England whom [he] was impatient to
see," "that kind and sensible woman," "the affectionate guardian of [his]
tender years," his Aunt Kitty (90-91). She still kept her boarding house in
College Street for the Westminster students. The evening was joyfully
spent, even though it included the dreaded visit to his father and his
father's new wife, in St. James' Square.

   Gibbon's account of his return in the *Memoirs* is quite candid. He was
very conscious of, and remembered with awe, his father's anger at their
last parting, an impression hardly dispelled by the tone, content, and
paucity of his father's letters, and because his "infancy, to speak the
truth, had been neglected at home" (91), Gibbon was not really acquainted
with his father's character and did not know what kind of reception to expect from him. He also had at least the ordinary apprehensions about his
unknown stepmother; indeed, even while writing the *Memoirs* after many
years' friendship with the lady, his smoothly self-mocking account of his
fears was marked in the manuscript by the accidental omission of a significant word, "bed": "the rival who had usurped my mother's [bed] appeared in the light of a personal and domestic enemy" (91).⁶ At the very
first meeting, however, he had to confess: "Her understanding her knowledge, and the elegant spirit of her conversation: her polite welcome, and
her assiduous care to study and gratify my wishes announced at least that
the surface would be smooth" (92). These words were written without
any expectation that his aged stepmother would ever read them.

   As for his father, Gibbon was surprised and gratified to be received "as
a man and a friend": "if my father remembered that *he* had trembled before
a stern parent, it was only to adopt with his own son an opposite mode of
behaviour" (91). This is, however, a description colored by wishful thinking. Such a reaction as Gibbon describes would indeed have been a rational
response to his dislike of his own father's sternness, but, as we know, most
people in fact repeat with their own children the behavior, good or bad,
that they experienced from their parents, and, in the event, Mr. Gibbon's
genial parental indulgence was rather less generous than his own father's
cold tyranny, if only because the South-sea director died earlier in his
son's life. Gibbon's father was, however, much more amiable in manner
than *his* father had been: "we ever afterwards continued on the same
terms of easy and equal politeness: he applauded the success of my education; every word and action was expressive of the most cordial affection;
and our lives would have passed without a cloud, if his œconomy had
been equal to his fortune, or if his fortune had been equal to his de-

sires" (91). Such is Gibbon's testimony, but the reservation so lightly expressed represented a powerful influence; Mr. Gibbon's actions, and even his words, often belied his avowed affection. Indeed, his welcome to his returning son was not altogether what it seemed.

Gibbon, unsuspicious of his father's motives, at first feared "art and falsehood" from Mrs. Gibbon, until he gradually discovered her "warm and exquisite sensibility." He was relieved to discover that she was past "the hopes of children." (92). The three Gibbons spent almost a month in London before visiting their country home at Beriton, and they did not settle there for the summer until July 1. Thus there was time for Gibbon to enjoy or at least to experience London life and for Mrs. Gibbon to overcome her stepson's initial reserve before they removed to the country. Soon Gibbon and his stepmother adopted "the tender names and genuine characters of mother and of son." The process apparently began even while they were living under different roofs; because the Gibbon family had no London house, the elder Gibbons stayed in lodgings, while Gibbon himself probably stayed with his aunt. Under these circumstances, he could hardly return to his scholarly activities; "The hurry of the journey and of the first weeks of my English life suspended all thoughts of serious application" (99).

The first object of this "hurry" must have induced a revision of his sanguine impression of his father. Three days after his arrival in London, on his twenty-first birthday, Gibbon discovered one reason that he had been permitted to return: his father's debts required that the entail that prevented sale or mortgage of the family estate without the consent of the next heir be broken. Such consent could not be given until the heir was of age. It was, of course, the first request of Gibbon's affectionate father.

Pleased by his welcome, unwilling to disoblige, gratified at the prospect of an assured allowance, hardly aware of the significance of his action, Gibbon consented. Later, he described himself, sardonically, as an innocent victim—in a religious sacrifice: "the priests and the altar had been prepared, and the victim was unconscious of the impending stroke" (90). But none of the contemporary records hints at a feeling of chagrin. Gibbon went through the required form, his father was able to raise £10,000 by means of a mortgage, and, in return, he recognized his son's adulthood, not to say cooperation, with an annuity of £300. This was half again as much as Gibbon's support in Switzerland had cost, and henceforth it could not legally be withheld or withdrawn from him; so much was clear gain. It was, however, no more than the eldest son of a man in Mr. Gibbon's position might have expected without any sacrifice of entailed property, and it was "inadequate to the style of a young Englishman of fashion in the most wealthy Metropolis of Europe" (90). Though Gibbon was indifferent or even averse to some of the expensive pleasures of London, the income had two serious limitations: (1) its buying power, measured against the needs of a serious scholar who had no connection with the universities, in an age when London did not yet have a great public library and when books cost often a pound or a guinea per volume (even when not rich or rare), was at least as limited as it was for a gentleman of fashion, and (2) it lasted only during his lifetime and therefore would offer a very shaky foundation for marriage. Despite the distractions of London and the discovery of parents, Gibbon had certainly not forgotten Suzanne: his third letter to her since leaving Lausanne was posted from London, although he had not heard from her, and she, as he later learned, had not yet received two of his letters.[7]

Vague if exciting prospects for Gibbon's future career were discussed in the evening by the family circle. Perhaps he could obtain the post of Secretary to a foreign embassy (a prospect that enticed him because it would take him back to the Continent); Mrs. Gibbon suggested that he study law. This suggestion, which he later regretted not having pursued, shows her early appreciation of Gibbon's rational and orderly mind; and, in a sense, he did study law when he "force[d his] way through the thorns and thickets of that gloomy labyrinth" (92) in the Roman Empire. At the time, however, he felt that the major barrier to his entering the profession of law was his lack of "the bold and ready eloquence which makes itself heard amidst the tumult of the bar...and I should probably have been diverted from...litterature without...[becoming] a successful pleader" (92).[8]

His annuity prevented his needing a profession to support himself; his talents and temperament prevented his needing one to occupy his time: he never knew "the tediousness of an idle life." London, he found, was "an astonishing and perpetual spectacle...each taste, each sense may be gratified by the variety of objects that will occur in the long circuit of a morning walk." The theater was also a never failing resource, "at a very prosperous æra of the stage, when a constellation of excellent actors . . . was eclipsed by the meridian brightness of Garrick" (93). Though he was sometimes "seduced" by example, he did not much enjoy the commonplace pleasures of town life—tavern, play, coffeehouse, bagnio—yet a "more elegant and rational society" was not within his reach. After twelve years' absence, his sociable father no longer had many useful acquaintances in London, and the shy son "found [him]self a foreigner in a vast and unknown city, and at my entrance into life I was reduced to some dull family parties, to some old Tories of the Cocoa-tree, and to some casual connections, such as my taste and esteem would never have selected" (M 245). There were, of course, the Mallets, with whom he was soon "domesticated" and who introduced him to Lady Hervey, a pleasant exception to his limited society. She had established a French house in St. James's place. At an advanced period of life, she was distinguished by her taste and politeness; her dinners were select: every evening her drawing-room was filled by a succession of the best company of both sexes and all nations; nor was I displeased at her preference and even affectation of the books, the language, and manners of the Continent. (M 245-46)

But his "solitary lodging in Bond Street"—he could not stay long in his aunt's house, which was crowded with schoolboys—"was destitute of books" (M 399), and his entry into society was on the whole left to his own efforts.

Those efforts were languid and slow. I had not been endowed by art or Nature with those happy gifts of confidence and address which unlock every door, and every bosom; nor would it be reasonable to complain of the just consequences of my sickly childhood, foreign education, and reserved temper. While coaches were rattling through Bond Street, I have passed many a solitary evening in my lodging with my books: my studies were sometimes interrupted by a sigh which I breathed towards Lausanne; and on the approach of spring I withdrew without reluctance from the noisy and expensive scene of crowds without company, and dissipation without pleasure. (94)

Even the world of scholarship was inaccessible:

I had promised myself the pleasure of conversing with every man of litterary fame; but our most eminent authors were remote in Scotland, or scattered in the country, or buried in the Universities, or busy in their callings, or unsocial in their tempers, or in a station too high or too low to meet the approaches of a solitary youth. (M 244-45)

One wonders whether Johnson, who after all had already published the *Dictionary* and the *Rambler* papers, and of whose preeminence Gibbon was aware, whatever the uncongeniality of their minds, was in one of those categories.[9] On the whole, in these early years, Gibbon found London lonely and disappointing, and he was not sorry to divide his time very unequally between the town and the country. Having received his first quarter's allowance (£75) on June 29, and having with never-to-be-forgotten "joy...exchanged a bank-note of twenty pounds for the twenty volumes of the Memoirs of the Academy of Inscriptions" (97), he went to Beriton on the first of July. He was highly pleased with his reception there.

The "old mansion...had been converted into the fashion and convenience of a modern house." The site was not well chosen, but the view was "various and chearful: the downs commanded a noble prospect, and the long hanging woods in sight of the house could not perhaps have been improved by art or expence" (94-95). He considered his "the most agreable apartment" of this pleasant house, and it was conveniently on the same floor with the library, which, although "stuffed with much trash of the last age," contained "some valuable Editions of the Classics and the fathers, the choice as it should seem of Mr Law; and many English publications of the times had been occasionally added" (97). So armed, he returned (on July 11) to his *Essai*: "I took in hand again my essay and in about six weeks finished it from C. 23–55 (except 27, 28, 29, 30, 31, 32, 33 and Note * to C. 38) besides a number of chapters from C. 55 to the end which are now struck out."[10] Actually the six-week estimate is generous,[11] because the manuscript is dated August 10, 1758, and either in the month between July 11 and August 10, or in the earlier flurry of travel and a new London life, he wrote four additional chapters, which he does not enumerate in the journal. Three chapters concern the advantages that the religion, politics, and methods of warfare of the ancients offered to their poets, compared to the moderns (chaps. XI–XIII), and one examines the remarkable slightness of the subject that Virgil transformed into a noble poem (chap. XVIII). These chapters, added to the manuscript on the facing pages originally left blank for notes, cannot be dated, but had been completed before the draft was divided into chapters and given chapter numbers.[12] After that process had been begun, and, of course, after the completion of the first draft of the *Essai,* Gibbon had another inspiration and added the chapters on the *Georgics*, which became chapters 20–23 of the draft (chaps. XIX–XXII of the published *Essai)*. The manuscript of these chapters is also dated August 10, 1758.[13] That manuscript begins on the page of Gibbon's notebook which he numbered "227" and is headed "Addition a page 182." The chapter numbers 20–23 had already been used, so that the chapter formerly numbered 20 had to be changed to 24. Several chapters were thus renumbered, but Gibbon then abandoned that dull task, trusting his copyist to be able to count. From "48" on, however, no renumbering was necessary, which makes it clear that it was after Gibbon had numbered the chapters that do not allow for the addition (the last such chapter was eventually published as chapter LII), as well as after he had written the remaining chapters of the draft, which occur on pp. 215–25 of the same notebook, that he stopped to write about the *Georgics*. Furthermore, before giving the manuscript to his copyist he had already written many of the notes and supplied most of the necessary references to sources.

Obviously his working speed had increased impressively, in spite of some new distractions. "By the habit of early rising I always secured a sacred portion of the day, and many scattered moments were stolen and employed by my studious industry" (96). But Mrs. Gibbon was a notable housewife, providing the "neatness and luxury of an English table" (95) for four long meals a day, unlike Mme. Pavillard's scant and "uncleanly" offerings twice a day, and "after breakfast Mrs Gibbon expected my company in her dressing-room: after tea my father claimed my conversation and the perusal of the newspapers" (96); in between, only too often, the visit of a friendly but idle neighbor would have to be politely received. The routine was pleasant, but it allowed Gibbon to discover that even pleasant family life could have its perils. Perhaps this discovery had some effect on his hopes of marriage. The issue, however, did not immediately arise.

Mr. Gibbon was an enthusiastic farmer and sportsman but, to his credit, did not attempt to force his slight and studious son to join him in these activities. "I never handled a gun, I seldom mounted a horse, and my walks were soon terminated by some shady bench of philosophic contemplation." (M 247). Nevertheless, dinners and visits had be to returned, and when the moon was full, so that return journeys after dark were practical, the Gibbons undertook the longer expeditions. Gibbon dreaded, therefore, the full of the moon—a romantic effect with a very prosaic cause.

On Sundays, the family's "pious or decent" custom was to attend church twice. Like other eighteenth-century rationalists, Gibbon was capable of appreciating the moral or literary value of a well-made sermon, but whatever the quality of the sermon, he could improve the hours of the church services by pursuing his Greek, "reading the lessons of the old and new testament every Sunday" (97). Otherwise he neglected his Greek, and even the completion of his series of Latin authors, in favor of the *Essai.*

The portion of the *Essai* conceived and written at Beriton in 1758 reveals a significantly expanded sense of his subject. Canceling the premature comparison of criticism and geometry which he had begun to write at Lausanne, he now went from a definition of criticism to a description of its scope: "Everything that man has been, everything that genius has created, everything that reason has pondered, all that labor has collected—that is the department of criticism."[14] The potential enthusiast suppressed in Gibbon by his painful experiences surely betrays itself for a moment in this exuberant paragraph, which concludes with a portrait of the man of letters at work in his study, "surrounded by the productions of every age" and overlooking nothing that can illuminate or correct his hypotheses. Several characters observe this scene with differing reactions: there is the "erudit," whose work is finished; the "'philosophe' of our time," who "stops there" and praises the memory of the compiler. There is the compiler himself, who sometimes mistakes the "materials for the building."[15]

And then, in the next paragraph, there is "the true critic," hero of the scene, who, unlike any of the others, "knows that his task has only begun."[16] Gibbon's ideal is hardly out of date, except that we might give this character the name of the true scholar or even the true scientist. Now, when he compares criticism to geometry as systems of logic, he can point out that geometry is limited to conclusions that apply within its own closed system, whereas criticism "balances the different degrees of probability."[17] Although an extensive discussion of the Pyrrhonists was added only in a later draft of the *Essai,* it is clear that young Gibbon had already rejected their conclusions. Criticism, he says, "searches for the kind of proofs appropriate to its subject and is content with them. [The critic], modest and sensible, does not display his conjectures as truths, his conclusions as facts, his probabilities as demonstrations."[18]

This approach to criticism, however, widened the material relevant to the essay so greatly as almost to overwhelm its original design. To know how to know what men have written, whether they wrote it well, and whether it was, to the best of their knowledge, true, however necessary such knowledge is to literary or cultural history—*l'histoire des sciences*—is obviously to undertake the task of the general historian; and the 1758 draft as a whole is no longer a reflection on the study of the classics, even in Gibbon's large sense of that term, but on the methods, purposes, and achievements of the study of the past, and on the general intellectual utility of the methods developed by the *érudits* to study it.

The divisions of the 1758 Beriton portion show this new conception. Though chapters 21-28 deal with criticism, they do not try to show that Virgil or Homer yields less delight and instruction to the man unfortified with the critical procedures of classical scholarship. Instead, after Gibbon's eloquent description of the province of criticism and the pointed distinction between the true critic and either *érudit* or *philosophe,* he chose to illustrate the process of balancing critical probabilities with a purely historical question: Was the office of *flamen dialis* vacant from the death of Merula to the time of Augustus? Tacitus, Suetonius, and Dion clearly say so, but they are not contemporary. Cicero, a contemporary, seems to say not, but his statement is ambiguous. "In short, does the probability that the historians knew this fact outweigh the probability that we understand Cicero, or yield to it?"[19] Gibbon did not care how the point was settled, he explained; he merely wished to indicate the sort of delicate question that criticism must and can decide. (This unresolved and limited example was, however, replaced in the published version.)

Criticism is not, he warned and illustrated in the remaining chapters, simply the application of general rules. It is not, unfortunately, a purely speculative discipline, one whose rules can be followed mechanically. "Would that all knowledge were *legum non hominum republica.*"[20] But in fact a critic must be not only "Master of rules, but also master of the reasons for the rules." Horace tells us that poets must portray heroes as history tells us they actually were. This rule, however, deprives the poet of the great power of fiction. We must remember the end of poetry—"To charm, to soften, to elevate the Spirit"—and accept deviations from history that are conducive to that end, but not those that are flagrant or pointless: "Let the reader always discover in [the poet's] fictions, the same degree of pleasure that truth and propriety would have offered him."[21]

The next section, chapters XXXIX–XLIII, does not at all reflect the organizational principle that influenced the Lausanne conception of the *Essai*. These chapters might have been placed elsewhere, so far as we can tell, yet they are ostensibly placed in sequence with the first two divisions by a roman numeral III. The subject of this section "III" is the natural sciences; its theme is that all knowledge is linked, and study of the classics is not useless even to the disciplines apparently most centered on the present, because all fields of knowledge have in common a need for reasoning—without which they are blind—and for facts—without which they are chimerical. The new principle of organization might be an enumeration of occasions for the study of the classics. But roman numeral IV will not fit this hypothesis. It is applied to the section called "L'Esprit Philosophique." Extending La Bruyère's figure, Gibbon finds it rarer than diamonds or pearls and rejects the views that it is the spirit of the age or of the geometers. No one, he wrote, knows how to acquire it; it may not be possible to do so. But belles-lettres, that is (according to his definition), classical studies, can develop that spirit, by requiring us to "escape from our own time and to live in the past"[22] and by revealing to us the unconscious relativity of our judgments, "which detest in the Barbarian what they admire in the Greek."[23] Chapters 38 and 39 of the 1758 draft, the last two chapters of the section, gave an example of this error that was replaced in the published version of the essay.

The combination of the philosophic spirit and the study of the classics led Gibbon to the idea of the philosophic historian, and the remainder of the 1758 *Essai* is devoted to discussion and illustration of the problems and procedures of the ideal historian, under two divisions labeled I. and II. and devoted respectively to issues of fact and theories of cause, until we reach chapter 60 and a section that surprisingly proclaims itself "V." and is devoted to "La Religion."

Under this heading Gibbon discussed, in chapters he later canceled, a subject of obvious interest to readers of the *Decline and Fall*: the emergence of Christianity in the pagan world. This section ends with an astonishingly but misleadingly familiar image: "The cross was erected on the ruins of the Capitol."[24] This section, it must be remembered, was written more than six years before the famous moment of October 15, 1764, when, according to Gibbon, as he "sat musing amidst the ruins of the Capitol while the barefooted fryars were singing Vespers in the temple of Jupiter,...the idea of writing the decline and fall of the City first started to [his] mind" (136, n.7). Had Gibbon precociously defined one of his themes in 1758, only to suppress it in a work published in hope of preferment? No. The specific discussion of Christianity occupies only one of these canceled chapters, which could have been suppressed or altered without affecting the others, if prudence had provoked the change. More significant is the fact that the passage is essentially admiring of Christianity—

not its goodness, but its potency. Readers of the *Decline and Fall* can assume, if they wish, that the admiration is grudging or even somewhat appalled, but perhaps an impartial reader would not make this inference, because the ruins that the Cross is erected upon are not portrayed as noble. The main portion of the passage argues that the study of antiquity can enable us to chart a moderate and accurate course between two extreme views. The first is that all the beauties of the most enlightened Christian ethics are innate in natural religion—"Christianity was not a new yoke imposed on men, but a system of duties known to all nations, adopted by priests, commanded by legislators, taught by philosophers, sung by poets."[25] The second is that without revelation all mankind is utterly vile—"vice and corruption flooded the earth when the legislator of the Christians came there to bring peace and light."[26]

Neither of these extreme views is the truth, said Gibbon. The truth is that "after having paid homage to the virtue of a few, we will shudder with horror at the general curruption," especially that of the emperors themselves. "It has been asked whether virtue could not be loved for itself. Would not anyone who has begun the disgusting history of these monsters cry out instead at every moment, did not these men love evil for itself?" The populace might well regret the memory of Augustus, whose "dissolute and cruel youth served only to put in relief the labours of the rest of his life," the "peace, abundance, and prosperity" of his reign. They could even worship him as a god. But that deification was only a political device of short-lived effectiveness. The real challenge to the evil of his successors was a different life and death. Despite its despised origin and continual persecutions, the teaching of this man is everywhere "reborn from its ashes" until "The Mage and the druid, the Stoic and the Epicurean, unite in believing a doctrine which dazzles reason and subdues it" (chaps. 63-67).[27]

Very much unlike chapters 15 and 16 of the *Decline and Fall,* this passage seems to marvel at the spread of the Christian religion, to find it inexplicable by natural causes. Furthermore, as in the final draft of the *Essai,* Gibbon seems clearly to believe that philosophy as well as revelation indicates the existence of a "Supreme Being." "The adversaries of the Supreme Being are few and hidden, perhaps they do not exist; those of revelation are numerous and bold."[28] By 1761, when he canceled these chapters, Gibbon may have realized that this passage raised more questions than it answered. He may have become more skeptical about the virtues or the inexplicableness of the spread of Christianity. He certainly became aware that one could not argue that its being beyond reason and yet believed, proved that it was extraordinary: "What is too absurd for mankind?" he asked rhetorically.[29] Anyone who reads the two passages together realizes that between August 1758 and April 1761, Gibbon's ironic scepticism considerably increased. The passage of 1761 already suggests the "solemn sneer" of the *Decline and Fall*; the passage of 1758 supports instead a wise observation of Low, at which he arrived on entirely different grounds, that "to assume that Gibbon was a complete sceptic from the time of his reconversion is to falsify both biography and history."[30]

Chapter 68 of this first complete version of the *Essai* sums up the somewhat inchoate whole with the sentence, "There we have some reflections which appear solid to me, on the different uses of classical studies."[31] Vague and loose, this is indeed the only organizational principle that accounts for his five sections or categories. It does not account for their proportions, for the surprising way in which "classical studies" becomes almost synonymous with Roman history after the Lausanne section, or for the real connection between his occasion and his conclusions, his real achievement in the *Essai*. Starting with the assumption that the *philosophes* were the judges of the value of intellectual activity, he began by defending to them the despised *érudits,* only to discover, as he looked at the idea of "criticism," that it led him to an ideal surpassing both, the true critic, whose particular task was the discovery of probabilities about the past. But the logic of the probable requires that one develop not only a science of facts (the contribution of the *érudits*) but also a theory of their significance, a goal that the *philosophes* were at least wise enough to desire, if not to achieve.[32] Thus the study of belles-lettres, history, literature can contribute even to those rival areas of esteem, natural sciences and religion. But this value is only incidental; their real value is the access they give us to a knowledge of times and places unlike our own, and the way of reasoning that is analogous to that needed in everyday life, a form of reasoning that permits recognition of something justly called truth although outside the closed system of a mathematical demonstration. This was, in brief, the *Essai* that was ready for a copyist in August 1758.

As Gibbon well remembered, and recorded three years later in his journal, it was August 24 when he hired M. Burdot, a French prisoner at Petersfield, to make a fair copy of the *Essai* for him.[33] It is not surprising that he remembered the exact date, because it also marked the effective end of another significant era in his life. It was the very day on which he "sighed as a lover" but "obeyed as a son" (85, n.7), or at least the day on which he brought himself to write to Suzanne to tell her that their fate had been determined.[34]

As Gibbon explained to Suzanne, he had approached his father about their love and their desire to marry. His father had told him that, being independent (i.e., receiving an annuity of £300), he could marry his "foreigner" if he liked, but before he did, he should remember that he was "a son and a Citizen" (*fils et Citoyen*). Then he had expatiated on the cruelty of abandoning him, of sending him early to his grave, and on the baseness *(lacheté)* of trampling underfoot all that he owed to his country.[35] Under this barrage from a father whose long-withheld approval he had enjoyed only a few months, conscious of the bitter penalty he had suffered for a previous romantic decision contrary to his father's will (his conversion to Catholicism), already aware that £300 a year was a narrow income for a gentleman-scholar, Gibbon could have resisted only if inspired by the sole love of his life. But in fact Suzanne had a rival, a "passion"—Gibbon's word—to which his love of her had always been second in time and which he might, especially in this moment of achieved composition, recognize as primary in power as well, "the love of Study."[36] The real choice was not between Suzanne and Gibbon's father, or even between Suzanne in Switzerland and his father in England, but between the life of a scholar and the life of a husband; his income could not support him as both, and his father made it plain that he would not increase it if Gibbon married contrary to his wishes. The choice does not necessarily imply that Gibbon's love of Suzanne Curchod was insincere or shallow; instead, it demonstrates that his love of scholarship was profound and inescapable.

The remainder of 1758 was inevitably anticlimactic. The surviving letters indicate a short trip to London in October as the only interruption to Gibbon's pastoral and studious life at Beriton before his going to London for the winter in mid-December.[37] That October visit probably had the important object of taking the *Essai* to its first external reader and critic, Matthew Maty, a librarian of the fledgling British Museum and erstwhile author of the *Journal Britannique*.[38] The account of the consultation of Maty which Gibbon gives in the *Memoirs* is quite misleadingly smooth and urbane: "His answer to my first letter was prompt and polite: after a careful examination he returned my Manuscript with some animadversion and much applause, and when I visited London, in the ensuing winter, we discussed the design and execution in several free and familiar conversations" (100). In fact, Maty was not particularly prompt and, to that extent, was less polite than Gibbon graciously asserts, although there may have been a (lost) letter of inquiry that received a (lost) prompt reply. Gibbon took or sent the manuscript to Maty in October. He was disagreeably surprised to have heard nothing from his selected mentor two months later, when he went to London again.[39]

While waiting, Gibbon allowed himself some leisure to enjoy the countryside. One fine November day, deserting his philosophic bench, he mounted a horse, summoned a groom, and rode out to enjoy "the beauty of the day and the pleasure of the ride," following wherever his groom led him. To his surprise, he was soon warned off a neighbor's manor as a suspected gentleman-poacher. His graceful but dignified note of explanation and apology survives to tell the tale.[40] Another story, possibly apocryphal, points to a lifelong interest in one aspect of country life, small animals. An old servant of the Gibbons recalled that the young man, aroused from scholarly contemplation by the cries of a dog that the servant was beating, intervened in the dog's behalf by beating the servant.

Gibbon loved and owned dogs throughout his life, but so physical a response, even to unwarranted abuse, does not seem characteristic of him. Perhaps the old servant improved his story.[41]

Even while his manuscript was out of his hands, Gibbon continued to think about his *Essai*. On October 2 he made some extracts from the *Mémoires de l'Académie des Inscriptions*, part of which he later incorporated in a note to his book. On November 2 he wrote an addition that was, again in part and after heavy revision, incorporated in the book. On December 5 he wrote another addition, which became chapter XLVII. Each of these revisions is keyed not to the fair copy, which, of course, was still in Maty's hands, but to the original manuscript.[42] Considering the habits of application he had now developed, it is likely that Gibbon found other work to do as well. Perhaps this was the period in which he began to work at reacquiring, as it were, his native language:

> The favourite companions of my leisure were our English writers since the Revolution: they breathe the spirit of reason and liberty, and they most seasonably contributed to restore the purity of my own language which had been corrupted by the long use of a foreign Idiom. By the judicious advice of Mr Mallet I was directed to the writings of Swift and Addison: wit and simplicity are their common attributes: but the style of Swift is supported by manly original vigour; that of Addision is adorned by the female graces of elegance and mildness; and the contrast of too coarse or too thin a texture is visible even in the defects of these celebrated authors. (98)

There is, in any event, little of the foreigner in the charming letter he wrote home on December 14. He had gone to his aunt's while looking for a lodging. The "hurry and noise and meazels" there made the day and half among her Westminster boys seem long. One of them was "Dr Maty's son a little odd cur, and by an unexampled generosity I tipped the boy with a crown and the father with a coal of fire."[43] It is pleasant to see the playful and easy relationship Gibbon now had—at least in letters—with his father.

He had been to the Westminster Scholars' Latin play the night before and

> proper allowances being made was very well entertained. All spoke justly enough and some (one or two) promised a good Deal. Harry Courtenay was one of these but he disapointed me before the end of the play. He came on with ease and enter[ed] well into his caracter. . . . From thence he sunk gradually tho' encouraged by repeated claps, dragged himself through the last scenes in the most dead and lifeless manner; my expectations were deceived, more than they ever were in my whole life.

As he wrote, he had just come from a visit to Dorothea Celesia, David

Mallet's daughter by his first marriage. Gibbon disliked her attire, enjoyed her conversation, and found her face not "pretty [but] something sweet enough."[44]

Naturally he described his new lodgings. They were in New Bond Street, at a linen draper's (appropriate for Matthew's great-grandson). For a guinea and a half a week, he had "a very good first floor, dining room bed-chamber and light closet with many conveniences." He had also acquired a chair (for which he paid 27 shillings) with the help of one Lee.[45] At relatively little expense, then, he had his town establishment of "a lodging, a servant, and a chair" (M 244), and a refuge in the country when his money ran out. Later, he prided himself on never having exceeded his allowance in the "seven years (1758-1760, 1765-1770) which [he] divided between London and Buriton" (M 243).

In the winter, as in the previous spring, his engagements, as far as they were recorded in the extant letters, were limited to his family, the Mallets, and their acquaintances. By December 21 he had visited Dr Maty: "I have seen Dr Maty. *Là Là*. He made little or no excuse for having deferred writing but has already criticised it with sense and severity. He finds it as I hoped. Good in general, but many faults in the detail."[46] His English here seems to have been contaminated by renewed contact with French. Although the meeting with Maty had not been fully satisfactory, he had hopes of a high intellectual treat when he wrote to his father on December 30: "I am also to meet at Mrs Celesia's the Great David Hume."[47] It is improbable, however, that he actually enjoyed this treat; so memorable an event would certainly have been recorded in his journal, in which he noted his reading of Hume's history.[48]

Literature and society were not his only preoccupations that winter. In Lausanne he had always found a little money to relieve an Englishman in distress; in England it was, logically enough, a Frenchman who engaged his compassion. The prisoners' allowances from France had ceased, and Burdot, the copyist of the *Essai*, had written to ask Gibbon's help. Gibbon not only answered his letter, but wrote to his father:

> I beg you would give him Five Guineas and deduct it upon the Christmas quarter of my Allowance. I do not doubt but you will do something for him, as I really think his situation deserves pity. This cessation of the prisoner's allowance shews I think better than fifty monitors to how low an Ebb the French are reduced. I cannot help pitying them too. I do not think it necessary to have no compassion, in order to be a good Englishman.[49]

The same letter reveals that Gibbon's scholarly affairs had received a check. He complained, "At last Maty and I have down-right quarelled. He behaved so very contempt[u]ously to me! Never made the least excuse for having eked out two weeks into two months."[50] We can picture

Gibbon giving the fair copy of his manuscript to the sometime editor of the distinguished journal, being told to expect a reply within two weeks, and returning home to await it—in vain. Most young scholars can sympathize! In completing the account of the matter to his father, however, Gibbon at least pretended to a philosophical calm. Maty had "left two letters I wrote him since without any answer, never came near me, [so] that at last I desired him to send back my manuscript. He did so. I then wrote him a letter to explain My behaviour. He answered it by another politely bitter. So *tout est fini.*"[51] In the event this proved to be merely a momentary rift, not a breach, with Maty, and, whatever his sense of injury at the time, Gibbon saw no reason to preserve his grievance in his memoirs.

If December was chilling, January was bleak. His sense of solitude and loneliness in the midst of the crowds and dissipation of the city continued, and it did not help that he considered the limitations to be imposed in large part by the faults of his own shy temperament or by the folly that had made him "a stranger in [his] own country" (M 399).

In February he went to Beriton again, with the fair copy of his *Essai,* retrieved from Maty. He improved it with the addition of chapters XXVII–XXXIII and the note* to chapter XXXVIII. He also wrote part of the preface. Yet he was in the country only "a few days" before, in the last week of February, he was back in London.[52] These new chapters replace a single chapter of the original draft (chap. 24) and amount to an attempt to *demonstrate* that the Pyrrhonist attack on historical certainty could be answered by methods the Pyrrhonists themselves used, that is, that we do not inevitably wind up in a state of helpless uncertainty as we dismiss layer after layer of error; the true *érudits* (not the mere compilers) have shown that we can reach relative though not absolute historical certainty, enough to base a narrative account upon. The problem was whether literary evidence was to be wholly rejected or merely reinterpreted. Gibbon worked out an example dealing with the date of the first treaty between Rome and Carthage and requiring consideration of the origin of the Roman navy. In the revised transitional chapter (XXXIV) in which he returned from this illustration to his discussion, Gibbon explained his purpose:

> I have especially wished to show by these reflections how delicate the discussions of criticism are, where it is not a question of grasping a demonstration, but of comparing the weight of opposed probabilities; and how necessary it is to distrust the most dazzling systems, since there are so few that withstand the test of a free and attentive examination.[53]

We may compare this with the much vaguer explanation in the canceled paragraph 24. This passage about the treaty has been condemned as a digression, even an "irrelevant digression,"[54] but it clearly has a logical place in the design of the essay, as an illustration. It gives the impression of a digression because the illustration grows so much larger than its occasion; a means appears here as if it were an end.

In two other alterations made in this 1759 visit to Beriton, Gibbon managed to retain a better proportion by confining his illustrations to notes. The note he referred to in the journal entry is a comment on Newton's ancient chronology. It is longer than many of his "chapters," but at least it is *called* a note. Also lengthy, though obviously of less importance in Gibbon's memory, was a note on Lucretius dated Feburary 5, 1759, which was added to the revision of chapter XLVII that he had made while Maty had his fair copy.

These are extensive changes; perhaps Maty discussed with him the dangers of an unresolved argument (in chap. 24) in a treatise intended to challenge the Pyrrhonists, among others. But the *Memoirs* give the false impression that Maty's advice and criticism immediately led Gibbon to put the *Essai* in virtually its final form. In the *Memoirs,* after mentioning his conversation with Maty, Gibbon continued: "In a short excursion to Buriton, I reviewed my Essay according to his friendly advice, and after suppressing a third, adding a third and altering a third, I consummated my first labour by a short preface, which is dated February 3^{d} 1759" (100). The labors of 1761 are underplayed as a "revisal" (101). In fact, most of this new material was not written until 1761, long after Maty's advice and influence could have been fresh in Gibbon's mind.

In the winter of 1759, he turned instead to other intellectual pursuits. The journal tells us of his reading, which included the four available volumes of Hume's history of England, Robertson's history of Scotland, and Freret's refutation of Newton's ancient chronology. Although Gibbon found Freret somewhat disappointing, the two British historians—who marked, to Gibbon's taste, a great advance over their English-language predecessors, both in manner and in matter—inspired him with ambition and despair: "The perfect composition, the nervous language, the well-turned periods of Dr Robertson inflamed me to the ambitious hope, that I might one day tread in his footsteps: the calm philosophy, the careless inimitable beauties of his friend and rival [Hume] often forced me to close the volume, with a mixed sensation of delight and despair" (99). It is the letters, however, that inform us of what no doubt seemed at the time the most significant developments of the winter. The first ominous note in the long series of financial crises in which Gibbon was involved with his father was sounded (had £10,000 already been dissipated?), and Suzanne's response to his letter of farewell reached him at last.

The financial shadow fell in actions, not words. The quarter's allowance due on December 29, or perhaps only some portion of it, seems not to have been paid. In a note that J. E. Norton has plausibly dated February 22, Gibbon had to write to his stepmother:

I am really concerned my father has not sent me a draught. I am really distressed for money. I have hardly a Guinea left and you know the unavoidable expences of London. I have tryed to borrow of Mrs Porten and of Harvey, my father's lawyer. But without success. Could you not send me a bank note by the Harting Post of Monday. I would run all the risk of its being lost; for, upon my word I shall hardly know what to do in three or four days.[55]

This letter is not really despairing, because the paragraph quoted is preceded and followed by cheerful chat. And it is amusing to recover the evidence that if Gibbon could claim "the singular merit of never having borrowed a shilling during the whole term of [his] filial dependence" (M 243), it was not for lack of trying. Mr. Gibbon's financial carelessness and delay would later occasion Gibbon many difficulties and some real distress, both before and after his father's death.

With the help of Suzanne's letter, Gibbon made another unpleasant discovery: his parents had been intercepting his mail. Suzanne's letter, dated November 5, tells how astonished she had been at having no reply to her letter of September 7 (and well she might have been surprised, if he cared for her, because hers was a very moving letter): "My regard for you, of which your tenderness formed one of the strongest links, was beginning to weaken," but she went on to say that she had eventually received a letter from his stepmother, informing her, with a delicacy and care that made Suzanne augur well of her character (this apparently without irony), that her letter to Gibbon had been intercepted, as others would be.[56] It had been suggested to Suzanne that Gibbon was a party to this action, but she did not believe it (she said, obviously seeking reassurance). She would not tell him how her personality had altered, how her gaiety had turned to melancholy, but her sentiments could not change, at least while she was unsure that his had. Knowing that her mother would be happy to live in England with her, she renewed a project that she had discussed with him before. Suzanne would stay in Switzerland only during the lifetime of her mother's husband (as she called her father in this context), "and if you could but make me one visit of some months in all that interval, I believe that I would prefer this plan to many others, if however M. Gibbon is inflexible, you know my views too well to need to tell me that nothing would oblige you to betray your duty."[57]

Gibbon's letter in reply, dated London, February 23, 1759, may employ an operatic rhetoric but nevertheless seems full of genuine emotion. He had had a hard time obeying Suzanne's command that he not let Mrs. Gibbon know that he knew about the intercepted letter; he wanted to reproach her. She had made him "languish Six months in painful suspense, devoured by troubles a burden to myself and others: uncertain of your sentiments, of your fate of all that interested me!" The breathless punctuation, normal for Suzanne, is in Gibbon's correspondence a sign of haste or strong feeling or both. And he added a pair of bitter sentences convincing to Suzanne: "These parents say however that they only desire our happiness. They believe it themselves."[58] The angry and ineloquent incredulity rings true.

He went on to tell her how much he loved her, how, despite all the distractions of his present life, despite never even hearing her name, he was always thinking of "the only woman who could have made me happy." When he received her letter he had gone to Beriton and raised the matter again with his father—shown all her merits, the sincerity and permanence of his attachment, the practicality of her proposal for their residence—but all in vain. His father was adamant, not only on the unreliability of lovers' judgments and the necessity that Gibbon marry advantageously, but especially on the problem of Suzanne's nationality. "You are already only too much inclined to foreign manners," he had said. Mlle. Curchod "would use her influence to induce you to expatriate yourself. Her action would be natural, but what a misfortune for me, what a crime for you." This refusal had given Gibbon moments of wanting to throw over all duty and be happy regardless of the cost—or at least to wait, hoping for eventual happiness. But the wait would be for that happy event, a father's death, and what a hope that would be. Besides, his father might outlive him—what then would Suzanne's state be? (She would have no claims on Gibbon's family and would have lost her chance of finding happiness or at least a home as another man's wife.)

He therefore concluded that they must forget each other, or remember each other only as friends. They must marry others, an idea he could hardly endure. "I fear that you cannot make this effort. I fear that you can. Alas, will I be able to do it myself?"[59]

He added a postscript to tell her how to write to him, and to send polite greetings to her parents. Unfortunately, he began the postscript by observing that he did not know whether it was "prudent" to continue the correspondence, though he could not bring himself to deprive himself of it. He might more accurately have said that he did not know whether continuing it, since they must relinquish all hope of happiness together, would cause them more pain than pleasure. But Suzanne, not unnaturally, responded to the worldly, unfeeling connotations of the word he chose, "prudence," and found the postcript "offensive." Her reply, in which she says as much and asks him (rather sarcastically) to spare her fifteen minutes of his leisure four times a year, is undated but is not earlier than April 1759, or later than January 1760.[60] If Gibbon answered it, she did not preserve the letter or reply to it. Gibbon's apparent fear that to continue their correspondence was to continue to torture themselves and each other was amply borne out by her letter. As in the case of his chosen religion, he was reconverted from his chosen love slowly, reluctantly, but in the end, completely. It could be a consolation to the woman, if not to the creed, that he never put another in their places.

When spring approached, the scene changed. Gibbon withdrew with his usual relief from London's noise and expense. In 1759, April 11 is recorded as the date of his return to Beriton. There he turned again to scholarship. His first efforts were devoted to an essay, "Sur le Nombre des habitans dans la cité des Sybarites."[61] In this brief piece he attempted to steer a course between Wallace's credulity about ancient statistics and Hume's equally off-hand skepticism about them. Gibbon tried instead to *demonstrate* that a particular statistic could not be accurate. His argument is dry, the issue is not very momentous, but both the logic and the data show what Gibbon could have done in antiquarian debate, had he chosen to make a career of it. The last sentence, however, reminds us of a more familiar Gibbon: "In everything—except religion—it is better not to believe enough, than to believe too much."[62] According to one draft of his memoirs, 1759 was the year in which a reading of Grotius's *De Veritate Religionis Christianae* "first engaged me in a regular tryal of the evidence of Christianity" (211, M 249), a trial, he implies, in which Christianity was not the victor.

His next scholarly undertaking was not, however, of so controversial a nature. "After having read Greaves, Arbuthnot, Hooper, de la Barre, Freret and Eisenschmidt, I resolved to write a treatise upon the ancient weights, coins and measures, the first two of which I finished."[63] Of this project he later remarked, "In my first Essay I had gathered some of the flowers, in my second I would have removed some of the thorns, of litterature" (M 251-52). In so saying he echoed his introduction to the work itself:

There are studies which do not increase knowledge, or at least increase it only in that they clear away those obstacles which the oddity of men has planted in its road on every side. Such is the study of languages.... The distinction of weights and measures is a new language, as barbarous as, and more ridiculous than, the others.... It will serve us as an interpreter in the geography, commerce, and economy of the ancients, interesting objects, the knowledge of which will prevent us from seeing in the ancients either savages or demi-gods.[64]

The next paragraph begins with a somewhat defensive comment on his decision to write in French and continues with a survey of the authorities consulted. The two parts or approaches to the subject which he completed are, as published in the *Miscellaneous Works,* longer than the *Essai,* and considerably longer than the *Essai* as he had then completed it. Obscured by Lord Sheffield's ingenious editing, however, is the fact that the material he published is really two drafts or approaches developing much the same material. The two manuscripts he conflated are differently numbered, differently placed on the paper, and in different stages of completeness. They are in strikingly different hands. It was only the first of these drafts that was written in 1759.[65]

The "completed" sections were composed under the title of "Remarques" on weights, money, and so forth, and that title was descriptive of the original approach. But the transitions are made even more arbitrary by Lord Sheffield's rearrangements. Because the two drafts involve repetitions, some rearrangement was forced upon him. Making such decisions, he also had to decide which notes to ignore and which to include. As a result, his version does not indicate how thoroughly Gibbon planned to document his conclusions. In short, Sheffield's heroic but misleading effort to make one readable text from two versions of a work that were composed several years apart must be reversed in order to determine Gibbon's scholarly activity in 1759. Gibbon's procedure seems to have been to make evaluative notes from his sources, then to employ these in loosely organized excursions of his own, and finally to try to incorporate them in a reasoned and polished argument. Furthermore, we can see that he carried on these different procedures simultaneously in different parts of his manuscript, that is, that he went on to the next section without finishing those that had gone before.

Perhaps we may infer a certain discomfort with this kind of scholarship on Gibbon's part. He clearly recognized that the *monumens*—the nonliterary sources of evidence—were his best authorities and that the problems he was addressing were petty in themselves, though useful or essential to more significant issues. He set himself an unglamorous but serviceable task of antiquarian research, for which he had neither first-hand materials nor a clear critical method. Common sense could and did serve him well, but it was not a substitute for original research in inscriptions and manuscripts and the like, and it did not amount to a systematic criticism of the published evidence. He could not make an original contribution to the subject and soon found that he could not content himself with extracting a useful handbook from the work of others. Nevertheless, he persevered and, as we shall see, even returned to the material. Yet it was perhaps with a certain relief that on June 12, 1759, he was interrupted "by the sound of the Militia drum" (M 252).

His first adult efforts to be his father's son in his father's world had met with mixed success. While he felt incorporated into, and comfortable in, his new-found family, he had neither found nor made a place for himself in the larger world of London, and the greatest virtue and happiness of the life of a country gentleman was for him the far from conventional resource of his books and his writing. He could not, it seemed, be happy in the life of a young Englishman of means and leisure, unless it was diluted with the challenges of scholarship. For a time, however, the new role he was about to undertake, as a comrade of his father, seemed satisfying.

CHAPTER 9

Soldier, Scholar,
Would-be Statesman

IN THE YEARS 1759-62, the contemplative Gibbon was converted, willy-nilly, to an active life: he became a citizen soldier. It was a role that he always respected in theory and that he carried out with dutiful diligence and some skill when, with the embodying of the Hampshire Militia, it was required of him; but it was totally foreign to his ordinary choices and abilities. Consequently, the first portion of his military life was marked by a hiatus in his scholarly activity.

As Gibbon explains in the *Memoirs,* he and his father had accepted their commissions (Gibbon as captain, his father as major) in the Hampshire Militia with sufficient patriotic fervor for the duties they expected, namely, monthly or weekly drills and a few meetings—the whole duty of militia officers when their units were not active.[1] They failed to anticipate that the militia would be embodied. After all, the Seven Years War had been carried on well enough without the active participation of the militia since 1756, and William Pitt, who had been in charge of the war since the end of 1757, would presumably already have made the changes he intended. And 1759 did not mark an increase in British peril, but rather was a year of numerous victories. True, there was a real threat of invasion, but before the end of the year, that too had been dispelled. Therefore, the call to arms surprised the unmilitant Gibbons.

The immediate effect of their gesture in joining the militia had simply been that "many tedious days were consumed at Petersfield, Alton, and Winchester, in our meetings of Justices and Deputy-Lieutenants" (M 247). Though boring, the new duties did not seem onerous, but, as Gibbon commented in 1761. "I knew not what I engaged in."[2] At the time, there was no need to give up other activities, serious or frivolous. That summer, Gibbon attended his father "to the races at Stockbridge, Reading, and Odiham, where he had entered a horse for the hunter's plate" (M 163); in September, they spent about a week with "M^r. Lethuillier at Red Rice," attending the Stockbridge races.[3] Gibbon remembered the occasion with pleasure; the color and excitement of "our Olympic games, the beauty of the spot,

the fleetness of the horses and the gay tumult of the numerous spectators" (M 163).

At home the distractions included a two-month visit from Mrs. Mallet
(September–October). Because Gibbon did not like her, perhaps he was
not sorry to be called away from home on other business. But the other
business was not confined to the militia. Gibbon and his father undertook
to support Simeon Stuart against Henry Legge as Member of Parliament
for Hampshire. They subscribed to his campaign—Mr. Gibbon £100, Gibbon £25—and, in November, Gibbon "constantly attended the meetings"
and helped in the canvass of Waltham, Portsmouth, and Gosport. The
campaigning failed, but for Gibbon it was not a total waste: "the interruption of my studies was compensated in some degree by the spectacle
of English manners, and the acquisition of some practical knowledge"
(M 163-64).

Toward the end of November, Gibbon went again to London for the
winter, traveling with a contemporary, Sir Gerald Aylmer, as he had done
the year before—for convenience, it would seem, not pleasure: the previous year Gibbon had had "a pretty tedious journey which [Aylmer's]
conversation did not render less so."[4] His town life was much as it had
been in the winter of 1758-59, except that he now found himself an Italian
master: "We read a grammar of his own and afterwards Machiavel's His-
toria Fiorentina and Discorsi sopra il Tito Livio and I came to read and
understand it pretty well but not to speak it at all."[5] This is not only the
only recorded intellectual activity of the winter, but the only recorded
activity of any kind, for there are no extant letters of the period.

On April 28, 1760, with the spring, Gibbon returned as usual to Beriton. There he settled down peacefully to work, reading dissertations by La
Bletterie and La Bastie on the powers and titles of the Roman emperors
and adding a note to his extracts from the former.[6] He even made approaches to his father—by letter, although they were living in the same
house—about a trip to Italy, land of his scholarly dreams.[7] So far, Captain
Gibbon's life had differed very little from that of Mr. Edward Gibbon, Jr.
But less than two weeks later, the South Battalion of the Hampshire Militia
was embodied. It was commanded by Lieutenant Colonel Sir Thomas
Worsley, Major Edward Gibbon, and Captain Edward Gibbon, Jr., and
consisted of 476 officers and men. There were four other captains, "seven
lieutenants, seven Ensigns [there were seven companies], twenty-one Ser-
jeants, fourteen drummers, and four hundred and twenty rank and file"
(M 183). Gibbon commanded a lieutenant, three sergeants, an ensign, two
drummers, and sixty men. It was not exactly a Roman legion, but it was
more than he had bargained for.[8]

"At the first outset I was dazzled and fired by the play of arms," he
admitted, "the exercise, the march, and the camp" (M 299). In another
account, he generalized:

A youth of any spirit is fired even by the play of arms, and my enthusiasm aspired to the character of a *real* soldier; but the martial feaver was cooled by the enjoyment of our mimic Bellona, who soon revealed to my eyes her naked deformity.... A larger introduction into the English World was a poor compensation for such company and such employment—for the loss of time and health in the daily and nocturnal exercises of the field and of the bottle. (M 401)

It is startling enough to think of Gibbon's small body in the saddle as he marched his sixty-five officers and men, not to mention his drummer boys, the ten miles or more from Alton to Alresford.[9] But there was more. The twenty-three-year-old scholar emerged from his books to find himself the acting executive of an independent battalion. The regular colonel of the South Battalion had resigned. Although the Duke of Bolton, commandant of the North Battalion, tried to elevate himself into the head of a two-battalion Hampshire regiment, the Gibbons, with their friend and Lieutenant Colonel Sir Thomas Worsley, successfully resisted this project and remained independent. The dispute on this issue occupied much of Gibbon's and his father's attention in the early months of the militia's active duty.

When that victory was obtained, however, Gibbon himself might well have regretted it, because although his "proper station was that of first Captain...as the Major was [his] father, and the Lieutenant-Colonel-Commandant...[his] friend, as they were often absent and always inattentive" (M 400), he had to supply their functions: "Every memorial and letter relative to our disputes was the work of my pen; the detachments or court-martials of any delicacy or importance were my extraordinary duties; and to supersede the Duke of Bolton's adjutant, I always exercised the Battalion in the field." On the positive side, "The habits of a sedentary life were usefully broken by the duties of an active profession: in the healthful exercise of the field I hunted with a battalion instead of a pack, and at that time I was ready, at any hour of the day or night, to fly from quarters to London, from London to quarters, on the slightest call of private or regimental business" (M 189-90). Nor was exercise the only or principal benefit:

My principal obligation to the militia was the making me an Englishman and a soldier....I should long have continued a stranger in my native country had I not been shaken in this various scene of new faces and new friends....The discipline and evolutions of a modern battalion gave me a clearer notion of the Phalanx and the Legion, and the Captain of the Hampshire grenadiers (the reader may smile) has not been useless to the historian of the Roman Empire. (117)

Gibbon's remarkable memory, operating on events little more than a year in the past, permitted him to record in his journal many of the comings and goings, the marches by day and debauches by night, of the first and worst months of his militia life. Although his duties never took him north of London, east of Dover, west of Blandford, or south of the Isle of Wight, he traveled hundreds of miles on horseback at all hours and in all weathers and experienced the irritations of bureaucracy, the responsibilities of caring for the health, welfare, and freedom of other men, and, albeit in a small way, something of the cruelties incidental to war even apart from the battlefield. No wonder he could deplore with fervor the Roman establishment that placed Horace, among others, in co-command of a legion "equal to eight or nine of our battalions....a worthy commander, of three and twenty from the schools of Athens!"[10]

The versions of this military life in the *Memoirs* vary significantly from one draft to another (the final draft was interrupted well before he reached this period of his life). The first and fullest version is introduced as follows:

> I shall now amuse myself with the recollection of an active scene which bears no affinity to any other period of my studious and social life. From the general idea of a militia I shall descend to the Militia of England in the war before the last; to the state of the Regiment in which I served, and to the influence of that service on my personal situation and character. (107)

It is obvious that Gibbon wanted to justify a full account of his militia life by treating it *en historien*; Lord Sheffield ruthlessly omitted all the result, and Bonnard called it a "digression." So it is, but a digression that indirectly reveals a good deal about the author's motivations and expectations, perhaps his pride and disappointments. For example:

> At a distance from their respective counties, these provincial corps were stationed, and removed, and encamped by the command of the Secretary of War; the officers and men were trained in the habits of subordination nor is it surprizing that some regiments should have assumed the discipline and appearance of veteran troops. With the skill they soon imbibed the spirit of mercenaries, the character of a militia was lost; and, under that specious name, the crown had acquired a second army more costly and less useful than the first. (111)[11]

The ironic significance of the final comment is clear.

In the subsequent drafts, Gibbon's account of his own service diminished and the larger historical perspective disappeared altogether. His first account of his own career requires about ten pages in Murray's edition of the drafts; about seven suffice for the second; two for the third; half a page for the last version, that of Draft E. The themes of the second version (Draft C) are two, respectively, "the history of my bloodless and inglorious campaigns....[which] have lost much of their importance in my own eyes" (M 253), and the interruption and resumption of his literary life, especially the good and bad effects of a different style of living, with the contribution of the captain of the Hampshire militia to the historian of the Roman Empire. In other words, Gibbon betrays some doubt as to the legitimacy of including material not needed to develop the account of the growth of the historian's mind. Drafts D and E achieved the subordination he approached in Draft C, and the lengthy period of Gibbon's life in which his intellectual aims were rivaled by ambitions and concerns of other kinds was effectively veiled.

That period is, however, intrinsically of interest to those who wish to know Gibbon himself—warts, contradictions, aborted possibilities or designs, and all. From it we learn that Gibbon could have been a useful public official or civil servant; he could even have found a welcome among his Hampshire neighbors as a convivial Tory squire. Before his militia service, his scholarship had been the only work he had ever had an opportunity to do; the alternatives had been love, poverty, and idleness. Afterward, the same scholarship was, in a new sense, a chosen life.

The first important experience of the militia period was the removal to Blandford "for the benefit of a foreign education" (112). The battalion took three days to march from Winchester. Gibbon found himself dining and drinking with companions whom he would never have known in his ordinary life as Hampshire gentleman or Continental scholar. The first station was almost too pleasant, "the weather fine, the quarters as good both for the officers and men as cheapness plenty and pleasantness could make them; the Battalion coming on every day under the care of Abbot. The Gentlemen of the County shewed us great hospitality . . . , but partly thro' their fault and partly thro' ours that hospitality was often debauch."[12]

The next assignment was not so happily arranged. In September, the battalion having been removed to Hilsea Barracks, Gibbon himself was sent with a detachment of "four subalterns...seven sergeants nine corporals and 214 private to guard about 3200 prisoners." Though the duty lasted only about a week and Gibbon recorded it nearly a year later, his account reproduced something of his concern at the time: "The place was agreable for the officers....But it was very bad for the men as we mounted 69 private every day, besides the piquet, and they were half that time on Sentry. The prison was very loathsome and the men's barracks not much better."[13]

Even more vividly remembered was an instance of army politics and discipline. The battalion's enemy, the Duke of Bolton, had insisted on depriving them of their excellent adjutant Abbot, and in September the duke decided to foist on them an ensign from his own battalion, one McCombe. A South Battalion sergeant said publicly that McCombe had been a prize fighter, as well as an alehouse keeper, and had been dismissed from another regiment "for having cheated his Captain as Paymaster Serjeant." Hearing this, McCombe demanded a court-martial of the sergeant. Numerous townspeople testified that McCombe's bad behavior was generally reported when he was discharged. On this evidence, the court-martial, of which Gibbon was president, acquitted the sergeant of the authorship of the story "without entering into the truth" of it. The officers of the South Battalion then wrote to ask to be relieved of such an adjutant, to which the duke replied "that our letter had made no manner of impression on him, and that to shew his approbation of M! McCombe in the strongest manner instead of an Ensign which he had made him at first, he had now appointed him a Lieutenant."[14]

The dispute dragged on for several months. On October 9, the South Battalion struck back by arresting McCombe for disobedience and applying to court-martial him (they had already been threatened with a court of enquiry on their court martial of the sergeant): the court-martial, delayed by the death of George II, finally met at Portsmouth, November 17-19, and dealt with both cases. The sentences, received on November 29, were "a publick reprimand for the Adjutant and a fortnight's suspension for Firth [the sergeant]." Probably no one was satisfied; certainly the justice-loving young Captain Gibbon was not. He recorded that the judge advocate "acted with the most notorious partiality."[15]

Gibbon also remembered in vivid detail the night of October 27, when, having been relieved in another stint at Portchester at 5 P.M., he and his men marched "thro' a dark night and heavy rain, not to the Barracks which the Battalion had quitted some few days before but to Fareham"—fortunately not far away. "The barracks within the Portsmouth lines are a square of low, ill-built huts, in a damp and dreary situation: on this unwholesome spot we lost many men by feavers and the small-pox" (M 185). He noted that the "Barracks had been very fatal...to the peace and discipline of the Corps," not only because of the disputes and court martials but also because of the duty itself. Their seven hundred men had replaced "two regular regiments," and their service was therefore "so hard that we could never have a field day, and finally we discharged and lost by sickness a great number of our men."[16]

Young Gibbon leading his men through a rainy night and worrying about their housing, sickness, and lack of military exercise is a surprising figure to those who know only the tranquil historian, cheerfully killing off battalions of Roman soldiers with his pen and only mildly curious about the prospects of the dawning French Revolution.[17] In a more familiar activity, he "retired" November 3 to Beriton "in the design of spending some days in solitude and quiet," but only to be carried off to the conviviality of Up Park the very next day.[18]

In December, the battalion received the surprising order to remove to Sissinghurst. They tried to "beg off," Gibbon says; they were told they must go on "but should soon be relieved."[19] The march to Sissinghurst, a long distance away for a militia company, required eleven days (December 2-12), of which three were rest days. The distance from Fareham to

Sissinghurst is perhaps 90 miles in a straight line, but their assigned route was far from a straight line, carrying them as far north as Greenwich before sending them east to Rochester and south again to Sissinghurst. Perhaps they averaged some 20 miles per day of marching, that is, traveled approximately 160 miles.

Gibbon's own route was, however, longer still, for from Rochester a political emergency sent him riding through the night—may we say galloping?—to London. He set out about 10 P.M. and reached London about 3 A.M. The political matter was only "some difficulties" about the advertising of a meeting at which the Gibbons' candidate for M.P. could address the electors. Thus Gibbon's nighttime ride of some 40 miles, not to mention the return journey necessary to catch up with the battalion at Maidstone, was indeed proof that he then "was ready at any hour of the day or night to fly...on the slightest call of private or regimental business."

In Kent the battalion had to guard more prisoners. "The duty was harder than at Portchester, the dirt most excessive thro' which the men from their wretched barracks had two miles to march everyday, & the officers three, from a Country town almost as miserable."[20] On the other hand, Gibbon's political dash was apparently useful. His prospective M.P., Stuart, was soon declared one of the Hampshire candidates, and, on the 21st, Gibbon was off to London again, where he and his father "went up with the address and kissed the King's hand."[21] On the 25th, the battalion was relieved and marched, without Gibbon, to Dover. They arrived December 27; the three Gibbons arrived January 9 (Mrs Gibbon accompanied the major and the captain). In his journal entry for January 11, 1761, Gibbon mused:

> From the day we marched from Blandford I had hardly a moment I could call my own, almost continually in motion, if I was fixed for a day, it was in the guard-room, a barrack, or an inn....At last I got to Dover....The charm was over, I was sick of so hateful a service, tired of companions who had neither the knowledge of scholars nor the manners of gentlemen. I was settled in a comparatively quiet situation. Once more I began to taste the pleasure of thinking.[22]

With the new year, then, fortune had smiled upon both the militia officer and the nascent scholar. Again there was reading and writing to record in the journal. Gibbon had thought of the speculations on the pagan gods with which he would later replace the last third of his *Essai* and had "resolved to read Tully de Natura Deorum, and finished it in about a month. I lost some days before I could recover my habit of application."[23] From February 9 to 23 he had a legitimate excuse for any delay that occurred in his studies, because he was on guard duty at Deal, which he confessed was easy, but, because he entertained a lot and "drank very hard," his study time was undoubtedly limited.

When he returned to Dover, he undertook the study of another book useful to his plans for the *Essai,* Beausobre's *Histoire du Manichéisme.* Between February 23 and March 20, he read the first four books of Beausobre and wrote some reflections on the method of making critical abstracts.[24] In those reflections he advises a mean between aimless reading and slavery to a project; he recommends varying one's records according to the type of books studied, and he says that one should reflect on one's own comprehension of, and response to, the material read. All this, he assumes, is advice of general application.

He also recommends—with the proviso that the method may be suitable only to his own mind—allowing the thoughts that arise in the course of reading to dictate the direction of inquiry, unless one is dealing with a subject altogether new to one, or "reading in order to write":

> The use of our reading is to aid us in thinking. The perusal of a particular work gives birth, perhaps, to ideas unconnected with the subject of which it treats. I wish to pursue these ideas; they withdraw me from my proposed plan of reading, and throw me into a new track, and from thence, perhaps, into a second, and a third. At length I begin to perceive whither my researches tend. Their result, perhaps, may be profitable; it is worth while to try: whereas, had I followed the high road, I should not have been able, at the end of my long journey, to retrace the progress of my thoughts.[25]

The extreme lucidity and order characteristic of Gibbon's writing is not, it would appear, a structure arduously imposed on his material, but often his own kind of organic unity, unrecognizable as associationistic because his train of thought is habitually logical, or at least orderly.

The *Memoirs* tell us that it was at this period of his life that he began his lifelong method of approaching new books:

> After glancing my eye over the design and order of a new book, I suspended the perusal till I had finished the task of self-examination, till I had resolved in a solitary walk all that I knew, or believed or had thought on the subject of the whole work, or of some particular chapter. I was then qualified to discern how much the author added to my original stock; and I was sometimes satisfied by the agreement, I was sometimes armed by the opposition of our ideas. (98)

In the early months of 1761, however, Beausobre and Cicero were put aside for the pursuit of a project that was rather Gibbon's father's than his own.

Almost from the moment of Gibbon's return from Switzerland, his father had desired that he enter Parliament, as he had done at Gibbon's age. Despite his financial problems, Mr. Gibbon was prepared to allot £1,500 to this purpose. While Gibbon himself could hardly object to the prospect of making history as a statesman, in "the true Station for historians of [one's] own times...acquainted with business of peace and war,"[26] he had a shrewd suspicion that he himself was not likely to shine in Parliament. Oral argument was not his forte; indeed, as we have noted, he even approached his father, living in the same house, with his pen, rather than his voice, when the question became urgent.

In an undated letter, convincingly attributed by Norton to the period between April 28 and May 10, Gibbon expresses gratitude for his father's generous proposal, but points out that "virtuous inclination unassisted by talents" could not make a seat in Parliament of much service to the country, and that he lacks the relevant talents:

> I never possessed that gift of speach, the first requisite of an Orator ... which nature can alone bestow.... my temper quiet, retired, somewhat reserved could neither acquire popularity, bear up against opposition, or mix with ease in the crowds of public life.... my genius, (if you will allow me any,) is better qualified for the deliberate compositions of the Closet, than for the extemporary discourses of the Parliament....I should be meditating, while I ought to be answering.

This is a candid and clear-sighted self-appraisal. Of course, his father might have argued in reply (and Gibbon went on to imagine his doing so) that not every M.P. need have so exalted an ambition; Gibbon did *not* imagine his father pointing out that he himself had hardly been a model legislator. But the letter suggests that if the Gibbons had had a borough at their command, or fortune sufficient to "despise" the expense, then Gibbon might well have been happy to enter Parliament with lesser hopes. "But with our private fortune is it worth while to purchase at so high a rate, a title honourable in itself but which I must share with every fellow that can lay out Fifteen hundred pounds? Besides, Dear Sir, a merchandize is of little value to the owner, when he is resolved not to sell it."[27]

His alternative proposal was, of course, that his father allow him that sum as an addition to his allowance, or keep it himself and increase his son's annuity, so that Gibbon might travel to Italy. This reasonable proposal was not immediately effective, and there is an unconscious pathos in Gibbon's careful and humble approach to a supposed friend as well as parent, especially because it came from an adult son. The implications, however, should be interpreted by the standards of the age, not of today— Fanny Burney, for example, was almost equally in awe of her loved and loving father, the genial Charles Burney. In the long run, Mr. Gibbon may have been moved by his son's argument, for though he insisted that Gibbon offer himself for a seat in Parliament in 1761, it was not a purchased seat. Some freeholders of Petersfield, the town nearest to Beriton and one in which the Gibbons had formerly been co-owners of the parliamentary interest, asked Major Gibbon to contest the seat of Joliffe, the long-time incumbent (he and the major had represented Petersfield in 1735). Joliffe was thought to have settled his votes on his wife and therefore to be defeatable. Gibbon's father declined the honor but proposed his son instead. "I never had any opinion of the affair," said Gibbon, who was comforted only by the reflection that it cost "hardly any thing. One Barnard of Alresford, made me lose the Election or rather gave me an opportunity of giving it up with honor."[28] The attempt was, nevertheless, certainly a primary occupation and source of excitement for Gibbon in March.

On April Fool's day—suitably, perhaps—Gibbon "in a set speech, thanked [his] friends, abused Barnard and declined a poll." This speech, printed by a Petersfield printer, is quite well designed for the purpose and suggests that the author might have acquitted himself well enough as an orator, had it been possible always to work from a prepared text. But Joliffe's power was too great for the "real Independent Freeholders," probably to the rival candidate's secret relief.[29] Gibbon quickly returned to his scholarly activities. On April 3, he made critical extracts from Bouhier's remarks on Cicero's *De Natura Deorum*; on the 14th, he abstracted two memoirs of M. de Foncemagne on a subject he had chosen for "an Historical composition," "the expedition of Charles VIII of France into Italy." He had also been writing and on this date concluded "10 folio pages besides large notes" on Charles VIII's title to the Crown of Naples.[30]

This piece forms an interesting contrast to Gibbon's premilitia inquiry into ancient weights and measures. If that essay was written *en érudit,* this one was written *en philosophe.* Gibbon says that it has "copious notes," but few of these notes validate evidence and fewer indicate Gibbon's sources; as he explains in the first note, "Being unable to cite the original historians, I think it better to trust to the notoriety of the transactions, than to refer the reader to compilations."[31] Most of the notes comment on or illustrate, rather than prove, the material in the text.

The object of the inquiry was, moreover, not utilitarian; Gibbon did not even attempt to settle the opposing claims he examined, and if he had settled them, he would of course have done nothing to assist historical inquiry in general, as he had hoped to do in the weights and measures treatise and in the *Essai.* The real theme of this discussion is not a question of history, but of political or legal philosophy, as the introduction and conclusion to the piece make clear.[32] In it, Gibbon asked by what rules *should* the succession to states be governed, and he eventually answered, "The right of conquest is made only for wild beasts. The laws of succession …are destitute of fixed principles. The only title not liable to objection, is the consenting voice of a free people."[33] These laudable propositions are, of course, totally independent not only of the inquiry he had just completed but also of specifically historical inquiry of any kind. Nevertheless, the intervening argument is truly historical, and it is interesting to see Gibbon's approach. Starting from a proposition acknowledged by both sides, he examined the issues of law and fact relevant to the claim of each and proposed arguments for and against each link in the chain. Most of the debatable issues were issues of law; he took the facts as given. But of course the existence of laws is itself a question of fact. At least once Gibbon's historical sense would not let him rely on the compilations, as he had intended to do, but sent him to a reliable predecessor: "In my compilation the consent of the states to this adoption is not mentioned....But I have since found, that the accurate Giannone is also silent respecting it."[34]

The greatest interest of the essay remains, however, its portrayal of the social and political views of the defeated candidate for Petersfield. One instance is his view of the justice of the stigma and legal disabilities suffered by bastards:

> Hereditary property in land implies the appropriation of women.... Whoever violates this law ought to be punished in his descendant, whose birth being an outrage to society, he cannot be considered as its child, nor participate in the property of which it secures the succession.... [Princes, however, may soften the action of laws; when] the repentance of his mother, or his own merit, have efficaciously pleaded for an illegitimate son, the clemency of a prince may...restore him to society and his rights.[35]

Gibbon forgot the possibility of matrilineal inheritance and was apparently unconscious of the masculine bias of his whole argument, but his principle—that those things or persons that threaten the existence of a society cannot claim the enjoyments of that society—was clear-headed, and his allowance for a means of relieving individuals from the rigor of that principle was pleasantly warm-hearted.

Similarly, he inquired whether European monarchs might dispose of their kingdoms by testament. This is an inquiry into the meaning of a word (king), but very different from some of the antiquarian investigations of his earlier years:

> Under [despotic Eastern Governments] a king can dispose of his people for the same reason that a shepherd can dispose of his flock. They are his property. But there are other nations, more deserving the name of men, who see in a sovereign nothing more than the first magistrate, appointed by the people for the purpose of promoting public happiness, and responsible to the people for his administration. Such a magistrate cannot transfer to another, a power with which he is entrusted only for his own life. At his demise, this power, if the government be elective, returns to the people; if the government be hereditary, the same power devolves on the nearest heir, according to the law of the land; and should the royal family be extinct, the people would resume all their rights.[36]

So speaks the newly recovered "Englishman," or at least the Anglophile à la Montesquieu.[37]

The next entry in the notebook he was now using is similarly a philosophic inquiry about a question of history: the new chapters for the *Essai*, those published as the second paragraph of chapter LV to chapter LXXIX.[38] Gibbon attributed this work to April 23 and to his father's advice that he publish his book:

> My private resolves were influenced by the state of Europe. About this time the Belligerent powers had made and accepted overtures of peace: our English plenipotentiaries were named to assist at the Congress of Augsbourg which never met; I wished to attend them as a Gentleman or a secretary, and my father fondly believed that the proof of some litterary talents might introduce me to public notice and second the recommendations of my friends. (101)

The manuscript of this final portion of the *Essai* is indeed dated April 23, but that date probably marked the conclusion, not the beginning, of its composition, for Gibbon had to make the fair copy himself, and the family left Beriton on April 27, yet the *Essai* was ready for the printer on April 30.[39]

These new chapters fit into the old scheme, in a way, because they replace the old section "La Religion," and they illustrate a key point in the old argument: a philosophic historian can and should aspire to a theory of general causes in some instances. According to the first of the new chapters, a Montesquieu would do so in the present instance, which is one of "those general events, whose influence, slow but sure, changes the face of the earth without its being possible to perceive the epoch of this change...especially in...religion."[40] But I, said Gibbon modestly, find in it only an opportunity to try to think, to mark some interesting facts, and then try to make sense of them. And so he did—for nearly a third of his book. An application so prolonged, an example so fully developed, cannot but overshadow its ostensible occasion.

Here is another reason, then, for the impression that the *Essai* as published lacked order. The order that it still possesses is invisible in the glare of the brilliant digressions to which it gives rise as illustrations. It is also easy to understand, however, why Gibbon later regarded this section with complacency and was moved to borrow Reynolds's reflection on the work of his youth:

> Upon the whole I may apply to the first labour of my pen the speech of a far superior Artist when he surveyed the first productions of his pencil.... my friend Sir Joshua Reynolds acknowledged to me, that he was rather humbled than flattered by the comparison with his present works; and that after so much time and study he had conceived his improvement to be much greater than he found it to have been. (105)

Gibbon's speculations on the origins of the pagan gods have indeed received approving notice from subsequent critics, though none is inclined to agree with his implication that they are almost as good as the *Decline and Fall.*[41]

On the other hand, in the *Memoirs* Gibbon reflected disparagingly on his youthful learning. He was thinking, of course, of his very limited Greek and perhaps of his nonexistence knowledge—later laboriously acquired—of the first centuries of the Church, Roman law, inscriptions, coins, and the like. But in 1761 he had mastered a whole area of learning with which he did not credit himself—perhaps he did not count it as learning. He was deeply versed in the writings not only of the French *philosophes* but also of the *érudits* of all nations who wrote in French, English, or Latin. The writers he knew thoroughly included d'Alembert, Bayle, Beaufort, Beausobre, Fenelon, Fontenelle, Huet, Hume, La Mothe le Vayer, Middleton, Montesquieu, and, of course, Voltaire. However, they also included Bentley, Casaubon, Freret, Le Clerc, Justus Lips, Massieu, Sallier, Gerard and Isaac Voss—not to mention La Bletterie. Mastering these modern writers, whether their works were antiquarian or philosophical or anything in between, required considerable time and labor, but was no substitute, in Gibbon's view, for the first-hand knowledge of antiquity he was later to acquire. We, however, can admire the intimacy of his knowledge of those Latin authors he had resolved to read through in the year 1757 and to whom he repeatedly returned in subsequent years. He agreed with Dr. Johnson, he said, that what is read twice is better remembered than what is transcribed (79). For Gibbon, the Latin authors were therefore always ready to hand, for allusions, for comparisons, for echoes, for bits of evidence.

At the end of April 1761, after arranging with Maty to correct his proofs, he had again to abandon the character of scholar and author and return to Dover and the militia.[42] May was filled with marches and diversified not so much by scholarship as by sailing, though he recorded having read several odes of Horace, which he compared "critically" with Dryden's translations; he also read books VI and VII of Beausobre on Manicheism.[43] And he wrote the dedication of the *Essai,* a "proper and pious address" (101) to his father. June was of far greater moment for both scholar and soldier: the scholar became a published author; the soldier, a grenadier.

The battalion was moved around a good deal in the first part of the month, and Captain Gibbon with it. He found time for some sightseeing in these journeys. While at Sevenoaks, he took a walk to Knole, which he admired very much although "the place want[ed] prospect and water." In Dorking a few days later, he visited "a whimsically pretty place of Jonathan Tyus in the style of Vauxhall." On the 10th, when the battalion went to Fareham, Gibbon went to London to give orders for the presentation copies of his book—twenty for Lausanne and twenty-one others: "great part of these were only my father's or Mallet's acquaintances."[44] Between June 12 and 23 the battalion waited at Alton for its new uniforms;

on the 23rd, properly attired, they marched to Alresford, where Gibbon received the first copy of his first book. Two days later, the battalion "marched into Winchester Camp....We had just formed a Company of Grenadiers with caps, swords and buff accoutrements." Although the grenadiers were not only the best but the tallest of the soldiers, Gibbon was appointed their captain and proposed their chosen motto, "Falces conflantur in enses." Meanwhile, the grenadier–captain-elect perservered with Manicheism and finished reading Beausobre's book.[45]

The four months of this Winchester encampment were, he tells us in the *Memoirs,*

> the most splendid and useful period of our military life. Our establish- ment amounted to near five thousand men, the thirty fourth regiment of foot, and six militia corps... [including] the Wiltshire the pride and pattern of the Militia....At our entrance into camp *we* were indispu- tably the last and worst: but we were excited by a generous shame... and such was our indefatigable labour, that in the general reviews, the South Hampshire were rather a credit than a disgrace to the line. A friendly emulation, ready to teach and eager to learn, assisted our mu- tual progress: but the great evolutions, the exercise of acting and mov- ing as an army which constitutes the best lessons of a camp never entered the thoughts of...our drowzy General. (114)

The soldier was, then, at his most successful; the fate of the scholar was somewhat more equivocal. Gibbon asserts that on the "loss of [his] litter- ary maidenhead," a student's "hopes and fears are multiplied by the idea of self-importance, and he believes for a while, that the eyes of mankind are fixed on his person and performance" (103).[46] Although in the course of time he was to be "delighted by the copious extracts, the warm commen- dations, and the flattering predictions of the Journals of Holland and France,"[47] and there were some gratifying letters from recipients of the author's presentation copies, the *Essai* failed to procure him the kind of appointment for which he and his father had hoped, and in "England it was received with cold indifference, little read and speedily forgotten" (102).[48] In July, the cares of the camp and the anxieties of authorship were pleas- antly varied with several excursions to Pylewell, a "charming place" with beautiful gardens.[49] Whatever his disappointments and satisfactions with his first book, Gibbon soon felt again the need or desire to write, and to write history. The new form this desire took was heralded in a letter of July 26 to his bookseller, Becket: "I should be glad if you sent me down as soon as you can the works of Sir Walter Raleigh published by Dr. Birch in 1751 in two Volumes in Octavo."[50]

Under the date of August 4, Gibbon recorded his new resolution in his journal. He and his father had returned to Beriton for a week "in harvest time." While there, Gibbon considered several possible historical subjects. Setting aside the Charles VIII project as "too remote from us, & rather an introduction to great events than great in itself," he proposed topics almost all of which are English, and almost all hero-centered: biographies, not general histories.[51] An exception to the latter principle was the "Barons Wars against John, & Henry III"; an interesting variation was a comparison—presumably parallel lives in the manner of Plutarch, or his youthful treatment of the Emperor Aurelian and Selim the Turkish Sultan—of the Emperor Titus and Henry V. But he settled at last on "Sir Walter Raleigh for my hero, and found in his life a subject important, interesting and various, with such a quantity of materials as I desired, and which had not yet been properly made use of." He had neither books nor leisure for such a work at the time; "however, to acquire a general insight of my subject and resources I read the life of Sir Walter by D! Birch, his long article in the General Dictionary...and the 2d. volume of Hume's history of England which contains the reign of Elizabeth."[52]

Recalled to camp on the 10th, Gibbon took with him the newly received volumes of the *Mémoires de l'Académie des Inscriptions* and found time to read two articles from them despite militia business and militia dinners before he returned on the 13th to Beriton. At home, he continued reading Hume for the Raleigh project. That book he was never to write; however, in this ten-day interlude he also began the work for what much later became his second book. He "perused the VIth Book of Virgil, and the System of Warburton upon it."[53] This was, of course, the subject of his *Critical Observations on the...Aeneid* (1770). On the 23rd he returned to camp, and on the 24th he began his journal. All the entries considered so far have been memorial reconstructions actually recorded on or after August 24, 1761.

Instead of beginning his journal *in medias res*, he decided to set down the circumstances and dates he could remember from his earlier life: "I have recollected them so much better than I imagined I could, that instead of four or six pages, which I at first thought of, they have filled between forty and fifty. The consequence has been that I could not bring myself even with the world before the 10th of September."[54] From August 24 to October 2, he kept a separate list of his readings on the next two sheets of the notebook he was using at the time for his miscellaneous writing.[55] (He added a final entry to this list on February 8, 1762.) This list permitted him to give precise page references when he eventually entered his reading in his journal, instead of leaving space in which to supply page references later, as was his usual custom. But all the other activities of the two weeks between August 24 and September 10 had to be remembered, including the record of his progress in writing the journal and, of course, the successes and failures of the battalion in its field exercises (on August 27, "Major, Officers, and men seemed to try which should do worst.")[56]

These additions include the story of one Miss Chetwynd, reminding one of Boswell's celebrated account of his conquest of Louisa not in its content or dramatic fullness, but in its care to portray each stage as it was at the time, uncontaminated by later knowledge.[57] On August 31, Gibbon dined with Lord Tracy at the Gloucestershire Mess. In his journal he enumerated all the guests, concluding with Miss Chetwynd: "The last, tho' perhaps not perfectly handsome, had something so pleasing to me in her person and manner, and won upon me so much that I felt some uneasiness at the moment we broke up, and some desire of seeing her again. An idle fear of appearing too particular prevented my inquiring who she was." On September 5 he "went to the play at Winchester," saw Miss Chetwynd, "bowed but did not speak." The next day, he "dined with Major Bragg; I had great hopes of meeting Miss Chetwynd but was disapointed. However, I found means to drink tea with her in the evening at Lord Tracy's tent."[58]

The next day Gibbon continued to record his reading in the *Mémoires* of the academy and his meetings with Miss Chetwynd. That night's meeting, unfortunately, was at the assembly, and even in the activity of his militia days, Gibbon never managed to become or to consider himself an adequate dancer. He

> saw Miss Chetwynd; but I bought that pleasure very dear. The disagreable figure I must have made to her by not dancing, and the necessity of resigning her to her partner, make me determined to seek other occasions of seeing her. This girl grows upon me. Tho' she has said nothing extraordinary, I am convinced she is sensible, perhaps its an illusion of passion, perhaps an effect of that sympathy by which people of understanding discover one another from the meerest trifles.

But poor Gibbon—and poor Miss Chetwynd perhaps—the entry ends with an ominous note: "I cannot yet find out who she is, she is no relation of Mrs Blackwell tho' a companion and I am afraid an inferior one." The next day Mrs. Gibbon came to Winchester. Miss Chetwynd appears only once more in the *Journal,* and that across a crowded theater: "The house was so full that I could not speak to her; she seemed to take notice of my assiduity in looking at her."[59]

The remainder of the encampment was not distinguished by scholarly accomplishments or romantic impulses. It is clear, however, that Gibbon had accepted as final his parting from Suzanne Curchod, but not from romance or the possibility of marriage. He had received Suzanne's letter objecting to his "offensive" postscript and requesting, or rather demanding, four letters a year, either shortly before accepting his militia commission or several months before the battalion was embodied. At least eighteen months of silence on both sides, not to mention a totally new life on his own part, perhaps excuses his regarding the episode as closed. He had been reliably informed, moreover, that the lady had consoled herself with other admirers and amusements.[60] He pictured her reigning as belle of Lausanne and flirting with any number of other suitors. But in fact, by 1761 Suzanne

had lost her father (in December 1759), she and her mother had not succeeded in obtaining any inheritance from her mother's family, and a year
and a half later, when she again wrote to Gibbon, she was to feel able to
claim, with whatever degree of self-deception, that her love had never
abated.[61] Meanwhile, Gibbon, unaware of this romantic constancy of hers,
did not aspire to any similar merit; his own form of constancy was only
the redefinition of "passion" into something much less than he had hoped
to know with Suzanne.

Writing retrospectively in his journal (for, once he had brought it up to
date in mid-September, he promptly left it off for six months), he remembered most powerfully the contrast between the pleasures of encampment
in the summer—"a new and very lively scene...a charming dry spot of
ground, our tents convenient and agreable by their novelty. Five counties
assembled and living in a mighty free friendly way"—and the miseries of
October—the "long cold evenings" and the "wet and cold" that made it
"uncomfortable [even] during the daytime to remain in our tents; so that
we were crouded from morning to night into the Suttling booth; where
reigned such noise and nonsense, as made it impracticable either to read or
think." His account concludes with a long, frank, soldierly review of the
qualities of the various regiments encamped together, including his own,
which learned "everything that was taught us, except cleanliness and
steadiness."[62] On October 23, the South Hampshire marched the whole
thirty miles from Andover, their first halt, to Devizes, their station until
early in March of the next year.

Devizes was not a pleasant station for officers or men. "The little civility
of the neighbouring Gentlemen gave us no opportunity of dining out,"
and the officers' only pleasure was "very good eating at the Bear."[63] As
for the men, strong beer, work, and the presence of an undisciplined,
newly formed rival regiment, the Black Musketeers, led to great disorder:
"We were obliged to hold one and twenty Court Martials in four months,
whereas at Dover we held only ten in five months. Numbers of our men
married, and bad claps and a pestilential fever grew...rife."[64]

In the midst of this enforced abstinence from social life, Gibbon set
himself to more self-education: the recovery of his Greek.[65] He began by
studying and memorizing Greek roots and by reading the first four books
of the *Iliad*. At the same time, he read Pope's translation and notes; Gibbon almost invariably made a point of reading modern versions and their
notes along with his classical reading, not, of course, to spare himself the
trouble of reading the original, but to acquire the benefit of another response to the literary qualities of the work. The translators thus served
him, as it were, as companions in his studies. For further aid—he was concerned, as usual, about the order of space—he read (in Latin translation)
the appropriate portions of Strabo's *Geography*. He was, of course, reading and commenting on other works besides Homer. He particularly

enjoyed the scholarly journals in which he found his own book favorably noticed, and it is interesting that he described Hume's Tudor volumes as *"Ingenious but superficial."*[66] The year ended with a hard-earned vacation from the militia for Captain Gibbon—six weeks starting on December 23.

There is a good deal of quiet warmth in his final words on 1761: "In the six weeks I passed at Beriton...my only ressources were myself, my books, and family conversations. But to me these were great ressources."[67] Thanks to Mrs. Gibbon, and to a temporary identity of aim with his father, companionship and comfort—which, throughout the rest of his life, were to replace the violence of passion or pleasure as the object of his hopes and the subject of his happiness—were for the moment available within his own family. With some free time and his books, it was now all he asked.

The events and projects of 1762 were fully recorded in the journal, which he resumed in March and for once maintained with fair regularity. As an officer, Gibbon was very active, often in awkward circumstances, but with obvious conscientiousness and success. "My present acquaintance will smile when I assure them that I was once a very tolerable officer" (M 299). Nevertheless, the other side of his character, the devoted and even passionate scholar, was never again totally lost. At Devizes, he wrote an *extrait raisonné* of Richard Hurd's studies of Horace, which he had begun to read in December on the road to Beriton. Perhaps the most important fact about this abstract is that it is written in English. "Tho' it took me up much more time than I imagined; by running into so unexpected a length, yet I don't regret it, as it started a new train of ideas upon many curious points of Criticism." Indeed, the abstract is much more a series of critical meditations inspired by Hurd and Horace than the collection of reading notes that the label might suggest.[68]

At this time and in this essay, Gibbon usually meant by the term *criticism* something much more specifically literary than he had meant in the *Essai.* He was less concerned with establishing probabilities from written evidence than with noting and explaining the effects of beauty in literary works. The concern foreshadows the aesthetic power of his own masterpiece, for it is neither a pious metaphor nor an accident of literary history that critics wish to credit the *Decline and Fall* with success as if in some fictional genre—epic, tragedy, novel.[69] Though Gibbon desired and labored to excel in that characteristic requirement of his chosen genre, factual accuracy, he was a literary artist in much more than the splendor of his prose. Perhaps only his lack of the painter's eye and the musician's ear prevented his at least trying to be a poet.

Militia business and Mr. Hurd were not, in the first months of 1762, his major preoccupations, however; on February 24, he received an important letter from his father, "containing two proposals" apparently complementary, not alternative: Mr. Gibbon would resign the majority of the regiment in Gibbon's favor (if the Duke of Bolton would consent), and he would add £100 per year to Gibbon's income, "and one hundred more for two years to be spent abroad; in consideration of the 700 in H— hands." Both propositions, but particularly the second, were of considerable interest to Gibbon and must have pleased him, not only for their intrinsic value but also as signs of his father's approval and understanding. It is appropriate that Gibbon felt moved to go to Beriton and "talk with him." [70] On the 28th, at Beriton, Gibbon talked over both proposals with his father and "absolutely agreed to the second." The first was not altogether in their hands, so on March 1, as they had decided, Gibbon saw Sir William Bennet, another of the captains, presumably in line for the majority, who "promised the earliest intelligence of his resignation, and . . . disclaimed any thoughts of the Majority." On the 6th, at his father's desire, Gibbon wrote a letter to be sent to the Duke of Bolton, "by which my father offers to resign, provided the Duke will promise me the Majority." [71] He had, therefore, clearly accepted both of his father's propositions and was prepared to continue his military career, as well as look forward to a Grand Tour. On the 9th, the South Hampshire was ordered back to its "beloved" Blandford.

There Gibbon again took up his journal and his Greek. From then on he recorded each day more or less as it occurred, especially his line-by-line progress in Homer and in the *Racines grecques,* which, beginning Sunday, March 28, he worked at faithfully: "The method I pursue is this. After reading [the Greek roots] attentively, I write them down from my memory, looking in the book as seldom as I can. I then repeat them twice, first mentioning the French word that answers to the Greek, then the Greek word that answers to the French. At last I repeat the French of every Greek root of the present, and two preceeding days. I find this method, tho' dry, helps me very much." [72] He worked in French, rather than in English, because French was dictated by the language of his chosen textbook.

Although the early charm of military life had long worn off, although he was to remember the work of these busy days with distaste, although he hoped, when the quarters were bad or the county inhospitable or the weather cold and wet, never to repeat that particular experience, Gibbon did not merely serve out his time; he actively sought more permanent engagement in the military. The scheme of 1762 most surprising to his later friends—in the twentieth as well as the eighteenth century—was his effort (on April 24) to become brigade major to the Earl of Effingham, who had commanded the 34th Foot, as well as seven militia regiments, and whose brigade major would have a very active, regular-army role. Gibbon pursued it "as a post I should be very fond of, and for which I am not unfit." A brigade major is "a staff officer attached to a brigade who assists the brigadier in command, and acts as the channel through which orders are issued and reports and correspondence transmitted" (*OED*). Eighteenth-century brigade majors often carried orders and correspondence in person. [73] Of course, when the brigade was disbanded, the office would cease to function, but it is certainly intriguing that Gibbon was sufficiently eager to serve as brigade major that he offered as a compromise to "do the duty without pay." [74] He did not give up the scheme until July, and then not by his own desire, but because another person had received the post. Gibbon's application, incidentally, preceded, and therefore was not influenced by, his discovery that his father had lost interest in resigning his majority. [75] Gibbon preferred the more active post of brigade major not only to idleness but also to being a major in the militia.

In the almost 150 pages of Gibbon's journal devoted to the events and experiences of the last nine months of his militia days, attributes of young Gibbon's mind, personality, taste, and abilities are revealed that are otherwise known, if at all, only through his letters to his most intimate friends. [76] It is impossible to note them all here. Low's introduction to the journal includes a valuable discussion of Gibbon's shrewd, pithy, and often witty accounts of people, places, and even *objets d'art*. (In these accounts, Gibbon again demonstrates "modern"—that is, neoclassical—tastes in the visual arts. [77]) As for his character, Gibbon himself summarized that, on his twenty-fifth birthday:

> It appeared to me, upon [impartial] ... enquiry, that my Character was virtuous, incapable of a base action, and formed for generous ones; but that it was proud, violent, and disagreable in society. These qualities I must endeavour to cultivate, extirpate, or restrain, according to their different tendency. Wit I have none. My imagination is rather strong than pleasing. My memory both capacious and retentive. The shining qualities of my understanding are extensiveness and penetration; but I want both quickness and exactness. As to my situation in life, tho' I may sometimes repine at it, it perhaps is the best adapted to my character. I can command all the conveniences of life, and I can command too that independence, (that first earthly blessing,) which is hardly to be met with in a higher or lower fortune. When I talk of my situation, I must exclude that temporary one, of being in the Militia. Tho' I go thro' it with spirit and application, it is both unfit for, and unworthy of me. [78]

Obviously he had not yet perceived the fetters imposed by his father's wasteful habits and demands upon him. He also appears either to have forgotten his desire to be a brigade major, or to expect the regular army to be quite different from the militia. We would hardly describe him as violent in temper or lacking in wit, but otherwise he seems to have had a good sense of his personal and mental qualities. It is unsurprising that he was unaware of his capacity for long-lasting and generous friendship: he had no real companion in the militia, and Deyverdun was far away. It is, on the whole, not a bad effort at impartial self-examination.

His strictures against his "wit" probably mean no more than that he did not aspire to "good things"—as Samuel Johnson called them—in conversation.[79] But a comic sense and what we would call a dry wit are often demonstrated in the journal. Recruiting in Alton, for example, he noted that "The present act exempts all poor men who have three Children and Alton is...I think the most prolific town I ever knew." Or "Keate and Stephens dined with us and to our immortal honor be it spoken we sent them both pretty drunk to the assembly." In similar vein, "Pleased to see him, we kept bumperizing till after Roll-Calling; Sir Thomas assuring us, every fresh bottle, how infinitely soberer he was grown." And (on the unlikely subject of Greek grammar), "If the *Vox media* is not very useful and ingenious, it is highly ridiculous."[80] Although none of these or the numberless other examples in the journal rank as immortal witticisms, they are certainly not the expressions of a humorless man.

In describing himself to himself, Gibbon naturally saw no reason to comment on his capacity for warm, even ardent, feeling. Similarly, he failed to mention his commonplace fault of drunkenness and was silent on the subject of his sex life, if any. The journal, however, supplies clues on each of these topics.

His strong emotions were now confined to the safe outlets of literature and friendship, but there they were artlessly and even charmingly evident on many occasions. He was "particularly pleased with the sorrow of Achilles's horses" in *Iliad* 17; he was excited by "the awful majesty in [Windsor's] Gothic pile," and, most strikingly, when Mrs. Gibbon, his stepmother and friend, came to visit, "I can't express the pleasure I had at seeing her, I love her as a companion, a friend, and a mother."[81] Few of his numerous acquaintances and companions in the militia were as truly friends as was his stepmother, but one of the South Hampshire subalterns, John Harrison, who became lieutenant of the grenadiers when Gibbon became captain, was an exception. They were, of course, constantly together, and, as long as they were working, all was well. A holiday at Beriton was less successful: "Tho' Harrison is a young man of honor, and good nature, yet when our common topicks about the Battalion are exhausted, he has not sufficient acquaintance either with books or the world to find any other." But "The virtues of his heart make amends for his not having those of the head." When Gibbon had a drunken quarrel with him, apparently about nothing in particular, Gibbon made haste to settle it as "soon as [he] had slept off the fumes of the wine."[82] There are a few cheerful references to him as "Prussy" in Gibbon's letters until 1767, when, in the midst of a congratulatory note to his friend John Baker Holroyd, whose marriage had just been announced, Gibbon could not forbear mentioning his grief over Harrison's death, though Holroyd did not even know him.[83]

During Gibbon's period with the militia, he seems to have recorded every letter he wrote or received in his journal. One of those he received was the occasion of the keenest expression of his strong feelings of friend-ship; it came from the long-silent Deyverdun. Gibbon wrote: "I had never forgot him but was afraid he had me....I shall answer his letter very soon, but that is a poor correspondence. D'Eyverdun from his character and way of thinking is the only friend I ever had who deserved that name. I wish I could find out any scheme of our living together, but I am afraid it is im-possible in my present state of dependance."[84] And a month later: "I fin-ished my letter of eight pages to d'Eyverdun, it is a kind of pleasure I have not had a great while, that of pouring out my whole soul to a real friend. *Why* I deferred writing and the *Schemes* I proposed to him are not to be trusted even to this paper."[85]

There is no evidence that this plan of living together was influenced by any sexual attachment to each other. On the contrary, both were in love with and hoping to marry various young women for some years to come. If Gibbon's unconscious desires played a role in his strong friendships, it was probably immunity from the pain, death, and grief he associated with sexuality on the model of his parents that he unconsciously sought. There is evidence that he preferred to satisfy his sexual needs without the emo-tional dangers of permanence or strong feeling, that is, by purchase. For instance, on April 20, he "lay at Pierrot's Bagnio." *Bagnio* meant either Turkish bath or brothel at the time, and it would seem impossible to "lie" at a bathhouse. Furthermore, on September 6, he consulted a sur-geon for "a complaint I had neglected for some time...a swelling in my left testicle."[86] This swelling, which persisted and worsened for the rest of his life, was, he told Lord Sheffield many years later, venereal in origin. The autopsy report made upon his body indicates that he was wrong in this assumption, but he could hardly have made the error had there been no opportunity for such an infection.[87] For the time being, this ailment improved without further medical attention.

In any case, it was plainly a companion for his mind, not his body, that he most wanted and valued in Deyverdun. Or, as Gibbon put it apropos of one Miss Fanny Page, who had been "talked of" for him: "a pretty, meek (but I am afraid) insipid Girl...tho' she will have a noble fortune, I must have a wife I can speak to." Miss Page improved slightly upon acquain-tance, but at last Gibbon said that she "discovers little understanding and less improvement."[88]

His best friends at the time were perhaps "among books," and the read-ing and study detailed in the journal during the remainder of the militia period would be impressive even if he had had no other occupation. Homer led him to Longinus, and Longinus to Burke; he sought out Black-well's "Life" of Homer and the Port-Royal Grammar.[89] He read and re-read the dissertations in the *Mémoires de l'Académie des Inscriptions* and the classical works to which they were relevant, often in groups, for example:

To understand the Genealogy of Dardanus, I read *Apollodori Biblioth. L. iii* . . . in Greek; I then consulted Strab[o] . . . and some difficulties arising about the word Υπωρεια, as Platon explained it . . . I read a dissertation upon the deluges of Ogyges and Deucalion, by the learned Freret . . . who . . . shews incontestably, that a deluge was unknown to Homer, Hesiod, and Herodotus . . . [and] that it obtained general credit before the time of Plutarch and Lucian.[90]

In the same entry, he recorded that he read, in the *Journal des savans*, "a better extract of the *Dissertations sur l'Ecriture Hiéroglyphique* than the Memoirs had given. I now see that the new System is absolutely indefensible."[91]

Gibbon's idea of light reading was Fontenelle, or Le Clerc's *Bibliothèques*. He made extensive and interesting comments upon modern works, not only those suggested by his classical reading, such as Burke's *On the Sublime*, but those read for mere pleasure, such as Voltaire's *Siècle de Louis XIV*. Gibbon's judgment of Voltaire as historian is clear in this entry:

When he treats of a distant period, [Voltaire] is not a man to turn over musty monkish writers to instruct himself. He follows some compilation, varnishes it over with the magick of his style, and produces a most agreable, superficial, inacurate performance. But [in the *Siècle*] the information both written and oral lay within his reach, and he seems to have taken great pains to consult it. Without any thing of the majesty of the great historians, he has comprized, in two small volumes, a variety of facts, told in an easy, clear, and lively style....His method (of treating every article in a distinct chapter) I think vicious, as they are all connected in human affairs, and as they are often the cause of each other, why seperate them in History?... [The second volume is the more interesting because] those detached particulars wanted less that art of narrating, which Voltaire never possessed, with all his other talents. I mean in prose, for there are some fine narrations in his tragedies.[92]

It is obvious that Gibbon's reading flourished.

His writing fared less well. He wrote one page of a French extract of Blackwell's life of Homer, but abandoned it.[93] He abandoned his proposed life of Raleigh, because Oldy's "infinite learning" and "collections" "disposed...in a pretty good method" left him nothing to aspire to, despite the myriad faults of Oldys's style, taste, and judgment, except "a good abridgement of Oldys." Besides, there were parts of "this copious life very barren of materials."[94]

In the same entry, he enumerated some other possible subjects for his writing: the history of Swiss liberty—"From such a subject, so full of real virtue, public spirit, military glory, and great lessons of gouvernment, the meanest writer must catch fire"—or that of Florence under the Medicis, an opportunity for the equally useful but opposite theme, the loss of liberty. "What makes this subject still more precious are two fine *morceaux* for a Philosophical historian, and which are essential parts of it, the Restoration of Learning in Europe by Lorenzo de Medicis and the character and fate of Savanarola."[95] Both the Swiss and Florentine topics recur later in his career, as we shall see.

The climax of the militia period was not, however, a scholarly achievement, a marriage, or even a military appointment. It was the reward of his satisfactory performance as a son and an Englishman. When the militia disbanded, his father gave him at last the means and opportunity to travel in Italy, and to prepare himself for the journey not merely with new clothes and socially acceptable introductions but also with preliminary sojourns in Paris and Lausanne. The latter was intended for additional intensive study, sufficient to make his first steps in Italy almost a homecoming. The parental approval and the prerogatives of his station, which in boyhood he had lost by passion and rebellion, as a young man he regained by patience and acquiescence. A natural distaste for excess he may indeed have had, but the history of his own life adequately instructed him in the dangers of zeal and the fruits of moderation.

Careful, then, to remain an English gentleman, especially in his letters home, Gibbon set off on the Continental journeys, literal and figurative, that he had long desired. He was almost twenty-six. He set sail from Dover on January 25, 1763, and reached Paris on the 28th, about 5 P.M.[96] The term of his first adult residence in his native country was three years, eight months, twenty days—more than a year less than his first absence had been. His first departure from England had been made in the heat of June and his father's wrath; this one was made in the cold of January, but in the warmth of familial approval.

CHAPTER 10

L'homme de Lettres,
L'homme de Qualité

REFLECTING ON his experiences in Paris in the retrospective account he decided to make in lieu of a regular journal, Gibbon noted that he had expected to see united in the Comte de Caylus "l'homme de Lettres et l'homme de qualité."[1] It is also clear that he desired to unite these roles in himself. To find a perfect balance between the two was not easy, however, and to get others to accept it was even more difficult. Until after his father's death, Gibbon continued to discover that he must act first in one role, then in the other, and win acceptance with most persons either as a man of letters or as a man of social standing and graces, but not as both: "I would not want the writer to eclipse the gentleman entirely," he said; but at Paris, that seemed to happen, just as for his companions in the militia or the visitors at Beriton, the gentleman completely eclipsed the scholar and author.[2]

Although Paris seemed to regard him as a man of letters—the author of the *Essai*—Gibbon spent most of his time there in the occupations of a gentleman traveler. The scholarly activities in which he managed to engage were few. Those few, however, proved useful eventually for his most significant role, that of historian of the Roman Empire. If fate or innate ideas did not really impose his subject on him, as he half wished to think (41), that subject was at least a natural fruit of the ground he was now cultivating. But a scholarly subject was not his primary aim in Paris. He found there a social milieu in which he felt comfortable. In the salons, therefore, he continued his ostensible search for a wife, and his real search for a nonthreatening substitute for a family. Unlike Boswell, who also felt rejected and defeated by his father, Gibbon never looked for a substitute father (at least not in his father's generation);[3] instead he looked ardently for persons of his own sex and generation, or the other sex and another generation, who could offer the kind of warm companionship, unadulterated by sexual or financial or legal demands, that had made him happy in the past, in the persons of his Aunt Kitty, his Westminster friend Lord Huntingtower, George Deyverdun, and his stepmother. Thus he welcomed brothers and "aunts," though the possibility of adoptive sisters, sons, and daughters had not, at age twenty-five, occurred to him. This search for a pseudofamily united not by bonds of blood or law, but only by affection, he thought successful in Paris; but it was not really so until he again reached Lausanne.

The crossing to France had been accomplished *en homme de condition*, in the company of "The Duke of Bridgewater, the Marquis of Tavistock, Lord Ossory and a Mr. Leigh." The peers, and probably Mr. Leigh as well, were all of Gibbon's own generation (they ranged in age from 18 to 27), and one of his mild disappointments at Paris was that he saw "very little of the English noblemen I came over with, beyond an exchange of visits."[4] Much more disappointing, and galling to his pride, was the neglect of the British ambassador, the Duke of Bedford. Gibbon had presented to him a letter of recommendation from a fellow duke who was also a member of the same political party. With such credentials, Gibbon confidently expected some invitations from the Duke of Bedford; instead, he received a conventional offer of assistance if an emergency should arise, a swift return of the formal visit, and no further response, not even admission to the duke's presence on some one of his numerous subsequent calls. To top it all off, Gibbon's father jumped to the conclusion that Gibbon was fool-ishly standing on ceremony with the great duke and rebuked him for it.[5]

The Comte de Caylus, because of his "odd" way of life, was also a dis-appointment: he got up early in the morning, spent the day in the artists' ateliers, and, returning home at six in the evening, put on his dressing gown and retired to his study. This was hardly the life of a gentleman of fashion! Gibbon had already complained, upon reading the Comte's account of ancient painting in the *Mémoires de l'Académie des Inscriptions*, that he wrote too technically, too much like a practitioner of the arts.[6] Because Caylus had expressed an extremely flattering opinion of the *Essai*, his inconvenient unsociability was a grave disappointment to the young author.[7]

The final disappointment was a M. de la Motte, upon whom history has revenged Gibbon by making him unidentifiable. Mrs. Mallet had appointed this gentleman (no doubt without consulting him) the worldly guardian of the still youthful traveler.[8] Gibbon and La Motte were, unfortunately, totally uncongenial, and although La Motte twice invited Gibbon to din-ner, he refused all Gibbon's overtures of friendship and requests for advice and then wrote to Mrs. Mallet that Gibbon had refused to follow his coun-sel. Gibbon's father, as usual, believed the complaint, which Mrs. Mallet hastened to report to him, and therefore La Motte did not merely fail to aid Gibbon but actively, if mildly, injured him. There is, however, no rea-son to suppose any malice in his action; probably he merely wished to excuse himself to Mrs. Mallet for neglecting her protégé.

He did Gibbon one material service, however; he introduced him to one

M. d'Augny, known as Mrs. Mallet's "son." For two or three months, Gibbon thought d'Augny might be another Deyverdun. He wrote to his stepmother:

> We are now very intimate, & I think I begin to know his character. It is astonishing for a Young French officer of the Guards. He is as reserved, as little a man of the world and as aukward as I can be. But he has a fine natural understanding, improved upon almost every subject, a clear unprejudiced head, and a heart which seems to be full of the noblest sentiments of honor probity and friendship. I will not decide too hastily but I believe and hope that I am forming a connection which will last as long as my life.[9]

It need hardly be said that he would not have written so frankly to his stepmother had he thought there was anything erotic in this attachment. In contrast, writing in the same letter of his friend Mme. Bontems, Gibbon was careful to represent his attachment to her, which he found both pleasant and excitingly equivocal, as safely placid and filial.

D'Augny and Mme. Bontems were the special friends always necessary to make Gibbon think permanent residence in a place desirable or even possible. In the *Memoirs* he tells us that had he been "rich and independent, [he would] have prolonged, and perhaps have fixed, [his] residence at Paris" (M 205). The way of life there was in general so pleasant as to interfere markedly with his activity as a scholar. For one thing, it was an excellent time to be an Englishman in Paris: "Our opinions, our fashions, even our games, were adopted in France; a ray of national glory illuminated each individual, and every Englishman was supposed to be born a patriot and a philosopher" (M 200). It may be supposed that Gibbon did not conceal his share of these merits, including his rank as captain of the Hampshire Grenadiers.

He soon found rooms on the third floor of a house in the Faubourg St. Germain. He had "an Antichamber, a dining room, a bed chamber, & a servant's room" for six guineas a month—not a bad bargain, apparently, and about what he had paid in London.[10] Unfortunately, transportation was at a premium in Paris, and Gibbon had to hire, instead of a chair at 27 shillings, "an elegant vis-a-vis" carriage for 16 guineas.[11] Gibbon was particularly pleased by the general hospitality. He observed that in England, people considered that they bestowed pleasure on their guests by receiving them; in Paris, they felt that they themselves received the pleasure. Indeed, he was soon welcome in more houses in Paris than in London. "The fact is not probable, but it is true."[12] He told Mrs. Gibbon that his invitations were chiefly for dinner and the evening, not for suppers,

> for Paris is divided into two Species who have but little communication with each other. The one who is chiefly connected with the men of letters dine very much at home, are glad to see their friends, & pass the

evenings till about nine in agreable & rational conversation. The others are the most fashionable, sup in numerous parties, and always play or rather game both before and after supper. You may easily guess which sort suits me best. Indeed, Madam, . . . in a fortnight passed at Paris I have heard more conversation worth remembring, & seen more men of letters amongst the people of fashion, than I had done in two or three winters in London.[13]

His preference for the more "rational" group was not so marked as he wished her to think, but this was the agreeable choice he saw as his in Paris society.

A material item in his pleasure was the dinners. Always attentive to the attractions of good cuisine, Gibbon particularly appreciated not having to pay for it. He and d'Augny, as bachelors, "had their living to get," that is, had to find for themselves the comforts of home outside their modest establishments if they were not to unbalance their budgets. It was therefore pleasant to have four regular dinners per week available, plus numerous other occasional invitations.[14]

The conversation was, however, a very real attraction as well. "Alone in a morning visit I commonly found the wits and authors of Paris less vain and more reasonable than in the circles of their equals, with whom they mingle in the houses of the rich" (127). Thanks to the *Essai*, Gibbon was received as a "recognized man of letters."[15] Except for Buffon, he made the acquaintance of nearly every man of learning or letters in Paris at the time. He found time, too, to visit the libraries and collections of manuscripts, coins, inscriptions, and so forth, which were of historical interest.

During the brief interval in which he kept a regular journal, he visited the Cabinet du Roi, where he saw the collection of about 25,000 ancient coins (and nearly as many modern ones) and felt "regret at being such a novice in this fine science. When I have finished my two Benedictines . . . I shall set myself to it seriously."[16] His two Benedictines were, of course, Jean Mabillon and Bernard de Montfaucon. This is the only reference to any serious study for the three or four months of this stay in Paris, but, if he had mastered the works of those two authors, the time would certainly have been well spent. In the *Memoirs*, however, he claims only to have "consulted" them (131), and it is perhaps significant that, in the notes to the first volume of the *Decline and Fall*, Mabillon does not appear at all, Montfaucon only three or four times. Of course, as Gibbon also says in the *Memoirs*, the time would have been of profit to him had his studies in Paris "been confined to the study of the World" (131).

In the afternoons, he dined and enjoyed the pleasures of intellectual conversation in the various salons in which he had become welcome. In the evening, there was the theater. It was almost a month before this regime left him time for sightseeing. The journal entries are for February 21–26, and the first words are, "Today I began my excursion to see the principal sights [lit., "the places worthy of attention"] of the city."[17] The reports on his sightseeing are reminiscent of those of his Swiss journey years before; that is, they are revelatory of his taste in the fine arts, but otherwise not very interesting. What is fascinating in this journal fragment are his descriptions of people and his reaction to a sermon.

Gibbon's comments on sermons in his earlier journal had revealed not only his taste in hortatory prose but also his sense that religion had a real and valuable role in society that its practitioners usually failed to live up to.[18] He disliked sermons that had "more imagination than soul" and that were "too full of comparaisons."[19] The fullest discussion of his views on the function of preaching is in a journal entry of August 22, 1762, in which he decided that the French effort to move the passions had the advantage of affecting "the sleeping sentiments of that heart [which "holds out"—his expression—against our known duty]," but "unluckily it is not so much acts, as habits of virtue" that we need, and an eloquent preacher "will dismiss his assembly full of emotions, which a variety of other objects, the coldness of our northern constitutions, and no immediate opportunity of their exerting their good resolutions, will dissipate in a few moments." Indeed, that very Sunday night Gibbon himself drank so much that the next day's journal entry begins,"I could do nothing this morning but spew."[20]

His Parisian consideration of sermons was prompted by a trip to hear a celebrated preacher. Gibbon complained, "On this doleful subject [death-bed repentance] he was more terrifying than touching; on a more consoling one, I think he would please rather than soften." What Gibbon wanted from a sermon was a moving call to human duties; when he praised a sermon it invariably had a topic such as "charity," not one such as "the Trinity." He wanted God to be represented as the "Common father of all nature," not as a "pitiless master," full of "anger and vengeance."[21] Though he claims in the *Memoirs* (M 211) that it was in 1759 that his theological reading led him to insuperable doubts of the historical and doctrinal claims of the Christian churches, it is apparent that in 1763 he had not yet become a complete skeptic, much less a convinced atheist. Indeed, he says that he could not "approve the intolerant zeal of the philosophers and Encyclopædists [he met in Paris] . . . ; they laughed at the scepticism of Hume, preached the tenets of Atheism with the bigotry of dogmatists, and damned all believers with ridicule and contempt" (127). Sheffield omitted this passage from his editions of the *Memoirs*; knowledge of it might have surprised those, both opponents and admirers of Gibbon, who have thought the last clause applicable to the *Decline and Fall*.

The persons he described in his Paris journal included the Marquis de Mirabeau: "He has enough imagination for ten others, and not enough plain sense for himself."[22] Most interesting of these sketches is, of course, that of Mme. Bontems. His retrospective view of her was discreetly deleted from the *Memoirs* by Lord Sheffield; it read:

> I have reserved for the last the most pleasing connection which I formed in Paris, the acquisition of a female friend by whom I was sure of being received every evening with the smile of confidence and joy. . . . Madame Bontems . . . had distinguished herself by a translation of Thomson's Seasons into French prose: at our first interview we felt a sympathy which banished all reserve, and opened our bosoms to each other. In every light, in every attitude, Madame B was a sensible and amiable Companion; an author careless of litterary honours, a devotee untainted with Religious gall. . . . In the middle season of life [she was born in 1718], her beauty was still an object of desire: the Marquis de Mirabeau, a celebrated name, was neither her first nor her last lover; but if her heart was tender, if her passions were warm, a veil of decency was cast over her frailties. (127-28)

This account enjoys the advantages of hindsight. In youth, Gibbon may not have realized that Mirabeau was her lover; Gibbon was certainly intrigued and confused by her behavior toward himself. "She was fond of me; I was her son and her friend," he began his summary of his Paris stay, with apparent confidence. These sentiments he reciprocated; indeed, he had seldom seen anyone so "aimable," with such tender and delicate sensibility, so "bonne, franche, et douce" (literally, so good, sincere, and sweet). He continued:

> First she began to attach herself to me, talked to me about her most secret affairs, gave me advice, and even reprimands. She sometimes even made overtures that I still do not understand too well. She spoke to me about the pleasures of the senses, encouraged me to talk about them, had me read stories about them by La Fontaine; and when, heated by these provocations, I emancipated myself a little, she repulsed me feebly and seemed moved. With a little more boldness, I would perhaps have succeeded. Perhaps, however, this conduct was only the effect of French liberty and of the openness of a character which acted without ceremony, because it acted without design.[23]

His further discussion of her abandoned this delicate issue, but continued to explore what he saw as the paradoxes of her nature. For instance, despite her excellent and well-known translation, she never behaved as a "femme savante," and indeed he could not even get her to engage in literary conversation. He noted with surprise that she was a fervent Catholic without losing her charity or good humor: "Madame Bontems can love God fanatically, but she cannot hate his enemies. She has admitted to me a hundred times that the damnation of heretics tried her faith severely."[24] Of course, the combination of devout faith and a charity that extended even to those outside the fold, though less common than it ought to be, is not really paradoxical or unique to Mme. Bontems, but it is significant that young Gibbon thought it was. An important aspect of his rejection of the Catholic Church was certainly a repugnance to the mental or physical tortures some adherents of that and other churches willingly inflicted on their enemies in this life, or gleefully anticipated for them in the next.

Mme. Bontems was a continual resource during Gibbon's first stay in Paris, not only for dinners and suppers—sometimes tête-à-tête—but also for introductions to others. Except for an incomplete sentence about La Motte, Gibbon's portrayal of Mme. Bontems concludes, as well as climaxes, his 1763 account of his Paris stay. He had planned to make that account much longer, but she was, after all, the most significant part of his worldly education there, and perhaps the rest would have seemed anticlimactic. He wrote to his father on April 5, "As I begin to have pretty well seen Paris, I propose (if you have no objection) setting out about the eigth of next month, & going thro' Dijon and Besançon to Lausanne to pass two or three quiet and cheap months with my old friends there in my way to Italy."[25]

Having prudently laid in a provision of "Cloaths, ruffles, silk stockings &c" at "this Capital of the Fashionable world," including a suit of "velvet of three colours, the ground blue," presumably in the new long-waisted style, Gibbon set out for Besançon, arriving there in mid-May.[26] His Acton cousins welcomed him with great hospitality and entertained him so well that he lingered there for a few extra days:

Not only they insisted upon my lodging in the house, but during the time I passed in it, the sole business of the family seemed to be finding out amusements for me. . . . What I saw of Besançon pleased me so much, that could I have stayed there without being an inconvenience to them I should have liked to have stayed a few days or even weeks longer.

Mr. Acton is admirable and well-respected, and as for his wife, "If she is a termagant I never saw such a Wolf in sheep's cloathing."[27] On May 25, he finally reached Lausanne. There he discovered with relief that the awkward problem of avoiding Mme. Pavillard's housekeeping without offending his old tutor would not arise, because the Pavillards' new house had no room for him. He settled in with some old acquaintances, Henri Crousaz de Mézery and his wife. "The apartments and table [were] both cheap and good,"[28] and Mme. de Mézery was an attraction in herself: nearly thirty years later, she was, in Gibbon's opinion at least, "still a graceful, I had almost said a handsome woman" (130).

Hardly was he settled in his new lodgings, with his books and papers, his evening visits and parties among the Swiss and "the Nation," as he called the English visitors, when the post brought a bombshell to his door. After four years of silence, during which she had been briefly engaged to another man, Suzanne had again written to Gibbon. He had never replied to her letter of 1759 reproaching him for the "offensive" postscript and requesting "four letters a year" of friendship. If he had been told of her father's death (she assumed that he had, but there is no evidence of it), he did not write to her on that occasion, and she was probably not one of the recipients of the *Essai*. Perhaps his only news of her, between 1759 and 1763, had been Deyverdun's letter of 1762.[29] This letter may have mentioned her father's death, but it may also have included the news of her acceptance of her wealthy Swiss suitor, M. de Montplaisir, and her flirtation with Deyverdun himself.[30] There is a considerable tradition in Gibbon studies of reproach to Gibbon and sympathy with Suzanne at this juncture of their affair.[31] Certainly Suzanne's case was pitiable, because she had lost not only a man she admired but also an opportunity for a comfortable home. Both of her parents were dead; she had bravely and creditably earned her own living and helped to support her mother by teaching. She had proved something by refusing eventually, despite her temporary weakening, to marry M. de Montplaisir, with whom she was not in love. Furthermore, she was accustomed, in matters of the heart, to the privileges of a belle; it had always been for her to decide when the end of an affair must come. Her pride, therefore, as well as her heart, had suffered a shock. And whatever his own wounded self-esteem, Gibbon ought to have tried to write a letter of condolance, however belated, when he learned of her father's death. Nevertheless, Gibbon's conduct is not so reprehensible, or Suzanne's so irreproachable, as some writers have suggested.

The letter she wrote to him in May was one of angry reproach. According to her informants in Lausanne, he was not inconsolable (he was flirting with other women). According to this letter, she had believed for five years that his "coldness" was only a sign of his "delicatesse," but she began to see her error. She demanded that he set her mind at rest by avowing his change of heart. She insisted that her heart had not wavered in its allegiance to him and that she had had reason to believe him still attached to her, despite his silence. She accused him of heartlessly and covertly breaking faith with her, whereas she had been a model of fidelity.[32]

It is quite possible, even plausible, considering Suzanne's ardent personality,[33] that she sincerely believed her heart never to have wavered, and yet that in fact it had. The strong feelings aroused by Gibbon's return, by such an unexpected and unexpectedly lost opportunity to return to her youthful hopes and security, might have made any intervening attractions or forgetfulness seem unimportant to her. She had been alone in the world only a few months. While in Geneva, she had certainly rejected some offers of marriage, although whether her rejections had anything to do with hopes of Gibbon, we cannot know. Certainly she could not rationally claim that he had given her such hopes, but rationality is not the determinant of such claims. Her behavior toward Montplaisir proves that she was not merely seeking an establishment, but she had been averse to his suit before Gibbon was in the picture, and that refusal therefore cannot be wholly attributed to false hopes or faithful love. Learning that Gibbon was to be again in Switzerland, never having understood the relationship between Gibbon and his father, she could easily persuade herself to hope for a renewed pledge of constancy if not a specific plan for the future. It would be for her a restoration of some portion of the happiness of those days when both Gibbon and her parents had doted on her.

But to Gibbon, who did know his father, who had half accepted that marriage was unlikely for him, and wholly accepted that marriage to Suzanne was impossible, her letter came as a surprise and an embarrassment. She demanded that he say to her what he could only regard as both unsayable and already fully, though tacitly, expressed—that he no longer found her loveable. Of course, she really wanted him to say that he continued to love her and expected, or at least hoped, one day to marry her; but he could not say that. So, reluctantly, he told her what she claimed to want to know. He resented having to do so; he considered her feelings feigned, and her behavior indelicate, in that she insisted on the spelling out of what had already been signified by the years of silence between them. His letter is missing—perhaps she tore it up—but her reply, dated June 4, suggests its content and proves its promptness.[34] She did not fail to seize the opportunity to reproach him for misleading her into follies and into thinking him a more loveable person than he was.

Nevertheless, she really was an admirable woman and had the sense to take up a theme that later made possible good relations between them. He had apparently said that he would always be her friend, and she, assuring him that she too would in the future be a friend but not a lover, asked his advice about the position of lady's companion in England. (One cannot help speculating that this inquiry was partly calculated to make him feel guilty.) She also sent along her critique of his *Essai*, which apparently she had recently read, and offered him a letter of introduction to Rousseau, if he wanted it. This last gesture might belie the dignified acceptance of the situation implied in the rest of the letter, for Rousseau, as Suzanne knew, had already been recruited by one of her friends to try to intercede for her with Gibbon.[35] But it is more probable that the offer was simply a sop to her pride; it could have soothed her wounded self-esteem to have made an impressive and magnanimous gesture toward the offender.

When Gibbon wrote a few days later to his stepmother, proposing to spend the winter in Lausanne, his annoyance or pique was clear between the lines: "Give me leave to add (for I am sensible you may have suspicions) that no woman is the least concerned in my desire, and that as to any old inclinations, they are so far from subsisting that no one can be more opposite to them at present than myself."[36] That Mrs. Gibbon might have suspected him, incidentally, proves that there had been no confederation between them in her interception of Suzanne's letter in 1758 and strongly suggests that his protestations to Suzanne in February 1759, were sincere.

His answer to Suzanne's second letter, that of June 4, was polite but cold; he seems to have been in some danger of losing patience with her refusal to accept reality. A friendly correspondence between them seemed both harmless and desirable to Suzanne—not so to Gibbon. Perhaps English manners regarded the liberty of correspondence differently from Swiss manners, perhaps Gibbon simply did not want to commit himself to more letter-writing, perhaps he was tired of her constant reproaches, but, in any case, he began: "Must you always offer me a happiness which reason obliges me to renounce? I have lost your affection; your friendship remains to me. . . . I receive it, Mademoiselle, as a precious exchange for my own. . . . But this correspondence, mademoiselle—I feel all its pleasures, but at the same time, all its danger."[37] He replied to her questions about the situation of companion, thanked her for her critique of the *Essai*, and ignored the offer of a letter of introduction to Rousseau (in whom he was not particularly interested). His letter, dated June 23, for a time silenced her.

In July, the course of Gibbon's life must be inferred from earlier or later accounts—"the little dissipations of the town, the tumult of Mesery [his landlord's country place], and the daily transfers from one to the other,"[38] a certain amount of work on his *Recueil géographique* or on Juvenal, the current objects of his literary study—because at the time he wrote no known letters and kept no journal. There is, however, one startling exception to this absence of direct evidence. As Gibbon put it in the *Memoirs*, "The habits of the militia and the example of my countrymen betrayed me into some riotous acts of intemperance; and before my departure, I had deservedly forfeited the public opinion which had been acquired by the virtues of my better days" (131). As a result, the name of "Guibon" appears in the records of the Conseil de Lausanne.[39]

On the last Sunday in June, complained a M. Bergier, around 10 P.M., at Ouchy, he had suffered "violence & bad treatment" at the hands of a M. Sidney and (as it appeared on further inquiry) two other foreigners.[40] Sidney and his "governor" boarded at the same pension as Gibbon, and William Guise, also a boarder there, was later cited in the same affair. The third foreigner was not identified. Sidney had to apologize and promise amendment, but Guise, claiming the frequenters of the Académie de Lausanne were not under the jurisdiction of the Council, succeeded in having the citation against him withdrawn. He was, however, asked to explain himself to the *Bourgmaître*, which he did to such good effect that the charges against him were declared erroneous. Gibbon's name was not mentioned, though he may well have been Guise's spokesman. But the affair did not end there.

The next phase was that the foreigners and their allies, who included "Monsieur le Justicier De Saussure," complained against the guards for exceeding their authority, mistreating and threatening them. There are two such cases in the records involving Gibbon and/or his friends: one took place on the night of July 14/15, the other on July 22/23. The first complainants were de Saussure and Clarke, the second were Clarke, Guise, Sidney, and "Guibon." By threatening to appeal over the heads of the Council to Berne, Gibbon, spokesman for the complainants, won a complete victory. The watchmen were reproved and the foreigners placated. So ended, on August 23, the "unhappy affair, which shows, on the part of the magistrate, an obstinacy, bad faith, and incapacity which render him very despicable; and on our part, too much passion in maintaining a trifle," recorded Gibbon in his journal.[41] The victory in law, however, was not one calculated to appeal to public opinion in Lausanne. Gibbon's part in the affair was not particularly embarrassing, so far as the archives record it. It could hardly add to his good reputation. Yet it may have been of value for him; the whole proceeding may have helped to prevent Gibbon and his friends from being called to account for an affair in September that *was* discreditable to them, as we shall see.

But even without extraordinary dissipations, Gibbon was wasting time. Bonnard's suggestion that he took up his journalizing again because he felt the need of keeping a strict account of his time in order to avoid losing it seems sound.[42] In December, looking back over the year, Gibbon noted that his first ardor in his geographic studies took him to the end of June. "It was then that a journey to Geneva somewhat interrupted my assiduousness, that the stay in Mézery offered me a thousand distractions, and that the society of de Saussure completed the process of making me lose my time. I took up my work with this journal in the middle of August."[43]

Early in August, he wrote a lively description of his visit to Geneva, or rather Fernay, to see Voltaire act and enjoy the supper he gave for a hundred guests afterward.[44] As Gibbon did *not* mention, one of his fellow guests was Suzanne Curchod. It was an awkward situation for him; on an earlier occasion he had hardly known what to do when two ladies with whom he was enjoying casual flirtations happened to appear at the same party,[45] and this was a much more serious encounter. Our only account of the meeting is Suzanne's; Gibbon seems to have handled it very badly. Gibbon assumed a gaiety that, she says, did not deceive her, but that struck her silent with its heartlessness, and told her, not in so many words, that he blushed for her conduct. In reply, she wrote to him some six weeks later—when she was about to leave Geneva and therefore did not hope or fear to see him again—vigorously defending her actions and recounting the whole story of their relationship from her perspective. In this letter she rejoiced in her escape and told him he would one day regret the loss of her affection. It is a good letter, if rather self-righteous, and both Bonnard and Norton take Suzanne's version at face value.[46] They condemn Gibbon not merely for clumsiness but also for heartlessness or cruelty. The accusation may be just, but two pieces of evidence suggest that the accusers have seen the case too one-sidedly (as, of course, Suzanne's avowed partisans do also).

The first piece of evidence is Gibbon's comment on the letter in his private journal. After calling Suzanne a "dangerous and artful girl" ("fille dangereuse et artificielle") he confessed to feeling some regrets and almost remorse at the air of candor, the sentiments of tenderness and "honnêteté" of her letter. But:

> Her trips to Lausanne, the adorers whom she had there and the complaisance with which she listened to them formed the article most difficult to justify. Neither d'Eyverdun (says she) nor anyone else effaced for an instant my image from her heart. She was amusing herself at Lausanne without forming attachments there. I wish it may be so. But still these amusements convict her of the most odious dissimulation, and if infidelity is sometimes a weakness, duplicity is always a vice. It was in July, 1758, that she wrote me from Crassy that extraordinary letter full of tenderness and despair, her eyes full of tears and her health weakened by grief. In the same month of July she was at Lausanne, full of health and charms. *The object of the jealousy of the women and the sighs of the men* (   ),[47] enjoying every pleasure, founding academies, distributing prizes, composing clever works herself, and playing at love if she was not engaged in it. Does not this contrast suffice to enlighten me about her. I say enlighten. It is only a question of ideas and not of feelings. The most complete justification, restoring her to my esteem, could not relight fires so entirely extinguished. Since she must soon leave Geneva, I shall not see her again, and all is over. This affair, singular in every respect, has been very useful to me. It has opened my eyes on the character of women and will long serve me as a preservative against the seduction of love.[48]

It seems clear that he was convinced he was the injured party, first deserted, then deceived by a false representation of her misery, and finally accused of being the faithless one. Her letter had shaken his confidence in his belief that she could have nothing to say on her side, but had not convinced him even that she was blameless, much less that the judgment he had reached was, given what he then knew, unjustifiable. Instead, he had decided to value the experience for the lesson it had taught him—to beware of women, presumably because they are fickle and dishonest, or at least confusing. Some readers have believed that he had actually achieved the kind of coolness he pretended to in calling the affair "very useful," but surely both his imagining that his experience was "singular" and his bombastic declaration of enlightenment on the character of women betrayed boyish posturing.

The other evidence against too severe a condemnation of Gibbon is the later course of his and Suzanne's relationship. In February 1764, Suzanne unexpectedly returned to Lausanne. Fortified with Pavillard's company, Gibbon called on her. "I was at first somewhat confused, but . . . we chatted a quarter of an hour with all the freedom of people who would see each other from time to time. How instructive for me was her tranquillity!"[49] Thereafter, they met with reasonable frequency in the confined society of Lausanne until, upon her departure in April, he paid her a farewell visit: "We chatted in a playful tone, which I easily redoubled to make her feel that I was indifferent to her departure. This sentiment was not feigned. Time, absence, but especially knowledge of the false and affected character of this girl have extinguished the last sparks of my passion."[50] The gentleman doth protest too much, and the appearance of friendship forced upon them in Lausanne might have given way to estrangement had either remained convinced of the unkindness and duplicity of the other. Instead, after a year's separation, they met as old friends in Paris. Both her heart and her pride had meanwhile enjoyed the solace of a brilliant marriage. In the larger sphere of Paris, if she had continued to think that he had injured her, she need not have continued the acquaintance, or could have chosen cold politeness if Gibbon retained a sense of injury. When their feelings cooled, however, each of the erstwhile lovers seems instead to have recognized some justice or excuse on the other's side, and both seem to have been happy to resume the friendship both had valued. In its new form, their relationship was concluded only by death.

The encounter with Suzanne was not the only important event in Gibbon's emotional life in August 1763. It was also the month in which he met the man who was to become the best of his English friends, his future literary executor, John Baker Holroyd, later Lord Sheffield. He also formed other valuable friendships, including one with Victor de Saussure, already mentioned, and he enjoyed numerous pleasant acquaintances and companions, including William Guise, with whom he would travel in Italy, and the young Prince Louis von Wirtemberg. The prince, some six years older than Gibbon, is the subject of a tart pencil portrait in the *Memoirs*. Perhaps Gibbon betrays some vanity of rank in singling out this acquaintance for recollection. But in 1763, Prince Louis singled himself out, for example, by inviting Gibbon to dine twice within three days; at the time, he was much more in Gibbon's mind than was Holroyd.

The August resumption of systematic scholarly work and critical reading of the classics represented the rekindling of a flame both prior to, and more permanent than, Gibbon's ardor for Suzanne. His reading of Juvenal's satires produced a few comments very useful in our understanding of his character, as well as his literary views. Despite the "solemn sneer" of his irony, despite the witty accusation that his charity slumbered only when Christians were persecuted or virgins ravished, and despite his admiration of Juvenal's "power, variety, and abundance," Gibbon neither held nor approved of a Juvenalian contempt for mankind. He disapproved of such contempt on both moral and pragmatic grounds; satire based on it was both false and ineffective:

> I would reproach him [Juvenal] for . . . a malignity of heart that makes him find vice everywhere. . . . Never does Juvenal permit himself the slightest praise of the virtuous (.)[51] even if only in contrast with vice. All other satirists—Horace, Boileau, Pope—understood that they should make their readers their friends, by representing themselves as friends of virtue and mankind; these are also, of all the poets, those whom we love most. But Juvenal would appear to detest mankind on principle.[52]

In the beginning of September, Gibbon's tranquillity suffered interruption from Beriton. His father wrote him a very disquieting letter about family finances. Apparently it complained of Gibbon's expenses, but the real difficulty was that it proposed an increase in the mortgage held by one Sir J. R—; the £5,000 so acquired was to be entirely at the disposal of Mr. Gibbon.[53] The letter represented this move as an opportunity to increase Gibbon's allowance, to allow him to continue his travels, and to bring him into Parliament. Gibbon's reply had to be very tactful but very firm. He well knew what would happen to any cash in his father's hands, but he had to evince gratitude for the good intentions toward himself, or lose this only opportunity to continue the journey that meant so much to him.

He proposed a scheme "which would set me entirely at my ease without costing you a shilling. It would be to change my annuity into a perpetual rent charge upon the Estate: this I would sell immediately for an annuity upon my own life, which . . . would enable me to travel . . . and to live afterwards in a very agreable manner in England. I think I may venture to say I shall never marry." He took the risk of adding, "In case this proposal should be disagreable to you, you have my full consent to the other. Only give me leave Dear Sir to mention one thing. . . . I am afraid (excuse the freedom) that Oeconomy is not the virtue of our family."[54] He proposed as another possibility the dividing of the sum borrowed between them, so that each might know the total of his resources and the limits necessary to his desires.

The probability of Gibbon's not marrying is a new note in his view of himself. It is impossible to say whether his disappointment with Suzanne, his recognition of the family financial straits, or his contentment in his life as a bachelor-scholar most influenced his decision; all probably had their effects. On August 10, he had written to Deyverdun to propose again their combining their resources and living together somewhere. Gibbon was too fond of company to plan a solitary existence, even if marriage were out of the question. In any event, his ideas about his future household were undoubtedly still open to change.

If the financial problems with his father were ominous indications of what was to come, the first hints of his acquaintance with Holroyd belied the happy future of that friendship. Holroyd "lacks neither intelligence nor knowledge but he seems to me very complacent. . . . [Holroyd and his traveling companion, Manners]are both military men, and they have adopted all the prejudices of that order against the militia."[55] We know that Holroyd, in the regular army, was amused by Gibbon's pride in his militia career. (We must again recall his description of Gibbon at Lausanne— short, thin, with a large head and red hair; round-faced, elaborately dressed, and already given to posing himself before the fire to take snuff in the characteristic gesture familiar in his later life.) Holroyd had told the hero of the bloodless campaigns of Hampshire about the new farce in London mocking Major Sturgeon, a vain militia officer.[56] Gibbon thought there could be no such farce, that Holroyd had invented it to make fun of him. Once this confusion was cleared up, however, Gibbon responded to Holroyd's teasing with good humor and soon began to value him highly.

After Gibbon again took up his journal, his studies—the *Recueil*, Juvenal's satires, the volumes of the *Bibliothèque raisonnée* he was systematically reading—settled into a pattern. On September 6, he recorded another element of the new pattern of his days, the "Cercle": "It is a society pleasant enough for passing one's spare time. They have a pretty room where one is sure of finding play, conversation, gazettes, journals, etc. . . . I count on going there rather often, especially during the winter."[57] Another resource, one he had enjoyed in his earlier stay in Lausanne, the "Société du Printems," no longer gave him much pleasure: "A silly group of young people who can do nothing but laugh, sing, and dance is not exactly what I need."[58]

One September day, or rather evening, was unfortunately singled out from the balanced regime he was establishing. It began propitiously enough with his receiving a letter from Deyverdun. "His letter gave me great pleasure, but his accepting my proposals now embarrasses me as much as his refusing them last year distressed me, as letters from my father have thrown me into an uncertainty that does not permit me to form projects." Gibbon then went to an assembly at the Chateau. "After leaving this assembly, why did I not retire immediately, instead of taking supper at Clarke's," he lamented, beginning a new page of his journal, having (understandably) skipped two in his agitation. At Clarke's, there were eleven young men (including the host), both Swiss and foreign. Among them they emptied twenty-five bottles of burgundy and then emerged into the quiet town with all the noise possible. Holroyd was not of the party, but Holroyd's friend Manners, "who is never so wise as when he is drunk," helped Gibbon to his room about 3 A.M. The others, moving to another room, grew quarrelsome; a pistol went off, and the ball broke a window. Worst of all, one Corsier, a Lausannois, had left earlier, and Guise and Clarke insisted on paying him a visit. When they were not welcomed at his house, they threatened to break down the door and were less than respectful (says Gibbon, perhaps euphemistically) to his sister, who had come to the window. In short, the whole group disgraced themselves publicly.

Though Gibbon was not involved in the worst parts of the escapade, his account of it takes up a full page in the manuscript journal and still more space in his recollections of this second sojourn in Lausanne, for this is the episode that might most fully justify his sense that he then lost his good reputation there. He ruefully concluded his account, "I would give a good deal for this commotion not to have occurred."[59] Still more eloquently, he reported the next day, "Is it necessary to speak of a day which did not exist? The morning for vomiting and sleeping, bouillon at noon. In the evening, a farewell meal [for Sidney]. Fatigue took the place of wisdom for us, and we retired very calmly at 11:30."[60] Perfect Augustans are made, not born, but in Gibbon's full, if wry, account of his own comedy, we can perhaps see foreshadowed the balance and detachment of the attitude later achieved by him.

At the end of this lost-day entry, he expressed his regret about the departure of de Salis, one of the visitors who had used his time in Lausanne to particularly good advantage. On the very next day, we can see, as it were, the first fruits of a new resolution to use his own time wisely. By the end of the week, he began to read Nardini's *Traité sur l'ancienne Rome* (in a Latin translation of the Italian original).[61] Pavillard had obtained the book for him from Geneva; it was, of course, essential to his *Recueil géographique*. Nardini's *Traité* and other such works, dinners or suppers and evenings of cards, rather than debauches, were the staples of Gibbon's autumn months at Lausanne. The card play was for very small stakes—"The greatest loss was that of time."[62] It was a much safer common ground for the young men of several nations and varying talents than were twenty-five bottles of burgundy.

But the damage to Gibbon's reputation had already been done. He was proposed as "Directeur des Etrangers" of the Cercle but lost the election. He felt sure that he could have rallied enough friends to win, "but at the same time, I know that three months ago I would have had it without a moment's effort. My reputation is sinking here with some reason, and I have enemies."[63] He could only try to live it down. The foreigners were daily departing, in any case; by September 21, only Holroyd and Manners, Guise and Gibbon, remained, of the numerous English visitors who had shared their pension. The household was fixed in town after the 23rd; the country house had been given up for the winter, to Gibbon's pleasure: "Although Mézery is pretty, it bored me very much: to avoid this misfortune I seldom went there and spent the night there even less often. Hence meals taken in town, the necessity of a carriage, and a great increase of expense, trouble, and dissipation."[64] He was glad to escape all three, for his change of manners had been noticed, and the notice was giving him pain. He called on Deyverdun's aunt, for example, after a lapse of ten days, and she, a particularly good friend, affected not to have noticed his absence. "I used to have an excellent reputation here for manners, but I see that they begin to confuse me with my compatriots, and to consider me a man who likes wine and disorder. Are they entirely wrong?"[65]

According to Bonnard, editor of this journal, such passages (not published, of course, by Sheffield) make it "certain that the reader of the complete text will form a less high opinion of Gibbon than the reader of Lord Sheffield's extracts only. In Gibbon, character and heart do not reach the height of the intelligence."[66] Considering that Gibbon was a genius, not a saint, this must be so, yet it seems a harsh judgment of a youth capable of such self-criticism, contrition, and amendment. It is true that he was a little old for fraternity-house follies, but also true that his faults of character were no more serious than such follies, and arguable that the alleged faults of his heart were no such thing. For instance, he had harsh things to say of Constant de Rebecque: "This man combines the most opposite bad qualities. Grossness and artifice, stupidity and cunning, prodigality and avarice."[67] These judgments may be ill-considered, but their warmth of indignation is not a symptom of heartlessness.

As for his behavior, Gibbon was wise enough by the end of September to reject temptations to further errors. Manners, Guise, Holroyd, and Clarke departed on a tour of Switzerland, pressing Gibbon to accompany them. "If only Guise and Holroyd had been in question, I would have gone with pleasure, but the two others are young fools, and with us, it is the fools who lead the wise and never the wise who govern the fools."[68] He therefore begged off on the grounds of the lateness of the season and his aversion to traveling on horseback, no doubt resisting much teasing on the latter account.[69]

While they were away, Gibbon's best Swiss friend then in Lausanne, Victor de Saussure, also departed: "I have lost this friend almost in the moment of acquiring him." Gibbon and de Saussure had been prepared to like each other by Deyverdun, their common friend; uncommonly enough they actually did like each other. "We found each other congenial, we passed rapidly to familiarity, to confidence, to friendship, and in six weeks, we had no secrets from each other. De Saussure's character justified all these feelings on my part."[70] To this entry, Gibbon added a shrewd character sketch—not a panegyric—of his friend. Gibbon's high idea of friendship had long been established; he could remark of another companion, "He is my 'friend,' not in the sense that I understand friendship with respect to de Saussure, or as I envisage it with respect to d'Eyverdun, but in the false and commonplace sense of the world" (they met often and always with pleasure).[71]

Finally, in mid-October, he began to make serious progress on the most important literary project of his Lausanne stay, the *Recueil géographique* of ancient Italy. Lord Sheffield's heroic editorial efforts (the printing of the *Nomina gentesque Italiae Antiquae*, as it was called, in the *Miscellaneous Works* is a story in itself)[72] made the *Recueil* publishable, but seriously obscured its method, its state of development, and the order of its composition, all of which can be deduced from the manuscript.[73] Essentially, Gibbon began as if he were producing a specialized commonplace book: he allotted two pages each to fifteen topics, except that to the fourth topic (Latium and Campania) he allotted four pages. If the second page became filled, he gave a new pair of pages the same title but a new "chapter" number. If he did not have enough information to write two pages on a given topic, he left the space blank or added to the entry later. Because each pair of pages (the first of each pair was the verso of one sheet, the second the recto of the next) had a different chapter number, he began with sixteen so-called chapters for his fifteen topics. Eventually there were forty-eight chapters, of which chapter 46 introduced a new topic, "Itineria."

The first expansion of his original sixteen-chapter plan (i.e., C. XVII) must have been required very early in his work, for it was no more than the continuation of the list of places in Latium and Campania, which in the Sheffield edition appear as subheadings to the subheading "Salernum" under the heading "PICENTINI" within the Latium and Campania section, but which were in fact Gibbon's first entries under that topic. This relegation of the list to an inconspicuous place is typical of the effects of Lord Sheffield's edition. Whatever the merits of his arrangement, it gives the false impression that the *Recueil* was from the beginnning a geographic essay, whereas at first it was only the framework and notes for such a study. Such misleading changes have effectively vitiated all previous efforts to discuss Gibbon's aims, accomplishments, and development in this work.[74]

His next supplementary chapter, for example, was required for an addition to C. II, the second topic, "Regiones Aer et Solum." Item nine in this section was an enumeration of the regions of Italy in the Augustan division. The addition began in the unfilled space at the end of the second page of C. II and continued as C. XVIII. It reads, "Constantine, who re-formed—shall I say—or who confounded all the ancient constitutions, made several changes in Italy."[75] A comparison of these two entries makes it obvious why it matters in what order Gibbon composed the parts of his *Recueil*. By the time he wrote the latter entry, he was already commenting like a historian, not just enumerating like a geographer. The second entry was written no earlier than October.[76]

Similarly, he soon had new information to add to the material on Latium and Campania; it required four pages (C. XIX and C. XX) and was no mere enumeration, but included quotations from poets as well as prose writers, and comments of Gibbon's own, for example, apropos of Lake Avernus, "Agrippa had the forests cut down, the surroundings of the lake were cleared and soon became inhabited, and all these fables disap-peared."[77]

He went on to make additions to C. XV, "Venetia and Istria"; to C. XVI, "Alpes et Gentes Inalpine et flumen Padus"; to C. XI, "Etruria," and to C. VIII, VII, VI, and I, in that order. After adding still more to his material on Latium and Campania and on the city of Rome, he added a new topic, "Itineria." This brought him to the end of his work on the project in Lausanne. The remaining two chapters (added to the entries on "Aemilia and Flamina" and "Etruria," respectively) were products of his Italian tour. The Sheffield edition conceals not only the accumulative nature of the entires but also their original order within the topics. It also changes the order among the topics. Gibbon, after the opening chapters on "the ancient appellations and inhabitants of Italy; its divisions, air, and soil,"[78] began at Rome, moved south through Latium, Campania, Lucania, and Brutium, then across the Gulf of Taranto to Apulia and Calabria, north through Samnium, Picenum, and Umbria; west again to Etruria, and only then out into Cisalpine Gaul. His account ended with the Alps, except for the later addition of the chapter on the roads. This is the order of a man with a Roman imagination; Sheffield replaced it with the itinerary of an English traveler, forgiveably enough, and then attributed that order to Gibbon, less forgiveably.

Because Gibbon prepared space for the first sixteen "chapters" before he began writing, dating them with respect to each other is not straight-forward. For example, we know that he wrote C. III, "Rome," on Octo-ber 15, because he recorded doing so in his journal.[79] Only four pages precede C. III in the manuscript, yet we know from journal entries of August and September that he had already written at least eight, probably nine or more, pages. Which pages were they? Certainly chapters IV and V and their continuation as C. XVII, but probably first C. I and C. II, which rely solely on materials he had read before coming to Lausanne.[80] That makes a total of nearly ten pages. None of the other chapters could have been written before he had read Cluverius's *Italia Antiqua,* which he did not begin until October 13, with the exception of the first paragraph of C. VIII.[81] Between August 6 and mid-October, his minimum production was about eight pages; the maximum, about fifteen. All the remainder of the ninety-two folio pages was therefore written between October 15 and his departure for Italy on April 18.[82] If we allow for reading and distractions, in fact, we can infer that much of this writing must belong to February and March.

To appreciate Gibbon's progress, we should retrace the stages in his writing; to understand the work he produced, we should read it in the divisions and the order he intended; Lord Sheffield's version permits us to do neither, and it is impractical to stop to do either here. Instead, we can examine a representative section, that on Samnium, C. VIII and C. XXVII–XXIX.[83] The first paragraph might have been written in the earliest stages of the *Recueil,* before Gibbon had begun reading Cluvier. It starts with a brief survey of the extent and boundaries of the region, derived from Deslisle's map of Italy and Pliny's *Natural History.* Gibbon concluded this factual paragraph with an enumeration of the principal cities—a pure, old-fashioned geography lesson.

He happened to record, on February 26, the topics of the three pages he wrote that day. As a result, it can be determined that on that date he wrote the remainder of C. VIII and the first half of C. XXVII.[84] He was developing his article on Samnium by proceeding through the principal cities and their surrounding dependencies in much the same fashion as he had introduced the whole article. He first surveyed the people, the boundaries, the language, and the principal towns of the Sabines, the first territory in his list of the principal cities of Samnium. The remainder of the article is less predictable. Although it mentions the shape and products of the state, it turns almost immediately to the effects of war in making once great towns into villages and hamlets and quotes Silius Italicus and Virgil to prove this point.

In a happier vein, Gibbon then attempted to identify the precise location of Horace's Sabine villa and quoted the poet's description of it. His next interest was the Sabines' great natural resource, the territory of Reate; Gibbon combined the testimonies of Varro, Cluvier, and Virgil (the *Georgics*) in its praise. He then turned to the second item on his Samnium list, the Marsi.

Owing to the small size and population of the Marsi area, his introductory survey is brief, but it is a miniature version of the same structure used for the Sabines. Without further discussion, however, he went on to quotations from the poets. He continued with the historians, from whom he could add that Rome sent a colony to Alba Fucentia in the Marsi territory

A.U.C. 459, that it was considered a safe place for important prisoners, such as kings and princes, and that two of them died there. This concluded the work of February 26.

Later, he added five more pages to the article on Samnium. All the new material fits smoothly into the territorial order, with the exception of two brief quotations, apparently omitted in their proper sequence and therefore added at the very end. For Gibbon his procedure—reading all his materials and relying on his memory to recall and arrange them before reducing them to paper—apparently was efficient. When he returned to this section, for example, he began easily enough with another topic relative to the Marsi, namely, a consideration of the great flood of Lake Celano (ancient Lacus Fucinus) in their territory, and the failure of the emperors to build an adequate canal to prevent destructive floods. Gibbon's historical understanding evidently extended to technology, in a way with which some modern historians may not fully credit him. Caesar planned the canal, but

> death halted the execution of this project, which Augustus, wiser or more timid, never dared to undertake. . . . Claudius finally had the courage to attempt it. . . . [He narrates the building of the canal and the spectacles at its opening.] After this entertainment the canal was opened, but it was soon apparent how imperfect the work was, and that the ignorance or negligence of the workers had not given it the necessary depth. . . . Is it then astonishing if Nero and Hadrian were obliged to restore this work and that in spite of their labors only vestiges of it remain? To facilitate and perfect this project the art of locks was necessary, which the ancients did not have.[85]

The page ends with the usual introduction—this one very brief—of the next group, the Aequi. Quotations from Virgil, Silius Italicus, Ovid, and Horace begin the next page, C. XXVIII. The date of the colony's founding ends the entry. The next entry, for the Peligni, is even shorter, and the entry for the Vestini, still on the same page, begins, rather irritably, "It is as difficult as it would be useless to mark with precision the boundaries of these little cities that are confused with one another."[86] Nevertheless, Gibbon gave a sentence to the Vestini boundaries, a sentence to their towns, and four lines of verse (of Silius Italicus) to record its glory, end the page, and end the entry.

The other page of C. XXVIII hurries on, after conscientious but brief entries for the Marrucini and Frentani, to the "celebrated people" that remains to be discussed, the Samnites themselves. They receive more than two pages of the *Recueil,* only ten lines of which are verse quotations. In his brief, but far from mechanical, survey of their heroic past and their dreadful fate, Gibbon seems to have forgotten that his was a geographical study, and he wrote entirely as a historian, seeing not merely isolated events but also their principles, causes, and connections. The Samnites' story is the tragedy or melodrama of the *Cité belligeuse,* at first subjugating their neighbors, waging war outside their own lands, then setting up laws and customs to preserve their warrior spirit, then contending for a long time with their more powerful and eventually invincible neighbors, the Romans. Gibbon says that "The Republic conquered them only after six bloody wars, or rather after a continual war of seventy years, in which Roman generals earned twenty-four triumphs, and suffered almost as many defeats." Then the Samnites spent an interval as the best of the Roman troops; finally, the deadly adventure of the civil wars began. The victorious Roman legions "carried steel and fire into their country, destroyed their cities to the last traces, and exterminated their inhabitants."[87] The country was no more than a desert in Tiberius's time and contained nothing more than villages in the modern era. Gibbon concluded the entry with a dutiful return to his established structure, with a list of principal towns and two quotations.

The remainder of his space was devoted to Beneventum. "All the ancients placed Beneventum in the Samnite territory. Why, in M. Delisle's map of ancient Italy, is it found in the country of the Hirpini, in Apulia?"[88] After discussing Bochat's learned account of the Celtic etymology of Beneventum's name, Gibbon abruptly began to examine the Middle Ages, giving a swift account of Beneventum's great days and their end A.D. 571–891. Like the Bochat reference, this material was recollected from Giannone, a favorite object of his youthful study.

Although from at least 1755 on, Gibbon's writing had a tendency to drop into history as easily as most of us drop into banality, Bonnard's seeing special signs, in this second sojourn at Lausanne, of his having unconsciously discovered his métier, and even his subject, is supported by close scrutiny of this *Recueil,* incomplete and inchoate though it is.[89] But Gibbon's progress toward the writing of the great history was so gradual, and accompanied by so many delays and detours, that a case can be made for other turning points as well. To examine the claims of this one has taken us far ahead of our story; in November the *Recueil* itself had far to go.

In November, Gibbon was without a particular friend in Lausanne, but not without pleasant distractions. His journal shows that he enjoyed numerous parties of pleasure during the interludes of his work (although he remarked, "It is strange how much I play Whist without liking or understanding it"!)[90] These relaxations did not, however, interfere with his reading, especially of the two folio volumes of the *Italia Antiqua,* a "truly laborious task," which he completed on December 3. "I do this reading, as I did that of Nardini, to prepare myself both for my journey to Italy and for my future studies."[91] Despite whist, disquieting and then reassuring letters from home, and other work, including the journal itself, which often contained quite substantial extracts and observations (e.g., the discussion of Hannibal's route over the Alps, the entry of October 24, almost ten pages in the manuscript journal), he completed the two folio volumes of Cluvier in about seven weeks.

Also of interest in the journal of this period is a lengthy essay, supplementing and correcting Vertot's conclusions and methods in his account of the Roman "social war"; it is worthy of the attention of those studying Gibbon's methods as a historian.[92] Most interesting, however, is a comparison to the body politic in which Gibbon then found himself: "I write in the Pays de Vaud. Its inhabitants must be content with their state. Let it be compared, however, with that of these peoples of Italy."[93] This guarded remark seems to be developed in his unpublished (until after his death), incomplete, but prudently pseudonymous criticism of the Bernese government, the "Lettre sur le gouvernement de Berne."[94]

When this piece was eventually published, it "made some impression among Vaudois patriots" and "subsequent historians of the Pays de Vaud have hailed [it] as a first raising of the banner of liberty in their midst."[95] Perhaps Gibbon intended this piece for publication; the pseudonym was hardly necessary or effective in a manuscript work. The "Lettre" rebukes the Vaudois for their complacent acceptance of the paternalistic stagnation imposed by the Bernese supremacy on the Pays de Vaud. Two hundred years of peace, the writer admits, is a great blessing, and the Pays de Vaud unites the virtues of London's philosophers and Paris's polished society: "It is the only country in which one both dares to think, and knows how to live. What do you lack? Liberty: and deprived of liberty, you lack everything."[96] He observes that whatever freedom of thought and speech the Vaudois claim, they must act as their masters require. The laws do not impartially serve the whole community. True, the ending of anarchy requires that liberty be confided to someone, but that someone should be a council representing "each part of the state." Prosperity is the counterargument of a slave, content although his comfort has no sounder foundation than "men's passions." It is not, however, the case that the public administration of the Bernese is unobjectionable. "Show me what truly useful establishment you owe to the Sovereign" (i.e., the rule of Berne).[97]

Gibbon criticized other omissions and actions of the Bernese government, paticularly the "Consensus."[98] He objected to the means of filling offices: "The burdens are common to all; the rewards should be also." But "talents, intelligence in your country are useless for anyone who was not born Bernese."[99]

Finally, against the argument that these disadvantages trouble only "gentlemen," he pointed out that the "tyranny" of the bailiffs applied to all. The bailiffs exercise, he said, the powers of legislator, executive, and judge. Although their authority is limited by that of the central government in Berne, a financial judgment of one hundred francs, which might be minor to a person of substance, would be a peasant's whole fortune; yet to appeal to Berne would be more expensive still.[100]

The author of the "Lettre" specifically disavowed advocating revolution, but he described it as a remedy "quicker, more complete, more glorious," than petitions and remonstrances, so his disavowal could easily be read as ironic. Perhaps it was so intended; almost certainly ironic is the comparison of a citizen to the Pauline description of charity, suffering long and hoping all things.[101] But later in the same paragraph, the tone is clearly not ironic as the "Swede" counsels (in Burkean mode) a preference of the known evils of submission over the greater and unknown evils of anarchy; he has no intention, he says, of persuading the people to shake off the "yoke of authority, in order to conduct them from complaint to sedition, from sedition to anarchy, and from anarchy, perhaps to despotism."[102] As usual, Gibbon objected to fighting even tyranny with anarchy, because he saw anarchy as leading again to tyranny.

But also as usual, in reality he espoused neither resignation to the present thralldom nor violent change, but rather a third option, which he described as dictated by reason, not by mythical fears. Unfortunately, he did not complete the "Lettre," and we cannot be sure exactly what he would have proposed, though it is possible to speculate, on the basis of the last sentence of the existing essay, that it would have involved action but not revolt against the Bernese authorities—what is now called "passive resistance" or "civil disobedience." The last sentence reads, "The Bernese have rights over your obedience; you are afraid of doing them an injustice by withdrawing it."[103] Obviously, the next word would have been some synonym of "but." But that word was never written.

Michel Baridon, who calls the "Lettre" Gibbon's most "advanced" statement, points out that nevertheless it is entirely explicable on the principles of Montesquieu: "One cannot . . . call this text particularly inflamed. Of the *Social Contract* . . . only the concept of general consent is retained. All the inspiration of the *Lettre* comes from Montesquieu: separation of powers, "Gothic" origin of liberty, explicit condemnation of despotism, apology for commerce and industry, so many running themes in the *Esprit des Lois*." It was its tone and the "discreet homage paid to Major Davel" that gave the "Lettre" a role in the Vaudois revolution.[104] To Baridon's astute summary may be added something of the place of this work in the history of Gibbon's political views. As we shall see, he was invariably outraged by violations of the "natural law" that the laborer is worthy of his hire; he invariably assumed that societies should curb one man's freedom no more than is necessary to safeguard that of other men; and he was consistently as unwilling to accept the tyranny of the many— what he sometimes called "wild" democracy, that is, mob rule or anarchy or, probably, pure democracy, but not representative democracies—as he was unwilling to accept the tyranny of the few or of one. The political theorist might question the logical consistency of some of these positions; if so, Gibbon was neither the first nor the last man to be guilty of illogical politics. Some students of his thought, notably Low and de Beer, think that from a youthful revolutionary he became a reactionary old man.[105] But the change of heart, if there was one, had to come between 1763/64 (the date of this essay) and 1765-67, when there are expressions of the later view, notably in his essay on Brutus and in his abstract of Blackstone.[106] Low cites Gibbon's comment in the *Memoirs* that "While the Aristocracy of Bern protects the happiness, it is superfluous to enquire whether it be founded in the rights, of man" (185) as proof that Gibbon had reversed his position. In context, however, it is proof only that when he wrote the *Memoirs,* he thought that the opposite extreme of the two he opposed was in danger of ascendancy and added his weight where it would assist the balance he thought proper. The context is, "Many . . . appear to be infected with the French disease, the wild theories of equal and boundless freedom: but . . . I am satisfied that the failure or success of a revolt would equally terminate in the ruin of the country." Whereas in 1763-64 Gibbon had seen the Vaudois gentry and bourgeoisie complacent in their stagnation and unaware of their impotence, in 1791 he saw the general populace preparing to replace order with anarchy. He objected to both, from the same intermediate position. The difference is, however, so marked as to seem a reversal, because his reaction to the rejected extreme, in each instance, was almost to applaud the alternative—to speak of "glorious" revolt, to scorn "superfluous" enquiry. While Gibbon would no doubt have acknowledged a change of spirit, perhaps have smiled at his own youthful impatience and enthusiasm, he would have repudiated the charge of a change of principle. Even in Gibbon's youth, his indignation did not last long enough for him to complete the essay. Instead, his time was soon again absorbed by the pleasures of society and the detachment of scholarship.

Despite its failure to mention the possibly dangerous "Lettre," the journal is our best evidence of Gibbon's thoughts and values, as well as his work, in this period of his life. He now recorded in it his reflections moral and psychological, not merely historical and critical. A good example is his consideration of Calvin's character as revealed by the burning at the stake of Servetus. In the *Decline and Fall,* Gibbon wrote as if Calvin's treatment of Servetus were simply and self-evidently inexcusable, worse in an enlightened reformer than even the atrocities committed by the Inquisition. In the *Journal,* he considered the psychology of Calvin's decision, the possibility that religious zeal might have led him to consent to the cruel deed without malice.[107] Gibbon concluded that malice was involved, but his own insight and toleration is much clearer in the journal than in the glib conclusions of the history.

As autumn ended, then, Gibbon's life was well regulated; he was making every effort to redeem his damaged reputation. He was enjoying excellent health. In November, however, he was ill enough to require rest (8th), blooding (9th), and "medicine," probably an emetic or purge (13th). His studies were reduced or delayed—no Cluvier for a week! Instead, he read a French imitation of Ariosto and volume 30 of the *Bibliothèque raisonnée*. Once he had recovered, his busy social and scholarly life continued despite the winter weather (there were eighteen inches of snow on November 19). He even attempted to make amends for a truly regrettable social gaffe, his failure during more than three months to call on the Prince de Wirtemberg, who had been so hospitable to him in August. Gibbon, Guise, Clarke, and M. de Mézery took a carriage to the prince's house, half a league outside Lausanne. The prince did not receive them. Gibbon confessed, "I was ashamed of my treatment of him; after the attentions I had received from him, I ought not to have passed three months without setting foot there."[108] The damage was irretrievable, as it turned out, to Gibbon's mild regret.

His greatest ardor, or at least that most freely expressed, was reserved for the intellectual intoxication of learning and the tributes of friendship. "I like this Boussens; everyone likes him. He is good-natured, cheerful, without artifice, and has much of that good humor that makes others laugh, no matter how solemn they are"—one is reminded of Johnson's delight in Goldsmith or even Foote.[109] And if one happened unsuspecting upon the following passage, would not one imagine that perhaps Rousseau, rather than Gibbon, was its author? "Yes, man is naturally good! I cite those Greenlanders, who know love in the midst of their frost, but who war only against animals. . . . Compared to a Greenlander, an Iroquois is already a civilized man. How I like to see nature!"[110]

During the first weeks of winter, little of his energy, emotional or intellectual, found its way into his writing, with the important exception of the journal. On December 7, he finally returned to work on the *Recueil géographique,* writing in the journal the equivalent of a proposal or preface for this work. Neither cumbersome, like Cluverius's *Italia antiqua,* nor superficial, like Cellarius, the work was to enjoy the advantages of modern discoveries ("two new types of erudition, the Etruscan monuments and those of Herculaneum") and of a modern language, and "in place of [Cluvier's] chain of citations . . . a narration, clear, methodical, and interesting." Preserving at times the very words of his sources, especially if they were poetic, Gibbon would follow Strabo rather than Pliny, by which he meant that he would aim not only at order and precision but also at casting "a philosophic eye" on his subject.[111]

The arrangement of such a work is necessarily arbitrary, he went on to say, but his choice would be (after the necessary preliminaries) to place himself on Mount Palatine with Romulus; then, in describing Italy, he would follow the progress of Roman conquests and pay particular attention to the country's division into regions by Augustus, with one exception: he would separate the Sabines from Samnium, and put that territory at the head of Latium. By this small alteration he would reconcile the two principles of his arrangement; and the reader would easily follow the progress of Roman arms and Livy's history. This revision of his *Nomina* remained visionary, perhaps because of his judgment of its probable fate:

> A work of this kind, well executed, would be favourably received by the public. It might enrich a bookseller, pass through ten editions, and become a classical book with students in colleges, travellers, and even men of letters. The author, however, would do wrong to value himself on a performance, which owed its whole success to the nature of the subject, industry, and method.
>
> To speak only of my own essay, the production of my youth, written in two months, and forgotten in four, yet it shews more originality of genius, than would be required for such a geographical performance. Of the two sources of literary fame, difficulty and utility, the second is the surest, though the least flattering to vanity.[112]

Not even Gibbon's most ardent admirers deny him his share of vanity.

As for his social life, an evening's deep play at whist and piquet led to a loss of forty louis and a resolution against playing for high stakes—as he remarked ruefully, "There is wisdom after the blow."[113] A less harmful dissipation was the reading of the Abbé Montgon's memoirs, in eight fat volumes of small print. The future autobiographer might have learned some important negative lessons from this work: "Everything concerning the Abbé appeared to him to deserve the attention of all Europe. He needs fifty pages for a conversation . . . a hundred pages for an intrigue."[114] But on the whole the gaps in and between his serious reading projects were not prolonged and were often bridged either by writing or by the *Bibliothèque raisonnée.* On December 19, he read Claudius Rutilius's poem about his journey in A.D. 416 along the coasts of Etruria and Liguria and wrote a lengthy account of it—a good day's work. This account contains an anticipation interesting to readers of the *Decline and Fall:* "It was not in the reign of Honorius that one should portray the power of the Roman Empire. Its powers had abandoned it long since; but its antiquity and its extent inspired a kind of veneration and even terror in its neighbors and sustained it still. This illusion had finally dissipated. Little by little the Barbarians knew it, despised it, and destroyed it."[115] This observation echoes a point made in the canceled section of his *Essai*[116] and anticipates the view expressed in the "General Observations on the Decline of the Empire in the West" (*Decline and Fall,* chap. 38), that it was not the fall of the Roman Empire so much as the delay of that fall which required explanation.

The Rutilius essay (for the entry is truly an essay) also contains a thoughtful statement about the difference between prose and verse, or, rather, poetry; given a subject unified and simple,

> it is almost impossible to preserve both the character of the material, and that of the verse. The former requires, in fact consists of, nothing more than propriety, ease, and a few ornaments disposed with art and managed with care. The latter, which presupposes enthusiasm in the poet and excites it in the reader, looks only for energy and harmony, and willingly sacrifices to them, all beauties of a lower order. Poetry has its own language. It is suitable only to the great motions of the soul. It is for them only, then, that it is made. The poet who seeks to employ it for a subject that leaves the soul quiet and without feeling, will find himself placed between two shoals that he cannot escape. He will be wrecked on each in turn. Here, the power of his colors will disfigure the simplicity of his object instead of embellishing it. There, the poet will be perceptible only in the harmony of the verse, while his expressions are cold and prosaic.[117]

This interesting discussion was so substantial that it caused Gibbon himself to recognize that, as a journal of his own life, his journal required reform. The remaining entries for December (beginning on the 20th) show the influence of this resolve, though he did not explain it until the last entry of the year.

In that entry, having reviewed the year ("how he had employed that portion of his existence that had flowed away and would return no more"), he included as an accomplishment "this journal itself, which has become a work 214 pages in four and a half months." He commented on it at length:

> There are some learned and well-reasoned dissertations in it. . . . But these pieces are too much extended, and the journal itself needs a reform which will remove a number of pieces that are foreign to its true plan. . . . Here are some rules . . . on the topics suitable to it. 1. All my social and private life, my amusements, my connections [*liaisons*], even my diversions, and all my reflections . . . on personal subjects. 2. Everything that I learn by observation or conversation . . . 3. . . . the material part of my studies: how many hours I have worked, how many pages I have written or read, with a brief notice of the subject. . . . 4. I would be sorry to read without reflecting on my readings, without forming reasoned judgments of my authors and without examining with care their ideas and expressions. But . . . there are some books that one runs through . . . some that one reads . . . some that one must study. My observations on those of the first class . . . short and detached . . . belong to the journal. Those on the second class will not enter it except insofar as they are of the same type. 5. My reflections on that small number of classic authors that one meditates with care will naturally be more profound and further pursued. For them, and for the more extensive

and original pieces to which reading or meditation may give rise, I will make a separate collection.[118]

The three entries of 1763 in that new collection, dated December 23, 24, and 25, indicate how rapidly Gibbon could work when he was not distracted by domestic problems or social pleasures. Each piece was preceded by at least two readings of the work that inspired it, and none was a mere collection of notes. The three entries dealt with the catalogues of armies of Virgil and Silius Italicus, and with Horace's and Cicero's journeys as a means of judging the speed of travel on Roman roads.[119]

By December 30, Gibbon was able to say with pardonable complacency that he had nothing left to read on the geography of ancient Italy, although he planned to reread Strabo. This he completed on the 31st, when he also went to the ball held for Miss Clarke (he did not dance, but amused himself with talk and with seven or eight rubbers of whist—"I would never have believed that I could like this game. Today I play a hand with pleasure") and reflected on his past accomplishments and plans for further study and journalizing.[120]

The latter resolution was instantly broken. Under the date of January 1, when he had intended to begin his journal on a new plan, he confessed instead to its being February 1, explaining the gap as resulting from work on his new *Recueil* (in which, however, there are no January entries) and on the *Recueil géographique,* from continual dissipations, and from his "inconstant and lazy humor."[121] Perhaps only Samuel Johnson so constantly, sincerely, and unjustly accused himself of laziness.

As usual, Gibbon filled the gap in his journal from memory. He had begun reading Ovid's *Fasti* and continued the *Bibliothèque raisonnée.* An article in the latter concerned Gibbon's old corespondent Allamand, whose character Gibbon sketched in the journal. Gibbon had also read Lady Mary Wortley Montague's *Letters* (he recommended them to his stepmother).[122] Otherwise, his recollections were of scandals, parties, and quarrels among the natives of Lausanne and the community of visitors. He reported engagements on the 4th, 9th, 10th, 12th, 14th, 20th, 24th, 26th, and 27th, in addition to the common run of calls, cards, and informal meals.

After this month's lapse, the occupations, dissipations, and accomplishments of the last two-and-a-half months in Lausanne were faithfully recorded in the *Journal.* One typically Gibbonian resource was theatrical performances, but in Lausanne his choices were few. They included a series of three amateur performances given by the Grand family and their circle, all very talented, which gave Gibbon considerable pleasure. He also attended some "'holy comedies' (Susann and the Sacrifice of Isaac) by the small children of the common people. The subject and the manner of treatment exactly resembled the Mystery Plays of the 15th century. These

plays were filled with obscenities and impieties . . . that the children repeated in a ludicrous tone of devotion."[123]

Most interesting of his diversions were his flirtation with "la petite
femme" (Mme. Philippe-Louis de Seigneux) and his renewed friendship
with Suzanne Curchod. Each entry about Suzanne suggests how attractive he continued to find her company, despite injured feelings and distrust on both sides. For example, on February 21, he mused, "I could
not help reflecting a good deal on Mlle. Curchod. She betrayed me, for
d'Eyverdun had no motive for doing so. . . . Her mind has very much developed and if we can forget the past, her company is charming."[124] The
"little woman" was a very different matter, a mere flirt about whom Gibbon sometimes wrote with an unattractive leering coyness. Clearly he
thought her ready for any degree of infidelity to her husband; in his
opinion, their relationship remained relatively virtuous only because he
himself was too prudent to risk a serious entanglement. "I have no intentions but if I had any I am sure that nothing but the opportunity would
be lacking."[125] It did not occur to him that she might recognize and welcome the safety of flirtation with him, though, of course, he might have
been quite accurate in his assessment of her character. February concluded with a ball to which Gibbon escorted Suzanne, but where "I kept
escaping to the little woman, and on this occasion my senses triumphed
over my mind."

He went on to describe the rest of the night's entertainment and the
next day's; he did not go to bed at all and concluded, "What a way of
life. At Paris I was a sage."[126] On another occasion, rather meanly pleased
to see Suzanne bested at her own games by another intelligent beauty, he
paid her the unintentional compliment of using her as his standard of reference. Ever more frank with each other, he and Suzanne "joke very
freely about our past tenderness, and I make it very clear to her that I am
aware of her inconstancy. She defends herself very strongly and maintains
that she always treated d'Eyverdun cruelly. What to believe? I confess that
my friend's conduct seems to me suspicious and I almost suspect that he
exaggerated matters."[127] As it happens, Deyverdun's extant letters to Suzanne appear to support her account of the matter, but Deyverdun might
have been honestly mistaken about her feelings toward him.[128] In any
case, if the reader is conscious of Gibbon's confusion and discomfort in
these entries, his remarks are not so "painful and unedifying" as Norton
considered them.[129] Gibbon's veneer of cynicism is thin, transparent, and
often broken. That he, Suzanne, and Deyverdun remained friends is evidence of genuine congeniality and good faith among them, whatever their
misunderstandings and changes of heart. As for his sophistication, it is
hard to see how any reader of his journal could be deceived by it, when
there are entries like the following: "I was very content with myself. I
carried on some rather pretty banter with the beauty [i.e., Suzanne],

I discussed *theatre* a great deal with Orosman. It so often happens that I feel that I am dull, that I ought readily to be permitted to say so when I am not. After all, the best company is here."[130]

The intellectual accomplishments of these months included considerable progress on the *Recueil géographique*—eventually it amounted to ninety-two folio pages—and systematic reading on numismatics, beginning with Addison's pleasant work, but concentrating on Spanheim's *De praestantia et usu Numismatum*. Also of interest for Gibbon's developing historical consciousness, as Giarrizzo points out, was his reaction to a work he thought of as a useless digression, fit for a lazy day (he had slept until 11 A.M.):

> I read a new work by Voltaire, *Treatise on Tolerance*. The end can only be praiseworthy—to awaken, to recall in every heart, the sentiments of humanity, and to describe the frightful consequences of superstition. But in the execution this is only a little collection of commonplaces in which the author speaks of everything except the great principles of his subject. I very much like his false and contradictory conclusions on ancient history. Ancient history (says he) is full of prodigies. They could not be true. Thus all is fable and conjecture. [Gibbon gives the reference.] Ancient history is full of prodigies. One can only adopt them. Thus men and nature itself had, in those remote times, nothing in common with us.[131]

Bonnard, editor of the journal, is uneasy about Gibbon's "arbitrary" treatment of Voltaire here and assumes that Gibbon overlooked Voltaire's irony in the second instance.[132] But as Giarrizzo suggests, that very arbitrariness or wilful misunderstanding is "a confirmation of the substantial diversity of their interests, and the spontaneity of their polemic."[133] For Gibbon, Voltaire's airy mining of history for fragments and anecdotes useful to his argument of the moment was an offense against the nature of history and an obstacle to belief in the case thus supported, however good the cause or brilliant the representation. Voltaire here presented the matter of chapter 16 of the *Decline and Fall*. However, far from welcoming "the rhapsodic exposition" of the material of which he would make a "closewrought problematic,"[134] Gibbon found it contemptible. It might be philosophic, but it was not history.

In mid-March, Gibbon received a letter from home giving him permission to continue his travels "on a respectable but not brilliant footing."[135] Typically, Gibbon began to set his house in order. The conscious efforts included attempts to mend his damaged reputation—for example, by calls on all the persons he had been neglecting—and completion of the *Recueil géographique* and the *Bibliothèque raisonnée*. Possibly an unconscious effect was his tiring of the game with the "little woman." Her husband had grown restless, and Gibbon's first satisfaction at always being expected to be her partner had waned, as indeed had his renewed interest in the Société du Printemps, to which she belonged. Suzanne was prettier and more intelligent; one March afternoon, moreover, in a serious conversation for once, she had talked to him "about [his] enemies at Lausanne who profitted from the little woman and the 14th of September [the evening of the great drunken scene] to portray [him] as a man without manners. The injustice is extreme: but when one begins by antagonizing public opinion, one must later stick to the straight and narrow path."[136] Hence, reforms.

Among his preparations for the journey itself was the acquisition of a traveling companion, William Guise. Guise, whom Gibbon had described to his stepmother (in a letter of December 7) as a "prudent worthy young man" and to his father (in a letter of April 14) as "a very sensible good-natured prudent Young man," but to his journal (April 6) as "worthy, loyal, and sensible, but with an impetuosity only the more dangerous because it is ordinarily suppressed," almost celebrated their departure from Lausanne with a duel.[137]

Guise, hopelessly in love with one Nanette de Illens and feeling threatened by a rival, had been so rude that the rival had sent him a challenge. Gibbon, Holroyd, and Pavillard spent a hectic day trying to reconcile the parties, and Gibbon dictated a letter for Guise to send to the rival, which managed to apologize with dignity and so avert the meeting. Gibbon was very pleased with himself, but it was no wonder that he decided that Guise could be dangerously impetuous.

The same journal entry contains a particularly significant sentence: "I have conceived a true friendship for Holroyd. He has a great deal of sense and feelings of honor, with the best of hearts."[138] Holroyd had not occupied a very large place in Gibbon's record of his sojourn in Lausanne, and Gibbon has no place at all in Holroyd's extant letters of the same period. But Gibbon's letters to his friend from Italy, and Holroyd's keeping them, show that strong roots for their life-long friendship had already been established. The anxious episode of the duel, in which each showed his character, feelings, and abilities, must have helped to establish those roots.

Despite the acquisition of such friends as de Saussure and Holroyd, Gibbon's retrospective look at his second sojourn in Switzerland was muted:

> I leave Lausanne with less regret than the first time. I leave there only acquaintances. [De Saussure was gone, and Holroyd was soon to go.] The other time I mourned the loss of a mistress and a friend. Besides, I saw Lausanne with the still fresh eyes of a young man who owed to it the reasonable part of his existence and who judged without objects of comparison. Today I see in it an ill-built city in the midst of a delicious country which enjoys peace and repose, and takes them for liberty. A numerous and well-brought-up people who love society

and who admit foreigners into their coteries with pleasure, which would be considerably more agreeable if conversation had not given way to play. The women are pretty, and in spite of their great liberty, they are very virtuous. . . . Affectation is the original sin of the Lausannois. Affectation of expense, affectation of nobility, affectation of intelligence, the first two are very common while the third is very rare.[139]

Gibbon, who had always doubted his own capacity to please, had managed some social success in the three differing milieus he frequented in Lausanne; that of the wild young men, hard-drinking and noisy; that of the giddy "printemps"; and that of the more sedate Chateau. Perhaps it was his own changes of role that made him see affectation as rife in Lausanne. Yet affectation is too harsh a word for Gibbon's whist-playing, flirting, and adaptations of conversation and drinking habits to fit his company. In the militia he had tried only one role; disliking it, he had settled for isolation. In Paris he had been comparatively "un sage," because that city had tolerated him in the combined role of gentleman and scholar, if not as both in the same salons, and had offered him no serious complications—intellectual, emotional, or even financial—in his brief sojourn. In a way, Lausanne, which had seen Gibbon through his intellectual adolescence, now helped him through a social awkward age. He had been intemperate, coy, ungenerous, vain, and salacious, at various times. Nevertheless, he judged himself severely, was open to evidence against his rash judgments of others, and was capable of self-discipline—impressively so with respect to study, high play, and drinking. It is pleasant, too, to see that he retained his warm friendships for Pavillard and Deyverdun—the latter friendship was expressed in attentions to Deyverdun's aunt, as well as in letters—and formed new ones of permanent significance. The major writing of the period, the *Recueil géographique*, did not become the humbly useful work he had hoped to produce, but it abundantly prepared him to be at home in his spiritual country, ancient Italy. And the "Lettre sur le gouvernement de Berne" is notable evidence not only of Gibbon's developing skill as a writer but also of the independence and acumen of his political observations.

On Wednesday, April 28, 1764, Gibbon, Guise, and four companions set out from Lausanne. Already operating as a wise traveler as he conceived that role,[140] Gibbon described the towns en route to Geneva in his journal, although of course he had seen them often before; and in Geneva itself he visited and described the library, noting with satisfaction its "fortunate newness that spares them all the scholastic rubbish with which the ancient libraries are inundated."[141] On April 20, the travelers left Geneva, bound for Italy.

CHAPTER 11

The Pilgrimage
of Italy

The PILGRIMAGE of Italy, which I now accomplished, had long been the object of my curious devotion," says the self-styled "Classic pilgrim" in his *Memoirs* (M 302). He kept a journal of this most momentous journey, but in some ways the record is disappointing. Lovingly edited by G. A. Bonnard, it was published in 1961, but it has not in itself added to Gibbon's reputation either as a writer or as an observer. The previous owner of my copy of Bonnard's edition stigmatized this journal as "unfortunately, terribly dull." This is hardly fair, but though the journal is not devoid of value or entertainment, it does omit several significant episodes of this eventful period. Gibbon's views of the Genoese republic, for example, are missing, with all their potential ethical and political interest, because he was interrupted by a visitor when he was about to write the entry. Almost the whole month of September, which might have told the story of an intrigue with one Mme. Gianni and which was marked by an encounter in which Gibbon nearly had to fight a duel, is left blank in the journal. Most regrettably and notoriously, there is no record of October 15, 1764, when, at Rome, "as [he] sat musing amidst the ruins of the Capitol while the barefooted fryars were singing Vespers in the temple of Jupiter...the idea of writing the decline and fall of the City first started to [his] mind" (136 n.7).

Indeed, the journal ends with his arrival at Rome on October 2, 1764, except for notes on various buildings, antiquities, and *objets d'art* seen there in December. Gibbon seems to have suffered the experience of many another journal keeper: he had least time to write when he might have had most to say. Of course, his travels after leaving Rome, which included Naples (where Gibbon's observations, informed by his reading of Giannone, would surely have been of interest), Venice, Turin, Lyons, and, once again, Paris (where he paid a visit to Suzanne Curchod and her wealthy husband, Jacques Necker), we know only from letters and his recollections in the *Memoirs*.

Nevertheless, the fourteen months between his departure from Lausanne and his return to England mark not only the era in which he found his life's work but also a period significant in his maturation as a person. Traveling with Guise and later with Holroyd as well, he tasted the freedom of his years and class, despite numerous reminders from his father—evident in the letters—that his hold on that freedom was precarious. Important as this foretaste of independence was, however, the experience of Italy itself was more important. Throughout Italy, but especially in Rome, the images of the past that had been so vivid to him— thanks to his strong visual and spatial imagination—even in the narrow confines of books, met, in all their power of physical presence, the looted and mutilated remains of that past. The result of the shock of confrontation is well known. But the result might not have been the *Decline and Fall,* had not Gibbon's travels in Italy allowed him to observe and judge the works both of the past and of the present, and, further, to see those of the past as exuding the melancholy grandeur of a lost romance, whereas those of the present were as measurable, explicable, and commonplace as every day. In the Cabinet du Roi at Paris, Gibbon had seen the series of Roman medals demonstrate the inexorable decline of the arts with the empire; in the same cabinet as these ancient medals, a series of modern medals representing the popes had invited him to inquire only whether they were actual likenesses.[1]

Even those staples of Romantic reveries, the Alps, did not escape the taint of actuality: "We have left perhaps the most beautiful countryside that exists under heaven, the delicious environs of Lake Leman, for the desert and craggy mountains of Savoy."[2] He took an expert interest in the local militia and an interest exactly comparable to that of his youthful Swiss tour in the principal manufactures, the architecture and town plan, the curiosities, and the government of the places that he and Guise passed through. Their means and difficulties of travel are also enumerated. Crossing the Alps, Guise tried a mule; Gibbon preferred a chair. Not yet corpulent, Gibbon required only one more bearer than the minimum (three), and two fewer than Boswell.[3] All this is minutely detailed in a matter-of-fact manner.

The first object to capture Gibbon's imagination was the triumphal arch of Suze—appropriately, a relic of the Empire:

I am astonished that a small Alpine canton, always poor and still half barbarous, could have conceived the idea of a monument in so grand a manner, for the execution of which a very considerable expense and some skilled workmen from Greece or Rome were necessary. Here is a conjecture. Augustus had a monument erected with an elaborate inscription, in which he recalled all the conquered peoples of the Alps. The cities of the Alpes Cottiae did not appear there. They were regarded less as conquered enemies than as voluntary subjects. These peoples must have felt the delicacy of this procedure. Love and gratitude wished, perhaps, to compensate Augustus for a glory that he had refused from the hands of victory. [4]

Gibbon made no such imaginative inquiry into the motives and feelings of present-day persons, his chair bearers, say, or even the "poor Slaves," as he called them, who were required to repair the road without pay. His pity for them was unaccompanied by curiosity. [5] Indeed, he rarely seems to think of himself as an actor in a present-day drama—differing markedly in this, as in other respects, from Boswell. Looking back on the journey after arriving in Turin, Gibbon observed, "Reading and conversation amused us, but it is difficult to take a road less agreeable than that of the mountains of Savoy." [6]

At Turin, Gibbon and Guise settled into the usual routine of Grand Tourists: presentation to the king of Sardinia, Carlo Emanuele III, and to socially eminent local citizens, exchanges of visits with the other Englishmen in the city, Italian lessons, and sightseeing, though of course the last was much more comprehensive and less concentrated than that of today's tourists. Eighteenth-century tourists, even in monument-filled Italy, visited not only great works of art, ancient buildings, and historic sites but also fine modern streets and buildings and such exercises as military drills. Gibbon and Guise, for example, took time to measure the size of a well-proportioned arcaded street they admired, "the famous rue de Po." [7] Gibbon was pleased to stand on a stone that, according to his guide, marked the very spot on which Vittorio Amedeo II stood with Prince Eugene to plan their successful effort to deliver Turin from the French siege: "I saw with pleasure the fertile plains of Piedmont beneath my feet, watered by the Po and the Doire, and bordered by mountains still covered with snow, the city of Turin in the center and the neighboring fields where I could follow the movements of the two armies and the theatre of combat." [8] Gibbon even accompanied Guise to the opera, although, because he did not understand the language, did not enjoy music, and could not escape until 11:30 P.M., he was "thoroughly bored." [9] Guise, who did not share Gibbon's strong background in French, may have been equally bored by their Italian lessons, which were scheduled from 7 to 9 A.M. daily.

Soon after reaching Turin, Gibbon made time for a dutiful letter home, a letter designed to please a father whose every letter, if we may judge from Gibbon's replies, contained complaints about money. Gibbon praised the pleasure and safety of the journey, tried to include material especially interesting to "the Major," and promised to stay strictly within the £700 his father had said he might have for the Italian journey. (Gibbon's calculations excluded the £200 for which he had had to draw at Lausanne to pay for his stay there and his journey as far as Turin; unless a letter has been lost, Gibbon did better than his word, confining his Italian expenses to £600.) He concluded this section of the letter, "Thus Dear Sir, you will in the two years and a half I may be abroad, have sacrificed about a thousand pounds extraordinary to the most agreable part of my life; a sacrifice I shall endeavour to repay by the behavior of my whole future life."[10] Gibbon was not quite twenty-seven when he wrote this letter; there is surely an unintended pathos in this resignation to having outlived his happiest years so early. Fortunately, of course, he was mistaken; there was much happiness yet to come.

He wrote to his father on the day before his and Guise's presentation at court. They were not looking forward to it with unmixed pleasure, because the court, "from one of the most polite in Europe is become bigotted, gloomy and covetous."[11] They found that they were not received into the king's chamber, a privilege reserved to "Peers and their sons" and that the king himself was only "a little old man...a bourgeois of a rather mean appearance." Gibbon was also disappointed that the king asked him only commonplace questions, though he was surely a "man of intelligence and a good politican."[12] It would be interesting to compare Gibbon's first impression of the other king he had met, George III, but unfortunately it is unrecorded.

The king did arouse Gibbon's interest in one respect: "Unfortunately for [the king], his father died in his prisons." Gibbon saw the king as suffering remorse, melancholy, and profound jealousy of his own son, who was thirty-eight, with many abilities, yet only "the first slave of the court." From the contemplation of this unnerving series of father-son conflicts, Gibbon moved to an unusual outburst of righteous indignation over social injustice:

> A court for me is simultaneously an object of curiosity and disgust. The servility of the courtiers revolts me, and I see with horror the magnificence of palaces cemented with the blood of the people. In a small, poor realm like this, it is necessary to crush the people to be on a par with other crowned heads and to sustain the appearance of grandeur. ...In each gilded panel I think I see a village of Savoyards ready to perish of hunger, cold, and misery.[13]

Gibbon's sentiments were always and genuinely humanitarian, though not democractic, but there is an operatic note here suggestive of stronger or less controlled emotion than his usual temperate and practical pity. Perhaps it is not too far-fetched to attribute this unusual fervor to an unconscious wish to distance himself from the troubled, patricidal king.

When Gibbon visited buildings and works of art, his response was his own, but not revelatory of aesthetic insight or eccentricity of taste. He was discontented to see brick where there might have been marble; he disliked twisted columns; he judged pictures by their literary content for the most part, with some attention to color. The most frequent adjective in his critical vocabulary is *propre* (suitable, appropriate, decorous, correct). Statues were praised for their workmanship or blamed for the choice of subjects too intricate for the medium, though Gibbon could praise "a Bacchus who is playing with a tiger. These two figures are well contrasted."[14] Of course, anachronisms were objectionable—even in the biography of gods: "I noticed with surprise that one of the Nymphs is offering a bunch of grapes to the God [Bacchus again], who has just been born and who could not yet have taught mankind to cultivate the vine."[15]

Not all antiquities aroused his interest: seeing the famous "Mensa Isaica," with its hieroglyphics, Gibbon admitted that Egypt, "curious as it is, is too far away, too obscure, and too enigmatic to interest me greatly"[16]—a surprising reaction in a man whose childhood toys had been the dynasties of Assyria and Asia. Much more characteristic, however, was his lengthy consideration of the manuscripts of the sixteenth-century antiquarian Piero Ligorio, who had spent his whole life collecting what he could of medals, inscriptions, and monuments. Whatever his faults of knowledge, said Gibbon, his industry was admirable. Gibbon was grateful for Ligorio's preservation of a record of many things that had since perished. Ligorio had been criticized for his inaccuracy and for supplying by guesswork what he did not know. But Gibbon noted "signs of candor" that made him doubt the justice of this censure: "I see a man who often doubts whether he has read well, who leaves gross faults in the monuments, noting only by a *sic* that he has observed them, and who leaves places blank that he could very easily have filled. I add, moreover, that he was only a compiler and had no system whose interests he needed to serve."[17] Gibbon's standards of judgment and independence of mind are clear in such a passage.

Gibbon's consistency on scholarly questions was perhaps not matched by his reactions to economic and social facts of the modern world. For example, all his objections to courts seem forgotten, when he actually visited that of Turin, in his admiration of its architectural magnificence: "This magnificence moderated by exact economy, but accompanied by an air of dignity, may be seen everywhere in this court."[18] This praise may, however, represent not inconsistency, but a genuine change of heart, responsive to the supposed or real economical methods of the court, for it was the favorable view that he remembered and reported in his memoirs. That Gibbon's pity for the peasants never became empathy is clear again in his reaction to the king's Flemish paintings: "This exact imitation of what is lowest and most disgusting in the manners of a gross populace interests my mind as little as their dry colors and black shadows displease my sight"[19]—the mixed construction is Gibbon's.

Gibbon's visit to Turin lasted some two-and-a-half weeks. Toward the end of that period his impatience with its evening amusements—the opera and *conversationi*—became marked. The *conversationi*, which provided rooms of beautifully dressed ladies not dancing but playing cards, might have been expected to please him, but although his principal hostess, the Contessa di S. Gillio, "professed a great predilection for...young Englishmen,"[20] apparently neither Gibbon nor Guise was one of her pets—indeed, she preferred the Tarot cards to either of them. To proceed from the tedium of the opera to the tedium of such an assembly was too much for Gibbon: "If it is pleasant to watch a game that one has no knowledge of, to hear a Piedmontese jargon that one does not understand at all, and to find oneself in the midst of a haughty and cringing nobility who will not address one word to you, we were very well entertained in this assembly."[21] He had time, either in lieu of such entertainments following supper on their last evening in Turin, or (probably) on the road, to write "two words"—closer to four pages—on the present state and sovereign of Turin, including an elaborate enumeration of Sardinia's military establishment. He took the long view: "When one sees the slow and successive accretions of the house of Savoy during eight hundred years, it must be admitted that its greatness is the work of prudence rather than fortune."[22]

Eye trouble prevented Gibbon from profiting fully from the journey to Milan, which required a day and a half and about £13.5 in post charges. The Milan cathedral had the distinction of being one of the few Gothic buildings given any praise by Gibbon: "It is one of the great efforts of Gothic architecture as it is one of the last." He disliked, however, the figures in high niches "where a man could never survive"; this violation of nature "wounded" the imagination. The exterior also suffered from that "aged air common to Gothic buildings...an idea of ruin and weakness, as the unity of the ancient proportions immediately inspires that of power and solidity."[23] He liked the marble, the silver statues, and the cloth of gold of the interior. He was also struck by the beauty of the colors of the great windows. He admired the great height of the dome, into which the travelers climbed (Gibbon's friends of later years would have found that hard to believe) and from which they went "by a very fine exterior stairway" to a platform on one of the towers, which gave them a spectacular view of Milan, and which gives us an unusual perspective on Edward Gibbon.[24]

The cathedral, capable of holding 20,000 people, clearly impressed Gibbon. As at Turin, however, he moved on to his characteristic interests of military discipline and libraries. Because Gibbon and Guise had only five days to spend in Milan, they visited tourist attractions there at a much faster rate than in Turin; on the very day on which they had climbed to the top of the Duomo, they went out again after dinner, to see the citadel. The next day, they visited the Ambrosian Library, the hospital, four more churches, and "the only remnant of Antiquity that still exists at Milan...a colonnade of sixteen great Columns."[25] Perhaps his most interesting aesthetic reaction was his obviously sincere pleasure in Breughel's paintings of the four elements: "I prefer Earth to all the others....It has been thought that Breughel wished to represent the golden age as well as the elements. An ox (it is a charming figure) who grazes without fear near a lion and a tiger who caress each other, is not an ox of this age of iron."[26]

Two of their days at Milan were actually spent in the Borromean islands nearby. Unfortunately, it rained. Gibbon used some of his enforced idleness to write to John Holroyd. This, his first known letter to his best friend, presents a side of his personality not so clearly visible even in his journals or letters to other friends.[27] It is light-hearted, entirely unstudied, and not only frank but even ribald. The beginning sets the tone: "Most certainly I am a puppy for not having wrote to you sooner; it is equally certain that you are an ass if you expected it." To "Leger" (his nickname for Holroyd), Gibbon could grumble about the old, dull court and the few women at the public assemblies—"a poor Englishman who can neither talk Piedmontois, nor play at Taro, stands by himself without one of their haughty nobility doing him the honor of speaking to him." He could also laugh at himself, as in the following vignette:

> The most sociable women I have met with are the King's daughters. I chatted for about a quarter of an hour with them, talked about Lausanne, & grew so very free and easy, that I drew my snuf-box, rapped it, took snuff, twice (a Crime never known before in the presence chamber,) & continued my discourse in my usual attitude of my body bent forwards, and my fore-finger stretched out.[28]

There is also, of course, a touch of boasting in this humorous confession.

Matters military were a bond, or at least a topic of common interest. Gibbon chose to conclude his letter, however, with a series of queries about Lausanne that abundantly illustrate the particular ease of his intimacy with Holroyd:

> How does the Bride look after her great revolution? As you have a liberty of saying what you please, pray ask her how often & &c the first night....We have drank the Dutchess's health not forgetting the little woman, on the top of Mont Cenis, in the middle of the Lago Maggiore &c &c. I expect some account of the said little woman, whether she talks bawdy as much as usual, and who is my successor. I think Montagny had begun to supplant me before I went. Salute all our friends... and don't forget to kick Constant & D'Hermanches before you come.

The letter ended, without a signature, "I expect your answer at Florence and your person at Rome, which the Lord of his infinite mercy grant. Amen."[29] That is probably Gibbon's only recorded prayer, and, even in jest, it is appropriate that it be for Holroyd.

The rain, which gave Gibbon the opportunity to write so long and cheerful a letter to Holroyd, did not spoil their excursion. Besides, even in bad weather, it offered unusual pleasures. Gibbon and Guise had been received as guests by the count's servants at the palace, so they had the singular sensation of being "at home, in a great palace, surrounded by a very extensive lake and thus separated from the rest of humanity." The next morning, the Crusoes were somewhat daunted to find that their island was hardly half a mile in circumference and had therefore "too much the air of a beautiful prison." Nevertheless, Gibbon admired the ingenuity, effort, and expense that had transformed a barren rock into a miniature paradise, particularly on the eastern side: "You walk in a beautiful avenue of orange trees, of a size and height that astonished me, and you leave it only to enter a charming little wood of laurels, where a thousand fountains appear to burst forth under your feet." On the west, however, the "paltry huts of fishermen" sorted ill with "a fairy palace. If it was necessary to leave [the huts], with a little expense the counts could have given them a very agreeable simplicity."[30] There is perhaps some humanitarian feeling in this observation, but there is as much aesthetic. In any event, satisfied with their interesting excursion despite the weather, Gibbon and Guise then returned to Milan.

When Gibbon thought of Milan after they had left it, he found it vast rather than beautiful and objected to its narrow, winding streets, especially at night, when they were not illuminated at all. Having had no letters of recommendation, he could say nothing about the customs or the people of Milan; he had seen only "things."[31]

Gibbon and Guise had intended to go straight on to Venice for the carnival, at which the Duke of York was expected, but their inadequate knowledge of the language and their want of cash made a change of plans desirable. They headed instead toward Genoa and planned to cross from there to Leghorn and spend the summer in Tuscany; "I hope to leave there master—or very nearly so—of the language," said Gibbon.[32] A visit en route to the Carthusian monastery of Pavia—which was decorated in marble, mosaic, jasper, agate, amethyst, and lapis lazuli; and where they also saw "the cell of one of the fathers"—caused Gibbon to reflect, "Most religious houses are distinguished by their extreme cleanliness, by the solidity of their works and by the richness of ornaments." A community "can but employ its revenues to satisfy the sole vanity that can remain to them."[33]

The travelers were delayed by high waters at the Po and thus took the opportunity to see Pavia. They also had to cross the Apennines: "The ascent . . . seems nothing when one has passed the Alps. The Apennines are rather a chain of rocks, than mountains."[34] They reached Genoa shortly after 8 A.M.—the inn at their last stop had been so bad as to prompt an early departure—on May 22. They had nearly three weeks in Genoa and the best of introductions: Gibbon's old friend, David Mallet's daughter Dorothea Celesia, was in Genoa with her husband, who was Genoese.

Celesia and Gibbon had a long discussion about current affairs, including the Corsican revolt and General Paoli. According to Celesia, Paoli, "this famous chief whose manners are still a little fierce, equals in natural talents the great men of antiquity." The Genoese view of the conflict, however, may surprise readers of Boswell's *Corsica*: "They would with pleasure leave the Corsicans to themselves, if they were not afraid of the King of Sardinia."[35]

Gibbon's energy as a sightseer began to flag somewhat in Genoa. Thursday, May 24, was a lost day (it was very hot), but visits to a church and to the Jesuit college and its library, followed by whist and company of "very good *ton*," made up for that on the following day. Another day was spent at the Celesias' country house, where Gibbon saw "a beautiful natural phenomenon, a mountain storm." The echoing thunder, the waters that poured down in a vast torrent into the road they had just passed, followed an hour later by an "open sky, the waters...rolled away, and...a charming freshness" gave him an almost romantic delight.[36] He also observed, with surprise, that the barefoot peasants had an air of health and contentment.

Gibbon's responses to art continued to produce occasional moments of individuality and interest. A predictably literary account of a painting of Perseus presenting Medusa's head to Cepheus is followed in the journal by an unexpected comment on what Poussin would have done with the subject. He dutifully admired a famous Veronese, but observed that he did not really like Veronese's work, owing to "an aridity in his manner and a bluish tint in his colors" and, in this case, a lack of unity of action in the composition of the painting.[37] He did like Rubens, especially an allegorical painting in the Palazzo Brignoletti representing Love threatened by War. Gibbon had been reading André Félibien's *Vies des peintres* and speculated that the painting alluded to Henri IV.[38]

He had also read a history of the revolutions of Genoa, in some "happy moments of repose, of which one does not know the value until one has lived in the whirlwind."[39] Disappointed that a political history gave such an imprecise notion of the constitution, laws, and customs of Genoa, Gibbon immediately improved the occasion of their presentation to the doge, "His Serenity": "This Serenity receives 5,000 Livres a year and spends at least 25,000, to have the pleasure of living in a very bad house, which he cannot leave without a permit from the Senate, of being dressed in red from head to foot, and of having twelve 60-year-old pages dressed in the Spanish manner."[40] As usual, Gibbon's thumbnail sketches of persons he had met or read about enliven the journal. Another Genoese sketch, that of the Abbé Imperiali, is as tart as this one of the doge.[41]

Although the travelers' departure from Genoa was delayed six days by contrary winds (indeed, they gave up and went by land), Gibbon profited by only one day of that delay. He wasted the others in "waiting, impatience, boredom and bad humor," reading a few of Horace's epistles, attempting some translations of his own *Recueils,* but not even writing the retrospective summary of Genoa (comparable to the one about Sardinia he had written in Turin) for which he left blank space in his journal.[42] He did spend one morning working further on the values of ancient money, the subject of his unfinished 1759 study.[43]

At 4 A.M. on June 12, Gibbon and Guise set out by land toward Plaisance. Bad roads and annoying officials delayed them; at 9 P.M. they stopped at Castel San Giovanni, eleven-and-one-half posts from Genoa and two from Plaisance. Gibbon had apparently been thinking of the importance of Piacenza and Cremona in his classical geography and was disappointed by the small population and economic decadence of Plaisance. Two equestrian statues were worth seeing, but "why must princes always be portrayed on horseback?" he complained. In this instance, the younger prince, "whose exploits, more peaceful and more useful, amounted to the building of theatres and the founding of libraries, could have appeared dressed as a citizen, and accompanied by those emblems of peace and the arts that appeared . . . on the bas-reliefs of the pedestal."[44] Gibbon's own dislike of riding perhaps influenced this call for a sedentary sculptured hero.

The travelers' next major destination was Florence, which they reached on June 19. Realizing that Bologna required an extended stay, they passed it by for the time being, but made the most of their opportunities en route in Parma, Reggio, and Modena. In his account of these places, Gibbon wrote primarily as a connoisseur, though his interest in antiquities or military establishments or court gossip is occasionally apparent. There were few encounters with either the natives or other visitors to vary his account. Gibbon and Guise met and for a time traveled with Reyman and Mersens, whom they had known in Lausanne; "We saw them again without pleasure and without pain."[45] But Gibbon's visits to these small states were too brief, and his acquaintances too few, to permit him to comment on their customs and governments. Scenery attracted little of his attention. He mentions that they chose to travel by night because the heat had become a problem. His tastes in scenery are, however, revealed only in his enthusiasm for the countryside, which "is but one continuous garden from Plaisance on, and as the cities and even the Capitals meet, it is less a journey than a most agreeable promenade," and in his response to his third crossing of the Apennines: "I know nothing sadder than their appearance: . . . you do not even see those pastures covered with flocks that enliven a little the spectacle of most mountains."[46] In spite of his momentary enthusiasm for the mountain storm, Gibbon's desire was for a peopled and fruitful nature.

As we have seen, art occasionally evoked a revealing personal response in Gibbon. He seems to have been genuinely moved, for example, by Correggio's *Madonna del S. Girolamo* at Parma. He remarked its anachronisms and objected to its unnecessary angels, but wrote: "I had never before known the power of painting. I would admire the art of the imitation without being touched by its truth. [But] here the character of peace and tenderness that breathes on the canvas communicates itself to the soul of the Spectator. Forced at last to tear himself away, he experiences the sad feeling of losing what he loves."[47] Subtract what we will for Gibbon's desire to play the role of art lover, both the length and the tone of this entry differ significantly from those for works he admired less sincerely. Equally sincere, if less extravagant, were his boredom with cabinets of natural curiosities, his objections to ceiling paintings, and his surprise at Guido Reni's achievement in painting St. Francis of Assisi. Guido, he says, "has to transform a madman canonized by superstition into a great man, without absolutely losing the resemblance. . . . Under his hands stupidity appears no more than humility and self-denial."[48] Gibbon's distaste for St. Francis is not surprising, but perhaps his grudging acknowledgment that stupidity and self-denial need not be synonymous, is.

Despite Gibbon's interest in the antiquities he saw, we do not have, in this part of his Italian tour, any sense of his viewing the present from the perspective of the Republic or even the Empire. But there are several reminders of his historical bent and of his particular mastery of the chronology and geography of Roman Italy. For example, discussing the monuments of Veleia, he noted that "most of these monuments pertain to the age of Claudius and even to the end of the reign of that prince. The inscription *Divo Augusto* also fits there. Until the consecration of Claudius himself there was only one *Divus Augustus,* whom one could designate absolutely."[49] More strikingly, he commented:

These years of the Tribune-ship [he had just noted an instance on a coin of Tiberius's] are the best guide we have for the chronology of the emperors; but it is a guide that is very difficult to follow, without the aid of a good table that is yet to be made, since the power of the Tribunate very often preceded the beginning of the reign. I would like to know, moreover, if they took possession of it on the anniversary of their accession, or if the Nones of December were always fixed for this ceremony, in the case of the emperors as well as for ordinary tribunes. . . . There is another difficulty for Tiberius; he is the only one whose term as tribune was interrupted.[50]

His lifelong "attention to the order of time" and his minute knowledge of Roman history are apparent here.

Following Addison's guide in his *Dialogues upon the Usefulness of Ancient Medals* (1721), which he had read, as we have seen, in preparing for his journey, Gibbon wished to examine the likenesses on the coins for evidence of the characters of their subjects: "I thought to read in the features of Agrippa this character of frankness, greatness, and simplicity . . . : but these sorts of observations . . . seem to me very hollow. Is it so common that the soul is legible in the features?"[51] When it is a question of Raphael's portrait of Pope Julian II, however, "The soul of this proud and ambitious pope is painted on the canvas. I see there all the sudden violence of the protector of Michelangelo, and the inflexible greatness of that old man who dared to chase the victorious French out of Italy. I contradict my maxim, but I believe I see an exception."[52]

Sometimes his responses may have been unconsciously affected by his previous problems with his father. On one such occasion, when his subject was gossip rather than art, there seemed to be such a touch of personal feeling in his perception of the experience of others. Was Gibbon altogether objective in finding the Duke of Modena, a father who constrained the obedience of an adult son, "hard and tyrannical," or in denying the sincerity of the son's acquiescence while that prince "did not enjoy the use of his own wealth"?[53] In June, however, Gibbon's relations with his own father were apparently tranquil. Though the £700 allowed for his journey was not enough for Venice in carnival time, the loss was a small one. When he reached Florence, he wrote to Mrs. Gibbon cheerfully:

> Every step I take in Italy, I am more and more sensible of the obligation I have to my father in allowing me to undertake the tour. Indeed, Dear Madam this tour is one of the very few things that exceed the most sanguine and flattering hopes. I do not pretend . . . there are no disagreable things in it. . . . But how amply is a traveller repaid for these little mortifications, by the pleasure and knowledge he finds in almost every place. The actual beauties and always the very great singularity of the Country, the different pieces of antiquity . . . and the variety of masterpieces of sculpture and painting have already made me pass some of the most entertaining days I have yet known and I have before me the pleasing reflexion that what I have yet seen is far inferior to what I shall find in this place as well as Rome and Naples.[54]

Florence, where he planned to spend two months and actually spent three, might have been expected to inspire him as a Renaissance historian, as Rome inspired him to write about the Empire. But though Florence caused him to react and comment *en historien*, it was the Roman antiquities in its galleries and libraries, not the memorials of more recent events in art or politics, that sparked his interest. For the first ten days, however, Gibbon and Guise were merely tourists, finding rooms (after some difficulties), hiring an Italian master, calling on the British consul, Sir Horace Mann, frequenting or at least sampling the fashionable promenades and amusements, and viewing the grand fete of St. John, protector of Florence. A principal feature of the feast was a horse race, la Course des Chevaux "Barbes" (though called barbarians, horses from any country were eligible, as Gibbon pointed out, and one of the favorites in the race was

English).[55] The horses ran without jockeys, and the race was a very old custom: "One sees that the Florentines cherish this custom as the sole vestige of their ancient freedom." Yet even while Gibbon was in Florence, his mind seemed to turn instinctively to the ancient past: "Since the games of the ancients this is perhaps the only pleasure spectacle for a whole State united to amuse itself by the care and under the eyes of its magistrates."[56]

After his previous instruction both in London and in Italy, Gibbon began at last to try to use Italian in speaking as well as reading; he had "the boldness to begin to speak a certain jargon that I would like to have people take for Italian. I was heard with kindness, . . . especially [by] a certain Madame Antinori who is very amiable."[57] Unfortunately, we hear no more of progress with either the language or the lady. There was an active and fairly congenial English colony at Florence, so Gibbon's need to use Italian, rather than English or French, was limited.

Even before he began his study of the treasures of Florence, Gibbon's historical sense led him to turn back to Rome. He procured Muratori's dissertation on the bronze "table," of the time of Trajan, which was found near Villeia. Gibbon had seen the tablet at Parma but had not been allowed to examine it closely or transcribe it. He now made up for that disappointment by reading and rereading Muratori's work. Of it, with unwitting prophecy, Gibbon said, "M. Muratori is not a mere erudite. He proves very well . . . that one can draw from this inscription . . . very useful lights on the history, geography, and economy of that age. I am of his opinion, but after mature reflection, I believe that he has not exhausted it."[58] In this instance, however, the fruit of his own further reflections on Muratori's materials was not a philosophic history, but a calculation of "the rents to which so great a number of the citizens of Villeia were subjected and the bases on which they were assigned. It is a dry and ungrateful work, but when one constructs an Edifice it is necessary to dig its foundations. One must play the role of mason as well as that of Architect."[59]

Finally, on July 4, Gibbon turned to the glories of present-day Florence—in a way—with his first visit to the Uffizi Gallery. He had prepared for his visit by reading a volume of A. F. Gori's *Florentine Museum,* an account of the antiquities in the gallery. Gori's work, already ten volumes long, was incomplete though "wise and curious." "To how many ideas have [his observations] given birth!"[60] Thereafter, the routine of Gibbon's days included long visits to the gallery, as well as an Italian lesson from 5 to 6 P.M., language study and journal-keeping, frequent dinners with "the Nation," and a promenade in the evening. Gibbon and Guise did not like the fashionable custom of "promenading" in carriages to the Porto S. Gallo, where the Florentine nobility came "to take the air or rather the dust." Instead, their chosen walk was the Cascine Gardens, "a lovely meadow surrounded with a wood."[61] This orderly and balanced regime gave Gibbon time to write some of the fullest and most interesting entries in the Italian journal; although much time was spent dutifully recording judgments inspired by his guidebooks, he also left there many fascinating instances of the working of his mind and his feelings.

In addition to visiting the Uffizi, the major project of July was the reading of the "Introduction" to P. H. Mallet's *Histoire du Dannemarck,* which dealt with the ancient religion of the Danes and included a translation of the Edda, "the sacred book of the ancient Celts. At present we have half a dozen of these bibles (counting our own)."[62] Formulas that Gibbon employs more than once in this journal are "A protestant might say, . . ." "As a protestant I should say, . . ." and the like. The implied detachment of such formulas is certainly visible in this unawed conjunction of Scripture and scriptures. In his consideration both of Mallet and of the gallery, some of Gibbon's most interesting remarks, predictably enough, dealt with history. The gallery also inspired valuable expressions of his aesthetic views, as again might be expected, and several unexpected personal revelations, for example, his appreciation of his stepmother and his desire to travel to Greece.

The gallery reports certainly convince us of Gibbon's capacity to respond to the beauty of the female form, at least of that which had "forgot [it] self to stone." The Venus de' Medici aroused him not only aesthetically but—at least figuratively—sensually:

> From my cradle I have always heard the Venus de Medici talked of; books, conversations, engravings, copies had put it [or *her*] before my eyes a thousand times and yet I had no idea of it. To know it one must see it. I have seen it, but the most faithful, the most vivid imagination, will it preserve the image that the senses gave me[?] It is the most voluptuous experience that my eye has ever experienced.[63]

Even if we take him literally, as I think we may, this response does not, of course, prove that his experience of voluptuousness has never been fleshly, but it may suggest either limited or imperfectly satisfying sexual experience. Possibly the most striking hint of sexual naïveté is his reaction to a statue ordinarily kept veiled lest it offend female visitors to the gallery, a priapus about three-and-a-half-feet high. Of "this enormous Machine . . . the veins are very well expressed, but nothing is understood about a certain bonnet that appears to cover its head." According to Bonnard's note, Charles de Brosses had no such difficulty comprehending the bonnet; according to de Brosses, the "handsome machine . . . is capped with the other machine, its usual companion."[64] Because de Brosses's assumption was possible, Gibbon's failure to think of it perhaps indicates that his sexual experience was limited or furtive. It also suggests that he did not inquire about the mysterious object at the gallery and that his objective statement, "nothing is understood," should read, "I do not understand."

This is, then, one more piece of evidence to suggest that Gibbon's sex life, if not entirely "confined to his footnotes" and not homosexual, had been limited to visits to brothels in his university and militia days.

But it was family financial problems that gave him occasion, now in letters from Italy, as earlier in letters from Lausanne, to assure his father that he never expected to marry.[65] He had almost accepted that, on his income, his prior marriage to scholarship was incompatible with marriage to a woman. Furthmore, l'affaire Suzanne had at least temporarily disillusioned him about romantic love. But his decision was also based, and this he told his father, on his "constitution." By this he presumably meant his fundamental qualities not only of body but also of mind and feelings. At the time he was only twenty-seven; his body, though small, was healthy, not yet obese and not yet visibly troubled with the hydrocele he later traced back to his militia days. Thus his viewing himself as "constitutionally" unmarriageable is surely an occasion for some compassion.

Despite the lack of self-esteem he felt in this respect, he thought himself generally an unusually fortunate person. A pleasant evidence of this attitude in his discussion of two sepulchral inscriptions relative to stepmothers: "I do not know which is the more injurious to stepmothers. . . . The hatred of stepmothers for their stepsons seems to me yet more marked [among the Romans] than in other nations. To the general motives I believe one should add the uncertain state of Roman wives and the unlimited power that the fathers had over their wealth." To this recognition, unexpected in a stepson, of the perils of the stepmother's lot, Gibbon added the comment, "How happy is our age, but I am still more so."[66] With the silent exception, perhaps, of a more financially and emotionally reliable father, Gibbon appeared to wish for no change in his life: even a trip to Greece was only something he "could like well enough (j'aimerois assez), though "A Greek journey cannot but spur the curiosity."[67]

These personal observations have the reliability of a private diary; Gibbon intended this journal for his own eyes only.[68] Seduced as usual, however, by the life of the mind, he strayed into miniature essays on aesthetic and historical subjects even in these private pages.

The aesthetic comments were largely, but not entirely, concerned with the visual arts. Many, of course, were inspired by the Uffizi treasures. Some are of interest only because they were his opinions, for example, speaking of a painting of a painter painting: "Generally I do not like these illusions within illusions, including the play in *Hamlet*. The attempt is too dangerous and the necessary resemblance between one illusion and the other serves only to dispell the spectator's intoxication," or a Reynolds-like comment on the servility of the species of imitation required for portraits, "imitation not of general nature, which is always the same, but of those particular natures that soon disappear, leaving us no means of comparing the original and the copy."[69] Other remarks are, however, interesting in themselves.

Gibbon speculated, for example, about why the earliest post-Renaissance masters in the fine arts had been surpassed by later masters, whereas no one had surpassed the early great poets:

> In these first painters I perceived minute and laborious work and a rigorous subjection to all the rules they knew, without genius and without any of that happy and original boldness which is the merit of the first poets, and which makes amends for all the flights of an unregulated imagination that wishes to command as a master language, history, and nature. I find the reason for this difference in the different origins of the two arts, sisters indeed, but whose fortunes have often varied. Poesy descended from heaven; painting arose from the earth. The first poets were prophets, men inspired, whose genius was heated by fanaticism, which silenced cold and feeble reason. The first painters were artisans: required to pass through a long and painful technique, they hardly dared deliver themselves to the flights of a talent that an ignorant age would have failed to recognize. They copied servilely because they saw little, and badly. The painter does not, like the poet, find his originals in the depths of his soul. [70]

In addition to the un-Augustan praise of the effects of fanaticism and the obvious interest this perspective on the "sister arts" has for the cultural historian, these remarks have value, in at least one respect, for the historian of art, as Baridon has pointed out: "Today no one would think of studying the Van Eycks without associating them with the corporation of Jewelers of which they were members; to link their style to their occupation is an anticipation of modern criticism that remains impressive two hundred years later!"[71] That Gibbon does not consider the probability that the "first" poets have not been preserved is irrelevant to this achievement.

Another remark still of interest for its own sake pertains to the artist's apprenticeship. The issue is the study of the sketches and preliminary studies of the masters: "I believe that a young artist would find it fruitful to study them and that in comparing them with the finished works of these Great men, he would discover how they had abandoned, perfected, or followed their first conceptions. It is especially for composition, *whether poetic or picturesque,* that this study would be most useful [emphasis added]."[72] In this advice Gibbon anticipates, of course, the practice and recommendations of his friend Reynolds, but Gibbon did not yet know him, and his emphasis on the study of the genesis of *composition* is distinct from that of those who recommend the study of masters for the sake of stylistic imitation or solutions to particular technical problems.

Another of Gibbon's responses distinguished him, as Baridon points out, from the ordinary run of travelers: his reaction to the series of busts of classical figures displayed at the Uffizi. [73] Seeing them, Gibbon attached to their appearances the psychological traits of the subjects that were known to him as a historian. "It is a very lively pleasure to follow the progress and the decadence of the arts and to run through this series of original portraits of the masters of the world," Gibbon mused as he began the account of "perhaps the most precious treasure of the Gallery" (he had not yet examined the Venus de' Medici). [74] Perhaps even more interesting than his search for the emperors' characters in their faces—after all, such speculations were contrary to his own maxim—is his consideration of the factual data implicit in the portraits—for example, about the age, fashionableness, beauty, or ugliness of the subjects. "If [Berenice] were no more beautiful than she is represented here, it is hard to comprehend Titus's passion." [75] Or his shrewd observation on the rarity of busts of Clodius Albinus: "When it is remembered that his shadow of royalty was followed by a twenty-year reign of a cruel and implacable Enemy, the reasons for this rarity are easy to conceive." [76] The intimacy of Gibbon's knowledge of the general history of the Empire, months before even the germ of the *Decline and Fall* entered his consciousness (for even if the famous story of the genesis of the history is a myth, [77] it obviously represents a psychological truth), is revelatory of the reason not only for his choice but also for his success in it.

Two other illustrations of Gibbon's historical talents and views as revealed in his Florentine journal must suffice. One is a comment on the armament of an Etruscan sculpture of a soldier:

> It seemed to me singular that he should be so badly provided with offensive weapons while nothing that might serve for his defense was forgotten. These two types of arms, however, have always been in proportion to each other among those nations in which prudence and valor were in equilibrium. The fierce peoples of the north thought only of striking their enemies. They often threw away their armor because they feared fatigue more than danger. The Etruscans, a rich and enervated people, would seem to have acted on a completely opposite principle. [78]

Perhaps this observation—certainly that of a "philosophic historian"—would in modern times be the province of a political scientist.

He also reacted as the future author of the *Decline and Fall* might have been expected to react to material he discovered in the course of his other major project of July, the reading of Mallet's *Denmark*. For example, he discussed a question that had interested him when he wrote the *Essai* and that would receive considerable attention in the *Decline and Fall,* the question of the spread of religion. Sheffield was sufficiently impressed by Gibbon's miniature essay on this subject to include it in the *Miscellaneous Works;* Baridon calls it, in a valuable discussion, "a piece of the greatest importance for the study of Gibbon's method."[79] From a biographical point of view, perhaps the most interesting passage is the one in which Gibbon examined the reason that the "inhabitants of the North should have so obstinately rejected Christianity, while their countrymen established in the empire embraced it with the utmost readiness." Rejecting two or three inadequate explanations, Gibbon concluded that the major difference was that of place: "All religions depend in some degree on local circumstances. The least superstitious Christian would feel more devotion on Mount Calvary than in London." The stay-at-home pagans would hardly desert the sacred places of their ancestors while the tradition-hallowed sites were in view, but new sacred places and objects would occupy the emigrants' senses and attention. Besides, a "barbarian, who had tasted the wine of Falernum, would not feel much desire of . . . Odin's [hydromel]; and when he panted under an African sun, a hell open to the north wind would not greatly excite his terror." Whether or not Gibbon had correctly interpreted the psychology of the Danes, he obviously expressed his own. It is therefore the more interesting that he went on to say, "Every cause would concur to make him quit a mode of worship founded on ignorance and barbarism, and to substitute . . . a religion connected with a science which he began to relish, and inculcating the virtues of humanity which he began to value."[80]

Turning back to the Danes who had remained at home, Gibbon noted that the missionaries to them, the "few Benedictines," had a very different task; they "travel[ed] into the woods of Sweden to preach patience, humility, and faith to numerous bands of pirates." Sheffield's excerpt concludes, "A Protestant would also observe, that the Christianity of the tenth century is of far more difficult digestion than that of the fifth. It certainly is so to a man who reasons." But Gibbon continued beyond this point: "but I believe that reasoning has had little enough part in these changes, and when one already believes the absurdities of his own sect, does he balk at a few mysteries more?"[81] Although this passage does not quite impute absurdity to Christian mysteries even of the impure tenth century, Lord Sheffield and his advisers thought it better suppressed.

Other passages of interest include an insight into the importance of pottery in estimating the state of a culture and one on the dangers of conjectural identifications.[82] But despite the constant activity of Gibbon's critical and historical intelligence in Florence, no subject presented itself to him for a composition of his own, and indeed no theme or story seemed to catch his imagination, except perhaps the characters of the emperors and the state of the arts that represented them.

After Gibbon and Guise completed their study of the Uffizi Gallery and visited a few libraries, they spent the last few days of July in diversions with the other English visitors and some of the hospitable Italians. The "wicked Lord Lyttelton," who had little to do with most English visitors, had attached himself to Gibbon and Guise.[83] In an interesting entry, Gibbon made a comparative sketch of Lyttelton and Lord Palmerston:

> The one [Lord Palmerson] composed, calm, somewhat cold, possessed of qualities of heart and mind that make him everywhere esteemed and which one sees that he has most earnestly cultivated. Lyttleton has in everything an impetuosity that knows no bounds, a vanity that makes him seek, without obtaining it, the applause of those for whom his pride inspires in him nothing but contempt, and a mad ambition that, not being accompanied with that constancy that alone can make it succeed, serves only to make him ridiculous. An air of philosophy without much logic and an affectation of knowledge sustained by aimless and superficial reading: such is that extraordinary man who everywhere attracts hatred or pity. I find in him, however, a stock of natural ability greatly superior to his rival's.[84]

The dispassionate portrayal in itself indicates how foreign Lyttelton's futile intemperance was to Gibbon's own personality.

In August and September, nothing in Gibbon's reading or his visits inspired him as had the Uffizi and P. H. Mallet, but the events of his social and emotional life are revealed both directly and in his comments on objects of art or antiquity. A remark about the "eternal spectacle of holy families" may only amuse us with its hint that Gibbon could weary of tourism, but in the same passage his analysis of ways of portraying the Virgin—as a being elevated by divine decrees almost above humanity, as a saint expressing pure humility and devotion, as a young person lifted far from the world, filled with the naive graces of innocence and sweetness—reveals that he considered these states of mind to be not merely distinguishable but distinct, that is, he thought that greatness and nobility were ordinarily incompatible not only with humility and devotion but even with innocence and sweetness. In the *Madonna della Sedia,* however, Raphael managed, Gibbon thought, "by a happy combination," to portray "a face noble, interesting, sweet and spiritual."[85] Of course, this view may apply only to portraiture and not to actual character, but Gibbon did not ordinarily make such a distinction.

Throughout this section of the journal, Gibbon characterized people, as well as persons portrayed in art, and by similar methods. When he deals with the historical figures portrayed on coins, it is sometimes impossible to say whether it is the emperor's "real or his stamped face" to which Gibbon's remarks apply, for example, of a coin of Nero's: "The occasion was indeed worthy of a public monument. But this prince, who little knew the dignity of such a ceremony, made it vile."[86] In fact or in representation?

Gibbon sketched, among people of his time, such varied characters as the antiquarian Cocchi, Sir Horace Mann's mistress, and the Damer brothers.[87] Although Gibbon and Guise were out almost every evening, and although for a while in August they were the only English visitors remaining in Florence, Gibbon made no friends among the Italians. A typical description: "We followed Sir Horace Mann to three assemblies, at the Comtesse de Gallo's, the Marquise Gerini's, and Duke Strozzi's. Only this swift succession could prevent me from being bored. I do not speak the language of the country. I do not know their games. The women are busy with their Cicisbeos and the men appear extremely indifferent."[88] In London, Gibbon missed the hospitality, the intelligent conversation, the smiling ladies, and even the whist, of Lausanne; he also missed them in Florence.

Gibbon's most memorable artistic observation of the period was undoubtedly his interpretation of the Arrotino of the Tribune. As Bonnard points out, Gibbon's interpretation "is now considered the only right one. But in 1764 it was not current. Gori does not mention it. Nor does Smollett who devotes two whole pages . . . to the discussion of the different theories."[89] It is also pleasant to note that Rembrandt, once at least, overcame Gibbon's prejudices against his subject matter: "Nature herself could not better portray Old Age itself . . . and assuredly in Nature I would see [it] with much less pleasure."[90] On the other hand, Gibbon seemed to admire rather the idea of Michelangelo than his works. He and Guise visited Santa Croce:

> The architecture is nothing considerable. But it was not without a secret respect that I contemplated the tombs of Galileo and Michelangelo, of the restorer of the Arts and that of Philosophy. Truly powerful and original geniuses, they adorned their country more than conquerors and politicians. The Tartars had a Jenghis Khan, and the Goths an Alaric, but we turn away our eyes from the blood-stained deserts of Scythia, to fix them with pleasure on Athens and on Florence.[91]

This is the style and sentiment of the *Essai,* of course, but, allowing for the language, one can hear in the last sentence especially an anticipation of the manner of the *Decline and Fall.* When Gibbon had fully pondered the history of Rome, however, he was no longer sure that his preference for the arts of peace was generally shared: "Trajan was ambitious of fame; and as long as mankind shall continue to bestow more liberal praise on their destroyers than on their benefactors, the thirst of military glory will ever be the vice of the most exalted characters."[92]

In keeping with his own principles, however, Gibbon felt and expressed admiration for such a "hero" as the librarian Magliabecchi, who, as a private citizen, had accumulated a library of 40,000–50,000 volumes, in addition to hundreds of volumes of letters from the "celebrated names" of Europe in his time, "which would have been a speaking index of great utility to a man of Genius occupied with some branch of literature."[93]

Gibbon felt also "a secret reverence" in the Riccardi palace, because it was the home of the Medicis when they were still citizens of the Republic of Florence. "They played a very much finer role, when, in their counting houses, they were the protectors of the arts and the arbiters of Italy, than later, when they elevated themselves to the rank of obscure sovereigns of a little state."[94] It is notable also that Gibbon's preference for republics and individual liberty was not only compatible with, but almost required, the benevolent control of great men over the populace, exercised, of course, for the benefit of the latter.

Missing from the journal, oddly enough, is any mention of Gibbon's only extensive writing during these two months—assuming that the manuscript date may be trusted—an account of a portion of the Cisalpine Gallic War, A.U.C. 529 (224 B.C.),[95] uniting Gibbon's own reflections on the subject and his information from a book by the Chevalier Lorenzo Guazzesi Aretino. Although Gibbon said modestly that the sketch would have been "less imperfect, had [he] a Polybius at hand," most of the geographic and strategic observations in this essay were his own. It begins, for instance, with consideration of the dangers to the Romans of a Gallic-Carthaginian alliance:

> But the cautious and narrow policy of the Carthaginians, and the lazy insensibility natural to improvident Barbarians, delivered the Romans from the danger of this alliance. The republic, I imagine, who knew how to dissemble her hatred as well as her ambition, was careful to keep on good terms with the Gauls; and, before provoking their resentment, patiently waited until they should have no other resource than in themselves.[96]

Turning then to narrative, Gibbon gave the antecedents of the conflict—with some puzzlement—and narrated the story to the point at which the defeated praetor was relieved by the consul Aemilius and the barbarians retreated: "The narrative of Polybius is clear; and if Casaubon had taken the sense of the passage as well as Mr. Guazzesi, the text of this great historian would no longer contain any geographical difficulties. . . . Thanks to the happy discovery of Mr. Guazzesi, the whole plan of the campaign is unravelled." Although the barbarians' route had been explained, however, their motive for choosing it had not:

> Mr. Guazzesi well explains these difficulties, by the changes which time has effected in the nature of the country, and by our ignorance whether this route was not the only one practicable for an army; by [the needs of] . . . their numerous cavalry, and by the hope of meeting [friendly shipping for their booty] . . . . But I believe it will be necessary to penetrate into the motives by which the Barbarians were actuated, before we can fairly appreciate their conduct. . . . The Gallic army was governed by two principles extremely different. The Cisalpine nations . . . fought

like men, who had their dearest interests at stake; but their allies the
Gesetae . . . not a nation, but rather an assemblage from different nations . . . had passed the Alps merely for the sake of plunder, and . . .
wished to secure their booty by a speedy retreat.[97]

But they did not know the country and chose the course allowed by the
swollen rivers. As a result, the Cisalpine Gauls could take advantage of
their ignorance to keep them in the combat area. Gibbon's analysis shows
perhaps the fruits of his militia experience and certainly a prejudice in
favor of the citizen-soldier.[98]

Similarly, Gibbon borrowed Guazzesi's explanation of the geography of
the final battle, but disputed the received notion that the arrival of the
second consul to assist Aemilius was pure chance, unexpected by either
consul. "Of all these circumstances, I find most difficulty in understanding the surprise of Atilius." Aemilius must have had orders to leave his
former post, those orders must have included the obtaining of intelligence
about the enemy's whereabouts, and that information would have been
easily obtained. Whatever the explanation of Atilius's surprise, "The Gallic
army, attacked in front and rear by two Roman consuls, advancing in contrary directions, will always, in my opinion, wear the aspect of a well-
combined project, rather than of a military neglect, hardly conceivable."[99]

Gibbon did not record the writing of this essay in his journal, despite
its obvious relevance not only to the future historian of Rome but also to
the former captain of the Hampshire Grenadiers. He did record, in passing,
that he had had no letters from home since March. Knowing his family,
however, he was unworried: "Only bad humor can conquer their laziness
and put the pen in their hands."[100] This ungracious plural was no doubt
actually intended only for his father; Mrs. Gibbon's letters always gave
him pleasure. The silence might have been more significant than he
realized, however, as we shall see.

In September, Gibbon omitted from his records three weeks of his life.
In the entry for September 2, he had "begun to establish an inclination.
It is a certain Madame Gianni."[101] The entry breaks off in mid-sentence.
Gibbon wrote no more until September 22, when he and Guise were departing for Pisa. The omitted entries would have included not only the
further account of the lady and a record of Gibbon's reunion with his
friend Holroyd (on September 15) but also an exciting affair—preserved,
fortunately, in Guise's journal:

Messrs Lyttleton, Damer's, Baron Wolfe, & Moula dined with us to
day. The dinner, and some time after, passed agreably, but the Evening
was spent much otherwise, owing to the Proud, obstinate, & quarel-
some, 'tho perhaps cowardly disposition of M^{r} . . . . [ellipsis Guise's]
who having very grosely abused the rest of the company, most gladly
excused himself to all, except Mr G. . . . with whom he was desirous of

continuing the quarel, first hopeing he would not be disposed to fight him; and next, that if he did, thinking he should have much more the advantage of him, than of any of the others. However after having exposed himself very much, and shew'd an ungenerous, *mean,* obstinacy, he thought proper to acknowledge the spirited, steady, and generous behaviour of Mr G. and to give him the satisfaction desired by himself and his friends.[102]

If Guise did not leave the quarrelsome guest's name off the list, or if the baron's "governor," Moula, did not act out of place and out of character, "M^r . . . ." was probably Lyttelton, whose character certainly fit the description. Poor Gibbon, probably the smallest and least quarrelsome, but not the least brave, man present, would certainly have had his negative opinion of Lyttelton confirmed by this episode. *But*—Gibbon and Guise dined the very next day with Lyttelton and the Damers, whereas Moula and the baron do not appear again in the travelers' journals. We cannot know whether Gibbon was magnanimous, or the sixty-year-old Moula lost his head, but I think the former theory much the more probable. Gibbon had forgiven and been forgiven for drunken quarrels in the past.

En route from Florence to Pisa, Gibbon once again attempted to reform his journal-keeping. He resolved to limit his entries to his own responses, omitting descripton of well-known objects. He also resolved, as usual, to keep the journal more faithfully. He then examined the country through which he and Guise passed with a military eye—for the campaigns of Antony, Metellus, and Catiline, of course: "The sight of this region sheds daylight on my ideas about this war." He analyzed the strategy, the advantages, and the use of the terrain; as Baridon notes, "This supple and penetrating type of imagination, which permits him to recompose the life of an army or the thought of its leaders, brings him closer to the historian than to the geographer."[103]

In Lucca, Gibbon reflected on the economic and political similarities between that republic and Geneva. "Industry constitutes their wealth, and their power is drawn from their very weakness, which gains them everyone's goodwill without exciting anyone's ambition."[104] Again he was writing as a historian. As a philosophic historian, he would have liked to spend some time at Lucca in order to study the constitution. "Republics always deserve attention. They are as different from one another as monarchies are similar to each other."[105] Of course, he meant formally different and similar. He had just described two republics that, de facto, were strikingly similar; and he was well aware that monarchies were as different as their monarchs. Hearing that Frederick the Great of Prussia despised any man who appeared intimidated by him, Gibbon complained:

Would he not distinguish between the Courtier who trembles before a King, and the man who feels the superiority of a Great Man? I have been presented to the kings of England and Sardinia, I have seen close at hand the King of France, and I have seen them all with as much indifference as the smallest of the petit bourgeois. There were even some for whom I felt only the most legitimate contempt.[106]

Such monarchs hardly resembled Frederick the Great; likewise, their monarchies differed.

From Lucca, Gibbon and Guise went to Pisa, where Gibbon met his Acton cousins. The commodore (commander of a "fleet" of three or four frigates) was very hospitable, somewhat embarrassingly so: he was ostracized by the English community for having become a Roman Catholic. Perhaps Gibbon saw with emotion what his own fate might have been, for he seemed to feel some pity for the old man, but he avoided all reminders of his own abortive conversion when he wrote to his father about the encounter: "Last winter [Acton] had a most violent attack of the Apoplexy; whilst in that situation he was persuaded either from motives of interest or devotion to change his religion. . . . I think from his manner and conversation that I never saw a more lively picture of an unhappy man."[107] Gibbon did not neglect his unhappy relative, but was careful to tell the other English visitors at Pisa and Leghorn why he maintained the acquaintance.

In Leghorn he noticed the good treatment of the Jews:

The interest of Commerce has almost silenced the proselytizing spirit of the Church of Rome. If a Jewish youth comes to declare to the priests that he wishes to become Catholic, he cannot be received until after having been left for three months in the hands of his father, who is obliged . . . to allow free access to priests as well as rabbis . . . . In this way proselytes are rarely made; the inconstancy of a child sustains his resolution with difficulty when all his family attempts to make him change it.[108]

Gibbon made no overt comparison between this procedure and his own experience, but he obviously approved of the religious liberty accorded to the Jews. This is in contrast to the anti-Semitism that marks most of his reference to Judaism in the *Decline and Fall*. In general, as we shall see, Gibbon's reactions to, and dealings with, Jews of his own time show no bias against them, despite his language and assumptions in the history.

From Leghorn, the travelers went on to Siena, where Gibbon admired the cathedral in spite of its Gothic lack of "simple forms and just proportions. . . . The pavement is covered with ancient pictures that represent the history of scripture and that of Siena. This taste is baroque, but I like it better than seeing a pavement painted with angels, and lions holding up a throne." He also preferred it to the population; "the women there were so ugly and the men so ignorant" that he had had no desire to stay in that vaunted society.[109]

Finally, on October 2, 1764, Guise and Gibbon arrived at Rome, at five o'clock in the evening. "Since the Pons Milvius I have been in a dream of antiquity," he said.[110] A week later, he wrote to his father:

> I have already found such a fund of entertainement for a mind some-what prepared for it by an acquaintance with the Romans, that I am really almost in a dream. Whatever ideas books may have given us of the greatness of that people, Their accounts of the most flourishing state of Rome fall infinitely short of the picture of its ruins. I am convinced there never never existed such a nation and I hope for the happiness of mankind that there never will again.[111]

A week later still, he would, again at evening, again in contemplation of the magnificence and uniqueness of the ruins, discover his great subject. According to his famous description, "It was at Rome on the fifteenth of October 1764, as [he] sat musing amidst the ruins of the Capitol while the barefooted fryars were singing Vespers in the temple of Jupiter, that the idea of writing the decline and fall of the City first started to [his] mind" (136, n.7). According to the diary of his friend Guise, however, it rained on the morning of the fifteenth, and he and Gibbon visited a collection of pictures. Although Guise says nothing about the afternoon's occupation, some have thought that this and other discrepancies proved that Gibbon's whole dramatic story was a fabrication.[112] But if the story in the *Memoirs* is an invention, Gibbon also invented the valedictory statement in the *Decline and Fall* itself: "It was among the ruins of the Capitol that I first conceived the idea" of the history. I cannot believe that he lied at the most solemn moment of his life. What he certainly did, in writing his account of his inspiration, was to improve the dramatic qualities of his narrative in each successive version. The facts he proposes in these various versions are: (1) the idea of writing a history of the decline of the city of Rome came to him on a particular occasion, albeit as the fruit of his long-standing interest in Rome and empire; (2) he was listening to the friars singing vespers at the time; (3) the friars' church occupied the site of the Temple of Jupiter on the Capitoline hill; (4) the occasion was not Gibbon's first visit to the Capitol, but it occurred fairly early in his visit to Rome. The most rhetorically effective version of these data is certainly that of the final draft, the famous version.

In Gibbon's journal, after the entry for October 2 and before those of December, there is nothing except two blank pages. Gibbon might have kept a pocket book, now lost, in which he recorded the "date and hour" of his inspiration, as he claimed to have done in one version of his memoirs, but we cannot know whether the famous scene is historically or only mythically true. That he was in a frame of mind in which it could have occurred, his letter to his father surely suggests. The coincidence that it was on October 15 that he made his first *in situ* historical discovery (Swiss tour 1755) and on October 15 that he had begun to write about the city of Rome in his *Recueil géographique* (Lausanne 1763) may have led him to imagine that he had recorded the date, or led him to choose it to make his myth precise. It was clearly important to him that posterity share his view that the confrontation of the ruins of the city and the rituals of present-day Catholicism inspired his writing of the *Decline and Fall.* My own opinion is that the incident really happened. Whether it did or not, we must in some sense respect his judgment of its symbolic importance: Rome, twilight, ruins, and friars in some sense caused the *Decline and Fall.*

At the time, of course, he did nothing about this inspiration. He and Guise set about visiting the antiquities and treasures of Rome in the approved manner, with the aid of their own antiquary. Throughout October and November, they accompanied their choice, a young Scotsman named James Byers, in visits to the famous sights of Rome.[113]

Halfway through November, Gibbon's dream of Rome was ominously interrupted by a letter from his father, after more than six months of silence. That letter no longer exists, but Gibbon's reply shows that his father's financial troubles, threatening in Lausanne, had continued and increased. Mr. Gibbon's new desire was to sell the Lenborough estate, an expedient Gibbon considered undesirable in itself and disastrous unless the funds remaining after clearing the mortgage and an old debt remaining from his grandfather's time could belong to them jointly and be handled for them by a banker. His father wanted to use the money to purchase more land. "Have not we enough already?" asked the son. Gibbon wanted to confine their views to "the happiness of your life, that of Mrs Gibbon's and of my own. Let us mutually consult what may the most contribute towards that object without calculating what estate may at last remain *for the Elliots.*"[114] He was more than ever convinced that he would never marry, and the letter was expressed with all his usual deference and tact. No doubt he hoped that it would suffice to achieve a happy settlement of the problem. His mind was sufficiently at ease to permit consideration and composition on more remote topics.

Late in November, he began an essay, in his nongeographical *Recueil*, on the laws, alleged and actual, governing the Roman triumphs. This essay, an exercise in constitutional history, provides some of the evidence for Giarrizzo's observation that "The Rome which he first seeks and responds to is the Rome of republican greatness, that divine place where liberty and virtue converged as in a golden age of human history."[115] Gibbon concluded in this essay that the only requirements for a triumph were that the general be a present or former magistrate and that he assemble the senators in a temple outside the walls and give them a sworn written narrative of the victory for which he hoped to be awarded a triumph. Two other inferred laws, that the victory include the killing of at least 5,000 enemies and extend the bounds of Roman territory, are refuted in fact and also in principle—these "laws" neither were, nor should have been, observed:

> It may be asked with greater probability . . . whether, . . . to demand the triumph, it was not necessary to terminate the war. . . . In such a regulation, I should perceive nothing but the wisdom of the senate, which was careful not to debase its honours by too lavish a prodigality; and which itself, always sovereign and free, knew how to refuse a presumptuous general, who courted the triumph by inglorious conquests over unworthy enemies. But in deciding according to facts, [as] we ought to decide, I perceive that the conduct of the senate varied in different ages of the republic; and that the cause of this variation depended on a circumstance altogether distinct from the merit of the general.[116]

One of the circumstances was the location and source of the soldiers. If they were returning citizens, the general whose success permitted their return usually deserved the triumph that permitted him to accompany them. If they were mercenaries who might remain at their stations, his triumph could be awarded or not without considering their desires, following "the maxims of policy rather than those of justice." In between, while Rome was growing, the fields of her victories were more remote, and neither soldiers nor general could return until the war was complete: "Triumphs in those wars were purchased only by conquests; and, in consequence of the excellence of those laws whose execution varies with the nature of things, rather than with the passions of men, the increasing majesty of the triumph kept pace with the growing greatness of the state."[117]

Despite the interest of its content and the cogency of its arguments, this essay, as an essay, lacks some of Gibbon's usual lucidity and shows that he had not yet fully mastered formal order. It concludes as if continuous with the essay on the route of the triumphal processions which Gibbon completed on December 13. Gibbon probably worked on the whole "chapter" throughout the two-week period, and the inevitable interruptions and distractions contributed to its fragmentation. However, the section of the essay devoted to the triumphal route, with its natural geographical order, is much more strongly organized than the rest, even where geography did not provide its structure. Before we can examine its argument, we must suffer, with Gibbon, an interruption from England still more serious than that of November.

On December 5, Gibbon wrote frantically to his father that his banker at Rome had received a letter from the banker at Lausanne, who had given me my general credit all over Italy, to recall that credit and to desire he would give me no more money. This can be only owing to the last draught from Florence having been protested and as the banker has probably sent the same advice to his other correspondents, my character is ruined in every great town in Italy, and what makes it more unfortunate is the draught I gave from hence about a week ago for £100 more at twenty days' sight, which will probably have the same fate. I feel my situation the more as I am not conscious of having deserved it by distressing you with extravagant draughts. After a mature deliberation you fixed upon 700 pounds for my tour of Italy. I have always advised you regularly before I drew, and I have never Dear Sir exceeded my proportion of the sum. To what then am I to attribute this unforeseen misfortune. In your last letter you say nothing and yet you must have then received mine from Florence. Forgive my warmth Dear Sir, I scarce know what to think write or do. . . . Till [you send me new credit] it will be impossible for me to stir from Rome, or to live with much pleasure in it, while I know there are people who may very naturally suspect me of being a rogue or an adventurer.

Once more Dear Sir forgive a man who scarce knows what he writes and believe me ever most sincerely Yours, E. G.
I beg Dear Sir a speedy answer.[118]

By the same post Gibbon sent his father a second letter to point out that new credit must also be sent to Naples, Bologna, Venice, and "one or two principal places in France or Germany according as you intend I should come home." Discreet and deferential as Gibbon was, he could not forbear ending this *cri de coeur* with a reproach: "How can it have happened Dear Sir that a letter can have had the time to go from London to Florence, from Florence to Lausanne and from Lausanne to Rome without my having had the smallest intimation of it from you."[119] A home question, that, and it or something apparently aroused his father to make amends, for Gibbon's next extant letter—dated Naples, January 29, and addressed to his stepmother—contains no mention of it, and was "recomandèe à M. Barazzi Banquier à Rome," the same banker to whom the Lausanne bank had written to cut off Gibbon's credit.[120] Although Mr. Gibbon had not yet written to explain himself or give directions for Gibbon's journey home, the last paragraph of the letter indicates that Gibbon's banker and his Cousin Darell had been in communication and restored Gibbon's credit. But once again, Gibbon's father had offered him the appearance of independence and security and then shattered the illusory gift.[121]

Despite the distress under which he labored, or perhaps partly because of it, the continuation of Gibbon's study of the Roman triumphs was tightly structured, clear, and well argued. He began with a statement of the position to be refuted: the route of the triumphal procession varied with the site of the victories. Then, interspersing a concrete scene as he does so often in the *Decline and Fall,* Gibbon introduced the contrary evidence of Cicero's portrayal of Piso's contemptible return, in obscurity, not through the "*'Porta triumphalis,* a gate always open to your predecessors.'"[122]

Cicero's evidence proved that there was a specific triumphal gate in his time; the nature of the thing, as well as human nature, suggested that it was not then a new custom, for in "enlightened ages, men seldom venture to establish customs which are respectable only in their end and purpose." Established by the example of Romulus, the fixed way must have been his route, because there would have been no motive to fix upon a specific route different from his.

Obviously, the next step was to establish what route Romulus took, and Gibbon proceeded to do so. Romulus's destination was the Capitoline Mount, and he was coming from Cenina. Cenina, called by some "Sabine," and by others, "Latin," was probably therefore in "that slip of ground on the banks of the Anio, where the [two] colonies" mingled. Lines from this district met in the Campus Martius, which faces the steep, inaccessible side of the Capitoline hill. Romulus would have had to go around it, either between the Capitoline and Quirinal hills, or on the plain between the Capitoline and the Tiber. "The gate of which we are in quest ought to be found within these limits. A chain of conjectural evidence leads me to this conclusion, which facts alone can substantiate."[123] One supporting fact was that it was proposed that Augustus's funeral procession should go through the triumphal gate in sight of his tomb. His tomb was in the Campus Martius.

The same narrative and geographical clarity, supported by ancient testimony, marks Gibbon's description of the triumphal route. Nardini and Donatus, however, differ from Gibbon and from each other on the location of the gate. According to Gibbon, he could use each authority against the other but instead chose to adduce his own arguments. He then enumerated his principles of judgment and used them to examine two sites, to eliminate one, and to propose that the other was the site and that the gate itself was identical with the so-called Temple of Janus, which Gibbon thought was instead an arcade with bronze gates, left open in times of war (when the triumphs also occurred) but closed in times of peace.

Lest his "chapter" grow into a book, Gibbon confined his remarks on the show itself to that fact of its being a natural, not an artificial, ceremony, making the spectators participants in a victory achieved in their name and for their glory. Led by association, Gibbon went on to wonder why the defeated monarchs suffered different fates, why Perseus was merely banished and honorably buried at last, whereas Jugurtha, whose crimes were equal or rather less, died in obscurity, hunger, and despair, in a Roman dungeon. "Perseus was a monument of the virtue of the republic . . . but, with Jugurtha, the Romans must have wished to bury for ever the memory of their own disgrace. . . . Such were the crimes of Jugurtha . . . for which the Romans could never possibly forgive him."[124] This foretaste of Gibbonian irony reminds us that that irony is not activated solely by a contempt for triumphs of barbarism and religion, as both his friends and his enemies sometimes think. Instead, it is the giving of pretty names to ignoble motives at which he "sneers."

The last known product of Gibbon's first visit to Rome was an "account" of a manuscript Gibbon had obtained from Mr. Byers, his antiquary, written by the Abbé G. V. Gravina and dealing with the *Governo Civile di Roma.*[125] Gibbon did not think much of this work and made only a few notes from it, but his introductory paragraph contains a remark that is another reason for believing that his vision of the *Decline and Fall* actually occurred: "its principal subject [is] the revolutions of the city after the fall of the empire [in the West] ; a subject which interests me much."[126]

After four months in Rome, a visit broken only by his January jaunt to Naples, where he was shocked by the squalor of the people's lives, Gibbon left Rome in February. Venice, as squalid as Naples, predictably displeased him, and at Lyons he found letters that made it clear that his father would be displeased if he toured southern France, as he and Guise had planned.[127] Therefore he headed home, by way of Paris.

It has more than once been suggested, and Baridon has persuasively argued, that the language of Gibbon's reference to Mme. Bontems in one of the drafts of his memoirs suggests that he eventually enjoyed her favors.[128] If so, that happy period must have been during the "ten delicious days" of his second Parisian visit.[129] The sexual satisfactions he enjoyed, if any, were not addictive, however; there is no evidence at all of Gibbon's setting up a mistress or engaging in an affair of any serious kind in the remainder of his life. But Mme. Bontems may help to account for his coming once again to consider marriage a possibility, and for his greater confidence in the company of women. In Paris, as we have already noted, he also ventured to renew his most dangerous female friendship, that with Suzanne Curchod, now Mme. Jacques Necker. His joking complaint to Holroyd that the Neckers' "impertinent" security when he visited them was "making an old lover of mighty little consequence" is as cheerful, unstrained, and unselfconscious in its good humor as his warning, in the same letter, to Holroyd the regular-army man, that he would not be allowed to "have the honor of reviewing my [Militia] troops next summer . . . I do not care to expose the chosen seed to the prophane mockery of the uncircumcised."[130]

Perhaps he was willing enough to forgo the rest of his tour. In retrospect he thought so:

The measure of absence and expence was filled; Rome and Italy had satiated my curious appetite, and the excessive heat of the weather decided the sage resolution of turning my face to the north. . . . After an happy fortnight, I tore myself from the embraces of Paris, embarked at Calais, again landed at Dover . . . and hastily drove through the summer dust and solitude of London. (M 271)

There he stopped to see his Aunt Kitty, finding her "in very good spirits and much better [health] than she had been."[131]

From London, the returned traveler proceeded quickly to the tranquillity of Beriton, which he reached "on the 25th of June, 1765" (M 271). Gibbon told Stanier Porten, his uncle, that his tour had made him a "better Englishman than [he] went out":

Tho' I have seen more elegant manners and more refined arts I have perceived so many real evils mixed with these tinsel advantages, that they have only served to make the plain honesty and blunt freedom of my own country appear still more valuable to me. What a mixture of pride vice, slavery and poverty have I seen in the short time I passed at Naples. . . . I am told great pains are taken to extinguish every ray of sense in the mind of their prince and to leave it as meer a blank as possible. I make no doubt of their success in so laudable a design.[132]

Gibbon's letters, like those of other thoughtful people, were biased by a sense of what would give the recipients pleasure (there were no interested reasons for cultivating Stanier Porten), but the sincerity of this response to Naples is indicated by its Gibbonian expression, while his being a better Englishman, in his political philosophy at least, is supported in his confident preference not only of the theory but of the practice of the English constitution above all others—so instructed, of course, by the French Anglophile *philosophes,* but contributing his own observations, as we shall see. Although his next letter to Holroyd betrayed some regret at having had to curtail his travels, apparently that regret was not severe.

His own description of the fruits of his pilgrimage to Italy omitted its most important results. He had acquired a subject, a theme, and an apparently inexhaustible stock of visual data from which to develop the scenes of his great work. That fruit could not be harvested immediately; the immediate fruit was the bitter one of a sense of thwarted independence. In his travels, he had learned what it was to live his own life, set his own limits on his time, money, and companions, and be accepted socially, personally, and intellectually as an English gentleman. He had been able to further his scholarly ambitions as well. In Italy, the banking crisis interrupted these dreams and reminded him that his independence was temporary and conditional. More subtly, it taught him that the true barrier to his freedom was not his father's power, but his father's weakness. For the next five-and-a-half years, the vision of the ruin of the Capitol was displaced willy-nilly by the specter of the ruin of the Hampshire gentleman.

CHAPTER 12

In Search
of a Subject

THE STORY of Gibbon's life in the
years 1765-67 is two-fold. This was the time when, doing his best to enter into the world and the concerns of his father—from lottery tickets to
Tory electioneering—he succeeded to such an extent that even Mr. Gibbon
seems to have come to love and trust him, while Dorothea Gibbon, his
stepmother, became virtually and happily a mother to him. At the same
time, no longer a boy, unable to anticipate an end to the current term of
his life (except the one that he tried to think unthinkable, his father's
death), he tried to create a life of the mind for himself within the geographical, temporal, and emotional confines of his father's world. He
knew, however, that the vision he had glimpsed of the *Decline and Fall*
could not be realized on a part-time basis; he searched, therefore, for a
satisfying project or subject not demanding such concentrated labor and
attention.

In the projects he now undertook, he had a new and welcome ally, his
Lausanne friend George Deyverdun, who had left an unhappy romance and
a German court to seek solace and a living in England.[1] As soon as Gibbon
had returned to Beriton, he was allowed to invite Deyverdun to join him
there. Perhaps he confided to Deyverdun his eventual plans for a history of
Rome; he asserts in the *Memoirs* (M 303) that he had already begun to do
the necessary preliminary reading and rereading for it. But even the confidence and companionship of Deyverdun was no adequate substitute for
adult independence and for the prospect of accomplishing his real work;
this period was "the portion of [his] life which [he] passed with the
least enjoyment, and . . . remember[ed] with the least satisfaction" (137).

Regretted and slighted by the autobiographer, the period has also been
passed over hastily by biographers, even Low. The scantiness of the evidence
about Gibbon's personal and social life is irremediable, but the study of
the manuscripts of his miscellaneous writing makes it possible to correct
Lord Sheffield's datings, to establish a rough chronology of Gibbon's work
in this period, and thereby to discover significant developments in his

intellectual life hitherto underestimated or ignored. The rhythm of his life returned to that of the nonmilitia days before he went to Italy—summers and autumns at Beriton, winter and spring in London. The neglected era began, of course, with the summer of 1765.

Deyverdun's arrival, welcome though it was, was in one respect embarrassing to Gibbon. He longed to assist his friend in some practical way, by influence or recommendation, to obtain a position by means of which he could earn his living. But, whatever Gibbon's prospects and the one-time importance of his family, he was unable to find any post for his friend. His first literary project was, probably deliberately, a means of at least solacing his friend's pride by making him useful to Gibbon's own literary labors. That project was the "history of Swiss liberty," long thought of but put aside for the excellent reason that most of the sources were in a language unknown to the would-be historian.[2] Deyverdun's presence and knowledge of German made the project a possibility and undoubtedly influenced Gibbon's return to it, rather than to his alternative topics, the Medicis (surely stimulated by his Florentine stay) and Rome.[3]

Gibbon also had unfinished business in hand, the studies of weights and measures and of ancient geography begun before the tour of Italy. Both were touched up with minor additions while Gibbon was traveling.[4] A grander scheme for the ancient geography had already been projected;[5] the scope of the "Weights and Measures" study was now reconsidered.[6] This reconsideration is in a much more mature hand than the 1759 version; it might, however, be attributed to Gibbon's militia days or his 1763 stay in Lausanne, except that so important a study would certainly have been recorded in the journals he kept during those periods. But it is not recorded in the journals—not surprising, if it were written in 1765, when he kept no journal.

This argument, though not impregnable, warrants a tentative dating of this new approach to his old project in the early period after his return from Italy. Because Gibbon and Deyverdun soon discovered that Deyverdun's excerpts and translations would have to be made before Gibbon could work on the Swiss project, Gibbon himself needed something else to do. He returned to his old project with a new approach. No longer content simply to extract a handbook from other scholars' work, Gibbon now proposed to use his synthesis of their labors in a study of "the history of men, rather than that of kings," by an "extensive collection of all the interesting facts" about the "economic language" and about the matters it assists us to interpret.[7] One page of an earlier attempt at this "avant-propos" survives.[8] The differences between that draft, which led nowhere, and this one, which led to further work, are instructive.

In the middle draft, as we may call the single-page version, Gibbon clearly assumed that he would publish his work; in the last draft, he added a sentence indicating uncertainty as to whether he was working for the public or merely for his own convenience: "This work will grow larger without design and without effort, and will enrich itself insensibly with the fruit of all my studies."[9] The final draft omits, on the other hand, an optimistic paragraph about his predecessors, which begins: "I shall not copy the great works we already have. The researches of so many scholars on all that regards the ancients, those of Fleetwood, Lowndes, Nicholson and Arbuthnot on the English, and those of La Blanc etc. on the French, leave little to desire with respect to the weights, measures, and money of these peoples."[10] To the four special objects of his attention enumerated in the next paragraph of both drafts, that is, revenue and taxes, prices of necessities, prices of labor, and interest rates, he added, in the final draft, "the use of money, and consequently. . . manners, luxury, and the arts."[11] The object of his work was thus converted from economic history to social history. Because this version was to be a "collection" rather than a discursive argument, with seven headings under which useful data could be recorded as they were discovered, it was structurally much less demanding than the "principles and tables" format he had planned in 1759. On the other hand, the now vast range made its incompletion quite predictable. Lord Sheffield's edition appears to separate, but actually mixes, material from the various drafts.[12] The only sustained discussion certainly written in 1765 is the appreciation of Hooper's *Inquiry*; the comments on Herodotus and other notes from the "Antiquities" section might have been made at the time of the middle draft, at the time of the final draft, or both. Gibbon never ceased to feel the utility of this kind of scholarship, as numerous grateful notes to the *Decline and Fall* attest, but he soon ceased to devote his own efforts to it.

Instead, he undertook a discrete project from his Florentine subject, the "Relation des Noces de Charles Duc de Bourgogne."[13] Compared with the labors of the "weights and measures" discussion, this essay was almost a mere amusement, an exercise in pure narrative, or rather, a fragment of one. Though Lord Sheffield did not date this study, the manuscript makes it possible to date it confidently in 1765.[14] It was the result of Gibbon's reading (or rereading) of Olivier de la Marche, encountered in his preparation for the Swiss history.[15] The narrative, with its vivid appreciation of the magnificence of the spectacle, is drawn from Olivier alone, and therefore, in spite of its adaptation to Gibbon's own ends and its recasting from his particular perspective, it is not surprising that he chose not to fulfill the promise of this leisurely beginning.

But his desire to attempt so modern a subject,[16] and the historiographical observation with which he began it, are of interest: "A sort of gratitude is due to the historians who have preserved for us the details, often minute, which paint for us the manners of an age, its artistic tastes, and the kind and extent of its commerce. There is more variety and often more instruction in these objects than in the relation of a battle or of a peace treaty."[17] Such a recognition of the instructiveness, as well as the pleasures, of cultural and economic history followed easily from his recent contribution to the history of men, rather than kings, and is consistent with Gibbon's views wherever they are recorded. The sum of such scattered historiographical comments is, to some extent, a substitute for the formal treatise on his art and craft that Gibbon never wrote.

We do not know whether lack of materials, lack of time, or failure of inclination caused him to leave the "Relation des Noces" incomplete; we do know what interest took its place. He observed in the *Memoirs* that he now found himself restless in the circumstances to which he had submitted fairly easily before his tour (139). Despite his library, despite Deyverdun, despite his mature age, despite his small but unrestricted allowance, he was powerless to order his own life, and he now felt acutely the absence of that power. Hours of chitchat with his parents, two church services on Sunday, tedious visits from neighboring sportsmen and gentlemen farmers, were not painful duties, but they marked an unrewarding and aimless way of life. He could see his patrimony slipping through his father's hapless hands, without the power to amend the situation, or the will to rebel against it, for at last his father was offering him a measure of affection and approval appropriate to their relationship: "My growing years abolished the distance that might yet remain between a parent and a son, and my behaviour satisfied my father, who was proud of the success, however imperfect in his own lifetime, of my litterary talents" (138). Although Gibbon recognized his father's good intentions ("his labours were useful, his pleasures innocent, his wishes moderate" [149]) and responded to his father's sociable virtues—"graceful person, polite address, gentle manners, and unaffected chearfulness" (150), he could not fail to see ominous signs of the family's failing fortunes. Gibbon did what he could to deal with the problem: he consented to another mortgage, he was careful to live within his own allowance, and he returned to his father (in the form of a loan) the one monetary gift he had received from him.[18] But the farm did not pay under his father's management, and the load of debt continued to increase.

Even worse than the apparition of poverty was the present state of overextended boyhood. Though he approached and passed the age of thirty, he was still in tutelage. "The most gentle authority will sometimes frown without reason, the most chearful submission will sometimes murmur without cause," he observed moderately, and (what is perhaps more telling) he assumed that it is an attribute of human nature to be unable to feel ourselves free, without knowing that others are dependent upon and obedient to us (139). This perhaps surprising axiom is obviously derived from his own case.

His father's control would have seemed less galling, or might not have existed, had Gibbon had the power over his own destiny conferred by a profession. "While so many of my acquaintance were married, or in parliament, or advancing. . . in the various roads of honours and fortune, I stood, alone, immoveable and insignificant" (139-40).[19] Marriage was not the road to independence for him, unpressed by parents or passions to propagate the Gibbons, as he drily observed. Parliament was out of reach while the family finances were in difficulty. But "I lamented, that . . . I had not embraced the lucrative pursuits of the law or of trade, the chances of civil office or India adventure, or even the fat slumbers of the Church; and my repentance became more lively as the loss of time was more irretrievable" (140). Lack of capital, influence, or a university degree inhibited even the belated pursuit of these professions, with one possible exception: law. It is striking that two well-attested activities of this period in his life were connected with the law, as if Gibbon wished to discover whether his talents might yet be applied in that direction.[20]

One was the study of the Theodosian code, with Godefroy's notes, but this probably came at the latter end of the period. The other was the "triple perusal of [Sir William] Blackstone's commentaries, and a copious and critical abstract of that English work was my first serious production in my native language" (148). In making this statement, Gibbon had either forgotten or undervalued his 1762 commentary on Richard Hurd's edition of Horace, but the abstract from Blackstone is indeed copious, critical, serious, and—despite Lord Sheffield's opinion that these remarks were mere extracts—his own.[21] Of course, Gibbon both quoted and paraphrased Blackstone from time to time, and he arranged his abstract according to the sections of Blackstone's work, but both Gibbon's text and his notes were expressed in his own style, governed by his judgment both in proportions and in emphasis, and representative of his independent opinions on numerous occasions. For example, although Blackstone was the source of Gibbon's data and even his image for the role of foreign clery in establishing the canon law beside the common law in England, the difference in their tones and judgments is obvious from a comparison. Blackstone had written:

> The common law of England, being not committed to writing, but only handed down by tradition, use, and experience, was not so heartily relished by the foreign clergy; who came over hither in shoals during the reign of the conqueror. . . . From this time the nation seems to have been divided into two parties; the bishops and clergy . . . who applied themselves wholly to the study of the civil and canon laws. . . ; and the nobility and laity, who adhered with equal pertinacity to the old common law; both of them reciprocally jealous of what they were unacquainted with, and neither of them perhaps allowing the opposite system that real merit which is abundantly to be found in each.[22]

This, on the other hand, is Gibbon:

> Unfortunately for this usefull science, the foreign Clergy who poured
> in shoals into England after the Norman conquest had little relish for
> the old Common law of this Country; they had formed the design of
> erecting upon it's ruins the new System of Civil and Canon Law which
> had just began to revive in the Court of Rome and the Italian Univer-
> sities. The artfull designs of these Ecclesiastics were however con-
> stantly disapointed by the steady opposition of the Nobility and Laity
> who supported the Municipal Law of England against these innova-
> tions; till at last despairing of sucess the Clergy affected to despise what
> they were unable to destroy & withdrew almost entirely from the
> secular tribunals. [23]

Gibbon's responses to Blackstone were sometimes more neutral or more
similar to Blackstone's concepts than in this example, but sometimes considerably more distinct. Unlike a collection of extracts, moreover, Gibbon's
abstract had its own coherent structure.

Some of this order was derived from the logic of Blackstone's argument,
but the preservation of that argument in a succinct essay drawn from a five-
hundred-page volume would not have been automatic, and in fact Gibbon
did more: he improved upon, modified, or replaced it. For example, he
observed:

> The first chapter upon the absolute rights of individuals is rather
> perplexed from a method which seems inverted. All societies must re-
> trench from the natural liberties of each individual. Free societies
> retrench as little as possible. The restrictions imposed by the laws of
> England will be diffused throughout the whole work and this chapter
> would I think have appeared with more propriety as an appendix
> than as a preface. [24]

In his own version of this chapter, then, Gibbon did not so much discuss
the nature of those rights as the securities for them: a representative
legislature, an independent but not arbitrary judiciary, and the rights of
habeas corpus, petition, and arms for one's own defense against private
injuries. It is noteworthy that Gibbon inserted the specific provisions
of the habeas corpus bill, which were not given by Blackstone. According to Gibbon's note, Blackstone, like other lawyers, had a preference
for common over statute law that an "impartial reader" could not share. [25]
The contributions from his own thought and reading already evident
early in this abstract suggest that he was following his usual procedure
when approaching a new work, the one he recommended to students in
the *Memoirs* (98).

Within the neglected essay on Blackstone, there is ample evidence not
only of the capacity for grasping and presenting the intricacies of a legal
system so brilliantly to be demonstrated in chapter 42 of the *Decline*

and Fall but also of the attractive and distasteful qualities, as Gibbon then saw them, of the practice of law. The essay contains many revealing comments, for example, on influence in elections, "It is far easier to exclude open violence than the silent pleasing power of interest"; on the king's loss of independent property, "A vast revenue of which he is the sole manager, and a regular standing army of which he is the perpetual general have made ample amends for these losses. The reign of interest, is less odious than that of fear & more solid than that of prejudice"; "Mr B laments the condition of the unhappy soldiers, the only slaves in a free country. But when as in modern institutions, the defence of the nation is entrusted to the vilest part of it: such wild beasts must either tremble themselves; or else they will soon make their masters tremble."[26]

Examples could be multiplied, but these perhaps suffice to illustrate Gibbon's concern with and for the common weal of his own country, and his political views, which were far from the vanguard of pure democracy. Gibbon's satisfaction with a Burkean view of the English constitution was not, as some have thought, a retreat in his old age from a youthful preference for more liberal views. He always regarded both mobs and kings as requiring restraint and considered "interest" the best *available* safeguard of a well-regulated state. Gibbon never mistook such states for utopias: "the power. . . of pressing [for example] is contrary to reason, humanity and every principle of freedom, and is suffered only from the still more powerfull plea of necessity."[27] He was not deaf to the demands of freedom and humanity and preferred that they be satisfied, but he could also be moved by the argument of necessity. Necessity was not, however, to be confused with mere convenience: Gibbon's view was, for instance, that slavery, even in the adulterated form (tolerated, according to Blackstone, by the British constitution) of a "right to the perpetual service of John or Thomas," is "scarce reconciliable with any notions of equity: since it is founded upon no voluntary contract, nor compensated by any just equivalent." [28] (It is obvious that Gibbon takes as axiomatic an "original contract" view of equity, not evoked here in Blackstone in any way.) Gibbon even seems to have had a dim sense of the inequity of England's marriage laws, noting that annulment and separation were the "sole redress which our laws afford to the complaints of ill temper or even adultery; unless the Legislature should interpose."[29] Blackstone proposed the problems a marriage might encounter, but did not appear to see any inadequacy in the redress provided by the law.[30]

From a biographical point of view, perhaps the most interesting section is "Of Parent and Child." Proportionately, Gibbon devoted twice as much space to this topic as did Blackstone, and he added a good deal to what he found in the *Commentaries.* Blackstone provided a remark on the deficiency of the laws in not requiring much from parents in respect to education or at least subsistence, as well as a contrast between the limits of English and Roman paternal power. Gibbon picked up these hints, but his fullness and fervor were all his own, in particular his observation on the effect of natural affection with respect to English and Roman paternal powers:

> [Here] a father is at liberty to regulate or neglect the education of his children, as he thinks fit. . . . Our laws seem to have reposed a entire confidence in the powers of natural affection; at least when they are not checked by religious zeal. . . . Our laws indulge the parent in the un-restrained disposal of his fortune; which he may totally deprive his children of; unless he is restrained by particular family compacts: a dread-full power indeed: since the momentary caprice of old age may by a rash but irrevocable sentence make an indiscreet perhaps an innocent youth for ever miserable. A Medium might surely be discovered: and the Child tho' not liable to want from the tyranny of his parent might yet find it his interest as well as his duty to deserve his favor. The absolute power which the Roman father enjoyed over the life of his child . . . might be a usefull supplement to publick justice, and nature which may often be too careless or injust towards her offspring, would always start with horror at the thoughts of destroying it. In this case . . . the greater trust seems of less dangerous consequence, than the lesser.[31]

The connections between these sentiments and Gibbon's own situation are inescapable. Gibbon's current understanding with his father rested, as he obviously felt, on the shaky foundation of that changeable character's continuing favor and justice. Though he had received an adequate education, it was so almost by chance. At this era in his life, moreover, he could not help feeling that some regular profession would have been preferable even to the advantages he had managed to obtain from his sojourn in Lausanne. He might further have reflected that nature, however generous in the provision of parental affection, might fatally fail to provide parental discretion.

No notes survive from Gibbon's other excursion into law, his reading of Godefroy's edition of the Theodosian code, with, of course, the all-important exception of its use in the *Decline and Fall*. Much of his miscellaneous reading of the period 1765-67 left traces, however, in two collections of notes he called "Hints" and "Index Expurgatorious," respectively.[32] These notes were not, for the most part, contributions to the collections for the *Decline and Fall* he described in the *Memoirs*, as he "investigated, with [his] pen almost always in [his] hand, the original records, both Greek and Latin, from Dion Cassius to Ammianus Marcellinus, from the reign of Trajan to the last age of the western Cæsars" (146-47). Such notes must have been lost or destroyed as they were superseded. They probably resembled the very sketchy materials we possess for the last three volumes of the history, that is, cue words and references for books he possessed, with a few paraphrases and quotations from those he had had to borrow.[33] The two collections he preserved, on the other hand, had other purposes; the "Hints," in particular, resemble rather the sketchbook of an artist than the laboratory records of a scientist. The artist in question was, however, clearly a historian. There are approximately fourteen topics in the seventeen hints (he numbered the entries by folios). Of these topics, nine are clearly historical; of the three that are literary, two are as relevant to the historian as to the literary critic; and the other two are "freedom of thought" and "the Popish worship like the Pagan." All the hints are interesting, but most of them are so fragmentary as rather to tease than to inform the reader. What, for instance, did Gibbon hope to make of La Bruyère's "very just" maxim about governments, "when quiet how ever disturbed! when disturbed how ever quiet"?

> Supported by the interest of a few, Courtiers Priests Soldiers—real power of the Latter—honor and attachment [this qualification inserted as an afterthought]—despotic government more secure in large states— Indolence, prejudices &c of the Multitude—chain of imitation—power of habit—necessity of order—Every conspiracy a new Society——Danger of each Individual—Extreme danger Strong passions and great talents— When the charm is once broke every man feels his real strength and despises the Idol——Hopes succeed to fears—The bond of faction grows stronger, that of government weaker——Vicissitude [34]

This is obviously a preliminary outline for an essay, perhaps one of general theory, on the causes of revolutions. It is tempting and possible to see it as the germ of his "General Observations on the Decline of the Empire in the West," written in 1774 and included in the third volume of the *Decline and Fall*.[35] Certainly this inertial principle accounts for the fall of an overextended state from the instability of its own growth, as do the "General Observations." But the crucial point, the one abbreviated as "Every conspiracy a new society," is too cryptically expressed to provide a clear guide. Perhaps Gibbon himself was already aware that this change remained mysterious to him, as the question-begging terms "Vicissitude" and "charm . . . once broke" suggest.

Other "hints" are clearer, but were never pursued, for example, "Historians friends to Virtue? yes—with exceptions. 1. Allow great Latitude in the means. 2. Incline more to personal than Social virtues. 3. Moderns if religious, pervert their natural Ideas."[36] The last of these observations is a commonplace in Gibbon, but the other two are propositions that a historian of historical writing might profitably pursue, for if they are accurate, they are surprising, and if they are not, Gibbon's error is a revealing one. Similarly, we can infer the drift of the essays Gibbon would have written on the "vanity" of the "science of politicks" and on the similarities and differences of the French and English civil wars, but if he ever wrote either of these essays, they have been lost.[37]

Happily, one of the longest entries, that on the "Character and conduct of Brutus," was developed into an essay that still exists. Presumably it was written in this period of his life, although he does not mention it in the *Memoirs*. The manuscript is in the hand of a copyist but has holograph corrections; it was obviously and carefully prepared for publication, presumably in England, because it was written in English.[38] Why, one wonders, did he do nothing with it?

The argument of the essay was that Brutus's character little deserved the praise it has received from history, first because he himself, as a creditor, was as oppressive as Caesar could be, second because he had sinned against gratitude by profiting from Caesar's patronage before he attacked him ("True Patriotism would have instructed him not to cancel but to refuse Obligations . . . from the declared Enemy of Cato and the Liberty of Rome"), and finally because assassination is an unacceptable instrument of social change, not commendable even in the intent unless the motive is absolutely disinterested.[39]

Gibbon's own political views are again evident, and strongly so, in this essay. He described himself an as "Enemy of Tyranny, under every Shape: who will neither be awed by the Frown of Power, nor silenced by the hoarse Voice of popular Applause. The Monarch and the Patriot are alike amenable to the severe but candid Inquisition of Truth."[40] He almost explicitly disavowed allegiance both with high Tories and with Radical Whigs, and friends might have counseled the suppression of an essay that might have been read as insufficiently detached from the affairs of his own time. Gibbon strongly opposed "foreign or domestic slavery" and therefore esteemed the "Patriots, who by a bold and well concerted Enterprize," delivered their countries from such oppression.[41] But there is no evidence of his distrusting, much less opposing, institutions, simply because they could be tyrannically exercised. He had therefore no serious objections to the institutions of monarchy or even dictatorship, unless they were used oppressively. "It was only for usurping the Power of the People that Caesar could deserve the Epithet of Tyrant. He used the power with more Moderation and Ability than the People was capable of exerting; and the Romans already began to experience all the Happiness and Glory compatible with a Monarchical Form of Government."[42] Restoration of a true commonwealth, if possible, nevertheless might have been more desirable, but only a *successful* attempt, or one "the calm Result of consistent and well grounded Virtue . . . tender of the Rights of Mankind," is justifiable.[43] Gibbon suspected that many "high and active Spirits, who deem the Loss of Liberty . . . the worst of misfortunes" were actually objecting to their own "Loss of Power."[44] He did not agree that the end justified the means. He added, moreover, the pragmatic view that an incompetent revolution was worse than none.

Thus this interesting essay is not just an exercise in historical reconstructionism, though it is certainly careful and ingenious as such. It is an inquiry about the nature of good government which assumes that:(1) a good government is one under which power is used for the people's benefit, regardless of who wields the power; (2) bad acts do not produce good governments; (3) incompetence defeats the merits of a political act; (4) the greatest quantity of individual liberty is not an absolute good. Only point three is at all original, but it is interesting to see Gibbon so early ally himself with these positions, and perhaps also interesting that he kept his views to himself.

The other collection from his miscellaneous readings, the "Index Expurgatorious," is, as the title implies, a series of corrections of blunders, large and small, observed in the books he was reading. These tart and entertaining remarks are not fragments, but complete, usually neatly or even epigrammatically expressed, arguments. The prose and the occasions are, however, informal; they resemble the notes to the *Decline and Fall*, but may really be addressed to himself alone.[45] Perhaps their greatest interest today is the range of the authorities cited—most often to be corrected—and the effortless command of the minutiae of Roman chronology, geography, and biography, not just in the period of the Empire, but virtually from the founding of the city. Some of the observations, for example the correction of Muratori in number 13, are obvious fruits of his antiquarian treatises on weights and measures and Italian geography.

Others are more general, for example, "M. de Beaufort (Republique Romaine Tom ii. p. 220) talks & quotes so very idly about the Consulars & Correctors of Italy; as to shew, he had mighty little idea of the Constantinean Scheme."[46] This entry also illustrates the sometimes casual tone of the "Index Expurgatorious." The reader unaware of Gibbon's comic sense[47] can find many surprises in these entries: "Sir William Temple. . . has discovered a fundamental law in the Mamluk Empire; which the Mamluks themselves were totally unacquainted with" or (apropos of Warton's lament that the age when Pericles and Plato might walk in a portico built by Phidias and painted by Appelles, then go to hear Demosthenes or a tragedy of Sophocles, would never return), "It will never return because it never existed. Pericles. . . could enjoy no very great pleasure in the conversation of Plato who was born the same year that he himself died."[48]

The work is by no means entirely frivolous; many of the errors Gibbon regarded as serious, though he chose to treat them in this informal way, for example, the limitations of Buffon and P. H. Mallet as classical scholars, which damaged their otherwise admirable works. Complaints of a different kind were leveled against Addison: "the blind or perhaps artfull Credulity, with which Mr Addison composed his admired little treatise of the Christian Religion" and (on Addison's inference of the truth of orthodox Christianity from the alleged absence of heretic martyrs),

"To connect different degrees of persuasion with different modes of opinion appeared to me highly unphilosophical."[49] Gibbon was equally offended, however, by Voltaire's anti-Christian bigotry; "Tho his objections [to the evidence for a Christian church in China in the Middle Ages] are very contemptible, yet I am still more offended at the haughtiness of his unbelief, than at his unbelief itself."[50] Although it is not clear whether Gibbon's religious sentiments had yet reached their final degree of skepticism, his attitude toward Addison suggests that it was not merely the errors of popery from which he disassociated himself. Yet he remained, throughout his career, capable of recognizing and praising the scholarly merits even of members of Catholic religious orders: "Father Pagi to whom good letters have many obligations" was given praise, even though he "read history like a monk."[51]

Among them, these three English pieces show that Gibbon had read or was reading at least the following between 1765 and 1768 or 1769: Blackstone's *Commentaries,* Mably's *Observations on the History of France,* Pope, Molière, Shakespeare, Huet, Middleton, Warburton, Muratori, La Bruyère, Montesquieu, Corneille, Warton, de Retz, Simler's *De Republica Helvetica,* Guilliman's *De Rebus Helveticus,* Tschudi's *Chronicum Helveticum,* Hume, all Latin authors who refer to Brutus, Dacier's edition of Horace, Wallace's *Numbers of Mankind,* Beaufort, Guichardt, Temple, Maillet's *Description of Egypt,* Voltaire, Pascal, Addison, Cave, Mosheim, Fontenelle, Christopher Smart, Horace Walpole, Buffon, and King Frederick II of Prussia. In this list, the Swiss items were, of course, part of his and Deyverdun's preparation for the Swiss history. Other items were probably designed to prepare for the *Mémoires littéraires* (see below), or for the *Decline and Fall.* Many, however, including the considerable project of reading Buffon (or at least the first eleven volumes of the *Histoire naturelle*) simply testify to Gibbon's wide-ranging intellectual curiosity.

Thus Gibbon not only read and reread the Latin, French, and Italian classics for pleasure, and the Greek ones to improve his command of the language as well as for delight; he not only attempted to keep up with new English publications for the benefit of *Mémoires littéraires;* he also read attentively new French works from the Continent, especially, but not exclusively, those from France itself. Furthermore, this multilingual reading and the English writing discussed so far were not his only activities between the end of the dissertation on weights and measures and the beginning of the Swiss history. He continued to write extensively in French as well. And all this was the produce of only a portion of the year, in a house where his leisure for scholarship was more apparent than real, except for the hours obtained by early rising.

The letters from this period are regrettably few; in the *Memoirs,* he tells us that he spent "the winters" in London, but that elastic term is not further defined. He seems to have been at Beriton until at least the end of October, and in London from January to March or April (though he might have made excursions to Beriton). May was spent at Southhampton with the militia. Where he spent November or December, and whether the summer at home began in June or not, we do not know. Whenever he was away from Beriton, he was "destitute of books" (148) and rich in distractions. In London, he fully engaged himself in the life of society, insofar as it was accessible to him. Though limited by his narrow allowance (and perhaps by his distaste for dancing), he set his sights on the social station proper to a Hampshire gentleman of means, taste, and an acceptable, if not noble, family.

In the first winter, Gibbon had the pleasure of seeing Deyverdun and introducing him to other friends, but in spite of this and of his increased age and experience, he continued to suffer from a feeling of inadequacy and isolation in London. "I hardly know myself as yet in this immense City; & to speak honestly am not as yet very highly entertained," he wrote to his stepmother on January 18, 1766. "I have had some invitations & expect more, but I must acknowledge I sometimes regret the small parties where an acquaintance may pass the evening & sup without form or invitation." In different ways, he had, of course, enjoyed such evenings freely not only in Lausanne but also in Paris and even in Italy. He added, "I have however candor enough to lay these defects rather upon the confined circle of my friends than on the general manners of the Metropolis. Society (no doubt) may be very agreable here, but the avenues to it are fortified with some care and I wish I may be able to muster up that modest assurance which is so necessary to force them."[52] He had already encountered his traveling companion William Guise and his family, and "an old Putney friend," Mary Comarque.[53] Of course, he had visited and frequently dined with his Aunt Kitty, but staying with her (and her fifty Westminster boys) was no longer possible; his lodgings were at "Miss Lake's St James's Place." Besides, his aunt had been unwell and Gibbon himself had suffered an attack of "Rhumatism" in his shoulder.[54]

The Mallets, his former avenue to London acquaintance, were no longer available. David had died in 1765, and Gibbon's opinion of the widow was not high. But "several more of [his] acquaintance" were expected in town soon and might "serve to enliven it. The public diversions are a great ressource, and the Cocoa tree serves now and then to take off an idle hour." As Norton explains, the Cocoa Tree, a Tory club in St. James's Street, was an affiliation inherited from Edward II. She adds that "about this time G[ibbon] joined Boodles, recently formed and. . . [also] in St. James's Street."[55] A clubbable man in spite of his diffidence and mannerisms, Gibbon joined with other travelers he had known in Italy to form a new club, the Roman, which apparently preceded his entrance into Boodles (M 273). The Romans had a "weekly convivial meeting" (there were nineteen members, including Gibbon, so even when some were absent, there were enough for a cheerful gathering).

Boodles was, especially while Gibbon lived in St. James's Street, even more useful as a diversion, or dangerous as a distraction. It provided the "daily ressource of excellent dinners, mixed company and moderate play. I must own, however, with a blush," he added—the passage was prudently suppressed by Lord Sheffield—"that my virtues of temperance and sobriety had not compleatly recovered themselves from the wounds of the militia, that my connections were much less among women, than men; and that these men, though far from contemptible in rank and fortune, were not of the first eminence in the litterary or political World" (139) . In the letter to his stepmother quoted above, Gibbon mentioned his hopes of joining the "School of Vice," that is, White's junior branch, "which notwithstanding the terrors of it's name" (he told her) "is as an agreable and I believe as innocent a Club as any in this Metropolis."[56] These hopes were never realized, and he perforce settled for the "School of Virtue," Boodles. His most famous club, Johnson's Literary Club, had been formed in 1764, but of course Gibbon was not yet considered for membership in it.

These contributions to the "hurry" of London made no amends for his lack of independence, emphasized the narrowness of his income, and prevented his pursuit of his literary interests. Yet he continued to spend a significant portion of each year in London. Probably it was a necessary respite from the pressures of being his father's son in his father's house, and of course he enjoyed certain genuine pleasures there, such as the theater of Garrick and the companionship of his friend Godfrey Clarke, who was "more than an acquaintance" (139) and might have ranked with Deyverdun, Lord Sheffield, and the de Severy family had he not died very early, of smallpox. Gibbon probably enjoyed also the continued hospitality of Lady Hervey, until her death in 1768, and perhaps he met with a certain "society of litterary foreigners" who would become the judges of his Swiss history (141). But the reason for continuing these London visits which he gave to his stepmother, and which was at least part of the truth, was that he thought he was preparing the way for the London life he really desired, one that would be appropriate to his tastes, abilities, and station: "An acquaintance must be formed and I shall not think this winter ill spent if it lays a good foundation for next."[57] Present sacrifice was worthwhile to maintain his role as gentleman of leisure in society; he did not intend to become a monk or hermit, even in the delightful cloister of scholarship.

When May returned, Gibbon had yet another role to play, that of major of the Hampshire militia. His interest in matters military persisted for a long time—indeed, it was apparent in the supplement he planned for the completed *Decline and Fall* in 1790-91.[58] But he regarded the twenty-eight days of active duty with less and less enthusiasm, until in 1770 he resigned. In 1766, he could still write to Holroyd, "I Need not desire you to pay a most minute attention to the Austrian and Prussian discipline. You have been bit by a mad Serjeant as well as myself."[59]

After Southampton and his twenty-ninth birthday, Gibbon returned to Beriton, where he again had the pleasure of welcoming Deyverdun. The work on the Swiss history continued, and, by the end of September, the two had done enough to realize that an ally in Switzerland was necessary, or at least desirable. Gibbon wrote to their common friend Victor de Saussure to request his aid. The letter is not fully preserved, and much of it is devoted to other subjects, especially de Saussure's love life, but Gibbon had much to say about his project and its needs: "I have heard of a manuscript in your vicinity which could be very useful to me. It is at Neufchâtel in the Bibliothèque des Pasteurs . . . and contains a very much esteemed history of the war of Burgundy."[60] Norton points out that Gibbon would have seen a reference to this manuscript in Leu's *Helvetisches Lexicon*, one of the works from which Deyverdun made "large extracts" for Gibbon's use (141).[61] References within this letter make it clear that his and Deyverdun's studies had certainly already included Diebold Schilling's *Beschreibung der Burgundischen Kriegen* (his chronicle of Bern, which was written in the fifteenth century) and probably also at least some of the nineteen volumes of J. J. Lauffer's modern work (1736–39), *Genaue u. Umständliche Beschreibung Helvetischer Geschichte.* Translations from these two works, written in Deyverdun's hand and annotated by Gibbon, still exist and show us how the friends worked together.[62]

Carefully recording his page references, Deyverdun seems to have chosen the extracts without Gibbon's immediate directions and then to have given his manuscript to Gibbon, who read it through, adding comments of his own or from sources he commanded, in this case primarily Philippe de Commines. For example, Deyverdun translated Lauffer's statement that "In 1473 from time to time sparks appeared in the air, preludes of the great conflagration by which they were menaced." Gibbon added a comment:

C[harle]s's negotiation with the Swiss must be placed here, although Lauffer puts it later. It certainly preceded the taking of Hagenbach. One can remark. 1. That Charles sent deputies there only through the mediation of the Comte de Romant and 2. That the Swiss (except those of Berne and Soleure) complained of nothing 3. That those of Lucerne complained that the D[uke] had taken Sigismond under his guard.—It was true, but another instruction of Charles's shows that he had rejected the D. d'Autriche's propositions that he make war on the Swiss.[63]

Gibbon's authority was two references to Philippe de Commines.[64]

The passage is concerned with a portion of Swiss history outside the scope of the part of the book that Gibbon actually wrote, so we cannot see how he moved from this weighing and comparison of the source and authority to his own narrative. We can, however, see that Deyverdun was required to exercise selectivity and, of course, to translate, but that he did not otherwise interpret his material, even by reducing figures of speech to literal statements. Gibbon's contribution, on the other hand, seems inefficient, if he annotated the excerpts by means of one source at a time. Perhaps this expedient was not used long. The archives of Lausanne contain other fragments of Lauffer with parallel passages from Tschudi inserted on facing pages. But this laborious practice was abandoned and was not used in Deyverdun's extracts from Leu and Schilling.[65]

Gibbon elaborately explained to de Saussure how to decide whether a transcript of, or extracts from, the Neufchâtel manuscript would be useful. He went on to list several other desiderata: plans of the battles, detailed maps of the area, copies of the military and ecclesiastical codes, and several printed books, including Barnaud's *Mémoires . . . des troubles arrives . . . à l'occasion du consensus,* which Gibbon had read as long ago as 1755, but of which he apparently owned no copy. After proposing "these commissions . . . with so little modesty or pity," Gibbon begged his friend not to execute them unless he could do so without difficulty: "With the exception of the Neufchâtel manuscript, there is nothing in all I have pointed out to you which is of the first necessity. There are even some items that are only the fruit of an avid curiosity, which seeks to extend itself beyond its object."[66] It is clear that Gibbon was deeply engrossed in the Swiss project, but there is evidence of his digressing not only to Swiss materials far outside the scheme of his work but also to other historical projects.

The earliest of these is his essay "Du Gouvernement féodal," inspired by reading Gabriel Bonnet de Mably's *Observations sur l'histoire de France* (1765). As has several times been noted, Lord Sheffield's guess that this piece was composed between 1758 and 1763 cannot be correct. The evidence of both hand and content suggests a date in the 1765–70 period, probably before 1767.[67] This essay, ignored by Gibbon himself and slighted by most of his readers, is short but complete and seems to deserve fuller study, if for no other reason than that it contains Gibbon's first recorded coupling of the themes of decline and fall: "I glimpse a new scope more vast and useful still, the decadence of this [feudal] system, and those that were elevated on its ruins, its rapid and terrible fall in Italy, its slow and tranquil sinking in England and in France, and the solidity that it achieved in Germany."[68] In contrast to other musings inspired by Montesquieu's combination of "Grandeur et Decadence," this essay distinguished the decline from the fall, and distinguished that subject from the increasing and flourishing portion of the system's history.

In the essay itself, however, Gibbon "glimpsed" this subject, but that was all. He contented himself with recalling a few policies of the French kings, from Louis le Gros to Charles VII, which opposed the riches of commerce to those of the land, and replaced the feudal militia with regular troops. In an admirable exception to the neglect of this small work, Michel Baridon shows how Gibbon combined the structure of Mably's account with observations from Montesquieu; he adds: "It should be emphasized . . . that in distinction from his illustrious predecessors, the young historian seeks to express his ideas without ever allowing himself the violence of tone that until then had marked the debate on the origin of the feudal institutions."[69] Giarrizzo is more general in his discussion of Gibbon's relation to his predecessors (among whom he counts Hume and William Robertson) and credits Gibbon with here discovering his new theme of decline and fall.[70] Yet even Baridon and Giarrizzo fail to discuss this essay's peculiar perspective on Montesquieu's paradox that republics permit civilization, which in turn undermines their primitive virtue by divorcing the cultivated citizen from his arms. Giarrizzo notes the importance of Gibbon's remark that, from the fifth to the eighth centuries, "the barbarians (I speak especially of the Franks) had become more corrupt without being more civilized." They had lost their "warrior humor" without gaining a compensatory improvement in their civil government.[71] Baridon stresses that neither the concept of the enslavement of the people nor the eloquent tone of Gibbon's discussion "could come from the *Esprit des lois*."[72] But neither writer suggests that Gibbon was already, at least as much as in the *Decline and Fall*, "destroying the myth . . . by whose means feudal society had so often been equated with the primitive republic of warrior free-holders,"[73] and he did so while standing respectfully in the presence of Montesquieu.

The historian of ideas might therefore do well to examine this essay, not for its sources in other writers, but for its representation of the movement of Gibbon's mind from the admiring distrust of systems of the *Essai* to the "sociologist of Empire," who escapes from the paradoxes of theory by a firm attachment to material reality.[74] Peter Brown has noted that in Gibbon's introduction to this essay, he described his saving pragmatism when he "declared his methods: 'Je combine l'experience avec le raisonnement. J'ouvre les codes de ces peuples. . . . J'ouvre leurs annales. . . . Enfin j'aperçois l'aurore de la nouvelle institution.'" ("I combine experience with reason. I open the codes of these people. . . . I open their annals. . . . Finally I perceive the dawn of the new institution.")[75] If this intellectual development occurs only in Gibbon, it is at least of biographical interest, but it might well suggest a means of integrating the achievements of the artists and scientists of the age with the speculations of their philosophical contemporaries.

On the verso of the last page of this medieval excursion, Gibbon began yet another historical essay, one that he considered worthy, in part, of preparation for publication, though he never published it. It is the "Mémoire sur la Monarchie des Medes," which was begun, according to its subtitle, "to serve as a supplement to the dissertations of MM. Fréret and de Bougainville," and "supplement" is an apt though vague label for the first sixty-six of its ninety-four pages.[76] It was, however, the last portion, "an Essay on the Cyropædia which in my own judgement is not unhappily laboured" (148) that, either at the time or later, he considered publishing. He obviously thought of this study as an indulgence: "After a certain age the new publications of merit are the sole food of the many: and the most austere student," he commented apologetically, "will be often tempted to break the line for the sake of indulging his curiosity and of providing the topics of fashionable currency" (148). He sounds as if he had stopped to write a sensational novel!

So lengthy an essay as this has not been ignored by Gibbon's readers, but Lord Sheffield's misdating—he thought it was written between 1758 and 1763—has led to confusion about its place in his development, or encouraged its summary dismissal. Gibbon himself was responsible for some of the confusion. Few or none of his readers have recognized his reference to this essay in the *Memoirs*, and his discussion of his two major historical projects prior to the *Decline and Fall*, the Florentine and Swiss histories, leaves no apparent place for this "memoir," which is actually longer than the work done on either of those subjects. Perhaps it is overlooked because the memoir is really two nearly distinct essays; in any event, the first section did not aspire to the dignity of independent work. Joseph Swain mentions that "Sur la Monarchie des Medes" includes "various reasons for the decline and fall of the Median Empire" and "is important for us as his first attempt to write formal history," but he does not discuss it further.[77] The fullest discussion, Baridon's, is handicapped by the assumption that the memoir was written before the Italian journey. In the text itself, Gibbon made clearer than any of his critics the scope and purpose of this study as he first conceived it. He began very much in the spirit and language of his *Essai*, "nearer," as Baridon observes, "to the French *philosophes* than he had ever been."[78] According to Gibbon, Nicholas Fréret, as erudite as Sir John Marsham and J. J. Scaliger, replaced their limited views, their partial and defective hypotheses and conjectures, with "a spirit of system, of criticism, and of philosophy. . . . From this work he saw emerging a quantity of light that illuminates without dazzling us. I shall present his system." Despite this enthusiasm, Gibbon added immediately, with his own characteristic and significant reservation, "In these sorts of study we ought to seek truth and be content with probability."[79]

After the enumeration of the chronological data, which, as Fréret had shown, must be reconciled to determine the era of the Medes, Gibbon states, "We have reached the dawn, but this dawn is covered with clouds. M. Fréret has not tried to dispel them. But . . . M. de Bougainville . . . wished to complete this great work." Bougainville converted the conjecture that the Median empires of Ctesias and Herodotus were different, Gibbon thought, into a "reasoned system," but he never had an opportunity to write a second memoir, in which he had proposed to "develop the origin, connections, and revolutions of the two dynasties, and . . . to show that this distinction [between the two] would give ancient history an accord and a harmony that would otherwise be sought in vain."[80] Gibbon intended to carry out this project for him. If he had done only that, the content of the essay would, of course, be of little interest, though its existence would be worthy of notice. But in addition to its superseded account of the Medes, Gibbon's memoir contains a number of observations on the practice of historical writing and historical judgment, which retain their interest and even their value.

Gibbon first discussed "the degree of faith" owed to Ctesias: "It can be established in a few words. Ctesias used excellent materials rather badly."[81] The *Oxford Classical Dictionary* dismisses Ctesias as "far from trustworthy," though it confirms that he held the position at court that was Gibbon's reason for saying that Ctesias had excellent materials available to him. Of course, modern historians would not attempt to discover Median history from Greek literary sources alone; thus Gibbon's subsequent discussion of how to separate wheat from chaff in the fragments of Ctesias preserved in the extracts of much later writers is not of interest in its results. But his method is interesting. First, he classifies the various kinds of material one may find in a single source; he remarks that "a critic . . . could separate the fabric of these accounts," and distinguish six types of statement: "truly historical references" (drawn from annals), "fabulous traditions," the historian's "interpretations of his materials," "digressions . . . linked with his principal subject [by a] connection existing in the mind of the historian [and not] fundamentally in the material," "fictions," and copyists' errors.[82] This set of distinctions served Gibbon in his judgment of his sources and of his own task throughout his career, although they were altered and refined, of course, to meet various occasions.

Gibbon argued, apropos of the second point, that the reader could detach such fables "without difficulty from the body of the history, and Constantine's cross does not make one reject the defeat of Maxentius." He would, of course, discover that this distinction was not always so effortless as he here assumed, but at least he did not propose to reject out of hand all testimony that had an accretion of fable. He also distinguished between fables and fictions in an interesting way. The former are pious and patriotic additions to a historical circumstance, useful to its mythic function in a people's tradition; the latter arise from the historian's personal ambition to forsake his proper sphere for that of "orator and even poet." Gibbon's example made it clear that he was talking not of merely formal or narrative temptations, such as interpolated speeches, but of temptations to improve the facts in the direction of instruction. How poetically just, for example, that the king of Assyria should send aid to Troy, and how unhistorical. These fictions, then, are what we may think of as errors of bias. In Gibbon's terms, the historian's "interpretations" are his historiographical methods, by which he represents as factual the material that he infers by combining genuinely factual material into arguments. Gibbon pointed out that even when the historian was conscientious and accurate in reporting his data, he might be misled by errors in geography, chronology, identification of proper names, or even weights and measures; and that truth "authorizes us to distinguish between the particular facts that he reports, and the . . . system . . . by which he draws them together."[83]

Gibbon's survey of the Assyrian realm, with his account of the fall of Sardanapalus, is a narrative of the traditions preserved by historians, rather than history proper, but it is the locus of his few reflections on doomed empires in this work and illustrates the beginnings of his own characteristic narrative manner, for example, in the combination of "philosophic" generalization—"Arbaces had employed in vain all the resources of politics; but those of superstition are inexhaustible"— with dramatic scenes and psychological analysis of the actors; of specific, even (in the notes) minute, concrete details with swift, sweeping chronological progression.[84]

In Arbaces, Gibbon even had a hero to his mind, one whose moderation spared the conquered and rewarded his allies with their promised liberty. "But it is well to establish the precise sense of a word [liberty] always vague in itself, and rather foreign to the language of the Orientals," added Gibbon, sounding very like the historian of the _Decline and Fall_; and he proceeded to enumerate and explain the privileges indicated by "liberty" under Arbaces.[85]

A king list from 898-790 B.C. afforded Gibbon few opportunities, but it was perhaps relatively ingenious to turn for light to the modern Orientalist d'Herbelot (Gibbon's boyhood favorite), specifically to his report of Persian classical literature. Gibbon was, however, very much discontented with what he found in the Persian writings: "no geography, no chronology, [but] paladins, genies, fairies, and monsters." Exactly what had attracted him to these studies as a child. Now, however, he wished to reduce the romantic domain in which he had once sought refuge to "some useful truths": "General events engrave themselves in human memory; the idea of great establishments passes to posterity, and the limited and sterile imagination of this singular creature, who can endure neither truth nor falsehood, alters more facts than it invents."[86]

Many other acute, or at least characteristic, observations on aspects of the historian's task appear in these pages, as Gibbon moved with diminishing degrees of probability (as he explained in a note) through the centuries until he reached the relatively secure ground of Cyrus's career. Low has noted how an approving description of Herodotus, who saw great objects with "sang froid" and painted them warmly, foreshadowed Gibbon's own aim and achievement.[87] A reference to Newton (in his capacity as chronologer, not scientist), "who had studied the prophets only too well," preceded by the tongue-in-cheek statement that a Christian owes a blind respect to the holy books, which is coupled with the straightforward statement that even "the enlightened but prophane critic" must prefer their testimony in eastern matters to that of the Greeks, foreshadows Gibbon's tone in religious history, including his capacity to make skillful use of the Christian records despite his contempt for their authors.[88]

In passing, Gibbon's understanding of political theory was also revealed, for example, in his quip about "this solemn compact which the philosophers presume universal . . . but which the historian finds only in the election of Deioces," or in his doubt that Media returned to a state of original anarchy following its revolt against the Assyrians: "a vast country . . . could never return to the state of nature after having for more than five centuries borne the yoke of laws. Revolutions change the political contract but they have never broken the bonds of the social contract. The first is founded only on fear or prejudice. The habits and interests of all assure the eternal duration of the second."[89] Even these first sixty-odd pages sufficiently justify Low's hint, oddly neglected by many Gibbonians, that this "very remarkable incursion into Oriental history . . . shows how deeply [Gibbon] had meditated on both the style and method of historical composition."[90]

The most interesting section, however, as Gibbon himself correctly judged, was the discussion of Cyrus and the *Cyropaedia*. Among other things, this essay contains the sequel to Gibbon's views on the "philosophic historian" he had so lauded in the *Essai*.

> When it is a question of a history whose variations permit some liberty to criticism and even to conjecture; the philosophic historian will choose, among the contested facts, those that best accord with his principles . . . and the logic of the heart will only too often prevail over that of the mind. When chronology proscribed a moral trait, Plutarch despised chronology, and Voltaire is not very particular about his authorities when it is a matter of painting the artifices of priests, the oddities of superstition, and the contradictions of the human spirit. There were several accounts of Cyrus's life; the one most consistent with Xenophon's views no doubt appeared the most probable to him.[91]

This position, which is both aware of a characteristic source of error in historians who were more than chroniclers and tolerant of, or at least polite about, the human weakness that produced such errors, marks

Gibbon's mature historical thought. In a comment easily applicable to his own work, he noted, "Every man of genius who writes history, expresses in it, perhaps without perceiving it, the character of his spirit."[92]

The specific criticism of the *Cyropaedia* is revelatory not so much of historical acumen as of Gibbon's assumptions about genres of historical writing and about human nature. He did not consider the *Cyropaedia* a philosophical allegory or romance, because it included many details of historical import that, in Gibbon's view, no writer of romance would have thought of, for example, the observation that the terms of a particular treaty were still in force. Further, Cyrus could not be an allegory of justice, because his character was humanly flawed: he behaved well, but only because he reasoned well, and "this reason had nothing in common with that of Marcus Aurelius, which would consult the will of the gods, the nature of man, and the order of the universe, and which preferred virtue: Cyrus's reason was only the knowledge of his own interests."[93] Gibbon granted that Xenophon's Cyrus had many virtues, but denied that he had the perfection to be expected in a figure in an allegory; nothing, in Gibbon's view, could make amends for Cyrus's "cold character."[94]

The composition of this lengthy essay may have taken some time and may not have preceded even in part the composition of the Swiss history, but whether the essay was written early or late in the period 1765–70, it is certainly further evidence that both Gibbon and his biographers underestimated the value of his work in this period of his life. Each fruitful summer and autumn gave way, however, in November or December or January, to the demands and pleasures of the London life to which an English gentleman was born. Although greedy posterity may deplore the time wasted in these interludes of distraction, such distractions may have been a necessary relief not only to the strain and restrictions of the family circle but also to the formidable demands of the scholarly pace Gibbon set for himself.

January 1767, however, was no relief. Instead, it began a series of difficulties for him which took away his pleasure in London and required his presence in Beriton. As a result, when he wrote to his friend Holroyd in April, Gibbon was looking forward to the twenty-eight days of militia training in Southampton with more than usually mixed emotions. After congratulating Holroyd on his recent marriage, he explained that he had been confined at Beriton ever since Christmas by a succession of "melancholy occupations." First his stepmother's brother had died.

> We were scarce recovered from the confusion . . . when my father was taken dangerously ill & with some intervalls has continued so ever since. I can assure you, my dear Holroyd that the same event appears in a very different light when the danger is serious & immediate or when in the gayety of a tavern dinner we affect an insensibility which would do us no great honor, were it real.[95]

This passage reveals precisely the ambivalence of Gibbon's feelings toward his father. On the one hand, he could not avoid knowing how much easier his own life would be if his feckless father were dead; on the other hand, he felt, somewhat to his own surprise, not only guilt about such anticipation but also pain in the sight of his father's helplessness, and at the prospect of so drastic a change in his own situation. He felt no need of pretense with Holroyd; thus his remarking on this feeling is reliable evidence both that he really felt the distress he mentioned and that the feelings were sufficiently unexpected to him to require remark. The sincerity of the whole letter is patent and easily distinguishable from *pro forma* expressions in other letters of a less intimate or more interested character.

As he immediately went on to say, moreover, the somber mood of this letter of congratulations (after the complicated pleasantries of the beginning, with their Rasselas-like conclusion—"celibacy is exposed to fewer miseries; [but] marriage can alone promise real happiness") had another cause:

> My father is now much better; but I have since been assailed even by a severer stroke; the loss of a friend [John Butler Harrison]. You remember perhaps an Officer of our Militia, whom I sometimes used to compare to yourself. . . . You will excuse my having said so much of a man you had not the least knowledge of; but my mind is just now so very full of him [he had died two-and-a-half weeks earlier] that I cannot easily talk or even think of any thing else.[96]

The prospect of returning to the milita life he had shared with his lost friend was a source of particular "uneasiness." These strong feelings were called forth, it should be remembered, not by the death of one of his most prized and intimate friends, but by the loss of the least uncongenial of his militia associates. Nor was this his first intimation of mortality in the form of the death of a contemporary. However contained Gibbon's emotional life with respect to the dangerous channels of sexual love, or the blocked ones of parental and filial attachment, it flowed fully and warmly in the outlet of friendship. His mind was still full of his lost friend in the only record of that stay in Southampton in 1767, a letter to his stepmother, expressing his pleasure in the news of his father's good health and reporting his friend's widow's safe delivery of a son. The letter ends cheerfully, though with some unintended pathos, "Southampton. May the 8th 1767. My birth-day. May I have many happy ones. Amen."[97]

In the summer of 1767, his intellectual labors took a new and less rigorous, less isolated direction. Not only were the preparatory studies for the first volume of the Swiss history near completion, but he and Deyverdun had another joint project under way. This one, they confidently expected, could supply their want of fortune, as well as their desire for occupation. It was the production of a literary review, similar to Maty's earlier successful *Journal Britannique*. The only post their combined efforts had secured for Deyverdun was a clerkship in the office of the secretary of state. Appointed a month (March 4, 1767) after the great David Hume became undersecretary in the same office, Deyverdun was known to Hume because Deyverdun had involved himself in the quarrel between Rousseau and Hume during the previous winter. But as Low points out, Stanier Porten, Gibbon's uncle, was the probable source of Deyverdun's appointment.[98] It gave Deyverdun welcome employment; however, as Gibbon wrote to G. L. Scott, that "dull mechanic labour" left him both time and mental energy for another task.[99] Thus the proposed journal, the *Mémoires littéraires de la Grand Bretagne.*

Their idea was to begin with the "English Litterature of the year 67" (as usual, by "literature" Gibbon meant anything in words, not just belles-lettres); they would continue the journal at quarterly intervals, unless the public demand encouraged expansion to a monthly: "The Journal will as usual give an account of the best books of every kind which come out during each period; with a short mention of the rest." Novelties would include "Curious anecdotes . . . which will entertain foreigners," "The English Theatre," "The State & progress of the polite Arts," "Translation from English poets," "& here & there a good extract from a German writer."[100] The journal would be published in French and was intended primarily for a Continental audience.

If, like Maty, Gibbon and Deyverdun had had a Continental publisher, or even an English publisher who promoted his productions abroad, they might have had a chance of success.[101] Recruiting G. L. Scott to review works on natural science, they planned a pleasantly varied and useful volume; "Various stomachs, we think, require various food. Some can support nothing but novels, others can digest even divinity."[102] As Gibbon wrote this letter (October 19, 1767), the plan was complete, but the execution was only "in great forwardness"; the first volume did not appear until April of the following year.

Instead, the climactic literary achievement for Gibbon in 1767 was undoubtedly the completion of the first book of his proposed history of Swiss liberty. That achievement was capped by a kind letter from Hume, who "exhort[ed]" Gibbon to carry on with it, but his hopes for the work were then dashed by the "free strictures and unfavourable sentence" of the "litterary society of foreigners" to whom he anonymously submitted it for judgment.[103]

The work itself has received more attention than any other posthumously published work of Gibbon, thanks not only to his own emphasis on it but also, since 1948, to the admirable if not altogether sympathetic study of it made by H. S. Offler.[104] Gibbon's own condemnation of his Swiss history as superficial, "an abridgement rather than a history, a declamation rather than an abridgement" (M408), is softened by this modern critic, who also rejects, however, hopeful claims that its skepticism about the William Tell myth or its supposition of a "directing *elite* in early Swiss history" demonstrates Gibbon's capacity for shrewd historical criticism: "We may feel that Gibbon got a hit somewhere on the target by a lucky shot in the dark."[105] But Offler proves that Gibbon's work was not superficial, if by "superficial" we imply either that it was a total waste of time or that his preparatory labors were either slight or trivial. Gibbon failed, not merely because he wrote in the wrong language, not merely because much of Switzerland was unknown or uninviting to him, but because he had "deficient materials, a dubious guide [Tschudi, not Deyverdun], an [even today] impossible goal." Yet

> in writing the Swiss History Gibbon was learning an essential part of his trade: how to sweat at the sheer collar work of his profession. . . . Slight and superficial it may have been by Gibbon's mature standards— but the effort involved had a part in making those standards—and by ordinary standards [of the time] the Swiss History was a very learned work.

Gibbon "owned almost every book of consequence which had been published on Swiss history" and, as we have seen, labored to acquire even manuscript materials. Offler adds that Gibbon had mastered these authorities, as "we can be sure by taking a little of the pains which Porson took in a larger matter," that is, by comparing Gibbon's product with its sources.[106]

After doing so, Offler concludes that Gibbon's effort failed

> because the authorities were not good enough. . . . But within the eighteenth century convention of historiography which was tied to the printed book they were all that was available, and Gibbon conscientiously exhausted them. If the result was thin, it was not because Gibbon had disregarded any opportunity of making it richer—short of anticipating the nineteenth century and exploring the archives.[107]

To Offler's appreciation of the Swiss history might be added recognition of many incidental glimpses of Gibbon's mind and feelings at the time, valuable to those interested in his development. In the second chapter, which is a pure narrative not yet supported with references to authorities, such observations constitute almost the only notes that Gibbon produced at the same time as the main body of his text.[108] The two chapters illustrate two characteristic stages of Gibbon's historical compositions. As he tells us in the *Memoirs* (159), he first planned his sentences and paragraphs in his head and then committed the polished phrases to paper. Occasionally a reflection had to be relegated to a note, and as he wrote, he kept his place (as it were) by running dates in the margin. But it was only on revising his work that he buttressed it with references to his authorities, antiquarian analyses, and criticism of his sources. The two stages exist side by side in this case, because the work was prepared for "publication" only in part and then abandoned, unfinished.

Offler credits Gibbon with the recognition that his authorities were not strong enough to warrant continuation of the history.[109] This theory is perhaps too generous, for Gibbon's own accounts stress other motives: his chagrin at the verdict of the foreigners and his failure to find, in French, an adequate historical style (141-42). Certainly Gibbon did recognize eventually the weakness of his data, the need for better materials than he could obtain (see, for example, M 408). But in 1767, the other influences were at least equally strong in his decision to abandon the Swiss history.

The problem of style for Gibbon was not merely a matter of successful or unsuccessful decoration, but of fulfilling or failing to fulfill the demands of genre. "I was conscious myself, that my style, above prose and below poetry, degenerated into a verbose and turgid declamation" (142), yet, as he had just noted in dealing with Xenophon, if one aspired to write history, instead of learned dissertations or patriotic fiction, one's expression" must not be "feeble." Gibbon's criticism of Xenophon, that he "describes the passions more than he paints them, and paints them more than he feels them," shows what he expected of a historical work that was "a work of taste."[110] The triple rewriting of the first chapter of the *Decline and Fall,* the first draft of which he could usually send directly to the printer, demonstrates similarly that Gibbon did not think that he had portrayed history accurately until he had found the proper language for it.

His account of his only "publication" of the Swiss history is interesting:

> . . . the first book, was read the following winter in a litterary society of foreigners in London: and as the author was unknown, I listened without observation, to the free strictures and unfavourable sentence of my judges. The momentary sensation was painful; but their condemnation was ratified by my cooler thoughts; I delivered my imperfect sheets to the flames. (141-42)

"The momentary sensation was painful" must be a considerable understatement. We do not know whether he listened "without observation" by playing the role of a disinterested hearer or by sitting behind a door or screen; we do not know how the manuscript was introduced to the group, or by whom. We cannot guess what tone their strictures were delivered in, and whether they expressed merely objections or contempt, whether they condemned the substance, the style, or both. But that he put the work out of his mind so thoroughly as to think the manuscript literally destroyed is surely suggestive, especially because the group's objections nullified, in his opinion, Hume's letter of praise. Some of Gibbon's modern detractors have tried to see some ulterior motive in his misstatement here, but it is impossible to imagine any advantage for Gibbon in deliberate misrepresentation of the fate of this, as distinct from others among his immature works. Instead, his trick of memory, if it has any significance, is likely to have the usual defensive value, protecting his conscious mind from discomfort it preferred not to re-experience. It was probably a relief, perhaps a great relief, to take on instead the safe and congenial role of critic, in the further shelter, as we shall see, of anonymity.

CHAPTER 13

Critical
Observations

THREE MORE YEARS of Gibbon's state of tutelage were yet to pass. Despite his increasing years and his father's relative good will, he could not be independent until his father's death. In the interval, he "twice gave [his] thoughts, without giving [his] name, to the public" (M 303). "Edward Gibbon" was not yet *his* name.

There were, of course, other reasons for not giving his name to the first of these works, the *Mémoires littéraires*. In this project he intended to subordinate himself to Deyverdun, as Deyverdun had subordinated himself to Gibbon in the Swiss history. In later years, Gibbon acknowledged only two particular contributions to the *Mémoires littéraires*: the review of Lord Lyttelton's history of Henry II, and that of Horace Walpole's *Historic Doubts on the Life and Reign of King Richard the Third*. Because Walpole was still alive when Gibbon wrote his *Memoirs*, Gibbon did not state his authorship of the negative review of his friend's book; we can only infer his acknowledgment of it from Lord Sheffield's flat statement that the essay was Gibbon's.

Gibbonians have variously speculated on Gibbon's further contributions to these volumes.[1] The task is undoubtedly complicated by instances of genuine collaboration when "in [their] social labours [Gibbon and Deyverdun] composed and corrected by turns" (143), and also by their community of interests and of books: book orders and books later owned by Gibbon might have been acquired for the use of either reviewer, for Deyverdun's financial resources were more limited than Gibbon's. However, one clue to their respective contributions seems to have been neglected: Gibbon's habit of framing his discourses within statements of principle or general perspectives and conclusions, a habit not shared by Deyverdun in the work known to be certainly his. While such evidence is hardly conclusive, it can contribute something to our distinguishing among the works primarily Gibbon's, those primarily Deyverdun's, and those either collaborative or indistinguishably the produce of both.

All readers agree that Gibbon's hand is much more apparent in volume one of the *Mémoires littéraires* than in volume two. In addition to the acknowledged review of Lyttelton (in any case, patently Gibbonian even in French), most readers consider Gibbon the probable reviewer of Nathaniel Lardner's *Jewish and Heathen Testimonies,* despite its incorporation into the article on "theology," which they planned to trust to an assistant,[2] and of Adam Ferguson's *History of Civil Society.* If they had a theological ally,[3] it nevertheless seems probable that it was Gibbon who supplied a reference in Scaliger that Lardner could not find,[4] and who commented on Gibbon's once and future subject, Julian the Apostate.[5]

The Julian section begins with a characteristically Gibbonian topic statement, framing and judging the subject as it was introduced: "The history and character of the Emperor Julian form one of the most interesting topics of Ecclesiastical Antiquity. Lardner devotes to this singular Prince a very extensive article, which does honor to his knowledge and to his moderation. In the vices of the Apostate and the follies of the man, he does not forget the great qualities of the Warrior, the Writer, and the Emperor."[6] In Deyverdun's articles, he seems to have favored a chronological rather than an analytical presentation; he tended to begin his essays with a simple description of the first chapters or scenes of the work in hand. Of course, the only piece definitely attributed to Deyverdun by Gibbon in this first volume was the *New Bath Guide,* which was not reviewed but translated (143). But the article on the theater was virtually ascribed to his friend by Gibbon—"few of our country men could enjoy the Theatre of Shakespeare and Garrick with more exquisite feeling, and discernment" (142), and this article contains a remark about the writer's learning to read English as a second language, which is either evidence that the author was Deyverdun, or a pointlessly elaborate subterfuge. Other articles can be attributed to him by similar arguments.

In the Lardner review, however, the magisterial beginning, the subject matter, the style, and Gibbon's known familiarity with the work are not the only signs of his authorship. Perhaps the most significant signs are the attitudes and arguments expressed. Several of them deserve to be better known, for example, the argument that Julian's not denying Christian miracles would be stronger evidence of their truth if it were not also the case that the Fathers had testified similarly to the truth of the pagan oracles and miracles: "Omens, magic, the existence and power of evil Demons, were doctrines common to the two parties," or (on Jerome's, Prudentius's, and Orosius's failures to discuss the "miraculous" prevention of the rebuilding of the Temple of Jerusalem): Lardner "could have added that in the matter of miracles, the silence of three theologians of a superstitious age is much less natural than the testimony of twenty of their contemporaries."[7]

More unexpected but after all very characteristic of Gibbon's paradoxically fair-minded prejudice, is the observation, "One has often done these Writers [certain post-Christian pagans] the honor of believing them Philosophers. Alas, they were far from it. Incredulous about Christianity, they were superstitious about everything else."[8] Gibbon's authorship of this review has been doubted, but the weight of the evidence is surely that it is at least in large part his.

Gibbon's authorship of the Ferguson review is usually assumed, largely on the basis of the subject. But if he contributed to it, it seems unlikely to be wholly his. The rhetoric leans heavily upon the rhetorical question, characteristic of Gibbon's style neither in English nor in French,[9] but part of Deyverdun's livelier and more familiar manner; and the attacks on Rousseau are similar not only in content but also in manner to Deyverdun's earlier objections to "Jean-Jacques."[10] On the other hand, such a sentence as "One does not see in it that spirit of system, in which the imagination leads us from chimera to chimera; all is built on facts and supported by reasons, almost always just," could easily be Gibbon's. Two sentences later, however, the review concludes in Deyverdun's manner: "And have you not yet seen enough of these colored Globes, toys of a childish imagination, which a breath of reason can cause to vanish?"[11] It may therefore be wiser to consider this review a collaboration than to attribute its style and sentiments to Gibbon alone.

Similarly, the review of the *Memoirs of Miss Sidney Biddulph* has been assumed to be by the frivolous, novel-translating Deyverdun.[12] But the essay begins with an overview of English fiction very much in Gibbon's manner, which expresses sentiments similar to his on the subject of Fielding and Richardson. Of course, these sentiments might have been shared or admitted by Deyverdun, but it seems probable that Gibbon's views, if not his language, are represented in this review. The most striking instance is the objection not merely to the insertion of digressive matter—anyone might condemn Fielding's "Man of the Hill" narrative—but to the interruption of an action with a narration of its antecedents, the objection Gibbon had dared to bring against the "law" that epics must begin *in medias res*.[13] According to the reviewer or reviewers of *Miss Sidney Biddulph,* "The narration is here awkwardly interrupted by the Episode of a girl seduced by Audly. . . . It is high time that Authors renounce these Episodes, which disfigure the best novels. He who thinks he needs one to revive the reader's curiosity by suspending it, is self-condemned to throw his work into the fire."[14] The principle is definitely Gibbon's; the expression is probably Deyverdun's. How Gibbon reconciled this principle with his delight in Spenser and Ariosto, I do not know. But he did not extend the same tolerance to the novel.

The brief, "over-smart"[15] notices of relatively unimportant works seem also the products of both writers. Of a worthless novel, one says, "This novel lacks only interest, probability, and style."[16] Either Gibbon

or Deyverdun might have written that one. But on a translation of Vega-
tius's *Military Institutions* by one Lieutenant John Clarke, it is surely the
major in the Hampshire Grenadiers who commented, "Let us praise this
soldier for having so well employed the moments that are lost by most
Officers."[17] The most interesting comments in the brief notices are an appreciation of Stubbs's splendid *Anatomy of the Horse* and the following
notice of book nine of *Tristram Shandy* (to which full justice would be
done in the reviewers' second volume): "The wits compare the Author to
Cervantes, to Rabelais, or with perhaps yet more reason, to Harlequin."[18]

If we assume that they carried out their plan to obtain a theological
assistant, who contributed the reviews of the theological section (except
Lardner) and of the *Confessional,* we thus may assign one each of the first
six items in the first volume of the *Mémoires littéraires* to each of the
collaborators, two to their combined efforts, part of another (the Lardner review) to Gibbon, and one and a half to the assistant. The seventh
item, "Transactions Philosophiques," and its supplement, the review of
John Harrison's *Montre Marine,* were probably contributed by their
science specialist, G. L. Scott, according to Gibbon's request. The final
department, "Nouvelles Littéraires," the short notices, was probably a
joint effort. It is not surprising, then, that the eighth article and the
departments preceding the final one seem to be largely Deyverdun's.
His departments were "Spectacles," "Beaux Arts," and "Moeurs" (customs or manners); his article was a review of a work on education, *Le
Gouverneur,* which waxes eloquent on the subject of the virtues of travel
and the importance of the proper selection of a traveling tutor.[19] A useful
but not infallible guide to attribution is that Deyverdun seems to have
kept—at least in print—a running tally of the pages being reviewed in the
margins of his (and the collaborative) contributions; Gibbon, who was
writing, as it were, review articles rather than page-by-page accounts, did
not. Thus marginal page references appear for the *Bath Guide,* for *Le
Gouverneur,* for the *Memoirs of Miss Sidney Biddulph,* and for the Ferguson review—where each comment by the reviewer is labeled in the
margin "R. de J.," that is, "remark of the journalist"—but do not appear
in the margins of the Lardner or Lyttelton reviews.

The Lyttelton review is perhaps the most neglected of the works of
Gibbon published in his lifetime. It was not reprinted by Lord Sheffield,
and, as a mere review, may seem to Gibbonians of no independent value,
not worth the effort necessary to obtain access to the fairly rare volumes.[20] It is, however, yet another concealed but valuable source of Gibbon's historiographical views. Is it not the author of the Swiss history who
begins the review of Lord Lyttelton's book with the generalization (sadly
inapplicable to the writer of the *Decline and Fall*), "It is pleasant for a
historian to be able to begin his course with a reference glorious to the
nation whose annals he has undertaken to traverse"?[21] Gibbon also

commented here on the continued English tradition of "great men" who were also men of letters, a tradition he was, of course, interested in belonging to.

He suggests that Lord Lyttelton's indefatigable pen might exhaust his readers, pointing out that three volumes had dealt with only sixteen years of Henry II's thirty-five-year reign, and "Our curiosity about facts grows weaker as they are more remote from our time, and it inspires only a rather feeble interest in the minute details of the twelfth century."[22] This sentiment suggests a temporary detour in Gibbon's view of history, one consistent with the pure narrative of his Swiss history, but belied by his later practice. Or perhaps this principle led him, not to dismiss minute facts, but to see his responsibility for giving them significance (as opposed to relying on his readers' curiosity). His conduct in the review supports a compromise interpretation: it reveals a taste for the grandeur of generalities even when unsupported by the concrete details that, in his later work, typically buttress his abstract or summary statements. But the review also indicates pleasure in many "facts" when they are presented as, or interpretable as, more than interesting curiosities. For an example of the first tendency, there is his description of William the Conqueror, who "for twenty years governed the Normans by esteem and the English by terror, and history, which cites so many crimes against him, reproaches him with only one weakness; his unbridled passion for hunting."[23] Or "The fashion in which Lord L. describes this civil war does honor to his heart and to his spirit. He expresses himself as a man and as an Englishman, attached to his Kings, but still more attached to liberty, of which they are only the prime ministers."[24] While such pronouncements sound like those of "le grand Gibbon" of the *Decline and Fall,* he did not accompany them with the precise and concrete illustrations and evidence so characteristic of his mature writing, and we do not yet see his characteristic use of metonymy, which in later work bridges the distance between abstract and concrete statement.

On the other hand, the lengthy account of Henry's encounter with Thomas à Beckett is interlaced with precise and vivid details; in it, Gibbon several times noted inaccuracies in dates or statistics.[25] Beckett was apparently an object of aversion to both historian and reviewer. "The fanaticism that this skillful Politician had long inspired in others had finally seized on him, & the Cheat [*Fourbe*] was no more than an Enthusiast. A Philosopher," Gibbon continued, "who had seen close up the progress of this fanaticism in the soul of the Prelate, could have enriched the history of the human spirit with a very curious piece."[26]

Gibbon assumed that Lord Lyttelton did not aspire to the ranks of the "philosophic" historians; his patronizing praise was hardly likely, therefore, to satisfy that author:

The other nations of Europe had outstripped the English in the progress of History. England possessed poets and philosophers, but she was
reproached with having only cold Annalists or impassioned Declaimers.
Two great men have silenced this reproach. A Robertson has adorned
the annals of his homeland with all the graces of the most vigorous eloquence. A Hume, born to instruct and judge mankind, has carried into
history the light of a profound and elegant philosophy. We will never
waste on rank the reward of talents: Lord L. must not pretend to the
glory of these men of genius, but he retains the qualities of a good citizen, a very enlightened scholar, an exact and impartial writer.[27]

Young Gibbon's magisterial confidence in his judgment is obvious, and (as
noted in the *Memoirs*) it was in the event entirely justified by the verdict
of the public. These opinions are so characteristic, and so characteristically
expressed, that no one can doubt their disinterestedness, though it would
theoretically have been possible that Gibbon's somewhat uncomfortable
acquaintance with Lord Lyttelton's son might have colored his response
to Lord Lyttelton's book.

The first volume of *Mémoires littéraires* appeared in April. Its reception
may be inferred from the editors' having to seek another publisher for
their next volume, which came out not in the following quarter, but in the
following year.[28] It was presumably the principal occupation of Gibbon's
and Deyverdun's summer at Beriton, though Gibbon perhaps made additions to his "Index Expurgatorious" and continued his Roman readings—
certainly William Warburton's *Divine Legation of Moses Demonstrated*,
briefly noted in the 1767 volume of *Mémoires littéraires*, was in his
thoughts.[29] In public affairs, he took an interest in the Wilkes case, but
of course he had no active role to play in it, and his one recorded comment shows no very strong feeling on the matter: "I shall say nothing of
Wilkes; every man has his story and his opinion, which mutually destroy
each other."[30] In the same letter in which he made this comment, he
sounded jaded in his responses to the election and to London entertainments as well; by the end of the year 1768, however, the possible tedium
of his way of life was painfully and effectively interrupted. A letter to
James Scott, a relative of Dorothea Gibbon's and a good man of business,
gives notice of the new state of affairs. Dated from Beriton December 20,
1768, it requests Scott's presence for "particular and very urgent reasons";
the reason was the family's need of his assistance in the Herculean task of
extracting Gibbon's father from his now almost hopeless thicket of
debts.[31] For the next two years, all Gibbon's tact and ingenuity, patience
and kindness, were called upon, as he tried to rescue his sick and frightened
father from these financial distresses.

Thus it is not surprising that Gibbon contributed less to the second volume of *Mémoires littéraires* than he had to the first. Indeed, H. H. Milman
saw nothing of Gibbon in it, with the possible exception of the "review of

the dialogue ascribed to Lord Herbert of Chirbury [which] approaches the nearest to his manner, but I doubt his authorship of this."[32] Milman overlooked the review of Walpole's *Historic Doubts,* which would not have been attributed to Gibbon so unreservedly by Lord Sheffield without Gibbon's positive acknowledgment; and, as Low correctly notes, the review of Boswell's *Corsica* contains erudite information almost certainly provided, if not expressed, by Gibbon.[33] The Walpole review, which is followed by, and deferential to, a brief note by Hume, seems rather inhibited by that deference; perhaps that diffidence explains Milman's tacit rejection of it.

Gibbon's criticism of Walpole's argument—the "historic doubts" were, of course, about the guilt of Richard III—stresses the probity of Thomas More (Gibbon assumes that the testimony of the "More" biography of Richard III is More's own) and the weakness of Walpole's case in favor of the supposed survival of the younger of the two princes in the tower as Perkin Warbeck. This aspect of Walpole's hypothesis was readily defeated, and, in so doing, Gibbon neglected the possibility that Walpole could have been right about Richard though wrong about Perkin. Nevertheless, the Walpole review has many internal signs of Gibbonian authorship, including the numbered series of parts of his argument, and such a sequence as the following:

> It is difficult to leave Mr. Walpole, but it is necessary to do so. Let us merely observe that he reduces Richard's monstrous deformity to some rather slight defects. . . . A very ancient drawing that Mr. Walpole has had engraved, and the testimony of a monk very impassioned with respect to Richard, furnished him these softened traits. The old Countess of Desmond depicted him still more favorably. She remembered having danced with him and recalled that next to his brother Edward, he was the best made man of the assembly.[34]

This *reductio ad absurdum* method, in which Gibbon allowed his description and arrangement of the opposition's evidence to undermine itself without overt commentary, is exactly the procedure so often described as hypocritical or underhanded—memorably as "sapping a solemn creed with solemn sneer."[35] But the obvious good humor of his tone here, and the absence of any possible self-serving motive in his choice of approach, may affect our response to the same tone and method when used in the controversial chapters of the *Decline and Fall.* Gibbon concluded this review, fairly enough, by stating that "the arguments of Mr. Walpole dazzled without convincing us. The following reflections returned us to the common opinion; they are Mr. Hume's."[36]

The other items reviewed in the second volume, in addition to Priestley on electricity, no doubt contributed by Scott or another scientific expert, and the three departments—"Spectacles," "Beaux Arts," and "Nouvelles

Littéraires"—include Baretti's *Account of the Manners and Customs of Italy,* Lord Herbert of Chirbury's autobiography and a dialogue on education, Sterne's *Sentimental Journey,* and Boswell's *Corsica.* The review of Baretti is essentially an account of his literary quarrel with a critic of Italy aptly named Samuel Sharp. The journalist seems to see nothing wrong in Sharp's writing from books as if from his own observations, and this, together with the abrupt beginning, the large proportion of quotations or paraphrases, and the limitation of commentary to moral or whimsically comical remarks, makes an attribution to Deyverdun probable. For example, Baretti had argued the *cicisbeos* were only disinterested friends. "It is thus that Mr. B. has judged it proper to refute Mr. S.—An Italian was telling me the other day: we are not very much obliged to Mr. B for justifying our women; he would make all of us pass for simpletons."[37] This technique of criticism by anecdote was distinctively Deyverdun's.

On the other hand, a reply to Baretti's deploring the praise given to Goldoni might have been contributed by Gibbon:

> I cannot persuade myself that Goldoni is absolutely without talent. I shall not enter into a dispute with Mr. B about the literature of his Country, but it does not seem to me very probable that a highly cultivated people would have applauded for many years works devoid of all merit. The Italian language is not so difficult as the English. If M. de Voltaire does not understand Shakespeare, Mr. B. will at least admit that he can understand Goldoni, & although he should not be very much prepossessed in favor of that man of Genius, I hope that he will readily admit also that he knows a little about the theatre. Would he have praised such an Author as Goldoni has been depicted to be?[38]

We are reminded of Gibbon's comment about the Italian adulation of Petrarch:

> Whatever may be the private taste of a stranger, his slight and superficial knowledge should humbly acquiesce in the taste of a learned nation; yet I may hope or presume, that the Italians do not compare the tedious uniformity of sonnets and elegies with the sublime compositions of their epic muse, the original wildness of Dante, the regular beauties of Tasso, and the boundless variety of the incomparable Ariosto.[39]

Despite the gestures of deference to the native speakers, both the journalist and the historian seem very confident in their assessment of Italian literature. But the former supported his views with the opinions of others; the latter, with a description of the characteristics of his favorites. Of course, it is not impossible that Deyverdun knew Italian—we know he knew French, German, and English—and was similarly confident of his literary judgment.

The account of Herbert of Chirbury's autobiography does not seem at all like Gibbon: it is a summary, neutral to respectful in tone, and almost without commentary. An exception occurs when Herbert, aged twenty-seven, threatens to duel with a Frenchman over a quarrel about a young girl's ribbons. The journalist says: "The reader will undoubtedly be astonished that a Statesman, a Philosopher, the father of four children, had such adventures; he will be still more astonished that he so seriously recounts it at the age of 60. But the customs of his time were very different from ours. What would now be ridiculous, even extravagant, was then scruples, delicacy, honor."[40] Not Gibbonian in manner or rhythm, this comment could nevertheless represent his sentiment as easily as it could represent Deyverdun's. Another comment is, however, so obviously not Gibbon's that to disprove his authorship it need only be quoted: "But it is time to say a little word to my Readers. If there is one among them who is not interested in the simple and naive picture of Mr. H. and the manners of his time, I advise him, as a friend, to throw away this Book."[41] The reviewers also considered a dialogue that, on the grounds of style and content, they attributed to Herbert. It includes five articles of religion ostensibly approved by reason and, one suspects, also by the journalist. Because the articles[42] were deistic but not atheistic, it would be interesting and possible to see their inclusion as at least approved, if not sponsored, by Gibbon. They included a doctrine of rewards and punishments "in this world, & in the other." Of course, Gibbon came to be very doubtful of the latter. The journalist concluded, "Monsieur says, finally, some beautiful things in favor of the idea of one sole God, & loses himself a little in the infinite." The hand may have continued to be that of Deyverdun, but the voice was either the voice of Gibbon or an echo of it.

The final section of the Herbert review is an evaluative description of his entire *oeuvre*. Despite the judgments it contains, this section too is more like Deyverdun than Gibbon. It has no topic statement, and no structure except chronological enumeration. When Herbert's historical work, the *Life and Reign of Henry VIII*, was reached, the writer allowed Walpole to speak "with much justice" for him. If Gibbon had a hand in this section, it was probably in the concluding reflections:

> In many respects he deserves to be at the head of the deistical writers. His style is superior to that of most authors of his time; it is in general clear, simple & sometimes agreeable. The lack of method is the greatest defect of M. H.'s works. . . . [His penchant] for judicial astrology, magic, &c. . . . is the homage that this man of genius pays to his age. M. H. was a philosopher; but a too vivid imagination sometimes spoiled his Philosophy.[43]

But I suspect that Deyverdun reentered here to speak as the man of feeling: "One cannot read the Memoirs of Lord Herbert, without feeling that one respects, that one loves this man. With what amiable ingenuousness he lets us see his defects, with what noble sincerity does he speak of his virtues."[44]

It was probably Deyverdun alone who produced an account of Sterne's *Sentimental Journey* which was made up almost entirely of quotations—it was he, after all, who had dared to translate the *Bath Guide*. After this series of translated excerpts, the writer noted that Sterne had died and quoted "with pleasure" a sympathetic obituary from the *Monthly Review:*

> The Journalist knew all the merit of Mr. Sterne's Work. . . . Mind does not suffice for that; it is necessary also to have a soul. Another Journalist [not cited] neither saw nor felt anything in Mr. S.'s work. . . . Perhaps it will be said, to excuse him, that reasons foreign to taste conducted his pen. What an excuse! Is there some reason that can make one affect to have no soul?"[45]

Gibbon admired Sterne and tender-heartedness, but this rhetoric of souls was not like him. More like him, though possibly Deyverdun's, was the comment on *Tristram Shandy,* with its independence of critical commonplace and its moderate position:

> This Work, which had something natural, lively, and especially, greatly original, was extremely well received; but little by little, the disorder, the indecencies, the obscurity disgusted the Reader, who criticized as much as he had praised, and who believed he saw a great difference between the first and the last Volumes. This difference is not so apparent to me. I see throughout the Work beauties and defects . . . & if it did not merit the eulogies it received in the beginning, it deserved still less the way in which it has been treated since. Not a volume but has beauties, not a volume also in which one does not purchase somewhat dearly the sight of those beauties.[46]

The eloquent call for originality that concludes the account of Sterne is certainly Deyverdun's: "People of taste cannot too much regret the loss of an original . . . writer, in times when Imitation tries to smother talents. . . . I said to the Actors, I said to the Painters, I repeat to the Writers, Imitation restricts genius; you will never be great by it."[47] The journalist had indeed given this advice to actors and painters in articles that were, as we have seen, probably by Deyverdun.[48]

It seems clear that although both friends probably read the major works they were considering in this volume, Deyverdun was the principal author of all the pieces mentioned so far, except the Walpole review. It would seem that Deyverdun determined the structure and the approach to the chosen works. But Gibbon probably discussed the works and authors with him, perhaps contributing brief essays and observations—similar to those he had included in his various journals and commonplace books—which Deyverdun worked into his own text.

The remaining major review in the volume is that of Boswell's *Corsica.*

It was probably approached in the same way as the others. It includes an argument by comic anecdote like the one discussed above, probably Deyverdun's.[49] But Gibbon no doubt contributed the geographical correction in which Boswell was advised to consult Muratori.[50] The particular objections to Boswell's account of the politics, exports, etc., may also owe something to Gibbon's erudition or to his conversations with Celesia in Italy.[51] But the bulk of the amused or patronizing criticism of the part of Boswell's work that was a "description of Corsica" could be pure Deyverdun.

Then the reviewer reached Boswell's journal:

Here is the brilliant part, which has made the fortune of the whole work. . . . The fire, the vivacity of the narration, amused those who sought only pleasure, and through a certain fog of enthusiasm, the Philosopher will have glimpsed with satisfaction the traits of a Great Man in Paoli; all, finally, will have seen with pleasure that sort of ingenuousness which interests us in favor of the Writer or which makes us laugh at his expense.

In addition to this double-edged tribute, the reviewer specifically commented on Boswell's likeableness: "If the Author portrays himself in his work, the Account of M. B. must inspire in the Reader the desire of knowing him." Boswell is credited with producing much aid for Paoli by "his writings & . . . his efforts," but, it is asserted, "we still lack a History of Corsica."[52] The review is not by any means altogether negative and shows no personal acquaintance with Boswell, much less personal bias against him. A continuing quarrel with Rousseau and his supporters is indicated in a note, undoubtedly by Deyverdun, and one or both of the journalists obviously either disliked Johnson, or disliked Boswell's adulation of Johnson. In 1768, however, neither Deyverdun nor Gibbon had any personal acquaintance with Johnson, and the "impish condensation" of Johnson's famous quip against the infidel philosophers seems to represent impersonal resentment of Johnson's attack on thinkers both reviewers revered, especially Hume.[53] In short, if Boswell had seen this review, he would indeed have resented it, but he would have found moments of pleasure in reading it, and he might have been forced to admit the legitimacy of some of the criticism. The truly objectionable aspect of the account is a long extract from a silly anti-Johnsonian pamphlet by one "K," which counters Boswell's parallel of Paoli and Johnson by a parallel of Paoli and Wilkes—a strained and dull joke. The reviewer fills three pages with this parallel, on the grounds that "some strokes" in it "could amuse our readers for a moment."[54] It is a very long moment.

If Gibbon had any hand in this review, it was probably of the same sort as his contribution to the other articles, that is, discrete points or brief observations, which were inserted by Deyverdun in an article essentially his.

Similarly, Gibbon may have contributed to Deyverdun's regular departments on spectacles, beaux-arts, and literary news. The section on plays includes reviews of Hugh Kelly's *False Delicacy* and Oliver Goldsmith's *Good Natured Man,* with an interesting account of the (according to the reviewer) untranslatably English concept of "good nature." In this review article critical skills are demonstrated which one might like to claim for Gibbon, but there is no reason to do so, and Deyverdun's great interest in the theater was of long standing.[55]

Among the brief notices in the *Nouvelles littéraires* there is a comment on a projected history of England by John Wilkes,

> which probably will never be written. Our author has much other business and does not enjoy very much of that tranquillity of mind which permits an historian to amass materials, to compare, judge them, and join to them just and impartial reflections. Reading the introduction is a very good way of consoling ourselves for the loss of the history. In it we saw that the English nation enjoyed complete Liberty under the reign of Elizabeth. Every reader somewhat instructed in the History of England, knows the Despotism of that Queen; but it is not for instructed Readers that Mr. Wilkes has worked.[56]

Short of a signature, this notice could hardly proclaim its author more clearly. In fact, Gibbon probably contributed most or all of the notices in the history section of the *Nouvelles littéraires.* Thus, though his contribution to the second volume of the journal was undoubtedly less than that to the first, his participation was sufficiently great to explain his claiming a role in it as in the other volume.

Though Gibbon had acquired a new responsibility, that of justice of the peace (August 20, 1768), the major cause for the reduction in his contribution to the journal was probably the developing familial crisis.[57] To it, from late December on, Gibbon had to devote most of his time and energy, and more and more acute symptoms of it must have appeared before the crisis itself was acknowledged. As Norton explains, the final straw seems to have been some new difficulty in a long-standing chancery suit, perhaps going back to a claim against Gibbon's grandfather's estate.[58] The resettling of Mrs. Gibbon's jointure because the security for it had to be mortgaged, and the acute discomfort that both the elder Gibbons seemed to be suffering in the early months of 1769 from the importunities of a Hampshire tradesman, indicate to what extremes Mr. Gibbon's financial difficulties had gone.[59] Sometime during the Christmas holidays, Mr. Gibbon finally decided to confide his problems to his son's care. Typically, he was most anxious about his wife's welfare; whatever his faults as a provider and his weaknesses of temper, Mr. Gibbon was a tender husband to both of his devoted wives. His son reassured him, and in a letter alluded comfortingly to their conference: "I shall not *forget* the conversation we had in the Study. It is my duty as well as my inclination to consider her in the light of a real Mother."[60]

Mr. Gibbon had to rely on his son because his own indiscretions had been such that drastic measures were necessary to appease his creditors. James Scott, their businesslike kinsman, wrote to Mr. Gibbon, "You must excuse me Sir for saying a harsh thing but as you have forfeited your word several times, no prudent Man would take it again."[61] One might exclaim, as Johnson did of Goldsmith's debts, "Was ever [bad businessman] so trusted before?" That Mr. Gibbon had had the opportunity *several* times to prove his word worthless was certainly a tribute to his powers of pleasing, but it made it necessary to take all his business affairs out of his hands, entrusting them in larger matters to trustees, in small matters to his wife.

Mr. Gibbon replied to Scott, in a letter aptly described as "almost hysterically contrite," that he wanted only

> [to] make you and my son easy . . . it is no great matter what comes of me. . . . I stand fully convicted of the heavy charge you accuse me; and have noth[ing] to say in my justification. I will most readily come into the [deed] of trust, for to get rid of this place is most desired by me, for fear of making bad worse by my living here, but what gives me as much uneasiness as anything is the distant prospect of it . . . and everything carried on as usual, tho I promise with the least expense possible.

These good intentions were instantly, though undoubtedly unconsciously, belied by conditions: "The Deed I should think must be limited to you & my Son, & not extended to Heirs and Executors."[62]

Before this exchange, Gibbon's own good intentions and efforts in the emergency had been signaled by three letters home in four days. The first two simply reported, respectively, his arrival in town and his first meeting with their new attorney, Southouse. Yet the second of these notes shows his anxiety not only to cope but also to comfort: "I am glad to assure you that the Chancery affair is of a much slower progress than we imagined. . . . Southouse can retard it & thinks the money (on a proper plan) may be procured. He . . . hopes every thing may be settled." In the third and longest letter (January 5), Gibbon began the long process of pressing his father for the necessary documents. The immediate proposal, the sale of the Putney property, required, first, proof that the estate, once held copyhold, was now freehold, and second, presentation of the deed of ownership, which would have been deposited with any creditor who accepted the estate as security for a loan and which therefore would have to be delivered to any prospective purchaser. Gibbon explained this to his parents: "for says [Southouse] any purchaser would . . . be allarmed at it's not being to be found, and would immediately suspect that some incumbrance (perhaps for your life only) had been contracted on that security. I hope and sincerely believe," Gibbon added, betraying, even in his denial, a fear or suspicion "that meer accident or neglect has deprived us of this important writing, but as it is so important We must beg, you would recollect all you can about it, and if possible give us some clue which may lead to a discovery of it."[63] He went on to list other necessary or useful documents.

Scott's letter of January 10 and Mr. Gibbon's reply indicate some of the difficulties Gibbon and Scott continued to encounter. There is no sign of Mr. Gibbon's complying with any of their requests, though he was obviously deeply concerned; he concluded his letter to Scott:

> I hope you or my son will send me as often as possible a line of comfort as we have a post every day, and that you will take a little care as to the fastening your letters, for whether by accident or villainy your last night was open—Dear Sir, excuse the [incor]rectness of my writing for my mind is kept in continual [?agita]tion and I am sometimes under terrible apprehensions from it, but God keep me right, that I may be able to make to My Son to you & every body else all the reparation & satisfaction in my power. I can say no more, but with a heart full of the greatest Gratitude remain My Dear Sir your most obliged tho most Unhappy Friend.[64]

Gibbon's letter of January 14 seems to reply to a different letter:

> I think Dear Sir you must be easy after what he said of the Chancery affair. I asked with some anxiety how long it could be staved off. What does that signify (answered he) We shall have the Money before it is wanted.
> Depend on it, Dear Sir, we do not wish to flatter you with vain hopes . . . and let this consideration dispell the Fantom which torments you and makes me so unhappy.[65]

Clearly Mr. Gibbon had expressed his continuing distress about the chancery suit and his fear that they were making light of it to comfort him. He had probably also mentioned Gibbon's promises about Mrs. Gibbon, for this is the letter in which Gibbon said he would not "*forget*" their conversation, and Gibbon's emphasis on "forget" implies a contrast with something. In the same letter, Gibbon included a progress report and again requested the papers for want of which they could not progress further. Gibbon mentioned in passing that he could not be one of the trustees for his father and proposed Stanier Porten, his uncle, as Scott's co-trustee.

The letter concludes with a description of Gibbon's own position, possibly in response to a question: "As for myself, I shall only say that as I cannot be happy, without your being so I am willing to make every reasonable sacrifice to your tranquillity. The only restraints I shall wish to impose on you are such as will be conducive to our common Good. Perhaps it had been better for us all, had I insisted on them some years sooner."[66] The good will is apparent, but the recognition of his father's errors is tactlessly visible as well. Meanwhile, Mrs. Gibbon had become active in the affair, writing to Scott on January 15—apparently they had not yet received Gibbon's letter—that she was sending all the papers she could find "in a basket with a hare," so that they would not be so small a package as to get lost. Loyally she told her cousin, "if Mr. Gibbon was made easy in his mind his advice would be usefull, he never will be so, till he knows the money is ready.... I dread the Consequence of his Anxiety."[67]

Mr. Gibbon himself apparently replied to his son's letter, for a week later, writing a note to his stepmother by the same post as a long letter to his father, Gibbon asked her to "send me some particular account of my poor father, his style makes me very unhappy: perhaps not the least so of the three, for it is very irksome to wear a perpetuall mask of gaiety." One can imagine the letter that called forth the reply Gibbon wrote to his father, which says, "I fear you will even magnify every difficulty, and really make things worse by the state of your own mind." This was his mask of gaiety. Gibbon was too much distressed to watch every word, and he let drop the phrase, "your neglecting either to keep or to send us the necessary writings." To his stepmother, he spoke with undisguised fervor, "For Gods sake for all our sakes press my father to recollect every thing, to look out every thing & to send us every thing that he can."[68]

Dorothea Gibbon's reply, addressed not to Gibbon (as Norton thought),[69] but to Scott, makes it clear that her husband's health was steadily deteriorating and that she found the pressure of their demands from London excessive:

> He grows very thin, the Consequence of fretting day and night. You told us ... Mr. Southouse had got every thing he wanted, but the Deed of infranchisement, but Mr. Edward Gibbon names several things in a letter we received Asunday; as the probate of the Will, which need not occation any delay, as a copy may be got from the Commons; as to all the other things he asks about, they must be of little Consequence, as no debts of my Mr Gibbon's could affect an estate intailed, as his is, without the concurence of his Son.[70]

Watching her husband's distress of mind and body, Mrs. Gibbon was naturally impatient of any demand that could be met in any other way than by pressing him with business; in their efforts to preserve the estate from ruin, the London committee tried to avoid the extra expenditures and inadequate expedients that could, it seemed, so easily be avoided by just a little effort from Mr. Gibbon. That all the parties emerged with their affection and forbearance intact is a tribute to all concerned—the invalid himself excepted, of course.

On January 31, Gibbon was forced to write to Mrs. Gibbon: "My father's last letter distressed me very much. He talks of my ... doubts & suspicions. Whatever unguarded expressions may have dropped from me,

I hope my past conduct & my present designs are far from deserving the reproach of doubts & suspicions."[71] In February, matters grew still worse, in all respects. The London committee required not only the missing deed of enfranchisement but also a schedule of Mr. Gibbon's debts. Mr. Gibbon, so nervous that he could neither eat nor sleep, awaited every post with impatience and apparently feared a creditor with every knock at the door. His letters loaded his son with reproaches. On February 9, Gibbon wrote to his father, and Scott wrote, much more bluntly, to his cousin Dorothea. She had suggested that Gibbon and Scott give a reward to Williamson, who had inherited the papers of Joseph Taylor, long-time attorney for the Gibbon family, to encourage him to produce the missing documents. Gibbon had already mentioned that expedient (January 31); he now found that it was insufficient. His father had proposed that they borrow money on the security of a farm he did not yet own, a project totally unacceptable, given his credit record. Gibbon's patience was severely tried. He wrote to his father:

> You have more than once reproached me with want of confidence [i.e., in him]. The subject of that reproach makes me very uneasy in whatever light I consider it. I must leave my Apology to your cooler moments. However in the present circumstances, the just confidence I shall place in your honor can be of no use to us, as the Deed of Trust must be finished before any money can be had.

Nevertheless, he repeated again and again the reassurances his father needed: "You are in no immediate danger from Chancery . . . your credit is unhurt, and should Heather &c make any present application, Mr S will send down to Petersfield a Clerk for You to execute Mr Scott's bond, &c. [Scott was lending them £900 for immediate needs] & then you may draw on me for *those particular sums*. This will be better & surely more agreable to you than coming twice to London."[72]

Meanwhile, Scott wrote to Mrs. Gibbon:

> I know it goes very hard with Mr G to make a deed of Trust, but there is an absolute necessity to do it, and every debt that he owes must be mentioned in it. . . . To paliate and stop a present gap, has been the ruin of most Men, and I see Mr G. would be easy for the present [i.e., regardless of the method or the future], if he could do it, but that would be the way for him to fall into the same again.[73]

This frankness seemed brutal to Mrs. Gibbon, and a draft reply exists in which she expressed indignation not only against Scott but also against her stepson's supposed anxiety about his own welfare: "When E Gibbon will have the power in his own hands he cannot be cheated."[74] But she recognized either the injustice or the indiscretion of such complaints against the persons upon whom she depended for aid and thus sent a less angry reply, in which, however, she complained that the listing of all the debts would "be attended with great & unnecessary expences as none of them can touch the estates but the mortgages & a list of them given in to Mr E Gibbon must answer all his purposes as well."[75] Her argument was somewhat inconsistent, because of course making up a list of debts for Gibbon would have required exactly the same trouble as making up the list for the deed of trust, but it perhaps occurred to her as she wrote that Gibbon's desire to clear the family of all debts, not just those the law could exact from the estates, could hardly be met without that trouble. She was much mollified to learn that the list of debts could indeed be kept a private matter.

The criticism from home was very painful to Gibbon. On February 23, replying to a missing letter from his father, he wrote:

> The displeasure your last letter expressed, convinced me that the meer blows of fortune are trifling when compared with the unexpected reproaches of those we love. . . .
> So far from wishing to expose your name I consulted S on the practicability of omitting the particular Schedule, and a method has been agreed on. . . . I shall execute writings by which I make myself liable to near eight thousand pounds Debt, you will then be able to make use of Mr Scott's money, & we shall find means to answer the Chancery Demands. . . . After this Dear Sir give me leave to ask whether your last expression that you are *still affectionately &c* was not somewhat severe. . . .
> I have wrote Dear Sir from a full heart, for which I make no apology. It is by actions not by words that I shall ever seek to prove how truly I feel for yourself and poor Mrs G, and how ardently I wish to make you, if possible, happy.[76]

Scott had written to Mr. Gibbon the day before to propose the plan the London committee had evolved for settling the Gibbon affairs. It included sale of some of the entailed property to pay Mr. Gibbon's debts, and—the new proposal—placement of the remaining estate, that in Buckinghamshire, in his son's name, with all the income to go to Mr. Gibbon and with Mrs. Gibbon's jointure charged against it. It was a proposal in no way damaging to Mr. Gibbon's financial position, but very trying to his pride, and Gibbon asked Scott to broach it. Scott's forte was clarity, not tact:

> The reasons why he chuse to have it in his own name [are that] he thinks your great indolence may make you be guilty of neglects, that may run you into farther difficulty. . . . as he gives up every thing on your account, and has agreed to discharge all your debts, nor has ever given you any trouble by calling you to account for any real or personal Estate or effects that he has been entitled to from his Grand Father's Will nor ever intends to make you uneasy in any thing he can prevent with any safety to himself. He thinks you cannot help complying with this. . . . I don't think you can refuse it. I am sure when you promise you intend to perform, but I think you *can* not, or

ought to trust yourself, therefore you can not take it amiss, if he puts every thing out of your power to hurt him for the future, as he is so great a sufferer already. [77]

If Mr. Gibbon had already received this letter when he wrote the one by which Gibbon was so much hurt, it is not surprising that, sick and frightened, he had feelings of guilt and wounded pride to vent on someone. It is clear, however, that a dispassionate and well-informed observer—Scott, Mrs. Gibbon's cousin, had no reason to be partial to Gibbon's cause— thought Gibbon's injury from his father's imprudence extraordinary, and his generosity in responding to those injuries admirable. [78]

The tension was somewhat relieved, early in March, by the finding of the missing papers among the effects of Joseph Taylor. However, Mr. Gibbon continued to wish to guard his dignity as a landed proprietor regardless of the effect on his son. Gibbon explained once more on March 4:

The only proposed alteration was that you should allow me to have the nominal possession of the Buckinghamshire Estate, subject to pay You the whole neat profits of it.... The very harsh Reception this proposal has met with from you has given me the deepest concern as I am conscious of the rectitude of my intentions, & ... the propriety of the measure.... I am willing, nay desirous to put it absolutely [out] of my power to sell mortgage or alienate the smallest portion of it, and wish to bind myself by the severest ties that the Law can invent, to pay you regularly half yearly, a method which must be easy to you, and may sometimes be inconvenient to me—But I shall proceed no farther on a Subject which appears so disagreable to you. . . . I have endeavoured to have the approbation of my own conscience, and of our real friends Mr Porten, and Mr Scott. I flatter myself, that I shall one day obtain your's. [79]

Mr. Gibbon responded by asking Gibbon to have the property revert to him in fee, if Gibbon predeceased him. This eventuality was to everyone but Mr. Gibbon obviously highly unlikely, but Gibbon agreed to humor him, only to learn from their lawyer that to do so would leave Gibbon unable ever to control the property: "My *supposed* future children must be put in this *new* Entail before you, the consequence of which contingency would leave me for my whole life, (even after your decease) a meer Tenant for life; a much worse situation, than my grandfather's will & former settlements placed me in; which indeed I consented to alter without being made acquainted with what I was doing." In the same letter, Gibbon made a new proposal, that he increase Mrs. Gibbon's jointure from £200 to £300: "Not that I claim any merit from *thence*; I shall sign with pleasure whatever it is in my power to do for a person, whose conduct & sentiments have always been to me those of *a real Mother*." [80]

Mr. Gibbon reached a new pitch of fury in his reply to this letter, as we can judge from Scott's response, written after Gibbon had showed it to him. Mr. Gibbon claimed that Gibbon had upbraided him for their former transactions, that he would rather "bear Mr Wilks company" (i.e., go to prison? or just to the devil?) than comply with his son's proposals, that his son was trying to keep the Buckinghamshire estate from him even in the event of his predeceasing his father, and that his son was "go[ing] about to expose [him]."[81] Scott defended Gibbon warmly on all counts:

> You certainly wrote that letter in a very ill temper. You look all on your own side and nothing on your Sons, you seem to forget how much he has given you and how much he does now, it is not a Son in a thousand that would have done as much. . . . I dare say Sir that when you think coolly and put yourself in his place, you will alter your way of thinking and will not drive him to do that that he would not willingly do, without your forceing him to it.[82]

Either the rational argument or the implied threat—might Gibbon have been forced to disavow his father's debts?—apparently prevailed. Soon the problems with Mr. Gibbon were relatively minor. On March 31, Gibbon gently rejected a visionary and belated proposal that would have involved starting over again from scratch, and, on April 4, he pointed out sympathetically but firmly that Mrs. Gibbon must indeed come to London when the documents were signed, because her consent to a different security from her jointure was required. These were trivial problems, easily resolved.

Gibbon's regard for his stepmother continued to increase. On April 13, he wrote to his father:

> Mrs G distresses me in every way—I am truly concerned that it should be necessary for her to come up, at a time when I can easily conceive the state of her mind and spirits: but I am still more embarassed from her generous obstinacy. The sum of her Jointure is left in blank [in the deed]. Should she still object to [its] encrease . . . I must leave it as an engagement not of law, but of honor, of gratitude and of inclination.[83]

She did persist in refusing the increase, and he did pay the larger amount on the voluntary and affectionate basis he mentions, entirely to the credit of both parties.[84]

Thereafter, the only hitch in the settlement of the financial affairs of the Gibbons was Mr. Gibbon's genteel unwillingness to advertise the property they wished to sell. Unlike the agent of Jane Austen's Sir Walter Elliot, the helpers of Mr. Gibbon eventually had to violate his delicacy by advertising the property, though in deference to him they omitted the location of the estate in their description of it, an obvious handicap in an attempt to interest a buyer. For the remainder of 1769, the correspondence between Scott and Mrs. Gibbon, and that between Gibbon and his parents, were largely concerned with the hopes and disappointments about the sale. Gibbon did not have to deal with prospective buyers until they were ready to make an offer; thus he had leisure for an entirely different project, the writing of a book, the first he published in English.

He delayed his return to Beriton until after the annual militia meeting, probably until the end of June; then, despite the demands of business, and possibly because of a further crisis in his father's health (a problem with his eyes), removed to Beriton.[85] Perhaps Deyverdun accompanied him: Gibbon tells us in the *Memoirs* that, undaunted by the ill success of volumes 1 and 2 of the *Mémoires littéraires,* the friends had prepared almost enough materials for a third volume before they were interrupted by Deyverdun's departure for the continent as traveling tutor to Sir Richard Worsley (144). That departure must have occurred before the end of September 1769, because, by September 22, Deyverdun was in Germany.[86]

Some of Gibbon's scholarly leisure at Beriton in 1769 might therefore have been available for a work of criticism unconnnected with any of his other projects. Written in English, it found both a publisher and an audience, but we may wonder why this, of all the projects he attempted between 1765 and 1770, was the only one he independently carried to full fruition.

The project was a reply to a portion of William Warburton's *Divine Legation,* which Gibbon considered a "monument, already crumbling into dust, of the vigour and weakness of the human mind" (M 305). Gibbon might have completed and published this book simply because Warburton's view was one of those fashionable topics by which he confessed himself to be tempted. But it may also be significant that it is a purely analytical study, in which Gibbon could rest on the relatively firm ground of confutation, without having to risk proposals of his own—in this the work resembled his contributions to the *Mémoires littéraires.* Moreover, Warburton, whom Gibbon in many respects admired, was of Mr. Gibbon's generation and temperament—passionate, intolerant, enthusiastic. Perhaps it was some relief to Gibbon, constrained both by prudence and by compassion in his dealing with his father, to attack another rash and damaging elder.

It was also true that Warburton's hypothesis genuinely offended Gibbon, because of the view it required one to take of Virgil. Gibbon's feeling about his own work, as Low points out, was clearly "complacency, in spite of the professed contrition for the 'cowardly concealment of my name and character.'"[87] In a revealing metaphor, Gibbon commented, "In this short Essay . . . I aimed my strokes against the person and the Hypothesis of Bishop Warburton." He had already asserted that "The real merit of

Warburton was degraded by the pride and presumption with which he pronounced his infallible decrees. . . . In a land of liberty, such despotism must provoke a general opposition. . . . *I* too . . . was ambitious of breaking a lance against the Giant's shield." Only after such remarks did he aver that he could "not forgive [him] self the contemptuous treatment of a man, who, with all his faults, was entitled to . . . esteem; and I can less forgive, in a personal attack," its anonymous publication (145-46).

He probably did regret the timidity that was at least one of his motives for anonymous publication. If he had been as confident personally as he was confident in his judgment, he would have acknowledged his work—there was, of course, no question of fear of legal or physical reprisal, as in the Pope-Curll disputes of an earlier generation. It seems at least possible, however, that he concealed his name for one reason of which he himself was not aware, that is, that this was another instance of his inability to claim as his own the power of the name he still shared with his father.

However that may be, he did complete, and expose to the public, this "accidental sally of love and resentment; of my reverence for modest Genius, and my aversion for insolent pedantry" (144). Warburton wished to prove the general principle that paganism was deliberately instituted by the "Antient lawgivers for the support and benefit of Society" and that the mysteries informed the initiated of the actual "vanity of Polytheism and the Unity of the First Cause."[88] In the process, he claimed to find in four hundred authors and eighteen centuries evidence to support this principle. One of these authors was Virgil, who allegorically portrayed, in book 6 of the *Aeneid,* the initiation into the Eleusinian mysteries of his ideal legislator, Aeneas.

In the *Memoirs,* Gibbon summarized his reply to this argument with rather more lucidity than his book itself possesses:

> I proved, at least to my own satisfaction, *that* the ancient Lawgivers did not invent the mysteries, and *that* Aeneas was never invested with the office of lawgiver. *That,* there is not any argument, any circumstance, which can melt a fable into allegory, or remove the scene from the lake Avernus to the temple of Ceres. *That* such a wild supposition is equally injurious to the poet and the man. *That* if Virgil was not initiated he could not, if he were, he would not, reveal the secrets of initiation. *That* the anathema of Horace *(Vetabo qui Cereris sacrum, vulgârit &c)* at once attests his own ignorance and the innocence of his friend (145).

The most modern discussions of Warburton's hypothesis discovered by Michel Baridon, who most recently investigated the subsequent history of the controversy, seem to favor Warburton's view, not Gibbon's.[89] Yet it is easy to see why Virgilians of Gibbon's day, professional and amateur, admired and preferred Gibbon's case, even those who deplored the pertness of his manner.[90] In the first place, his book is embellished by digressions to point out virtues of Virgil's masterpiece that Gibbon thought insufficiently noticed, for example, his approbation, in a republican spirit, of the Etruscans' desire to "punish as well as to resist a Tyrant."[91] And it is hard to resist the powerful common sense of Gibbon's approach to some of Warburton's extravagances. For once explicitly Johnsonian in his criticism (Gibbon quotes the *Rambler*), he objected to Warburton's converting Aeneas from hero to lawgiver: "The naked eye of common sense cannot reach so far....Virgil seems as ignorant as myself of [Aeneas's] political character. . . . There is another public occurrence, at least as much in the character of a LAWGIVER as either voyaging or fighting; I mean, GIVING LAWS."[92] Gibbon pointed out that Aeneas "gives laws" in only one line of the poem and specifically disavows the role of lawgiver in favor of Acestes and Latinus. Granted that the fable of the *Aeneid* is the foundation of an empire, the founder need not be represented as a legislator: "as if Virgil had a design against the Bishop's System, at that very moment [when the hero's labors would give way to the lawgiver's] the Aeneid ends."[93] In contrast, Gibbon says, we possess in Fénelon's *Télémaque* and Xenophon's *Cyropaedia* actual examples of the kind of work Warburton would like to make of the *Aeneid,* not epics but "political institutes."

Gibbon's real quarrel with Warburton's hypothesis, however, had a religious and moral basis. Though he felt the "sublime Poetry" of Virgil's description of the "mind of the universe," Gibbon objected to Virgil's materialism in it:

> The poverty of human language, and the obscurity of human ideas, makes it difficult to speak worthily of THE GREAT FIRST CAUSE. Our most religious Poets, in striving to express the presence and energy of the Deity, in every part of the Universe, deviate unwarily into images, which are scarcely distinguished from Materialism. Thus our Ethic Poet:
> "All are but parts of one stupendous Whole,
> "Whose body Nature is, and God the soul;"
> and several passages of Thomson require a like favourable construction. But these writers deserve that favour, by the sublime manner in which they celebrate the great Father of the Universe, and by those effusions of love and gratitude, which are inconsistent with the Materialist's System. Virgil has no such claim to our indulgence. THE MIND of the UNIVERSE is rather a Metaphysical than a Theological Being. His intellectual qualities are faintly distinguished from the Powers of Matter, and his moral Attributes, the source of all religious worship, form no part of Virgil's creed.[94]

Gibbon may simply have objected to Warburton's misrepresentation of Virgil's position. We cannot infer that he thought materialism a false view. But in context, the whole passage suggests that he found a materialistic philosophy unpoetic and demeaning to human nature. For sublimity, love, and gratitude, the universe needed a Father.

Gibbon certainly regarded Warburton's interpretation of Virgil's work as morally demeaning to that beloved author. Gibbon granted that the Eleusinian mysteries "exhibited a theatrical representation . . . of the lower world . . . and that a warm Enthusiast, in describing these awful Spectacles, might express himself as if he had actually visited the infernal Regions." But that did not establish whether Virgil described the religious imitation of a descent into hell, or an actual descent:

> Lear and Garrick, when on the stage, are the same; nor is it possible to distinguish the Player from the Monarch. In the Green-room, or after the representation, we easily perceive, what the warmth of fancy and the justness of imitation had concealed from us. In the same manner it is from extrinsical circumstances, that we may expect the discovery of Virgil's Allegory. Every one of those circumstances persuades me, that Virgil described a real, not a mimic world, and that the Scene lay in the Infernal Shades, and not in the Temple of Ceres.[95]

Gibbon proceeded to point out the distinctions between the real and the mimic scenes. For instance, real death is easy to go to, difficult to return from, possible at any time; the mysteries were difficult to go to, easy to return from, possible "a few days at most in the course of the year." He quoted the "Facilis decensus Averni" passage from the *Aeneid* (6. 126–29) to show that Virgil was describing the former. Gibbon's method, he claimed, was to "lay aside Hypothesis, and read Virgil." Whatever the value of its results, its theoretical virtues are undeniable. Further (again Johnsonian), Gibbon urged that everything "animated . . . terrible . . . pathetic, evaporates" if this description is only that of a show, into "lifeless Allegory." True, the gate of ivory presents a difficulty, but "I had much rather reproach my favourite Poet [Gibbon had temporarily forsaken Homer; one may say he had sided with the son rather than the father] with want of care in one line, than with want of taste throughout a whole Book."[96]

Even this was not Gibbon's climactic point. Reverting from critic to historian, he pointed out the lack of evidence that Virgil had been initiated and then came to the vital point: "None but the Initiated COULD reveal the secret of the Mysteries; and THE INITIATED COULD NOT REVEAL IT, WITHOUT VIOLATING THE LAWS, AS WELL OF HONOR AS OF RELIGION."[97] Gibbon's capitals by no means exaggerate the importance of this argument to him. If the evasions of apology and allegory could have "saved [Virgil] from the sentence of the Areopagus, had some zealous or interested Priest denounced him . . . [for] publishing A BLASPHEMOUS POEM," yet by the "Laws of Honor . . . Guilt is aggravated, not protected, by artful Evasions."[98] Warburton's system made Virgil less than a man of honor, and Gibbon could not forgive that aspersion.

Gibbon granted equal emphasis in capitals and the pride of concluding place to a rather labored argument depending on the date and sense of one of Horace's odes. "The detestation of the Wretch who reveals the Mysteries of Ceres . . . must be applied [on Warburton's hypothesis] by all Rome to the Author of the Sixth Book of the Aeneid." Would Horace have so defamed his admired friend? No, of course not. Gibbon's fondness for this argument was perhaps derived from the chronological aspect of its proof and from the epigrammatic conclusion it permitted him: "Nothing remains to say, except that Horace was himself ignorant of his friend's allegorical meaning which the Bishop of Glocester has since revealed to the World. It may be so; yet, for my own part, I should be very well satisfied with understanding Virgil no better than Horace did."[99]

Unfortunately, Gibbon added a sarcastic paragraph about Hurd's adulation of Warburton and appended an argument from John Jortin's criticism of Warburton's thesis, which he had not read until his own book was in press, together with a last-minute thought of his own about the ivory gate passage. Only the last of these additions contributes to his character as a critic, and all of them, of course, mar the structure of the essay.

Gibbon's little book, or rather pamphlet, entitled *Critical Observations on the Design of the Sixth Book of the Aeneid,* was published by Elmsley on February 3, 1770. It received quite favorable notice from the reviewers and the more important compliment of acceptance by scholars such as Christian Heyne and Samuel Parr.[100] Gibbon must have been well pleased by his success. But he had little time to relish it. Mr. Gibbon's health, which had improved with summer and solvency, began again to worsen. The sale of Putney had been accomplished in August 1769; in October, Gibbon anticipated (in a letter to Holroyd) that he could complete some "particular business" in London about November 6, but it required two weeks longer in Beriton and a month in London. Norton plausibly suggests that the business was the publication of *Critical Observations.*[101] On Christmas day, Gibbon wrote again to Holroyd, "I received a letter this day from my father, which irresistibly draws me to Beriton for about ten days."[102] The book was presumably in press, and Gibbon wrote cheerfully about the prospect of visiting Holroyd at Sheffield Place. Mr. Gibbon's sight was still sufficient for letter writing. But by February, when the book appeared, he was no longer capable of any business.

On February 20, Stanier Porten wrote to Mrs. Gibbon, explaining that he and Gibbon agreed that they should henceforth avoid troubling Mr. Gibbon with business.[103] This resolution was necessary despite relatively satisfactory news from Beriton and hopes for Mr. Gibbon to consult a famous eye surgeon.[104] That consultation had to be postponed until the surgeon was less overwhelmed with patients.

A month later, Gibbon

was a good deal alarmed with [Mrs. Gibbon's] letter of yesterday, and as much pleased with that of to-day which dispelled my uneasiness.... I have seen [the surgeon] who very obligingly took my guinea to tell me that he could tell me nothing about my father's case without seeing him. On that head he was very cool and very fair; a decay of the Optic nerve, he said was sometimes tho' seldom to be removed.[105]

Gibbon was in the process of resigning from the militia at the time; he did not mention his book.

By mid-April, when the first review appeared, poor Mrs. Gibbon was writing to Scott of her husband's "nervous asthma" and saying that the doctor "advised him as a friend to bring his mind to be satisfyd with the degree of Sight he has."[106] It was advice not likely to have been followed by the volatile Mr. Gibbon, and, in any event, his sight continued to worsen, until he was almost totally blind. "With his sight he lost almost every pleasure of life as he could no longer enjoy the Country nor attend to the business of the farm . . . his chief amusement and occupation. . . . last spring we were still more terrified by the Symptoms of an approaching dropsy; a shortness of breath, swelling of the legs and body, and the loss of rest, strength and appetite."[107] This account, written to Hester Gibbon some months after Mr. Gibbon's death, does not really convey the length and severity of his final illness. In July, Gibbon had already been at home in attendance on his father for "some time"; Mrs. Gibbon's mind was fully occupied with the doctor's reports and the patient's care, but Gibbon was also troubled by the family business. To Scott he wrote, "There are other subjects, which it is as cruel to press, as inconvenient to neglect."[108] A month later he wrote to Holroyd:

There is but one way that [my father's illness] can be decided: a confirmed Dropsy & Asthma . . . allows us no hope of his recovery.

You may easily suppose that I am in a very improper frame of Mind, for the easy flow of a familiar Epistle.[109]

In August 1770, however, a new medication produced "a great evacuation of Water" and with it, some hope. But in November, "If I had wrote last week, I should have said that he was better than when you left Beriton. . . . Now, on the contrary I think him much worse. His breath[ing] is very bad, he is greatly swelled, and this morning had a fainting fit, which alarmed us exceedingly."[110] The fainting fit was followed by others, albeit with lucid and conscious intervals, in one of which he received the sacrament. On November 12, 1770, he died.

In his letter to Holroyd on this occasion, Gibbon said that "The expectation itself [of his father's death] thro' the course of a very painfull illness had in some measure prepared [him] for it. Yet notwithstanding these just motives of Consolation, it has been a very severe shock."[111] He added that he would have to be in London in the following week for a ten-day stay and would "think [him] self very lucky" if anything called Holroyd to London during his stay there. An identical letter (except for the closing compliment) of the same date, without an address or salutation, is in the British Museum, as Norton points out.[112] The existence of two such letters may cast doubt on the sincerity of his shock or grief. Yet the most likely recipient of the unaddressed letter would have been Scott, and it would have been difficult for Gibbon to say something different to two such good friends on such an occasion. Gibbon's description of his own reaction was precise and honest when, two weeks later, he wrote to Deyverdun:

> Throughout his illness, I was never away from Beriton a single day, I hardly left his room a single instant: everything, even my reading, was interrupted, and I feel the sad consolation of having fulfilled my duties as a son, until the moment when they ceased. There remain to me, I know, many other motives for consolation. I see them, but to feel them I require that time add its powers to those of reason.[113]

For weeks, even months, his every effort and thought had been engrossed with his father; for many years, since Gibbon had been detached from the household of his mothering aunt, his father, however difficult and unstable in himself, had been the one human constant in Gibbon's life. It had all ended. No longer "Mr. Edward Gibbon" or "young Gibbon," but the only Gibbon, master not only of himself but of all the family name and estate, it was no wonder that he was preoccupied with the lost father. The sense of lost opportunities—so strong a part of the guilt of any grief—could be appeased only by concentrating on the one fully satisfactory relationship he had had with his father, that connected with the melancholy duties of the deathbed. This consolation was not enough, however, to unshadow the years it concluded.

In spite of the publications, the praise, the productivity that, as we have seen, characterized Gibbon's intellectual life in these years from 1765 to 1770, he thought of them as frustrated and empty. There were two reasons for his so perceiving and so representing these years.

One was that, so long as his father lived, he could not emerge as Mr. Gibbon, English gentleman; like his father before him, he could only be Mr. Gibbon's son, and the negligible son of a successful father. For, failure at fathering and farming though he was, Mr. Gibbon had succeeded in ways his son could not rival. He was physically attractive. He was popular among his contemporaries of all social classes and both sexes. He was active in the governing class and had more than once been an M.P. He had, until the financial crises of his last years, a cheerful, comfortable, conventional niche in the social and economic life appropriate to his breeding; it was his vocation as well as his birthright. And he had had not one, but two, deeply satisfying marriages. Perhaps his son did not covet these blessings, but he could not fail to recognize that he had no adequate substitutes for them.

The other reason for dissatisfaction with the years in question was that in them he *completed* no work that seemed, in retrospect, a significant step toward his history of the Roman Empire. His completed pieces were either brief (and unpublished), like the Brutus essay and the "Index Expurgatorious," or digressions into his former role as man of letters in the narrow sense: they were mere literary criticism, not Criticism in the sense that he had established in the *Essai*. Though there were, as we have seen, substantial ways in which his discoveries and experiments in these critical pieces and in the unfinished works helped to form the Roman historian, he was unaware of them.

His transformation into the grand Gibbon, to whose story he would dedicate his *Memoirs,* required some two more years. In those years, he took two further steps toward his long-delayed adulthood: he set up his house, and he wrote the first rough sketch of the *Decline and Fall.*

CHAPTER 14

The Tears
of a Son

THE TEARS of a son are seldom lasting," reflected Gibbon in his *Memoirs* (though Lord Sheffield concealed the sentiment): "Few, perhaps, are the children who, after the expiration of some months or years, would sincerely rejoyce in the resurrection of their parents; and it is a melancholy truth, that my father's death, not unhappy for himself, was the only event that could save me from an hopeless life of obscurity and indigence" (150). Those of us blessed with loving and lovable parents can pity the son who thought this a general truth, and Gibbon himself came to sense what he had lacked, when he observed sons who lost a friend when they lost a father. Less than four years after Mr. Gibbon's death, Gibbon's friend Godfrey Clarke lost his father. Gibbon wrote to Holroyd, "If my esteem and friendship for Godfrey had been capable of any addition, it would have been very much encreased by the manner in which he felt and lamented his father's death: incredible as it sounds to the generality of sons, and as it ought to sound to most fathers, he considered the old Gentleman as a friend."[1] The pathos of this wistful incredulity is heightened by Gibbon's unconscious inconsistency in considering it virtuous—not merely natural—in a friend, so to love a father.[2]

In his own case, the removal of his father was a necessary, though not a sufficient, condition for mature achievement. For the first few days after Mr. Gibbon's death, indeed, Gibbon was all son—all his stepmother's son, because he was fond of her and she needed him. Her handwriting, in a letter she wrote to a cousin more than three weeks after her husband's death, sufficiently evidences her shock and distress, and her hand had not recovered when she wrote to him in January. A constant theme of her letters was Gibbon's goodness: "Mr. Edward Gibbon is in town I expect him to Morrow. he is very kind & good to me," she wrote in that first note—not yet really aware that there was no longer any need to distinguish him as Mr. *Edward* Gibbon.[3] He had gone to town, eight days after his father's death, only after arranging for her to stay with friends (the

Joseph Baylys) during his absence.[4] Though she was apparently worried about his health and wanted him to see a doctor, his major purposes were to arrange for her mourning (and presumably his own) and to begin the work of administering the estate—his father had, predictably, died intestate.

On a frigid November morning, no later than 6:30, Gibbon started on the ten-hour journey to London, arriving about 4:30 in the afternoon. He either inquired for Dr. Turton or pretended to (he told his stepmother that "Turton was not to be found, but I will endeavour to see him tomorrow") and made his way from his lodgings in Pall Mall to his Aunt Kitty's house in Dean's Yard, where he dined. He conveyed his stepmother's commission to his aunt and, less than five hours after his arrival, wrote her a letter. He concluded this note, "Let me entreat you, my dearest Mrs Gibbon to try to divert thoughts, which cannot be suppressed, and believe me that I can only be easy, as I have reason to think that you are so."[5]

One of his objects in London was to find a female friend to stay with his stepmother. When he wrote again, after six days in the city, he had made inquiries about two of her friends and arrangements to bring one of them (David Mallet's daughter Arabella Williams) to her whenever Mrs. Gibbon wanted her to come. He had already sent the mourning to Beriton and apologized because, lacking her measurements, the things could not be sent ready-made (Dorothea Gibbon was no merry widow, enjoying the prospect and styling of her weeds).

The next day, Gibbon sent her, together with a proxy for her to sign, most affectionate good advice about her health:

> I am sorry to find by a letter from Mr Bayly, that you have not yet left your own room. Let me intreat you, Dear Madam, to allow your friends to see you, and not to refuse the reliefs of air and change of place. As to myself they have so good an effect on *my* health, that were I to consult a Physician I should be at a loss what bodily complaint to alledge.[6]

The intention of this last comment was undoubtedly to assuage her anxiety about him; she was always concerned about his health. But the tone suggests that he had "obtained from time and reason a tolerable composure of mind," as he says in the *Memoirs* (151), and therefore was ready to begin "to form the plan of an independent life most adapted to [his] circumstances and inclination." But as the (previously cited) letter that he wrote the day after to Deyverdun suggests, he was by no means fully recovered from the fact of his father's death, and of course, there remained many matters to settle before he could complete and carry out such a plan of life. "Yet so intricate was the net: my efforts were so awkward and feeble, that near two years (November 1770–October 1772) were suffered to elapse before I could disentangle myself from the management of the farm, and transfer my residence from Buriton to an house in London" (151).

In retrospect, this delay seemed to him an entanglement and a digression in the history of the historian, but in this relationship with his stepmother, we see that he had already made the transition from dependent to protector that he himself felt to be prerequisite to adulthood. [7] It was a relationship of choice, required neither by blood nor by law, and far exceeding what was required by custom or "decency." Like his chosen brothers, sisters, and son, [8] his chosen mothers (Dorothea Gibbon and Catherine Porten) found him a thoughtful, active, and tender friend. His care of Dorothea in this crisis brought him no closer to the *Decline and Fall,* but it was an important step toward his becoming the man whose life work it indeed was, but whose life was more than his work.

The immediate difficulties were to arrange to pay the interest on the mortgage and to bring a companion for Mrs. Gibbon to Beriton. The latter turned out to be rather the more time-consuming task, and Gibbon seems to have been genuinely impatient to return to Beriton—partly, indeed, because he planned to spend a month there, "looking into the state of it: the profits and expences of the farm, the value of the Estate, and the probable encrease of it in respect to timber," as he, with just a touch of naive self-importance in the new role of landowner, wrote to Scott. [9] It is significant, moreover, that none of those activities had been possible while Mr. Gibbon lived. But Gibbon's impatience was also to be with "Dearest Mrs. Gibbon," whose shock and grief he sincerely pitied, and whose company he genuinely valued. Responding gratefully to Gibbon's affection, she wrote to Scott in January, "I told you in my last that Mr Gibbon [no longer "Mr. Edward Gibbon"] was very kind and obliging to me, indeed more considerate than you could imagin." [10] Although Gibbon had to return to London sooner than he had planned and stay longer than he had intended, her improved spirits, as well as their comradely relationship, are aptly illustrated by a letter he wrote to her around January 22: "Nothing was ever more judicious than your advice of getting my Writings out of the Old fox's den [Attorney Southouse's office]," he began the letter, abruptly and flatteringly. "The difficulty he gives me shews the necessity of it. I have not yet been able either to get a word or a line from him; and Mr Porten . . . strongly dissuades me from leaving town till they are in my own power." He concluded with a postscript, which remains unexplained, but must under any interpretation be playful, "My Compliments to the Calf." [11]

There was only one interlude of strain between them, and it was caused by false witness and quickly cured. Gibbon's regard for Mrs. Gibbon's judgment is clear in his requesting her advice, for example, in a letter of February 2, 1771, not merely *pro forma,* but urgently, by stagecoach. [12] About the end of February, however, she apparently sent him a letter not merely of advice but of rebuke. Gibbon's draft reply accepted the advice—somewhat stiffly—but elaborately and convincingly rejected the charges of extravagance and gambling that had accompanied it:

I am much obliged to your friendship for the advice you have given me with regard to my future Conduct and shall always pay the most sincere deference to it. Both prudence and inclination will engage me to get rid of the farm as soon as such a complicated piece of business can be transacted. With respect to my expences they shall always be proportioned to my income and I am already preparing to discharge a Cook, a Groom, and other unnecessary Servants.—There is one part of your letter which has given me, Dear Madam very great uneasiness. You say that you have heard from undoubted authority that my own imprudences had so much embarassed me, as to oblige me to make concessions which otherwise I might not have done. Were I conscious of these imprudencies, I should fairly acknowledge them, and endeavour by my future behaviour to make some amends for past follies. But an innocent person has a right to speak a very different language.

He then pointed out that his income was no extravagant provision, but merely a moderate allowance, within which he had lived, except for the permitted period of Continental travel. On the issue of gambling, "I have never lost at play a hundred pounds at any one time; perhaps not in the course of my life. Play, I neither love nor understand."[13] This statement implies either that she had specifically mentioned his losing £100 on some occasion, or that he regarded a £100 loss as a metonymy for moderation in gaming losses. On an income of £300, the former is the more probable, though compared to the thousands of pounds others lost in Gibbon's time, sometimes in a single evening, never to have lost so much as £100 at once was indeed modest. Of course, in his youth in Lausanne, in the unfortunate episode with Mr. Gee,[14] Gibbon had in fact lost 110 guineas, possibly in one evening, certainly in no more than two, but clearly he was defending not his whole life, but his way of life in London.

Possibly this formal case seemed too much for the occasion; Norton suggests that as a substitute, he might have sent the note dated February 23, 1771, in which he apologized for not writing more, promised to write again by the next post, and urged Mrs. Gibbon not to "suffer [her] spirits to sink at the apprehension of, I hope imaginary evils."[15] On February 27, he went down to Beriton for a fortnight's stay, during which he and Mrs. Gibbon recovered their usual excellent understanding.

They also began to think not merely of settling the debts and problems of the past but also of establishing a new way of life. On March 15, Mrs. Gibbon wrote to Scott that, though she could not make any decision about her own way of life until the estates were sold or let (in effect, she was managing Beriton—very efficiently—for Gibbon), "if in the mean time you should see a house either at Bath or anywhere else, that you might think would suit me I should be much obliged to you to let me know." She added, with, as Gibbon would say, a sigh, "My brother . . . is another perplexity to me when I think of the future."[16]

It is clear from this comment and from Gibbon's friendly messages that Dorothea's brother, William, was now living with her at Beriton, but it is also clear, from her continued appeals to Scott and from Gibbon's concern to provide company for her whenever he was not at Beriton, that William was neither a help nor a companion for her. Various schemes for her settling in Bath were raised in Dorothea's letters to Scott and Gibbon's letters to Dorothea; eventually she did settle there. In one such discussion of the house she might want, Mrs. Gibbon remarked spontaneously to Scott: "I know you will be glad to hear that Mr Gibbon is most excessively good to me. I think there never was a more worthy man, in the transactions that has called upon him to show an exactness both of Duty & honor, there are few I believe that would have the same notions he has."[17]

In mid-April, Gibbon wrote of his pleasure in an invitation his stepmother had received, "as I am persuaded that Bath if you can settle there in a manner agreable to yourself will be a very proper and a very convenient place. I must add, tho' I hope there is no occasion to say it, that nothing in my power shall be wanting to make it so." He then (in the unaccustomed role of "Farmer Gibbon") asked her about sheep rot and wheat harvests, concluding "and I should think—but I have no sort of business to think, and am sure you will give your order with a much more enlightened zeal for our Interest than I could possibly do myself."[18] An even more marked tribute to her acumen as manager of the farm occurred later, when he humorously boasted to Holroyd that he had sold the hops at a price better than anyone else would have done, "even Mrs G."[19] He also shared with his stepmother an attitude toward at least the more sensational public events of the day, such as the arrest of a Lord Mayor;[20] toward new books of general interest; and toward the Gibbon relatives, particularly the peculiarities of Hester Gibbon and the stiffness of the Eliot cousins. If this friendship with his stepmother had not quite the fervor of Gibbon's attachments to the men and women he singled out for himself, it was nevertheless warm and firm.

The most important friendship of his life, that with John Holroyd and his family, was now resumed in all its strength; and from now till, and in a sense long after, Gibbon's death, it continued not merely to endure but to grow. Gibbon's letter to Holroyd informing him of his father's death and hoping to see him in town was met with the swift and generous compliance that was thereafter typical of "my friend Holroyd who is a most invaluable Counsellor," as Gibbon described him as early as February 2.[21]

Holroyd, an excellent man of business, was invaluable because Gibbon had acquired a whole new set of duties and responsibilities. No longer simply the junior member of a committee of trustees, Gibbon was now himself a man of property and affairs. In the *Memoirs,* he admitted that he actually enjoyed this uncharacteristic period of his life, in which, in effect, he tried out his father's role unadulterated by his own literary goals:

"That home, the house and estate at Buriton were now my own: I could invite without controul the persons most agreable to my taste: the horses and servants were at my disposal: and in all their operations my rustic ministers solicited the commands, and smiled at the ignorance of their master" (151). Even at the time he smiled at his own pretensions:

> I set down to answer your Epistle, after taking a very pleasant ride— *A Ride! and upon what?* —upon a horse— *You lye* —I do'nt—I have got a droll little Poney, and intend to renew the long-forgotten practice of Equitation. . . .
> What do you mean by presuming to affirm, that I am of no use here? Farmer Gibbon of no use? *Last weak* I sold all my Hops. . . . *This week* I let a little Farm . . . raising it from £25, to 35 pr annum. and Farmer Gibbon of no use?[22]

Although he smiled, it is doubtful that he was then fully aware of the amusement his agricultural pose might have caused the servants and tenants: "I will not deny that my pride was flattered by the local importance of a country gentleman: the busy scene of the farm, productive of seeming plenty, was embellished in my eyes by the partial sentiment of property" (151-52). With such pleasures, however, and the pleasure of Mrs. Gibbon's company, he could "without much impatience" await an adequate tenant and postpone the beginning of his new way of life.

But as a note to the *Decline and Fall* informs us, even in 1771 he had returned to his true role long enough to produce a rough sketch for his great history, part of which apparently has been preserved in the "Outlines of the History of the World 800-1500."[23] These "Outlines" represent the surviving fragment of the structure of his subject as he first conceived it, with three divisions: Trajan to Justinian, Justinian to Charlemagne, Charlemagne to the fall of Constantinople.[24] These divisions are not those of the *Decline and Fall* as he actually wrote it, but this outline, which deals with the third division only, is enlightening both for its information about his knowledge and views in 1771 and for its implications about his procedure as a working historian.

We know that before he read a new book or studied a new subject, he tried to recollect and order all that he already knew on the subject. We know also of his "early and rational" adherence to the order of time and place, and every reader has been awed by his capacity to comprehend, clarify, and keep in proportion, an enormous mass of information. This outline is one glimpse of his procedure. Because the manuscript has its own separate title, we may infer that the "Outlines" for the two earlier parts were written as distinct projects, perhaps at different times. Within the "Outlines," each century has its own subheading, and there are shoulder notes to indicate specific dates within each. In each century, Gibbon devoted a paragraph or two to each nation or topic, usually more or less in the divisions established by the topic statement for the ninth century, that is, Franks and Germans, Normans, England, Arabs, Greeks. For the eleventh and thirteenth centuries, however, he did not hesitate to establish more appropriate divisions, and for the latter, which was given much more space than the earlier centuries, he introduced geographical and topical shoulder captions. This method he continued for the fourteenth and fifteenth centuries, and he developed these centuries at length, as he had the thirteenth.

Obviously, his state of knowledge was reflected in these two different treatments. Having not yet moved to London or begun his research specifically directed to this period, he had to rely on his historical background; he knew relatively little about the period 800–1200 and was necessarily detached, or relatively so, in dealing with it. Thus there are comparatively few editorial comments in this section of the "Outlines," though it is by no means a mere chronicle—for example, "A powerfull Party was unable to resist the Right and the Arms of Henry," or "[Suger was] a Monk without the prejudices of the Convent."[25] With the conclusion of the account of the twelfth century, however, the manner became that characteristic of the remainder of the "Outlines":

> Under the Feudal System the rights, natural as well as civil, of Mankind, were enjoyed only by the Nobles and Ecclesiastics who scarcely formed the thousanth part of the Community. In this Century they were gradually diffused among the Body of the People. The Cities of Italy acquired full Liberty: the great towns of Germany, England France and Spain became legal Corporations, and purchased Immunities more or less considerable; even the Peasant began to be distinguished from the rest of the Cattle on his Lord's estate.
>
> With the Liberty of Europe, it's Genius awoke; but the first efforts of it's growing strength were consumed in vain and fruitless pursuits. Ignorance was succeeded by error. The Civil and Canon Jurisprudence were blindly adopted, and laboriously perverted. Romances of Chivalry, and Monkish Legends still more fabulous, supplied the place of History. The dreams of Astrology were dignified with the name of Astronomy. To discover the Philosopher's stone was the only end of Chymistry. Superstition, instead of flying before the light of true Philosophy, was involved in thicker darkness by the Scholastic Phantom which usurped it's honours. The two great sources of Knowledge, Nature and Antiquity, were neglected and forgotten.[26]

We may surmise that his greater expansiveness for the remainder of the "Outlines" was dictated not only by greater knowledge but also by greater interest in his subject: "We may now contemplate two of the greatest powers, that have ever given laws to Mankind; the one founded on force, the other on opinion: I mean the Tarter Conquerors, and the Roman Pontifs."[27] There is, however, a clear and important distinction between the perspective of the *Decline and Fall* and that of these "Outlines"; in the former, the controlling issue is the fortunes of the Eastern Empire, and Gibbon writes, as it were, from Constantinople; in the latter, he writes of each aspect of Western European history from its own perspective and might be said to take a global view, had he had any interest in the Orient or the New World. And, of course, even when he expanded his treatment and commented on his material, this work remains a summary, not narration, description, or analysis. We can see, by comparing the "Outlines" with volumes 5 and 6 of the *Decline and Fall*, how the neat division into centuries and sovereigns had to be abandoned, how certain topics (e.g., the Norman Conquest) dwindled whereas others (e.g., the Turks) swelled as he mastered new materials and defined his subject. A small touch epitomizes the difference: in the "Outlines," he mentioned "our countryman Chaucer," "on this side the Alps"; in the *Decline and Fall*, "this side the Alps" is always the side toward Rome.[28]

We can reconstruct his usual procedure, then, somewhat as follows. First, he read and reread the general or fundamental sources for his subject. Then he collected the fruit of this general reading and reflection in a chronological survey, further organized geographically and/or thematically. He then studied every published work, primary or secondary, that could contribute to his knowledge of the branch of his subject he proposed to treat first, repeating this step, of course, for each new chapter, investigating "with [his] pen almost always in [his] hand . . . the subsidiary rays of Medals and inscriptions, of Geography and Chronology . . . the collections of Tillemont . . . to fix and arrange within [his] reach the loose and scattered atoms of historical information" (147). Such notes were at least sometimes ordered in an extremely elliptical list of items as a form of outline for a particular chapter,[29] but the data were recorded in full—if at all—in papers apart or in commonplace books; perhaps they were written down only if he did not own the work he was studying. He came to agree with Dr. Johnson, he has told us (79), that one remembered better what one read twice than what one transcribed; presumably, therefore, he tried and adopted the former method as well as the latter.

Finally, of course, he wrote each chapter, pacing around the room as he tried each sentence in his mind before committing it to paper (147). When a whole chapter was complete, he added the notes.[30] Only the first two stages of this procedure could be accomplished in the interregnum of 1771–72. Though the reader of the "Outlines" is afforded glimpses of the ideas, insights, prejudices, and style of the grand Gibbon to come, they were the only substantial literary product of this period in his life. A commonplace book datable between 1770 and 1777 might have been begun in 1771, but its entries are brief and few.[31]

The "Outlines" have been discussed by some of Gibbon's readers, though only Joseph Swain dated them correctly. In perhaps the most serious study, Giarrizzo sees in them evidence that the medieval section of the *Decline and Fall* was not simply "an enormous coda to the history . . . of the decline of the empire" and argues that in this sketch Gibbon's subject is the emergence of the modern spirit and modern freedom from the travails of medieval ignorance and superstition. As Giarrizzo describes the "Outlines":

> The pages are bare and thin, lighted up here and there by the dry point of invective or the determined energy of polemic; there is not a single sarcastic gesture, or a smile of satisfied irony [this statement is rather too strong]. We have not yet reached the Gibbon of the *History*: the stony austerity of Montesquieuan thought entirely holds and dominates him, he has not yet succeeded in overcoming it, in regarding it with detachment.[32]

Giarrizzo may have been influenced by his impression that the "Outlines" were contemporary with the "Feudal Government" and preceded the Swiss history, yet it is true enough that Gibbon's emphasis was not on the ruins of empire, but on the emerging nations of Europe. David Jordan, who is misled by Lord Sheffield's dating into some false inferences about the relationship between the "Outlines" and the *Decline and Fall*, sees their content as "practically a scenario" for the history, although he too is aware that the point pressed in the "Outlines" is the rise of Europe and that it was a concern that Gibbon shared with the "humanist historians of the Renaissance . . . and Montesquieu."[33] Swain, ingeniously dating the "Outlines" properly, asserts that in "these terse summaries we can distinguish many of [Gibbon's] characteristic ideas," but he contents himself with a very brief and disappointingly superficial list, including the dangerous half-truth that Gibbon "had much to say about liberty and despotism, but the liberty he praised is for the upper classes only, for Gibbon never trusted the populace."[34] Whereas Giarrizzo quotes only Gibbon's criticism of the limited "liberty" advanced by feudalism, Swain quotes only Gibbon's criticism of the "evils . . . of a wild democracy."[35] Gibbon's view, as we have seen most clearly in his "Brutus," was actually that individual liberty is endangered both by despots and by mobs. He opposed not the freedom of the individual members of the populace—he abhorred slavery and oppression—but the tyranny of their uncontrolled collective power. Another of Swain's points, that Gibbon's "pugnacity" in his attack on the medieval church, as in the attack on Warburton in the *Critical Observations*, "is best explained by the general feeling of frustration under which he suffered during his last years at Beriton," may be defensible as an explanation of the severity of the *Critical Observations* (though one need read only a few pages of Warburton to become quite as irritated as Gibbon seems to be), but it is contradicted in this case by his own dating, because in 1771 Gibbon was quite cheerful and not at all frustrated in his sojourn at Beriton.

It is interesting, in view of Gibbon's difficulty when he came to begin the actual writing of the history (he had to write the first chapter three times, the second and third twice "before [he] could hit the middle tone between a dull Chronicle and a Rhetorical declamation" [155]), that in one sense his style—his diction, tropes, sentence structure, and irony—was already fully developed in this piece. For example:

> By establishing the Doctrine of Transubstantiation, and the Tribunal of the Inquisition, [Pope Innocent III] obtained the two most memorable Victories over the common Sense, and common Rights of Mankind. . . . The Free Cities of Italy now delivered from the German yoke, began to enjoy and to abuse the blessings of Wealth and Liberty. . . . Every Gentleman exercised round his Castle a licentious Independance; the Cities were obliged to seek protection from their Walls and Confederacies; and from the Rhine and Danube to the Baltic, the names of Peace and Justice were unknown. . . . Their jealous caution successively fixed on Rodolph Count of Hapsburgh, and Adolph Count of Nassau; whose fortune was far inferior to their birth and personal merit.

These examples all come from the same two pages of the "Outlines,"[36] but *any* pair of pages dealing with the period 1200-1500 might have provided a similar wealth of sentences that proclaim their origin from the pen of the author of the *Decline and Fall.*

In what respect, then, did Gibbon need to develop a style? A preliminary answer is twofold: he had not yet developed the architectural unity and majesty within and between the long paragraphs characteristic of the *Decline and Fall,* and he had not found a technique—or could not use it until he worked on the ampler scale—for incorporating the concrete evidence and the dramatized scenes that are everywhere in the history. There is also little sense of specific time and setting in this survey, despite the chronological and geographical labels. His imagination was still in Beriton, though his wit and intelligence had traveled far. Already established in this 1771 sketch was the cordial yet formal relationship with his reader, which Giarrizzo neatly captures by comparing it to Gibbon's conversational mannerisms: "Bending the small, round body, looking around with an air of affected complacency, creasing the little round cheeks with a meaningful smile, and beginning—not without having given a discreet tap to an elegant snuff-box—'In the second century of the Christian Aera. . . . '"[37] We may surmise, however, that Gibbon found some difficulty in maintaining that relationship as he changed his scale of narrative; certainly it is lost, perhaps for the only time, in the long and tedious chapter (*Decline and Fall,* Chap. 48) in which he tried to survey 550 years of Byzantine sovereigns.

With due deference to the historians cited above, is it not really we who read the "ideas" of the *Decline and Fall* into this sketch? In a trivial sense, of course, they were there; Gibbon's general positions were already formed, but Gibbon's positions, the paraphrasable content, as it were, of his history, are not remarkable. It is the tissue of qualification, support, complication, relations, cautions, and reservations in which he embodies those positions that constitutes his particular statement, his true "ideas." The literary merits of his history are not just pleasant decorations for a set of insights that might have been expressed in other ways; they are inseparable from his discovery of the past and his re-creation of it. The larger literary merits, such as the discovery of character, of tragedy, of epic sweep, are necessarily lacking in the "Outlines."

Yet this sketch, deficient if considered as an independent work, is remarkable as a sign of progress toward the composition of the history, especially if the missing sections were equally substantial. That this is Gibbon's idea of a preliminary study, to be followed by five more years of research and writing before the publication of even the first volume, is evidence of his dedication to the craft and science of history, as well as its art, for it shows that he could have written a "philosophic" history or a merely literary one without further preparation. If Montesquieu and Hume had already prepared Gibbon's views of empires lost and Europe found, if time and Voltaire had already formed his style, more years were necessary for Muratori, Tillemont, the Augustan history, and all the others to assist him to produce the history's thousands of notes and the meticulous accuracy to which they testify.

His time, even at Beriton, though at his own disposal, was by no means entirely free for scholarship; and he was even less often at Beriton than he had been during his father's lifetime: "My stay in London was prolonged into the summer; and the uniformity of the summer was occasionally broken by visits and excursions at a distance from home" (151). On June 27, 1771, for example, he was still in London, and in July, though he was at Beriton and inviting both James Scott and Holroyd (at different times) to visit him there, he went to Sheffield Place at the end of the month and might have gone up to town briefly en route.[38] With the Holroyds he spent a few days at Brighton before returning on August 7 or 8, with John Holroyd, to Beriton. In November, he lingered at Beriton until about the 25th, but the delay was partly caused by his waiting for a letter of business from Holroyd. The charm of being Farmer and Proprietor Gibbon had already worn off to a considerable extent; he says as much to Holroyd in a letter of October 25, influenced, perhaps, by a ludicrous error he had recently made while carrying out that role:

> To shew that I am not an ungratefull Wretch I wrote immediately to Damer, and to shew that I am a very careless one, I directed the letter to another person, whose Epistle went to Damer. Lord Milton's heir was ordered to send me without delay a brown Ratteen Frock [he was apparently either out of mourning or preparing to be, on the anniversary of his father's death, i.e., November 10], and the Taylor was desired to use his interest with his cousin the Duke of Dorset. . . .

Plût au Ciel that I had neither Farm nor Tenants, they suit not my humour.[39]

His chagrin, if any, was not severe. The letters of this winter, both to Mrs. Gibbon and to Holroyd, are remarkable for their entire good cheer, in spite of their subjects, almost invariably the cold, the delays and misdeeds of the surveyor and other persons concerned with the Gibbons' affairs, and political sensations, such as the Danish scandal.[40]

For most of the following year (1772), Gibbon's papers are entirely those of the man of leisure and business; the man of letters seems entirely dormant. His concerns were financial, political, friendly, filial, or proprietal, but no one would guess that either his reading or his writing differed from that of any other man of fashion and position—indeed, he did not even write about the latest publications, as he had often done in the past. There is one major exception to this generalization, but though the plan of this exception might have been conceived as early as March, it did not manifest itself until summer, perhaps as late as August. It will therefore be discussed below.

Meanwhile, Gibbon was absorbed in his attempts to find a tenant for Beriton and a buyer for Lenborough, so that he might pay off his father's mortgage and his large debt, that to the Clarke estate.[41] The friendly intimacy between Gibbon and Holroyd grew stronger and stronger, not only in Holroyd's role as Gibbon's "Oracle" (unpaid business adviser), but in the friendliness between the two families—Gibbon's messages to Holroyd's children, Mrs. Gibbon's gift of a greyhound puppy to Holroyd. In June, Gibbon had the further pleasure and distraction of a two-week visit to England by Deyverdun, a correspondent even more dilatory than Gibbon himself, with whom, therefore, Gibbon had to some extent lost contact. Deyverdun "is not come back nor has he replied a syllable to six letters of mine and Sr R's," Gibbon complained.[42] When Deyverdun did reach England, however, he "explained fully to my satisfaction the reasons of his whole conduct; tho' they are such as it is not permitted me to reveal."[43] Whatever they were, they must have satisfied Lord Chesterfield as well as Gibbon, because Chesterfield, as he had long intended, made Deyverdun his godson's tutor and traveling companion (M 280).

In the letter just quoted, Gibbon also mentioned, for the first time, eye trouble, "which is now perfectly removed." Perhaps it was, though Gibbon always made light of his illnesses, especially when writing, as here, to his stepmother. At approximately this period in his life, however, he found it necessary to begin wearing eyeglasses.[44] There is an extant pair, an analysis of which shows that Gibbon suffered from far-sightedness, which meant that he would have required glasses for reading earlier and more urgently than those who simply grow far-sighted with age.[45] He never mentioned his spectacles in his letters, or wore them in the portraits and sketches made of him, which we might interpret as a sign of his vanity about his personal appearance if we chose, but which is more probably a sign that the glasses were sufficiently strong to blur his vision for purposes other than reading.

A clearer evidence of his vanity is his clothing bills. Though few bills remain for this period, we can discover that his mourning outfit included a sword and that less than a year after his father's death he was ordering colored clothes.[46] His use of the "droll little poney," although soon ended, suggests that he had not yet attained the corpulence characteristic of his later years, and his girth was not too great to be adorned by Mrs. Gibbon's handiwork: "Your Wastecoat is most universally admired, and I shall be much obliged to you for another exactly the same."[47]

In July, his cheerfulness was seriously interrupted by a friend's unhappiness. John Holroyd's only son died on July 12. Gibbon was so distressed that he wrote at first not to Holroyd himself, but to Holroyd's mother:

> I so truly sympat[h]ize with them, that I know not how to write to Holroyd; but must beg to be informed of the state of the family by a line from you. I have some Company and business here but would gladly quit them [if] I had the least reason to think that my presence at Sheffield would afford the least comfort or satisfaction to the man in the world whom I love and esteem the most.[48]

This heart-felt sympathy and eagerness to comfort is very characteristic of Gibbon the friend; it was one role in which he felt no need for restraint or moderation. When he received Holroyd's reply to this letter, desiring his company, he planned to set out at once; "I hoped to have been with [you] to day: but walking very carelessly yesterday morning I fell down and put out a small bone in my ancle. I am now under the Surgeon's hands, but think and most earnestly hope that this little accident will not delay my journey longer than the middle of next week."[49] Indeed, he did not allow it to do so; four days later he wrote to Scott (with a revealing repetition), "I am going next Wednesday . . . to condole with my friend Holroyd to condole with him on the loss of his only son."[50] It was a two-day journey, and he wrote to Mrs. Gibbon from Sheffield Place on August 7, so he was as good as his word.

He had planned only a two-week stay, but on the 21st he wrote to Mrs. Gibbon: "my friend who is still very low expresses so much uneasiness at the Idea of my quitting him, that I cannot refuse him the remainder of the month."[51] He mentioned trying to persuade the Holroyds to an excursion to Portsmouth, the Isle of Wight, Southampton, which would include a few days at Beriton; and in his next letter home he announced their coming "[We] shall dine at Beriton [Friday, August 28], and stay there most probably three or four days. A Farm house without either Cook or Housekeeper[52] will afford but indifferent entertainment, but we must *exert*, and they must *excuse*."[53] The further plans included some ten more days of travel and Gibbon's return with the Holroyds to Sheffield Place. Thus throughout August Gibbon was preoccupied with the Holroyds' bereavement, and much of the month was spent in travel. Yet on August 29, Richard Hurd replied to a pseudonymous correspondent who had written an elaborate and polite controversial letter to him, denying the antiquity of the Book of Daniel.[54] That correspondent was Edward Gibbon; Norton dates his letter to Hurd August 1772. Obviously, it was written after March, when Hurd's book to which it replies was published, and before August 29, the date of Hurd's reply to it. But surely it is more likely that Gibbon wrote it in the first two weeks of July, in the tranquillity of Beriton, rather than in his weeks of worry and travel with the Holroyds.

However that may be, the letter survives to prove that the historian of the Roman Empire was not utterly lost in the Hampshire gentleman, even in this least scholarly year of Gibbon's adulthood. The neat epistle is, in both structure and manner, very Gibbonian, and its arguments are illustrated from topics recently canvassed by Gibbon: the state of the Median Empire and the writings of Virgil. Gibbon's case—long since won—has not received much attention from recent historians interested in his work, but, although its tone is much better designed to avoid offending the orthodox than is that of the *Decline and Fall* (if indeed he was genuinely surprised that his tone there gave offense[55]), it is clearly the work of the same mind. His attitude is portrayed as that of a reasonable man, but *not* that of a zealous atheist or even deist. He withheld his assent to the antiquity of the Book of Daniel because: "I. The author of the Book of Daniel is too well informed of the revolutions of the Persian and Macedonian empires, which are supposed to have happened long after his death. II. He is too ignorant of the transactions of his own times. In a word, he is too exact for a Prophet, and too fabulous for a contemporary historian."[56] Gibbon acknowledged that a counterargument to the first objection is that the prophecies were uncommonly skillful, but he asked:

> May I not assume as a principle equally consonant to experience, to reason, and even to true religion; 'That we ought not to admit any thing as the immediate work of God, which can possibly be the work of man; and that whatever is said to deviate from the ordinary course of nature, should be ascribed to accident, to fraud, or to fiction; till we are fully satisfied, that it lies beyond the reach of those causes?' If we cast away this buckler, the blind fury of superstition, from every age of the world, and every corner of the globe, will invade us naked and unarmed.[57]

He went on to argue that a *sine qua non* for assuming accurate prophecy rather than hindsight should be the well-attested existence of the prophecy previous to the event; Virgil's ending his account of the fate of Rome

(*Aeneid* 6) with the death of Marcellus is an instance of such easy "prophecy," though, of course, not intended to deceive. If we did not know when Virgil lived, Gibbon concluded, we should, from that episode alone, be "authorized to infer, that Virgil lived in the Augustan age; and the sixth book was composed during the yet recent grief for the loss of young Marcellus." Hurd replied that Gibbon required as minimum evidence, the best evidence that the case admits of; and his point was well taken, if only because Gibbon did not deal with the testimony urged by the supporters of the antiquity of the Book of Daniel, that Jesus' "appeal to it supposes and implies that reception [of the book by the Jews] to have been constant and general."[58]

Gibbon's second argument was presented more elaborately and obviously weighed more heavily. He maintained that "Daniel's" account of his own life did not jibe with historical fact in five respects. Four of these are not so much matters of fact as matters of political and psychological probability:

1. It is unlikely that skill in astrology would have led to Daniel's being made a minister;

2. It is unlikely that the jealous rivals, seeing Daniel supported by miracles, would have dared to entrap him, even though it is remarkable (a touch of the "solemn sneer" here) how indifferent the ancients were to the miracles vouchsafed to their era—"Although the hand of the Almighty was almost perpetually employed in tracing out those divine characters; they were no sooner formed, than they were obliterated from the minds of men";[59]

3. The irrevocability of the laws of the Medes and the Persians is too much of a check on the reigning despot to be probable;

4. The edict of Darius prohibiting all worship for thirty days is too sweeping to be plausible: the ministers of Darius could not possibly represent it as beneficial, because "to suspend during thirty days the most universal propensity of mankind, is a strain of wanton despotism unparalleled in the history of the world."[60]

Hurd disposed of the first point neatly, as Gibbon acknowledged in his draft reply, by arguing that skill in soothsaying, though not a sufficient cause for a ministerial appointment, was no deterrent to one, just as, in modern times, clerics have been ministers for their merits, not because of their clerical standing. On the second point, Hurd suggested that the most rational fears may be, and often are, overruled by "inflamed selfish passions."[61] This telling point induced a very interesting response from Gibbon, in which he denied the power of passion to blind quite so thoroughly as it is alleged to do. The draft reply is incomplete, but Gibbon seems to have thought that "ruling passions" operate only by degrees and only on individually trifling, though collectively crushing, instances. We think that our merit will permit us to engineer good fortune for ourselves, and it is that false reasoning, rather than irresistible passion, that leads us to repeat an error we can easily observe in others. In the case of disregarding miracles, it is easy to be indifferent where the belief is not strong. But (he must have intended to continue), were there overpowering evidence that, on some important occasion, we could not possibly overcome our opponents, as in the case of those who had witnessed a visible miracle on their opponent's behalf, passion could not overcome fear. Hurd's case seems truer to human experience in general, but Gibbon's own power over irrational impulse is undoubtedly reflected in his inability to think mankind as unreasonable as it often is.

Hurd conceded some weight to Gibbon's fourth argument, but countered that the pagans would not be so shocked by the deprivation of prayer as Christians would be, and, in any case, the law could not suppress mental and even, in private, oral prayer. Gibbon seems to have understood the polytheists' feelings rather more thoroughly than Hurd, here, for if one really lived in a world inhabited by powerful beings who could be propitiated only by sacrifices to particular images or in particular shrines, no amount of private prayer would make up for being unable to placate or supplicate them. If a god lives in a particular temple and likes to sniff incense or feed on burnt offerings, that god will be dangerously angry if no one feeds him for a month. On the other hand, Hurd suggested that a despot might be flattered to think that for a month he alone was to be worshipped;[62] and, given enough hubris, a despot might indeed enjoy such an exclusive privilege. Gibbon's reply to this point either was not composed or has not survived.

Gibbon's fifth argument was a matter of fact: there may have been no "Darius the Mede." Gibbon used in part the conclusions of his study of the *Cyropaedia*,[63] and without his presenting them at length, it is not surprising that Hurd was not convinced. Hurd conceded that the *Cyropaedia*, even if a romance, was well grounded in history, but argued that if Cyaxares was Darius, and Cyaxares never reigned at Babylon, nevertheless there might be ways of reconciling Xenophon's account and a "reign" of Darius in some sense of the term.

He added that, even if there are errors and fables in some parts of the Book of Daniel, "it would be too precipitate to conclude that therefore the whole book was of no authority," and concluded:

And now, Sir, I have only to commit these hasty reflections to your candour; a virtue which cannot be separated from the love of truth, and of which I observe many traces in your agreeable letter; and if you should indulge this quality still further, so as to conceive the possibility of that being *true and reasonable,* in matters of religion, which may seem strange, or, to so lively a fancy as yours, even ridiculous, you would not hurt the credit of your excellent understanding, and would thus remove one, perhaps a principal, occasion of those

mists which, as you complain, *hang over these nice and difficult subjects.* [64]

The whole debate was carried on in a gentlemanly and rational manner
that is a credit to both participants. Such a spirit is not common, on
either side, in Gibbon's encounters with his clerical opponents.

Hurd began his letter by saying that Gibbon's had been "just now received," but we may assume that Gibbon wrote the letter some time before he sent it, or that Hurd's expression is not to be strictly construed, or
that the letter was delayed in transit. In his *Memoirs,* Gibbon implies that
this letter to Hurd was an amusement, the fruit of the studies of the Bible
with which he entertained himself during church services (M 211). Obviously, it was more than that; it was another trial effort as a historian, and
like the writings between 1765 and 1770, it was essentially negative criticism, not positive assertion; it was fragmentary; and it was anonymous.
Especially after the achievement of the "Outlines," it was a symptom of
incomplete recovery from, or of relapse into, the impotence of prolonged
adolescence. In attempting to be his father, he had again delayed his emergence as himself. But he knew that he must escape, and, with the aid of
Holroyd, he knew how to do so.

A difficulty was the objection of Mrs. Gibbon to the disposal of Beriton.
One infers that she rather enjoyed farming;[65] she certainly thought of
Beriton as her home, and although Gibbon was entirely willing to leave
her the use of the house, it was impossible to let the farms without giving
the tenants permission to cross the grounds in front of the house to get to
the barns, and those in back to get to the fields. Mrs. Gibbon did not like
that prospect. When Gibbon wrote (September 25, 1772) to Holroyd to
tell him with delight that Beriton had been let, he said:

> I should think it one of the most agreable days of my life, were it not
> embittered by the uneasiness I feel on Mrs G.'s account. She refused to
> yield an iota of her pretensions ... [though she] was repeatedly told
> that every farmer did and ever would reject the farm on such terms. At
> length she gave [their agent] authority to say that she had given up all
> thoughts of the place: but her temper both then and since has been
> very different from what I could wish it. She is angry if she is not con-
> stantly consulted and yet takes up every thing with such absolute
> quickness that we all dread to consult her. She is at present, I fear,
> equally offended with me with [the agent] and Mr Scott. Nothing shall
> however abate my regard for her, and as soon as I can discover whether
> she will fix on Bath [or] some Country place, she may command
> every service within my power. All this *sub sigillo amicitiae.* [66]

Mrs. Gibbon's temper or mood soon grew sunny again, and, on October
3, Gibbon wrote, "Mrs G is now chearfull, and I hope satisfied"; after completing the sale of the farm produce and excess household furniture, he

would take her to Bath to find a house, and then return, "impatient to examine London in quest of a comfortable habitation."[67] It is from this month, in the *Memoirs,* that he dated his emancipation, although the sale of Lenborough and settlement of the mortgage were not even illusorily accomplished until June 1773 (in reality, that sale was never completed, and the mortgage was not fully paid off until 1785), and he did not move into his own house until February 1773. But after October, he was no longer in the shadow of that life of the country gentleman, which his father in some ways had graced, in others had failed at, but which was financially and perhaps emotionally incompatible with Gibbon's own desire for a town establishment. Appropriately enough, when he was clearing up papers in November, preparing for the move to town, he found and burned the manuscript of his first childish effort at authorship, the "Age of Sesostris" (56). He preserved the family portraits that had hung at Beriton, but he found nowhere to hang them in his new house.[68]

If his father had made few inroads on the family resources, perhaps Gibbon would have continued to maintain the country estate as well as his town house, but if he had done so, he might have found too little leisure or energy for the great history. Well might he

> believe and even assert that in circumstances more indigent or more wealthy, I should never have accomplished the task, or acquired the fame, of an historian; that my spirit would have been broken by poverty and contempt; and that my industry might have been relaxed in the labour and luxury of a superfluous fortune. Few works of merit and importance have been executed either in a garret or a palace. A gentleman, possessed of leisure and independence, of books and talents, may be encouraged to write by the distant prospect of honour and reward: but wretched is the author, and wretched will be the work, where daily diligence is stimulated by daily hunger. (153-54)

He probably had in mind a range of income that would have included enough to retain the landed estates, for his terms for their sale—"amputation," "sacrifice"—are not those of a man who thought their possession would have left him too rich to achieve his life's work; nevertheless, it was precisely and only the "clear untainted remains of [his] patrimony" that supported for him "the rank of a Gentleman, and . . . the desires of a philosopher" (154).

The house he found in London was No. 7, Bentinck Street. A modern house (only some eleven years old when he took it), which he redecorated according to his own taste, it was regarded by him with great pride and affection. The decoration and furnishing of it concerned him for the remainder of 1772; it was his principal occupation, though he was briefly delayed by the death of Mrs. Gibbon's brother. That brother had long been an invalid, and Mrs. Gibbon was apparently relieved, as well as grieved, by the event.[69] Another diversion in his London activities was the responsiblity of finding a house, stables, and a footman for the Holroyds' use during their stay in the city. But his own house was his major interest. He liked Bentinck Street when he first saw it, despite its "offices and two pairs of stairs," but as he consulted with the upholsterer, planning his "book-room" in particular ("The paper . . . will be a fine shag flock-paper, light blue with a gold border, the Bookcases painted white, ornamented with a light frize"), he grew more and more possessive of it.[70]

Two more interruptions conspired with the upholsterer to delay his actual occupancy. One was the unexpected death of his old friend and financial adviser, James Scott, who died intestate and whose property descended to Dorothea Gibbon as his next of kin. Gibbon wrote to tell her of the event, assisted her when she came to town, but neither went to her nor carried out the immediate arrangements himself; the invaluable Stanier Porten took on that task at Gibbon's request. Gibbon's behavior was kind and proper, but not comparable to his active sympathy in the Holroyds' bereavement, or that he had felt toward Mrs. Gibbon herself when his father died. We may infer either that Gibbon underestimated Mrs. Gibbon's affection for Scott, or that Mrs. Gibbon herself did not feel deeply affected by his death, however much his generous assistance over the years may have deserved attachment. Certainly Gibbon's letter to Sheffield after seeing her in London suggests that both he and his stepmother were more concerned with Scott's estate than with his loss.[71] They had, of course, seen relatively little of him since 1770.

Gibbon's second distraction was less momentous at the time, but of greater future influence on his comfort:

> On Thursday the third of December in the present year of our Lord one Thousand seven hundred and seventy-two, between the hours of one and two in the Afternoon, as I was crossing St James's Church Yard, I stumbled, and *again sprained my foot* [emphases throughout are Holroyd's], but alas after two days pain and Confinement, a horrid Monster *ycleped the Gout made me* a short Visit.[72]

Though a short visit, it would not be its last.

Gibbon spent Christmas and New Year's at Sheffield Place, except for the brief trip to London occasioned by Scott's death. Both before leaving town, and after returning, he spent numerous evenings with his faithful Aunt Kitty, though he continued to stay in his Pall Mall lodgings. On February 11, he could at last write to Mrs. Gibbon from his "own house in Bentinck Street."[73] Reminiscing affectionately about it in the *Memoirs* (one of Gibbon's most endearing traits is his capacity to enjoy fully the homely comforts life provided to him), he said, "I had now attained the solid comforts of life, a convenient well-furnished house, a domestic table, half a dozen chosen servants, my own carriage, and all those decent luxuries whose value is the more sensibly felt the longer they are enjoyed"

(154). Lord Sheffield thought these sentiments unfit for publication—too much concerned with creature comforts, perhaps. Gibbon himself omitted, in first writing this sentence, the table and the servants. His idea of practical bliss required the house, and the carriage with which to leave it; the servants and the table were delightful afterthoughts, lost at first among the other "decent luxuries" in which he took so much satisfaction and pleasure.

Thus lodged, he could feel himself at last truly independent, "absolute master of [his] hours and actions," able to "divide [his] day between Study and Society." At last, the history of the youngest Edward Gibbon was securely that of the historian of the Roman Empire. It had been a very long apprenticeship, filled with apparent failures. Successively he lost his mother, his home, his religion, his father, and his country; in Switzerland, he found a new home, a new language, a new identity, a true, life-long friend, and his education flowered; but he lost his capacity for zeal and his first and only love—not to mention all those guineas to Mr. Gee. Back in England, he regained a place in his father's house and enjoyed the limited triumphs of the militia and the *Essai,* but he gave up his rights under his grandfather's will and lost the Petersfield election; he found no circle of friends to replace those of Lausanne; and he increasingly fretted at his failure to put to use his real vocation—scholarship, writing, history. He felt the loss of time and finally won the opportunity to complete his self-education both as a gentleman and as a scholar by means of the Grand Tour.

It was a unique Grand Tour, carried out as much in books at Lausanne as in the roads, cities, and monuments of France and Italy. Prepared intellectually and emotionally to enter the past whose setting he traveled through, he found instead the petty intricacies of modern states and politics, and the melancholy grandeur of antiquity in ruins. He found, or ever afterward retained the conviction that he had found, the germ of his great subject in that confrontation. At the same time, however, the illusion of a secure status as his father's son was shattered by his father's financial betrayal. He returned, therefore, to a life of tutelage, in which his time was divided between London—where he was homeless, houseless, and bookless—and Beriton—where his writing, under the literal and emotional limitations of his father's roof and his father's name, was incomplete or brief or unpublished or anonymous. Toward the end of the period, he had to form a coalition with his uncle and his stepmother's cousin to rescue his sick and frightened—and thence unwilling and ungrateful—father from himself, particularly his good name, which was threatened by unmet debts. This thankless, difficult, and uncongenial work required most of his time and energy until the last few weeks of his father's life, when his presence at his father's side became his constant duty.

All of this period seemed to him so much lost time, but in it we have seen him build on the foundations of his historical studies and perfect his craft through exercise. Most significantly, however, he matured as a person in ways of which he himself seemed unconscious. The facing of economic reality, the study in patience and charity, the rewards of generous friendship, the acceptance of friendship's vulnerability to his old enemy, death, despite its invulnerability to time and distance, and simply the long period of endeavoring to find contentment in the better moments of an unsatisfactory way of life—all these prepared him for the labor of his great work, for the keen enjoyment of the possible that ever afterward characterized his way of life, for the distrust of passion that forced his emotional life into the untainted outlets of friendship and writing; prepared him, in a word, to be the "luminous historian" Sheridan called him [74] and a man who could think "the historian of the Roman Empire" a full and acceptable definition of his life.

From infancy his frail and malformed body had taught him to experience the relief of pain as a positive pleasure, but the "moderate sensibility" of the man developed over time, and at a cost even he dimly perceived: "Some flowers of fancy, some grateful errors, [may] have . . . been eradicated with the weeds of prejudice. . . . The warm desires, the long expectations of youth are founded on the ignorance of themselves and of the World: they are gradually damped by time and experience, by disappointment or possession " (186, 189). So it had been with him.

The suffering infant, the romantic schoolboy, the ardent young man (his heart fatally divided between Suzanne and scholarship), the enthusiastic and intemperate militia officer, the learned but sociable traveler, the dutiful son, now give way to the rational historian. But they survive in the fervor of his friendships and in the tragic sense of the *Decline and Fall*.

Appendix

T

HE ORDER in which works entered in Gibbon's commonplace book were read by him can be reconstructed because the entries are only loosely alphabetical; each entry is assigned to a category determined by its initial letter and the first subsequent vowel, but the entries are chronological within categories, and the categories are set up only as they are needed. In the course of one's reading, as one came upon an entry that fitted into a particular alphabetical category, for example, CA, one simply assigned the first empty page in one's commonplace book to that category, made the entry, and recorded in a table of contents the number of the page that was henceforth to be used for entries beginning with those letters. If a page had already been assigned to the desired category, of course one made the new entry on the page assigned earlier. When a page was filled, the entry or category was continued, if necessary, on the first page that was still blank at the time it was needed. Gibbon assigned pages in pairs. For example, pp. 16–17 (his numbers) were devoted to "Co" entries. In the midst of an entry at the bottom of p. 17, however, he exhausted the page, so he continued that entry, and made subsequent "Co" entries, on pp. 100–101.

Within each category, then, the entries are chronological. Furthermore, at least the first entry on each pair of pages was made earlier than the entries on subsequent pages. And when an entry is continued from a full page, all the entries on the filled page preceded all the entries on pages later than the one on which the entry is continued, but the first item, at least, on the page preceding the continuation was written before at least the entry that had to be continued, for if that page had been blank, the continuation would have been placed on it. Similarly, pages must have been filled in the order in which they required continuations; for example, the entry that exhausted p. 51 and was continued on p. 96 must have been made prior to the entry that exhausted p. 17 and was continued on p. 101.

These clues allow one to establish the relative order of the entries and therefore of Gibbon's reading; other clues permit us to relate this order to the calendar. The three most important are a reference to his September 21–October 20 tour of Switzerland, a citation of the November 1755 issue of the *Mercure de France*, and an entry in another notebook, dated January 19, 1756, in which Gibbon recorded and implemented a reading plan to which some of the commonplace book entries can be referred. The inferences from each clue require explanation.

Gibbon made an entry, on p. 134 (fol. 71v) of the commonplace book, from Watteville's *Histoire de la confédération helvétique,* referring to an inscription at Coucy. A cue in the continuously written text, that is, a cue that must have been written at the same time as the text, not a later addition, leads the reader to the marginal note, "Je le vis le 15 Octobre 1755" ("I saw it, October 15, 1755"). Sir Gavin de Beer, modern editor of Gibbon's journal of this tour, assumed that Gibbon had read Watteville before setting out: "Gibbon avait . . . préparé son voyage, et après l'avoir fait il nota dans son livre de raison, en face du relevé de l'inscription: 'Je le vis, Oct. 15, 1755.'" (MG, p. 83.) (Gibbon had . . . prepared for his journey, and after he had made it, he noted in his commonplace book, opposite the transcription of the inscription: 'I saw it, Oct. 15, 1755.') If de Beer is correct, Gibbon must have read not only Watteville, but all the works he read before reading Watteville, in the six months between March 19 and September 21. But de Beer's only reason for the assumption that Gibbon read Watteville prior to his tour turns out to be that the commonplace book itself was dated March 19, an obviously inadequate argument. Instead, it seems probable that Gibbon wrote the entry after returning from the tour, smoothly signaling the reference to his visit as he wrote. Thus all entries later than Watteville can be dated after October 20, 1755.

It is possible that Gibbon had read, but not yet made extracts from, Watteville's recent book (Bern, 1754) before going on his tour. But it is equally probable that he read it after he returned or during the journey—perhaps he even bought it while he was in Bern. Pavillard's draft account (Magdalen College, Oxford, mss. 359, fol. 6) includes a payment to "Mr. Muret pr la Confederation helv.," but his letter to Mr. Gibbon does not list this expense (*Memoirs*, p. 222), which might mean that it was treated as part of the expenses of the tour, separately billed. In any case, the writing of the entry must be subsequent to October 20. Entries beginning pp. 136–46 (from *Mémoires sur les troubles arrivés en Suisse à l'occasion du consensus*, from La Mothe le Vayer, and from Cornelius Nepos) were therefore made not earlier than the last eleven weeks of the year. The first entry on p. 146 is from the *Mercure de France* of November 1755. Swiss schoolboys were unlikely to have instant access to French journals; thus this and entries subsequent to it cannot be earlier than November 1755, and are probably later.

The next pair of pages begins with an entry on a topic (King) begun on pp. 6–7, from Du Bos's history of the French monarchy. The remaining entries are all from Latin poets, except the second (and last) entry on p. 154, which is from Fontenelle. Like the entry from Du Bos, it deals with the Middle Ages, but with troubadours, not kings. The entries from the Latin poets can be placed in 1756, for they represent his reading in the Latin classics, according to his plan of January 19, 1756 (see Chapter 6). Entries in the commonplace book related to this project can be identified because they took the form of lists of references without comment or context. Other entries intermingled with or subsequent to such entries can, therefore, also be attributed to 1756 or later.

Notes

CHAPTER 1

1. *Memoirs*, p. 27. References to this, the standard edition of Gibbon's autobiography, will hereafter be indicated by page numbers in the text.

Parliament was dissolved on April 28, 1741 (N.S.), and Edward Gibbon II was returned for the next Parliament, summoned for June 25, 1741. Robert Beatson, *A Chronological Register of Both Houses of the British Parliament*, 3 vols. (London, 1807).

2. The description is that of Gibbon's friend and literary executor, John Baker Holroyd, Lord Sheffield (*MW* 1814, 1: 82); we know that Gibbon had red hair from Meredith Read, *Historic Studies in Vaud, Berne, and Savoy*, 2 vols. (London, 1897), 2: 348.

3. So striking is this moderation and temperateness that he has been portrayed as a "born" Augustan. See chap. 9 of J. W. Johnson's *The Formation of Neo-Classical Thought* (Princeton, 1967). While I acknowledge the metaphoric aptness of this description, I suggest that it is not literally true. Instead of being born Augustan, Gibbon both achieved Augustanism and had it thrust upon him.

4. Edmund Malone to the Earl of Charlemont, February 20, 1794, MSS. of the Earl of Charlemont, *Historical Manuscriptions Commission Thirteenth Report*, appendix, pt. 8 (vol. 28, pt. 2), pp. 230-31.

5. *The Autobiographies of Edward Gibbon*, ed. John Murray (London, 1896), pp. 417-18. The manuscript of the drafts is Add. MSS. 34874. References to the Murray edition will be indicated in the text by the prefix "M."

6. See especially Gibbon's account in the first draft of his memoirs, M 356. The correction of his genealogical information was made by Sir Samuel Edgerton Brydges in a series of notes in the *Gentleman's Magazine*, 1788-96, especially the issue of August 1788 (vol. 48): 698, which Gibbon saw (*Letters*, 3: 246).

7. Parish Register of St. Helen's Bishopsgate; *London Marriage Licenses* (London, 1887).

8. D. M. Low, *Edward Gibbon, 1737-1794* (London, 1937), p. 8.

9. For the Acton connection, see M 372-74, reprinted in *Memoirs*, pp. 201-2.

10. Parish Register of St. Andrew Undershaft.

11. Low, *Gibbon*, p. 9.

12. Robert B. Gardiner, *Records of St. Paul's School*, London, 1884.

13. *Calendar of State Papers*, Treasury Books, 8: 997, 1033 (November 1686).

14. Ibid., 9:394, 629, 668-69, etc.

15. Brydges gives the date as 1709; it is obvious that this is wrong, because Matthew's widow remarried in 1698.

16. Add. MSS. 44085, fol. 32.

17. E.g., *Calendar of State Papers*, Treasury Books, 7: 139.

18. See M 366; corroborated, of course, by Hester Gibbon's letter, quoted previously, and another fol. 34 of the same B.L. MS.

19. *Faculty Office Marriage Licenses* and the Parish Register of St. Peter Cornhill.

20. For date, see *London Marriage Licenses*; jewelry is listed in *Particular and Inventory of Edward Gibbon, Esq.* (London, 1721), p. 7. Hereafter *P & I*.

21. *P & I*, pp. 3–4.

22. Parish Register of St. Helen's Bishopsgate. Noted by George Sherwood as a curiosity in *Notes and Queries* 171 (Dec. 12, 1936); 421.

23. According to Gibbon. *Memoirs*, p. 13. Accepted by Low.

24. The actual date was January 18, 1711/12. Narcissus Luttrell, *Brief Historical Relation of State Affairs from September 1678 to April 1714* (London, 1857), 6:717.

25. *Victoria County History* (henceforth *VCH*), *Surrey*, 4: i, 81n.

26. G.F.R. Barker and A. H. Stenning, *Record of Old Westminsters* (London, 1928).

27. *VCH, Buckinghamshire*, 3: 484. *P & I*, p. 2.

28. *VCH, Hampshire*, 3: 87. *P & I*, p. 1.

29. See John Patrick Carswell, *The South Sea Bubble* (London, 1960), esp. pp. 102–240.

30. *P & I*, p. 2.

31. Dates of birth for Catherine and Mary are from the genealogical table prepared for Low by Captain C.M.H. Pearce, *Edward Gibbon*, pp. 357–58. No date is given for Judith's birth, but Gibbon says she was in her thirty-eighth year when she died. She died in December 1746, but he thought she died in 1747. She was therefore born in 1709 or 1710. Captain Pearce unfortunately did not supply his authority for the statement that Catherine was born December 6, 1706. Her burial is recorded in the Putney Parish Register on April 29, 1786; she was said to have been eighty.

32. Putney Parish Register.

33. James Porten, Merchant and Insurer, is listed in London directories as late as 1744; he figures in Treasury Book entries.

34. Pearce in Low, *Gibbon*, p. 357, n.(e).

35. *P & I*, "Abstract," p. [3].

36. Michel Baridon, *Edward Gibbon et le mythe de Rome* (Paris, 1977), argues that Gibbon exaggerates this loss by overlooking the fact that £30,000 of the £106,000 were in South-sea Company stock, for whose loss of value Parliament was not responsible. Moreover, the property reserved for his wife amounted to £35,971; therefore he lost not £96,000, but about £30,000, by Act of Parliament. Gibbon did indeed neglect to consider the revised value of the stock, but the £35,971 mentioned in the *Particular and Inventory* was Edward Gibbon I's *life interest* in the property made over to his wife, plus property not assigned to her. The life interest amounted to an estimated £15,000, on the assumption that he would live for ten years; the other £21,000 was certainly lost, and the whole sum was if the fine was levied as a fixed sum, instead of as confiscation of assets. Furthermore, the stock that he held in the South-sea Company and that was confiscated or charged against him by the act, did not become worthless; it merely dropped to some 10–12 percent of its maximum value. The difference between Edward Gibbon I's estimate of its value in April 1721, and its value at a price of 135 is less than £3,000. Gibbon therefore probably estimated his grandfather's loss fairly accurately, at £96,000, though it might have been as low as £78,000.

37. Walton MSS. 186.10.2. Dr. Williams's Library, London.

38. Walton MSS. 186.8.8.

39. Catherine and Edward were married by another cousin, Williams Gibbon, at St.

Paul's Cathedral. Edward Elliston was the son of Edward Gibbon I's sister Hester; Williams Gibbon, the son of his brother Thomas. (*Marriages at St. Paul's Cathedral*). Catherine is usually said to have died "about 1737," but she was still alive in 1743, when she wrote a letter that her sister preserved; Catherine died some time before her husband, however, who was buried at Putney, June 13, 1747. Walton MSS. 186.6.41.

40. John and J. A. Venn, comps., *Alumni Cantabrigiensis* (Cambridge, 1922-26).

41. John Byrom, *Private Journal and Literary Remains*, ed. R. Parkinson, 2 vols. (Manchester: Chetham Society, 1854-57).

42. Law's character of Flatus is quoted and discussed by Gibbon (M 382-83), who comments that, because his father was only twenty-five when the second edition of the *Serious Call* was published, "the prophetic eye of the tutor must have discerned the butterfly in the caterpillar. But our family tradition attests his laudable or malicious design."

43. Byrom, *Private Journal*, 1, pt. 2, p. 398.

44. Ibid., pp. 422, 424.

45. Ibid., pp. 425-35.

46. Robert's younger brother, John, later married Katherine Acton of Besançon, a cousin of the Gibbons. Robert and Mary's sons became successful merchants, respectively directors of the Bank of England and the South-sea Company. See *Letters*, 3, and Norton's source, F. A. Crisp and J. J. Howard, *Visitations of England and Wales*, vol. 12, *Notes* (London, 1917).

47. Walton MSS. 186.10.3.

48. *Letters*, 1: 146-47.

49. Beatson, *Register of Parliament*.

50. This correspondence is now at Magdalen College, Oxford, MSS. 363,B.II. It has never been published. I have preserved spelling, punctuation, and capitalization because these details sometimes appeared to have expressive purpose or effect, but superscript letters in abbreviations have been leveled, and *th* written *y* is expanded to *th*. My quotations are, in order, from his letter "1st" (Jan. 18, 1734/5); her letter incorrectly dated on the back "Jan 17," but actually a reply to his letter of January 21; a letter of hers labeled "Feby" that begins "I look upon my self to be very happy"; his "5th" (Jan. 28, 1734/5); his 11th (April 24, 1735); his 18th (May 29, 1735); two May letters of hers ("according to promise I'm come" and "I'm determined to run all hazards"); her letter of March 2, 1735/6, and her letter of April 7, 1736.

51. *Spectator*, no. 15 (Addison): "*Aurelia*, tho' a Woman of Great Quality, delights in the Privacy of a Country Life, and passes away a great part of her Time in her own Walks and Gardens. Her Husband, who is her Bosom Friend, and Companion in her Solitudes, has been in Love with her ever since he knew her. They both abound with good Sense, consummate Virtue, and a mutual Esteem; and are a perpetual Entertainment to one another. . . . They often go into Company, that they may return with the greater Delight to one another." *The Spectator*, ed. Donald F. Bond (Oxford, 1965), 1: 68.

52. Joseph Taylor (d. 1759—Norton), the Gibbon family lawyer.

53. Parish Register of St. Christopher-le-Stocks. Williams Gibbon performed about half the marriages there from 1731/2-1736. Williams Gibbon was a favorite nephew of Edward Gibbon I, who mentioned him in his will. Perhaps this connection explains Law's being welcomed at the church and hence the place of Edward and Judith's wedding, which puzzled Low, *Gibbon*, p. 18, n.2.

54. Now in the Public Record Office.

55. Low, *Gibbon*, pp. 18-19.

56. Public Record Office, B 11, 1681.

57. By Christopher Walton, would-be biographer of Law, in his *Notes and Materials for an Adequate Biography of* . . . *William Law* (privately printed, 1854), p. 429.

58. Walton MSS. 186.10.7.

CHAPTER 2

1. D. M. Low, *Edward Gibbon, 1737-1794* (London, 1937), p. 24.

2. See above, chap. 1, n.31.

3. Magdalen College, Oxford, MSS. 363,B.II. Edward's letter of January 21, 1734/5.

4. Judith's reply, endorsed (erroneously) January 17.

5. The first quotation is from Judith's reply to Edward's letter of May 29, 1735 ("according to promise I'm come"); the second is Gibbon.

6. *Letters*, 1: 3, introductory note.

7. Byrom, *Private Journal*, 2, pt. 1, p. 104.

8. William Cadogan, as quoted in G. F. Still, *The History of Paediatrics* (London, 1931), p. 350.

9. Still, *History of Paediatrics*, p. 389.

10. Ibid., p. 379.

11. Putney Parish Register, which is also the source for the christening and burial dates, and for birth and death dates, where given, for all Gibbon's siblings.

12. Byrom, *Private Journal*, 2, pt. 1, p. 138. The landlady's remark perhaps refers to the Gibbons' Sunday attendance at the local church. It surely does not refer to the young couple's wedding, because that would have been the office of Judith's father, and the wedding took place in London, not Putney.

13. *Letters*, 3: 46.

14. Compare Samuel Johnson, *Rambler*, no. 72, on the success of persons of good humor, who "without any extraordinary qualities or attainments, are the universal favourites of both sexes."

15. Walton MSS. 186.10.16. Dr. Williams's Library, London.

16. Christopher Walton says that the death of Edward Gibbon I "necessarily led to a change in [Law's] domestic circumstances, though he did not finally retire from the town until about four years after that event." (The date would have been late 1740 or early 1741.) Christopher Walton, *Notes and Materials for an Adequate Biography of* . . . *William Law* (privately printed, 1854), p. 364. A letter to Hester Gibbon dated July 25, 1741, and addressed to Bear's Street, Coldbath Fields, London, is among the Walton MSS. (186.8.7).

17. Hester and another pious lady, Mrs. Archibald Hutchinson, joined Law at his house at King's Cliffe in 1744, according to Walton, *Notes and Materials*, p. 428.

18. Still, *History of Paediatrics*, p. 298.

19. Ibid., p. 224.

20. Ibid. Still explains that bleeding was debated as a treatment for children from the time of Celsus (first century A.D.) until the general discontinuation of the treatment. Either lancets or leeches were used; the former were somewhat preferred.

21. For Sloane, see *DNB*.

22. F. H. Garrison, *History of Medicine*, 4th ed. (London, 1929), p. 391.

23. For Ward and Taylor, see *Notes and Queries*, ser. 7, vol. 7 (Feb. 2, 1889): 83. Gibbon's future stepmother suggested the consultation of Ward (see a letter of Edward Gibbon II to Gibbon, Add. MSS. 34886, fol. 1r; printed by Low, *Gibbon*, p. 60).

24. Low, *Gibbon*, p. 27.

25. For Emerson, see Evelyn Barish's forthcoming book, "Emerson and the Allegory of Death."

NOTES TO PAGES 27-36

26. *Letters*, 3: 46.

27. Gibbon's fragmentary note identifying his favorite story is expanded by Bonnard in *Memoirs*, p. 247.

28. Ellen Emma Guthrie, *The Old Houses of Putney* (Putney, 1870), p. 11.

29. For John Kirkby, see *DNB*.

30. Add. MSS. 37772, *Journal A*, p. xlvii.

31. Gibbon believed his father's political sympathies to be very similar to Kirkby's; see *Memoirs*, p. 26.

32. The authority for this reminiscence (Add. MSS. 34887, fol. 40v) was probably Dorothea Gibbon, Gibbon's stepmother.

CHAPTER 3

1. W. D. Biden, *The History and Antiquities of the Ancient and Royal Town of Kingston-upon-Thames* (Kingston, 1852), p. 75.

2. *Memoirs of the Life of Gilbert Wakefield* (London, 1804), 1: 41. Add. MSS. 34882, fol. 218v.

3. Samuel Johnson, *Diaries, Prayers, and Annals*, ed. E. L. McAdam, Jr., et al. (New Haven, 1958), p. 14.

4. James Boswell, *The Life of Samuel Johnson, LL. D.*, ed. G. B. Hill and L. F. Powell (Oxford, 1934-50), 1: 46.

5. Ovid *Ars Amatoria* 1. 159. (Small matters affect light minds.)

6. Boswell, *Life*, 1: 46, 461.

7. W. Jackson Bate, *Samuel Johnson* (New York, 1975, 1977), p. 26.

8. William Hayley, *Memoirs of the Life and Writings*, ed. John Johnson (London, 1823), 1: 16.

9. According to one of his school fellows, as reported by D.P. (Daniel Prince, according to G. B. Hill in his edition of Gibbon's *Memoirs* [London, 1900], p. 34 n.3; Daniel Parker, according to D. M. Low, *Edward Gibbon, 1737-1794* [London, 1937], p. 32), in the *Gentleman's Magazine* (Feb. 4, 1794): 119.

10. Letter of Edward Gibbon II dated November 18, 1746. Walton MSS. 186.10.5. Dr. Williams's Library, London. Putney Parish Register.

11. Catherine Elliston, daughter of Edward Gibbon II's sister Catherine, letter of January 5, 1747. Walton MSS. 186.10.6. Catherine was born in 1735.

12. Catherine Elliston's letter; baptism and burial dates from Putney Parish Register.

13. In the same letter (it was to her aunt Hester Gibbon), Catherine said that she had "heard" that her "Uncle [was] as well as can be expected; & [her] Cousin Ted very well."

14. Walton MSS. 186.10.7.

15. 1748.

16. Walton MSS. 186.10.8.

17. Gibbon says that family tradition considered Law's portrait of Flatus, "always uneasy and always searching after happiness . . . [in] some new project," a portrayal of his father's "natural inconstancy." (*Memoirs*, appendix 1, p. 205.)

18. Walton MSS. 186.10.9. This letter was franked by Edward Gibbon II.

19. Walton MSS. 186.10.13,14.

20. E.g., *Letters*, 1: 9, 37.

21. See William Holdsworth, *History of English Law*, 10.

22. See his will, Prerogative Court of Canterbury, 175 Prob 11/789, fol. 217.

23. Stanier Porten, born 1716, figures frequently in the Gibbon family papers as a reliable adviser and aide.

24. Add. MSS. 34887, fol. 40v.

25. *MW* 1814, 1: 36.

26. F. Markham, *Recollections of a Town Boy at Westminster* (London, 1903), pp. 11, 7, 11.

27. Ibid., p. 3.

28. J. Sargeaunt, *Annals of Westminster School* (London, 1898), p. 160.

29. Markham, *Recollections*, pp. 2-3.

30. Ibid., pp. 60-61, 48.

31. When Gibbon arrived at Lausanne he already knew a little French ("In my childhood I had once studied the French Grammar," *Memoirs*, p. 69); this appears to have been his best opportunity for that study.

32. Sargeaunt, *Annals*, p. 38.

33. Ibid.

34. Ibid., p. 39.

35. Markham, *Recollections*, p. 95.

36. Hers was one of the largest houses. Sargeaunt, *Annals*, p. 159.

37. Lionel Tollemache, third viscount Huntingtower (1734-99).

38. Add. MSS. 37772, fol. 43r. Another occasion of note may have occurred on November 6, 1749, for there is a copy of the *Dramatick Works* of Richard Steele labeled, in Gibbon's unmistakable hand, "Edward Gibbon/Nov^br 6th 1749." It is in the possession of Professor Charles C. Nickerson of Bridgewater State College, Mass., who most kindly showed this copy to me. See his discussion of it in the *Book Collector* 13 (Summer 1964): 207. The copyright date is given as MDCCLI, possibly a misprint, as Professor Nickerson points out, for MDCCIL. It is tempting to speculate that the book was given to Gibbon as a reward for his only academic achievement at Westminster, i.e., his advancement from the second form to the third. Although that promotion could have come earlier in his career there, it could not have come much later: the autumn term ended at Christmas, and the winter term of 1750 (Gibbon's last at Westminster) was cut short by serious illness. Another possibility is that Gibbon had been taken to the theatre to see a performance of one of the plays in the volume.

39. W.A.G. in *Notes and Queries*, ser. 7, vol. 7 (Feb. 2, 1889): 83.

40. See above, n.22.

41. Putney Parish Register.

42. *Letters*, 1: 1.

43. So given in G.F.R. Barker and A. H. Stenning, *Record of Old Westminsters* (London, 1928), 1: 371.

44. Add. MSS. 37772, fol. 43r.

45. *Journal B*, p. 166.

46. John Hutton remembered, "When I was a Winchester Schoolboy I had often repeated an Ode of Horace to Mr Gibbon the Historian." Letter of 3 August 1818. B.L. Add. MSS. 34888, fol. 85r.

47. *EE*, pp. 5-8. He seems to include this list, however, in an account of his "first litterary attempts" after his arrival at Oxford: "a new plan of Chronological tables, the paralel lives of Aurelian and Selim, and a critical enquiry into the age of Sesostris" (M 224). In other accounts only the two latter projects are attributed to his time at Oxford (M 122; *Memoirs* p. 55).

48. See Bonnard's notes, *Memoirs*, p. 251.

49. Low, in appendix to *Letters*, 1: 389.

50. The letters of the experts called in by Lord Sheffield to help him prepare Gibbon's rough manuscripts for publication (these letters are in the Sheffield Papers, Beinecke Library, Yale University) constantly comment on Gibbon's many errors,

not only in Greek but also in Latin and even in French. The works that were examined were not merely juvenilia; they included materials from his maturity.

51. H. A. Mason, *To Homer through Pope* (New York, 1972), pp. 3-10.

CHAPTER 4

1. D.P. in *Gentleman's Magazine*, p. 199. (See above, Chap. 3, n.9.) See also *Memoirs*, p. 53.

2. "Since the days of Pocock [1604-91] and Hyde [1636-1703], Oriental learning has always been the pride of Oxford." *Memoirs*, p. 53.

3. Oxford's defenders sprang to their pens as soon as Gibbon's memoirs were published, but even they had to admit that the university was at its lowest ebb during Gibbon's days. See especially a privately printed pamphlet attributed to J. Hurdis called "A Word or Two in Vindication of the University of Oxford and of Magdalen College in Particular from the Posthumous Aspersions of Mr. Gibbon" (1800?). He describes the reading list for the terminal examinations but then admits, "it may be true that the terminal exercises, upon their present plan, may not have been in force more than *thirty* years" (p. 17).

4. Gibbon's fragmentary note cites the well-known instance of Thomas Gray at Cambridge. Hurdis's defence now seems as damaging as Gibbon's attack. He assured his readers that Fellows of Magdalen were then required to present three lectures per term, and tutors to meet their students an hour a day. Ibid., pp. 18-19, 24.

5. Thomas Waldegrave (d. 1784) is said by Murray to have been born in 1721, but he is also said to have been a Fellow of Magdalen in 1733; perhaps the latter date should be 1743 (M 77n.).

6. Unlike Samuel Johnson's tutor, Waldegrave did not awaken his pupil's penitence by this forebearance. James Boswell, *The Life of Samuel Johnson, LL. D.*, ed. G. B. Hill and L. F. Powell (Oxford, 1934-50), 1: 272. Perhaps Gibbon's conscience, even at a tender age, was less susceptible than Johnson's.

7. Add. MSS. 37772, fol. 43.

8. D.P., *Gentleman's Magazine*, p. 199.

9. J. R. Bloxam to G. B. Hill (January 22, 1889), information of President Routh of Magdalen, communicated to Milman. Edward Gibbon, *Memoirs*, ed. G. B. Hill (London, 1900), p. 283.

10. Hill, ed., *Memoirs*, p. 283, from the College Books.

11. Bloxam in Hill, ed., *Memoirs*, p. 283.

12. H. H. Milman, note to his edition of the *Decline and Fall* (London, 1834), 1: 32. Communication from Finden to Routh to Milman.

13. According to Hearne. See Hill, ed., *Memoirs*, p. 61, n.3.

14. *The Works of Samuel Parr*, ed. John Johnston (London, 1828), 2: 528.

15. George Simon, Earl Harcourt, born August 1, 1736, educated at Westminster School, styled Viscount Nuneham (Burke's Peerage). They would meet again in Lausanne.

16. September 24-October 6. Add. MSS. 37772.

17. Murray's note, derived from J. R. Bloxam, *Register of the Members of Magdalen College, Oxford* (Oxford, 1853), 1: 150 ff., depicts Winchester more favorably, but in Draft B of his memoirs, Gibbon had been even more critical: Winchester's "only science was supposed to be that of a broker and salesman" (M 126).

18. Joseph Foster, ed., *Alumni Oxonienses 1715-1886* (Oxford, 1891-92).

19. Add. MSS. 37772.

20. Ibid.

21. In the text of *MW* 1814, 1: 62. But as G. B. Hill pointed out, there is no record of a Molesworth among Gibbon's contemporaries at Oxford. Hill, ed., *Memoirs*, p. 69, n.5.

22. For Conyers Middleton, see *DNB* and Gibbon's notes and remarks in the *Decline and Fall*, the *Vindication*, and his "Hints" and "Index Expurgatorius" (*EE*, pp. 88-128).

23. *MW* 1814, 1: 62, Sheffield's note; Bossuet in *Memoirs*, p. 59, with Bonnard's note, p. 264.

24. He supplies "March, 1753" as the date of his "stumbl[ing] on some books of Popish controversy" in the margin of Draft E of his memoirs (M 296).

25. Gibbon habitually miswrites this word, though his self-corrections indicate that he did know the correct spelling. Perhaps the error indicates some residual discomfort, either with his former belief or with his current rejection of it.

26. Edward Hutton, "Gibbon's Conversion," *Nineteenth Century and After* 3 (March 1932): 365-75, retells in detail the slow process of reclaiming Gibbon from Catholicism, primarily from the letters of Gibbon's Swiss tutor to Edward Gibbon II. Hutton supplies the full names and backgrounds of the priests concerned in Gibbon's conversion from the publications of the Catholic Record Society.

27. Gibbon quotes this description from Clarendon's *Life* (Oxford, 1857), 1: 53. I owe this reference to the kindness of Professor Joan Hartman of the College of Staten Island, City University of New York. Gibbon's fragmentary notes for the draft of the memoirs do not exist for this final section. He bought the Clarendon papers, three volumes in large paper, in 1788. B.L. Add. MSS. 34888, fol. 12.

28. *MW* 1814, 1, 63n.

29. See Sir Gavin de Beer, *Gibbon and His World* (New York, 1968), pp. 18-19.

30. Magdalen College, Oxford, MSS. 359, B.II.3.6. fol. 1. The knife cost 12 livres (half a guinea).

31. For Pavillard, see Bonnard's note, *Memoirs*, p. 270, and J. Meredith Read, *Historic Studies in Vaud, Berne, and Savoy*, 2 vols. (London, 1897), 2: 274.

32. *Letters*, 1: 2. In the outline for this section of the final version of his memoirs (a section never actually written), Gibbon's description was "First aspect horrid—house, slavery, ignorance, exile" (M 416).

33. *Letters*, 1: 1-2.

34. "[I]l est plus particulierement attaché à Mylord Huntinghtower . . . qui paroit l'aimer beaucoup." *Memoirs*, p. 215; Add. MSS. 34887.

35. The letter is not extant, but of it Pavillard says, "Vous souhaittez que je tienne Monsieur votre Fils à la maison attaché à ses études, et qu'il sorte peu." *Memoirs*, p. 216.

36. ". . . comme venant d'un homme qui est dans les idées qu'il desaprouve, et qui veut cependant les lui faire recevoir parce qu'il est paié pour cela." Ibid.

37. "Quelque jours après son arrivée il me demanda de l'argent . . . je le priai de me dire combien il en souhaittoit, il me demanda deux Louis neufs. Est-ce là, lui dis-je, ce que Monsieur votre Pere a accoutumé de vous donner, il me repondait qu'ouï, et même que vous lui en donniez davantage." *Memoirs*, p. 217.

38. See Bonnard's note, based on the Magdalen College accounts, *Memoirs*, p. 273.

39. Disputation on religious topics would have been part of Pavillard's training as a Swiss clergyman, as Gibbon points out. See also Michel Baridon, *Edward Gibbon et le mythe de Rome* (Paris, 1977), pp. 47-48.

40. Add. MSS. 37772. The journey is not mentioned in the accounts sent to Edward Gibbon II. Magdalen College MSS. 359, B.II.3.6. fol. 1.

41. Born March 14, 1734/5, Lord Mountjoy died in Paris on February 2, 1754 and was buried February 29, 1754 (Burke's Peerage).

42. Read, *Historic Studies*, 2: 276-77.

43. Transcription from Deyverdun's unpublished journal, in the Deyverdun *Fonds*, ACV. Entries of May 31, 1754, and July 14, 1754.

44. Add. MSS. 37772. It was also recorded in Gibbon's commonplace book of 1755. *EE*, p. 23.

45. Deyverdun journal, June 1, 1754: "Sorti à 5 heures . . . pour une promenade sur la Terass. Recontre M. de Guibon."

46. Read, *Historic Studies*, 2: 298–302.

47. Caryll Family Papers. Add. MSS. 28237, fol. 43.

48. Add. MSS. 28237, fols. 41, 44.

49. *Memoirs*, pp. 218–20.

50. "[I]l m'a fallu un tems considerable pour le detromper & lui faire comprendre qu'il avoit tort de s'assujetir à la pratique d'une Eglise qu'il ne reconnoissoit plus pour infaillible." *Memoirs*, p. 219.

51. D. M. Low, *Edward Gibbon, 1737–1794* (London, 1937), p. 52.

52. C. S. Lewis's term for the tenets and attributes of Christianity agreed upon by most persons who consider themselves Christians.

CHAPTER 5

1. *Letters*, 1: 3.

2. D. M. Low, *Edward Gibbon, 1737–1794* (London, 1937), p. 51.

3. Three senses told him that the Host at Communion remained unchanged; only one informed him that Christ said that the Bread was His Body. But of course the taste, texture, and appearance of the Host is the same by either hypothesis; according to the doctrine of transsubstantiation, it is only the invisible essence that is changed.

4. Low, *Gibbon*, p. 51.

5. *Letters*, 1: 3.

6. *Letters*, 1: 4. Was his debt for 110 or for 150 (40 plus 110) guineas? Low (*Gibbon*, p. 54) assumes the former but also assumes that there was only one night of gambling, which seems an impossible interpretation.

7. Magdalen College, Oxford, MSS. 359, B.II.3.6.

8. Low, *Gibbon*, p. 55.

9. *Letters*, 1: 4. For date, see *Journal A*, pp. 3–4.

10. *Letters*, 1: 4–5.

11. *Letters*, 1: 5–6.

12. *Letters*, 1: 6.

13. For the repayment, see *Letters*, 1: 7, and Low's note in *Gibbon*, p. 57.

14. Pavillard's letters were published by Bonnard as appendix 2 to his edition of the *Memoirs*.

15. "1. a Mon Francois. Je sais qu'il s'en faut de beaucoup que je ne possede cette langue aussi bien que je pourrois le faire. Mais j'ose dire pourtant sans craindre d'en etre dementi par Monsieur Pavilliard que je la sais mieux que la plupart des Anglois que j'ai vu a Lausanne. 2. Mes Langues mortes. Vous savez mieux que Personne ma foiblesse par rapport au Latin lorsque j'ai quitté l'Angleterre. Il n'y avoit alors point d'Auteur que je pusse lire avec facilité ni par consequent avec plaisir. A present il n'y en [a] aucun que je ne lise coulamment. J'en ai lu plusieurs depuis quelque peu de tems tels que la plus grande partie des Ouvrages de Ciceron, Virgile Saluste les Epitres de Pline deux fois, les Comedies de Terence autant, Velleius Patercule, et je me propose de les lire tous avec le tems. Pour ce qui est du Grec comme je n'ai commencé à l'aprendre que depuis un mois ou Six Semaines, vous sentez bien que j'en suis encore aux Premiers Principes. 3. Ma Philosophie. J'ai achevé la Logique de Monsieur de Crousaz laquelle est fort estiméé dans ce pays-ci en partie avec Mons: Pavilliard et en

parti dans mon Particulier. Je vais lire pour la seconde fois l'Entendement Humain, et aussitot que Je l'aurai fini je commencerai l'Algebre que vous me recommandez tant. 4. Ma Danse et Mon Dessein. Je crois que vous ne serez pas mécontent de mes progrés dans la derniere de ces choses. Pour ce de la premiere je fais tout ce que je puis." *Letters*, 1: 12-13.

16. *Journal A*, pp. 4-5.

17. ". . . deux ou trois bevues de ce celebre Historien." Add. MSS. 34880, fol. 38r.

18. *Letters*, 1: 12, n.3. The CPB is in Add. MSS. 34880, fols. 2v-82v.

19. All published in *EE*, pp. 9-24.

20. *EE*, p. 18.

21. Voltaire, *Annales de l'empire depuis Charlemagne* (La Haye and Berlin, 1754), 1: 8.

22. Abbé Banier, *Mythologie et les fables expliqués par l'histoire,* 3 vols. (Paris, 1738). This is the edition in which I have verified Gibbon's quotations. It is not the edition Gibbon cited, which he did not identify and which I have been unable to identify.

23. First entries from Banier occur in the following order, on the versos of fols. 22, 23, 26, 27, 28, 31, and 32: 2: 155; 2: 39-51; 1: 227; 1: 487; 3: 35; 3: 253.

24. The portion of Gibbon's *Essai sur l'étude de la littérature* that deals with the origins of pagan religions was not written until 1761 (see below, chap. 9).

25. CPB, fols. 27v, 26v, 18v.

26. CPB, fols. 28v, 20v.

27. CPB, fols. 18v, 22v.

28. Banier, *Mythologie*, 2: 39-51; "Monsieur l'Abbé Banier nous donne le precis de ce qu'on a dit pour et contre l'existence des Geans." CPB, fol. 23v.

29. CPB, fol. 23v.

30. "L'auteur de l'avertissement devant la traduction Francoise de son histoire dit que cet evenement arriva l'an 1736."

31. "Mons: Giannone refute solidement la fabuleuse donation que quelques ecrivains pretendent que Constantine fit de l'Italie a Silvestre Eveque de Rome l'an 324 quatre jours apres avoir recu le Bateme de sa main. On la demontre fausse, par les raisons suivantes

1me. Parceque ni Eusebe ni les auteurs ecrivains qui ont ecrit la vie de Constantine avec un si grand detail n'en ont point parlè.

ii. Parceque Euseube nous apprend que Constantine se fit baptiser a Nicomedie, quelques jours avant sa mort (selon une mauvaise coutume assez frequente parmi les grands de ce siecle) & non pas a Rome l'an 324.

iii. Parceque nous scavons par les dates des Edits de Constantine que pendant tout le cours de l'an 324 en question, il ne mit point le pied en Italie, mais qu'il le passa tout entier a Thessalonique.

iv. Mais ce qui prouve hors de toute doute la faussetè de cette donation, c'est que toutes les provinces d'Italie demeurerent sujettes aux successeurs de Constantine qui y commandoient en maitre jusqua la destruction de l'Empire de l'Occident." [In the left-hand margin, in addition to the title of the entry, "Constantine (Donation of)," Gibbon gave his source:] *Giannone: Hist Civ: du Royaume de Naples Tom i p. 123.* [He underlined it to distinguish it from the sources he recorded that had been utilized by the authors he read. CPB, fol. 12v.]

32. Michel Baridon (*Edward Gibbon et le mythe de Rome* [Paris, 1977], p. 412) points out that Gibbon could have observed such arguments in Bayle's notes to his great *Dictionnaire*, which Gibbon had begun to consult even before reading Giannone. But there is no evidence that Gibbon appreciated the superior power of such arguments until he saw their effect in the extended and systematic work of Giannone.

Indeed, as Baridon himself notes, Gibbon's comment, as late as 1762, suggests that he thought Bayle's method rather carefree and arbitrary: "He could pitch on what articles he pleased and say what he pleased on these articles." *Journal A*, pp. 108-9.

33. The interesting subject of Gibbon's relationships to his predecessors has often been discussed; two writers, Baridon and G. Giarrizzo (*Edward Gibbon e la cultura europea del settocento* [Naples, 1954]), include considerable attention to the juvenilia and minor works in their studies. But because the CPB was largely excluded from Lord Sheffield's editions of Gibbon's *Miscellaneous Works*, the evidence it provides remains undiscussed.

34. *EE*, p. 24.

35. CPB, fols. 7, 11, 12, 18, 20, 22, 23, 27, 29, 30, 31, 33, 35, 36, 37-40, 42, 44-47, 49, 53, 55, 70, and/or on the recto of the next succeeding odd-numbered folios.

36. *DF*, chap. 20, n.111 (the note number is the same in the quarto editions and in J. B. Bury [7 vols., London, 1896-1900, and all subsequent editions].

37. *DF*, chap. 56; CPB, fol. 30v. "Mons: Giannone nous donne une Idee tres avantageuse de Roger 1."

38. "Je marquerai ~~deux~~ ~~trois~~ deux petites meprises de ce jeune savant." CPB, fol. 33v.

39. *DF* (chap. 53, n.28; Bury, n.29).

40. "Ex Antiquissimo M. S. Codice nuper in Abrosianà Bibliotheca reperto." CPB, fol. 14v.

41. "Le R P Etienne Souciet naquit a Bourges l'an 1671. Son pere etoit Avocat au Parlement de Paris . . . il entra dans la societé de Jesus a l'age de dix-neuf ans . . . et il mourut à Paris l'an 1744 dans la 73me anneé de son age. . . . Son Esprit vaste et etendu ne lui permit pas de se borner a un seul genre d'etude, il embrassa toutes les sciences et se rendit egalement habile dans chacune. Erudition sacrée et profane, Histoire ancienne et Moderne, Geometrie, Astronomie, Chronologie, Geographie, Mythologie Medailles, Inscriptions &ct toutes ces connoissances etoit de son ressort, il nous a donné des preuves qu'il les possedoit en Maitre." CPE, fol. 43v.

42. CPB, fol. 57v.

43. "Cependant il y auroit un passage de Donat: qui feroit croire que ces habits de diverses Couleurs etoient en usage parmi les jeunes Gens." CPB, fol. 56v.

44. The Magdalen College accounts, for example, include such items as a "blue & buff figured silk waistcoat laced with gold & silver" and an "orange zigzag printed corded dimity waistcoat." MSS. 359.91.

45. CPB, fols. 7, 18, 21, 45, 49.

46. "Christianisme [*sic*; the *i* is, however, undotted].

Julien l'Apostat avait pour grand but de detruire la religion Chretienne et certainement il s'y prenait bien. C'etait le persecuteur le plus doux le plus Sytematique et en meme tems le plus dangereux de tous. Il avait senti que les X Grandes Persecutions n avaient fait qu'augmenter le nombre de Chretiens, il resolut de se conduire autrement pour les abattre. Voila quelqu'unes de ses mesures que j'ai tiré du nouvel Historien de la vie de Julien.

I. Il affectait de parler des Chretiens quelqufois avec pitie (1) quelquefois avec mepris (2) jamais avec haine et faisait parade souvent d'une grande moderation a leur egard. (3)

II. Tous les Emplois Civils et militaires etaient donnés a des Payens, tous les convertis etaient recu avec empressement et bien recompenséz. (4) et pour obliger tout ceux qui approchaient sa personne d'etre Payens il faisait entrer des actes d'Idolatrie par tout. (5)

III. Il defendit aux Chretiens de tenir ecôle et d'expliquer les auteurs Payens a la jeunesse, qu'il permit de frequenter les Ecoles des Payens (6)

IV. Il rapella tous les Eveque soit Ariens soit Orthodoxes (qui avaient eté chassés de leurs sieges,) et sous un masque de moderation, tachait d'entretenir la division entre eux. (7)

V. Il travaillait a reformer les moeurs et le culte des Payens (8)

VI. Il permit quelqfois aux habitans des provinces d'exercer des violences contre les Chretiens, mais toujours tacha tacitement et se faisant un merite du pardon qu'il leur en accordait. (9)

VII. Quand il faisait mourir quelque Chretien il employait toujours quelque raison pour prouvér que ce n'etait pas a cause de sa religion. (10)." *CPB*, fol. 8r.

[A transcription, differing in several minor respects, including normalized punctuation, from my microfilm, was published in Pierre Ducrey et al., eds., *Gibbon et Rome* (Geneva: 1977), pp. 212–13.]

47. *DF*, chap. 23.

48. "Julien voulant oter aux Chretiens les arguments qu'ils tirent de la dispersion des Juifs et la destruction de leur temple, ordonna qu'on la [*sic*] rebatit. On assemblait pour cet effet un quantité prodigieuse de Materiaux on travaillait jour et nuit á nettoyer l'emplacement de l'ancien Temple et a demolir les vieux fondemens. . . . La demolition etoit acheveé et sans y penser on avait accompli dans la derniere rigeur la parole de Jesus Christ, 'qu'il ne resterait pas pierre sur pierre.' On voulut placer les nouveaux fondemons. Mais il sortit de l'endroit meme d'effroyables tourbillons de flammes, dont les élancemens redoublés consumerent les ouvriers. La meme chose arriva a diverses reprises, et l'opiniatreté du feu rendant la place inaccessible, obligea d'abandonner pour toujours l'ouvrage. Ce fait e[s]t certain par le temoignage (pour ne rien dire de ceux de Rufin, Theodoret, Sozomene, Socrate, et Philostorge, et de ceux de St Gregoire de Nanianzen, de St Chrysostome, et de St Ambrose) par celle celui (dis-je) d'Ammien Marcellin, Payen et Cotemporain (1), et est meme insinué par Julien lui-meme (2)." CPB, fol. 49v.

49. *EE*, pp. 308–9, provides an example.

50. CPB, fol. 54v.

51. CPB, fol. 41v.

52. *EE*, p. 117.

53. "N'ayant jamais vu les ouvrages de Velsirus, je ne sai point de quels argumens il s'est servi, mais en voici Quatre qui en demontrent la fausseté." CPB, fol. 37v.

54. "Peut-on s'imagine qu Vell: Paterculus eut fait des bevues si grossieres sur des evenemens qui touchaient de si pres a son tems."

55. *Letters*, 1: 8.

56. See the Appendix.

57. C. G. Loys de Bochat, *Mémoires sur l'histoire ancienne de la Suisse*, 3 vols. (Lausanne, 1747).

58. Baridon calls Loys de Bochat an "historien original et profond du Droit naturel." *Mythe*, p. 52. Loys de Bochat received a eulogistic account in the *NBG* and a respectful notice in the *BU*.

59. Loys de Bochat, *Mémoires sur l'histoire ancienne*, 2: 315.

60. "Les curateurs (a prendre l'idéé que M de Bochat nous donne sur ce sujet) etoient les magistrats des villes municipales du tems de l'Empire Romain. Il est difficile de prononcer d'une façon bien exacte sur leurs fonctions et leur pouvoir; cela varioit selon la constitution des endroits differens. dans quelques villes ils avoient de la jurisdiction, dans des autres ils n'en avoient point. Ici c'etoient les magistrats principaux, lá ils n'etoient que subordonnés." CPB, fol. 25v.

61. "On ne pouvoit point les obliger de l'exercer plus d'une anneé. Et les Citoyens qui l'avoient acceptér plus d'une fois avoient grand soin de le mettre parmi leurs titres

sur les monumens publics. Quelques Savans ont cru qu'il falloit etre citoyen Romain pour y parvenir, mais Mons: de Bochat renda fort vraisemble tant par des autorités que par des raisonnemens, que les Provinciaux en jouissoient egalement." Ibid.

62. CPB, fols. 33v-34r.

63. "Journal de mon voyage dans quelques endroits de la Suisse" (henceforth *Tour*), p. 66: "On suppose et même avec beaucoup de vraisemblance que c'etoit l'Aventicum des Anciens que Tacite appelle la Capitale de la Nation. . . . Monsieur De Bochat dont je vous ai deja parlé comme d'un savant Antiquaire, dérivoit le nom d'Aventicum de celui des Avantici, peuples des provinces meridionales de France, qui selon lui ont fondé Avanche."

64. "Cette remarque est de M. de Bochat; mais j'en avois fait la premiere partie avant d'avoir lu son ouvrage." CPB, fol. 59v.

65. *Letters*, 1: 10.

66. ". . . quoiqu'il n'y ait personne de fort riche tout le monde est a son aise." *Tour*, p. 11.

67. "Cette fameuse journéé ne fait pas moins d'honneur aux Annales des Suisses que celles de Marathon, de Salamine, de Platée, de Mycale aux Grecs." *Tour*, p. 12.

68. "Nous arrivames a Neufchatel apres avoir passé au travers d'un pays des plus beaux que j'ai vu. On y voit un air riant qui marque l'opulence at la prosperité de ses habitans. Il y a partout des manufactures, les villages pour ainsi dire se touchent, et excepte les Environs de Londres je n'ai jamais vu dans une pareille etendue de terrain un aussi grand nombre de maisons de campagne, la plupart fort jolies." *Tour*, p. 13.

69. Jane Austen, *Sense and Sensibility*, ed. R. W. Chapman (Oxford, 1933), p. 98. See also Sir Gavin de Beer's commentary on this tour. *Tour*, p. 81.

70. "Elle est fort laide. Sa maison de ville est des plus pitoyables." *Tour*, p. 15.

71. I quote Fodor's *Switzerland* (New York: 1977).

72. For further examples, see his journal of his tour of Italy, *Gibbon's Journey from Geneva to Rome*, ed. Georges A. Bonnard (London, 1961).

73. "Je n'y ai rien vu qui meritât beaucoup l'attention d'un voyageur." *Tour*, p. 22. ". . . ces fameux dez." P. 23.

74. So I infer, from its having been left to Pavillard's discretion. Mr. Gibbon paid a lump sum of 35 louis for the expenses of the tour (Add. MSS. 34886, fol. 1), i.e., 560 Swiss livres. Gibbon's usual monthly pocket money was 32 livres, some of which presumably went to pay off his gambling debt. See Bonnard's discussion of this confusing matter, *Memoirs*, p. 271; the accounts in Magdalen College Library; and Low, *Gibbon*, p. 56, n.1.

75. "nous firent mille politesses pendant le jour et demi que nous y avons passé. Ils ne voulurent point que nous eussions d'autre table que la leur." *Tour*, p. 23.

76. Compare Gibbon's reflections while in Genoa, *Journey*, p. 79.

77. "Au lieu de ce coteau riant, peuplé, et cultivé, nous nous trouvames dans un pays egalement abandonné par l'art et par la nature. . . . Le moindre faux-pas d'un cheval eut pu nous precipiter dans les precipices a coté que nous ne regardions qu'en tremblant. Ce chemin etoit bordé de Sapins qui par leur epaisseur et leur noirceur relevoient l'horreur de la perspective. Si quelque fois nous decouvrions des objets au dela de ce bois, ce n'etoit que pour entrevoir des Rochers arides et les cabanes de quelques miserables vachers." *Tour*, p. 27.

78. "En effet il faut un esprit, bien ferré a Glace par la bonne Philosophie pour n'y pas sentir un certain tremoussement, un certain—(en Anglois je dirois Awe) mieux senti, que defini. Tel est la force de prejugé et si grand le pouvoir de notre imagination." *Tour*, p. 28.

79. "La ville de Zurich est située dans un des plus beaux Emplacemens du monde, a la tete d'un beau lac qui y fait venir toutes denréés du Pays a fort bon marché. . . .

Tous le Bord du lac est parsemé de maisons et de village et la vue n'est terminéé par les hautes montagnes de Schwitz que lorsqu'elle ne peut plus s'etendre." *Tour*, p. 35.

80. "Cette rue toute belle qu'elle est a trop l'air d'un beau village." *Tour*, p. 36.

81. "Pendant que notre bon Roi Henri VIII pendoit les Catholiques pour ne vouloir pas le reconnoitre Chef de l'Eglise Anglicane et bruloit les Protestans pour refuser de souscrire aux Cinq Articles, beaucoup de chaque Communion . . . se retirerent dans les pays Etrangers." *Tour*, p. 37.

82. "Il n'est ouvert que du coté de la France, le seul a la verité d'ou il a quelque chose a craindre." *Tour*, p. 46.

83. "Pourquoi donc rester si long-tems dans un Endroit que j'avois deja suffisament vu? . . . femme de la Personne a qui vous m'aviez confié, Madame (dis-je) . . . vouloit que son Mari passat quelque tems avec sa belle sœur." *Tour*, p. 46.

84. ". . . qui a certainement bien du Genie . . . a toujours rodé par le monde mettant le feu de la discorde (au dire de ses ennemis) par-tout . . . ont cessé de l'etre." *Tour*, p. 47.

85. Published *MW* 1814, 2: 1-32, where Lord Sheffield dated it c. 1758; see Low, *Gibbon*, p. 66; Giarrizzo, *Edward Gibbon e la cultura europea*, p. 38; modern edition by Louis Junod, *MG*, pp. 123-41. Add. MSS. 34882.

86. The date that Lord Sheffield read and printed was 1722. Junod read 1712 (although he admitted that the text was obscure), because Stanyon was ambassador from 1705-1713. The MS. (fol. 10r) looks as if it had *originally* read 1712, but had been changed to something else in ink, which ran to a blot. It might more easily be read as 1702 than as 1722; it might even be a series: 1712-1722-1712. Junod points out that Gibbon says that the Bernois have held the Pays de Vaud "212" years from 1536 and that he speaks of 200 years of Vaudois fidelity to Berne, possibly alluding to the treaty of 1564, or again to the conquest in 1536 (*MG*, p. 118). Junod suggests that Gibbon may have been deliberately misleading with these dates. Because "212" is not a round number, it must be meant to fix a dramatic date for the Swedish traveler; and if Gibbon intended to write *1702* as the date of Stanyon's estimate, a possible reading of the manuscript, he could have intended to suggest that the *Lettre* was composed in the 1740s.

Junod also sees Gibbon's journal entry of November 1, 1763, as pointing, for a Vaudois, directly to the government of Berne, with its talk of governors "dont l'insolence egaloit l'avarice" and of "un mur d'airain qui separoit a jamais le Citoyen et le sujet" *MG*, p. 119. But compare E. Badian, "Gibbon on War," *Gibbon et Rome*, p. 116 n.18, and an exchange there with Michel Baridon, pp. 131-32.

87. "Les Bernois ont lû l'histoire, pourquoi n'ont ils point remarqué que les mêmes causes produisent les mêmes effets? La reponse est facile mais delicate, c'est que la Cupidité particuliere éteint les lumieres de la raison." *Tour*, p. 53.

88. ". . . seuls maitres de l'Etat. . . . Ils ont jusqu'au pouvoir de dégrader un Conseiller sans en rendre raison. . . . Le Conseil secret a Berne, ressemble assés au Conseil de dix a Venise, excepté qu'il n'exerce point son autorité avec la sévérité du dernier." *Tour*, p. 57.

89. "Cent Pauvres entretenus selon leur Etat, me plaisent bien plus que cinquante dans un Palais . . . il faut etre Bourgeois de Berne, pour etre digne qu'on ne vous laisse pas mourir de misère, ou de maladie. Dans celui-ci de quel Païs, de quelle Religion que vous soyés, le titre de Pauvre ou de Malade vous suffit." *Tour*, pp. 62-63.

90. ". . . jusqu'à avoir une maison de campagne pour ceux à qui les medecins conseillent un changement d'air." *Tour*, p. 63.

91. "C'est un homme d'assés bonne façon, mais d'un embonpoint excessif." *Tour*, p. 60. De Beer suggests that this meeting with an author showed the young Gibbon that books were not mysterious products that came to bookstores ready-made. P. 83; Baridon (*Mythe*, p. 56) points out that though the meeting should have had that effect,

in fact Gibbon did not react to it as revelatory: "Il semblerait même que ce portrait cache quelque animosité." Perhaps Gibbon was neither awed nor angry, but simply more struck by Haller's size than his ability.

92. ". . . qui fera un jour figure dans la Republique des Lettres. Depuis son Enfance il a toujours montré un gout décidé pour les Etudes de l'antiquité. A l'age de quatorze ans il composa une dissertation Latine sur les monumens qu'on avoit découvert a Avanche, dans laquelle il osa attaquer les sentimens de Monsieur De Bochat, le plus savant antiquaire qu'il y eut alors en Suisse, et l'attaqua si bien, que M^r De Bochat lui même . . . fut fort content d'avoir trouvé un si savant adversaire. Cette année il a remporté le second prix á l'academie de Besançon." *Tour,* pp. 61-62.

93. ". . . de peur que vous ne me reprochiés que c'etoit la tout le profit que j'avois fait de mon voyage . . . la profession de Cabaretier est bien plus honorable en Suisse que partout ailleurs. . . . [A] Zurich, a Basle, a Berne, nos cabaretiers ont toujours été des gens a cinq cent mille Francs ou deux cent mille Ecus, des gens honorés et considerés de tout le monde." *Tour,* p. 65. Young Boswell, on a similar tour in the same period, but not writing for his father, had a great deal more to say on this topic. See F. A. Pottle, ed., *Boswell on the Grand Tour: Germany and Switzerland* (New York, 1953).

94. "Car a Grandson il perdit ses tresors, a Morat ses troupes, et a Nancy sa vie." *Tour,* p. 66.

95. *Letters,* 1: 9.

96. *Letters,* 1: 8.

97. Ibid.

98. Ibid., p. 8n. Her jointure was £200 (p. 243), which suggests a dowry of about £2,000.

99. Walton MSS. 186.10.13. Dr. Williams's Library, London.

100. Her letters, both in the Walton MSS. and in the collections formed after she knew Gibbon, sufficiently attest her good qualities, though Gibbon's affection for her is the best evidence. For Phoebe Ford, see A. L. Reade, *Johnsonian Gleanings* (London, 1909-52), 4: 46-49.

101. Walton MSS. 186.10.14.

102. His suggested revisions are inserted parenthetically in the draft.

103. Gibbon wrote a careful letter to his aunt, no doubt on his father's orders, on his return to England. *Letters,* 1: 105.

104. Add. MSS. 34886, fol. 1.

105. The last work, published anonymously, is identified in Geoffrey Keynes, *The Library of Edward Gibbon* (Oxford, 1940).

106. So described in Dominique Joseph Garat, *Mémoires historiques sur la vie de M. Suard* (Paris, 1821), 2: 191-92. But Fanny Burney, *Memoirs of Dr. Burney* (London, 1832), 2: 224, says that his feet were small.

107. "Justa igitur statura estimatione Romana Sexum pedum circiter fuit." CPB, fol. 58r.

108. Add. MSS. 34886, fol. 1.

CHAPTER 6

1. M 416-17. This outline takes up where Draft F of the *Memoirs* leaves off and is on a scale commensurate with it. Furthermore, Draft F alone ends each chapter with a section that might aptly be labeled "Recall and Estimate," and the accounts of his life in Lausanne in Drafts B-E do not adhere to this outline. Such an outline does not exist for the period up to June 1753, which is the period Gibbon wrote of in Draft F. He usually destroyed his preliminary sketches for works as soon as he had completed the

works themselves. I therefore think that this outline was intended as a sketch for the next chapters of the unfinished Draft F.

2. "J'ai pris la Résolution de lire de suite tous les Classiques Latins les partageant suivant les matieres qu'ils ont traité en I.^{me} Les Historiens. IIme Les Poetes. IIIme Les Orateurs dan laquelle Classe je renfermerai tous les autres Auteurs qui ont ecrit en Prose sans etre si Philosophes ni Historiens. IVme Les Philosophes." Add. MSS. 34880, fol. 141v.

3. J. W. Moss, *Manual of Classical Bibliography*. Kennikat Press 1969 reissue of 1837 edition.

4. Etienne André Philippe de Prétot (c. 1710-87). See *BU*.

5. Add. MSS. 34880, fol. 141v; *MW* 1814, 4: 401.

6. "Tout le monde sait que Salluste s'est distingué dans le genre concis, mais peut-être tous n'ont pas fait la remarque que l'usage fréquent qu'il fait des infinitifs absolus y contribue beaucoup." *MW* 1814, 4: 403.

7. ". . . assez propre pour l'histoire, puisqu'il cache en quelque façon les circonstances peu intéressantes qui pèsent de tems à autre sur la plume de l'historien" *MW* 1814, 4: 403.

8. ". . . ce qui est du fonds de l'histoire" *MW* 1814, 4: 404.

9. Bell. Catilin. C. 14. *MW* 1814, 4: 405.

10. ". . . a cat a cat" *MW* 1814, 4: 406.

11. "M. Thyon se trompe lorsqu'il nous dit que le pére de Pompée mourut pendant son consulat. Il n'y a rien de plus certain que qu'il ne mourut que . . . deux ans après." *MW* 1814, 4: 407.

12. For the influence of Montesquieu on Gibbon, see especially Michel Baridon, *Edward Gibbon et le mythe de Rome* (Paris, 1977); G. Giarrizzo, *Edward Gibbon e la cultura europea del settocento* (Naples, 1954); and David P. Jordan, *Gibbon and His Roman Empire* (Urbana, Ill., 1971).

13. ". . . un grand mérite de l'écrivain . . . et non des Mémoires mêmes . . . une façon juste et élégante . . . Des plagiats peuvent bien faire le mérite d'un livre, quoique jamais de son auteur. . . . Mauvaise réflexion pour l'amour-propre des auteurs!" *MW* 1814, 4: 411-12.

14. "Let's go back to our goats."

15. *MW* 1814, 4: 414. Cf. *EE*, p. 91, and *DF*, chapter 28.

16. "Les Clerges de tous les Sectes et les peuples de tous les Siecles se ressemblent assez, c'est a dire que les premiers sont toujours fourbes, et les autres toujours betes." Add. MSS. 34880, fol. 145v.

17. *Memoirs*, p. 33.

18. "Comme je ne sais point s'ils se trouvent dans toutes les éditions, les voici." *MW* 1814, 4: 420.

19. "Comme je compte que l'article de son histoire, que je vais commencer à présent, me mènera un peu plus loin que les autres, je partagerai ce que j'ai à dire dans quelques portions; j'en ferai quatre: I. Dans la première, je dirai quelque chose de la personne et de l'ouvrage de Tite Live. II. Dans la seconde, je donnerai quelques des qualités qui distinguent son histoire de la plûpart des autres. III. Dans la troisième, je considererai les objections et les accusations qu'on fait contre lui; et IV. dans la dernière, je ferai quelques remarques détachées sur quelques endroits de cet historien." *MW* 1814, 4: 422-23.

20. "[O]n ne peut guères concevoir un point de vue plus magnifique que celui-là, où toute la terre connue étoit le théâtre, et une foule de grands hommes, que la nature pour l'ordinaire ne produit qu'à l'éloignement de quelques siècles, mais qu'elle avoit alors fait contemporains, étoient les acteurs. . . . Un pinceau tel que le sien, sans se jetter, comme Salluste, dans des déclamations continuelles contre les moeurs de son

tems, et sans donner, comme Tacite, à l'esprit des hommes ce qui étoit à leur coeur, auroit décrit les moeurs du siècle de Lucullus avec le même sangfroid qu'il l'a fait de ceux de celui de Fabricius, voyant que les unes et les autres étoient des états différens de la république, et que vouloir qu'un peuple maître du monde fût animé du même esprit que les habitans de Rome naissante, étoit vouloir une république de Platon. Semblable aux observateurs de la nature il auroit reconnu que les expériences valoient mieux que les systèmes, et . . . il auroit expliqué le caractère de l'homme par ses actions (. . . avec bien des précautions,) non point les actions suivant l'idée qu'on s'étoit formé d'avance du caractère. Il auroit vu que bien loin que le caractère qu'on pose à la base de la narration soit uniforme, que bien loin, dis-je, qu'il puisse nous rendre raison de la conduite d'une vie entière, rien n'est plus dissemblable à l'homme de hier que l'homme d'aujourd'hui." *MW* 1814, 4: 428-29.

21. *Essai*, chap. 52. "L'un a écrit l'histoire en rhéteur, et l'autre en philosophe." *MW* 1814, 4: 66.

22. *MW* 1814, 4: 67.

23. "Patience pour que dans les mille ans que leur règne a duré ils n'ayent point avancé les sciences, s'ils nous avoient au moins laissé dans le même état où se trouvoit le monde littéraire vers l'an 400, quand ils ont commencé tout de bon leurs inondations." *MW* 1814, 4: 430.

24. Unidentified.

25. "Les Grecs modernes sont à la fois si ignorans et si pauvres." *MW* 1814, 4: 434.

26. To his entry on Vertot in his CPB, Gibbon added a long paragraph (Add. MSS. 34880, fol. 76v) with the words, "Depuis que j'avois ecrit ces remarques, on m'a attaqué sur la premiere." His opponent, i.e., the person with whom he had discussed his work, might have been Pavillard, but if not, he was surely Deyverdun.

27. *Journal A*, p. 5.

28. *Letters*, 1: 23-5. In it Gibbon reminds his father that he had mentioned reading Tacitus in his previous letter.

29. Respectively fols. 62v, 63r, and 71v of Add. MSS. 34880.

30. J.B.L. Crevier, ed., *Livy* (Paris 1736-41); his letter was printed in *MW* 1814, 1: 433-35. " . . . souvent de pareils secours."

31. "Je saisis avec joie quelques momens de repos pour m'entretenir, Monsieur, avec vous: ce sera, s'il vous plait, sans faire de trop grands efforts sur l'article des idées innées que vous me proposez." *MW* 1814, 1: 436.

32. D. M. Low, appendix to *Letters*, 1: 389-90.

33. John Matthias Gesner, in Gibbon, *MW* 1814, 1: 507-9. *Letters*, 1: 16, n.6; Low's appendix, p. 388.

34. Low, *Letters*, appendix, p. 388.

35. Low, *Gibbon*, p. 64; *Letters*, 1: 389.

36. "Il a presque lu la moitié de l'Iliade d'Homere." *Memoirs*, appendix 2, p. 223.

37. Magdalen College, Oxford, MSS. 359.

38. *Essai*, chap. 26. "La géométrie s'occupe de démonstrations qui ne se trouvent que chez elle; la critique balance les différens dégrés de vraisemblance. C'est en les comparant que nous réglons tous les jours nos actions." *MW* 1814, 4: 40.

39. "Which require rather the rein than the spur" (Sheffield translation). *MW* 1814, 1: 477-78.

40. ". . . ont quelquefois eu le bonheur de plaire aux personnes à qui je les ai montré . . . attraper [le caractere distinctif] de [chaque] Siecle et . . . pays." *Letters*, 1: 24.

41. *Essai*, chap. 47. *MW* 1814, 4: 59.

42. *Letters*, 1: 35-36. John Clive's essay "Gibbon's Humor" indicates both in its text and by its very existence the failure of some readers to observe that Gibbon

is not limited to "silly witticisms" or a "solemn sneer." See *Daedalus* 105, no. 3 (Summer 1976): 27-35.

43. *Letters*, 1: 36-37.

44. *Letters*, 1: 37-38.

45. We cannot infer, from the loss of most of Gibbon's letters to his Aunt Kitty, her failure to keep them. Gibbon was in Switzerland when his aunt died, and her effects were therefore dealt with by her surviving brother and his family, who presumably would have had no reason to preserve papers of merely sentimental interest.

46. Add. MSS. 34880, fol. 101r. *Journal A*, p. 6. This essay has never been published.

47. *MW* 1814, 4: 441-46. Add. MSS. 34880, fols. 90-92.

48. *MW* 1814, 4: 446-66. Add. MSS. 34880, fols. 93-100.

49. ". . . suivi des routes différentes; on a rapproché la Perse du Nil; on a reculé le Nil jusqu'à la Perse. Voyons quel sentiment il nous convient le mieux d'embrasser." *MW* 1814, 4: 447.

50. Cf. *Essai*, chap. 10. *MW* 1814, 4: 23-24.

51. "J'y aurois voulu plus de choix dans ses citations, plus de netteté dans ses idées, plus de méthode dans son plan; j'y cherchois l'esprit philosophique qui rassemble, je n'y ai trouvé que l'esprit compilateur qui ramasse." *MW* 1814, 4: 453-54.

52. J. B. Black, *The Art of History* (London, 1926), p. 162.

53. "M. Huet n'observe point une précaution très nécessaire à prendre. Il cite indifféremment tous ceux qui paroissent contenir quelque chose de favorable à sa cause, sans faire attention au tems où ils ont vécu, comme si c'étoit rendre vraisemblable l'erreur de Virgile en déterrant quelque chose de pareil dans un écrivain qui a vécu six cens ans avant ou après lui." *MW* 1814, 4: 456.

54. "Les voyages, les conquêtes, le commerce, les étendent: les transmigrations, le partage des états, la barbarie, les rétrécissent. Les occidentaux ont eu là-dessus leur aurore, leur midi, et leur couchant." *MW* 1814, 4: 457.

55. Add. MSS. 34880, fols. 104-6.

56. *Journal A*, p. 5.

57. *Letters*, 1: 74. It cost 16 louis neufs.

58. Add. MSS. 34880, fols. 107-9; 34880, fols. 111-12 and *MW* 1814, 5: 53-60; 34880, fols. 113-14 and *MW* 1814, 6: 61-65.

CHAPTER 7

1. "Quand pourrois je esperer de vous les temoigner, ces sentiments en Angleterre. Quatre ans se sont deja ecoulés depuis qu'un arret de votre part m'a fixé dans ce pais. Ils m'ont paru autant de siecles. Ce n'est pas que je me plaigne du pays meme ni de ses habitans. Je leur ai des obligations essentielles. Je dois au sejour que j'y ai fait mont gout pour la culture de mon Esprit, les progrés quelqu'ils soient que j'ai fait dans quelques genres d'Etudes. Je me suis meme acquis un petit nombre d'amis qui meritent mon Estime, et dont le souvenir me sera toujours cher. Mais ces amis que sont ils au prix d'un pere à qui je dois tout, d'une mere qui a autant de droit sur ma reconnoissance que sur mon respect, d'une Tante que j'aimai des que je la connus, et que je connûs aussi-tot que moi meme. . . . Je ne repasserai pas toutes les raisons dont je me suis deja servi pour faire voir que quelques soient vos intentions un plus long sejour à Lausanne ne me peut etre que nuisible. . . . Mais permettez moi Mon trés Cher Pere de vous prier de reflechir serieusement quel effet le different emploi de mes plus belles années peut avoir sur le reste de ma vie." *Letters*, 1: 56-57.

2. Magdalen College, Oxford, MSS. 359.

3. D. M. Low (*Edward Gibbon, 1737-1794* [London, 1937], p. 70) provides a charming re-creation of the scene.

4. Samuel Deyverdun, George's father, seems to have dissipated the family fortunes and sent his son to live with an aunt. He attempted to secure professional posts for his three sons—e.g., George had some training in the law—but even after their inheritance of 2,000 livres each in 1759, they were persistently in financial difficulties. Not only was George forced to earn his living as a tutor and government clerk, but a younger brother sought his fortune and lost his life in India. George Deyverdun was nineteen in 1753, i.e., about three years older than Gibbon. See Meredith Read, *Historic Studies in Vaud, Berne, and Savoy*, 2 vols. (London, 1897), 2: 293-98.

5. For Gibbon's notes, see *EE*, pp. 202-3, 327-29, 367.

6. *Journal A*, p. 6. Virgil, *Eclogues* 10, 69. (Love conquers all; and yield we to love.)

7. ". . . taille, grande et proportionée, [est] privée de cette elegance enchanteresse qui en augmente le prix . . . un air villageois . . . brusquerie." G.P.O. de Cléron, comte d'Haussonville, *Le Salon de Madame Necker*, 2 vols. (Paris, 1882), 1: 16.

8. This is how J. W. Johnson designates him. See *The Formation of Neo-Classical Thought* (Princeton, 1967), chap. 1, n.3.

9. "Lorsque j'etudiois en belle-lettres, à Lausanne, M. Darney notre professeur, nous disoit que vous étiés une exception de votre sexe par vos lumières, et vous proposoit pour notre modèle. Lorsque vous passiés dans les rues, toujours entourée d'un cortège d'admirateurs, j'entendois le public qui disoit: 'Voilà la belle Curchod!' et je courois aussitôt sur votre passage, où je demeurois le plus longtemps qu'il m'etoit possible. J'eus même l'honneur de danser avec vous au bal des étudiants, dont vous étiés la reine." d'Haussonville, *Madame Necker*, 1: 23-24.

10. "Pendant ces trois années . . . ces accés d'humeur même hélas! je les avois contre toi, parce que tu étois la source de toute ma félicité sur la terre." "que de larmes, que de tendresse, que de sentiments, que de transports ont racheté ces instants d'humeur!" Ibid., pp. 88, 87.

11. "Vos Genevois sont bien injustes, et je n'ai jamais cru que le plus grand effort de vertu dont je fusse capable dût etre regardé comme avilissant. Je parle de ces leçons; personne ne sais tout ce qu'elles ont coûté à ma fierté." Ibid., p. 105.

12. "J'ai des amis athées, disait elle, pourquoi non? Ce sont des amis malheureux." Ibid., p. 165.

13. "lui répondit d'abord avec vivacité; puis . . . elle perdit tout empire sur ses nerfs et fondit en larmes devant tous ses convives un peu décontenancés." Ibid., p. 150.

14. See, for example, in d'Haussonville's second volume, an intimate letter to Necker before their marriage (pp. 7-8) and many passages indicating her passionate fears that he no longer loves her (pp. 16-17).

15. Magdalen College, MSS. 359.

16. See Norton's analysis in *Letters*, 1, appendix 2.

17. *Journal A*, pp. lxiv-lxxxii; Low, *Gibbon*, pp. 73-91, 137-48.

18. d'Haussonville, *Madame Necker*, 1: 36.

19. "Si spirituelle et singuliere. . . . En un mot c'est une de ces physiognomies si extraordinaire qu'on ne se lasse point de l'examiner de le peindre, de le contrefaire." Ibid.

20. "Son esprit varie prodigeusement." Ibid.

21. James Boswell, *The Life of Samuel Johnson, LL. D.*, ed. G. B. Hill and L. F. Powell (Oxford, 1934-50), 1: 95.

22. Rousseau, notoriously, was one of those who condemned Gibbon's heartlessness in consenting to give up Suzanne (M 298).

23. "Le lieu que [votre genie] habite est prodigieusement orageux, sujet à la gréle, aux brouillards, aux vents, aux tonneres, et aux eclairs, pays charmant cependant l'orsqu'il est tranquille, pays qui peut produire dans un instant des fleurs d'une beauté

surprenante (ces contrées etoient precisément dans cet etat enchanteur lorsque vous composiés votre lettre, la ridicule parenthése!)." *Letters,* 1: 72.

24. *Letters,* 1: 70.

25. *Journal A*, p. 6.

26. Julie de Bondeli, a friend of Suzanne's, told this anecdote to a correspondent, four years after the incident. E. Bodeman, *Julie von Bondeli und ihr Freundeskreis,* cited by Low, *Gibbon*, p. 77.

27. "Voulez vous Mademoiselle que je vous parle naturellement? je vous ai toujours infinément estimé mais l'heureuse Semaine que j'ai passé à Crassie, vous a donné un Relief dans mon Esprit que vous n'aviez point auparavant. J'ai vu tous les trésors de la plus belle ame que je connois. L'Esprit et l'humeur toujours egale, et toujours la preuve d'une Ame contente d'elle meme. De la Dignité jusque dans le badinage, des agrémens dans le serieux méme. Je vous ai vu faire et dire les choses les plus grandes, sans vous en appercevoir audela de ce qui etoit necessaire pour les dire et pour les faire avec connoissance de cause. Votre passion dominante. On le voit assez, c'est la plus vive tendresse pour les meilleurs des parens; elle eclate partout et fait voir à tous ceux qui vous approchent combien vous avez le coeur susceptible des plus nobles sentimens. Toutes les fois que cette reflexion s'est presentéé à mon Esprit, elle m'a toujours emportée bien loin des Objets qui l'avoient fait naitre. Je reflechis dans ce moment meme au bonheur d'un homme qui possesseur d'un Tel Coeur vous trouvât sensible à sa tendresse, qui pût vous assurer mille fois le jour combien il vous aimoit et qui ne cessât de vous en assurer qu'en cessant de Vivre." *Letters,* 1: 77.

28. "Autrefois mon sort etoit plutot ennuyeux que affligeant. Une fortune honete, quelques amis une certaine reputation; Voila peut-etre à quoi je devois m'attendre mais tous ces biens reels sans doute n'etoient point accompagnés du pouvoir d'en jouir. Je portois un Coeur capable de beaucoup de Sentimens; je n'en avois eprouvé aucun. Et Tout me faisoit ressentir que les sensations les plus douleureuses ne sont pas aussi facheuses à l'ame que ce vuide, cette inaction totale ou elle languit isolée dans l'univers. . . . Voila Mademoiselle un affreux tableau. Cependant voila une Idéé que j'ai souvent eprouvé, Etat d'autant plus penible qu'on n'a pas meme la consolation de se repandre au dehors. . . Je vous ai connu Mademoiselle, tout est changé pour moi. Une felicité au-dessus de l'Empire au dessus meme de la Philosophie peut m'attendre mais aussi, Un supplice reiteré chaque jour, et aggravé toujours par la reflexion de ce que j'ai perdu peut me tomber en partage. Cependant Socrate remerciat les Dieux de l'avoir fait naitre Grec; je les remercierai toujours de m'avoir fait naitre dans un Siecle, de m'avoir plaçé dans un pays où j'ai connu une femme que mon Esprit me fera respecter comme la plus estimable de son Sexe pendant que mon Coeur me fera sentir qu'elle en est la plus charmante. Voila direz vous du serieux du lugubre du Tragique meme. L'Ennuyeux personnage, peut on s'empecher de bailler en le lisant. Baillez Mademoiselle je sens que je l'ai merité, mais j'ai merité aussi que vous ajoutez, Il seroit cependant à souhaiter que tous les predicateurs fussent aussi convaincus de ce qu'ils disent." *Letters,* 1: 78-79.

29. *Letters,* 1: 90.

30. J. W. Swain (*Edward Gibbon the Historian* [London, 1966], p. 36) says that "Gibbon certainly took no such trip," on the basis of the dates of Gibbon's studies of Newton. His conclusion is too hasty and much too positive. Michel Baridon hesitantly follows him in it (*Edward Gibbon et le mythe de Rome* [Paris: 1977], p. 62). But Bonnard, Low, and Norton all believe that Gibbon made the journey and that the evidence to the contrary requires another explanation. Low, *Gibbon*, p. 78, n.1. *Journal B*, p. 289, n.1. *Letters,* 1, appendix 2, pp. 396-97, n.30.

31. Add. MSS. 34880, fols. 116-23.

32. Published in *Memoirs*, appendix 2, p. 225.

33. *Letters*, 1: 91.

34. ". . . ceux de l'Inegalité de fortune."

35. "Il voudra mon bonheur et s'il [le] veut il ne songera pas à m'eloigner de vous. . . . L'amour de l'Etude faisoit ma seule passion jusqu'au tems où vous m'avez fait sentir que le Coeur avoit ses besoins aussi bien que l'Esprit, qu'ils consistoient dans un amour reciproque." *Letters*, 1: 91.

36. *Letters*, 1: 92-93.

37. *Journal A*, p. 7.

38. As Low points out in *Gibbon*, p. 102.

39. *Letters*, 1: 94-95.

40. The *Essai* was published in 1761. It was reprinted in Paris and in London in 1762 and pirated in Dublin in 1767. An English translation was published (London, 1764) and pirated (Dublin, 1788). J. E. Norton, *A Bibliography of the Works of Edward Gibbon* (Oxford, 1940), pp. 1-10. Manuscript drafts are available in Add. MSS. 34880, fols. 129v-141r, 149v-159r, 175r-185r.

41. Add. MSS. 34880, fols. 124r-129r. The notes for the *Essai* were begun on the verso of the last sheet of this study. The sheets had probably not yet been bound together, so this does not necessarily imply that the *Essai* followed the La Bletterie extract immediately. The extract is in *MW* 1814, 3: 169-77.

42. "Je veux me faire une Idéé nette du Systeme de M. de la Barre. Il en vaut la peine comme il est propre à jetter beaucoup de Lumiere sur les Anciens. Il en a besoin; car l'Esprit de son auteur n'est pas aussi lumineux qu'il est profond, et d'ailleurs sa Grande Erudition lui suggere à tous momens des Digressions auxquelles il n'a pas le courage de se refuser." Add. MSS. 34880, fol. 124r.

43. "Porter un Esprit de netteté dans les Tenèbres de l'Antiquité suffit pour l'homme de lettres qui veut s'instruire; joncher des fleurs sur les Epines de la Science arrête le Bel Esprit qui ne cherche qu'à s'amuser. Réunir l'utile à l'agreable: violà tout ce que le Lecteur le plus difficile peut demander: Qu'il le demande hardiment à M. de la Bletterie." Add. MSS. 34880, fol. 126r. *MW* 1814, 3: 169.

44. "Qui me paroît incontestable. C'est que le témoignage d'un historien Contemporain est d'une toute autre autorité dans ces matieres que les inductions que nous autres François pouvons tirer des faits qui se rencontrent dans leurs Ecrits. La raison en est claire. C est que nous ne voyons l'Histoire de ces tems qu'en gros, au lieu qu'ils la voyoient en détail: Et c'est de ce détail que tout dépend dans des discussions aussi délicates que celles-ci." Add. MSS. 34880, fol. 127r. *MW* 1814, 3: 172.

45. "En attendant que M. de la Bletterie éclaircisse ces difficultés, tenons nous toujours à son Systeme. Il est clair, plausible, et bien lié. Si c'est une Erreur c'est une de ces erreurs qui eclairent l'Esprit en le trompant. En le supposant prouvé je vais hazarder quelques idées sur la part qu'avoient les Soldats au choix des Empereurs." Add. MSS. 34880, fol. 128r. *MW* 1814, 3: 174.

46. "Nouvel exemple de l'attachement des hommes aux noms, et de leur négligence pour les idées qu'ils renferment." Add. MSS. 34880, fol. 129r. *MW* 1814, 3: 174.

47. *Letters*, 1: 95-101.

48. Add. MSS. 34880, fol. 130r, left margin, adjacent to title: "Commencéés à Lausanne. environ le 20 Mars. 1758." *Journal A*, p. 7.

49. *Letters*, 1: 102.

50. This draft has never been published.

51. A footnote to the original title, not included in the published version because the term belles-lettres was no longer used, defined that term and his topic explicitly: "Pour eviter toute equivoque, j'avertis une fois pour tout que j'entends par *l'Etude de Belles Lettres, celle des Anciens, et de l'Antiquité Grecque et Latine.*" Add. MSS. 34880, fol. 129v.

52. "La connoissance de l'antiquité, voilà notre vrai commentaire: mais ce qui est plus nécessaire encore, c'est un certain esprit qui en est le résultat; esprit qui non seulement nous fait connoître les choses, mais qui nous familiarise avec elles, et nous donne à leur égard les yeux des anciens." *Essai*, chap. 14. *MW* 1814, 4: 27.

My collaborator in a forthcoming edition and translation of the *Essai* is Professor Nelly Murstein of Connecticut College.

53. ". . . presqu'inintelligibles à quiconque n'a pas appris à vivre et à penser comme le peuple Romain." *Essai*, chap. 16. *MW* 1814, 4: 28.

54. ". . . profondement instruit." Add. MSS. 34880, fol. 134r.

55. ". . . fade aux yeux de celui qui n'apporte à la lecture de Virgile, d'autre préparation qu'un goût naturel, et quelque connoissance de la langue Latine!" *Essai*, chap. 17. *MW* 1814, 4: 31.

56. "La nature des choses et dans la connoissance du coeur humain. Il les a éclaircies par les exemples des plus grands modèles." *Essai*, chap. 23. *MW* 1814, 4: 37.

57. "L'art de juger des écrits et des écrivains, ce qu'ils ont dit, s'ils l'ont bien dit, s'ils ont dit vrai . . . vrai historique . . . de leurs témoignages, et non de leurs opinions." *Essai*, chap. 23. *MW* 1814, 4: 38.

58. Magdalen College, MSS. 359.

59. James Boswell, *London Journal*, ed. F. A. Pottle (New York, 1950), pp. 41-42.

60. *Journal A*, p. 7.

CHAPTER 8

1. *Journal A*, pp. 7-8. All information about the towns passed through in this journey is recorded in these two pages.

2. ". . . le langage du Coeur [et] de l'Esprit" ". . . les Chemins les Voituriers et les Cabarets." ". . . dispensez moi d'achever." *Letters*, 1: 104, 103.

3. *Letters*, appendix 2, table 1, p. 394.

4. *Letters*, 1: 104.

5. *Journal A*, p. 8.

6. Though not recorded in Bonnard's edition, this textual peculiarity is clearly visible in the manuscript. Add. MSS. 34874, fol. 40v.

7. *Letters*, 1: 107.

8. He clearly assumed that he would have had to plead cases. The possibility of being a solicitor was theoretically open to him, but it did not occur to him to enter that less glamorous branch of the legal profession.

9. D. M. Low, "Edward Gibbon and the Johnsonian Circle," *New Rambler* (June 1960), thinks they were unacquainted until the 1770s.

10. *Journal A*, p. 9.

11. Several scholars, notably David Jordan and G. A. Bonnard, overlook the fact that Gibbon says here that this was the time required to *complete* the draft (rather than to compose it), and also the fact that he did complete the original fifty-five chapter *Essai*, exactly as he said he did, even though he later canceled parts of this draft and replaced them with other chapters. They incorrectly allege that Gibbon misrepresents his work on the *Essai* and therefore draw unreliable inferences about his attitude toward it. David P. Jordan, *Gibbon and His Roman Empire* (Urbana, Ill., 1971), p. 10. *Journal B*, p. 170 n.1.

12. Add. MSS. 34880, fols. 132v-133v.

13. Add. MSS. 34880, fols. 156r, 157r.

14. "Tout ce qu'ont eté les hommes, tout ce que le Genie [a] créé tout ce que la raison a pesé; tout ce Que le travail [a] recueilli, voila le departement de la Critique." Add. MSS. 34880, fol. 135r. MS. has "à" before *recueilli* and *créé*.

15. ". . . entouré des productions de tous les Siecles . . . le philosophe de nos jours . . . s'y arrete . . . materiaux pour l'edifice."

16. ". . . le vrai critique . . . sent que sa tache ne fait que commencer."

17. ". . . balance les differens degrés de Vraisemblance."

18. ". . . cherche le genre de preuves qui convient à son sujet et s'en contente. Modeste et sensé, il n'etale point ses conjectures comme des Verités, ses inductions comme des faits ses Vraisemblances comme des demonstrations."

19. "En un mot la probabilité que les Historiens savoient ce fait l'emporte t'elle sur celle que nous entendons Ciceron ou bien lui cede t'elle?" Add. MSS. 34880, fol. 136r.

20. "Que toutes les sciences fussent *legum non hominum republica*." The Latin means "a republic of laws, not men."

21. "Maitre des regles, mais maitre aussi des raisons des regles. . . . Charmer, attendrir Elever l'Esprit. . . . Que le Lecteur retrouve toujours dans [les] fictions [du poete], ce meme degré de plaisir, que la Verité et les convenances lui eussent offert."

22. Jordan, *Gibbon and His Roman Empire*, p. 88. Jordan's account of the *Essai* as a statement of "Gibbon's highly original speculations on the nature of history and the role of the historian," p. 81, is valuable, though perhaps he somewhat overstates the importance of Montesquieu's influence on the content (as opposed to the style) of the work. Gibbon had several masters.

23. ". . . qui detestent chez le Barbare ce qu'ils admirent chez le Grec." Add. MSS. 34880, fol. 140r.

24. "On erige la croix sur les debris du Capitole." Add. MSS. 34880, fol. 155r.

25. "Le Christianisme n'etoit point un nouveau joug imposé aux hommes mais un Systeme de devoirs connu de toutes les nations, adopté par les prètres, ordonné par les legislateurs enseigné par les Philosophes, chanté par les poetes" Add. MSS. 34880, fol. 154r.

26. "Le vice et la corruption . . . innondoi[en]t la terre quand le législateur des Chrétiens y vint apporter la paix et la lumiere." Add. MSS. 34880, fol. 154r.

27. "Apres avoir rendu hommage a la vertû d'un petit nombre on fremira d'horreur à la corruption Generale." "On a demandé si l'on ne pouvoit pas aimer la vertû pour elle meme, celui qui s'est engagé dans l'histoire degoutante de ces monstres ne s'ecriera t'il plutot pas a tout moment, Ces hommes n'ont ils point aimé le mal pour luimeme?" ". . . jeunesse dissolue et cruelle ne servit qu'a donner du relief aux travaux du reste de sa vie." ". . . la paix, l'abondance et la prosperité." ". . . renait de ses cendres." "Le Mage et le Druide le Stoicien et l'Epicurien se reunissent à croire une doctrine qui etonne la raison et qui amortit." Add. MSS. 34880, fols. 154r, 155r.

28. "Les adversaires de l'Etre supreme sont en petit nombre et cachés, peutetre n'existent-ils nulle part, ceux de la révelation sont nombreux et hardis" (chap. 61). Add. MSS. 34880, fol. 154r.

29. "Qu'y a-t'il de trop absurde pour les hommes?" (chap. 58). *MW* 1814, 4: 72.

30. D. M. Low, *Edward Gibbon, 1737–1794* (London, 1937), pp. 52–53.

31. "Voila quelques reflexions qui m'ont parues solides sur les differentes utilités des Belles-Lettres." Add. MSS. 34880, fol. 155r.

32. Giarrizzo points out that Gibbon seems less than just to the similarity of his views to those of d'Alembert. G. Giarrizzo, *Edward Gibbon e la cultura europea del settocento* (Naples, 1954), pp. 98–99.

33. *Journal A*, p. 9.

34. *Letters*, 1: 106–7.

35. "Voici sa reponse. Epousez votre Etrangere . . . mais souvenez vous avant de le faire que vous etes fils et Citoyen."

36. *Letters*, 1: 91.

37. *Letters*, 1: 109, 112.

38. For Maty, see Uta Janssens, *Matthieu Maty and the Journal Britannique 1750-1755* (Amsterdam, 1975).

39. *Journal A*, p. 9; *Letters*, 1: 115.

40. *Letters*, 1: 112.

41. *Notes and Queries*, ser. 2, vol. 3 (Feb. 21, 1857): 145-46.

42. Add. MSS. 34880, fol. 155v-157v.

43. *Letters*, 1: 113.

44. *Letters*, 1: 113-14.

45. Assumed by Norton to be a servant in *Letters*, 3, index 1, p. 389, but Gibbon mentions a Mrs. Lee (1: 277) who is a creditor, possibly a neighbor or a tenant.

46. *Letters*, 1: 115.

47. *Letters*, 1: 117. He adds, not altogether clearly, "I shall seek his acquaintance without being discouraged by Maty." By Maty's advice, or his example?

48. *Journal A*, p. 9.

49. *Letters*, 1: 117.

50. *Letters*, 1: 116.

51. Ibid.

52. *Journal A*, p. 9.

53. "J'ai voulu surtout montrer par ces réflexions, combien sont délicates les discussions de la critique, où il ne s'agit pas de saisir la démonstration, mais de comparer le poids des vraisemblances opposées; et combien il faut se défier des systêmes les plus éblouissans, puisqu'il y en a si peu qui soutiennent l'épreuve d'un examen libre et attentif." *MW* 1814, 4: 45. Chapter 24 is Add. MSS. 34880, fol. 135r.

54. Arnaldo Momigliano, *Studies in Historiography* (London, 1966), p. 45.

55. *Letters*, 1: 118.

56. "Mes sentiments pour vous dont votre tendresse faisoit un des plus forts liens, commençoient à s'affoiblir." *Letters*, 1: 110.

57. "Et ne me fissiés vous qu'une visite de quelques mois dans tout cet intervalle, je crois que je prefererois ce partit à bien d'autres, si cependant Monsieur Gibbon est inflexible, vous connoissés trop mes idées pour avoir besoin de me faire sentir que rien ne vous obligeroit à trahir votre devoir." *Letters*, 1: 111.

58. ". . . languir Six mois dans une attente penible, devoré d'ennuis à charge à moi-meme et aux autres: incertain de vos sentimens, de votre sort de tout ce qui m'interessoit! *Ces parens disent cependant qu'ils ne veulent que notre bonheur. Ils le croyent eux-memes.*" *Letters*, 1: 119. Norton believes that this underlining was Suzanne's.

59. ". . . *la seule femme qui eut pu me rendre heureux*" (emphasis Suzanne's). "Vous n'avez deja que trop de penchant pour les moeurs Etrangéres." ". . . se serviroit de son ascendant pour vous engager à vous expatrier. Son procedé seroit naturel, mais quel malheur pour moi, quel crime pour vous." "Je crains que vous ne puissiez pas faire cet effort. Je crains que vous le puissiez. Helas le pourrai-je moi meme." *Letters*, 1: 120-21.

60. For the date see *Letters*, 1, appendix 2, p. 399.

61. Published in *MW* 1814, 3: 178-82, the essay is in Add. MSS. 34881, fols. 61v-64r. Notes belonging to, and contemporaneous with, the first page of the "treatise upon the ancient weights coins and measures"—attributed to the summer of 1759 in *Journal A*, p. 10—are on fol. 64v.

62. "En tout, hormis la religion, il vaut mieux ne pas croire assez, que de croire trop." *MW* 1814, 3: 182.

63. *Journal A*, p. 10.

64. "Il est des études qui n'augmentent point les connoissances, ou du moins ne

les augmentent, qu'en écartant ces obstacles dont la bizarrerie des hommes en a hérissés la route de toutes parts. Telle est l'étude des langues. . . . La différence des poids et des mesures est un nouveau langage, aussi barbare et plus ridicule que les autres. . . . Elle nous servira d'interprète dans la géographie, le commerce, et l'économique des anciens, objets intéressans dont la connoissance nous empêchera de voir dans les anciens des sauvages ou des demi-dieux." *MW* 1814, 5: 66.

65. See Add. MSS. 34881, fols. 1-60. Lord Sheffield's version is in *MW* 1814, 5: 66-169.

CHAPTER 9

1. The colonel, Sir Thomas Worsley, was an old friend of Mr. Gibbon's.
2. *Journal A*, p. 10.
3. *Journal A*, pp. 10 and 184.
4. *Letters*, 1: 109.
5. *Journal A*, p. 10.
6. See above, p. 115.
7. *Letters*, 1: 123.
8. He was twenty-three, the same age at which Horace became commander of a legion. See below.
9. June 2-3, 1760; *Journal A*, p. 11.
10. *EE*, p. 340.
11. Compare the interesting discussion by J.G.A. Pocock, "Between Machiavelli and Hume: Gibbon as Civic Humanist and Philosophical Historian," (*Daedalus* 105, no. 3 [summer 1976]), of Gibbon's treatment of the relationship between military virtues and civilization in the *DF*, esp. pp. 157-64. Perhaps not only Machiavelli but also experience instructed Gibbon that the more professional the citizen-soldier became as a soldier, the more corrupt he became as a citizen.
12. *Journal A*, p. 12.
13. *Journal A*, p. 14.
14. *Journal A*, p. 16.
15. *Journal A*, p. 18.
16. *Journal A*, p. 17.
17. *Letters*, 2: 32; 3: 161.
18. *Journal A*, p. 17.
19. *Journal A*, p. 20.
20. *Journal A*, p. 21.
21. Ibid.
22. *Journal A*, p. 22.
23. Ibid.
24. Published in *MW* 1814, 5: 209-13. Sheffield translation.
25. "Ne devons lire que pour nous aider a penser. En lisant quelque ouvrage la lecture me fait naitre [maitre?] des Idees mais des idees un peu differentes du sujet de cet ouvrage; je veux les pousser, je m'ecarte de mon plan et je me jette dans une autre lecture qui m'est necessaire, de la peutetre a une seconde et un troisieme. Enfin Je vois ou mes pensees me menent c'est peut etre à quelque chose qui en vaut la peine mais toujours faut il essayer. Si j'avois suivi mon grand chemin, au bout de ma longue carriere, j'aurois a peine pu retrouver les traces de mes idéés." Add. MSS. 34880, fol. 161.
26. *EE*, p. 94.
27. *Letters*, 1: 125.

28. *Journal A*, p. 23.

29. *EE*, pp. 25-26. It is possible that this speech is not really Gibbon's; it was not published until after his death.

30. *MW* 1814, 3: 206. Add. MSS. 34880, fols. 163v-174r.

31. *MW* 1814, 3: 206, 222.

32. Baridon points out that Gibbon's conclusion to this essay "le place nettement dans la lignée orthodoxe des théoriciens du droit naturel: les différents titres de possession mentionnés [conquest, inheritance, people's choice] sont repris de Locke qui les avait tirés de Grotius et de Pufendorf." ("places it squarely in the orthodox line of theoreticians of natural law. The various titles of possession mentioned are recapitulated from Locke, who had drawn them from Grotius and Pufendorf.") Michel Baridon, *Edward Gibbon et le mythe de Rome* (Paris, 1977), p. 290.

33. Sheffield translation. Original (Add. MSS. 34880, fol. 174r) is "Le Droit de conquéte n'est fait que pour les bêtes feroces. Le droit de succession . . . n'a pas des fins des principes fixes. Le seul droit au-dessus de toutes les objections est celui qui sort de la voix d'un peuple libre."

34. *MW* 1814, 3: 217-19. "Dans mes Compilations, le consentement des Etats à cette adoption ne paroissoit point. . . . Mais j'ai vu depuis que l'exact Giannone n'en dit rien non plûs." Add. MSS. 34880, fol. 169v.

35. *MW* 1814, 3: 208-9. "La propriété des terres entraine celle des femmes. . . . Quiconque viole cet ordre de la societé en doit etre puni dans son enfant et cet enfant dont la naissance est un outrage fait aux loix, n'est point enfant de la societé; et ne doit pas participer aux biens dont elle garantit la succession. . . . Lorsque le malheur de la mére, ou le merite du fils ont plaidé pour lui, la Clémence du souverain le rend à la societé en effaçant la tâche de sa naissance et lui rendant ses droits." Add. MSS. 34880, fols. 164-65.

36. *MW* 1814, 3: 217. "Sous un tel gouvernement le souverain peut donner ses etats par la meme raison qu'un berger peut donner son troupeâu. Ils lui appartiennent. Mais il y a d'autres nations plus dignes du nom d'hommes, qui ne voyent dans le souverain que le premier magistrat etabli par le peuple pour le rendre heureux, et comptable à lui de sa conduite. Un tel magistrat ne pouvoit transferer à un autre un pouvoir dont il n'etoit que l'usufruitier. A sa mort il etoit devolû au peuple si le gouvernement etoit electif; s'il etoit hereditaire au plus proche heritier suivant les loix que la nation avoit etablies, et si la maison royale devenoit eteinte le peuple rentroit dans tous ses droits." Add. MSS. 34880, fols. 170r-171r.

37. "Montesquieu apparaît clairement dans la distinction . . . entre les sujets d'un despote, qui sont sa propriété, et ceux d'un 'Prince européen'" Baridon, *Mythe*, p. 290.

38. In the first edition, which had two chapters numbered LVI. In reprint editions, the equivalent chapter numbers are therefore LV-LXXX.

39. Add. MSS. 34880, fol. 175. The date "23 Avril" looks as if the numbers were once different, perhaps "15." *Journal A*, pp. 24-25.

40. ". . . ces événemens généraux, dont l'influence lente mais sûre change la face de la terre, sans qu'on puisse s'appercevoir de l'époque de ce changement, et surtout dans . . . les religions." *MW* 1814, 4: 69.

41. See, e.g., Robert Shackleton, "The Impact of French Literature on Gibbon," *Daedalus* 105, no. 3 (Summer 1976): 40, and G. Giarrizzo, *Edward Gibbon e la cultura europea del settocento*, pp. 121-22. Most useful is Baridon, *Mythe*, pp. 284-85, especially for his discussion of Gibbon's relationship to de Brosses and to Hume (*Natural History of Religion*).

42. *Journal A*, p. 25.

43. *Journal A*, pp. 25-26.

44. *Journal A*, p. 27.

45. *Journal A*, p. 28. The officers of the South Hampshire wore "swords and silver lace, a brass gorget when on duty, a red-and-silver waistcoat, white kerseymere breeches and white stockings with black garters . . . powdered hair and pigtails."C. P. Hawkes, *Authors-at-Arms* (London, 1934), pp. 59-60. He provides a drawing of Gibbon (facing p. 49) as "the Captain of the Hampshire Grenadiers." It is to be hoped that his military information is more reliable than his knowledge of Gibbon.

46. Gibbon reminds us here of the hero of *Rambler*, no. 146, though, of course, he need not have recalled Johnson's essay to arrive at so obvious a conclusion. However, that they shared both the response and a wry amusement about it is another instance of similarity between these two "polar" figures of the age.

47. G. A. Bonnard, "Gibbon's 'Essai sur l'étude de la littérature' as Judged by Contemporary Reviewers and Gibbon Himself," *English Studies* 32 (1952): 145-53. Baridon (*Mythe*, p. 268n.) adds that the French notices of the *Essai* are far from equally valuable, only the *Journal étranger* being truly a critical appreciation.

48. See J. E. Norton, *A Bibliography of the Works of Edward Gibbon* (Oxford, 1940), pp. 1-10.

49. *Journal A*, p. 28.

50. *Bodleian Library Record* 9, 6 (Jan. 1978): 374.

51. Cf. Lynn White, Jr., ed., *The Transformation of the Roman World* (Berkeley and Los Angeles, 1966), pp. 15-16.

52. *Journal A*, p. 30.

53. *Journal A*, p. 32.

54. Ibid.; see also p. 36.

55. Add. MSS. 34880, fols. 187-88.

56. *Journal A*, p. 33.

57. James Boswell, *London Journal 1762-1763*, ed. F. A. Pottle (New York: 1951), pp. 84-161, 174-87, and Pottle's introduction, pp. 12-13.

58. *Journal A*, pp. 34-35.

59. *Journal A*, pp. 35-36.

60. Deyverdun was probably Gibbon's informant. He had been flirting with Suzanne himself, he had written to Gibbon, and, in a late reflection on the whole question, Gibbon mused that Suzanne "m'a trahi, puisque d'Eyverdun n'avoit aucun motif de le faire." *Journal B*, p. 222. In context, it is clear that the "betrayal" he has in mind is deception, not infidelity.

61. See below, chapter 10.

62. *Journal A*, p. 50.

63. *Journal A*, pp. 38-40.

64. *Journal A*, p. 41.

65. *Journal A*, p. 47.

66. *Journal A*, p. 42.

67. *Journal A*, p. 44.

68. See Hoyt Trowbridge, "Edward Gibbon, Literary Critic," *Eighteenth Century Studies* 4 (1971): 403-19.

69. E.g., E.M.W. Tillyard, *The English Epic and Its Background* (London, 1954), and Leo Braudy, *Narrative Form in History and Fiction* (Princeton, 1970).

70. *Journal A*, p. 46.

71. *Journal A*, p. 48.

72. *Journal A*, p. 52. For a description of the books Gibbon used in his study of Greek, see Giarrizzo, *Edward Gibbon e la cultura europea*, p. 158.

73. For the duties of a brigade major, see J. W. Fortescue, *History of the British Army*, 2.

74. *Journal A*, pp. 64-65.

75. We do not know why Mr. Gibbon changed his mind about giving up the majority; perhaps, given his changeable character, it would have been constancy on his part that required explanation, not change.

76. Especially Lord Sheffield. See Patricia B. Craddock, "Edward Gibbon: The Man in His Letters," in *The Familiar Letter in the Eighteenth Century*, ed. H. Anderson, P. Daghlian, and I. Ehrenpreis (Lawrence, Kans., 1966), pp. 238-42.

77. He notes at least once, however, a preference for decor consistently "in the old style," in contrast to a mixture of old and new. *Journal A*, p. 71.

78. *Journal A*, pp. 69-70.

79. This impression of Gibbon's conversation may be, however, unduly influenced by Boswell. See D. M. Low, *Edward Gibbon, 1737-1794* (London, 1937), p. 225; cf. Henry, Baron Brougham, *Lives of Men of Letters . . . in the Time of George III* (London, 1845-46), 2: 316-17.

80. *Journal A*, pp. 88, 132, 130, 137.

81. *Journal A*, pp. 88, 62, 72.

82. *Journal A*, pp. 84, 194, 150.

83. See *Letters*, 1: 214.

84. *Journal A*, p. 82.

85. *Journal A*, pp. 92-93.

86. *Journal A*, pp. 63, 136.

87. See G. R. de Beer, "The Malady of Edward Gibbon," *Notes and Records of the Royal Society* 7 (1949); 71-80. After proving that Gibbon's illness could not have originated in a venereal disease, de Beer argues that Gibbon was not making an honest error in attributing the hydrocele to a venereal origin, but rather "used this expedient to silence the reproaches which . . . Lord Sheffield cannot have failed to make to him on account of the culpably long neglect of his condition, and at the same time perhaps to gratify a point of vanity." I fail to see why Lord Sheffield would have been supposed to approve of his friend's neglecting a venereal complaint, but be that as it may, de Beer's argument rests on the shaky grounds (1) that Gibbon knew too much about anatomy and physiology to err in such a point and (2) that Gibbon had had no sexual experience of any kind. De Beer quotes a visitor to Lausanne in 1802 who wrote, "I have been assured by a person who enjoyed the confidence of that distinguished man, that the historian of the Decline and Fall of the Roman Empire, though he has frequently described in glowing colors, and perhaps in some pages with lascivious freedom, the passion of love, was a stranger to its pleasures" (p. 80). De Beer recognizes, of course, the slightness of such evidence; the wording of the anecdote makes it clear what the reporter wished to believe, and why. Even if it is accurate, however, it need not imply that Gibbon never experienced sexual intercourse. Indeed, it may imply nothing more than Gibbon's own statement in the *Memoirs*, "I was not very strongly pressed by my family or my passions to propagate the name and race of the Gibbons" (p. 140).

88. *Journal A*, pp. 83, 99.

89. *Journal A*, p. 95.

90. *Journal A*, pp. 95-96.

91. *Journal A*, p. 96.

92. *Journal A*, pp. 129-30.

93. Add. MSS. 34880, fol. 219.

94. *Journal A*, pp. 102-3.

95. *Journal A*, pp. 103-4.

96. *Journal A*, p. 204. His retrospective summary of the period in the militia is echoed in the *Memoirs* in most respects. It concludes: "The General system of our government . . . [has] been impressed in my mind, not by vain theory, but by the

indelible lessons of action and experience. I . . . am myself much better known, than (with my reserved character) I should have been in ten years. . . . So that the sum of all is, that I am glad the militia has been, and glad that it is no more." Pp. 194-95.

CHAPTER 10

1. *MG*, p. 104.

2. "Je ne voulois pas que l'ecrivain fit totalement disparoitre le Gentilhomme." *MG*, p. 106. Michel Baridon points out that if Reynolds had painted Gibbon in an allegorical fashion, he might have shown him between "le monde modest et austère de l'étude [et] . . . celui de la haute société et de la politique, celui de Deyverdun et celui de Lord Sheffield. Deux tentations qui furent longtems rivales dans l'esprit de l'historien et qu'il n'arriva pas toujours à concilier." *Edward Gibbon et le mythe de Rome* (Paris, 1977), p. 60.

3. Pavillard and, to a lesser extent, Gibbon's first tutor at Oxford, may be thought of as counterinstances. But Gibbon *chose* neither of these elders as intimates, though he valued their friendship when it was offered to him; and his relationship with both was exactly like his relationship with his contemporaries—they were not mentors, or sources of either rewards or punishments. Gibbon later gratefully accepted the care and advice of two or three men of business who were older than he, but he was dependent on them only with respect to their special expertise, as we shall see.

4. *Letters*, 1: 132; 137-38.

5. Though Mr. Gibbon's letter is not extant, its content may easily be inferred from Gibbon's reply. *Letters*, 1: 141-44.

6. *Journal A*, p. 35.

7. *MW* 1814, 2: 43-44.

8. *MG*, p. 104.

9. *Letters*, 1: 138.

10. According to W. Cole, *Journal of a Journey to Paris*, ed. Stokes (1931), p. 62, Horace Walpole paid 14 guineas for the same kind of accommodations two years later. *Letters*, 1: 135, n.3.

11. *Letters*, 1: 135.

12. "Le fait n'est pas vraisemblable, mais il est vrai." *MG*, p. 104.

13. *Letters*, 1: 133.

14. *Letters*, 1: 139.

15. ". . . homme de lettres reconnû." *MG*, p. 105.

16. ". . . regret d'etre si neuf dans cette belle science. Desque j'aurai fini mes deux Benedictins . . . je m'y mettrai serieusement." *MG*, pp. 98-99.

17. "Aujourd hui j'ai commencè ma tournèè pour voir les endroits dignes d'attention dans la ville." *MG*, p. 94.

18. Compare his famous dictum, "The various modes of worship which prevailed in the Roman world were all considered by the people as equally true, by the philosopher as equally false, and by the magistrate as equally useful." *DF*, chapter 2. See also Robert Shackleton, "The Impact of French Literature on Gibbon," *Daedalus* 105, no. 3 (Summer 1976), p. 45, and Owen Chadwick, "Gibbon and the Church Historians," *Daedalus*, p. 115.

19. *Journal A*, p. 98.

20. *Journal A*, pp. 127-28.

21. "Père commun de toute la nature . . . maitre impitoyable . . . la colère et la vengeance." *MG*, pp. 96-97.

22. "Il a assez d'imagination pour dix autres, et pas assez de sens rassis pour lui seul." *MG*, p. 99.

23. "Elle m'aimoit; j'etois son fils et son ami. . . . Elle commença d'abord à s'attacher

à moi, me parloit de ses affaires les plus secrettes, me donnoit des conseils, et jusqu'à des reprimandes. Elle avoit même quelquefois des Ouvertures que je ne comprends pas trop encore. Elle me parloit des plaisirs des sens, m'encourageoit à en parler, m'en tendoit lire les contes de la Fontaine; et lorsqu'èchauffè par ces agaceries, je m'emancipois un peu, elle me repoussoit foiblement et paroissoit emûe Avec un peu plus de hardiesse j'aurois peut etre reussi. Peut-etre aussi cette conduite n'etoit l'effet que de la libertè Francoise et de la franchise d'un Caractère que agissoit [sans] façon, parcequ'il agissoit sans dessein." *MG*, p. 106.

24. "Madame Bontems peut aimer Dieu en Fanatique, mais elle ne peut hair ses ennemis. Elle m'a avouè cent fois que la damnation des heretiques exerçoit beaucoup sa foi." *MG*, p. 107.

25. *Letters*, 1: 144.

26. *Letters*, 1: 114, 135.

27. *Letters*, 1: 146-47.

28. *Letters*, 1: 151.

29. See above, Chapter 9, n.60.

30. Suzanne's letter giving the history of the affair as it appeared to her admits these two points even as it extenuates them. *Letters*, 1: 159-62.

31. Including Bonnard (*Journal B*, introduction), Norton (*Letters*, 1, appendix 2), and, of course, Suzanne's most ardent supporter, d'Haussonville, to whom Gibbon is incidental but culpable.

32. *Letters*, 1: 145-46.

33. See, e.g., G.P.O. de Cléron, comte d'Haussonville, *Le Salon de Madame Necker*, 2 vols. (Paris, 1882): 1: 104-6, or 2: 4-5.

34. *Letters*, 1: 148-49.

35. d'Haussonville, *Madame Necker*, 1: 65 ff.

36. *Letters*, 1: 151.

37. "Faudroit il toujours que vous m'offriez un bonheur auquel la raison m'oblige de renoncer? J'ai perdu votre tendresse; votre amitiè me demeure. . . . Je la reçois Mademoiselle, comme un echange precieux de la mienne. . . . Mais cette correspondence Mademoiselle—j'en sens tous les agrèmens, mais en mème tems j'en sens tout le danger." *Letters*, 1: 152.

38. "Les petites dissipations de la ville, le tumulte de Mesery, et les changemens journaliers de l'un à l'autre." *Journal B*, p. 3.

39. See *Journal B*, appendix, pp. 273-80.

40. "Extraits du Registre du Conseil de Lausanne . . . 1761 à 1764," fol. 239r, quoted in *Journal B*, p. 273: ". . . des violences & mauvais traitemens."

41. ". . . affaire malheureuse, qui montre de la part du Magistrat un entêtement, une mauvaise foi et une incapacité qui le rendent tres meprisable; et de la notre trop de passion à soutenir une bagatelle." *Journal B*, p. 7.

42. *Journal B*, preface, p. ix.

43. "Ce fut alors qu'un voyage de Genève interrompit un peu mon assiduité, que le sejour de Mesery m'offrit mille distractions, et que la societé de Saussure acheva de me faire perdre mon tems. Je repris mon travail avec ce journal au milieu *d'Août*." *Journal B*, p. 189.

44. See *Letters*, 1: 155.

45. *Journal B*, p. 3. He devotes a paragraph to the situation, ending, with an irony for once probably unconscious, "Avec quel serieux la vanité des *femmes* traite ces miseres" (emphasis added).

46. See *Journal B*, preface; and *Letters*, 1, appendix 2, p. 401.

47. The parentheses, signalling his intention to supply a reference, were never filled. Bonnard plausibly suggests that Gibbon intended to refer to a phrase in Suzanne's

own letter, "tous, dis-je, m'engageoit à m'attirer la jalousie des femmes et des critiques des hommes que je ne goutais pas." *Journal B*, p. 5.

48. "Ses Voyages à Lausanne, les adorateurs qu'elle y a eû et la complaisance avec laquelle elle les a ecoutés, formoient l'article le plus difficile à justifier. Ni d'Eyverdun (dit elle) ni personne n'ont effacé pendant un instant mon image de son coeur. Elle s'amusoit a Lausanne sans s'y attacher. Je le veux. Mais ces amusemens la convainquent toujours de la dissimulation la plus odieuse et si l'infidelité est quelquefois une foiblesse, la duplicité est toujours un vice. C'est pendant le mois de Juillet 1758, qu'elle m'ecrivoit de Crassie cette singuliere lettre pleine de tendresse et de desespoir, ses yeux remplis de larmes, et sa santé affoiblie par la douleur. Au meme mois de Juillet elle etoit a Lausanne pleine de santé, et de charmes. *L'objet de la jalousie des femmes et des soupirs des hommes* (   ), goutant tous les plaisirs, fondant des Academies, distribuant les prix, composant elle meme des ouvrages d'Esprit, et se jouant de l'amour si elle ne s'en occupoit pas. Ce contraste ne suffit il pas pour m'eclairer sur son compte. Je dis eclairer. Il n'est question que d'idées et nullement de sentimens. La justification la plus complette en lui rendant mon estime, ne pourroit plus rallumer des feux si parfaitement eteints. Comme elle . . . doit bientot quitter Geneve, je ne la reverrai plus, et tout est fini. Cette affair[e] singuliere dans toutes ses parties m'a eté très utile; Elle m'a ouvert les yeux sur le caractère des femmes—, et elle me servira longtems de preservatif contre les seductions de l'amour." *Journal B*, pp. 51-52.

49. "J'ai eté d'abord un peu confûs, mais . . . nous avons causé un quart d'heure avec toute la liberté de gens qui se seroient quelquefois vûs. Que cette tranquillité de sa part est instructive pour moi." *Journal B*, p. 217. He continued the entry, with further uncharacteristically unconscious irony, "J'ai passé l'Après midi avec la petite femme chez Madame Fornerey. Rien de nouveau."

50. "Nous avons causé sur un ton de plaisanterie, que j'ai redoublé sans peine pour lui faire sentir que je la voyois partir avec indifference. Ce sentiment n'est point joué. Le tems, l'absence, mais surtout la connoissance du caractere faux, et affecté de cette fille ont eteint jusqu'aux dernieres etincelles de ma passion." *Journal B*, p. 257.

51. Gibbon's note: "J'entend de ses contemporains"—I mean, among his contemporaries.

52. ". . . force . . . varieté et . . . abondance." "Je lui reprocherois . . . une malignité de coeur qui lui fait trouver le vice partout. . . . Jamais Juvenal ne se permet la moindre louange des vertueux(.) quand ce ne seroit que pour contraster avec le vice. Tous les autres Satyriques, un Horace, un Boileau, un Pope ont compris qu'ils devoient se faire des amis de leurs lecteurs, en se representant comme ceux de la Vertû et des hommes; ce sont aussi de tous les poètes, ceux que nous aimons le plus. Mais Juvenal paroit detester les hommes par principe." *Journal B*, pp. 12-13.

53. *Letters*, 1: 162.

54. *Letters*, 1: 157-58.

55. ". . . ne manque pas d'esprit, ni de connoissances mais il me paroit très suffisant. . . . ils sont tous les deux militaires, et ils ont adopté tous les prejugés de leur etat contre la milice." *Journal B*, p. 21.

56. D. M. Low, *Edward Gibbon, 1737-1794* (London, 1937), pp. 155-56.

57. "C'est une societé assez agreable pour y passer ses momens perdûs. . . . Ils ont un joli apartement ou l'on est sur de trouver du jeu, de la conversation, les gazettes, les journaux etc. . . . Je comte d'y aller assez souvent, surtout pendant l'hyver." *Journal B*, pp. 25-26.

58. "Une jeunesse folatre qui ne sait que rire, chanter et danser n'est pas precisément ce qu'il me faut." *Journal B*, p. 29. Low (*Gibbon*, p. 161) quotes the more favorable description of the youthful Lord Sheffield, who attended the Sunday meetings "most devoutly." He had occasion to note that the young women of the

Société du Printemps "are not so reserved as English misses, but are extremely shy of pawing and handling" Add. MSS. 34887.

59. "Sa lettre m'a fait grand plaisir, mais autant qu'il m'a chagriné en refusant mes propositions l'année passée, autant m'embarasse t-il en les acceptant à present, que les lettres de mon père m'ont jetté dans une incertitude qui ne me permet pas trop de former des projets." ". . . qui n'est jamais si sage que lorsqu'il est gris." *Journal B*, p. 31. "Je donnerois beaucoup que tout ce tintamarre ne fût pas arrivé." P. 32.

60. "Est il necessaire de parler d'un jour qui n'a pas existé. Le matin à vomir et à dormir, un bouillon à midi. Le soir . . . repas d'adieu. La fatigue nous a tenû lieu de sagesse, et nous nous [sommes] retirés fort tranquillement à onze heures et demi." *Journal B*, p. 33.

61. This treatise was included in Graevius's *Thesaurus Antiquitatum Romanarum*, the fourth volume of twelve, folio. Gibbon eventually read several other treatises in the volume.

62. "La plus grosse perte a eté celle du tems." *Journal B*, p. 47.

63. ". . . mais je sai en même tems que je l'aurôis eu (il y a trois mois) sans y songer un moment. Ma reputation baisse ici avec quelque raison, et j'ai des Ennèmis." *Journal B*, p. 50.

64. "Quoique Mesery est joli, je m'y ennuyois beaucoup: pour eviter ce malheur, j'y allois peu, et j'y couchois encore moins. De là des repas faits en ville, la necessité d'avoir un Cabriolet, et un grand surcroit de depense, d'embarras et de dissipation." *Journal B*, p. 63.

65. "J'avois une très belle reputation ici pour les moeurs, mais je vois qu'on commence à me confondre avec mes Compatriotes, et à me regarder comme un homme qui aime le vin et le desordre. Ont-ils tout à fait tort?" *Journal B*, p. 58.

66. ". . . certain que le lecteur du texte complet se fera une moins haute idée de Gibbon que celui des seuls extraits publiés par Lord Sheffield. Chez Gibbon, le caractère et le coeur ne sont pas à la hauteur de l'intelligence," said Bonnard. *Journal B*, p. xiv.

67. "Cet homme reunit les mauvaises qualités les plus opposées. La grossiereté, et l'artifice, la betise et la mechanceté; la prodigalité, et l'avarice." *Journal B*, p. 59.

68. "S'il n'avoit eté question que de Guise et de Holroyd je l'aurois fait avec plaisir, mais les deux autres sont de jeunes fous, et parmi nous ce sont les fous qui entrainent les sages et jamais les sages qui gouvernent les fous." *Journal B*, p. 65.

69. He had apparently already established his dislike of riding: he told Holroyd that he intended "to renew the long-forgotten practice of Equitation as it was known in the World before the 2d of June, of the year of our Lord, one thousand seven hundred sixty three." *Letters*, 1: 294.

70. "J'ai perdû cet ami, presqu'au meme instant que je l'avois acquis." "Nous nous goutames reciproquement, nous passames rapidement à la familiarité, à la confiance, à l'amitié, et dans six semaines, nous n'avions rien de caché l'un pour l'autre. Le Caractère de Saussure meritoit tous ces sentiments de ma part." *Journal B*, p. 81.

71. "Il est mon ami, non pas dans le sens que je l'entens par rapport à de Saussure, ou comme je l'envisage par rapport à d'Eyverdun, mais dans le sens faux et banal du monde." *Journal B*, p. 84.

72. An interleaved copy of the *Miscellaneous Works* of 1796, used by Lord Sheffield and his assistants to prepare the 1814 edition, and much correspondence about Gibbon's papers and the publication of the *Miscellaneous Works* are in the Beinecke Library at Yale.

73. Add. MSS. 34881, fols. 121-68.

74. They are few and brief. Giarrizzo, 179, and Giarrizzo, "Towards the *Decline and Fall:* Gibbon's Other Historical Interests," *Daedalus* 105, no. 3 (Summer 1976):

57–58; Joseph Swain, *Edward Gibbon the Historian* (New York, 1966), pp. 106–7; David P. Jordan, *Gibbon and His Roman Empire* (Urbana, Ill., 1971), p. 16; Baridon, *Mythe*, pp. 305–8.

75. "Constantin, qui réforma dirai-je, ou qui confondit toutes les anciennes constitutions, fit plusieurs changemens en Italie." *MW* 1814, 4: 167. Add. MSS. 34881, fol. 125r.

76. It required knowledge of Cluverius's *Italia Antiqua*, which he did not begin reading until October.

77. "Agrippa fit couper ces bois, les environs du lac se défrichèrent et se peuplèrent bientôt, et toutes ces fables disparurent." *MW* 1814, 4: 264. Add. MSS. 34881, fol. 154v. Chapters XIX–XX were published as *MW* 1814, 4: 258–65 and 225–27, respectively.

78. Lord Sheffield's description, *MW* 1814, 4: 155.

79. The coincidence that October 15 is the date, noted, he said, in his journal, of his famous vision of his Roman subject (p. 136), cannot be dismissed without comment. There is in fact no extant journal entry for October 15, 1764, when he was literally in Rome; but this entry of October 15, 1763, when he was mentally in Rome, might explain why he thought he had recorded the other date, or why he remembered or chose to set October 15 as the date of his *Decline and Fall* vision.

80. C. IV–V and C. XVII published as *MW* 1814, 4: 247–58; C. I, ibid., pp. 157–60; II, ibid., pp. 164–67. Add. MSS. 34881, fols. 141v, 152r–v, 153r, 129v, 124v, 126v, 122r–v, 125r.

81. *Journal B*, p. 90. *MW* 1814, 4: 287–88. Add. MSS. 34881, fol. 159v.

82. The probable order (after I, II, IV, V, XVII) is III, XVIII, XII, XV, XIII, XIV, XVI, XI, X, VIII, IX, VII, VI, with XIX and XX possibly interspersed, but probably after VI. As soon as XVI and XX had been written, XXI was possible, and so on; i.e., chapters after the first sixteen suppose the completion of the chapters they continue and at least the commencement of any chapters numbered XVII or higher which have a lower number than theirs. It follows that C. V was the first *filled*, and that the others filled, in order, were: II, XVII, XIX, XV, XI, XXIII–XXV, VIII, XXVII–XXVIII, VII, VI, XXXII–XXXIII, I, XX, XXXVI–XL, III, XLII–XLIV, XIV, XXVI.

83. *MW* 1814, 4: 287–302. Add. MSS. 34881, fols. 159v, 162r, 138v, 163r–v, 164r–v, 160r, 162r, 165r.

84. *Journal B*, p. 226.

85. "La mort arrêta l'exécution de ce projet qu'Auguste, plus sage ou plus timide, n'osa jamais entreprendre. . . . Claude enfin eut le courage de la tenter. . . . Après ce spectacle on ouvrit le canal, mais on s'appercut bientôt combien l'ouvrage étoit imparfait, et que l'ignorance ou la négligence des ouvriers ne lui avoit pas donné la profondeur nécessaire. . . . Faut-il donc s'étonner si Néron et Hadrien n'ont été obligés de rétablir cet ouvrage, et que malgré leurs travaux il n'en reste plus de vestiges? Pour les faciliter et les perfectionner il falloit l'art des écluses que les anciens n'avoient point." *MW* 1814, 4: 293–94. Add. MSS. 34881, fol. 163r.

86. "Il est aussi difficile qu'il seroit inutile de marquer avec précision les bornes de ces petites cités qui se confondoient les unes dans les autres." *MW* 1814, 4: 296. Add. MSS. 34881, fol. 163v.

87. "La republique ne les subjugua qu'après six guerres sanglantes, ou plutôt après une guerre continue de soixante-dix ans, où leurs généraux méritèrent vingt-quatre triomphes, et essuyèrent presqu' autant de revers . . . les légions Romaines victorieuses par tout portèrent le fer et le feu dans leur pays, détruisirent jusqu'aux vestiges de leur villes, et exterminèrent leurs habitans." *MW* 1814, 4: 299. Add. MSS. 34881, fol. 164r–v.

88. "Tous les anciens ont placé Beneventum dans le Samnium. Pourquoi dans la

carte de l'Italie ancienne de M. Delisle le trouve-t-on dans le pays des Hirpini et dans la région d'Apulia?" *MW* 1814, 4: 300. Add. MSS. 34881, fol. 164v.

89. G. A. Bonnard, "L'Importance du deuxième séjour de Gibbon à Lausanne," in *Mélanges d'histoire et de littérature offerts à Charles Gilliard* (Lausanne, 1944).

90. "Il est singulier combien je joue au Whist sans l'aimer ni l'entendre." *Journal B*, p. 88.

91. ". . . une tache vraiment laborieuse." *Journal B*, p. 163. "C'est pour me preparer à la fois à mon voyage d'Italie, et à mes etudes futures que [j'ai fait] cette lecture comme j'avois fait celle de Nardini." P. 90.

92. See *Journal B*, pp. 122-30.

93. "J'ecris dans le pays de Vaud. Ses habitans doivent etre contens de leur etat. Qu'on le compare cependant à celui de ces peuples d'Italie." *Journal B*, p. 127. For a contrasting interpretation see E. Badian, "Gibbon on War," *Gibbon et Rome à la lumière de l'historiographie moderne* (Geneva, 1977), p. 116, n.18.

94. In *MG*. *MW* 1814, 2: 1-32. On November 8 (*Journal B*, p. 142), Pavillard lent Gibbon a book called *Lettres écrites de la Campagne*, which discussed Genevan politics (and, of course, supported the magistrates). Might not this inspire the form and be the immediate occasion of Gibbon's *Lettre*?

95. Low, *Gibbon*, p. 66, and note.

96. "Il est le seul [pays] où à la fois l'on ose penser et l'on sache vivre. Que vous manque t il [?] la liberté: et privés d'elle, tout vous manque." *MG*, p. 124.

97. ". . . chaque partie de l'etat." *MG*, p. 126. ". . . les passions des hommes." P. 130. "Indiquez-moi quelque etablissement vrayment utile que vous devez au Souverain." P. 132.

98. On the "Consensus," Read is useful. Meredith Read, *Historic Studies in Vaud, Berne, and Savoy*, 2 vols. (London, 1897), 1: 366-71.

99. "Les fardeaux leur sont communs à tous, les recompenses doivent l'etre aussi." *MG*, p. 135. "Les talens, les lumieres dans votres pays sont inutiles pour quiconque n'est pas né Bernois." P. 136.

100. *MG*, pp. 137-38.

101. ". . . plus prompt[,] plus entier, plus glorieux." *MG*, p. 141.

102. ". . . joug de l'autorité, pour le conduire du murmure à la sedition; de la sedition à l'anarchie, et de l'anarchie peut-etre au despotisme." Ibid.

103. "Les Bernois ont des droits sur votre obeissance; vous craignez de leur faire une injustice en la retirant." Ibid.

104. "On ne peut . . . pas dire de ce texte qu'il soit particulièrement enflammé. Du *Contrat social* . . . seul est retenu le concept de volonté générale. Toute l'inspiration de la *Lettre* vient de Montesquieu: séparation des pouvoirs, origine 'gothique' de la liberté, condamnation expresse du despotisme, apologie du commerce et de l'industrie, autant de thèmes courants dans l'*Esprit des Lois*." ". . . hommage discret rendu au Major Davel." Baridon, *Mythe*, p. 102.

105. Low, *Gibbon*, p. 66. G. R. de Beer, *Edward Gibbon and His World* (New York, 1968), p. 117.

106. *EE*, pp. 59-87, 96-106.

107. *Journal B*, p. 151.

108. "Jai eu honte de mon procedé à son egard; après les politesses que j'en avois reçues je n'aurois pas dû etre trois mois sans y remettre le pied." Ibid.

109. Louis-André Saussure de Boussins (1706-77)—Bonnard. "J'aime ce Boussens; tout le monde l'aime. Il est bon, gai, sans façon, et [a] beaucoup de cette bonne plaisanterie qui fait rire les autres du plus grand serieux du monde." *Journal B*, p. 152.

110. "Oui, l'homme est naturellement bon! J'en appelle à ces Groenlandois, qui connoissent l'amour au milieu de leur[s] frimats, mais qui ne connoissent la guerre

qu'envers les animaux. . . . Comparé au Groenlandois, [l'Iroquois] est deja homme civilisé. Que j'aime a voir la nature!" *Journal B*, p. 154.

111. ". . . deux nouveaux genres d'erudition, les monumens Etrusques, et ceux d'Herculaneum." ". . . au lieu de cette chaine de citations . . . une narration claire, methodique et interessante." *Journal B*, p. 168.

112. The translation is that of *MW* 1814, 5: 431. "Un ouvrage de cette espèce, s'il etoit bien executé, seroit sans doute accueilli du public. Il pourroit enrichir un libraire, passer à la dixieme Edition ( ) et devenir un livre Classique pour les Colleges, les Voyageurs et meme pour les gens de lettres. L'auteur cependant auroit tort de s'enorgueillir d'un succès qu'il ne devroit qu'à la nature de son sujet, à son travail et qu'à un Esprit juste et methodique.

"Pour ne parler que de moi-mème, mon Essai ouvrage de jeunesse fait dans deux Mois et oublié dans quatre, annonce plus de genie original que ne pourroit faire un pareil traité. Des deux pivots de la reputation, la difficulté et l'utilité de travail, Celui-ci est le plus sur mais le moins flateur." *Journal B*, pp. 169-70. The parenthesis remained unfilled.

113. "Voila de la sagesse après coup." *Journal B*, p. 173.

114. "Tout ce qui regardoit l'Abbé de Montgon lui paroissoit meriter l'attention de l'Europe entiere. Il lui faut cinquante pages pour une conversation . . . cent pages pour une intrigue." *Journal B*, p. 175.

115. "Ce n'etoit pas sous le regne d'Honorius qu'il falloit peindre la force de l'Empire Romain. Ses forces l'avoient abandonné depuis longtems; Mais son antiquité et son etendue, inspiroient une sorte de veneration et meme de terreur à ses voisins et le soutinrent encore. Cette illusion s'etoit enfin dissipée. Peu à peu les Barbares le connurent, le mepriserent et le detruisirent." *Journal B*, p. 178.

116. Chapter 56, Add. MSS. 34880, fol. 152.

117. "Il n'est presque pas possible de conserver à la fois le ton des choses, et celui de la versification. Celui là ne demande, il ne comporte meme que la netteté, la facilité et quelques ornemens disposés avec art et menagés avec soin. Celui ci qui doit supposer l'enthousiasme chez le poete et l'exciter chez le lecteur ne cherche que l'energie & l'harmonie; et leur sacrifie sans peine toutes les beautés d'un ordre inferieur. La poesie a son langage particulier. Il ne convient qu'aux grands mouvemens de l'ame. Ce n'est donc que pour eux qu'elle est faite. Le poete qui cherche à l'employer dans un sujet qui laissera l'ame tranquille et sans sensation, se trouvera placé entre deux ecueils qu'il ne pourroit guères eviter. Il echouera tour à tour contre l'un et l'autre. Ici la force de son coloris defigurera la simplicité de son objet au lieu de l'embellir. Là, le poete ne se fera sentir que par l'harmonie des vers, pendant que les expressions sont froides et prosaiques." *Journal B*, p. 180.

118. ". . . comment [il a] employé cette portion de [s]on existence qui s'est ecoulée et qui ne reviendra plûs . . . ce journal meme qui est devenû un ouvrage 214 pages en quatre mois et demi." "Il s'y trouve des dissertations savantes et raisonées. . . . Mais ces morceaux sont trop etendus, et le journal meme a besoin d'une reforme qui lui retranche quantité de pieces qui sont assez etrangeres à son veritable plan. . . . Voici quelques regles . . . sur les objets qui lui conviennent. 1. Toute ma vie civile et privée, mes amusemens, mes liaisons, mes ecarts meme, et toutes mes reflexions . . . sur des sujets . . . personnels. . . . II.ment Tout ce que j'apprens par l'observation ou la conversation. . . . III.ment . . . la partie materielle de mes etudes. Combien d'heures j'ai travaillé, combien de pages j'ai ecrites ou lûes, avec une courte notice du sujet. . . . IV.ment Je serois faché de lire sans reflechir sur mes lectures, sans porter des jugemens raisonnés sur mes auteurs, et sans eplucher avec soin leurs idées et leurs expressions. Mais . . . [i]l y a des livres qu'on parcourt . . . qu'on lit . . . qu'on doit etudier. Mes observations sur ceux de la premiere classe . . . courtes et detachés . . . conviennent

au journal. Celles . . . [sur] la seconde des classes n'y entreront qu'autant qu'elles ont le même caractère. V.^ment Mes reflexions sur ce petit nombre d'auteurs Classiques qu'on medite avec soin seront naturellement plus approfondies et plus suivies. C'est pour elles, et pour les pieces plus etendues et plus originales auxquelles la lecture ou la meditation peut donner lieu, que je ferai un recueil separé." *Journal B*, pp. 190–91.

119. *MW* 1814, 4: 327-54. They were published in French in the 1796 edition, 2: 313–41. All three entries were published in English translation by Lord Sheffield.

120. "Je n'aurois jamais crû que je pusse aimer ce jeu. Aujourdhui je fais ma partie avec plaisir." *Journal B*, p. 187.

121. ". . . humeur inconstante et paresseuse." *Journal B*, p. 193.

122. *Letters*, 1: 169.

123. ". . . des Comedies saintes (Susanne et le sacrifice d'Isac) par des petits enfans du peuple. Le sujet et la maniere de les traiter ressembloient parfaitement aux Mystères du XVme Siecle. Ces pieces etoient remplies d'obscenités et d'impietés . . . que ces petits enfans repetoient avec un ton de devotion tout à fait risible." *Journal B*, p. 211.

124. "Je n'ai pû m'empecher de reflechir beaucoup sur Mdlle Curchod. Elle m'a trahi, puisque d'Eyverdun n'avoit aucun motif de le faire. . . . Son esprit a beaucoup acquis et si nous pouvons oublier le passé, Son commerce est charmant." *Journal B*, p. 222.

125. "Je n'ai point de vues mais si j'en avois je suis [sûr] qu'il ne manqueroit que l'occasion." *Journal B*, p. 225.

126. "Je m'echappois toujours vers la petite femme et pour cette fois les sens ont triomphé chez moi sur l'esprit." "Quel train de vie. A Paris j'etois un sage." *Journal B*, pp. 228-29.

127. ". . . badin[ent] très librement sur notre tendresse passée, et je lui fais comprendre très clairement que je suis au fait de son inconstance. Elle se defend fort bien et soutient qu'elle a toujours crualisé d'Eyverdun. Qu'en croire? J'avoue que la conduite de mon ami me paroit louche, et je soupconne presque qu'il aura outré les choses." *Journal B*, p. 232.

128. See d'Haussonville, *Madame Necker*, 1: 70-76.

129. *Letters*, 1: 401.

130. "J'ai eté très content de moi. J'ai soutenu un assez joli badinage avec la belle, j'ai beaucoup raisonné *théatre* avec Orosmane. Il m'arrive si souvent de sentir que je suis maussade, qu'il doit bien m'etre permis de dire quand je ne le suis pas. Apres tout c'est ici la meilleure Compagnie." *Journal B*, p. 243.

131. See Giarrizzo, *Edward Gibbon e la cultura europea*, pp. 169-73. "J'ai lû un ouvrage nouveau de Voltaire, *Traité sur la Tolerance*. Le but ne peut qu'etre louable. Reveiller, rappeler dans tous les coeurs, les sentimens de l'humanité et developper les suites affreuses de la superstition. Mais dans l'execution ce n'est qu'un petit recueil de lieux communs ou l'auteur parle de tout que des grands principes de son sujet. J'aime beaucoup ses conclusions fausses et contradictoires sur l'histoire ancienne. L'histoire ancienne (dit il) est remplie de prodiges: Ils ne sauroient etre vrais. Donc tout y est fable et conjectures. . . . L'histoire ancienne est remplie de prodiges: on ne peut que les adopter. Donc les hommes et la nature meme n'avoit dans ces tems reculés rien de commun avec nous." *Journal B*, p. 239.

132. See Bonnard's notes 1 and 3 to this passage.

133. ". . . una conferma della sostanziale diversità dei loro interessi, e della spontaneità della loro polemica." Giarrizzo, *Edward Gibbon e la cultura europea*, p. 172, n.133.

134. Giarrizzo's phrases are "la rapsodica esposizione" and "una impegnata problematica."

135. ". . . sur un pied honnete sans etre brillant." *Journal B*, p. 242.

136. ". . . de mes Ennemis à Lausanne qui profitoient de la petite femme et du 14 Septem pour me faire passer pour un homme sans moeurs. L'Injustice est extrème; mais quand on commence par indisposer les esprits, il faut ensuite marcher droit." *Journal B*, p. 247.

137. ". . . brave, vrai, et sensé, mais d'une impetuosité qui n'est que plus dangereuse pour etre supprimée à l'ordinaire." *Journal B*, p. 259. *Letters*, 1: 165; 170.

138. "J'ai conçu une veritable amitié pour Holroyd. Il a beaucoup de raison et de sentimens d'honneur, avec un coeur des mieux placés." *Journal B*, p. 259.

139. "Je quitte Lausanne avec moins de regret que la premiere fois. Je n'y laisse plus que de[s] connoissances. C'etoit [l'autre fois] la maitresse et l'ami dont je pleurois la perte. D'ailleurs je voyois Lausanne avec les yeux encore novices d'un jeune homme qui lui devoit la partie raisonnable de son existence et qui jugeoit sans objets de comparaison. Aujourd hui j'y vois une ville mal-batie au milieu d'un pays delicieux qui jouit de la paix et du repos, et qui les prend pour la liberté. Un peuple nombreux et bien-elevé qui aime la societé . . . et qui admet avec plaisir les Etrangers dans ses cotteries, qui seroient bien plus agréable si la Conversation n'avoit pas cedé la place au jeu. Les femmes sont jolies, et malgré leur grande liberté, elles sont très sages. . . . L'Affectation est le peché original des Lausannois. Affectation de depense, affectation de noblesse, affectation d'esprit, les deux premieres sont fort repandues pendant que la troisieme est fort rare." *Journal B*, p. 263.

140. See *Memoirs*, pp. 135–36.

141. ". . . heureuse nouveauté [qui] leur epargne tout le fatras des Scholastiques dont les anciennes bibliothèques sont inondés." *Journal B*, p. 266.

CHAPTER 11

1. *MG*, pp. 98–99. Compare Francis Haskell, "Gibbon and the History of Art," *Daedalus* 105, no. 3 (Summer 1976): p. 224.

2. "Nous avons quittè le plus beau paysage qui soit peut-etre sous le ciel, les bords delicieux du Lac Leman pour les montagnes desertes et escarpèès de la Savoye." *Journey*, p. 1.

3. *Journey*, p. 5, nn.4 and 5.

4. "Je m'etonne qu'un petit canton des Alpes, toujours pauvre et encore à moitiè barbare ait pû concevoir l'idèe d'un monument dans un aussi grand gout, pour l'execution duquel il a fallû une depense très considerable et des bons ouvriers de la Grèce ou de Rome. Voici une conjecture. Auguste avoit fait elever un monument avec une inscription fastueuse, où il rapelloit tous les peuples vaincûs des Alpes. Les Citès des Alpes Cottiennes n'y paroissoient point. On les regardoit moins comme des Ennemis vaincus que comme des sujets volontaires. Ces peuples ont du sentir la delicatesse de ce procedè. L'amour et la reconnoissance ont peut-etre voulû dedommager Auguste d'une gloire qu'il avoit refusèe des mains de la victoire." *Journey*, p. 10. See Bonnard's note 5 for the inscription Gibbon had in mind.

5. *Journey*, pp. 3, 6.

6. "La lecture et la conversation nous ont amusè, mais il est difficile de faire une route moins agreable que celle-ci dans les montagnes de la Savoye." *Journey*, p. 11.

7. ". . . la fameuse rue de Po." *Journey*, p. 15.

8. "J'ai vû avec plaisir sous mes pieds la plaine fertile de Piemont, arrosèe par le Po et la Doire, et bornèe par des montagnes encore couvertes de niege, la ville de Turin au centre et les champs voisins où j'ai pû suivre les mouvemens des deux armèes et le thèatre du combat." *Journey*, p. 17.

9. ". . . très bien ennuyè." *Journey*, p. 16.

10. *Letters*, 1: 172.

11. Ibid.

12. ". . . les Pairs et leurs fils." *Journey*, p. 17. ". . . un petit Viellard . . . un bourgeois qui a assez mauvaise façon . . . homme d'Esprit et bon politique." Ibid., p. 18.

13. "Malheureusement pour lui, son père est mort dans ses prisons . . . le premier Esclave de la Cour. . . . Une Cour est à la fois pour moi un objet de curiosité et de degout. La servilitè des courtisans me revolte, et je vois avec horreur la magnificence des palais qui sont cimentès du sang des peuples. Dans un Royaume petit et pauvre comme celui-ci il faut ecraser le peuple pour aller de pair avec les autres tetes couronnèès, et pour soutenir l'air de grandeur. . . . Dans chaque lambris dorè je crois voir un village de Savoyards prèts à perir de faim, de froid et de misère." *Journey*, p. 18.

14. ". . . un Bacchus qui badine avec un tigre. Ces deux figures sont bien contrastèes." *Journey*, p. 21.

15. "J'ai remarquè avec surprise qu'une des Nymphes offre une grappe de raisins au Dieu qui vient de naitre et qui n'avoit point encore pu enseigner aux hommes la culture de la vigne." *Journey*, pp. 22-23.

16. ". . . toute curieuse qu'elle est, est trop eloignèè, trop obscure et trop enigmatique pour m'interesser beaucoup." *Journey*, p. 28.

17. "Je vois un homme qui doute souvent s'il a bien lû, qui laisse des fautes grossieres dans les monumens, en avertissant seulement par un *sic* qu'il les avoit remarquèès, et qui laisse des endroits en blanc qu'il lui etoit très facile de remplir. J'ajoute encore qu'il n'etoit que Compilateur et qu'il n'avoit aucun systeme dont il falloit servir les interets." *Journey*, p. 29.

18. "Cette magnificence moderèè par une economie exacte, mais accompagnèè d'un air de dignitè se voit partout dans cette cour." *Journey*, p. 31.

19. "Cette imitation exacte de ce qu'il y a de plus bas et de plus degoutant dans les moeurs d'une populace grossiere interesse aussi peu mon Esprit, que leur coloris sec et leurs ombres noircis me deplaisent à la vue." *Journey*, p. 32.

20. Louis Dutens (1730-1812), *Mémoires* (Paris, 1806), p. 181, quoted and cited in *Journey*, p. 13, n.2: ". . . professoit sur-tout une grande prédilection pour nos jeunes Anglois."

21. "S'il est agreable de regarder un jeu qu'on n'entend point, d'ecouter un jargon Piedmontois où l'on ne comprend goutte et de se trouver au milieu d'une noblesse orgueilleuse et rampante qui ne vous addressera pas la parole; nous nous sommes très bien amusès dans cette assemblèè." *Journey*, p. 34.

22. "Quand on voit les accroissemens lents et successifs de la maison de Savoye pendant huit cens ans, il faut convenir que sa grandeur est plutot l'ouvrage de la prudence que de la fortune." *Journey*, p. 41.

23. "Il est un des grands efforts de l'architecture Gothique comme c'en est un des derniers . . . où jamais homme ne pourroit se soutenir . . . un air de viellesse commun aux batimens Gothiques . . . une idèè de ruine et de foiblesse, comme l'unitè des proportions anciennes inspire d'abord celle de force et de soliditè." *Journey*, p. 45.

24. ". . . un très joli escalier en l'air." *Journey*, p. 48.

25. ". . . le seul reste de l'Antiquitè qui subsiste encore à Milan . . . une colonnade de seize grandes Colonnes." *Journey*, p. 52.

26. "Je prefere la terre à tous les autres. . . . On croiroit que Breughels a voulû representer le siecle d'or aussi bien que les element[s]. Un buef (c'est une figure charmante,) qui rumine sans crainte auprès d'un lion et d'un tigre qui se caressent, n'est pas un buef de ce siecle de fer." *Journey*, pp. 51-52.

27. See Patricia B. Craddock, "Edward Gibbon: The Man in His Letters," in *The Familiar Letter in the Eighteenth Century*, ed. H. Anderson, P. Daghlian, and I. Ehrenpreis (Lawrence, Kans., 1966), pp. 238-42.

28. *Letters*, 1: 174-75.

29. *Letters*, 1: 176-77.

30. "Chez nous, dans un grand palais, entourè d'un lac très etendû et separès ainsi du reste des humains . . . trop l'air d'une belle prison. . . . Vous vous promenez dans une belle allèè d orangers d'une grosseur et d'une hauteur qui m'ont etonnè, et vous n'en sortez que pour entrer dans un charmant petit bois de lauriers où mille fontaines paroissent jaillir sous vos pieds . . . mechantes cabanes de pecheurs . . . un palais des fèès. S'il falloit les laisser, les Comtes les auroient pu rendre avec peu de depense d'une simplicitè très agreable." *Journey*, pp. 54-56.

31. ". . . les choses." *Journey*, p. 59.

32. "J'espère d'en sortir maitre ou peu s'en faut de la langue." Ibid.

33. ". . . la cellule d'un des peres. . . . La plupart des maisons religieuses se distinguent par leur extreme propretè, par la soliditè de leurs ouvrages et par la richesse des ornemens. . . . ne peut employer ses revenûs qu'à satisfaire le seul orgueil qui puisse leur rester encore." *Journey*, pp. 61-62.

34. "La montèè . . . paroit rien quand on a passè les Alpes. L'Apennin est plutot une chaine de rochers que de montagnes." *Journey*, p. 64.

35. "Ce chef fameux dont les moeurs sont encore un peu feroces, egale par ses talens naturels les grands hommes de l'antiquitè. . . . On abandonneroit avec plaisir les Corses à eux-memes si on ne craignoit pas le Roi de Sardaigne." *Journey*, p. 66.

36. ". . . un beau Phenomene de la nature, un orage dans les montagnes . . . le ciel . . . eclairci, les eaux . . . ecoulèès, et . . . une fraicheur charmante." *Journey*, p. 69.

37. ". . . une secheresse dans sa maniere et un teint bleuatre dans son coloris." *Journey*, p. 71.

38. André Félibien, *Entretiens sur les vies et sur les ouvrages des plus excellens peintres anciens et modernes* (London, 1705). *Journey*, p. 75, n.4.

39. "Heureux momens de repos, dont on ne sent le prix que lorsqu'on a vecû dans le tourbillon." The history is identified by Bonnard, n.2. The historian who disappointed Gibbon was the author of "important historical works." *Journey*, p. 81.

40. "Cette Serenitè reçoit 5000 Livres par an et en depense au moins 25000, pour avoir le plaisir de demeurer dans une très vilaine maison, dont il ne peut sortir sans une permission du Senat, d'etre vetû de rouge depuis les pieds jusqu'à la tète, et d'avoir douze pages de 60 ans habillès à l'Espagnole." *Journey*, pp. 81-82.

41. *Journey*, p. 82.

42. ". . . l'attente, l'impatience, l'ennui et la mauvaise humeur." *Journey*, p. 86.

43. *Journey*, pp. 86-87. This material was never incorporated in his manuscripts of the "weights and measures" studies. In the same interlude, he also "fait des Essais de traductions Angloises sur quelques endroits de mes Recueils, qui m'ont donnè lieu de faire plusieurs observations sur l'idiome different des deux langues, et sur l'extreme difficultè d'ecrire bien dans l'une et l'autre, sans que leur puretè soit alterèe par le melange reciproque."

44. "Pourquoi faut il toujours mettre les princes à cheval . . . les exploits plus pacifiques et plus utiles se reduisoient à batir des thèatres et à fonder des bibliothèque[s] auroit dû paroitre, vetû en citoyen, et accompagnè de ces emblèmes de la paix et des arts qui paroissent . . . sur les bas-reliefs du piedestal." *Journey*, pp. 89-90.

45. "Nous les avons revûs sans plaisir et sans peine." *Journey*, p. 92.

46. ". . . un seul jardin depuis Plaisance, et comme les villes et meme les Capitales se touchent, c'est moins un voyage qu'une promenade des plus agrèables. . . . Je ne connois rien de plus triste que leur coup d'oeil: . . . vous ne voyez pas mème de ces paturages couverts de troupeaux qui egayent un peu le spectacle de la plupart des montagnes." *Journey*, pp. 117-18.

47. "Jamais je n'avois connû auparavant le pouvoir de la peinture. J'admirois l'art

de l'imitation sans etre touchè de sa veritè. Le caractere de paix & de tendresse qui respire ici sur la toile se communique à l'ame du Spectateur. Forcè enfin de s'en arracher il eprouve le sentiment douleureux de perdre ce qu'il aime." *Journey*, p. 97.

48. ". . . doit convertir un fou que la superstition a canonisè dans un grand homme; sans absolument perdre la ressemblance. . . . Sous ses mains la betise ne paroit plus que l'humilitè et le renoncement à soi-meme." *Journey*, p. 115.

49. "La plupart de ces monumens se rapportent au siecle de Claude et meme à la fin du Regne de ce prince. L'inscription *Divo Augusto* y convient encore. Jusqu'à la consecration de Claude lui-meme il n'y avoit qu'un seul *Divus Augustus* qu'on pouvoit bien designer absolument." *Journey*, p. 99.

50. "Ces annèes de la puissance Tribunitienne sont le meilleur guide que nous ayons pour la Chronologie des Empereurs; mais c'est un guide qu'il est très difficile de suivre, sans le secours d'une bonne table qui est encore à faire puisque la puissance de Tribunat a très souvent precedè le commencement du regne. Je voudrois savoir encore s'ils en prenoient possession l'anniversaire de leur avenement, ou si les Nones de Decembre etoient toujours fixèes pour cette ceremonie à l'egard des Empereurs aussi-bien que pour les Tribuns ordinaires. . . . Il y a encore une difficultè pour Tibère, il est le seul dont la puissance Tribunitienne ai etè interrompûe." *Journey*, pp. 112-13.

51. "J'ai crû lire dans les traits d'Agrippa ce caractère de franchise, de grandeur et de simplicitè qui distinguoient cet homme respectable: mais ces sortes d'observations quoiqu'elles ayent eu la sanction d'un Addison . . . me paroissent bien creuses. Est il si commun que l'ame se lise dans les traits?" *Journey*, p. 112.

52. "L'ame de ce pape fier et ambitieux est peinte sur la toile. J'y vois toute la brusque violence du protecteur de Michel Ange, et la grandeur inflexible de ce Viellard qui osa chasser de l'Italie les François victorieux. Je contredis ma maxime, mais je crois voir une exception." *Journey*, p. 138.

53. ". . . dur et tyrannique" ". . . ne jouit point de ce bien qui lui appartient." *Journey*, p. 102.

54. *Letters*, 1: 180-81.

55. *Journey*, p. 127.

56. "On voit que les Florentins cherissent cet usage comme le seul vestige de leur libertè ancienne . . . depuis les jeux des anciens c'est peut-etre le seul spectacle des plaisir[s] de tout un Etat reuni pour s'amuser par les soins et sous les yeux de ses magistrats." *Journey*, p. 128.

57. ". . . la hardiesse de commencer à parler un certain jargon que je voulois que l'on prit pour l'Italien. On m'ecouta avec bontè, et surtout une certaine Madame Antinori qui est très aimable." *Journey*, pp. 128-29.

58. "M. Muratori n'est point un simple *Erudit*. Il prouve très bien . . qu'on peut tirer de cette inscription . . . des lumieres très utiles, sur l'histoire, la Geographie, et l'Economie de ce siecle. Je le pense avec lui mais apres y avoir murement reflechi, je crois qu'il ne les a pas toutes tirèes." *Journey*, p. 122.

59. ". . . les rentes auxquelles un si grand nombre des Citoyens de Veleia s'etoient assujetis et les fonds sur lesquels on les avoit assignèes. C'est un travail sec et ingrat, mais quand on construit un Edifice il faut en creuser les fondemens. L'on est obligè de faire le role de macon aussi bien que celui d'Architecte." *Journey*, p. 129.

60. ". . . savantes et curieuses. Combien d'idèes n'ont elles pas fait naitre!" *Journey*, p. 130.

61. ". . . promenès en Carosse . . . prendre de l'air ou plutot de la poussiere." *Journey*, p. 119. ". . . un beau prè entourè d'un bois." P. 122.

62. ". . . le livre sacrè des anciens Celtes. Nous avons à present une demie douzaine de ces bibles, (en y comprenant les notres)." *Journey*, p. 159.

63. "Dès mon berceau j'avois toujours entendû parler de la Venus de Medicis; les livres, les conversations, les estampes, les modeles me l'avoient mille fois mis devant

les yeux et cependant je n'en avois aucune idee. Pour la connoitre il faut la voir. Je l'ai vue: mais l'imagination la plus fidèle, la plus vive conservera t'elle l'image que les sens m'en ont donnèe[?] C'est la sensation la plus voluptueuse que mon oeil ait jamais eprouvè." *Journey*, p. 179.

64. "Cette Machine enorme. . . . Les veines y sont fort bien exprimèes mais on ne comprend rien à une certaine calotte qui paroit lui couvrir la tète." ". . . belle machine . . . est coiffée de l'autre machine sa compagne ordinarie." *Journey*, p. 145, and n.1. Charles de Brosses, *Lettres familières sur l'Italie*, ed. Y. Bezard (1740; Paris, 1931), 1: 337.

65. *Letters*, 1: 187.

66. "Je ne sai laquelle est la plus injurieuse aux belles meres. . . . La haine des belles Meres pour leurs beaux-fils me paroit encore plus marquèe que dans les autres nations. Aux motifs generaux je crois qu'on doit ajouter l'etat incertain des femmes Romaines et le pouvoir illimitè qu'avoient les pères sur leurs biens. . . . Que notre siecle est heureux, mais que je le suis encore plus." *Journey*, pp. 156-57.

67. "Un voyage de la Grèce ne peut que piquer la curiositè." *Journey*, p. 143.

68. Or possibly for his eyes and those of Guise, his traveling companion. This is a possible explanation of the *"contrat"* made at the beginning of the journey to which both Gibbon and Guise refer in their journals. Guise says: "Aiguebelles. It is a very poor, small place, and affords nothing for my pen; however an agreement made there between Mr Gibbon, and myself will most probably remind me of it, and a thing we did there, tho uninteresting at that time, will one of these days become much more interesting to both." *Journey*, p. 3, n.1.

69. "En general je n'aime point ces illusions dans une autre illusion, à commencer par la comedie dans Hamlet. L'Essai est trop dangereux et la ressemblance necessaire entre l'une et l'autre ne sert qu'à tirer le Spectateur de son yvresse." "imitation non pas de la nature en general qui est toujours la mème, mais de ces natures particulieres qui disparoissent bientot, sans nous laisser les moyens de comparer l'original et la copie." *Journey*, pp. 131, 132.

70. "Parmi ces premiers peintres j'appercois un travail minutieux et timide, et un assujetissement rigoureux à toutes les regles qu'ils connoissoient, sans genie et sans aucune de ces hardiesses heureuses et originales qui font le merite des premiers poetes, et qui rachetent tous les ecarts d'une imagination dereglèe qui veut disposer en maitre de la langue, de l'histoire et de la nature. Je trouve la raison de cette difference dans l'origine differente des deux arts, soeurs à la veritè, mais dont la fortune a souvent variè. La poesie est descendue du ciel, la peinture s'est elevèe de la terre. Les premiers poetes etoient des prophètes, des hommes inspirès dont le genie etoit echauffè par le Fanatisme, qui faisoit taire la froide et foible raison. Les premiers peintres etoient des artisans: obligès de passer par une Mechanique longue et penible, ils osoient à peine se livrer aux essors d'un talent qu'un siecle ignorant auroit meconnû. Ils copioient servilement parce qu'ils voyoient peu de chose, et mal. Le peintre ne trouve point comme le poète ses originaux au fond de son ame." *Journey*, p. 138.

71. "Nul ne penserait aujourd'hui à étudier les frères Van Eyck en les dissociant de la corporation des joaillers dont ils étaient membres; lier leur style à leur metier est une anticipation sur la critique moderne qui demeure impressionnante à deux cents ans de distance!" Michel Baridon, *Edward Gibbon et le mythe de Rome* (Paris, 1977), p. 114.

72. "Je crois qu'un jeune artiste les etudieroit avec fruit et qu'en les comparant avec les ouvrages achevès de ces Grands hommes, il rechercheroit comment ils ont abandonnè, perfectionnè ou suivi leurs premieres idèes. C'est surtout pour la composition soit poetique soit pittoresque que cette etude seroit des plus utiles." *Journey*, p. 141.

73. Baridon, *Mythe*, p. 115.

74. "C'est un plaisir bien vif que de suivre les progrès et la decadence des arts et de parcourir cettes suite des portraits originaux des maitres du monde" "peut etre le tresor le plus precieux de la galerie." *Journey*, p. 166. See also Frank Haskell, "Gibbon and the History of Art," pp. 217-29.

75. "Si [Bérénice] n'etoit pas plus belle qu'elle n'est representèe ici, on a peine à comprendre la passion de Titus." *Journey*, p. 168.

76. "Quand on se rappelle que son ombre de royautè a etè suivie d'un regne de vint ans d'un Ennemi implacable et cruel, on concoit bien les raisons de cette raretè." *Journey*, p. 170.

77. The various arguments to this effect are conveniently summarized by David P. Jordan, *Gibbon and His Roman Empire* (Urbana, Ill., 1971), pp. 18-23. He concludes, "As a picture of his feelings, the vision is accurate. . . . It is not so important that the vision is not strictly true. What is important is that Gibbon wanted it to be true."

78. "Il me paroit singulier qu'il soit si mal pourvû d'armes offensives pendant qu'on n'a rien oubliè de ce qui peut servir à sa defense. Ces deux sortes d'armes ont etè cependant toujours en raison l'une de l'autre, parmi ces nations où la prudence et la valeur etoient en equilibre. Les feroces peuples du nord ne songeoient qu'à frapper leurs ennemis. Ils jettoient souvent leurs cuirasses parce qu'ils craignoient plus la fatigue que les dangers. Les Etrusques peuple riche et amolli me paroissent avoir agi par un principe tout à fair opposè." *Journey*, p. 134. See *MW* 1814, 3: 231-38, Sheffield translation.

79. ". . . un morceau du première importance pour l'étude de la méthode de Gibbon." Baridon, *Mythe*, p. 117.

80. "Peuples du nord ont rebutè le Christianisme avec tant d'opiniatretè pendant que leurs Compatriotes etablis dans l'Empire l'ont embrassè avec une si grande facilitè." *Journey*, p. 162. *MW* 1814, 3: 235. "Toutes les religions sont locales jusqu'à un certain point. Le Chretien le moins superstitieux sentiroit plus de devotion sur le Mont Calvaire qu'à Londres." *Journey*, p. 163. *MW* 1814, 3: 236. "Un barbare qui avoit goutè le vin de Falerne, se soucioit assez peu de s'enyvrer d'hydromel aux festins d'Odin, et quand il souffroit toute l'ardeur d'un soleil Africain, un Enfer dont les fenetres seroient ouvertes du cotè du nord ne lui paroissoit plus bien redoutable." *Journey*, p. 164. *MW* 1814, 3: 237. "Tout contribuoit à le detacher d'un culte qui n'est fondé que sur la barbarie et sur l'ignorance pendant qu'il le disposoit en faveur de celui contenoit la foible [word omitted in Sheffield translation] science du siecle qu'il commencoit à gouter et qui n'enseignoit que cette humanitè dont il sentoit deja le prix." *Journey*, p. 164. *MW* 1814, 3: 237.

81. ". . . quelques Benedictins . . . vont dans les forets de la Suede precher la patience, l'humilitè et la foi à des nations nombreuses de pirates. . . . Un protestant diroit encore que le Christianisme du Xme Siecle etoit bien plus difficile à digerer que celui du Vme; il l'est assurement pour un raisonneur." *Journey*, p. 165. *MW* 1814, 3: 238. ". . . mais je crois que le raisonnement a eu assez peu de part dans ces changemens et quand on croit deja aux absurditès de sa propre secte, se rebute t'on pour quelques mystères de plus?" *Journey*, p. 165. *MW* 1814, 3: 238.

82. *Journey*, pp. 145, 158.

83. Thomas Lyttelton (1744-79). See *DNB*. Bonnard quotes an interesting description in a letter of Sir Horace Mann to Walpole; see *Journey*, p. 119, n.1.

84. "L'un posè, tranquille, un peu froid possede des qualitès du coeur et de l'esprit qui le font estimer partout et l'on voit qu'il a mis l'attention la plus serieuse à les cultiver. Lyttleton est en tout d'une impetuositè qui ne connoit point de bornes, d'une Vanitè qui lui fait rechercher sans l'obtenir l'applaudissement de ceux pour qui son orgueil ne lui inspire que du mepris & d'une Ambition folle qui ne sert qu'à le rendre ridicule sans etre accompagnèe de cette constance qui peut seule la faire reussir.

Un Air de philosophie sans beaucoup de logique et une affectation de savoir soutenue par une lecture vague et superficielle. Voila cet homme extraordinaire qui s'attire partout la haine ou la pitiè. Je lui trouve cependant un fonds de genie naturel très au-dessus de son rival." *Journey*, p. 188.

85. ". . . spectacle eternel des saintes familles." ". . . un heureux melange une physionomie noble, interessante, douce et spirituelle." *Journey*, p. 191.

86. "L'occasion etoit digne en effet d'un monument public. Mais ce prince qui connoissoit peu la dignitè d'une pareille ceremonie l'avilissoit." *Journey*, p. 194.

87. *Journey*, pp. 193, 220, 218.

88. "Nous avons suivi le Chevalier Mann à trois assemblèes chez la Comtesse de Gallo, chez la Marquise Gerini, et chez le Duc Strozzi. Cette succession rapide peut seule m'empecher de m'ennuyer. Je ne parle point la langue du pays. J'ignore leurs jeux. Les femmes sont occupèes de leurs Cicisbèes et les hommes paroissent d'une indifference extrème." *Journey*, p. 204.

89. *Journey*, p. 199, n.4.

90. "La Nature elle meme ne rendroit mieux la Vielle-elle-meme . . . et assurèment dans la nature je les verrois avec bien moins de plaisir." *Journey*, p. 205.

91. "L'Architecture n'a rien de considerable. Mais ce n'a pas etè sans un respect secret que j'ai considerè les tombeaux de Galilèe et de Michel Ange, du Restaurateur des Arts et de celui de la Philosophie. Genies vrayment puissans et originaux, ils ont illustrè leur patrie mieux que les Conquerans et les Politiques. Les Tartares ont eu un Jenghiz Khan, et les Goths un Alaric, mais nous detournons nos yeux des deserts ensanglantès de la Scythie pour les fixer avec plaisir sur Athenes et sur Florence." *Journey*, p. 213.

92. *DF* (chap. 1), 1: 1, in first edition (1776).

93. ". . . qui auroit etè un Indice parlant des plus utiles à un homme de Genie occupè de quelque branche de litterature." *Journey*, p. 212.

94. ". . . une reverence secrette." "Ils jouoient un role bien plus beau, lorsque dans leurs comptoirs ils etoient les protecteurs des arts et les arbitres de l'Italie, que dans la suite qu'ils s'eleverent au grade de souverains obscurs d'un petit Etat." *Journey*, p. 204.

95. 284 B.C., according to the *Oxford Classical Dictionary*.

96. "Moins imparfaite si j'avois un Polybe sous les yeux." "Mais la politique timide et bornee des Carthaginois et l'insensibilitè paresseuse si naturelle à une nation de barbares qui ne prevoit jamais les dangers, epargnerent aux Romains tous les perils de cette alliance. Je pense que cette Republique qui savoit dissimuler et son ambition et sa vengeance menageoit les Barbares avec soin et qu'elle attendoit tranquillement pour les irriter le moment quand ils n'auroient de ressource qu'en eux memes." Add. MSS. 34880, fol. 227v. *MW* 1814, 3: 223-24, Sheffield translation.

97. "Ce recit est clair et si Casaubon avoit aussi bien pris le sens de Polybe que M. Guazzesi, le texte de ce grand historien n'offriroit plus de difficultès Geographiques. . . . Graces à cette idèe heureuse de M. Guazzesi le Systeme entier de cette campagne se devoile à nos yeux. . . . M. Guazzesi repond très bien à ces difficultès par les changemens que le tems a apporté au pays; et par l'ignorance ou nous sommes si cette route n'etoit pas la seule praticable pour une armèe, par . . . leur cavalerie nombreuse, et par l'esperance de se servir des vaissaux. . . . Mais je crois qu'il faut penetrer jusqu'aux ressorts qui ont fait mouvoir les Conseils Gaulois pour bien apprecier une conduite. . . . Les Gaulois etoient gouvernès en effet par deux esprits tres differens. Les peuples Cisalpins . . . combattoient avec cette ardeur qu'inspirent les plus grands interets; mais . . . les Gesatae leurs allies . . . etoient moins une nation qu'un Corps d'Avanturiers rassemblès de plusieurs peuples differens n'avoient d'autre motif pour passer les Alpes que l'esperance du butin & ne songeoient qu'à conserver

ce butin par une prompte retraite sans s'exposer d'avantage." Add. MSS. 34880, fols. 228r-v, 229r. *MW* 1814, 3: 227-28.

98. J.G.A. Pocock, "Between Machiavelli and Hume: Gibbon as Civic Humanist and Philosophical Historian," *Daedalus* 105, no. 3 (Summer 1976): 159.

99. "De toutes ces circonstances il n'y a que la surprise d'Atilius qui me paroit inconcevable." "Les Gaulois pris en front et par derriere par deux armées Romaines qui arrivent des deux cotès opposès m'a plutot l'air d'un projet très bien entendû que d'une negligence á peine concevable." Add. MSS. 34880, fol. 229r-v. *MW* 1814, 3: 230.

100. "Ce n'est guères qu'un accès de mauvaise humeur qui puisse vaincre leur paresse et leur mettre la plume à la main." *Journey*, p. 219.

101. ". . . commencè à me faire une inclination. C'est une certaine Madame Gianni." *Journey*, p. 223.

102. *Journey*, appendix, p. 256.

103. "Le coup d'oeil de ce pays repand du jour sur les idèes que j'ai de cette guerre." *Journey*, p. 224; Baridon, *Mythe*, 119: "Cette forme d'imagination souple et pénétrante qui lui permet de recomposer la vie d'une armée ou la pensée de ses chefs le rapproche de l'historien plus que du géographe."

104. "L'industrie fait leur richesse, et leur force se tire de leur foiblesse mème, qui leur concilie la bienveillance de tout le monde sans exciter l'ambition de personne." *Journey*, pp. 225-26.

105. "Les Republiques meritent toujours de l'attention. Elles sont aussi differentes que les Monarchies sont semblables les unes aux autres." *Journey*, p. 226.

106. "Ne distingueroit il point entre le Courtisan qui tremble devant un Roi, et l'homme qui sent la superioritè d'un Grand homme?. J'ai etè presentè aux Rois d'Angleterre et de Sardaigne, j'ai vû de près celui de France et je les ai vus avec autant d'indifference que le plus petit bourgeois. Il y en a meme eu pour qui je n'ai senti qu'un mepris des plus legitimes." *Journey*, pp. 222-23.

107. *Letters*, 1: 183-84.

108. "L'Interet du commerce a presque fait taire l'Esprit convertisseur de l'Eglise de Rome. Si un enfant Juif vient declarer au Clergè qu'il souhaite de se faire Catholique on ne peut le recevoir qu'après l'avoir laissè trois mois entre les mains de son père, qui est obligè . . . d'accorder un accès libre aux pretres aussi bien qu'aux Rabbins. . . . De cette façon on fait rarement des proselytes; l'inconstance d'un Enfant soutient difficilement sa resolution que toute sa famille tente de lui faire changer." *Journey*, pp. 230-31.

109. ". . . la simplicitè des formes et la justesse des proportions. . . . Le pavè e[s]t couvert de peintures anciennes qui representent l'histoire de l'Ecriture et celle de Sienne. Ce Gout est baroque mais je l'aime encore mieux que de voir un pavè peint en Angles, et des Lions qui soutiennent une Chaire." [He certainly meant to write "Anges."] "Les femmes y etoient si laides et les hommes si ignorans." *Journey*, pp. 233-34.

110. "Depuis le Pons Milvius j'ai etè dans un songe d'antiquitè." *Journey*, p. 235.

111. *Letters*, 1: 184.

112. See Bonnard's discussion, *Memoirs*, pp. 304-5, and, for views of the episode as essentially fictional, H. R. Trevor-Roper, "Edward Gibbon after Two Hundred Years," *Listener* 72 (1964): 617-19, 657-59, and E. Badian, "Gibbon and War," *Gibbon et Rome* (Geneva, 1977), p. 103.

113. On Byers, see Bonnard's note, *Journey*, p. 237.

114. *Letters*, 1: 187.

115. "La prima Roma che egli cerca e sente è la Roma della grandezza republicana, quel luogo divino ove *liberté* e *vertu* convissero come in un' età d'oro della storia umana." G. Giarrizzo, *Edward Gibbon e la cultura europea del settocento* (Naples, 1954), p. 192.

116. "On demanderoit avec plus de vraisemblance . . . s'il ne falloit pas achever la guerre. . . . Je ne verrois dans un pareil reglement que la sagesse d'un Senat qui craignoit d'avilir ses recompenses en les prodiguant mais qui toujours libre et souverain savoit aussi refuser cet honneur à un General presomptueux qui ne lui auroit offert que des ennemis et des conquetes indignes de ses armes. Mais en interrogeant les faits (et ce sont les faits qu'il faut interroger,) je vois que la conduite du Senat a variè dans les differens siecles de la republique, et je trouve la cause de cette variation dans un usage accessoire et etrange au merite du Chef." Add. MSS. 34880, fol. 233r. *MW* 1814, 4: 372, Sheffield translation. French published in *MW* 1796, 2: 361-401.

117. ". . . la politique plutot que la justice." "Le triomphe ne s'achetoit que par les conquetes, et par un effet admirable de ces loix qui s'executent par la nature des choses plutot que par les passions des hommes, la majestè du triomphe s'elevoit avec la grandeur de l'Etat." Add. MSS. 34880, fol. 233r. *MW* 1814, 4: 374, Sheffield translation.

118. *Letters*, 1: 188-89.

119. *Letters*, 1: 189.

120. *Letters*, 1: 190.

121. David P. Jordan, following a misleading statement of Low's, seems to think that Gibbon was without credit in Venice, but it is clear that steps to restore his credit had been taken by the end of January. The Venetian banker's objection was to giving credit where it had ever been questioned, not to its being presently questioned. See Jordan, *Gibbon and His Roman Empire*, p. 33; D. M. Low, *Edward Gibbon, 1737-1794* (London, 1937), p. 189. Gibbon's "several months of very real distress" were at most less than eight weeks.

122. ". . . la porte Triomphale porte qui a toujours ete ouverte à vos predecesseurs." Add. MSS. 34880, fol. 235r. *MW* 1814, 4: 382, Sheffield translation.

123. "Cette lisiere des deux cotês de l'Anio où les colonies." "Un enchainement de conjectures m'a conduit à cette conclusion. C'est aux faits seuls à la justifier." Add. MSS. 34880, fol. 235r-v. *MW* 1814, 4: 384.

124. "Persèe etoit un monument de la vertù des Romains . . . pendant qu'ils auroient voulû ensevelir avec Jugurthe la memoire de leur honte . . . voila les forfaits de Jugurthe, et ceux que Rome ne pouvoit jamais lui pardonner." Add. MSS. 34880, fol. 238r. *MW* 1814, 4: 397-98.

125. Add. MSS. 34880, fol. 238v. *MW* 1814, 5: 39-41. *MW* 1796, 2: 402-4 (French).

126. ". . . [il] traite principalement des revolutions qu'a eprouvèes cette ville depuis la chute de l'Empire Romain, sujet qui m'interesse beaucoup." Sheffield translation. Add. MSS. 34880, fol. 238v. *MW* 1814, 5: 39. *MW* 1796, 2: 402-4.

127. *Letters*, 1: 194-95.

128. Baridon, *Mythe*, p. 123.

129. *Letters*, 1: 199.

130. *Letters*, 1: 201, 200.

131. *Letters*, 1: 198.

132. *Letters*, 1: 197-98.

CHAPTER 12

1. Deyverdun's recent adventures are recounted by Gibbon, *Memoirs*, p. 138.

2. As early as July 26, 1762: *Journal A*, pp. 103-4.

3. Compare G. Giarrizzo, *Edward Gibbon e la cultura europea del settocento* (Naples, 1954), p. 154.

4. See above, pp. 185 and 207.

5. *Journal B*, p. 169.

6. Add. MSS. 34881, fol. 24r; "Avant Propos" marks the beginning of this new draft. See *MW* 1814, 5: 120.

7. ". . . l'histoire des hommes plutôt que celle des rois." ". . . un recueil étendu de tous les faits intéressans auxquels [elle] nous serviroit d'interprète." [Sheffield substitutes "il," but Gibbon intends his pronoun to refer to "cette langue économique," hence his "elle"].

8. Add. MSS. 34881, fol. 50r.

9. "Cet ouvrage se grossira sans dessein et sans effort, et s'enrichera insensiblement du fruit de toutes mes études." *MW* 1814, 5: 120.

10. "Je ne copierai point les grands ouvrages que nous avons deja. Les recherches de tant de savans sur tout ce qui regarde les anciens, celles de Fleetwood, de Lowndes de Nicholson et d'Arbuthnot sur les anglois, et celles de le Blanc &c sur les Francois laissent peu de choses à desirer sur les poids les mesures et les monnoyes de ces peuples." Add. MSS. 34881, fol. 50r.

11. ". . . l'emploi de l'argent, et par conséquent aux moeurs, au luxe et aux arts." *MW* 1814, 5: 121.

12. The 1759 draft occupies Add. MSS. 34881, fol. 64v (unpublished), fols. 1-3, 58, 53, 55, 60, 4, 8-9, 5-7, 10-23, in that order. Lord Sheffield published the rectos in the order in which they are now assembled (through the first 35 sheets), but because he had reordered the sections, the notes, from the facing versos, are not necessarily in numerical order. This manuscript was sent to the printer; directions to the printer are frequent and must have been necessary. His version continues: 37, 38r, 39r-v, 38v, 41r, 42v, 43r, 41v, 45v, 52r, 45r, 46r.

13. *MW* 1814, 3: 202-6. Add. MSS. 34881, fols. 215-16.

14. The verso of fol. 216 discusses a book published in 1765.

15. In Gibbon's "Index Expurgatorius" (*EE*, p. 123), he refers to Olivier's *Chronique de Bourgogne*, published in Philippe de Commines, *Mémoires* (London and Paris, 1747), 4 vols. Gibbon used Philippe de Commines to annotate some of Deyverdun's translations from German sources (manuscripts in the Archives Cantonales Vaudoises).

16. See Giarrizzo, *Edward Gibbon e la cultura europea*, p. 195 ff.

17. "On doit une sorte de reconnoissance aux historiens qui nous ont conservé les détails souvent minutieux, mais qui nous peignent les moeurs d'un siècle, son goût pour les arts, et le genre et l'étendue de son commerce. Il y a plus de variété et souvent plus d'instruction dans ces objets que dans la relation d'une bataille, ou d'un traité de paix." *MW* 1814, 3: 202-3.

18. *Letters*, 1: 405 and n.11. Freedom from debts, M 413. Return of money, *Letters*, 1: 281.

19. The sentence structure of this and the other drafts in which the point is made stresses "alone"; he might have written "I alone stood" had not loneliness seemed a disadvantage parallel to immobility and insignificance. I owe this observation to Professor Joan Hartman of the College of Staten Island.

20. He had studied "the law of nations" on his own in Lausanne; see *Memoirs*, p. 78.

21. Portions published by Sheffield, *MW* 1814, 5: 545-47. Published in full in *EE*, pp. 59-87.

22. Sir William Blackstone, *Commentaries on the Laws of England* (Oxford, 1765), 1: 17, 19.

23. *EE*, p. 59.

24. *EE*, pp. 63-64.

25. *EE*, p. 63.

26. *EE*, pp. 66, 77, 81. See also a mysterious page in French, defending the view that the Roman constitution was free under the emperors, who were only the "first magistrates." Add. MSS. 34881, fol 59. The hand of this piece is that of the mid-sixties.

27. *EE*, p. 82.

28. Blackstone, *Commentaries*, 1: 412; *EE*, p. 82.

29. *EE*, p. 83.

30. Blackstone, *Commentaries*, 1: 428.

31. *EE*, pp. 84-85.

32. *EE*, pp. 88-95, 107-29.

33. See examples in *EE*, pp. 214-17, 319-37.

34. *EE*, pp. 92-93.

35. Although a note published by Lord Sheffield and written by Gibbon clearly declares that "The concluding observations of [his] third Volume were written before his accession to the throne [1774]" (175), many scholars hastily assume that they were written in 1781. The error is sometimes significant.

36. *EE*, p. 88.

37. *EE*, pp. 88-90.

38. Add. MSS. 34880, fols. 264-72. Because the essay is called a "Digression" on the character of Brutus, it is remotely possible that it was copied, translated, or even written for the "seventh volume" Gibbon thought of writing in 1790-91. See *EE*, p. 587.

39. *MW* 1814, 4: 95-112; *EE*, pp. 96-106.

40. *EE*, p. 104.

41. *EE*, p. 96.

42. *EE*, p. 103.

43. *EE*, p. 98.

44. Ibid.

45. He made an index to the "Index Expurgatorius" (*EE*, pp. 128-29), which served principally to aid his own use of it.

46. *EE*, p. 108.

47. See John Clive, "Gibbon's Humor," *Daedalus* 105, no. 3 (Summer, 1976): 27-35.

48. *EE*, pp. 112, 119.

49. *EE*, pp. 114-15.

50. *EE*, p. 117.

51. *EE*, p. 125.

52. *Letters*, 1: 203-4.

53. *Letters*, 1: 202, n.2.

54. *Letters*, 1: 202-3.

55. *Letters*, 1: 204, and n.2.

56. *Letters*, 1: 204.

57. Ibid.

58. *EE*, pp. 338-52.

59. *Letters*, 1: 200.

60. "On m'annonce une pièce manuscrite dans votre voisinage et qui pourrait m'être très utile. Elle se trouve à Neufchatel dans la Bibliothèque des Pasteurs de cette ville et contient une histoire fort estimée de la guerre de Bourgogne." *Letters*, 1: 209.

61. *Letters*, 1: 209-10, n.13.

62. ACV. Gibbon papers. Box 3.

63. "En 1743 il parut de tems en tems des Etincelles en l'air préludes du Grand incendie dont on etait menacé." "Il faut placer ici le negociation de C avec les Suisses, quoique Lauffer la mette plus bas. Elle eut certainement lieu avant la prise d'Hagenbach. On peut remarquer. 1. Que Charles n'y envoya ses deputès que par la mediation du Comte de Romant et 2. Que la Suisse (à l'exception de ceux de Berne et de Soleure) ne se plaignoient de rien 3. Que ceux de Lucerne se plaigneroient, que le D avoit

pris Sismond sous sa garde.—La chose etoit vraie mais on voit par une autre instruction de Charles qu'il avoit rejettè les propositions du D. d'Autriche pour l'engager à faire la guerre aux Suisse." Ibid., fol. 3.

64. For the major point, de Commines, *Mémoires*, iii, pp. 347-56; for the final point, iii, 238-46.

65. Also in the Gibbon papers, ACV. Gibbon papers. Box 3.

66. ". . . ces commissions dont je vous ai chargé avec si peu de modestie ou de pitié. . . . A l'exception du M. S. de Neufchatel il n'y a rien dans tout ce que je vous ai marqué qui soit de première nécessité. Il y en a même quelques articles qui ne sont le fruit que d'une curiosité avide qui cherche à s'étendre au delà de son objet." *Letters*, 1: 212.

67. Add. MSS. 34881, fols. 65v-75r (text on rectos, notes and additions on facing versos, as usual). The study of the Median monarchy, which Gibbon dates in 1768 or 1769 (*Memoirs*, pp. 146-48), begins on fol. 76v. *MW* 1814, 3: 183-202.

68. "J'entrevois une nouvelle carrière plus vaste et plus utile encore: la décadence de ce systême, et ceux qui se sont élevés sur ses débris, sa chute rapide et terrible en Italie, son dépérissement lent et tranquille en Angleterre et en France, et la solidité qu'il s'est procuré en Allemagne." *MW* 1814, 3: 202.

69. "Il faut souligner . . . qu'à la différence de ses illustres devanciers, le jeune historien cherche à exprimer ses idées sans jamais se laisser aller aux violences de ton qui avaient marqué jusque là le débat sur l'origine des institutions féodales." Michel Baridon, *Edward Gibbon et le mythe de Rome* (Paris: 1977), p. 294.

70. Giarrizzo, *Edward Gibbon e la cultura europea*, p. 206.

71. "Les barbares (je parle surtout des François) étoient dévenus plus corrompus sans être plus civilisés." ". . . humeur guerrière." *MW* 1814, 3: 190.

72. ". . . ne pourraient venir de l'*Esprit des lois*." Baridon, *Mythe*, p. 203.

73. J.G.A. Pocock, "Gibbon's *Decline and Fall* and the World View of the Late Enlightenment," *Eighteenth-Century Studies* 10 (Spring 1977): 297.

74. Peter Brown, "Gibbon's Views on Culture and Society," *Daedalus* 105, no. 3 (Summer 1976): 75.

75. Ibid., p. 85.

76. ". . . pour servir de supplément aux Dissertations de MM. Freret et de Bougain-ville" Add. MSS. 34881, fols. 75v-120r. *MW* 1814, 3: 56-149.

77. Joseph Swain, *Edward Gibbon the Historian* (New York, 1966), p. 109.

78. ". . . plus près des philosophes français qu'il ne le fut jamais." Baridon, *Mythe*, p. 265.

79. ". . . un esprit de systême, de critique, et de philosophie. . . . De ce travail il a vu sortir une masse de lumière qui éclaire sans nous éblouir. Je vais exposer son systême. Dans ces sortes d'étude nous devons chercher la vérité et nous contenter de la vrai-semblance." *MW* 1814, 3: 56.

80. "Nous sommes parvenus à l'aurore, mais cette aurore est couverte de nuages. M. Freret n'a point essayé de les dissiper. Mais . . . M. de Bougainville . . . a voulu consommer ce grand ouvrage." ". . . systême raisonné." ". . . développer l'origine, la liaison, et les révolutions des deux dynasties, et de montrer que cette distinction mettoit dans l'histoire ancienne un accord et une harmonie qu'on chercheroit vaine-ment ailleurs." *MW* 1814, 3: 57-58.

81. ". . . le dégré de foi. . . . On peut le fixer en peu de mots. Ctesias se servoit assez mal des excellens matériaux." *MW* 1814, 3: 58-59.

82. "Une critique . . . pourroit décomposer le tissu des récits," "traits vraiment historiques," "traditions fabuleuses" "interprétations que [l'historien a] données à ses matériaux," "des digressions . . . liées avec son sujet principal: mais cette liaison qui existe dans l'esprit de l'historien n'a point de fondement dans la nature des choses," "fictions." *MW* 1814, 3: 59-61.

83. ". . . nous autorise à distinguer entre les faits particuliers qu'il rapporte, et le systême de chronologie par lequel il les rassemble." *MW* 1814, 3: 60.

84. "Arbace avoit inutilement employé toutes les ressources de la politique; mais celles de la superstition sont inépuisables." *MW* 1814, 3: 66, 66-68.

85. "Mais il est bon de fixer l'idée précise d'un mot toujours vague en lui-même, et assez étranger au langage des Orientaux." *MW* 1814, 3: 71.

86. "Nulle géographie, nulle chronologie, des paladins, des génies, des fées et des monstres." *MW* 1814, 3: 75. ". . . quelques vérités utiles." "Les événemens généraux se gravent dans le souvenir des hommes, l'idée des grands établissemens passe à la postérité, et l'imagination bornée et stérile de cette créature singulière, qui ne peut souffrir ni la vérité ni le mensonge, altère plus de faits qu'elle n'en invente." P. 76.

87. D. M. Low, *Edward Gibbon, 1737-1794* (London, 1937), p. 327.

88. ". . . qui n'avoit que trop étudié les prophètes." "Le Chrétien doit un respect aveugle aux livres saints. . . . Le critique éclairé mais profane doit préférer leur témoignage des affaires d'orient à celui des premiers historiens de la Grèce." *MW* 1814, 3: 102.

89. ". . . ce pacte solennel entre le prince et le peuple, que les philosophes supposent partout ailleurs, mais que l'historien ne trouve que dans l'élection de Déjoce." *MW* 1814, 3: 112. "Un vaste pays tel que la Médie, n'a jamais pu rentrer dans l'état de la nature après avoir porté pendant plus de cinq siècles le joug des loix. Les révolutions changent le contrat politique, mais elles n'ont jamais brisé les liens du contrat social. Le premier n'est appuyé que sur la crainte ou le préjugé. L'habitude et l'intérêt de chacun assurent la durée éternelle du second." Pp. 110-11.

90. Low, *Gibbon*, p. 206.

91. "Lorsqu'il s'agit d'une histoire, dont les variations permettent quelque liberté à la critique, et même à la conjecture; l'historien philosophe choisira parmi les faits contestés, ceux qui s'accordent le mieux avec ses principes, . . . et la logique du coeur ne l'emportera que trop souvent sur celle de l'esprit. Lorsque la chronologie proscrivoit un trait de morale, Plutarque méprisoit la chronologie; et Voltaire est peu difficile sur ses autorités, quand il s'agit de peindre les artifices des prêtres, les bisarreries de la superstition, et les contradictions de l'esprit humain. Il y avoit plusieurs relations de la vie de Cyrus; celle qui se prêtoit davantage aux vues de Xénophon lui parut sans doute la plus vraisemblable." *MW* 1814, 3: 128.

92. "Tout homme de génie qui écrit l'histoire, y répand, peut-être sans s'en appercevoir, le caractère de son esprit." *MW* 1814, 3: 126.

93. "Cette raison n'avoit rien de commun avec celle de Marc Aurèle; qui consultoit la volonté des dieux, la nature de l'homme, et l'ordre de l'univers, et qui préféroit la vertu: la raison de Cyrus n'étoit que la connoissance de ses inté[rêt]s." *MW* 1814, 3: 133.

94. ". . . caractère froid"—the contrast is with Henri IV, ". . . dont on n'a jamais lu l'histoire sans attendrissement." *MW* 1814, 3: 132. Peter Brown has high praise for this essay: "Getting behind the flat picture of Cyrus presented in the *Cyropaedia* of Xenophon, Gibbon is able to conjure up a three-dimensional picture of the creation of an absolute monarchy. The resultant portrait of Cyrus . . . is a triumph of binocular vision. . . . We are dealing, therefore, with a historian who treads with certainty and clear eyes on any ground where any empire has risen and declined in the Eurasian landmass." Brown, "Gibbon's Views on Culture and Society," p. 75.

95. *Letters*, 1: 214.

96. Ibid.

97. *Letters*, 1: 216.

98. Low, *Gibbon*, p. 198.

99. *Letters*, 1: 219.

100. *Letters*, 1: 217.

101. See Gibbon's and his publisher's misgivings, *Letters*, 1: 216. Maty's *Journal britannique* was published in Holland, at The Hague.

102. *Letters*, 1: 220.

103. Hume's letter is in Add. MSS. 34886, fol. 42. It was first published in *MW* 1814, 1: 204-5. *Memoirs*, pp. 141-42.

104. H. S. Offler, "Edward Gibbon and the Making of His 'Swiss History,'" *Durham University Journal* 41 (1949): 64-75.

105. Ibid., p. 69.

106. Ibid., pp. 73-74.

107. Ibid., p. 74.

108. The manuscript is in Add. MSS. 34881, fols. 169v-213r. The two "chapters" are very obviously in different stages of completeness, as may be seen even in the printed text (*MW* 1814, 3: 239-329), in which all the references are provided for pages 239-83, and only one, at the beginning, for pp. 283-329.

109. Offler, "Edward Gibbon," p. 74.

110. ". . . son expression est foible. Il décrit les passions plus qu'il ne les peint, et il les peint plus qu'il ne les sent." ". . . un ouvrage de goût." *MW* 1814, 3: 127, 125.

CHAPTER 13

1. V. P. Helming, "Gibbon and Georges Deyverdun Collaborators in the *Mémoires littéraires de la Grande-Bretagne*," *PMLA* 47 (1932): 1028-49, was the first and fullest of these considerations. For other extensive discussions, see D. M. Low, *Edward Gibbon, 1737-1794* (London, 1937), pp. 202-4; and G. Giarrizzo, *Edward Gibbon e la cultura europea del settocento* (Naples, 1954), pp. 218-22.

2. *Letters*, 1: 220.

3. Gibbon's term is *therogia*, a mistake, according to J. E. Norton, for *theoria*.

4. *ML*, 1: 98-99.

5. *ML*, 1: 99-108.

6. "L'histoire & le caractère de l'Empereur Julien forment un des morceaux les plus interessans de l'Antiquité Ecclesiastique. M. Lardner consacre à ce Prince singulier un article très etendu, & qui fait honneur à son savoir & à sa moderation. Dans les vices de l'Apostat & dans les ridicules de l'homme, il n'oublie point les grands qualités du Guerrier, de l'Ecrivain, & de l'Empereur." *ML*, 1: 99.

7. "Les prestiges, la magique, l'existance & la puissance des Demons malfaisans, etoient les doctrines communes aux deux partiss." *ML*, 1: 100. "Il auroit pû ajouter qu'en fait de miracles, le silence de trois Theologiens d'un siècle superstitieux, est bien moins naturel que le temoignage de vint de leurs contemporains." *ML*, 1: 103.

8. "On a souvent fait à ces Ecrivains l'honneur de les croire Philosophes. Hélas, ils en etoient bien eloignés. Incredules sur le Christianisme, ils etoient superstitieux sur tout le reste." *ML*, 1: 107.

9. For this aspect of Gibbon's style, see Patricia B. Craddock, "The Distinction of Similar Styles: Two English Historians," *Style* 2 (Summer 1968): 115.

10. *ML*, 1: 67.

11. "On n'y voit point cet esprit de systêmes, où l'imagination nous promène de chimères en chimères; tout est bâti sur des faits & appuié par des raisonnemens, presque toujours justes." "Et n'avez vous pas encore assez vûde ces Globes colorés jeux d'une imagination enfantine, & qu'un souffle de la raison fait evanouir?" *ML*, 1: 73.

12. Relatively frivolous. The novel Deyverdun translated was Goethe's *Werther*.

13. See his study of Hurd on Horace, *EE*, pp. 31-35.

14. "La narration est ici coupée maladroitement par l'Episode d'une fille seduite par Audley. . . . Il seroit bien tems que les auteurs renonçâssent à ces Episodes, qui

defigurent les meilleurs Romans. Celui qui pense en avoir besoin, pour reveiller la curiosité de Lecteur en la suspendant, se condamne lui-même à jetter son ouvrage au feu." *ML*, 1: 82.

15. Low, *Gibbon*, p. 203.

16. "Il ne manque à ce roman que l'interêt, de la vraisemblance, & du style" *ML*, 1: 221. The novel was *The Adventures of Emera, or the Beautiful American*.

17. "Louons ce Militaire d'avoir si bien employé des momens qui sont perdus pour la plupart des Officiers." *ML*, 1: 215.

18. "Les plaisans comparent l'Auteur à Cervantes, à Rabelais, ou avec encore plus de raison peut-etre, à Harlequin." *ML*, 1: 223. Stubbs notice, p. 217.

19. *ML*, 1: 147-55.

20. Giarrizzo, for example, was unable to obtain access to a copy of the second volume. *Edward Gibbon e la cultura europea*, p. 218, n. 127.

21. "Il est doux pour un historien de pouvoir commencer sa carriere par un trait glorieux à la nation dont il a entrepris de parcourir les annales." *ML*, 1: 1.

22. "La curiosité des faits s'affoiblit en s'eloignant de notre tems, & n'inspire plus qu'un interet assez foible pour les details minutieux du douzieme siecle." *ML*, 1: 2.

23. ". . . gouverna pendant vint ans les Normans par l'estime & les Anglois par la Terreur, & l'histoire qui cite contre lui tant de crimes ne lui reproche qu'une foiblesse; sa passion effrenée pour la chasse." *ML*, 1: 5.

24. "La façon dont Mylord L. decrit cette guerre civile fait honneur à son coeur & à son esprit. Il s'exprime en homme & en Anglois, attaché à ses Rois, mais plus attaché encore à la liberté, dont ils ne sont que les premiers ministres." *ML*, 1: 8.

25. *ML*, 1: 15-22.

26. "Le fanatisme que cet habile Politique avoit si longtems inspiré aux autres l'avoit enfin saisi, & le Fourbe n'etoit plus qu'un Enthousiaste. Un Philosophe, qui auroit vu de près le progrès de ce fanatisme dans l'ame du Prelat, eut pu enrichir d'un morceau très curieux l'histoire de l'esprit humain." *ML*, 1: 21-22.

27. "Les autres nations de l'Europe avoient devancé les Anglois dans la carriere de l'Histoire. L'Angleterre possedait des Poëtes & des Philosophes, mais on lui reprochait de n'avoir que de froids Annalistes, ou des Declamateurs passionés. Deux grands hommes ont fait taire ce reproche. Un Robertson a paré les annales de sa patrie de toutes les graces de l'eloquence la plus male. Un Hume, né pour eclairer & pour juger les hommes, a porté dans l'histoire la lumière d'une philosophie profonde & elegante. Nous ne prodiguerons jamais à la grandeur la recompense des talens: Mylord L. ne doit point pretendre à la gloire de ces hommes de genie, mais il lui reste les qualités d'un bon citoyen, d'un savant très eclairé, d'un ecrivain exact & impartial." *ML*, 1: 29.

28. ". . . presumably early in the year." J. E. Norton, *A Bibliography of the Works of Edward Gibbon* (Oxford, 1940), p. 13.

29. *ML*, 1: 91.

30. *Letters*, 1: 227.

31. *Letters*, 1: 228.

32. In G. B. Hill's edition of the *Memoirs* (London, 1900), p. 233n.

33. Low, *Gibbon*, p. 204.

34. "Il est difficile de quitter Mr. WALPOLE, mais il faut le quitter. Observons seulement qu'il réduit la difformité monstrueuse de Richard à quelques défauts assez légers. . . . Un dessein fort ancien que M. Walpole a fait graver, et le témoignage d'une moine très passioné à l'égard de Richard, lui fournissent ces traits adoucis. La Vielle Comtesse De Desmond le dépeignoit d'une manière encore plus favorable. Elle se souvenoit d'avoir dansé avec lui et se rappelloit qu'à son frère Edouard près, il etoit l'homme le mieux fait de l'assemblée." *ML*, 1: 25.

35. Byron, *Childe Harold*, bk. 3, canto 107.

36. "Les argumens de M. Walpole nous avoient ébloui sans nous convaincre. Les réflexions suivantes nous ont ramné au sentiment général. Elles sont de M. Hume." *ML*, 2: 25. Published in *MW* 1814, 3: 331–41, with Hume's remarks, pp. 341–49.

37. "C'est ainsi que Mr. B. a jugé a propos de refuter Mr. S.—Un Italien me disoit l'autre jour: nous n'avons pas beaucoup d'obligations à Mr. B. pour justifier nos femmes, il veut nous faire tous passer pour des sots." *ML*, 2: 41.

38. "Je ne saurois me persuader que Goldoni soit absolument sans talens. Je n'entrerai point en dispute avec Mr. B. sur la Littérature de son Pays, mais il me paroit peu vraisemblable qu'un peuple très-policé ait applaudi pendant plusiers années à des Ouvrages dénués de tout mérite. La Langue Italienne n'est pas aussi difficile que l'angloise. Si Mr. de Voltaire n'entend pas Shakespear, Mr. B. conviendra du moins, qu'il peut entendre Goldoni, & quoiqu'il ne soit pas trop prévenu en faveur de cet homme de Génie, j'espère qu'il voudra bien convenir aussi qu'il connoit un peu le Théatre. Comment auroit-il donné des éloges à un Auteur tel qu'on nous depeint Goldoni." *ML*, 2: 45.

39. *DF*, chapter 70.

40. "Le Lecteur s'étonnera sans doute qu'un Homme d'Etat, un Philosophe, le pere de 4. enfans eut de pareilles avantures: il s'etonnera encore plus qu'il le raconte aussi sérieusement à l'âge de 60, ans. Mais les moeurs de son tems étoient bien différentes des nôtres, ce qui seroit maintenant ridicule, extravagant même, étoir alors scrupule, délicatesse, honneur." *ML*, 2: 63.

41. "Mais il est tems de dire un petit mot à mes Lecteurs. S'il est quelqu'un d'entre eux que la peinture simple & naive de caractère de M. H. & des moeurs de son tems, n'intéresse point, je lui conseille en ami, de jeter ce Livre." *ML*, 2: 70.

42. The articles are: that there is one supreme God; that He alone should be adored; that the best adoration is virtue, piety, and charity joined to faith and love; that if we violate these rules, we must repent and reform; that there are rewards and punishments in this world and the next. *ML*, 2: 81.

43. "M. dit ensuite de belles choses en faveur de l'opinion d'un seul Dieu, & s'égare un peu dans l'infini." *ML*, 2: 81, 89. ". . . avec bien de justice." P. 100. "A bien des égards il mérite d'être à la tête des Ecrivains Déistes. Son stile est supérieur à celui de la plupart des Auteurs de son tems: il est en général clair, simple & quelquefois agréable. Le manque de méthode est le plus grand défaut des Ouvrages de M. H. . . . pour l'Astrologie judiciaire, la Magie, &c. . . . est l'hommage que cet homme de génie rend a son siécle. M. H. étoit Philosophe; mais une imagination trop vive égara quelquefois sa Philosophie." P. 101.

44. "On ne peut lire les Mémoires de Milord Herbert, sans sentir qu'on respecte, qu'on aime cet homme. Avec quelle aimable ingénuité ne nous laisse-t-il pas voir ses défauts, avec quelle noble sincerité ne nous parle-t-il pas de ses vertus." *ML*, 2: 101–2.

45. ". . . avec plaisir. . . . Le Journaliste a connu tout le mérite de l'Ouvrage de Mr. Sterne. . . . L'esprit seul ne suffit pas pour cela, il faut encore avoir de l'ame. Un autre Journaliste n'a rien vu ni senti dans l'Ouvrage de M. S. . . . Peut-être dira-t-on pour l'excuser que des raisons étrangeres au goût ont conduit sa plume. Quelle excuse! y a-t-il quelque raison qui puisse faire affecter de n'avoir point d'ame?" *ML*, 2: 122–23.

46. "Cet Ouvrage, qui avoit quelque chose de naturel, de vif, & surtout de fort original, fut extrêment accueilli; mais peu à peu, le désordre, les indécences, l'obscurité dégoûterent le Lecteur, qui critiqua autant qu'il avoit loué, & qui crut voir une grande différence entre les premiers & les derniers Volumes. Cette différence ne m'est point aussi sensible, je vois dans tout le cours de l'Ouvrage les beautés & les defauts . . . & s'il ne méritoit pas les éloges qu'on lui donna au commencement, il méritoit encore moins la maniere dont on l'a traité ensuite. Point de volume où il n'y ait des beautés, point de volume aussi où on n'achète un peu cher la vue de ces beautés." *ML*, 2:124.

47. "Les gens de goût ne sauroient trop regretter la perte d'un Ecrivain . . . original, dans des tems où l'imitation semble vouloir étouffer les talens. . . . Je l'ai dit aux Acteurs, je l'ai dit aux Peintres, je le répéte aux Ecrivains, l'imitation resserre le génie, vous ne serez jamais grands par elle." *ML*, 2: 133.

48. See above, apropos of the reviews of Sharp and Baretti. See *ML*, 1: 183.

49. *ML*, 2: 138.

50. *ML*, 2: 141-42.

51. See above, Chapter 11.

52. "Voici le morceau brillant, & celui qui a fait la fortune de l'Ouvrage entier. . . . Le feu, la vivacité de la narration, ont amusé ceux qui ne cherchent que l'agrément, & à travers certain brouillard formé par l'enthousiasme, le Philosophe aura entrevu avec satisfaction les traits d'un Grand Homme dans Paoli, tous enfin, auront vu avec plaisir cette sorte d'ingénuité qui nous intéresse en faveur de l'Ecrivain, ou qui nous fait rire à ses dépens." "Si l'Auteur se retrace dans son ouvrage, la Rélation de M. B. doit inspirer au Lecteur le désir de le connoitre," "ses écrits & . . . ses soins." ". . . il nous manque encore une Histoire de Corse." *ML*, 2: 147-48, 161, 163, 164.

53. D. M. Low, "Edward Gibbon and the Johnson Circle," *New Rambler* (June 1960), p. 5.

54. "quelques traits pourront amuser un moment nos Lecteurs" *ML*, 2: 164. The parallel occupies pp. 165-67.

55. See Meredith Read, *Historic Studies in Vaud, Berne, and Savoy*, 2 vols. (London, 1897), 2: 300-304.

56. ". . . qui vraisemblablement ne sera jamais écrite. Nôtre Auteur a bien d'autres affaires, & ne jouit pas trop de cette tranquilité d'esprit, qui permet à un Historien d'amasser des matériaux, de les comparer, juger, & d'y joindre des réflexions justes & impartiales. La lecture de l'Introduction est très-propre à nous consoler de la perte de l'histoire. Nous y avons vu que la Nation Angloise jouissoit d'une pleine Liberté sous le regne d'Elizabeth. Tout Lecteur un peu instruit de l'Histoire d'Angleterre, connoit le Despotisme de cette Reine; mais ce n'est pas pour les Lecteurs instruits que M. Wilkes a travaillé." *ML*, 2: 252.

57. Gibbon's declaration upon being appointed J.P. was located by Norton in the Hampshire archives. *Letters*, 1: 275, n.1.

58. See *Letters*, 1, appendix 3, pp. 402-7, especially p. 404.

59. See, e.g., *Letters*, 1: 237, 238, for Heather. Heather was a Petersfield draper. P. 404.

60. *Letters*, 1: 232.

61. DGP, sec. 2, no. 1.

62. DGP, sec. 2, no. 2.

63. *Letters*, 1: 229-30.

64. DGP, sec. 2, no. 2.

65. *Letters*, 1: 233.

66. Ibid.

67. DGP, sec. 2, no. 3.

68. *Letters*, 1: 235.

69. *Letters*, 1: 236, n.1. Norton had not seen the actual letter, but only the catalogue of the papers, Add. MSS. 11907, dd, 25/2.

70. DGP, sec. 2, no. 4.

71. *Letters*, 1: 236.

72. *Letters*, 1: 237-38.

73. DGP, sec. 2, no. 6.

74. DGP, sec. 2, no. 7a.

75. DGP, sec. 2, no. 7.

76. *Letters*, 1: 239-40.

77. DGP, sec. 2, no. 9.

78. Scott was also probably of the generation of Gibbon's parents (or older); he died in 1772.

79. *Letters*, 1: 241.

80. *Letters*, 1: 243.

81. DGP, sec. 2, no. 12.

82. Ibid.

83. *Letters*, 1: 247.

84. E. Badian's assertion (*New York Review of Books* 24 [Sept. 13, 1977]: 9) that Gibbon treated his stepmother shabbily in financial affairs is entirely without foundation.

85. See *Letters*, 1: 252-53.

86. Read, *Historic Studies*, 2: 381.

87. Low, *Gibbon*, p. 204.

88. Gibbon's summary, *EE*, p. 134.

89. Michel Baridon, *Edward Gibbon et le mythe de Rome* (Paris, 1977), p. 321.

90. See Gibbon's allusion, *Memoirs*, 145-46, and Bonnard's note, p. 310.

91. *EE*, p. 139.

92. *EE*, p. 141.

93. *EE*, p. 142.

94. *EE*, pp. 146-47.

95. *EE*, pp. 148-49.

96. *EE*, pp. 149-51.

97. *EE*, p. 155.

98. Ibid.

99. *EE*, p. 159.

100. See Norton, *Bibliography*, pp. 19-20.

101. *Letters*, 1: 253-54, and Norton's n.2 to no. 108.

102. *Letters*, 1: 255.

103. DGP, sec. 2, no. 19.

104. See *Letters*, 1: 256-59; and DGP, sec. 2, no. 20.

105. *Letters*, 1: 258-59.

106. DGP, sec. 2, no. 21.

107. *Letters*, 1: 272.

108. *Letters*, 1: 261.

109. Ibid.

110. *Letters*, 1: 262.

111. *Letters*, 1: 263.

112. Ibid., n.1.

113. "Dans toute sa maladie, je ne me suis jamais absente de Beriton un seul jour, à peine ai je quittè sa Chambre un seul instant: tout, jusqu'à mes lectures, a etè interrompû, et je goutte la triste consolation d'avoir rempli mes devoirs de fils, jusqu'au moment où ils ont cessè. Il me reste, je le sai, bien d'autres motifs de consolation. Je les vois, mais pour les sentir, j'ai besoin due le tems ajoute ses forces à celles de la raison." *Letters*, 1: 267.

CHAPTER 14

1. *Letters*, 2: 12.

2. Compare his sensitivity in the case of Wilhelm de Severy, when his father died; see Patricia B. Craddock, "Edward Gibbon: The Man in His Letters," in *Familiar Letter in*

the Eighteenth Century, ed. H. Anderson, P. Daghlian, and I. Ehrenpreis (Lawrence, Kans., 1966), p. 234.

3. DGP, sec. 3, no. 1.

4. *Letters*, 1: 264. There are several subsequent references to the Baylys.

5. Ibid.

6. *Letters*, 1: 265.

7. See above, Chapter 12.

8. Deyverdun, the Holroyds, the de Severys, and Wilhelm de Severy.

9. *Letters*, 1: 270.

10. DGP, sec. 3, no. 2.

11. *Letters*, 1: 275.

12. *Letters*, 1: 276, and n.2.

13. *Letters*, 1: 280-81.

14. See above, Chapter 5.

15. *Letters*, 1: 282, and 280n.

16. DGP, sec. 3, no. 3.

17. DGP, sec. 3, no. 4.

18. *Letters*, 1: 285.

19. *Letters*, 1: 296.

20. *Letters*, 1: 283 and n.1, 287, 285.

21. *Letters*, 1: 277.

22. *Letters*, 1: 294-95.

23. *EE*, pp. 163-98; for date, *EE*, p. 57, and Joseph Swain, *Edward Gibbon the Historian* (New York, 1966), pp. 122-23.

24. See *DF*, 1, preface, p. iii.

25. *EE*, p. 172.

26. *EE*, pp. 174-75.

27. *EE*, p. 175.

28. *EE*, p. 188.

29. See some notes for the *Memoirs*, e.g., Add. MSS. 34880, fol. 284.

30. See above, Chapter 13.

31. *EE*, pp. 199-203.

32. "Una coda enorme alla storia . . . della decadenza dall'impero." G. Giarrizzo, *Edward Gibbon e la cultura europea del settocento* (Naples, 1954), p. 208. "Son pagine nude e scarne, dove traluce qua e là la punta secca dell'invettiva o la risoluta energia della polemica; non c'è un solo gesto di sarcasmo, o un sorriso di soddisfatta ironia. Non siamo ancora al Gibbon della *History*: la severità granitica del pensiero montesquieuiano lo tiene tutto e lo domina, egli non è riuscito ancora a superarlo, a guardarlo con distacco." P. 211.

33. David P. Jordan, *Gibbon and His Roman Empire* (Urbana, Ill., 1971), p. 22.

34. Swain, *Edward Gibbon the Historian*, p. 123.

35. Giarrizzo, *Edward Gibbon e la cultura europea*, p. 211; Swain, *Edward Gibbon the Historian*, p. 123.

36. *EE*, pp. 176-77.

37. ". . . ergere la persona piccola et rotonda, guardarsi attorno con aria di affettuosa compiacenza, incrinar le gote rotondette ad un sorriso accennato, et cominciare, non senza aver dato un colpetto discreto all'elegante tabacchiera. . . . 'In the second century of the Christian Aera. . .'." Giarrizzo, *Edward Gibbon e la cultura europea*, p. 223.

38. *Letters*, 1: 291, 293, and n.

39. *Letters*, 1: 296.

40. *Letters*, 1: 299-322. The king's sister, wife of the King of Denmark, had been

arrested for plotting against him. A particularly enjoyable political letter is no. 168, the "Victory of our Dear Mamma the Church of England" against a petition against the Thirty-Nine Articles. P. 305.

41. *Letters*, 1: 320 and countless other references. See also appendix 3, p. 405.

42. *Letters*, 1: 320.

43. Ibid.

44. He wore a type of glasses not made before 1770. See J. H. Doggart, "Gibbon's Eyesight," *Transactions of the Cambridge Bibliographical Society* 3 (1963): 407. The glasses and their case were repaired in 1775. Ambrose Heal, *Notes and Queries*, 194 (Oct. 29, 1949): 475.

45. Doggart, "Gibbon's Eyesight," p. 408.

46. Magdalen College Accounts, Oxford, MSS. 359, items 12 and 15.

47. *Letters*, 1: 322.

48. *Letters*, 1: 323.

49. *Letters*, 1: 324.

50. *Letters*, 1: 324-25.

51. *Letters*, 1: 326.

52. Norton mistakenly refers the reader to a letter about Gibbon's planned economies to explain the lack of a cook; in fact, however, the missing cook had been discharged by Dorothea Gibbon: "I have parted with my Cook, and ford says She has not spirits to take charge of the family so I am in danger of being my own Housekeeper." Dorothea Gibbon to James Scott, January 23, 1772. DGP, sec. 3, no. 10.

53. *Letters*, 1: 326.

54. Hurd was asked to direct his answer "*To Daniel Freeman, Esq. at the Cocoa Tree, Pall Mall:* but if you have any scruple of engaging with a mask, I am ready, by the same channel, to disclose my real name and place of abode; and to pledge myself for the same *discretion*, which, in my turn, I shall have a right to expect." *Letters*, 1: 338-39.

55. Readers differ in their interpretation of the tone of Gibbon's assertion that he was "startled at the first vollies of this Ecclesiastical ordnance" and had not foreseen that "the pious, the timid and the prudent would feel or affect to feel with such exquisite sensibility." *Memoirs*, pp. 160, 159.

56. *Letters*, 1: 328.

57. *Letters*, 1: 328-29.

58. *MW* 1814, 2: 85.

59. *Letters*, 1: 333.

60. *Letters*, 1: 335.

61. *MW* 1814, 2: 86-87.

62. *MW* 1814, 2: 90.

63. But he now emphasizes the possibility that the *Cyropaedia* is a romance: "Their hypothesis . . . falls to the ground if the Cyropaedia is a romance; and is overthrown by it, should that noble performance be received as a genuine history." *Letters*, 1: 336.

64. *MW* 1814, 2: 93-94.

65. DGP, sec. 3, no. 11. If Beriton were her own, she thinks she could manage it "to great advantage."

66. *Letters*, 1: 340.

67. *Letters*, 1: 342.

68. See *Letters*, 1: 364-65, and n.3, p. 364.

69. *Letters*, 1: 246.

70. *Letters*, 1: 353. J. W. Johnson calls attention to Gibbon's architectural interests, literal and figurative. Like the captain in the Hampshire Grenadiers, the designer

of Bentinck Street was not "useless to the historian of the Decline and Fall." "Gibbon's Architectural Metaphor," *Journal of British Studies* 13 (Nov. 1973): 54.

71. *Letters*, 1: 359.

72. *Letters*, 1: 351-52.

73. *Letters*, 1: 360.

74. He alluded to Gibbon in these flattering words during his speech of June 13, 1788. R. F. Rae, *Sheridan* (London, 1896), 2: 69.

Indexes

I: General Index

Abbot, Charles, 145
Acton, Catherine, 171
Acton, Edward, 10–11, 171
Acton, Elizabeth Gibbon, 3
Acton, Francis, 4, 7
Acton, Hester Gibbon. *See* Gibbon, Hester Abrahall
Acton, John 221
Acton, Richard, 3, 4
Addison, Joseph, *Spectator* of, alluded to, 13–14. *See also* Index II
Allamand, François-Luis, correspondence with Gibbon of, 96, 193
Arabian Nights, 30, 44, 99, 110–11
Augny, M. d' (Parisian friend), 167–68
Aylmer, Sir Gerald, 142

Baridon, Michel, 188, 213, 214–15, 227, 246, 247, 277
Barnard, Sir John, 150
Bayly, Joseph, 285–86
Beaufort, Louis de, 121. *See also* Index II
Becket, Thomas, 154
Beckett, Thomas à, 261
Bedford, John Russell, Duke of, 166
Beer, Sir Gavin de, 189
Bennet, Sir William, 159
Bergier, M. (Lausanne resident), 174
Bochat. *See* Loys de Bochat, C. G.
Bolton, Charles Paulet, Duke of, 143, 145–46, 158–59
Bonnard, Georges A., 27, 144, 176, 181, 195, 198, 211, 217
Bontems, Marie-Jeanne, 167, 170–71, 227
Boswell, James, 120, 155–56, 165, 199, 200, 263
Boussens (Boussins), Louis-André Saussure de, 190

Bragg, Major Charles, 156
Breitinger, Johann Jakob, correspondence with Gibbon of, 85, 96–99, 103
Bridgewater, Francis Egerton, Duke of, 166
Brignole-Sale, Rodolfo, Doge of Genoa, 206
Brosses, Charles de, 211
Brown, Peter, 246
Burdot, M. (copyist), 131, 134
Burney, Charles, 149
Burney, Frances, 149
Bury, J. B., 97
Byers, James, 223, 227
Byrom, John, 9–10, 22–23
Byron, George Gordon, Sixth Baron, quoted, 263

Calvin, John, and Servetus, 189
Cambridge, University of, 3, 9–10
Carlo Emmanuele III (King of Sardinia), 200–201
Caylus, A.C.P. de Tubières, Comte de, 165–66
Celesia, Dorothea Mallet, 133–34, 205
Celesia, Pietro Paolo, 205–6, 267
Charles the Bold (Duke of Burgundy), 84–85
Chesterfield, Philip Dormer Stanhope, Earl of, 295
Chetwynd, Miss (interest of Gibbon), 155–56
Chillingsworth, William, 51
Clarke, George Hyde, 180-81, 190
Clarke, Godfrey, 243, 284
Clarke, Miss (sister of George Hyde), 193
Cobham, Richard Grenville-Temple, Viscount, 49

II: Gibbon's Reading

III: Gibbon's Writings

Patricia B. Craddock is professor and chairman of the Department of English at Boston University. She is the editor of The English Essays of Edward Gibbon.

The Johns Hopkins University Press

Young Edward Gibbon: Gentleman of Letters

*This book was composed in Baskerville text and display type
by Horne Associates, Inc., from a design by Lisa S. Mirski.
It was printed on S. D. Warren's 50-lb. Sebago Eggshell paper
and bound in Holliston Roxite A by the Maple Press Company.
The manuscript was edited by Jane Warth.*